Peter Akinola: Who Blinks First?

─────────────────────────────────────

Peter Akinola: Who Blinks First?

Biblical Fidelity Against the Gay Agenda
in the Global Anglican Communion

Gbenga Gbesan

Foreword by Peter Jensen
Preface by Foley Beach

RESOURCE *Publications* · Eugene, Oregon

PETER AKINOLA: WHO BLINKS FIRST?
Biblical Fidelity Against the Gay Agenda in the Global Anglican Communion

Resource Publications
An Imprint of Wipf and Stock Publishers
199 W. 8th Ave., Suite 3
Eugene, OR 97401

www.wipfandstock.com

PAPERBACK ISBN: 978-1-7252-6463-2
HARDCOVER ISBN: 978-1-7252-6464-9
EBOOK ISBN: 978-1-7252-6465-6

Manufactured in the U.S.A.   03/16/20

To
All past and present Anglican leaders worldwide,
Steadfast in courage and stout in commitment,
Defenders of Truth and protectors of the Gospel,
The bold advocates of Faith as once delivered to the saints

Contents

Foreword

The Church of Jesus Christ is One, Holy, Catholic and Apostolic.

It is "built on the foundation of the apostles and prophets, Christ Jesus himself being the cornerstone" (Eph 2:20). The Church is one, for the Lord prayed that it would be one, and as a result it is described as "one new man" (Eph 2:16). Through Christ both Jew and Gentile, male and female, slave and free have access to the Father in one Spirit (Eph 2:18). It is catholic because, as it stems from the apostolic gospel, so it reaches out to every nation on earth. It is holy, because it belongs to Christ and comprises saints who are in Christ and who are destined to be with him and like him in glory.

It is all four things—one, holy, apostolic, and catholic. But in this age, it must forever strive to be those things. Just because there is one body and one Spirit, one call and one hope, one Lord, one faith, one baptism, and one Father of us all, so we are to bear with one another in love, "eager to maintain the unity of the Spirit in the bond of peace" (Eph 4:1–6).

Archbishop Peter Akinola has been engaged as a key leader in a huge struggle to maintain both the apostolic gospel of Jesus Christ and the unity of the church. He did not choose to be involved. But he saw that if he did not speak and act, many of the Lord's sheep would be left without an effective witness to the truth. His was the path which love dictated.

Some would see his actions involved with GAFCON (Global Anglican Future Conference) as divisive. I see them as arising from a longing for the oneness of God's people. Those who left the denominational Anglican churches over a major doctrinal matter, especially in North America, had no desire to be anything else than Anglican. They had not changed. They still believed what the Church Catholic had believed for two thousand years. They were true to what the Lambeth Conference had affirmed as recently as 1998.

So, the ministry of Archbishop Akinola was to stand true to the apostolic faith, as revealed in Scripture, and to help gather up the fragments and to make sure that the faithful remained in fellowship with the majority of Anglicans around the world. This was achieved.

It was my privilege to work under and with the archbishop during these crucial years. Personally, I experienced him as a decisive, insightful, faithful, and visionary Christian leader. His impact has been extraordinary. I am glad that a book has been written about him. I look forward to reading it and hope you will too.

I can only say that my personal debt to the archbishop could never be repaid.

Peter Jensen
    Former Archbishop of Sydney and
    General Secretary of GAFCON (2008–2018)

Preface

If you abide in my word, you are truly my disciples, and you will know the truth, and the truth will set you free (Jesus in John 8:31, 32, ESV).

The truth. It should come as no surprise that fake news, rewritten histories, and new spin about all kinds of topics has crept from the world into the modern Church. The truth seems less important than the position one takes on the latest hot issue of the day.

What happened to the truth? What happened to the actual facts? Sometimes these are lost because people and personnel change and institutional memory is forgotten. Sometimes these are lost because it is more convenient to the political agenda being pursued. Sometimes it is intentionally changed for propaganda purposes.

Sadly, this loss of truthful history is happening in the Anglican Communion as the Anglican establishment has failed again and again to remember discussions, agreements, and the basic truths of Scripture and Anglican history. A neo-pagan Anglicanism has emerged embracing theologies and moral practices more in line with what was once considered paganism than with historic Christianity. All dressed up with the spiritual language of love, inclusiveness, and unity, the Anglican establishment has welcomed into its midst those who have walked away from historic Christianity and the clear teaching of the Bible, making it normative for leaders to live in immorality, sensuality, and licentiousness.

Into this chaos and confusion came Global South leaders like Peter Akinola, a modern lion of the faith, who challenged the colonial and patronizing arrogance of the Anglican establishment and other western leaders. Akinola, the archbishop and primate of the Anglican Church in Nigeria, led an effort by Global South leaders to stop the manipulation and unbiblical practices being forced upon them at their meetings and agencies throughout the Communion.

The issues of gay and lesbian relationships, ordination, and same-sex marriage within the Anglican Communion brought western colonialism to the forefront. The Episcopal Church (USA) consecrated a non-celibate gay man, and the Anglican Church of Canada permitted married gay clergy to be ordained. These actions destroyed the fellowship of the Anglican Communion at its core. In addressing these actions, the Anglican establishment would not honor agreements of the Primates Meetings, thinking with a colonial mind-set that the colonies (or commonwealth) would eventually fall in line—"After all, they need our money!"

Akinola and other Global leaders said enough is enough. Knowing they could not lead their sheep down immoral pathways, they formed the Global Anglican Future Conference (GAFCON) as a place to not only resist these heretical teachings, but to call the Anglican Communion to repentance, revival, renewal, and reform.

Years have passed and new bishops and primates have risen. Many of these godly leaders do not know the history of recent years, and others like the Archbishop of Canterbury are rewriting recent history with their own narratives. These revisions of history picture those who stand for historic Christianity as the ones who are unchristian because they will not join hands with those who are living in immoral relationships. This makes *Who Blinks First?* such an important book! Akinola was there. He stood tall when so many would not. He had these conversations. He spoke the words. His stories can be verified by other leaders who were present and have not yet fallen asleep in the Lord. He is telling the truth. Documents and minutes of the meetings verify the book's content, and the conversations.

Whatever happens with the Anglican Communion in the future, it cannot be said that there were not men of God like Peter Akinola who spoke out, who sought to save it from its current destructive path, and who called it back to its biblical foundation. This history brings out the truth about what has happened, and sadly, the hypocrisy and abandonment of Christian principles by so many.

Why is all this important? Souls. Millions of souls are being taught a false gospel and led away from Jesus for all eternity—all in the name of the Church. We are to teach the biblical faith, and make disciples of all nations, baptizing them in the Name of the Father, the Son, and the Holy Spirit, and teaching them the Word of God as Jesus taught it.

The Most Rev. Dr. Foley Beach
Archbishop and Primate, Anglican Church in North America
Chairman, Global Anglican Future Conference

Acknowledgments

When interest arose in 2007 for a biography of The Most Rev. Peter Akinola, the plan was for a trilogy. There was so much to the Nigerian primate, and even then, he was already evolving in many ways. He had taken the world by storm. Initially, the archbishop did not seem like a person who could sneeze and cause the world to catch cold. At the turn of the twenty-first century, however, his name and voice became a bugle rising peoples and nations to attention. Born humbly, the bulk of Akinola's life and ministry had been lived in anonymity. This ceased when perversion of the Bible in the Anglican Communion reared its ugly head through the homosexuality crisis. The Church was divided. The calamity brought him out—introduced, demonstrated, and tested his leadership before the world.

Akinola brought out his natural endowments and exhibited his unknown leadership qualities and virtues for the world to see. Becoming one of Time magazine's 100 most influential people in the world—twice in a row—confirmed the power of his influence as one of the important Christian leaders to emerge from the developing countries of the South in the twenty-first century. As an apolitical priest not given to self-promotion and advertising, a lot is obscure about him. And there have been many untruths, misconceptions, and deliberate falsehoods expressed and written about him. There is need, therefore, for honest and truthful accounts of the real Akinola—to know and synthesize the man, the priest, and the world church leader. A book cannot unpack adequately the many strata of Akinola's life, especially in the light of the complications and complexities of the homosexuality crisis in the Anglican Church. Hence the idea of a trilogy.

The first in the series of the three-part biography was published in 2009. *Peter Jasper Akinola: Before the Mission—A Biography* provided an account of his birth, childhood, family, and how he became a priest, as well as his life as a young ordained priest. The second volume, *Peter Akinola—Born for a Time Like This*, and the third serial, *Peter Akinola: Who Blinks First?*, were written simultaneously. The latter two volumes took about eighteen months to complete and were written ten years after the first. The larger part of that intervening decade was spent gathering materials from primary and secondary sources for the two volumes. Information had to be updated and cross-checked as the worldwide Anglican Communion changed rapidly. The homosexuality crisis yielded many documents that demanded thorough and painstaking examination. Caution and circumspection were exercised in processing information obtained from the varied and divergent sources. Consequently, no information, opinion, or document was taken at face value. Rather, they were tested for accuracy and reliability. The manuscript itself went through and benefitted from this same painstaking and meticulous exercise.

It is in this regard that I owe extreme gratitude to Dr. Mark Coppenger. He employed every gift at his disposal to benefit the work. Incidentally, we have not met, but distance didn't prove to be a barrier. He lent the book his scholarly, intellectual, and skillful craftsmanship. The result is what you are reading. Without Emmanuel and Camille Kampouris, the paths of Coppenger and I would have not crossed. They were the bridge and ensured that the link did not break or collapse till the end. I wish English had better inventions than a mere thank you to express appreciation for all of your self-sacrifice for the cause of Scripture. Bless you.

And, of course, The Most Rev. Peter Akinola, the former Nigerian primate and subject of the biography must be included in the long list of those to whom appreciation is due. Without his collaboration and support, the book would lack much rich, first-hand information. The archbishop was a delightful curator and a meticulous preserver of information. That helped the task tremendously, along with the other support and encouragement he cheerfully gave. The assistance is much appreciated. Similar helpfulness was exhibited by The Rt Rev. Prof. Dapo Asaju, bishop theologian and vice chancellor of the Church of Nigeria-owned Ajayi Crowther University in Oyo, Oyo State, Nigeria. An erudite scholar and distinguished academic, he benefitted the book with his characteristic thorough analysis and meticulous attention to details. As with the others I have mentioned, "thank you" is an inadequate payment for his help.

The "primate's men"—The Most Rev. Prof. Adebayo Dada Akinde, the retired archbishop of Lagos and pioneer bishop of the Lagos Mainland Diocese of the Church of Nigeria (Anglican Communion); Mr. Yinka Fisher, Archbishop Akinola's "civilian chaplain"; and the retired The Rt Rev. Oluranti Odubogun—came a long way with the primate and refused to abandon him at any point, including seeing that the books were completed. There were other senior and leading citizens in and outside Nigeria who shaped his leadership one way or the other. They provided valuable information. In that group were people like the head of the interim government in Nigeria, Chief Ernest Sonekan; the former Nigerian primate and Akinola's predecessor, The Most Rev. Abiodun Adetiloye; his former boss in the Kaduna Diocese, The Rt. Rev. T. E. Ogbonyomi; his mate at the theological school, The Rt Rev. Christian Efobi; and The

Acknowledgments

Rt Rev. Ignatius Kattey, his fellow board member at the Peter Akinola Foundation. In this group also were The Rt Rev. and Mrs. Martyn Minns as well as The Rt Rev. Sosthenes Eze, bishop of the Enugu diocese.

People like Hon. Justice A. G. Karibi-Whyte, chancellor of the Abuja diocese; Abraham Yisa, registrar of the Church of Nigeria; Ms. Amma People, a former federal head of service and minister; and Mr. Ade Ademo deserve specific mention. They provided very useful information that forms the cornerstone of how Akinola played out his bishopric in Abuja. A big thank you to them and the many others who cannot be mentioned individually.

Colleagues, associates, friends, and family members directly and indirectly were part of this project. The list begins with my colleague Akin Enilolobo, who coordinated the books' research. He was as painstaking as he was meticulous. Besides that, he traversed the entire length and breadth of Nigeria, defying the dangers associated with the Nigerian roads in search of facts. I say a great thank you to him. Further assistance came from friends like Niyi Fasanmi, Biodun Odetoyinbo, Prof. Lai Oso, Waheed Kadiri, Demola Oladosu, Nike Lukan, Biade Coker, and Bose Muibi. Your support encouraged seeing the tasks through. In the same vein, were the Oluwoles—Sola and Rolayo—of Kent, England, and the Elemides—Koye and Yemisi—of Central London. During my month-long trip, these two cousins-in-law threw their homes and hospitality open in ways that enlivened the body and spirit when they were sagging from weariness. Thank you, cousins.

Lastly, is the home front, my family, beginning with the best partner I could have, my wife Oluremi Asake. Ever unassuming, she ensured I was free from all burdens throughout the writing process. She epitomized domestic efficiency, meeting my needs and those of the children. "Ori Aran," thank you. To my children, Bambo, Tunji, Ewa-Oluwa, and Kehinde, thanks for the understanding.

If this book deserves any credit, it goes to all those that have been mentioned, particularly Mark Coppenger. Any shortcoming, however, is mine alone.

Chronology Of Events

Surrounding Archbishop Peter Akinola's Life

1944	Peter Akinola born in Maga-Adeniregun, Abeokuta, Ogun State, Nigeria
1948	Death of Peter Akinola's father, Titus Adeniregun Akinola
1960	Works as a patent medicine dealer
1963	Begins training as carpenter specialising in cabinet making
1967	Completes carpentry training
1967	Also opens postal agency at Nguru in Northern Nigeria
1969	Selected for Catechist Course at Diocesan Training Centre, Zaria
1969	Marries Susan Atinuke (nee Adebesin)
1971	Finishes the Catechist Course
1973	Enrols at the Theological College of Northern Nigeria for ordination course
1978	Becomes a deacon under the Rt. Rev. Titus Ogbonyomi of Kaduna Diocese
1979	Becomes a priest of Kaduna Diocese under the Rt. Rev. Titus Ogbonyom
1979	Attends the Virginia Theological Seminary, USA, for his master's in theology
1981	Posted to Abuja to establish presence of Church of Nigeria in the new federal capital
1983	Preferred a canon by Rt. Rev. Titus Ogbonyomi
1989	Elected and consecrated the pioneer Bishop of Abuja Diocese.
1991	Anglican Church primates worldwide in Newcastle, Northern Ireland, at the first meeting with Archbishop George Carey, issue statement

concerning matters raised by Presiding Bishop Browning about homo-sexuality in the US Episcopal Church.

1993	Virginia Theological Seminary honours him with DD (*Honoris Causa*)
1995	Primates in Windsor, England, agree that human sexuality issue is deep and complex
1997	Becomes archbishop of Province 3, covering northern Nigeria
1997	Second Encounter of the Global South and issuance of the statement on human sexuality
1998	Lambeth Conference held, with Resolution 1:10 on Human Sexuality passed by majority vote of 526–70 as the standard position of the Church
1998	Minority comprising 185 bishops and 9 primates breaks away from the majority at the conference to write pastoral letter to the gays and lesbians in the Anglican Church promising action toward overturning the majority decision
1999	Anglican Consultative Council (ACC) meets in Dundee with protest and boycott from Archbishop Moses Tay of Singapore
1999	Nigeria returned to civil rule with swearing-in of Chief Olusegun Obasanjo as president
1999	Zamfara State introduces Sharia law, copied by Nigeria's other northern states
1999	Archbishop Abiodun Adetiloye retires as primate of Church of Nigeria
2000	Archbishop Peter Akinola elected as Nigerian primate
2000	Anglican Church primates in Oporto, Portugal, issue communique expressing concern over actions of certain provinces
2000	Canterbury's Archbishop Carey sends pastoral letter to all bishops, urging them to maintain "the Church's historic teaching"
2000	Episcopal Church General Convention in Denver, Colorado, passes resolution DO39 welcoming full inclusion of non-marital relationships
2001	Primates Meeting in Kanuga, North Carolina, USA, with Archbishops Drexel Gomez and Maurice Sinclair presenting "To Mend the Net" as the way forward for the Communion
2002	Primates in Canterbury; issue pastoral letter on the need for all bishops "to maintain the Church in truth"
2002	Diocese of Westminster, Canada, approves blessing of same-sex unions

2002	Archbishop Carey has last meeting as head of the worldwide Anglican Church
2002	Primates agree that unwritten law common to churches of the Communion constitutes the "Fifth Instrument of Unity" in the Communion
2002	Primates Meeting in Lambeth and Newport elect Rowan Williams as archbishop and express support for him to uphold the "faith once delivered to the saints"
2002	Archbishop Akinola becomes Chairman/President, Global South-South Encounter
2002	Archbishop Akinola becomes archbishop of Province of Abuja
2003	Archbishop Rowan Williams installed as the 104th Archbishop of Canterbury
2003	Primates in Brazil, the first official meeting with Dr. Rowan Williams as the archbishop of Canterbury, issues clear statement that they cannot support same-sex unions
2003	Archbishop Akinola elected as the President of the Christian Association of Nigeria (CAN)
2003	Jeffrey John proposed as the bishop of Reading while living in openly-gay relationship
2003	Worldwide Anglican Mainstream Leaders meet in Fairfax, Vancouver
2003	Archbishop Akinola chairs meeting at Truro Church; warning given to the Episcopal Church regarding the proposed election of openly gay Gene Robinson as bishop
2003	Jeffrey John's consideration as bishop withdrawn by Archbishop Rowan Williams after public protests
2003	American Episcopal Church's General Convention supports election of Gene Robinson as bishop and passes resolution C051 on same-sex blessings
2003	Archbishop Akinola becomes Chairman, Council of Anglican Provinces in Africa (CAPA)
2003	Archbishop Rowan Williams calls special primates' meeting over election of Gene Robinson; facing opposition from other primates, American Presiding Bishop Frank Griswold remains intransigent; pastoral statement issued condemning the church's action and calling for "adequate provision for Episcopal oversight" for those dissenting from the Episcopal Church's action
2003	Despite all pressures and persuasions, Gene Robinson consecrated as the Bishop of New Hampshire

2003	Archbishop Akinola on behalf of Global South issues strongly-worded statement declaring "impaired communion" with ECUSA
2003	Archbishop Akinola receives one of Nigeria's national honors, the Commander of the Order of the Niger (CON)
2004	Anglican Communion Network (ACN) launched in the USA as a network for confessing dioceses and congregations
2004	Archbishop Rowan Williams convenes Lambeth Commission chaired by Archbishop Robin Eames
2004	Archbishop Akinola in Atlanta, Georgia, in relation to the plight of Nigerian congregations in the USA
2004	Archbishop Akinola arranges extensive tour of Nigeria for Canon Minns and wife
2004	Archbishop Akinola presides over meeting of the Global South Primates; statement issued concerning the work of the Lambeth Commission
2004	Former Canterbury Archbishop Carey conducts confirmation at Truro Church
2004	Lambeth Commission releases its *Windsor Report*, which reaffirmed Lambeth 1.10 and the authority of Scripture as central to the Anglican common life; also called for moratorium on same-sex blessing as well as the election and consent of any bishop candidate living in same-sex union
2004	First African Anglican Bishops Conference meets in Lagos, Nigeria
2005	Archbishop Akinola presides over meeting of the GS/CAPA Primates in Nairobi; both groups issue statements commending the work of Archbishop Eames and the Windsor Report
2005	Archbishop Akinola writes to Archbishop Williams on behalf of the 14 primates in anticipation of the Dromantine meeting, raising issues about the continued intransigence of the American and Canadian churches
2005	Anglican Primates from all over the world in Dromantine to consider the Windsor Report; ask America and Canada to withdraw their representatives from the ACC till 2008; also asked ACC to give "hearing" to two churches at its June 2008 meeting to know the "thinking behind their recent actions"
2005	American Episcopal Church replies to Communion leaders; insists they will send their delegation to the ACC June meeting for observation instead of official participation

2005   Archbishop Akinola writes to House of Bishops of Church of Nigeria in response to statement from the American House of Bishops on proposed Anglican Covenant

2005   The ACC, with 13, meets in Nottingham, England; Lambeth Resolution 1.10 on human sexuality upheld; endorses the decision of primates asking America and Canada to withdraw representatives until 2008 Lambeth Conference

2005   Archbishop Akinola issues statement denouncing the Church of England's House of Bishops' acceptance of civil partnerships; insists it contravenes extant Anglican Church position

2005   Church of Nigeria synod votes to amend its constitution; redefines its relationship in the Communion around shared faith rather than allegiance to the see of Canterbury

2005   Third Anglican South-to-South Encounter held in Egypt; calls for common "Anglican Covenant" among churches remaining true to biblical Christianity and historic Anglicanism

2005   Anglican Communion Network holds *"Hope and Future Conference"* at Pittsburgh

2005   Archbishop Akinola signs Concordat with Reformed Episcopal Church

2006   Archbishop Akinola at Singapore for the installation of Archbishop John Chew as the South East Asia Primate; presides over meeting of Global South and formation of GS Primates Steering Committee

2006   Archbishop Akinola in Nairobi presides over meeting of the CAPA Primates; meeting re-emphasises seriousness of the crisis within the Communion; again asks American Episcopal Church to repent and comply with the Windsor Report.

2006   American Church changes its name from the Episcopal Church in the United States of America (ECUSA) to The Episcopal Church (TEC); approves resolution A167 that "pledged inclusion of openly homosexual persons on every committee, commission or task force dealing with sexuality issues"

2006   Bishop Katharine Jefferts Schori elected as Presiding Bishop of TEC

2006   Archbishop Akinola presided over the meeting of CAPA Primates in Kampala, Uganda. The meeting issued the statement on increasing influence of Islam in Europe

2006   Election and consecration of Canon Martyn Minns as Bishop by the Church of Nigeria House of Bishops

2006   Archbishop Akinola presides over Global South Primates in Kigali, Rwanda; communique asserts "that the time has come to take initial steps towards the formation of a separate ecclesiastical structure of the Anglican Communion in USA"; receives report, "The Road to Lambeth"

2006   Archbishop Akinola meets in Northern Virginia with US Diocese seeking "Alternative Primatial Oversight"

2006   Eight Virginia parishes vote to depart TEC and affiliate with Convocation of Anglicans in North America (CANA)

2007   Archbishop Akinola writes to Archbishop Rowan Williams on the Primates Meeting coming up in Dar es Salam, raising serious questions about the meeting

2007   Archbishop Akinola writes to Global South Primates Steering Committee about plans for "separate ecclesiastical structure of the Anglican Communion in the USA"

2007   Archbishop Akinola presides over Global South and CAPA Primates meeting in Dar es Salam before global Anglican Primates Meeting; both meetings express serious worry about dilemma facing the Communion

2007   Anglican Primates worldwide in Dar es Salam; meeting highly contentious; Archbishop Akinola refuses to sign communique until rewritten; some fellow primates entreat him to sign, and he does eventually; guards protect the primates from gay groups; Archbishop Williams challenges Akinola with the question of "Who blinks first?"; assembly calls on TEC House of Bishops "to make an unequivocal common covenant" that they will not authorize rites of blessing for same-sex unions and shall not confirm "a candidate for Episcopal orders living in a same-sex union"; September 30, 2007, set for the American HOB to reply; Primates called to establish a five-member "pastoral council" to work with TEC to set up this structure and recommend course of action should TEC fail to comply; group also asks TEC and congregations involved in property disputes to suspend lawsuits

2007   Archbishop Akinola presides over installation of Martyn Minns as missionary bishop of CANA in Woodbridge, Virginia

2007   Lambeth unilaterally announces denial of some bishops' invitations to 2008 Lambeth Conference

2007   TEC Bishops respond to primates' communique in Dar es Salam; response doesn't provide categorical statement on the expected moratorium on same-sex blessings and election of homosexual bishops; at the same time,

HOB rejects the Primates' Pastoral Scheme and calls for participation of Gene Robinson, who was being excluded from the Lambeth Conference

2007   Archbishop Rowan Williams visits America along with members of the Joint Standing Committee and the ACC.

2007   Joint Standing Committee of the Primates and ACC declares that American Episcopal Church has "cleared all outstanding questions" and has "given the necessary assurance sought of them"; minority group issues a counter-statement describing American church's response as a "superficial shift" rather than a change in the position taken in 2003

2007   Archbishop Akinola releases "A Most Agonizing Journey," a paper on the crisis in the Communion and fruitless efforts at resolving it

2007   Archbishop Akinola's tenure as CAPA chairman ends; group elects new chairman, the Most Rev. Ian Ernest, bishop of Mauritius and archbishop of Indian Ocean

2007   Archbishop Akinola presides over Global South Primates in Shanghai, China; communique asserts that what's at stake in crisis is the very nature of Anglicanism; primates "reject the religion of accommodation and cultural conformity"

2007   Archbishop Akinola calls meeting of Global South leaders in Nairobi, Kenya; leaders decide to hold the Global Anglican Future Conference (GAFCON) in Jerusalem in 2008

2007   Archbishops Akinola and Rowan Williams have private, one-on-one meeting at insistence of the Anglican Church leader in Holiday Inn near Heathrow Airport, London

2008   Church of Nigeria House of Bishops issues strongly-worded communique on the forthcoming Lambeth Conference after retreat at Ibru Retreat Centre at Agbhara-Otor

2008   Archbishop Akinola presides over Global South Primates meeting; differences of opinion reconciled; no bar for those wishing to attend both GAFCON and Lambeth

2008   Church of Nigeria meets in Nnewi, Anambra State, Nigeria, and expresses strong support for GAFCON

2008   Archbishop Akinola denied entry into Jordan for GAFCON's pre-conference summit

2008   First GAFCON convenes; biblically-orthodox Anglicans numbering 1,184, from 19 provinces, congregate in Jerusalem; pass the "Jerusalem Declaration" and form Fellowship of Confessing Anglicans (FCA);

Primates Council consisting of seven primates established and call made for the formation and recognition of new North American province for members of the Common Cause Partnership

2008   Lambeth Conference organized at University of Kent; gay groups hold party outside and within the venue; more than 200 bishops boycott conference; conference adopts "Indaba" style, producing no resolutions or decisions

2008   Windsor Continuation Group calls for continued moratoria on same-sex blessings, election of non-celibate homosexuals, and cross-boundary interventions; recommends Faith and Order Commission to serve as Fifth Instrument of Communion

2008   First meeting of GAFCON Primates' Council, held at Marriot Hotel, Heathrow, London; GAFCON was reviewed and plans made for future

2008   Anglican Church in North America (ACNA) established under the leadership of Bishop Bob Duncan

2009   Church of Nigeria House of Bishops again issues statement giving strong support to GAFCON

2009   Global Anglican Communion Primates meet in Alexandria, Egypt; reaffirm Lambeth 1.10; ask for restraint on all three moratoria called for in Windsor Report; call for a professionally-mediated conversation to resolve disagreement in North America; affirm plan for Pastoral Council and Pastoral Visitors; request ACNA to neither "recruit" nor "proselytize" to expand membership

2009   Church of Nigeria Standing Committee meets at Ile-Ife, Osun State, Nigeria; welcomes Bishop Bob Duncan and declares full communion with nascent North American province.

2009   Archbishop Akinola presides over GAFCON/FCA Primates Council in London; group gives full recognition to ACNA

2009   ACNA holds its first Provincial Assembly in Bedford, Texas, USA, to mark official launch

2009   General Convention of the TEC held in Anaheim, California

2009   GAFCON Primates Council meets at Renaissance Hotel, Heathrow

2009   Archbishop Akinola takes part in the signing of Manhattan Declaration

2009   Archbishop Akinola in Singapore for Global South Steering Committee meeting

2009   Awarded LL.D [Honoris Causa] by Ajay Crowther University and installed as the first Chancellor of the University

2009   Inducted into the Ogun State Hall of Fame, first Christian leader whether from the state or outside it to be given such an honor

2010   Global South Primates Steering Committee meets in Nairobi, Kenya

2010   Archbishop Akinola presides over the GAFCON Primates Council in Bermuda

2010   Global South Fourth Encounter held in Singapore and 4th Trumpet issued

2010   Second All Africa Bishops Conference takes place in Entebbe, Uganda

2010   Archbishop Akinola retires as Primate of Church of Nigeria

2010   Archbishop Nicholas Okoh installed as the Primate of Church of Nigeria

2010   Archbishop Akinola returns home to hero's welcome in Abeokuta

2010   Establishes Peter Akinola Foundation (PAF)

2012   First set of trainees at PAF's Centre of Youth Industrial Training graduates

2013   Archbishop Akinola abducted in Abeokuta at gunpoint and released later that day without payment of any ransom

2014   Celebrates silver jubilee anniversary in ministry

2015   Archbishop Akinola's mother Janet Amoke Akinola dies at age 100 and is buried on December 18, 2015, in Abeokuta.

Introduction

The Rise of Faithless and Godless Society

At no time in human history can man ever hope to conquer God. Thousands of human armies, no matter how sophisticated, can never wage a successful war against the tiniest finger of the Almighty. God is immutable and unconquerable, the author of divine law. Yet, man in total illusion, speaking foolishness, will not abandon his dream of conquering the Omniscient. The conceited human nature continues to blind humanity to the mercy of God and often sees it as a weakness of the Divine. This is notwithstanding reminders of the repercussions of man's iniquities in history. The lessons have been forcefully taught over the millennia of human existence. Nations have arisen and collapsed. Vibrant empires of yesterday have gone into ruins, lost to history. Numberless inventions were recorded as challenges were overcome. But immortality remains the exclusive preserve of God. God is the only being with no comparison. He has no competitor or rival. He can neither be cloned nor photocopied. He is immortal, invincible, and indivisible; the omnipotent, singularly Omni-divine and omnipresent Lord with no earthly comparison. Man's ingenious adventures might have led to the conquest of space and travel to the moon, but human effort has failed to bring man to near equal status with God.

Man's existence is marked by endless folly. The struggle of faithlessness and godlessness has been ceaseless and endemic both in the individual life and in the society that humans have created for themselves. Of historical significance was the Lutheran Reformation that was the touchstone of freedom in Europe. From that fresh burst of opportunity was birthed the era of Enlightenment. The ultimate effect was the replacement of traditional Christian orthodoxy with secular philosophy. Critical thinking and rational philosophical thought gained ascendancy. The free reign of ideas culminated in massive injury to people's faith in God. No longer hallowed was the authority of the Holy Bible. The Scripture's significance as the bedrock of ordered private life and the guardian of collective public life in societies and nations suffered massive erosion.

Departure from the pristine biblical standard opened the way to the age of atheistic communism and secularism and their variant forms. The Word and fear of God began taking flight from families, communities, schools, governments, and societies in general. Humanity began losing its soul to the extent that the Christian faith and church attendance were being mortgaged. What the Holy Book commanded became merely a matter of personal preference on the part of individuals. This was followed by profound indulgence in epicurean lifestyles, with people's priorities and values shifting dramatically. Religious fervor was seriously eroded and corroded, and materialism was on the upswing. Instead of emphasizing godly and righteous existence, society embraced a decadent celebration of mundane and sensual pleasures. New gods like sports, entertainment, and the wayward indulgence of homosexuality took over. Nations founded upon Christian traditions witnessed a gradual and systematic compromising of their Christian identities and heritage. Not only was there open demonstration of faithlessness and godlessness; the Church itself had an internal fight on its hands as many believers found the Christian lifestyle abhorrent and old fashioned.

Sin is blind to color and race, but Satan was targeting Western society in particular. The agent of darkness, having been given an inch of space to tempt modern man like he did Eve and Adam, is now in the full trot. Satanic forces are leaping in every direction and attacking the foundation of the Church. A major casualty of the satanic attack has been theological education. Theology is the heart of religion; it gives meaning to the belief and practice of the religion, including what it worships. A religion that has had its theology corrupted loses its soul. This is one of the tragedies befalling Christianity because of the West's consuming obsession to pervert the undiluted Word of God.

It is beyond ordinary mischief when theological seminaries and university departments for theological studies begin to subvert and replace orthodox doctrines meant to serve as ingredients for the spiritual formation of clergy. Serious and unpardonable transgressions arise when teachers seek to break down biblical fundamentals and aim at rewriting the Scripture. Nothing endangers Christianity more than this devilish perversion. Seminarians and postulants, who genuinely and eagerly want to train for God's service and go to seminaries full of faith for evangelism and missions, become victims with no faith at all in God, due to evil indoctrination. The corruption leads them to not believe in the inspiration and authority of the Holy Bible, makes them doubt core doctrines relating to Heaven and Hell, and subjects them to a poor account of biblical ethics. The clergy resulting from such an obnoxious system will only pollute and destroy the Church.

The rise of faithless and godless society is not a fairytale or fiction. That age and time is here. Agents and disciples of Satan (camouflaging as angels of light) rose in ranks and took over church leadership. They are entrenched in powerful places and positions in important countries around the world. The battle that has emerged, accordingly, is one between the Kingdom of God and the Kingdom of Satan. And man's rescue will come only from uncompromising faith and complete submission to renewal and the restoration of godliness. Pretentious claims to the light of knowledge that has cast no illumination on human miseries are dishonest. The struggle is for reclamation of the lost possession—faith—with which the church would surely make a comeback. Sad to say, humanity is still chasing the wild goose of continuing in the perfidious direction it has been heading. False piety, like pews in the churches, has continued to speak the same language—emptiness and nothingness. Churches have been going up for sale, and, where there is still a measure of worship, materialism has overtaken spirituality. The demography of every country in Europe and of the United States of America continues to show that they have become post-Christian nations. Today, these societies, once preserved by Christian values and ethics, have almost yielded to the yoke of occultism, the glorification of Satan worship, atheism, and the insurgence of immigrant Islam.

The worse development was the descent to a form of sinful behavior which the Bible has proscribed explicitly—homosexuality. Under the ideology of progress, society and the Church are being driven towards embracing what God and Bible have unequivocally proclaimed as a sin. Unfortunately, the Anglican Communion has allowed itself to be dragged into the debauchery, making the Church the center of this embarrassing crisis. No reason justifies why the Anglican Communion should be bedevilled by this scandalous catastrophe. Homosexuality and same-sex marriage ought not to have been contemplated in the first place by the Church. The Church's existence had been based on genuine and unadulterated Christianity. Regrettably, the so-called agents of the Church are among those promoting this sinful act! Ichabod! It is religious debauchery at its worst, this unimaginable and unashamed celebration of an abomination. Even the least-informed on Holy Scriptures know that God judged Sodom and Gomorrah on this sinful act as far back as Abraham's patriarchal era. Driving the Church towards homosexuality is, therefore, mortgaging her glory and making worshipers depart from such an unholy environment. Quite evidently, leaders and churches on this dangerous path suffer from amnesia, the loss of a sense of history. They are denying their connection with God and the Almighty's authority based on the Holy Scripture. The repercussions are obvious—spiritual euthanasia.

The supremacy of God assures that in history, good will ultimately triumph over evil. The wisdom of Satan never amounts to more than the futility of wiles, intrigues, and machinations. Each clash with God's divine will results in a resounding failure. Satan lacks the overcoming power of God's salvific program in human affairs. God, at times, uses surprising tools against Satan's folly (the way Elijah arose against the false prophets of Baal upon Mount Carmel), lifting up advocates to champion the cause of righteousness. And the African church is playing such a role. God has used them to defend the faith and renew hope for the Church's survival under serious threat and persecution. And he has used bold and courageous leaders to accomplish this, none more effectual than the Most Rev. Dr. Peter Jasper Akinola, the Nigerian archbishop and primate.

The Most Rev. Akinola was not the activist type. He was born on January 27, 1944, in Abeokuta, Ogun state, in Southwest Nigeria. Four years later, he lost his father, who was the breadwinner of the family. Life became a series of daunting survival struggles with his mother, the single parent and sole provider. Akinola's education suffered as a result. He went where the family's little resources could take him and not toward opportunities befitting someone of his ability and intellect. He was a sharp-witted and intelligent young man. After his secondary education, Akinola took to carpentry and furniture making. Leaving home at the age 15, he practised the trade in Nguru, a town in the far northeastern part of Nigeria. Modest and humble success attended his efforts. He was rising in his business when the elders of his church in Nguru nominated him for a catechist course. After initially declining it, he eventually accepted the offer.

From that initial step, which he took in 1974, emerged a reverend in 1978. He attended the American Virginia Theological Seminary in 1979 for his post-graduate study. And then, back home, Akinola was saddled with the responsibility of establishing the Church of Nigeria's presence in Abuja, Nigeria's new federal capital city. In 1983, the Kaduna Diocese made him a canon. Singlehandedly, he built Abuja into a diocese and was consecrated as its first bishop in 1989. Ten years later, in 1999, he succeeded The Most Rev. Abiodun Adetiloye as the third archbishop and primate of the Church of Nigeria.

Nationally and internationally, little was known about him when he emerged as the leader of Anglicans in Nigeria. He was the self-effacing and apolitical type. As a result, people tended to underrate him. As previously stated, God is always ahead of Satan in the latter's machinations. So it was no accident that, at that time, somebody of the nature and character of Archbishop Akinola was elected to lead the most populous church in the Anglican Communion. By the same Omnipotent's design, he was called upon to lead all Anglicans from outside Europe and America. That honor was bestowed on him as the elected chairperson of the Conference of Anglican Provinces in Africa (CAPA). Through all of this, Akinola employed no guile or subterfuge. He inherited the noble legacy left by his predecessor, The Most Rev. Abiodun Adetiloye, who had also held all of these positions.

For the discerning, it will be understandable why, at that point in history, God decided to thrust into international church leadership this relatively unknown Nigerian. His leadership began when the Anglican Communion was under ferocious attack by forces of homosexuality determined to overrun the Church. He had not fought international battles before. Neither did he have resources to match the mighty war chest of the West. God seemed, however, to have chosen Akinola, to have raised him as a prophetic voice to galvanize, prepare, and lead confessing Anglicans to take the Lord's side against the forces hell bent on thwarting the Gospel and bringing God to shame. The battle was daunting. But God made Akinola a strong leader. The war was vile, foul, and ferocious. God accordingly strengthened Akinola to be bold, undaunted, and indomitable. The contending forces dared him, asking, "Who blinks first?" Would it be them—the well-heeled and better-positioned homosexual movements and their collaborators in the Anglican Church—or him, the unknown, poor church leader from Nigeria? "Who blinks first?" Arrogant as it sounded, the question was asked with a confident conviction that Akinola was no match for his powerful opponents. Did Akinola blink in the end? This is the story. It is told here honestly and authentically, to set the record straight on how the gay crisis that rocked the Anglican Communion was fought.

1

The Start of Rumblings in the House

Canada, 2002

In 2002, Archbishop Peter Akinola was in his second year as head of the Church of Nigeria. His cup was overflowing. Confronting his nascent administration was how to give the church a focused direction. Shortly after his inauguration, he had convened a meeting of church leaders from all over Nigeria to develop a vision for the church. The conference had ended with the emergence and approval of a blueprint entitled the "Church of Nigeria Vision Document."[1] So many duties were entrusted to him by the Vision. Coupled with the allocated duties was his work as the see of Abuja, along with the added responsibility of an archbishop. Akinola had many demanding tasks tugging at his sleeve. Yet, amid the demanding jobs competing for his limited time, he was dragged irresistibly into a global maelstrom.

Akinola had never gone to school on international politics or advocacy. Neither had he engaged in an international cause or campaign. But he had no choice other than to respond to the challenge when it was thrust upon him. He was forced into the crisis that sharply divided the worldwide Anglican Communion, and subsequently turned out to be a major international, politico-religious upheaval. Few incidents have shaken the foundations of the global Church more than this threat to the continued stability of the world's third most populous Christian denomination.

It began with the Anglican Church of Canada (ACC). In 2002, the ACC's Diocese of Westminster took a unilateral step to bless same-sex unions. The diocese was one of the five-finger bishoprics in the Ecclesiastical Province of British Columbia and the Yukon. It had age and history behind it. The diocese, founded in 1879, possessed

---

1. Accounts of establishing the Church of Nigeria's vision are drawn from interviews conducted with the Most Revd. Peter J. Akinola at various times in 2006 and 2007 in Abuja and Abeokuta; an interview with Chief Ernest Sonekan, former head of the interim government, Federal Republic of Nigeria, at his Ikoyi residence in May 2007; "Vision 2010 Report Full Text" (nigeriaworld.com/focus/documents/vision2101.html); and "Visioning Exercise for the Church of Nigeria" (www.anglican-nig.org/Vision.php).

a tradition of electing into its episcopacy priests of traditional hue. Every one of Westminster's bishops, up to that time, had been a full-time priest, their entire career devoted to life in the ministry. Michael Ingham was no exception. He was Westminster's eighth bishop and its episcopal authority at the time. Ingham was ordained at the Anglican Diocese of Ottawa at age of 25. He came into his calling with a cultivated mind grounded in politics, philosophy, and divinity. He studied those disciplines beginning at the University of Edinburgh, where he earned a master's degree, proceeding to Harvard University for postgraduate studies, and ending at the Hebrew University in Jerusalem, where he crystallized his precocity with knowledge of divinity. His acquired learning positioned him at the center of three often-conflicting, concentrically-revolving subjects: politics, philosophy, and religion. Ingham put his fertile mind at work in the field of theology. Some theologians assume they know the inner mind of God; they presume they can reconstruct the hidden meaning of the Word in the Scripture. Ingham had a proud membership card from that school of religious eggheads. Additionally, he had bosses favorably disposed to his idealism.

Ingham began his pastoral call working in parishes of the Diocese of Ottawa, where he was ordained. Thereafter, he moved to the Diocese of Westminster. From Westminster, he became the principal secretary to Michael Peers, the then-primate of Anglican Church of Canada. Peers himself was an atypical church leader. His initial inclination was for work as a diplomat rather than as a minister of God. Brought up with no background in religious nurturing, Peers moved to God's work through self-will. He was a gifted man. Languages come naturally to him; he had a flair for them, an aptitude enhanced by study at the University of British Columbia, where he received a diploma in translation in 1957. Fluent in five languages—English, French, Spanish, German, and Russian—he seemed perfectly poised for diplomatic career, which would have been a handsome reward for his natural gifts. But Peers opted for God's work. In return, God rewarded him. Two years into his fifties, and twenty-three years after re-ordering his career path into the priesthood, which he began as a curate at the Holy Trinity Church, Ottawa, he assumed leadership of the Anglican Church of Canada. He became its primate in 1986. That same year, Peers made Michael Ingham his principal secretary.

They apparently held similar worldviews; their chemistry was in accord, as was their disposition toward the Anglican practice they'd inherited. Ingham was like a loaded gun waiting to fire, and Peers was willing to indulge his protégé.

Hardly had Ingham settled in his new position in 1986 when he authored a book, *Rites for a New Age: Understanding the Book of Alternative Services.* The book ignited controversy, sparking protest within a portion of the Anglican community in the ACC, most notably the Prayer Book Society of Canada. Ingham's book was promoted as a supplement to the *Book of Common Prayer,* the venerable liturgy of the worldwide Anglican Communion, but *Rites for a New Age* was a perfidious betrayal, out to annul the historic liturgical book. The Prayer Book Society of Canada (PBSC) therefore launched a spirited fight to see the displeasing publication thrown away before it could contaminate their cherished Christian heritage.

The matter was brought before the ecclesiastical court of the church. Unfortunately, the battle was not against Ingham but against Peers, and, regrettably, he had the weapons to fight back. As acting primate, he decided to preside over the ecclesiastical court that tried the matter. In a secular judicial system, this would have been deemed inappropriate. It would have contravened one of the essential principles of justice, not allowing the accused to serve as judge in his own case, and the PBSC failed to get a fair hearing. The case kept bouncing against a brick wall as the ecclesiastical court ensured the PBSC was unsuccessful. Peers, however, was not the only one to blame for spreading indulgent acts and toxic ideas within the ACC. He had only pushed his feet deeper in the shoes left behind by his predecessor, Archbishop Ted Scott.

Edward Walter Scott contrasted sharply with Michael Peers. Scott did not have an irreligious background like Peers. Indeed, he was draped in the shawl of Christianity from birth. His father was a rector in Vancouver, British Columbia, Scott's birthplace, where he spent his childhood. Scott simply followed his father's vocation, entering the priesthood in 1949 at age 23. This followed his acquisition of theological education from the Anglican Theological College.

The young Scott was destined to attain clerical heights greater than his father did. Two decades after beginning his ministry, he became a bishop. After five years in the episcopacy, he rose further, arriving at the peak of the ecclesiastical offices in the ACC, the position of primate, which he occupied for 15 years (1971–1986). His service brought him national and international attention within the ecumenical fold, on the stage of international politics, and in the worldwide Anglican Communion. He became a leading light in the World Council of Churches, serving as moderator of the organization's Central Committee.

The 1980s saw unprecedented, worldwide condemnation of the apartheid regime in South Africa. In this context, Scott was appointed a member of the "Eminent Persons" constituted by the Commonwealth (the association of former colonies of Britain) to look at ways to make the obnoxious, South African regime respect worldwide opinion. Scott lent his voice to imposing sanctions on the apartheid government, and the group concurred.

Within the worldwide Anglican Communion, he was also an advocate for the ordination of women. The subject made its first noticeable entry into the agenda of the decennial gathering of worldwide Anglican bishops in 1948 and reappeared five times at the Lambeth Conference before a resolution in 1988 affirmed the "legal right of each Church to make its final decision about women priests." A prudent leader, Scott knew the limit of idealism. He acted in a measured fashion as the larger worldwide Anglican Communion considered female ordination.

His leadership of the ACC resulted in neither polarization of the church nor international offense. Yet, his period as the church's helmsman did coincide with a time of a serious shift in the ethical mores of Canadian society. Until the late 1960s, Canada did not permit homosexuality. Rather, it counted the practice as a serious sexual offence punishable by indefinite imprisonment. By 1969, Canada's parliament effected a change in the legislation. Homosexuality ceased to be a criminal offence. Two years later, the slate was wiped clean. The last convicted homosexual criminal was released from prison. It was the same year as Scott's inauguration as the primate of the ACC, the third largest church in Canada, surpassed only by the Roman Catholic Church and the United Church of Canada. The ACC was no mere footnote in the emergence of Canada as a sovereign country. Initially, the church was known as the "Church of England in Canada." From funding to appointment of bishops to supply of priests, the Church of England met all the needs of the infant church. Beginning in 1893, the church began the process of establishing its autonomy. The first change of its name was in 1955. It continued the progression until 1989, when it formally adopted its present name—the Anglican Church of Canada. The Canadian Anglican church had a sort of osmotic relationship with its sister church in the United States, with deep historical connections between the two North American churches. Indeed, the American Revolution caused a split in what was formerly known as the Church of England in North America.

A consequence was that a large percentage of the US emigrants to Canada after the Revolution were Anglicans. One of them was Charles Inglis, the rector of Trinity Church in New York. Inglis and Samuel Seabury, the first Anglican bishop in North America, were close allies. They knew each other well and appreciated each other's work. On two different occasions, March 8 and 21, 1783, both were among eighteen prominent clergy that met in New York to determine the future of Nova Scotia, the Canadian province with the first North American bishop appointed by the Church of England. Inglis was to become the first occupier of that office on August 12, 1787, three years after Seabury had been consecrated bishop by the Scottish Episcopal Church.

Though administratively separated, the Canadian and English Anglican Churches were joined by an umbilical cord, which continued strong in many ways, but not so as to rob the Canadian church of its independent mind. In 1979, for instance, the Canadian House of Bishops decided on the same-sex blessing question, issuing guidelines on the matter and declaring, "We do not accept the blessing of homosexual unions."[2] This was under Ted Scott's leadership. And the position was maintained until his retirement in 1986. Scott could be a "liberal," a "progressive voice," and "an advocate of reforms in the church" (the media's various descriptors of him), yet he refrained from being priggish. He drew the bounds between personal quest and collective stance. He honored and respected the mutual decision on homosexual unions until the end of his tenure.

This was the position of the church that Michael Peers inherited. And, so it was that, in 1992, six years into his administration of the church, Peers was confronted

2. "Global Realignment—A Canadian Chronology," www.anglicannetwork.ca.

with a test of will. He had either to renounce or reaffirm the Canadian bishops' guidelines on homosexuality. An Anglican priest, James Ferry, had been arraigned before a bishop's court for violating the church's stand. He was accused of being in a same-sex relationship. Ferry was found guilty and was sanctioned. His "licence" was revoked and he was "inhibited" from functioning as a priest. Not even a feeble plea was made by Ferry over his predicament. Instead, he abandoned the ACC to join a church accommodating his way of life.

The curious development was that, in 1998, Ferry was back in ACC—partially reinstated!—even though a year earlier, the House of Bishops had reaffirmed its position on the question that warranted Ferry's indictment in the first instance. The 1997 Canadian bishops' pastoral statement had clearly reiterated, "We are not ready to authorize the blessing of relationships between persons of the same sex." A further puzzle was the timing of Ferry's "pardon." It coincided with the Lambeth Conference, the once-in-ten-years gathering of the worldwide Anglican bishops. The 1998 Conference turned out to be one of special significance. This had to do with the pressure building on the Communion to take a decisive stand on the controversial homosexual issue.

At the Conference, opinions among the church leaders were so sharply divided that a vote was necessary. With 749 bishops in attendance, 596 voted on the issue, while 153 abstained or were absent from the session. There was no doubt as to the majority opinion. The vote against homosexuality was massive—526—as against the tiny minority—70—who wanted the Communion to adopt a dramatic change in its teaching and liturgy. The vast voice from the Conference was clear. To every "Yes" vote on homosexuality, eight thundering voices rose against it in a chorus of resounding "No's!" Accordingly, the Communion passed Resolution 1.10, stating that "homosexuality is incompatible with scripture" and that the church "could not advise the legitimising or blessing of same sex unions or ordaining those involved in same gender unions."[3]

Apparently, there was a group within the body of Anglican world leaders who had assumed the assembly could be stampeded into approving their position on the homosexuality question. The vote proved to be an ego-crushing defeat for them. Initially, it seemed they were caught unawares. But, quickly, they recovered. Politics became the game. They conceived an attempt to incite contempt and ill feeling toward their majority colleagues who wanted the Communion to maintain a cautious approach on the issue for the time being.

The Lambeth Conference was scheduled to last from July 18 to August 9, 1998. On Thursday, August 5, four days before the formal closing of the Conference, they rushed a public statement to the media, this despite the fact that the Conference was

3. "Lambeth Conference," https://en.wikipedia.org/wiki/Lambeth_Conference#Fourteenth:_2008; "Section H: Human Sexuality," http://www.anglicancommunion.org/resources/document-library/lambeth-conference/2008/section-h-human-sexuality?author=Lambeth+Conference&year=2008; The Oxford Centre for Mission Studies and The American Anglican Council, (1998) *Lambeth Directory—The Worldwide Anglican Communion 1998.*

yet to conclude its deliberations or draw up its official communique. Claiming responsibility for the rebellious publication was a small renegade group styling itself as "some members of the Lambeth Conference." Dubbed "A Pastoral Letter," the message was specifically directed "To Lesbian and Gay Anglicans." The group declared that three weeks of deliberations on human sexuality at the Conference had shown "enormous diversity" of views. They were however disgruntled regarding the "limitations of this Conference," which had rendered it impossible "to hear adequately [the homosexuals'] voices." Usurping the power of the collective body, they tendentiously intoned, "We apologise for any sense of rejection that has occurred because of this reality."[4]

The intention of the group was clear: "This letter," the group claimed, "is a sign of our commitment to listen to you and reflect with you theologically and spiritually on your lives and ministries." The direction in which they wanted to take their crusade was explicit: "We pledge that we will continue to reflect, pray and work for your full inclusion in the life of the church." They were determined to achieve their aim. Like all propaganda, playing on the emotions of its targets to create the impression of victimhood and oppression, theirs was part of a disingenuous strategy: "You, our sisters and brothers in Christ, deserve a more thorough hearing than you received over the past three weeks."

Evidently, the Lambeth 1998 dissident group was not sending an empty threat. They were serious. By November 24, 1998, a total of 185 bishops had signed on to the letter. Of the 38 primates in the Anglican Communion, nine identified with the scheme. But if figures measure strength, the dissident group was still a tiny minority. Nine out of the Communion's 38 primates, a tiny fraction, was purported to be on their side. The overall figure of 185 bishops, given by the group as being disgruntled with the view of the Communion, even if doubled, would still not have equalled the 526-bishop majority that preferred caution in handling the issue. Paradoxically, the tiny clique was not only vocal and powerful, but also stubbornly determined to subdue the majority. They had pledged, "We will work to make it so."

Two conspicuous names in the group were the Canadian twin Michaels—Michael Peers, the Canadian primate, and Michael Ingham, his protégé and principal secretary. Without doubt, the ACC seemed to have made a turnaround from the 1979 House of Bishops Guidelines and its 1992 stand that had led to the sanctioning of James Ferry. Canada had the third largest number of the bishops signing onto the "Pastoral Statement." Its share of the recalcitrant bishops numbered 17. The USA topped the group with 76, while United Kingdom was in the second place with 42. Evidently, among the three countries—Canada, the United Kingdom, and the United States—were to be found the masterminds behind the plot to subvert the will of the Anglican Communion on the homosexual issue. The three countries collectively

---

4. "A Pastoral Statement to Lesbian and Gay Anglicans from Some Member Bishops of the Lambeth Conference," http:justus.anglican.org/resources/Lambeth1998/pasttment.html.

accounted for the largest chunk of the dissenting bishops, a whopping 135 out of the total of 185, which represented 73 percent of the anti-Lambeth, rebellious group.

Peers didn't get to the list by accident. Based on available evidence, he supported the ordination of gays and lesbians. Perhaps like others pushing the idea, he had thought the 1998 Lambeth Conference could be manipulated in that direction. But their wish had become unattainable in the face of the majority decision. That had not, however, stopped his cultivation of a much closer relationship between the Anglican Church of Canada and the Episcopal Church of the United States. Peers had tangible benefits from the chummy relationship. Courtesy of the American church, he became the president of the Metropolitan Council of Cuba, the council overseeing the epis-copal work of the Protestant Episcopal Church of Cuba, which was once a part of the American church.

This was an outworking of the "Cold War" period in which the relationship be-tween capitalist America and its communist neighbor was at its lowest ebb. In fact, the US government's official policy was to treat Cuba as a "pariah" country denied any form of contact. And that included all forms of interaction—governmental, organiza-tional, business, civil, and even religious. The result was for the Episcopal Church of United States to cede to Peers the control of the Cuban church.

The other Michael—Michael Ingham—Peers' principal secretary, had also moved up in status and position. After six years of working with Peers, he returned, in 1992, to pastoral care and parish work, back to Vancouver as the rector of the Christ Church Cathedral as well as dean of New Westminster. Two years later, at age 45, Ingham was elected the bishop of New Westminster, a historic diocese dating back to 1879, with 67 parishes, 68 active congregations, and membership plateaued at a relatively low 18,000.

Over the years, Westminster had acquired a reputation for ecclesiastical revo-lutionary activism. Supporters lauded the diocese's ability to be at the forefront of progressive causes in the Anglican Communion, irrespective of whether it affronted Anglican teaching or not. Under the diocese's sixth bishop, the image of ultra-radical-ism persisted.

The Most Rev. Thomas David Somerville was a harbinger of ground-breaking change. He was one of the first Canadian bishops to ordain women. Indeed, he led the revolt that gave the Anglican Church in Canada its first-ever female priests. And he had every reason to feel triumphant when on November 30, 1976, he ordained the first set, including Elspeth Alley, a friend he had made a deacon in 1972. He assured her of more. He promised to "make her a full priest as soon as he could." In fulfilling his pledge, he helped her enter the Anglican Theological College. Somerville's muscle could buy his ward a space in the theological school but not the warm affection of her fellow students. Alley was derided, and he was humiliated often with verbal abuse. It was not a time when women were welcomed in the clergy. Alley felt unwanted and insecure, which dismayed Somerville. Somehow, the experience rekindled the agony of his troubled childhood.

Somerville had become a partial orphan when he was two years old. He lost his father, a police officer, to a flu epidemic. He grew under the care of his mother, Martha, who immigrated with the young Somerville to England. There, the toddler was jolted by the heartlessness of his young peers. He loved going to the Sunday school, but the other children often shunned him, refusing to allow him to play with them. He toughed it out with a show of confidence, and he grew strong. But the experience left a psychological mark on him.

Later, there was the matter of career. Initially, he had wanted to be a doctor, but, instead, he became a priest, inspired by a local priest's ministry to the poor and sick. Indeed, the medical and clerical vocations both serve the poor and the sick. Both save life also—the former physically and the latter spiritually—while the latter is more amenable to social causes. Somerville's humanist ideals seemed incompatible with the quietness of the life of a doctor imprisoned in a consulting room. Surgical rooms were also not forums or platforms for advancing revolutionary ideas. He loved causes and desired to change the world, perhaps, to compensate for his unforgettable childhood experiences.

The priesthood offered a suitable platform. It fit his nature and purpose. Orthodoxy does not typically belong to crusaders. Conformism, thus, was not one of Somerville's cultivated virtues. He abhorred traditional values, and by extension toed the line. He was not a man inclined to abide by the rules.

Somerville promised to make Elspeth Alley a full priest as soon as he could, and four years later, he delivered on his vow. He employed every means to push the idea through within the ACC, and he won. The General Synod with its processes was manipulated. The end ultimately justified the means. Somerville faced antagonism, but he silenced the opposition. "Having come so far and worked so hard," as he reportedly said years later, "I was determined to proceed."[5] In every other area where he held strong convictions, he railroaded his decisions as he wished. For instance, he granted children the right to Eucharist, the freedom to be served bread and wine during the Holy Communion. Unorthodox and unconventional as the idea was, he ensured that it passed.

Before his retirement in 1980, he opened the church to overtly gay men and women. Nothing seemed wrong about it to him. He defended the decision by arguing that the Canadian House of Bishops' 1979 guidelines only forbade the "blessing of homosexual unions." Somerville became one of the most influential and powerful church leaders in Canada. He was the dictionary and thesaurus of his calling, interpreting canons and doctrines as he deemed fit. As the metropolitan archbishop of the Ecclesiastical Province of British Columbia and the Yukon, which he became in 1975, he had had the leeway to do as he pleased. His style was that of dominating episcopal power and authority in the Diocese of New Westminster.

---

5. Carriere, "Archbishop, Agent of Change," www.bullzip,com.

His successor, Douglas William Hambidge, was to bring a more calming influ-ence to the diocese with a sort of measured and mature headship. During his tenure (1980 to 1993), Westminster neither fought battles locally nor championed offensive causes internationally. Hambidge shepherded the flock with humble integrity.

Hambidge was more or less an outsider. He was "translated," that is, transferred from somewhere else to the Westminster. He was the seventh bishop in the line of succession at the Caledonia diocese, from whence he came, and had the unique honor of also being the seventh bishop of Westminster. Both Caledonia and West-minster dioceses were part of the Ecclesiastical Province of British Columbia and the Yukon. Hambidge's episcopacy in Caledonia lasted eleven years, from 1969 to 1980, and he left with a reputation for being a man committed to ensuring the wider spread of the gospel.

Born in London on March 6, 1927, educated at London University, and ordained at 23, Hambidge took to missionary work with a sizzling passion. He became something of a missionary cult hero among one of Canada's minority groups, the Nisga'a Nation. Hambidge was revered for his work in the community. The Nisga'a First Nation, as the group was called, numbered about 6,000. Their language, known by the same name of Nisga'a (formerly spelled Nishga), was on its way to extinction, with only about 700 native speakers. Yet, the autochthonous population, situated in northwestern British Columbia near the Nass River, had had long, close ties with the Anglican Church. As far back as 1890, *A Nishga Version of Portions of the Book of Common Prayer* had been published. It owed its origin to the pioneering work of James Benjamin McCullagh, the Nisga'a's earliest missionary. The publication combined liturgical material as well as hymns. If McCullagh had the honor of being the pioneer of this worthy missionary adventure, Hambidge had the credit of sustaining and consolidating the noble past.

Hambidge's episcopacy at Westminster didn't seem to be eventful. If it had any remarkable aspect, he seemed willing to downplay it. Yet, for 13 years, he served as metropolitan of the Ecclesiastical Province of British Columbia and the Yukon, with a concurrence as the bishop of the Westminster diocese, the so-called center of pro-gressive causes in the Anglican Communion. It was something of a surprise when Hambidge resigned in 1993. From a position that could be said to be plum, he went on to take the less prestigious office of principal at the Saint Mark's Theological Col-lege—not in any of the American or European capitals but tucked away in the African city of Dar es Salaam in Tanzania. He dropped everything, including high-sounding names, titles, and designations. He chose to work simply and in a challenging environ-ment with the unassuming title of assistant bishop, determined to bring his wealth of experience to the training of a new generation of African priests.

It was into the shoes of this mission enthusiast that Michael Ingham stepped in 1994. Was Ingham's election deliberate? Was it coincidental? One fact is clear: Be-fore his arrival at Westminster, Ingham was no stranger to controversy. His publica-tion, *Rites for a New Age,* had provoked a serious uproar. It had taken the authority of Archbishop Michael Peers to stave off the controversy. He was also conspicuous among the 185 bishops at the 1998 Lambeth Conference for this advocacy of the full inclusion of gays and lesbians in the life of the Communion. Returning to Westminster from the Lambeth Conference, Ingham's initial preoccupation seemed to be with sundry concerns, including the promotion of inter-faith dialogue. He was immersed in the subject, culminating in his second book, *Mansions of the Spirit.* Luckily, he made no tongues to wag by his literary effort. The unavoidable question was whether Ingham was deliberately playing for time. Was he waiting for an auspicious opportunity to raise more dust? It seems the answer was yes, as unfolding events would demonstrate in 2002. This was a new century, with a big alteration in the power configuration within the Anglican Communion.

The archbishop of Canterbury, the Most Rev. George Carey, who had stymied the pro-homosexual element within the Communion at the 1998 Lambeth Conference, was on his way out. It was at this critical period of succession in the Anglican Communion that Ingham delivered his blow below the belt, catching everyone off guard.

On June 2002, unilaterally, with the pretext that his diocese had autonomy and that his synod had so approved, he evoked his power as the bishop to authorize formal blessing of same-sex unions. Ingham knew he had transgressed against the 1998 Lambeth Resolution that had, without any ambiguity, forbidden such an action. Nowhere else in the entire Anglican Communion had the step been taken. It was an act of brazen contempt. Within the Canadian Anglican Church community, there were gasps. Internationally, Church leaders expressed shock. All over, within and outside the Communion, there was general consternation. Anglican leaders, particularly from the Global South, found bewildering the humongous leg of an elephant that Ingham had scornfully jammed into the room! The rumblings in the house that accompanied this aberration were serious.

2

Trumpet from the South

Kuala Lumpur, 1997

The Global South, as the group was called within the Anglican Communion, was conceived as a forum to bring together Anglican leaders from the southern hemisphere to meet, relate, share ideas, and develop strategies for meeting issues of common concern in the mission and general life of the Church. The idea dates back to 1986 when, at the meeting of the Anglican Mission Agencies' Conference in Brisbane, Australia, Anglican leaders from the South decided to establish the platform. Yet ideas, no matter how progressive, remain only dreams until birthed successfully, and the Global South lacked a dynamic vision and focus. So, for almost a decade, nothing concrete happened with the organization.

Then, in 1994, the first meeting of The Anglican Encounter in the South was convened in Limuru, Nairobi, Kenya, where, 23 years earlier, the Anglican Consultative Council (ACC) was born. The ACC was one of the four governing instruments of the Communion. It usually brings together the clergy and laity from all over the world to make decisions on issues affecting the Church. For the inaugural meeting of the Global South, 72 delegates, males and females, bishops and other priests, as well as members of the laity from 23 provinces of the Church, had come together, representing 22 nations in the Global South.[1] Either as a matter of prophetic irony or a development of historical coincidence, the Nigerian archbishop and primate, The Most Rev. Abiodun Adetiloye, played not only a prominent role in the birth of the organization but also emerged as one of its leading figures. He was selected as chairman of the group as well as the keynote speaker at the inaugural meeting. Adetiloye was an unwavering disciple of the Scripture. He was also a leader committed to church planting, evangelism, and expansion of the Christian faith to unreached places. The first Anglican Encounter in the South was held under the theme, "Maturity: Its Challenges and Responsibilities."

---

1. Taiwo, *Joseph Abiodun Adetiloye.*

Adetiloye shook his colleagues to reality with an address that was both incisive and instructive in opening the summit. He reflected on the past and inspired a new future course that he felt the Global South should take: "The first responsibility we must take on and which, thankfully, is built into the theme of our consultation is the challenge to take on the mantle of leadership and mission in our context."[2] He felt that in a world where values and virtues were undergoing challenge by "socio-political antagonisms," with identities and group cohesion being undermined seriously by "cultural revivals," the "onus for evangelising our part of the world rests squarely on us—local Christians." He added, "The world is watching us."

The map he drew of the road ahead involved the Global South coming to terms with some practical realities that it must face. The first such burden was for the leaders to realize the obligations imposed on them by virtue of their position in the Church:

> We, therefore, owe a great debt of responsibility to our people and to the world at large to enrich the theology and worship, including the liturgy of the Church with the unique insight which is ours because we are not Western.

The closing portion of his remarks was no less pithy:

> . . . I see a vision which suggests that we are at the threshold of the final gathering. I see the Church engaged in a mission which is freed from racio-political and economic bigotry and the ugliness of denomination rivalry. A mission in which the power of God is real and the love of God is the driving force. A mission in which all the people of God are united irrespective of race or class, from north or south, east and west. *But a mission in which the churches of the south will hence forth* (sic) *set the pace and decide the agenda* (Emphasis by the author).

The five-day gathering of the Global South in Kenya (January 31 to February 5, 1994) afforded examination of the broad, Christian worldwide perspectives through the narrow prisms of peculiarities and experiences common to the countries of the South. Finally, on February 5, 1994, the group issued the "First Trumpet." This was more or less its official communique, dealing with a range of issues—global, regional, continental, and national—and expressing the common understanding of the Global South. Covering nearly five pages, it expressed the minds of the Anglican Communion global leaders from the South regarding world affairs and on issues pertaining to the worldwide Anglican Communion.

The leaders stated that while they were not oblivious to the differences that the divergence of their contexts might entail, still they must not compromise the unity of action among the churches. In unison, they proclaimed, "We in the South believe that God has given us distinct gifts to offer the Communion," adding, "Just as we were once the objects of mission, so now we wish to offer ourselves to the Communion." What

---

2. Adetiloye, "Maturity: Its Challenges and Responsibilities," in *Joseph Abiodun Adetiloye.*

they wanted seen and were determined to propagate was "the message of repentance, forgiveness and reconciliation and [a return] to apostolic patterns of ministry." Loudly, they blew the trumpet. Though they cherished their Anglican identity and tradition, a point they expressed in the document, they insisted, "'Being Anglican' is not our final goal." Their highest aim was to work "for the Kingdom of God," and this meant they wanted to see "inclusion of the South's input in the planning of the Lambeth and other Communion-wide meetings or events."[3] They agreed also to "encourage the planning of a further 'Encounter in the South' before the Lambeth 1998." And these Encounters weren't meant to be ineffectual meetings. Rather, as observed in the Trumpet, the next Encounter "should include . . . a specific message to Lambeth." Furthermore, in a radical departure from the past, they insisted that the "holding of regional Encounters . . . should be self-financed."

In 1997, Adetiloye convened the second *Global South Encounter*. From February 10–15, the delegates met in the Malaysian capital of Kuala Lumpur. And it's significant that they met exactly as scheduled, demonstrating a strength of vision and resolve they lacked at the beginning. Adetiloye was assured of bearing the voice of the Global South at the Lambeth Conference. Attendance was good, with about 80 delegates, a slightly bigger turnout than the first conference.[4] The number of archbishops and bishops who attended personally this time around was encouraging.

The 1997 Encounter was critical in relation to the world milieu at the time. For most countries of the global south, the outgoing millennium had been one of lost hope. Many of the countries and peoples were in poor, pathetic, and pitiable conditions. Most regions these countries inhabited were "overflowing [with] refugees as a result of war and sometimes natural disasters." Hunger, poverty, and the burden of debt imposed by the Western countries continued to inflict the worst dehumanizing misery on the hapless populations. The overwhelming consequences were tragic, with the struggle for human survival enveloping nearly two-thirds of this part of the world. The Global South Anglican Church leaders were at pains to note the horrors that had become a "common experience of life" in their dioceses. Their lands were "overshadowed by ethnic hatred, political instability, neo-colonialism, social injustice, marginalisation, crippling international debt, spiralling inflation, environmental damage and pollution, religious strife and intolerance, unbridled materialism and pervasive corruption." The monumental tragedies were a serious challenge to their social conscience and Christian charity.[5]

---

3. Adetiloye, "A Trumpet from the South," "Maturity: Its Challenges and Responsibilities," "A Pastoral Letter," and "Lambeth Palace Letter to the Most Rev. Joseph A. Adetiloye," in Taiwo, *Joseph Abiodun Adetiloye*.

4. Adetiloye, "A Place of Scripture in the life and Mission of the Church in the 21st Century" and "A Second Trumpet from the South," in Taiwo, *Joseph Abiodun Adetiloye*.

5. The following papers and documents were obtained from the private papers and collections of Archbishop Peter Akinola: "Trumpet 1: From the First Anglican Encounter in the South", 5 February 1994; "A Pastoral Letter from The Most Rev. Joseph A. Adetiloye on the 1st Encounter—5 Feb. 1994";

Accordingly, the "Second Trumpet" from the Encounter called the world's attention to the issue of inequality between the North and the South. The South had given much in exploited labor and resources to the development of the North. It wasn't just a matter of inequality, but also one of injustice. The South had paid the price while the North reaped the benefits. Consequently, the "Second Trumpet" made strenuous appeal to "churches of the West to put pressure on their governments and on the World Bank and the IMF to respond to the many appeals coming from various quarters worldwide, to make the year 2000, a year of Jubilee, to remit two-thirds of the World debt." The Global South leaders also implored the "Communion to return to mission as the pivot of our life and ministry in the world," and "to return to faithfulness and to reliance on the Holy in the interpretation and application of Scripture." They maintained that the "life of the Communion is impoverished by the lack of direct input from the South," and they urged "the Communion to explore ways of intentionally encouraging direct South input for the enrichment of the life and mission of the whole Church."

Perhaps the weightiest of all the issues before the Encounter were the interlinked subjects of Scripture, family, and human sexuality. The Global South was already having some serious concerns about them despite the inaudibility of conversations surrounding the subject, and it is difficult to deny that the controversial issues had begun to trigger apprehensions in the Communion. In spite of the fact that the theme chosen for the Encounter, "The place of Scripture in the life and mission of the Church in the 21st century," did not reflect any direct link with the subject, the angle to which the opinion of the Global South tilted was not in doubt. They devoted lengthy discussion to the subject at their meeting and arrived at a common decision. In "Trumpet II: The Encounter Statement," the official communique of the conference, the threefold subject of Scripture, the family, and human sexuality occupied a major section. With no ambiguity, Global South leaders outlined the principles on which they stood, and to which they were irrevocably committed—their "resolve to uphold the authority of scripture in every aspect of life, including the family and human sexuality." From this, they enumerated the five key principles that would determine and guide their approach to the subject of homosexuality.

The first was to "call on the Anglican Communion as a Church claiming to be rooted in the Apostolic and Reformed tradition to remain true to Scripture as the final authority in all manners of faith and conduct." Next was their affirmation that "the scripture upholds marriage as sacred relationship between a man and a woman in the creation ordinance." Thirdly, they declared that "the only sexual expression, as

---

"The Kuala Lumpur Statement on Human Sexuality—2nd Encounter in the South, 10–15 Feb. 1997"; "Second Trumpet from the 2nd Anglican Encounter in the South, Kuala Lumpur, 10–15 February 1997"; "South-South Encounter" email exchange between Abp Akinola and Bishop Dr. John Chew on 08 June 2003; "Minutes Notes" (Archbishop Peter Akinola & Bishop John Chew" at Sheraton Hotel & Tower, Lagos, on Saturday, July 12, 2003); "We are Appalled," Public Statement by the Most Rev. Peter J. Akinola DD, for the working committee for the primates of the Global South, with attachment of the [i] "Primates Statement October 16, 2003, [ii] Commission's Mandate October 29, 2003 Paragraph 2.

taught by scripture, which honours God and upholds human dignity is that between a *man* and a *woman* (emphasis from source) within the ordinance of marriage." The fourth plank on which they stood was the conviction that "scripture maintains that any other form of sexual expression is at once sinful, selfish, dishonouring to God and abuse of human dignity." Last but not least was their acknowledgement of "the scourge of sexual promiscuity, including homosexuality, rape and child abuses in our time."

They observed, "These are pastoral problems, and we call on the churches to seek to find a pastoral and scriptural way to bring healing and restoration to those who are affected by any of these harrowing tragedies." Copious and cogent as the Encounter's views on the human sexuality question were, the Kuala Lumpur conference did not lay the issue to rest.[6] Indeed, it would have been naïve to expect it might be so. Developments within the worldwide Anglican Communion did not reassure the Global South leaders. No sooner than the Second Trumpet was blown, the group issued another pronouncement—"The Kuala Lumpur Statement"—with a rider, "Statement on Human Sexuality."

In turn, nearly two-thirds of the leaders in the Anglican Communion brought out another eleven-point declaration dealing specifically with the issue of human sexuality. There was no doubt that Church leaders were becoming agitated. They were destressed by cases of flagrant disobedience of the Church's stand and Scriptural teachings in the West with regard to the homosexuality issue. The "Kuala Lumpur Statement on Human Sexuality" made specific reference to the aberrations.

Though disturbed by the unsavoury developments, the Global South leaders chose to maintain a peaceful stance in the face of the deliberate provocation, simply expressing "profound concern about recent development relating to Church discipline and moral teaching in the North, specifically, the ordination of practising homosexuals and the blessing of same-sex unions." Meekly, they drew attention once again to the fact that the unlawful practice and action "calls into question the authority of the Holy Scriptures." With no equivocation, they asserted, "This is totally unacceptable to us." Nevertheless, they pleaded for "mutual accountability and interdependence," in a manner that would lead provinces and dioceses to "seek each other's counsel and wisdom," so that they could always "reach a common mind" before "embarking on radical changes" touching on Church discipline and moral teaching.

The Kuala Lumpur declaration was the Global South's response to the 1998 Lambeth Conference. They had succeeded in rallying the majority to their side at the Conference, which adopted Resolution 1.10 as the Communion's stand, with these four essential declarations of conviction and resolve. The group of Global South leaders stated that it:

6. "Scripture, the family and human sexuality" and "A Second Trumpet from the South" in Taiwo, *Joseph Abiodun Adetiloye.*

a. in view of the teaching of Scripture, upholds faithfulness in marriage between a man and a woman in lifelong union, and believes that abstinence is right for those who are not called to marriage;

b. recognises that there are among us persons who experience themselves as having a homosexual orientation. Many of these are members of the Church and are seeking the pastoral care, moral direction of the Church, and God's transforming power for the living of their lives and the ordering of relationships. We commit ourselves to listen to the experience of homosexual persons and we wish to assure them that they are loved by God and that all baptised, believing and faithful persons regardless of sexual orientation, are full members of the Body of Christ;

c. while rejecting homosexual practice as incompatible with Scripture, calls on all our people to minister pastorally and sensitively to all irrespective of sexual orientation . . . ;

d. cannot advise the legitimising or blessing of same sex unions nor ordaining those involved in same gender unions.[7]

The resolution was commended to every part, group, and section of the Church. Ironically, it was still the subsisting position of the Communion when the New Westminster diocese of the Anglican Church of Canada unilaterally decided in 2002 to bless same-sex unions.

It was a pity that, at this critical time, the Global South was losing its initial vibrancy. By the time the New Westminster diocese's aberrant behavior surfaced, indeed for the five-year period after the 1998 Lambeth Conference, the Global South organization appeared to have gone to slumber. No Encounter took place and no Trumpet sounded. Maybe part of the 1998 Lambeth Conference pro-homosexuality, rebellious group's strategy was to take advantage of the laid-back attitude of the Global South to present its position to the Communion as a *fait accompli*. And they were aided by two more developments. There arose, from the most surprising of places in the Communion, the Church of England, the seat of the Archbishop of Canterbury and a place to which all Anglicans worldwide look up as their home, a second attempt (after the one in Canada) at perverting the majority decision reached at the Lambeth Conference.

An openly gay priest, Jeffery John, was appointed as a bishop to the shock of all. If the New Westminster diocese's unilateral decision to bless same-sex marriage caused rumblings in the house, what followed Canterbury's action was an eruption with reverberations throughout the Communion. Yet, hardly had the London commotion died when America struck with her own quake. The General Convention of the Episcopal Church in the United States of America (ECUSA) confirmed an openly gay priest, Gene Robinson, for the position of bishop. A lone event might have been

7. www.anglicancommunion.org/resources/documentation/library/lambeth-conference/1998/section-i-called-to-full-humanity/section-:10-human sexuality?author=lambethconference &year=1998.

construed as an accident. Had there been just two, perhaps it would be right to refer to them as a mere coincidence. But with three of them happening in a row as they did, it would not be inappropriate to say they suggested conspiracy. The timing and progression were very suspicious.

The 2002 Canadian rebellion took place on the eve of Archbishop George Carey's departure from Canterbury. On the other hand, the 2003 British and American perfidies that occurred months apart were part of the baggage accompanying his successor, The Most Rev. Dr. Rowan Williams, to the Canterbury. Even though the Global South leaders at the time did not address the notion of conspiracy, they did not take the incidents as coincidental either. They were not only shocked by the impunity but were ruffled by the apparent condescending arrogance of their Western counterparts. The irony, however, was that the Global South leaders were their own enemies. They were sulking, toothless bulldogs. They lacked the ability to organize themselves and move in a practical way to contain the superciliousness of their Canadian, British, and American brethren.

In contrast, their Western colleagues were adroit in politics. They knew how to exploit such vulnerabilities to their advantage; they had the means to manipulate and control their adversaries, with years of experience in subduing the hapless Third World leaders. Though the Global South primates were riled by the unfolding provocative actions of their colleagues from the West, they lacked any effective response. In fact, prior to the developments, efforts were made twice to revive the Global South and return the organization to its former vibrancy. But it was in vain. The first attempt, made in Cairo, Egypt, in 2001, was a failure as was the second endeavor in the following year, 2002, in Oxford. So, from 1998 to 2003, the Global South leaders had no organization to serve as their rallying point. Inertia and vulnerability plagued them.

Things began to turn as the worldwide leaders of the Anglican Church met in Gramado, Brazil, February 19–26, 2003. It was meant to be a routine "Primates Meeting"—a formal association as well as one of the four key organs that administered the Church globally. But Global South leaders used the opportunity to renew efforts at resuscitating their platform. In the midst of their hectic schedules, they organized a side meeting. The labors paid off as twenty-two primates of the Global South attended. Fortune smiled on the efforts at reviving the group because the Brazilian meeting turned out to be highly productive. The primates opened their minds, unanimously reviving the Global South. They also wanted the Encounter back, better and sustained.

Some within the group, however, had misgivings about the previous Encounters. They came out into the open with their complaints and grievances, some upset because they were largely excluded from the earlier Encounters. To mollify them, the group agreed that all documents and other necessary records pertaining to the earlier Encounters should be shared with them. In the end, a common agreement was reached regarding administration and management of the Global South and return of the Encounter as the voice and platform for Anglicans in the South.

One byproduct of the meeting was the constitution of a coordinating committee to implement the objectives. Archbishop Akinola was appointed to head the committee. It so happened, he was replacing the Most Rev. Abiodun Adetiloye, his predecessor as the Nigerian primate and pioneer chair of the Global South Encounter as well. Three other persons were appointed to the Committee—Archbishop Gregory Venables of the Southern Cone; Archbishop Drexel Gomez of the Bahamas; and Archbishop Yong Ping Chung of Southeast Asia. Small as the committee was, these men were leaders of strength, character, and remarkable pedigrees in the administration of the Church and mission efforts.

Venables, for instance, was British-born. He had his entire education in the British-cultural environment. Venables attended Chatham House Grammar School, Kingston University, and Christ Church University College, Canterbury. He qualified and worked successfully as a computer system officer. Afterwards, he dropped the plum job for teaching and rose to become the headmaster of St. Andrew's College, Asuncion, which he managed from 1978 to 1989. He was enticed by the process of shaping the young to embrace higher ideals, of adding value to the lives of both the young and the old. While still a headmaster, he was ordained as a deacon in 1984. The following year, he became a priest.

He served in Paraguay, Bolivia, and Argentina, often volatile countries of the South American region. Venables was consecrated bishop in 1993. Eventually, he rose to become primate of the Southern Cone province of the Anglican Church in South America in 2001. The Southern Cone, formed in 1981, encompasses Argentina, Bolivia, Chile, Paraguay, Peru, and Uruguay.

The oldest member of the quartet, Archbishop Drexel Gomez, had a reputation for bluntness. His tongue was as sharp as a razor, and he had fearlessness for telling the truth piercingly. He neither measured nor diluted his words. To him, a spade was either a spade or nothing else. Gomez was born in the Berry Islands of the Bahamas, a chain of about 30 islands. It was a community where wealthy individuals displayed affluence as landed gentry and controlled the resources. The archbishop must have fought tough battles growing up, for the islands were populated by slaves freed in 1836 by William Colebrook, the British colonial lieutenant governor in charge of the Bahamas when the slave trade was abolished. The archbishop broke barriers constraining development of a colonized people.

He went on to graduate from St. Chad's College, Durham University, in 1959, and then found his way to the priesthood. Perhaps the past shaped his ideals for the future, solidifying within his mind the equality of all humans before God. Whatever the case, on June 25, 1972, at age of 35, he was consecrated as the bishop of Barbados. Twenty-five years later, he was elected the bishop of Bahamas and the Turks and Caicos Islands. In 1998, he became the archbishop and primate of the Church of the West Indies. His ecclesiastical positions might have changed, but not his characteristic frankness. Gomez remained known for his sharp-shooting tongue. He accommodated no untruth nor spared anybody his biting view of things, no matter how highly placed they might be.

The same applied also to Datuk Yong Ping Chung, archbishop of the Province of South East Asia.[8] Archbishop Moses Tay could not have had a more worthy successor. Chung wasn't born into Christianity. He converted from Chinese traditional religion. But Chung was known for his steadfastness. He held tenaciously to Christianity after he had received it. He was the youngest member ever elected to sit in the Diocesan Standing Committee when the Diocese of Sabah was inaugurated in 1963. He was, then, a high school student. That achievement determined Chung's eventual course in life. The following year, 1964, he left Sabah for Newfoundland in Canada with one goal, to pursue theological education. He attended Memorial University, where he graduated with a B.A., and then Queen's College, where he earned a Licentiate of Theology (L.Th). Away from home, at the request of his bishop in Sabah, he was ordained a deacon in May 1969 at Newfoundland, Canada. The year after, he returned home to become a full priest. From 1970 on, Chung worked as a diligent, dedicated, and devoted pastor. He was selfless, always driven by the need to apply Christian tenets to people's lives. He worked with the same relentlessness in promoting the higher ideals of Christianity even as a bishop. Average Sunday attendance doubled in his diocese in the 1990s. When Tay retired, the choice of a replacement was not difficult; Chung was available, his records impeccable, and his character unimpeachable. At a meeting of the Synod of the Province of the Anglican Church in South East Asia, held in Singapore in November 1999, he was elected unanimously as the second archbishop of the province.

There was a snag, however, with the four-man team constituted to resuscitate the Global South. The four men had a kind of "CIV"—an abbreviation for the pedigree of conviction, integrity, and valor. They had all registered themselves as Christian soldiers. They had planted churches, built congregations, and advanced the inherited past in their respective countries through courageous Christian leadership. They had worked in volatile and violent environments. Time had tested them, and they had acquitted themselves well. The problem was that none of them had prior experience with the Global South as an organization. That disadvantage wasn't a big hurdle, but it was still a setback. It could potentially curtail the speed with which they pursued the assignment. There were, however, two men with experience who could assist in fast-tracking of the task: Mouneer Anis, the bishop of Egypt, and his Singaporean counterpart, John Chew, who had stepped into the fearless Moses Tay's shoes as the bishop of Singapore.

The revitalization meeting therefore culminated in an observation that it was necessary to include these two names among the committee membership. From the initial figure of four, the committee's membership rose to six as Mouneer Anis was

8. "The Most Reverend Datuk Yong Ping Chung," http://www.anglicannews.org/news/2000/02/biography-of-the-new-archbishop-of-south-east-asia.aspx.

included to serve as the treasurer and John Chew was selected to be the secretary. Chew had previously occupied the same position, but Anis had no background in accounting. Rather, he had trained and served as a medical doctor, becoming the director of the Harpour Memorial Hospital, Menouf, a city located in the Nile Delta area of Egypt. The nearest that Anis had come to the financial or general management discipline was his acquisition of a certificate in hospital management and administration from the University of California's School of Public Health in the United States. But he was endowed with the attributes of a good manager. He could be trusted with the management of men, money, and materials. Anis was also imbued with honesty of purpose.

Incidentally, he didn't choose the priesthood as a vocation until later in life, ordained at age 49. Quickly, however, he registered his presence. He was committed to and manifested a serious zeal for learning. Down to Sydney, Australia, he went for theological and practical training at Moore Theological College, and then to England for hands-on experience, where he worked with the Diocese of Canterbury, and finally to Nashotah House in the United State. Anis brought his experience to bear in his service at Cairo's All Saints Cathedral and later as administrator of the diocese of Egypt.

Egypt was a hotspot of Islamic fundamentalism, yet Anis was undeterred. He stood firmly in the midst of Islamic extremism and refused to be subjugated. On May 15, 2000, he became the third national bishop of the Diocese of Egypt. Anis might have joined the work of faith late, but he remained dedicated to the calling that had brought him to proclaim the faith.

In contrast, John Chew charted an early course toward the ministry. He was ordained as a deacon at 30, in 1977. The year after, he became a full priest. He had received his bachelor of arts degree in 1969 from Nanyang University, Singapore. Eight years later, he was back to school for his master's degree and that same year, 1977, earned a bachelor of divinity from the University of London, which he obtained with honors. His capacity for rigorous learning seemed limitless. In 1983, he obtained his doctorate degree from the University of Sheffield, England. He chose Old Testament as the area of his scholarly interest. Chew's ministry was devoted to teaching and imparting the word. He spent the bulk of his career at the Trinity Theological College, Singapore, where he was a lecturer from 1982 to 1999. He was appointed principal of the college in 1991, maintaining the position until 1999. The searchlight beamed on him in 2000 as a replacement for Moses Tay, who had spent a short but eventful episcopate from 1996 to 2000 as bishop of Singapore.

Unfortunately, initial efforts to establish contact between Chew and Akinola suffered from frustrations common with communication in the global south. On one occasion, June 8, 2003, Chew tried desperately and unsuccessfully to contact the archbishop, for he was 800 kilometres away from his base in Abuja. Chew had left telephone and email messages for him. Somehow, the messages were rerouted to Akinola, and he responded swiftly as soon he got them. Archbishop Akinola had written to brief Chew about the outcome of the Global South's primates meeting, the enthusiasm, the agreement to see the forum revived, the constitution of the committee, and other minor but essential details. "The task before us now," Akinola wrote, "is to agree on a suitable date when the six of us can meet to make recommendations to the Primates." He advised a cost-saving venue, a location that the committee members would find central enough and reasonable for their expenses. The sanguine Akinola, who loved to hit the ground running, added, "My dear brother, we need to work fast."[9]

Fortunately, the two had the opportunity for a one-on-one meeting a month later. Chew had made the tortuous journey to Lagos, and Akinola had flown down from Abuja to warmly receive his guest. The July 12, 2003, meeting enabled the men map out how to take the assignment forward. Akinola and Chew shared the same opinion about the general coming together of the Global South. They were also united on the need to have a rallying body for Africa. The Global South Encounter, however, would remain sacrosanct. Its existence had become non-negotiable. The forum must be independent, truly owned by the Global South. Financially, it had to be self-reliant, with a view to making it a prophetic voice for the Anglican Communion. The two men agreed on the important work to be done to ensure that the Global South attained its objectives.

They were much encouraged by the endorsement of everything done so far by the primates at the Brazil meeting. Even South Africa, whose lukewarm attitude was evident at the primates meeting, had overcome its half-heartedness by canvassing for inclusion of other issues in the focus of the forum. Against South Africa's tepid outlook was the inspiring, enthusiastic, and heart-warming report coming from dioceses that were not even located within the geographic South. They were fervent, not shy or reluctant, about seeing that the 1998 Lambeth Conference's decisions were respected. After reviewing all of the developments, Archbishop Akinola and Bishop Chew saw the new lights emerging as positive indicators for the Global South's future.

Akinola and Chew considered it mandatory that the body be proactive—both in its orientation and operation. They also agreed that the Global South should be rational and reasonable, not impetuous. They believed the body "must respect the jurisdiction of other churches in the Communion in the spirit of Anglicanism to ensure integrity, accountability and mutual respect." Nevertheless, they believed that the Global South should maintain resoluteness on its convictions and not countenance compromise. They resolved that at no time should the Global South fail to express itself boldly, clearly, and unambiguously, especially where the points at issue had been settled. Also, they believed the Global South must not allow itself to be stereotyped or misconceived as a single-issue movement. Indeed, it should aim "to strengthen the Communion by contributing positively to it." And so the two of them continued to think together on their approach.

9. "South-South Encounter" email exchange between Akinola and Chew; "Minutes Notes" (Archbishop Peter Akinola & Bishop John Chew at Sheraton Hotel & Tower, Lagos, on Saturday, July 12, 2003).

The two agreed that the Global South must be financially independent—not only that it should have financial autonomy, but also that the body must have an abiding principle of being averse to taking of "Greek gifts" (as with the Trojan horse). To avoid being vulnerable and weak financially, they believed it was important to establish "a pool of funds where contributions from various dioceses and friends of the body could be deposited." Furthermore, if for any unavoidable reason the Global South had to be a beggar, it should be a beggar with a choice, ensuring that donations coming its way "should not be with strings attached." Akinola and Chew were categorical in maintaining that "the body *must not* look to the *West* for funding" (emphasis in the original).

The remaining part of the meeting was spent on routine administrative matters that such a global forum would entail. The two agreed, for instance, that it had become desirable and appropriate that the leaders of the "Global South should meet annually." A major implication was the cost of holding such meetings. In view of this, "it was suggested that [the] meetings should be held more often in Africa so as to reduce the cost." Akinola and Chew presumed the impact of that decision would be to boost "participation [of the leaders] and thereby ensure the continuity of the body." The duo also felt the time had come for the Global South "to set up a theological network, that is, commissioning of groups of theologians to focus on specific issues and articulate clear and well-researched positions" that could support and strengthen the leadership of the Global South and its primates. Another miscellaneous matter was the idea of developing a "priestly code of conduct . . . to strengthen the performance of priests and bishops." Finally, the two leaders agreed on "the need for a third Encounter." As far as they were concerned, the time was overripe for a "Third Trumpet" to sound from the Global South.

Both Akinola and Chew were men accustomed to hard work, and they compressed a great deal of discussion into the little time they had had to meet. What remained was action—practical and effective action to assure that the Global South had a new orientation with men of vision at the helm. Between themselves, the two men apportioned the different tasks.

Chew was saddled with developing "operational guidelines" for the forum. He was to craft the process whereby "The Primates will be the driving force (of the *Global South*) with a small committee reporting to the Primates." Archbishop Akinola was to provide a summary of the Brazil meeting, a sort of *aide-memoire* for the twenty-two primates, including those who were not in attendance but belonged geographically to the Global South. He was also to convene a meeting of the committee charged with resuscitating the forum, "preferably in Canterbury." The aim was to have the Canterbury archbishop, Dr. Rowan Williams, in attendance. Having cleared the issues on the agenda of their consultative meeting, Akinola and Chew took their leave. Both left ensconced in their belief that "the time for rhetoric is over."

By the time of their Lagos meeting, developments in the Communion were moving at a fast pace. The advances had begun to spin chaotically with an alarming impact.

Akinola and Chew met in Lagos on July 12, 2003. Eleven days later, Akinola was air bound to Fairfax, Virginia, and Vancouver, British Columbia, on a trouble-shooting mission. He was to lead the gathering of the "Worldwide Anglican Mainstream Leaders." The July 23, 2003, meeting was to plead with the American church's General Convention not to proceed with confirmation of the election of Gene Robinson, the openly gay priest who had already been elected a bishop.

Defiantly, America was inflexible in her stand. There was not to be a compromise by the church and no apology or regrets. So all eyes were fixed on London, the home and center of affairs of the Anglican Communion in the world. The Anglican Church was heading fast toward a global crisis.

3

A Choice to Make

London, 1998

The Church of England (CoE) enjoys enormous status and stature within the global Anglican Communion and is respected as the center, "mother church," umbilical cord, and spiritual head of one of the world's major religious faiths—Protestantism. In the United Kingdom, the CoE's dignity is incomparable. Furthermore, the CoE is to Anglican churches worldwide what Britain is to her previous colonies and overseas dependencies. Britain exercises influence over these countries as members of the Commonwealth of Nations, the association that brings together the colonies of the former imperial power. Similarly, the relationship holds between the CoE and all other Anglican Churches worldwide. Claims to national sovereignty by the countries of these churches might have led to their becoming autonomous and self-governing, but the CoE remains, nevertheless, the connecting bond between Anglicans worldwide.

One might say that as the British monarch, out of mutual respect based on historical connections, is the head of the Commonwealth association, the same privilege is extended to the archbishop of Canterbury. Canterbury and its presiding archbishop remains the focus of unity for the wider Anglican Communion. Furthermore, the Canterbury archbishop retains the functions of the primate of all England, performing the duties of the spiritual head of the Church of England. Parallel as well to the queen's position as the sovereign of Great Britain, the archbishop of Canterbury has international recognition as the spiritual leader of the Anglican Communion worldwide. He bears the burden to lead in "good faith," engendering trust and confidence across the entire Communion. As a global leader, under whom a diversity of races, cultures, views, and opinions are united, he must exhibit extreme sensitivity and sensibility. And indeed, it's a challenge to find the right balance, a balanced position among the sharply conflicting opinions that are bound to occur in the life of a diversified organization.

Peter Akinola: Who Blinks First?

In 1998, it was obvious that the archbishop of Canterbury, the Most Rev. George Carey, could not be spared a grave predicament surrounding that year's Lambeth Conference. As the 103rd archbishop of Canterbury, he convened the 13th Lambeth Conference, having developed the agenda, including discussion of human sexuality among the Church's global leaders.

Carey was not a man without personal beliefs or convictions. He was not shy or afraid to make his position clear. He was, however, a respecter of rules, and so his actions were orderly. He, for instance, strongly believed in the ordination of women, and at the 1978 Lambeth Conference, a consensus had emerged permitting "each church to make its own decision about women priests." Then, about two decades after the Lambeth Conference resolution, Carey became the first archbishop of the Church of England to ordain female priests. He was also tolerant of divorce, sympathetic to the divorced, and encouraging to divorced persons who desired to remarry. Cynicism often trailed Carey's soft spot for divorce and divorced people. Some insinuated that the divorce of one of his two sons was his underlying motive. Carey demonstrated, however, that his disposition toward divorce stemmed not merely from nepotism or selfish motive. He was, for instance, instrumental in encouraging the prince of Wales and Camilla Parker Bowles to formalize their relationship in a civil ceremony with a subsequent "blessing" at St. George's Chapel, Windsor Castle.

On the other hand, Carey did not indulge social trends that, in his estimation, conflicted with Scripture or with ecclesiastical canons. As an example, he was uncompromisingly opposed to homosexual relationships among the clergy. Yet he did not deny the existence of homosexual practice among Church of England priests, and he acknowledged the high profile that the homosexuality campaign had attained in British society, even long before he became the archbishop of Canterbury. In fact, Carey admitted that the issue accompanied him to office in 1991, and that he might well have mistakenly "consecrated two bishops whom he suspected of having same-sex partners." The problem was that at the time, he had no proof or convincing evidence to ground his suspicion.

In his seven years of leading the church, Carey had become a witness to the great height and volatility of the homosexual movement. He had become a target of desperate homosexual campaigners who engaged in a virulent effort that spread beyond British soil and emerged throughout a broad network of organizations across Europe and America. Though not a man given to provoking trouble, Carey had not been able to shield himself from encounter with aggressive homosexual groups in England. The timing of the fiasco was ironic, an assault on the eve of the 1998 Lambeth Conference and, infuriatingly, even during the Easter celebration. At the center of the humiliating attack was a British gay-rights advocacy group led by one Paul Tatchell.

Tatchell was not a minor figure in social causes. He had a solid reputation, a name, and political skills—a force to reckon with. He had engaged society on a wide range of issues, and he was as dogged as he could be in the crude pursuit of his goals.

Tatchell was neither a Briton nor a freeborn English citizen; born an Australian 1952, he'd later acquired British citizenship. He was the product of a divorced home and poverty, and his circumstances had forced him out of school early, at age 16. Education that was unavailable to him through formal learning he gained on the street. He did some menial work as a sign writer and a window dresser in department stores and developed skills that found expression in his irrepressible social activism. He had been raised a Christian and had not yet abandoned to become an atheist, an identity popular with revolutionaries.

One big problem was his aversion to authority. Instead of confronting authority in his native country, he fled conscription into the Australian Army, choosing to run to London in 1971 at age 19. No longer a child, he was not yet a man either. The teenager was unaccompanied to London by either of his parents. (His mother had remarried after the divorce from his father.) Nor was he entrusted to the guardianship or support of any relations. Tatchell was, however, a daring young man. He was bold, boisterous, and blessed with boundless energy—wired dynamite awaiting detonation.

Back in his secondary school days in Australia, he had taken on a big cause from which many an adult would have shrunk. Politics titillated him. He was an adolescent leader of his class and had launched a campaign in support of the Australian Aboriginal people. When he became the captain of the school, he extended the campaign to the highly sensitive political issue of land rights for indigenous people. His intrepid impetuosity led the school principal to say he was a communist lackey.

Arriving in London, he threw himself headlong into advancing the gay cause. The untrained, unlettered, and unskilled 19-year old thus had a ready occupation, a job requiring no certificate, no interview, and no employer to enforce organizational rules. Tatchell shone well.

In 1969, at 17, he had admitted to being gay. The London Gay Liberation Front, therefore, offered him the opportunity he wanted. From 1971 to 1974, when the organization collapsed, Tatchell was its leading member. He organized sit-ins at pubs discriminating against gays. Many times, police were on the receiving end of the protests he led. He also fought strenuously for removal of homosexuality from the medical list of illnesses. Within a year, the young arrival had transformed himself into an activist icon, and he celebrated his first anniversary of living in London (1972) in a big way, by joining with others to give Britain its first "Gay Pride" march.

Twenty-six years later, when Tatchell confronted Carey, the defiant teenager had evolved into a middle-aged man, known around the world as a rare breed of social-change warrior, championing nearly every kind of deviant behavior. He had been an activist, an agitator, a campaigner, a change agent, a catalyst, a reformer, a radical, a revolutionary, a rebel, and of course, an anarchist. Tatchell's strategies were without limits, involving all sorts of weapons to achieve his ends. He oscillated from pragmatism to irrationality, naiveté to realism, idealism to practicality, and sometimes wove his way around to thoughtlessness and flippancy.

These traits showed in all of his activities. He was a man perpetually driven by an uncontrollable ego. Always, he hated to fail. Narcissistic, he hated not having his way. In politics, it accounted for his movement from the Labour Party to the Green Party. It was his reason for switching allegiance from the defunct Gay Liberation Front to Outrage!, an organization he cofounded in the 1990s to continue the LGBT campaign. In this connection, he was involved with a 1991 blackmail threat to release the names of 200 leading British personalities who allegedly were homosexuals; in a 1994 threat to expose ten Church of England bishops for their duplicity in condemning homosexuality in public while allegedly leading secret gay lives; and in an attack on twenty members of Parliament, who were told to either shut up or be exposed as homosexuals. Perhaps as a result, Sir James Kilfedder died of heart attack two months later.

His schemes knew few limits. He attempted, in vain, a citizen's arrest of the late Zimbabwean President Robert Mugabe on two different occasions. Failure frustrated Tatchell, but every failure led to his becoming more daring, obsessive, and even a bit more destructive.

This was the backdrop for Tatchell's fracas with Carey on that Easter day of April 12, 1998. By Tatchell's admission, Carey had been a frustrating block to him and his cohorts—a "chaotic mix of anarchists, hippies, left wingers, feminists, liberals and counter-culturalists," as Tatchell described them. Their professed aim was "to change society's values and norms, rather than adapt to them." By his account, "We were sexual liberationists and social revolutionaries, out to turn the world upside down" and "to overturn centuries of male heterosexual domination." Tatchell found "Carey's opposition to legal equality for lesbian and gay people" "aggravating," and the archbishop had to be dealt with.

On that eventful day, Tatchell led a band of protesters from Outrage! to disrupt the Easter service Carey was conducting. It was bad enough that he and his "chaotic mix" had chosen a sacred day to launch his vile attack. Worse was the irreverence he displayed. Tatchell shoved the revered man of God aside as he mounted the pulpit, and in a torrent of vile and villainous invectives, he denounced what he claimed was Carey's sin. Of course, Carey's iniquity was not supporting the "chaotic mix's" malady. Theatrics excite the media, and they loved Tatchell's drama. The media feasted on the unusual, thrilling events, and their attention helped magnify his self-portrayed image as a fighter. Tatchell relished their celebration and adoration, which energized his extremism. And not surprisingly, the LGBT press beatified him as "Saint Peter Tatchell" leading the attack on religion.

Nevertheless, it seemed that "Saint Peter Tatchell" had overreached on that occasion. His behavior was not saintly. Britain might be respectful of individual liberty, rights, and freedoms, but it abhorred felonious intent and action. Tatchell broke a law, even if the regulation was seldom invoked because rarely had his type of reckless conduct occurred. The Ecclesiastical Courts Jurisdiction Act of 1860 (formerly part of the Brawling Act 1551) had prohibited any form of disruption or protest in a church. Tatchell was arraigned for violating the law.

Of course, he wanted to turn the case into another sensational, narcissistic event. He wanted Carey in the witness box. The plan was obvious, to scandalize the respected spiritual figure. But Tatchell failed. The court was not convinced that Carey was of any importance to his defence against the charge. Found guilty, he received a lenient fine of £18.60, an amount that corresponded symbolically to the year the law was enacted.

That event coincided with other happenings to foreshadow the 1998 Lambeth Conference. Carey was undeterred. He refused to falter in shepherding the Conference toward arriving at a decision which represented the majority in the worldwide Anglican Communion. Though a clique comprising a tiny but powerful minority tried to subvert the conference, Carey rebuffed the manipulation, spurned machinations, overcame calculated attempts to make him budge, and stoutly stood in defence of institutional integrity.

It's easy to underrate him. He had a quiet mien, but he possessed a tough, fighting spirit. Carey didn't rise to his eminent position through weakness, and he didn't employ pliability as a survival strategy. His journey had been rough and tough, yet he learned from his initial failures to make positive advances in life.

Carey had a troubled childhood. He was born in the East End of London on November 13, 1935, and his early years were unimpressive. He had learning difficulties and didn't do well in primary school. So he found himself at Bifrons Secondary Modern School in Barking. At 15, he was out of the school, and his best available opportunity was in blue-collar work. He sought employment with the London Electricity Board, and was given a job as an office boy. After three years of running errands in the office, he turned 18, the age at which he was expected to serve his country. Unlike Tatchell, Carey didn't evade the military; instead he patriotically enrolled for the National Service and served as a wireless operator in the Royal Air Force in Iraq.

Carey went to Iraq, however, with a major change occurring in his life. A year earlier, at 17, he had attended a church service with some friends and experienced a turning point. Carey was to say years later, "I had a conversion experience which was very real . . . There were no blinding lights, simply a quiet conviction that I had found something."[1] It was a captivating encounter, a total immersion. A turning point had come for the poor, early-starter teenager. He chose to become a priest.

He returned home after the national service and applied himself strenuously to his studies. Within 15 months, he reversed his past failure, passing six subjects at the ordinary level and writing an additional three papers at the advanced level. The dull, unimpressive child of yesterday gave way to a focused, admirable, pace-setting, and emerging youth. Initial failure didn't disorient him.

Carey's Christian conversion seemed to be a good tonic, one that put his life on the right course. He subsequently attended the King's College, London, graduating

1. http://en.wikipedia.org/w/index.php?title=George_Carey&oldid=672297572.

with a second-class-upper honors award in divinity, and he set out to earn master's and doctorate degrees. None of this made him conceited.

His faith became the defining guidance of his life and ministry, which were marked by hungry devotion. When, in 1975, for example, he became the vicar of St. Nicholas' Church, Durham, he left an imprint of abounding zeal. Within two years, he tripled the congregation, an achievement he later documented in his book, *The Church in the Market Place*. Perhaps through the apt title of his book, God was giving Carey a gift of vision for what was to come.

By 1998, the year of Carey's first and last Lambeth Conference as archbishop of Canterbury, the church was not just in the marketplace, but had become the marketplace itself, where anything goes and all wishy-washy sells! But God had preserved Carey for a special purpose. Carey succeeded Archbishop Robert Runcie, and the change bore the marks of providence. It didn't appear that the glitterati, the literati, and their cohorts in the ecclesiastical order of British society gave him a thought. The appointment came his way through the former private secretary to the prime minister, Michael Allison MP, who suggested him to Prime Minister Margaret Thatcher, while the latter simply forwarded his name to the queen, who out of tradition, concurred with his nomination.

Carey's selection broke records. He was the first archbishop of Canterbury in modern times not to have been from the two prima donna institutions, the Universities of Oxford and Cambridge, which seemed to hold the patent for supplying occupants to the venerated office. Some may have expected disaster for Carey, assuming him to be a modern-day Simon Sudbury (the archbishop who was lynched in the 14th century), but though externally taciturn, his resolve was unswerving. Push him, vilify him, excoriate him, he would always refuse to be intimidated.

Carey might not have known where the future would take the Anglican Church, but he had an understanding of past trajectories that had brought the church health. He was equally familiar with the contemporary leadership imperatives. He was well aware of the challenges. Because he was wearing the shoe, he knew where it was pinching. Carey was the man of the moment and for the moment.

On becoming archbishop, Carey introduced a decade of evangelism. Events foreshadowing the 1998 Lambeth Conference, however, overshadowed this mission—and indeed, every other contribution to the church—consigning them to insignificance. The Conference that would have been the crowning glory of his reign turned out to be a thorn in his flesh.

The air was thick with the human sexuality question. Peter Tatchell's attack was not an isolated or spontaneous incident. It was part of an organized offensive aimed at the church. Every attempt—civilized and crude—was made to stoke the fire, to keep this subject of debate in the public eye, and force the matter at the Conference. It happened, but the results were not to the activists' liking. Though the 1998 Lambeth Conference began in the usual way, with prayers, committee meetings, reports, plenary sessions, voting, and finally resolutions, the end proved who the losers were. Though vocal, tough and determined, the loud minority could not overwhelm the majority. Instead, the majority humbled the minority, and Lambeth Resolution 1.10 was an eloquent testimony to this fact.

After the Conference, Carey found himself in an unenviable catch-22. As the worldwide leader of the Communion, he had to decide between the two bitter, antagonistic positions confronting him. It was an honest, plain truth that Carey was not pro-homosexual. He was not favorably disposed to blessing and ordaining those involved in homosexuality. But that was his personal feeling. It was a sentiment that he had neither the power nor the authority to decree on the Anglican Church. He was lucky that his personal position accorded with the majority opinion of his fellow Anglican leaders. Could he have influenced the majority to toe the line of the minority? Not likely, given the passion the issue had sparked and the polarization it generated, much of it along geographical lines. In any case, his conviction went along with that of the majority.

Unfortunately, Carey's affirmation of an essential norm of democracy—upholding the decision of the majority—did not go down well with some of his colleagues. He stepped on a few big toes because of that. Some powers in the Church sent up flak and stirred furor. He was ridiculed for being pliable, chastized for "allowing himself to be used," and berated for being "a factor of disunity . . . disloyalty . . . and a divisive force." He was denounced as "the worst Archbishop for a media age." Richard Holloway, Carey's fellow primate, the primus of the Scottish Episcopal Church and bishop of Edinburgh, complained, "I feel gutted, I feel betrayed," and he promised the "turncoat" Carey that the "struggle [would] go on."[2]

Holloway was a man of resourceful, imaginative endowment. His knowledge was extensive, as was his prodigious output of creative, artistic, and scholarly works. Ordained at the age of 26, he served as a priest for 41 years, from 1959 to 2001. Twenty-seven years of work as a priest took him to various parishes in England, Scotland, and the United States before he became the bishop of Edinburgh in 1986. In 1992, he was elected primus of the Scottish Episcopal Church, the year after Carey had become archbishop of Canterbury.

It wasn't surprising that he was part of the dissenting minority group. As a bishop, and one of the nine rebellious primates to have signed the apology to homosexuals, Holloway was the patron of the organization LGBT Youth Scotland. His desire was to see "LGBT young people [in] the life of Scotland," and he was desperate to have the church legitimize homosexuality. He hoped that a favorable Lambeth decision would give his cause the high moral ground, since the church ranks high as a custodian of public morality. Unfortunately, for him, the 1998 Lambeth Conference only responded in a disappointing way. Holloway and his cohorts in the pro-homosexuality group were galled by the *coup de grâce*, and particularly infuriating was Carey's refusal to

2. http://en.wikipedia.org/w/index.php?title=Richard_Holloway &oldid=674394210.

accept a "condemnation of homophobia" contained in the original draft of the Conference's resolution. As the matter stood for Holloway, with the Communion's refusal to endorse homosexuality, he had nothing to take back home from London to the youth under his misdirection.

Holloway spared no effort to inject his venom, but Carey took the malicious bite nobly, and the attack had no effect. It didn't weaken his resolve to uphold the decision of the majority. Then, his steadfastness was tested anew in 1999, when the ink of Resolution 1.10 was still fresh on the paper. The irony, however, was that, in addition to the diatribes from Holloway, real pressure to abridge the majority's decision was to come from Carey's home front!

A group within the Church of England had conceived a scheme to subvert Resolution 1.10, one involving a spurious agreement called the "Cambridge Accord," whose intent was to bring English bishops to an "agreement on affirming certain human rights of homosexuals, notwithstanding [the] differences within the church on the morality of homosexual behaviour."[3] What was sought, in effect, was for the bishops to repudiate the Lambeth Conference's decision.

Carey bluntly refused to betray the Church. Three other bishops shared his stand and followed suit, shrugging off the revolting treachery. Integrity is at the heart of genuine leadership; a worthy leader must be consistent, constant, and dependable, uncompromising in honesty, truthfulness, and trustworthiness, both in private and public irrespective of the cost. Carey refused to act in the so-called "politically correct" manner. He shunned expediency.

At 67 years of age, having nearly reached the sunset of his archiepiscopal career, and with a total of 41 years' experience pastoring and leading the church, 14 of which he served as a bishop and eight as the head of the Scottish Episcopal Church, Holloway resigned from office. This was in 2000. By his own admission, he had all along lived a life of lying. He admitted to being a dissimulator and that he had concealed facts about himself. For a greater part of his life in the Church, he had nursed serious doubts about Christianity. The doctrine he believed was the very antithesis of the creed he was supposed to be propagating. In the end, he unveiled his agnostic and atheistic worldview. Furthermore, Holloway made the startling disclosure in his memoirs that "he secretly conducted his first of many of gay marriages as early as 1972." But he ended the life of charade in 2000.

Carey survived Holloway in the same way he outlasted all his foes' antics and machinations, except for one scheme, which occurred too late for a response. Perhaps it was meant to serve as his parting gift, or maybe to set the stage for his successor. It was the blatant breach of the Lambeth Resolution by the New Westminster diocese of the Anglican Church of Canada in its authorization of blessing same-sex unions. The diocese's misconduct occurred in June of 2002. Carey retired from office on October 31.

3. "Cambridge Accord" as quoted in http://en.wikipedia.org/w/index.php?title=George_Carey&oldid=672297572.

Whatever lay in store for Anglicans, Carey had made his choice, standing for the Lambeth resolution. Carey's place in Anglican Church history was that he inherited an undivided, unbroken, and unimpaired Communion, and he, in turn, passed on an untorn Anglican Church at his exit.

By February 27, 2003, a new archbishop of Canterbury had been installed, the Most Rev. Dr. Rowan Williams.[4] Formerly, he was the archbishop of Wales with episcopal concurrence as bishop of Monmouth, a diocese on the Welsh border. Williams received the vital votes of the Crown Nominations Commission (CNC), a body charged with overseeing the election of a new archbishop of Canterbury. It has 16 members in addition to the secretary general of the Anglican Communion, the prime minister's appointments secretary, and the archbishops' secretary for appointments. The latter group are non-voting members. The CNC's task is to present the name of a preferred candidate (and a second appointable candidate) to the prime minister. The prime minister's constitutional job is to submit the list to the queen and tender advice to her majesty, counsel she rarely rejects. And so, on December 2, 2002, he was confirmed, and two months later, enthroned at the Canterbury Cathedral.

For the new archbishop—and the worldwide Anglican Church—a new history was unfolding. Canterbury may lack a prepared office manual that teaches its elected leader how to perform the duties attached to his office, but Williams wasn't arriving as a neophyte. He had had hands-on experience as a bishop and an archbishop. For eleven years, Williams had worn the episcopal epaulette, while for three years before his ascension to the Canterbury seat, he supervised seven dioceses in the Church in Wales. Those three years also witnessed his being a primate, one of 38 in the Communion. This made him part of the collegiate body providing global leadership to the Anglican Church.

Besides, he had strong selling points to the public: He was a teacher, a theologian, a translator, a professor, a polyglot, a poet, an activist, and an international social crusader. These numerous roles had created an idealistic personality, one open to shifting identities. Williams came into office determined to break records and shatter myths.

Like Carey, the first modern-era non-graduate of Oxford or Cambridge to become archbishop of Canterbury, Williams was the first Welshman to ascend the Canterbury see from outside the English Church since the mid-thirteenth century. Unlike Carey but very much like Holloway, he participated in the rebellion during the 1998 Lambeth Conference as one of the minority bishops who authored the dissenting letter to gays and lesbians. And now it was time to make his mark.

---

4. On Williams' election as archbishop of Canterbury, see http://rowanwilliams.archbishopof-canterbury.org/articles.php/2403/outline-of-procedures-for-the-appointment-of-an-archbishop-of-canterbury.

4

Another Heat in the House

London, 2003

On May 20, 2003, ninety days into his nascent archbishopric, the Most Rev. Rowan Williams took the first wrong step, appointing Jeffrey John, an openly gay priest, as a bishop. Not surprisingly, this raised the temperature in an already-scorching Anglican house. Reactions came swiftly.

The selection of a candidate for the bishopric is governed by rules, procedures, and conventions. Any English bishop is an official of the crown, with the queen as the consenting authority to his appointment. A bishop's selection begins locally however. It starts with the process of setting up a diocesan vacancy-in-see committee. The committee identifies the needs of the diocese, articulates them, and then forwards its assessment as a "Statement of Needs" document to the Crown Nominations Commission (which at that time was known as the Crown Appointments Commission). Fourteen members sit in a kind of Electoral College saddled with the responsibility of deciding on a preferred and an alternate candidate whose nominations are to be put forward to the prime minister for official assent. The fourteen include the archbishops of Canterbury and York along with three representatives each from the clergy and laity, as well as six members elected from the diocesan vacancy-in-see committee. The two appointments secretaries (of the prime minister and the archbishop of Canterbury) join them. The two secretaries are like the search party supplying the committee with information on possible candidates.

Conventionally, the archbishop in whose province the vacancy exists presides over the selection process. A nomination is virtually a guarantee to installation. Part of the established convention is that the prime minister rarely rejects the names forwarded. Though the prime minister reserves the power to request additional names, this happens rarely. But it does happen. On political grounds, Margaret Thatcher, the "Iron Lady," opposed Jim Thompson's nomination as bishop of Birmingham, not pleased with what she perceived as the candidate's liberal and left-wing views. Except for that incident, the tradition of upholding nominations made by the commission had become an essentially sacrosanct practice. Consequently, the nomination of Jeffrey John as the bishop of Reading was seen as almost certain.

Jeffrey John would have replaced Dominic Walker as bishop of the diocese of Reading. Interestingly, the vacancy did not arise through the usual means, that is, by retirement, death, or resignation. Instead, Walker was translated to the diocese of Monmouth, in Wales, to replace Williams when the latter became the archbishop of Canterbury. Incidentally, the diocese of Monmouth had paired two churches that grew out of the Church in Wales when it gained autonomy from the Church of England in 1921.

Walker's translation was the climax of his silver jubilee in the priesthood, which began in 1997 with his appointment as bishop of Reading. The following year, 1998, he attended his first Lambeth. Like Williams, he joined ranks with the minority dissenting from the Church's stand on the human sexuality question. It is not clear whether the special needs of the Monmouth diocese made Walker the appropriate choice; none of his previous eight predecessors had come the way he did.

He was a man of broad experience in church work. Hardly was there any part of church life that he had not traversed. From service in the smallest urban parish to the challenging task of coordinating work as a rural dean, he had become a seasoned minister. Wales was also not a strange territory to Walker. He attended University of Wales after initial stints at three London Colleges—Plymouth, King's, and Heythrop.

Walker had a rare preoccupation with paranormal exploration, a subject on which he is considered a leading expert. Because he had an avid interest in supernatural phenomena, he delighted in studying arcane metaphysical matters like ghosts and extrasensory perception. And there was another peculiarity, membership of the Oratory of the Good Shepherd—a select, international organization within the Anglican community open to clergy and laity. Its aims included the encouragement of piety through meditative prayers, fellowship, and commitment to the rigorous application of the intellect. Walker wore his membership with pride, making sure the initials OGS followed his name.

He was elected bishop of Monmouth in December 2002 after Rowan Williams' confirmation as archbishop of Canterbury that same month. Then, a month after the enthronement of Williams, Walker was enthroned on March 30, 2003. Whatever deliberation and engineering went into Walker's translation, the Monmouth diocese's congregation welcomed him. No hair-splitting reaction came from within the Monmouth diocese or any other part of the Communion with his translation, but not so with the man chosen to replace him in Reading.

Trouble reared its head the moment Jeffrey John was named as the potential successor. Countless strident criticisms attended the announcement. The trouble was not with the position John was to occupy. Rather John himself was the trouble. John was an Oxford thoroughbred with a sharp mind. At age 18, he made a first class in classics and modern languages at Hertford College, Oxford. He returned to Oxford, this time to St. Stephen's House, to study theology, which he finished at a slightly lower grade of second-class honors. And then, at 27, he received the doctorate from Oxford, with special focus on Pauline theology.

His career encompassed sundry priestly appointments, beginning with a curacy at Penarth, the chaplaincy of Brasenose College, a vicarage at Holy Trinity, Eltham, in south London under the diocese of Southwark, the canon chancellorship and theologian position in Southwark Cathedral, and the deanship of divinity at Magdalen College, Oxford.

Obviously, John wasn't a classical, old-style preacher and teacher of the Word from the pulpit. Indeed, in mind and outlook, he didn't come near the archetypical Sunday school teacher. He advocated social causes of the time, including the ordination of women and the program of "affirming Catholicism" within the Anglican fold. But these were not the source of controversy in his appointment.

Rather, it was John's open involvement in a same-sex relationship. He and Grant Holmes, his same-sex partner and also a priest of the Church of England, had been in a committed long-term union. By the canon law of the Church of England, the Christian Scriptures serve as the foundation of its doctrine. More specifically, the House of Bishops of the Church of England in 1991 had issued a guideline about the Church's position on human sexuality. The instruction followed the 1988 Lambeth Conference, which had advised a decade-long reflection by all Anglican bishops on the human sexuality question. Categorically, the bishops maintained that ordained ministers "shall not only preach but also live the gospel." The consequence, as they outlined it, was that "certain possibilities were not open to the clergy by comparison with the laity," emphasizing that this was "a principle that has always been accepted." Those who disagreed with the stand were granted the concession to differ, but "what they are not free to do is to go against that mind in their practice." And this was what had provoked John's opponents.[1]

John had been in a same-sex relationship with Holmes as far back as 1976, about a year after his graduation from Oxford. In all likelihood, he was yet to be ordained at that time. But certainly, his decision to join the ecclesiastical order was why he enrolled in theological study.

Over the years, John had made his sexual preference known. Consistently, however, he maintained that the association was celibate. Though he succeeded in keeping the dark side of his sex life out of public scrutiny, it was not so with his view on gay issues. He remained an unrepentant advocate of so-called gay rights. Apparently, John didn't take to heart the wisdom that a heavy rain or a fierce wind doesn't eliminate or obliterate every footprint. He had stuck his feet too deep into the mud, with messy prints left everywhere.

1. "Issues in Human Sexuality—A Statement by the House of Bishops of the General Synod of the Church of England, December 1991."

John's opponents argued that his elevation would amount to laying disordered tracks, setting a most disagreeable precedent that could not be ignored. Apart from being a serious affront to the integrity of the Church of England, it amounted also to a big stain on the reputation of the worldwide Anglican Communion. The two bodies had both spoken clearly on the subject of human sexuality within the church, and they had neither reviewed nor renounced their positions.

For nine Church of England diocesan bishops, keeping quiet on such a grievous matter would mean consenting to the perfidy, so they rose publicly in opposition to John's nomination. They saw the nomination as contemptuous, offensive, and demeaning. It impugned the integrity of the Anglican Church, both nationally in Britain and in the world at large.

Their complaint, however, was not primarily against John. He hadn't nominated himself. Nor had he presided over the appointment process. The real culprit therefore was the new archbishop of Canterbury, the Most Rev. Rowan Williams. In their thinking, there was at least a *prima facie* case of culpability against the archbishop. In him was vested the power, the influence, and the authority of superintending the appointment. He was the metropolitan controlling the 30-plus dioceses of the province of Canterbury, among which was the diocese of Reading. Williams headed the Crown Nominations Commission responsible for the nomination. If he had put the interest of the church, nationally and internationally, above all other considerations, he would have blocked John's nomination. He had the prerogative.[2]

Even if others had made mistakes early in the nomination process, Williams had the opportunity to correct them. John's nomination was not a holy writ cast in stone. The error was human and could be rectified. So, acting in concert, the nine bishops wrote an open letter to Williams, drawing his attention to the lack of prudence in the decision and calling for reversal.

No sooner than their had letter gone public, they became objects of vile attacks from supporters of the homosexual movement. They were called all sorts of names in public, and various insinuations were made about their reputation and integrity. None of the nine bishops was spared. Some characterised "the nine" as "rebel bishops." One compared them to the "Nazgûl," the despicable nine characters in J. R. R. Tolkien's epic Middle-earth legend. The "Nazgûl" were Sauron's "most terrible servants," who submitted to him in order to acquire power, glory, and wealth. In the end, striving for possessions became the source of their undoing. It is a story about the futility of greedy grasping, a moral lesson on the emptiness of power. Of course, there's no comparison between the character of the bishops and Tolkien's fictional Nazgûl. Each of the bishops was a person of substance and distinction. Within the church and in the larger society, they held positions of honor and commanded healthy respect. And though they shared a common view on the inappropriateness of John's behavior, they

2. See "Criteria for Selection for the Ordained Ministry in the Church of England," https://www.churchofengland.org/media/1274926/criteria%20document%20-%20web.pdf.

would have expressed the same strong convictions had they stood as individuals, without the collective platform.

Graham Dow, the bishop of Carlisle, for instance, wasn't the home-grown, British, subtle type. He was blunt and bold, and his scalpel sharpness was never dulled by fear. He could stand and face a crowd alone, irrespective of the implications. Dow attended the 1998 Lambeth Conference, when he was bishop of Willesden, and distanced himself from the rebellious bishops wanting to subvert the majority's decision. A believer in cause and effect, he had strong conviction that divine retribution usually was the consequence of sin. The blunt Dow proclaimed a truth that many considered offensive—the steps that the United Kingdom had taken to introduce same-sex marriage made the country "liable for God's judgement."

There was also Peter Forster, bishop of Chester and a lord spiritual with a seat in the House of Lords. Forster was opposed to homosexuality, which nearly got him into trouble. He was accused of "hate speech" for calling for psychiatric tests of homosexuals. The subsequent police investigation however absolved his innocuous remarks of any criminal intent. James Jones, then-bishop of Liverpool, was of a different mold. Jones had an interesting public service record. He'd etched his name on a distinguished public service honor list by becoming a champion of community service and leading one of the first community service programs in schools. Jones' challenge, however, revolved around maintaining consistency, as he became the only bishop among the lot to recant his opposition of John. He was said to have later apologized to John for his action. Interestingly, Jones was at the 1998 Lambeth Conference and declined to be part of the 185 bishops opposing the majority decision. But one could not count on his unwavering support of biblical morality.

In sharp contrast was George Cassidy, bishop of Southwell and Nottingham. Cassidy maintained a forthright stand in opposition to homosexuality. During his time in the House of Lords, he opposed attempts at putting the aberrant relationship on equal footing with the normal man-woman partnership. Cassidy was unapologetic for his inflexible denial of ordination rites to openly gay priests like Jeffrey John.

Of equal disposition was John Hind, a theologian and a former bishop in Europe before assuming the episcopacy of Chichester in the Church of England. Unpretentious about his stand on homosexuality, Hind, ironically, had the responsibility of ministering in places with a sizeable percentage of gay residents. He was not shy, however, to make his stand known publicly. Any effort at protecting marriage in its traditional form enlisted his interest, and he needed no persuasion to sign a petition organized by the Coalition for Marriage opposing same-sex marriage.

David James was another of those courageous bishops, a man who preferred conscience to political correctness. He was bishop of Bradford, with very serious concern about the integrity of the church. He had no doubt that John's consecration would do irreparable damage to the church. He was convinced that it was far better to stop the lump from growing than to allow it to metastasise into a malignant tumor. James had no regrets over his action and he offered no apologies.

This left the "three Michaels," the first of which was Michael Scott-Joynt, bishop of Winchester, and thus one of the five senior bishops of the Church of England. He had both courage and conviction and could utter unpleasant truth with an inoffensive candor. Like the former archbishop of Canterbury, George Carey, Scott-Joynt urged that the church relax its position on remarriage of divorcees with a surviving spouse. But his disagreement with the church's position notwithstanding, he didn't act contemptuously or trade on his exalted episcopal position. He submitted himself to the established procedure. When opportunity arose in 2000 with the Church of England setting up a committee on the issue, he was appointed as the head of the panel. Scott-Joynt respected due diligence. The relevant organs of the church deliberated over the report that included Scott-Joynt's viewpoint, leading to a final decision to loosen restrictions on remarriage.

On same-sex relationships, however, Scott-Joynt did not favor social adventurism. Any attempt to upset the balance of the scale incurred his opposition. He was against the Equality Act as well as the civil partnership legislation. The two, as he saw them, were evil Siamese twins, devoid of sensitivity to religious conscience and the uniqueness of marriage. He didn't feel intimidated by all the developments around him. He made it clear that he "would closely question clergy in his diocese who entered [into] a civil partnership." He also predicted "no future for the Anglican Communion" unless there was "exclusion of Christians in same-sex relationships from positions of leadership."[3] That was his motive for teaming up with others to protest the nomination of Jeffrey John.

The second Michael was Michael Langrish. He was made bishop of Birkenhead in 1993 and remained in that position till 2000. Langrish attained the position of lord spiritual in 2005 by virtue of his 2000 appointment as bishop of Exeter. He was at the 1998 Lambeth Conference, and he too refrained from being dragged into the Lambeth's minority subversive group. His consistency of conviction for nearly half a decade shows the strength of his character and will. He believed the nomination of Jeffrey John portended a grave risk to the health of the church.

This left the last of the triple Michaels, Michael Nazir-Ali. One of two candidates nominated for the archbishopric of Canterbury in 2002, he was passed over by Prime Minister Tony Blair in favor of Rowan Williams. Nazir-Ali possessed impeccable credentials qualifying him for the job. His academic, scholarly, and church administration experience was distinguished, and he had the intellectual background and ability to confront a wide range of complex socio-cultural issues.

Nazir-Ali was a dual citizen of both Pakistan and Britain, and he had a similar mixed background in religion. His father was a Muslim convert to Christianity, and Nazir-Ali became a Christian at age 15. He received formative training at the Roman

---

3. https://en.wikipedia.org/wiki/Michael_Scott-Joynt.

Catholic-run St Patrick's College in Karachi, his birth place, and he began to attend Roman Catholic services.

At 20, he formally became a member of the Anglican Church of Pakistan. Everything thereafter followed the usual course: education, work, career, struggles, hard work, determination, ordination, devotion, and purposefulness—with these helping him become Pakistan's youngest bishop at 35. This gave him episcopal responsibility in one of the world's most volatile regions at the time. He was Raiwind's first bishop in 1984, serving a diocese in West Punjab. He advocated for the poor and was an unrelenting critic of the country's autocratic rule. This brought him into serious conflict with General Zia, Pakistan's despotic ruler. His life became threatened. As a result, then-Archbishop of Canterbury Robert Runcie arranged a safe harbor for him in England in 1986. The archbishop took him under his wings, making him his assistant at Lambeth.

Nazir-Ali had performed a range of duties. He assisted in planning the 1988 Lambeth Conference, and when it was over, he was appointed general secretary of the Church Mission Society. He served five years in that post, 1989–1994, and also was assistant bishop of Southwark. He assumed a full-fledged episcopal position in 1994 with his appointment as bishop of Rochester. The bishopric carried a seat in the House of Lords, and with attainment of the required seniority in 1999, he found his way to Britain's highest legislative chamber as one of the lords spiritual. He was the first religious leader from Asia to have been so privileged. Besides his work in varied capacities within the church, he had also integrated himself fully with British society.

Yet he was not the acquiescing kind, easily susceptible to intimidation or coercion. He was, for instance, the first bishop to appoint a woman archdeacon in the Church of England. However, he was opposed to the ordination of non-celibate homosexuals as clergy and the blessing of same-sex unions. Nazir-Ali did not hesitate to express his mind publicly, even when doing so elicited an acrimonious reaction, as when he called on homosexuals to "repent and be changed" during a gay pride parade in London. He received their accusations of "hate and homophobia" with equanimity, and the bullying neither changed nor mellowed Nazir-Ali's view of homosexuality, especially in the church. He remained resolute in his conviction that it was wrong for a priest to be a homosexual. Accordingly, Jeffrey John's nomination was inappropriate. John was gay, and openly so, which the church had said was not acceptable. Nazir-Ali and his like-minded colleagues were insistent that John had no place in the episcopal leadership of the church.

It's not clear what Archbishop Williams thought about this protest. What was discernible was his decision-making style: playing for time when decisive action was required. His leadership was marked by calculated delay, avoidance, resort to red-tapeism, and a predilection to hide under bureaucratic officialdom. Even when matters were simple and straightforward, it was common to see him prevaricate.

For forty-eight days, the fire lit by Jeffrey John's nomination raged. Canterbury was plunged into inaction. On his part, John didn't watch events sitting idly by. The inaction gave him opportunity to mount a counter-offensive. He decided to fight back. But he realized the vulnerability in fighting alone without organizational strength behind his struggle—thus, the founding of the Inclusive Church, an organization that advocates the full inclusion of homosexuals in the Church of England. The group was founded by Giles Fraser, then-vicar of St. Mary's, Putney.

Fraser became the first chair of the Inclusive Church at the pioneering meeting held at St. Mary's, Putney. Unlike Paul Tatchell, Fraser was not gay, but he shared Tatchell's razzmatazz for brinkmanship and showmanship. Also unlike Tatchell, he was well lettered, with excellent performance at a high level of academic learning. Fraser attended Newcastle University; Ripon College, Cuddesdon; and the University of Lancaster, where he obtained a doctorate in 1999. Afterwards, he taught, wrote, and lectured in various institutions while involved continually in social and political causes.

Journalism provided him the platform, power, and opportunity to influence public opinion. Media influence was bewitching to Fraser. Indeed, he confided in a newspaper article that he "would be the first to admit that he is fond of the sound of his own voice."[4] And the priestly calling afforded him extra status. Fraser was a Jew with a Christian mother. His father was part of a long line of Jewish immigrants to Britain who had adopted the new name of Fraser (from the original Friedburg) during the Second World War. Introduced to Jewish tradition at the early age, Fraser was influenced to adopt Christianity from the Christian education he received. Fraser decided to become a priest while studying politics at Oxford. Subsequently, he was ordained a deacon in 1993 and a year later certified as a freshly-minted minister. By 2000, he had moved up to be appointed "team rector" overseeing two churches, St Mary's and All Saints, in his southwest London parish.

Christianity proved an ally in furthering his political and societal goals, and his appointment as vicar of St. Mary's Church, Putney, was fortuitous. The church had a perfect history for the resurgence of libertarian values. The church sits close to the River Thames, by the southern approach to Putney Bridge. St. Mary's Church dates back to the thirteenth century and was host to the epochal 1647 Putney Debates during the English Civil War, a series of discussions about a new constitution for Britain. At the heart of the discussions were the members of the New Model Army, who, after seizing London from their Presbyterian opponents in August 1647, had encamped at Putney. In narrow perspective, the Putney Debates were a means of ensuring that the state discharged its responsibility to men bearing arms. But in wider context, they were about expanding the constitutional guarantees of liberty and freedom.

Fraser exploited the opportunity of teaching moral leadership to the British Army at the Defence Academy at Shrivenham to play off the Putney Debates, as if they served his cause. And from 2000 on, he started using the St. Mary's Church as the launch pad of his scheme, with Jeffrey John as *cause celebre*. Inclusive Church was therefore born in a historically incongruous place, for he had things backward. In

4. Thompson, "Giles Fraser: The Church's Own Radical Cleric Will Still Have a Voice."

the seventeenth century, St. Mary's Church celebrated democratic decision-making process. It highlighted common consent as the legitimate foundation of group decision making. Opinions and counter-opinions were traded in a free exchange of ideas. Everybody—the majority and the minority—had his or her say. But the final decisions of the day belonged to the majority. There was respect for institution, law, and order. In contrast, the church was now being used to provide a springboard for schemes to subject the majority to the tyranny of the minority, to hatch narrow and selfish plots. So the Inclusive Church was guilty of exploitation.

Jeffrey John and Giles Fraser shared the same vocation but were opposites in several ways. John was gay; Fraser was not. Indeed, the latter was married with two girls and a boy. John was embattled, the church disapproving of his chosen lifestyle. Fraser had no such burden. The duo had a commonality however. Both were disgruntled, bearing animosities against their vocation and faith. That led to the Inclusive Church. The organization didn't have to invent a new theory of social engagement. That was in existence already. The LGBT movement had a ready-made manual for public dissent. It had perfected its style and stratagem, tested and certified for effectiveness over time, a do-it-yourself kit for advancing the homosexual cause.

And success they had: The organization's petition in support of John garnered nearly 10,000 purported signatures. Unlike the nine bishops, however, whose identities were public, the supporters of John's cause were shrouded in secrecy, a mass of unknown, faceless, and obscure partisans. Had Inclusive Church truly gathered some 10,000 signatures? Or was this merely ingeniously fabricated propaganda? Either way, Canterbury felt the petition's weight. Frankly, the Jeffrey John debacle reinforced the maxim that "uneasy lies the head wearing a crown."

Archbishop Rowan Williams was in a tight spot. He had tied his own hands by signing the 1998 pro-gay and lesbian document. Now that the proverbial hen had come home to roost, he was trapped, sandwiched between two uncompromising parties. Unluckily for him, by virtue of his position, he was the only one who could douse the burning fire. He was required to make a categorical decision. He had to deliver either a yes or a no. Williams was in an unenviable condition. His choice was narrow, either to support Jeffrey John and incur the wrath of the majority of the Communion leaders, or stand by the majority and become a traitor to the rebelling minority. Prudently, he chose to vacillate initially. However, he could not hedge his bet forever.

Developments galloping at rapid rate foreclosed the luxury of continued delay. On the home front, John, Fraser, and Inclusive Church, had their media savvy, their activist swagger, and the hubris to dismiss their foes as inconsequential, but the crisis had become a Communion-wide global disagreement.[5]

Williams was confronted with a precarious situation, underscored by reactions from many parts of the Communion. Several leaders signified their readiness to "split from the Communion if the consecration went ahead." Williams had no alternative

---

5. Akinola, "Why I Object to Homosexuality."

but to grapple with the dangerous development, with little room for maneuvering. For the first time in the long history of the church, a new troubling and troublesome word—"split"—had crept into its lexicon. Williams made his choice, averting the split by siding with the majority. He dumped Jeffrey John. Even though he had supported the pro-gay and lesbian group at the Lambeth Conference and signed the dissenting document, he shied away from sacrificing the greater interest of the Communion. It seemed he had no choice but to defend a position and policy that the broader community of the church had arrived at and was willing to defend at all costs.

On Sunday, July 6, 2003, 48 days after the debacle had started, Williams reversed the nomination of John unceremoniously and publicly. The Inclusive Church's account was that John "had not agreed" to voluntarily stand down. In other words, Williams finally decided to wield the big stick.

John might have failed in achieving the bishopric. But he didn't end up a tragic hero or a humiliated loser. He was given a consolation prize. Nine months later, on April 19, 2004, he was appointed as the dean of St. Albans. Five months after the appointment, his induction took place on July 2, 2004.

John wasn't willing to forget the course of events. Nor did he throw in the towel admitting surrender. Formation of the Inclusive Church had given life, steam, and power to the homosexual movement. The question was merely when to push the elephant of the gay issue into the Anglican room. A new chapter opened in the life of the Communion, with the expression "endemic crisis" assuming a new meaning. The 2003 episode didn't make John eat humble pie, and the majority of leaders in the Anglican Church, particularly those from the Global South, were badly shaken by the incident and increasingly disturbed by the antics of their Western counterparts.

5

The Last Straw

America, 2003

Within eighteen days of the provocative nomination of Jeffrey John by the Church of England, the Anglican Communion was confronted with another case of similar nature. Could this be a coincidence? On June 7, 2003, the Episcopal Church in the United States of America (ECUSA, later TEC when it rebranded as The Episcopal Church) stoked the fire with appointment of an openly practicing gay priest as a bishop. TEC's action truly brought the Anglican house down. This was the last element of the three-pronged revolt—Canada and England being the other two—to upstage the 1998 Lambeth Conference's majority decision on homosexuality. Of the 142 American bishops who attended the conference, more than half, 54 percent (numbering 76 to be exact) signed the apology and assured that the Communion would hear from their group on the gay and lesbian issue.

The man at the center of the storm was Gene Robinson. At birth, the physician in charge of his delivery gave Robinson little chance of survival. Indeed, the odds were that the new infant was more likely to die than live. Consequently, the doctor requested two names from his parents—one name for the boy if he lived, the other for the statutory death certificate in case he died. Like every set of parents, the couple had expectations of the new addition to their family. Charles and Imogene Robinson were looking forward to a girl child. Confronted with the disconcerting news of a high possibility of infant mortality, the deeply religious Charles and Imogene accepted the pronouncement with equanimity. The baby was named Vicky, the female version of Charles' father's name, Victor, and also Gene, derived from the mother's name—Vicky Gene Robinson. Temporarily paralyzed at birth, his head was malformed. He fought serious battles with illness for the greater part of his childhood years. The family was poor, living on the margin of existence, ordinary tenant famers working on tobacco fields as sharecroppers. They doted on their new child, and he survived against the odds. But he never ceased striking fears in his parents, particularly his father, who wondered if each of the boy's steps might be his last.

Both parents were committed church attenders at their small Disciples of Christ congregation. Charles and Imogene inculcated that same virtue in Gene, as they fondly called him. They ensured his strict attendance at Sunday school, and every Sunday they towed him to church, doing their best to teach him Christian values.

Though born fragile, Robinson seemed blessed with a natural fighting spirit. His troubled childhood and financially challenged parents didn't diminish his growth. He grew up smart and sharp. At 18, he had found his way to college on a full scholarship, and he graduated in American studies. This was not his first choice for a major. He was previously considering a medical degree, but somehow philosophy and theology had begun to interest him. And so, the year of his gradation, 1969, Robinson found the ordained ministry to be of greater attraction. He proceeded to the Episcopal General Theological Seminary in New York for his master of divinity degree. This was the same institution attended by a host of earlier advocates of homosexuality in the Episcopal Church, people like Ellen Barret,[1] Paul Moore,[2] and Presiding Bishop Frank Griswold, the American church leader at the time of Robinson's appointment. Robinson received his degree in 1973, and that same year, he was ordained a deacon in the diocese of Newark. The ordaining bishop was the Rt. Rev. Leland Stark, who also made him a priest within six months. Stark might have been unaware of Robinson's sexual orientation, and it's a matter of speculation whether that would have made any difference.

Stark was a maverick of sorts himself. A nonconformist, he defied the orthodox views of his time, bringing his diocese along with him in the crusade for social change. He was the first bishop to make an African-American a dean of any Episcopal cathedral in the church. He was also a strong opponent of the Vietnam War, and he lent his voice and personality to the peace movement, even travelling to Vietnam and Africa for the cause.

Stark supported women's ordination to the priesthood just as he stood solidly behind the black power movement in the larger society. He defied New Jersey Governor Richard J. Hughes, who, fearing race riots, had cancelled a national black power conference in Newark a week before its opening. But Stark provided his Cathedral House and diocesan administrative office for the conference. He was also a power broker in the imbroglio between James Pike and the House of Bishops. Pike, a bishop who defied many orthodox Christian doctrines, was arraigned on heresy charges by the House of Bishops, but deftly, Stark worked out a truce that led to a compromise between the two sides. Stark was a man of exceptional negotiating skills, but did that

1. Rev. Ellen Barret was the first lesbian to be ordained as a priest in the Episcopal Church and the first president of Integrity USA, a group established in 1974 to advocate acceptance of homosexuality in the church.

2. Bishop Paul Moore of New York ordained Ellen Barrett despite his awareness that she was a lesbian, which was against the canon of the Episcopal Church itself and the larger Communion's policy.

qualify him to address the issue of Gene Robinson? Ordination had its own rules, very different from those of negotiation and compromise.

Robinson knew *ab initio* that he was *prima facie* disqualified from priesthood because of his sexual orientation. Homosexuality violated the doctrine of the church. Robinson claimed that as far back as his seminary days, he had been having homosexual thoughts. He sought counselling to rid himself of same-sex attraction, but it didn't go away. During that same period, he also began a heterosexual courtship with his future wife, Isabella "Boo" McDaniel. Robinson claimed he revealed his same-sex attraction to McDaniel one month into their relationship. He shared with her "his background and his fears about sexuality." Boo was a remarkably understanding young woman. She was in love too, perhaps. They planned to marry, and a month before their wedding, Robinson raised his fears again. He warned that their relationship might not last because of his homosexual tendencies. Nonetheless, they married in 1972, with Robinson at age 25. For thirteen years, the terror in Robinson's life was under strict control. The nagging sexual drive for a male partner seemed subdued. They even raised a family. Their first daughter, Jamee, came five years after their marriage in 1977, while Ella, followed four years later in 1981.

The Robinsons established The Sign of the Dove Retreat Centre, which combined business with ministry. During summer, the center was turned into a horse camp for children. In 1975, however, the couple decided to relocate to New Hampshire. Boo was born there, and the place suited them well. Unfortunately, their blissful life didn't last long. The ghost of Robinson's yesteryears re-emerged, and their marriage slipped into uncertainty. In 1985, during the couple's thirteenth year of marriage, Robinson came out to friends as a homosexual. He moved out of the family house, leaving his children aged eight and four. Boo became a single parent, though she and Robinson said they remained friends. The nuptial knot that tied him to Boo was finally broken in 1986, when they divorced.

Robinson didn't remain a divorcee for long. In 1987, he went on holidays to Saint Croix, an island in the Caribbean within the district of the United States Virgin Islands but with some measures of independence. There he met Mark Andrew, a staffer at the Peace Corps headquarters in Washington, DC, and a romance developed. Eight months later, they began life together. On July 2, 1988, Robinson and Andrew moved into a new house. The couple had the best wishes of Robinson's bishop, New Hampshire's Douglas Theuner, who was invited as their special guest to personally bless their new home.

Theuner was elected the bishop of the New Hampshire diocese in 1986, the year of Robinson's coming out. The Rt. Rev. Theuner wasn't a home-grown bishop. Previously serving in Connecticut, he was elected bishop coadjutor of New Hampshire in 1986. He rose quickly to assume full episcopal control of the diocese that same year. Theuner was neither a rookie priest nor an untested church administrator. He was ordained in 1962. After donning the collar, he had served congregations in Ohio and

Connecticut before landing in New Hampshire for nearly two dozen years of pastoral work, to which brought his social ideals and philosophy. His major concern was social justice, with AIDS, human sexuality, family planning, and Planned Parenthood topping his interests. Accordingly, he served on various boards and committees engaging these subjects.

A populist, Theuner's focus was on the poor, the insecure, the vulnerable, the socially disadvantaged, and the economically fragile. Enthusiastically, he advocated public action on their behalf. He was never afraid to state his convictions, nor reluctant to hold his position against all opposition, no matter his unpopularity. He facilitated the golden era in Robinson's clerical career, publicly endorsing Robinson's ways of life—his public declaration of being a homosexual, his divorce, his taking on a new gay partner, and his establishing a home with that same-sex partner. Robinson's conduct was incompatible with church doctrine, but it didn't seem to bother Theuner. Robinson was the subordinate "in whom Theuner was well pleased." It was a protective relationship with an impenetrable wall to shield Robinson. He brought him under his wings and made him canon to the ordinary, his executive assistant. From 1988 until Theuner's retirement 18 years later, Robinson worked in no position other than as Theuner's chief helper.

It appeared that the godfather wanted his godson to succeed him, and he was placed strategically to fulfill that wish, within the top hierarchy of the Episcopal Church. Within the regional block of the church, he was influential. He was the president of Province I, a position he occupied from 1994 to 2002. Nationally, he was also a member of the Presiding Bishop's Council of Advice, which for five years he led as its president. In terms of power, position, and influence, Theuner was ideally located to maneuver the process to Robinson's advantage.

However, the 1998 Lambeth Conference threw spanners into the works! Many of the gay and lesbian advocates were anticipating the conference's provision of moral authority for the ordination of homosexuals in the church. The crushing defeat collapsed their house of cards.

Theuner was among those who suffered the crushing blow, for he was one of the dissident bishops who signed the letter to gays and lesbians kicking against the Lambeth Conference's decision. In the end, he wasn't content with merely grumbling. Time was running against him, for in 2003, Theuner's tenure was going to expire, and he was due to retire. Another Lambeth Conference was not due to be held until 2008. He would be long gone by then—out of power, out of influence, and no longer in control of the lever to insure his protégé would be installed in office. It was now or never.

On June 7, 2003, at St. Paul's Church, Concord, Theuner achieved his goal. Robinson was elected bishop of the New Hampshire diocese. It wasn't smooth sailing however. He failed to win on the first ballot. The diocese's rules required 39 votes from clergy and 83 lay votes to guarantee the election of a bishop. Robinson didn't make that number. On the second ballot, however, he fared better, becoming the New

Hampshire bishop-elect. However, he had to cross one more hurdle before he could truly say the election was successful.

By the American church's law, the national church, the Episcopal Church, oversees the election of bishops. A part of the law gives authority to the national church for vetting and reviewing both the procedure and the candidate emerging from the process. Another law requires that, when the election of a bishop falls within 120 days of the General Convention of the church, its highest legislative body, the consent of the two constituent bodies of the national church—the House of Deputies and the House of Bishops—must be sought. So Robinson's election moved to the General Convention.

It would have been surprising if Robinson's election had occurred trouble-free at the Episcopal Church's General Convention in August 2003. Groups with divergent interests had dug trenches and positioned themselves ahead of the convention. First among the groups were the pro-gay dissenting bishops within the House of Bishops itself, those who had authored the apologia to homosexuals over the outcome of the 1998 Lambeth Conference with a promise to see the wrong righted. Against this group was the minority opposing them, which stood firm in its opposition to the step the church was taking. So, the Episcopal Church's upper legislative chamber was split as the bishops entered the convention. Each group was determined to show its strength. In spite of the outward concealment of conflict, its imminence was apparent.

Gene Robinson had a second line of backers at the Convention. There was no doubt about the election's outcome in the House of Deputies. With the work of pro-gay organizations like Integrity USA[3] and Oasis[4] within the American church, much infiltration by priests and lay members predisposed to advancement of the homosexual cause had been achieved within the House of Deputies. Many partisans in the House of Deputies were coming to the Convention to prove their might and strength within the church.

As the Convention approached, signals indicated a resolute will on the part of the pro-homosexual groups to see Robinson's election confirmed at all cost. Indeed, the in-house activists and external LGBT groups were united in that singular endeavor. Within and outside, the forces of pressure had been mustered. The 2003 General Convention of the American church was therefore going to be momentous, its events defining, the issues groundbreaking. The pro-Robinson rooters were formidable. They

3. Integrity USA was formed in 1974 to advance the homosexual agenda within the Episcopal Church. By 2003, it had acquired power, strength, and formidable influence within the church. As part of the organization's strategy, it changed its own Convention to coincide with the triennial Episcopal Church General Convention.

4. Oasis, an outreach organization for homosexuals within the Episcopal Church, was established in 1989 under the maverick and eccentric bishop of Newark, the Rt. Rev. John Spong, who condemned religion generally and specifically denounced the Christian faith in utter disregard of his canonical vow. Against the policy and rule of the American church and the global Anglican Communion, he founded Oasis and installed the first openly male gay priest, Robert Williams. Oasis became a powerful agent for rallying homosexuals to infiltrate the basic structure and governing organs of the church like the House of Deputies.

were better organized, better resourced, and better positioned. Even without a center to coordinate their activities, it was obvious that the confirmation was bound go through.

Weak as the small, vocal minority was, they refused to be intimidated by the power of the forces arrayed against them. Their convictions were the strength of their opposition. They argued that Robinson's election violated all the rules of the church—local and international—and especially 1998 Lambeth Resolution 1.10. They held that as a church, they were bound to uphold rules, respect regulations, and obey laws. They warned that defiance was bound to incite unwholesome reactions. The problem, however, was that the American church had seen the death of reason and rational argument. Decisions of the church were not about what the Scriptures said, or what the canons of the church prescribed, or what the worldwide Anglican Communion decided to be in the common interest of the Anglican Church. Rather, weight lay in what the cliques manipulating the church decided or felt. For nearly 40 years these powerful cabals had tilted the church as they pleased.

On August 3, 2003, Robinson's confirmation process began. At the House of Bishops, nothing unfavorable to him happened. Then the battle shifted to the House of Deputies. The first two of the three votes required to ratify his election were held, with Robinson winning. He was coasting home to victory. The road to becoming the first divorced, openly gay bishop elected in the history of the worldwide Anglican Communion lay before him. But suddenly, on August 4, a series of allegations, serious and scandalous accusations, charges difficult to ignore, was raised against him.

David Lewis, a male parishioner in Manchester, Vermont, a neighboring diocese to Robinson's, accused Robinson of inappropriately touching him in a suggestive way. Following that allegation was another that "Gene Robinson's website was linked by one click to 5,000 pornographic websites." The second accusation came from one David Virtue.[5] By the rules of the Episcopal Church, all outstanding allegations about an elected candidate must be resolved for his consideration to proceed to the House of Deputies for the consent vote. As a result, the Committee on the Consecration of Bishops was mandated to look into the allegations against Robinson. That same August 4, the committee began a two-day hearing. The enquiry was conducted in the open. Supporters and opponents alike were given the opportunity to present their case.

Robinson was a master in the art of wooing public sentiment to his advantage. He knew how to shift the burden to opponents and attract sympathy to his side. At that critical period when his reputation was at stake, he knew how valuable the image of a "family man" would be to boost his public perception. Thus, beside him stood Ella, who was 4 when Robinson divorced her mother. Ella Robinson, a fully-grown young woman in her early twenties, brought a letter from her mother, which she read in the open, expressing strong support for her ex-husband. With this invaluable character endorsement from Boo and Ella, Robinson was certainly on a good track. Robinson's trouble then evaporated when David Lewis recanted his story.

5. https://virtueonline.org/david-virtue.

Lewis had said he came across Robinson at an event involving Vermont and New Hampshire dioceses. Robinson was the executive secretary in charge of the province, and the occasion had provided opportunity for Robinson and Lewis to engage in conversation. Lewis had observed Robinson's "seductive arm-squeezing and back-stroking" friendliness. The same uncomfortable chumminess allegedly had been repeated with Lewis on another occasion. His impressions were based on the two incidents. The encounters left him to conclude that "as outstanding as Gene Robinson may have been thus far as a priest, my personal experience of him is that he does not maintain appropriate boundaries with men."

But when the Committee on the Consecration of Bishops, headed by the Rt. Rev. Gordon Scruton, bishop of Western Massachusetts, called Lewis to confirm an email he sent the presiding bishop, Lewis recanted. He retracted his claim. He was no longer sure about his interpretation of Robinson's actions. Perhaps he read too much meaning into the two incidents, he averred. He felt others might interpret those actions differently, seeing them as innocuous gestures expressing ordinary affability. He regretted his use of the word "harassment" in referring to Robinson's actions. Yet he would not deny that the two events left him disturbed. Pressed over whether he still wanted formal charges, he declined. So, the investigating committee acquitted Robinson.

David Virtue's accusation regarding pornography was not as easily dismissed. He was physically present at the Convention and had made the damaging allegation openly. Usually, routine press briefings were held during the Convention as sideline activities. It was during one such scheduled exchange with the media, on Monday, August 4, with Virtue in attendance, that the allegation surfaced. Virtue indicated his intention to speak, and he was invited to the podium. From the microphone, he posed a question for bishops Wendell Gibbs of Michigan and Ed Little, Gibbs's counterpart from Northern Indiana. The two were the spokespersons for the bishops at the Convention.

"Do you know that Gene Robinson's website is linked by one click to 5,000 pornographic websites?" He had dropped a bombshell. The media gathering was rocked by consternation.

"No," the bishops had replied him pointedly.

Virtue then steered the bishops to his real point: "Well, now that you do know this, will this change your vote on his election?"

It was Gibbs who replied, coolly: "I would doubt the veracity of such information at this moment."

Curtly, he dismissed the allegation as "a last-minute ploy." Flushed, Virtue found his way back to his seat shaking his head. Unfortunately, at that point in time, he couldn't have stepped on a more vicious rattlesnake. He became a marked man that must be brought down at all cost. Within hours of the press conference, the gay community went into hyper-frenzy, activating all of its connections and networks. The cult-like fury to undo the harm Virtue had unleashed was pursued with a rabid ferocity. There was only one desired outcome: to neutralise the damage to Robinson's reputation. The rescue mission had to be as fast as possible. Robinson had to be washed of the stain to which his character had been exposed. He must be made to look good before the Convention delegates. On the other hand, the opposite had to be done to Virtue. His credibility and integrity had to be torn to shreds, his moral standing brought into question; doubts had to be sown about his reputation both before the Convention delegates and in the wider public. Virtue must be discredited, tarnished as a malicious, spurious, and biased character assassin.

Gay movements thrive on a persecution complex. They treat anything uncomplimentary as an assault, a challenge to "war." Within a short time, an enormous volume of research was done on Virtue. The astounding results "brought out" a lot about him. Virtue was taken to the cleaners. Every medium that old and new technology permitted—newspapers, magazines, blogs, websites, etc.—was drafted as an assault weapon. The combined effect ensured saturation of the public information meant to discredit him. Virtue, as those in arms to support Robinson would want people to believe, had no virtues. He was an "academic fraud": "What are his degrees, and what institutions conferred them?" one of the pro-gay blogs wrote. Fortunately, another bitter critic provided the answer that David Virtue was educated at Scots College in Wellington, New Zealand, studied English literature and philosophy at Victoria University in Wellington, and ended at London Bible College, London, England, where he completed his diploma in theology. He was not a crass illiterate as portrayed. He even had theological education at Trinity Evangelical Divinity School in Deerfield, Illinois, before completing his master's in interdisciplinary studies at Regent College, University of British Columbia, Vancouver.

Those initial deprecatory onslaughts were, however, not enough. Thus, the second tack was to vilify Virtue as an "impostor." The question arose over what qualified him, a "Baptist minister, to comment so extensively on the beliefs and practices of the Anglican Communion/Episcopal Church-USA?" Yes, Virtue was an ordained Baptist minister (ABCUSA). He had served as the associate pastor of St. Paul's Baptist Church, Montclair, New Jersey, for two years. For over 20 years, however, he had worked as managing editor of the Virginia Churchman as well as a columnist, journalist, and writer on religious issues. The ten years preceding the Convention, he had been the president of a high tech media corporation and edited an Episcopal newsletter besides his production of *Episcopal/Anglican Online Newsletter* for mainstream Anglicans worldwide, with a reach of nearly 100,000 readers in 36 countries. If Virtue was not Anglican by denomination, his professional interaction gave him the capacity to make intelligent comments on Anglican affairs. Nevertheless, he was excoriated as "the notorious online source of [an] aggressive anti-women, anti-homosexual agenda," as the gay group asserted. It was wholesale character assassination.

But the substance of the charge remained: Did Robinson have links to pornography on his website? Whether by error of omission or commission, Robinson neglected the most obvious move that could have helped his case—bringing his daughters, Jamee and Ella, as character witnesses. They could have provided the corroborative evidence about his character and morals. Jamee and Ella could have torn to shreds any notion of Robinson's complicity with such an inappropriate behavior for a father of two girls. Their testimony would been taken as evidence of how respectable, responsible, and disciplined he was as a father and that it would have been inconceivable for him to expose other people's children to what he would not have permitted his own children to access. But Jamee and Ella made no appearance; nor was it read anywhere that they spoke on his behalf.

On the other hand, a number of organizations in the gay community rose in Robinson's defence. They came up with "evidence" to discredit David Virtue's allegation. First, was the review of Robinson's page on the Diocese of New Hampshire's website. No link to pornographic sites was found. Based on this, Virtue was dubbed a liar. He was challenged to provide the link's exact address. Virtue was forthcoming. He gave the precise address as http://www.outright.org/. He insisted that the link was still active as of the night before his making the allegation at the press briefing.

The investigators themselves discovered that an organization by the name that Virtue claimed actually existed. Accordingly, the next step was to review www.outright. org. There was no discovery of a connection to a pornographic site. The indisputable fact, however, was that www.outright.org belonged to a gay and lesbian organization. The organization, Outright, has the mission "to create safe, positive, and affirming environments for young gay, lesbian, bisexual, trans[gender] and questioning people ages 22 and under." These were young people the age of Robinson's children. Outright pursues "a youth-driven philosophy." It works to integrate "youth needs and beliefs" into a "decision, and [builds] a collaboration of youth and adults [to] provide support, education, advocacy, and social activities." In other words, its underlying motive is to catch them young, from 22 years and under. But what was the minimal age that "under" implied? That was the nagging question.

Yet, Robinson's defenders said the idea of Outright "sounds positive." They also "discovered" that "there was no evidence of the organization's relationship to Gene Robinson." But that was a lie. Indeed, they found that Robinson helped launch an Outright chapter in Concord, N.H. Quickly, they attempted to undermine the damage. They got the organization to make a statement. The disclaimer was that Robinson "has not been involved with their work in two years." But it was not denied that he initiated the Concord chapter.

Every new organization needs resources to nurture it. Where did the initial resources that fostered the Concord chapter of Outright come from? Were they from Robinson, the diocese, Province One, friends of the organization, or its young target audience? There was a desperate attempt to bury the facts, yet the ghost of truth kept haunting the facts. Virtue's crucifiers insisted that by characterising Ourtight's website as "Gene Robinson's website," Virtue has told an obvious lie. Well, that made sense.

Gene Robinson and Outright were two separate legal entities, even if one is the god-father and the other a godson. Another "falsehood," they claimed, was the "one click to porn allegation." Shamefacedly, they acknowledged that a "link to porn was found deeply embedded in the outright.org." The embarrassing argument, on the other hand, was that, instead of the one click claimed by Virtue, "it took six clicks from their home page to get to that link." Does that exculpate a father of two, a priest, a guardian, a shepherd, a counsellor, and a potential bishop from getting involved with an organiza-tion purveying pornography, whether by one, two, three or six clicks? To the Scruton Committee, the evidence was too tenuous, thin, watery, and wholly circumstantial. It lacked merit. Consequently, the case was dismissed.

Within 24 hours of giving the road-clear sign, Robinson's hearing was concluded. On August 5, 2003, he received the much-needed consent vote, with 62 of the 107 bishops voting in favour while 43, or 40 percent, were against. So Gene Robinson, a divorced, openly non-celibate, homosexual priest received consent to become the bishop-elect of the diocese of New Hampshire, as well as the first of such bishop-elect in the worldwide Anglican Communion. Admittedly, it stood out as quite a feat.

No one's joy at the Convention surpassed that of Bishop Douglas Theuner. The American church had done what Canterbury could not do. For 18 years, the calf had been under his care, nurtured, protected, and groomed painstakingly. He could bask with a sense of pride on what he made of the ox. The moment was an ecstatic, glorious end for Theuner, a befitting end to his career. The elephant now occupied the center of the room! It was now the main attraction at center stage of an international circus show. The election had certainly pushed the simmering crisis within the Anglican Communion to a serious climax. Consequently, predictable was the reaction that greeted the Convention's decision and its consent vote regarding Gene Robinson. It was sharp and strident in both content and tone. Everywhere, there was uproar. Even before the delegates to the 2003 Episcopal Church General Convention began dispers-ing to their various destinations, it was clear that Gene Robinson's confirmation would brew trouble.

6

A Huge Crisis Looming

Nigeria, 2003

In Abuja, Nigeria, Archbishop Peter Akinola was concerned about the unfolding events in the Anglican Communion. Particularly unsettling were the developments emanating from the Episcopal Church in the United States of America (ECUSA). He was unhappy with the situation. The unsavoury, unpalatable situations were becoming "three" much! Canada began it; England took it over; and now America was completing the triple revolt. Ruminating, he recalled the 1998 Lambeth Conference. The aberrations now occurring were contrary to the decisions reached by the Conference. At Lambeth, he had not been a benchwarmer. He took part fully in the deliberations and voted in all decisions reached. His vote and voice were with the majority. Consequently, his opinion was that no group, no matter how powerful, had the right to subvert the majority's will. Nor was it morally appropriate to employ underhanded maneuvers to thwart the agreed-upon resolution. The American church's attitude smacked of "I-don't-care" boorishness, showing a brazen contempt for the global Anglican Church leaders.

Even before his becoming primate of the Nigerian church, he knew the human sexuality question had not only been contentious but had also arisen often in deliberations of the Anglican Church primates. His predecessor, the Most Rev. Abiodun Adetiloye, had brought the issues back to the floor of the Nigerian House of Bishops after each meeting, providing them with the opportunity to learn about developments within the international arena of the Church. Adetiloye's briefings also offered the bishops a chance to suggest direction to their primate, their own representative, about the Nigerian church's position on the issues, which he was supposed to maintain at the primates' meeting. He knew that decisions had repeatedly been made on these issues by the global leaders. In one sense, he felt they were starting to sound like a broken record, merely reiterating and reaffirming positions that were stressed again and again.[1]

---

1. See from the private papers of Peter Akinola: "Pastoral Letter from the Primates Meeting,

For instance, nine years before Akinola became primate of Church of Nigeria, his predecessor along with other primates of the Anglican Church worldwide met on April 13, 1991, at Newcastle, Ireland. The meeting happened to be the first coming together of all the Anglican Church primates with the Most Rev. George Carey, the newly appointed archbishop of Canterbury. His colleagues warmly welcomed him and pledged their "wholehearted personal support." At the dawn of Carey's new era, however, the human sexuality matter arose. America's Presiding Bishop Edmond Browning had presented the issue like a bouquet of flowers to his colleagues. He had laid before them a report on human sexuality prepared by his church, which was to be presented to the American General Convention in July after the primates meeting.

Browning wanted his fellow primates' opinion on the report, and after reading it, they warned, "These are sensitive questions." They told him that the American church "needs to give full weight to the testimony of the Holy Scripture." They counselled that homosexuality should be studied in light of available scientific evidence; that he should be clear with the fact that opinions within the Anglican Communion on human sexuality differed considerably; and that discussion on the subject must be approached with "honesty, compassion and a genuine desire to seek the will of God." The primates insisted that

> it would not be faithful to the Gospel to ignore or simply label as homophobic the anguished cries of men and women who feel hurt, rejected, and angry that what they see as sin is not being reaffirmed as such.

Four years later, the 36 primates representing all national provinces into which the global Anglican Communion was divided assembled again in Windsor, England. The weeklong meeting began on March 10 and ended March 17, 1995. Human sexuality appeared on the agenda. Nothing had changed or weakened their earlier stand regarding issues of human sexuality, which they judged "deep and complex," a matter unlikely to "admit of easy [and] instant answers." In the end, they maintained that resolving a thorny issue like that demanded a "careful process of reflecting . . . [particularly] in the light of the scriptures and the Christian moral tradition." They counselled "every part of the Church to face the questions of sexuality with honesty and integrity." In addition, the Anglican leaders warned against "unnecessary confrontation and polarization."

The Windsor meeting was a prelude to the 1998 Lambeth Conference. In fact, there was another gathering on the eve of the Lambeth Conference, the Jerusalem meeting of March 18, 1997. The Holy Land gathering witnessed discussion and finalization of plans for the Lambeth Conference. In other words, no fewer than three

---

Newcastle, Ireland; Statement from the Primates Meeting in Windsor, England, March 17, 1995; "A Closing Statement from the Primates Meeting Jerusalem," Jerusalem, March 18, 1997; "Final Communique from the Primates Meeting in March 2000 in Portugal"; "A Pastoral Letter and Call to Prayer"; "On the Archbishop of Canterbury's Presidential Address at ACC 12"; "Report of the Meeting of the Anglican Communion."

times in six years—1991, 1995, and 1997—the second highest organ in the administration of the worldwide Anglican Church had discussed, debated, and decided on the issue of human sexuality. The stand of the Communion was made clear, explicit, and unequivocal. At the 1998 Lambeth Conference, bringing all bishops of the Communion together into a larger pool of global opinion, the subject again was examined and a majority decision reached. The steps the Canadian, British, and American churches were taking were obviously on the path of perfidy and outright revolt.

Archbishop Akinola became primate of Church of Nigeria in 2000, and he attended his first primates meeting in Portugal that same year, March 22–29. Two major issues surfaced from their talk, on which they had strong points of convergence. The first was an agreement to give "priority not simply to the proclamation of the gospel in words but to the 'holistic evangelism' that looks to transform the whole person." Secondly, there was acknowledgement of "the deep problems arising from conflicting teaching and practice in relation to sexual ethics in different provinces or parts of Provinces of the Communion." They also highlighted accountability as a cardinal principle binding their corporate union:

> When we see in each other what we believe to be failure or unfaithfulness, we
> expect honesty and challenge from each other.

They were talking about what ought to be, but the reality was that despite overwhelming adoption of Lambeth Resolution 1.10 as "the rule that was to be binding," it had "been rejected in some dioceses of [the] Church." "Such clear and public repudiation of those sections of the Resolution related to the public blessing of same-sex unions and the ordination of declared non-celibate homosexuals," the primates stated, "have come to threaten the unity of the communion in a profound way."

No previous meeting had witnessed such an overt warning. The stage had been set for a new phase in the crisis. Particularly telling was the statement that continued repudiation of the majority's decision would have only one possible consequence: a rupture of the church's unity.

The archbishop of Canterbury, the Most Rev. George Carey, had also been nursing his own anxiety over developments within the Communion, and so he penned a passionate appeal to all bishops of the Communion. He desperately struggled in the February 17, 2000, letter to straddle the middle, maintaining a conciliatory position between the two conflicting sides. On the side of the majority, he asserted that the "Church's historic teaching on this matter is so clearly evident in scripture as to be fixed and final." Nevertheless, he had no interest in squabbling with advocates of homosexuality. As far as he was concerned, they had the right to express their view as a group "not convinced that the Bible speaks at all clearly to the questions currently before us."

For him, however, there was a defining line: Resolution 1.10 and other issues tackled by the 1998 Lambeth Conference's Section Report on Human Sexuality. He saw no room for compromise on those issues because they were already settled. At the same time, he also considered unequivocal the injunction to listen to the experience of homosexuals within the Church, an action prescribed by the same report. Carey counselled his colleagues that, as primates, they possessed "first and foremost the responsibility to foster this engagement and to exercise pastoral care and support towards each other."

The Anglican leader was quick to identify two misconceptions he felt should not be allowed to interfere with or cloud the listening process: (1) that readiness to listen signalled moral leeway on the matter; and (2) that it gave the green light to publicly demonize, vilify, and brand those against homosexuality in the Church as "political opponents." The archbishop's pastoral letter and the March 2000 communique of the primates meeting were like two sides of the same coin in their rationality, logic, and gravity.

Archbishop Akinola shared the same view as the archbishop of Canterbury and supported his truce formula. For a leader confronted with such a crisis, and eager to preserve the unity of the Church entrusted to his care, peace and amicable resolution should be the first option.

Unfortunately, the next meeting of the Anglican primates gave no assurance that his entreaty would be respected. Hosted by the American Episcopal Church, Anglican Church leaders from all over the world assembled at the Kanuga Conference Centre in North Carolina on March 8, 2001. Though it had only been a year since the previous meeting, it was if it had never happened. The rebellious behavior of the American Episcopalians was transforming advocates of biblical sexual morality into "alienated groups within the church."[2]

Though the majority of the primates were saddened by what they were hearing, the meeting navigated the familiar ground of reticence, followed by the usual rhetoric enjoining peace and urging "responsibility toward each other." And so the pacification continued, with timid appeals to those breaching the standards to rethink their actions. The Pastoral Letter written subsequently asked every cadre of the Communion's leadership to avoid "actions that might damage [the Church's] credibility in the world."

Either the primates were victims of utopian thinking or were naïve, lacking ability to read the political atmosphere. They didn't seem to pick up on the air of deceit around them. Such was the situation when they gathered on April 17, 2002, at Canterbury, England, for what proved to be an epochal event. It coincided with Archbishop Carey's last meeting, the final time he would preside over the primates meeting. Carey was due to retire in five months, by the end of October 2002. The meeting was for the primates to bid farewell to the archbishop and his wife and to express appreciation for their contributions to the Church. For 11 years, Carey had weathered the storm as he piloted the global Anglican Communion. Inopportunely, his leadership was almost defined by the peculiarly sour issue of his time—homosexuality. At that valedictory meeting, however, his 37 colleagues from across the world viewed his legacy

2. "A Pastoral Letter and Call to Prayer."

appreciatively. If Carey had failed in his leadership of the Communion, it was not for want of ability. He was striving to walk the Communion's tight rope. He didn't promise what he could not deliver, and he didn't deliver what he did not promise.

The Canterbury meeting also afforded opportunity for the Anglican spiritual fathers to take stock of the Church, with a range of subjects competing for their attention. One was a report from the Consultation of Anglican Communion Legal Advisors, a group comprising more than 20 lawyers drawn from different parts of the Communion. Their meeting had been held ahead of the primates', March 6–13, 2002, and had centred on the "unwritten law common to the churches of the Communion." Incredibly, they discovered an "initial list of forty-four shared principles of canon law common to Anglican churches." Furthermore, they identified an additional fifteen legal issues needing more study. The primates naturally had insufficient time to deal with the report, so they deferred discussion on some aspects. Still, they did reach an important conclusion.

They resolved that "the unwritten law common to the churches of the Communion and expressed as shared principles of canon law may be understood to constitute a fifth 'instrument of unity' within the Church." In other words, these norms peculiar to Anglican churches worldwide should be seen as a further tool for regulating the conduct and affairs of the Church globally. The idea was an entirely novel concept, prompting theological reflection "on the nature of the Church and her mission in [the] world."

Two of the primates (both part of the minority, pro-homosexual 1998 Lambeth group) rose to share their thoughts on this vital subject. The first was Most Rev. Rowan Williams, the primate of Wales, while the second was his counterpart from Canada, the Most Rev. Michael Peers. The two broke new ground in their submission, calling mutually for "the possibility of developing new ecclesial or governing structures so as to free the Churches of the Communion for more effective mission." They requested their fellow "Primates to be open to the development of new patterns of ministry within the inherited legal framework" of the Anglican tradition. Relating their idea to a number of specific action areas, they suggested, for example, a "non-geographic network within the geographically structured dioceses, including, perhaps transcending diocesan boundaries along the lines of the work of religious orders with specific ministry commitments." The suggestions were opening a new frontier in the Anglican history. Given the important nature of the matter, the primates resolved that the issue could not be resolved in an ad hoc manner; the subject demanded time for examination and evaluation, so a think tank was constituted for this purpose. Sounding a note of optimism, their communique observed, "We leave the meeting determined to wrestle together with challenging issues." They would "steadfastly affirm" their commitment to work for "one Communion."

One encouraging sign at the meeting was the appearance of the archbishop's appointments secretary, Mr. Tony Sadler, along with his colleague from the prime minister's office, Mr. William Chapman. The two men were joint secretaries of the Crown Appointment Commission, which oversaw the process of appointing a new archbishop of Canterbury. Their work included consultation with Anglican global leaders regarding qualities required of the new leader. Every primate at the meeting received the *carte blanche* opportunity to share his thoughts on challenges facing the Anglican Communion and qualities desirable in the new leader, who would be called upon to address those issues. For this they were grateful, since it enabled them to make frank statements on the matter. They had made the mind of the Communion known regarding the type of archbishop desired. If all other things were equal, then the wish of the Communion would be fulfilled. So they departed Canterbury, hopeful that the Church would witness a rebirth and that the new leader would fulfill the promise of a united, cohesive Communion.

Archbishop Akinola was among the primates fed a dish of red herrings at the Canterbury meeting. The idyllic environment suffused with charm fooled them all. For barely two months after the meeting, the diocese of Westminster in the Anglican Church of Canada took the unilateral step of approving the blessing of same-sex unions. The coup was well-timed: Primate Michael Peers, along with his counterpart from Wales, the Most Rev. Rowan Williams, had made eloquent pleas for exploring a new ecclesial structure within the Communion, giving no hint of the impending rebellion, indeed, of a well-plotted conspiracy. Archbishop Akinola and others like him had a simple, trusting nature, and the Canadian incident shocked and mortified them. They discovered that they were neophytes in politicking, but they would prove to be quick studies as they came to terms with the style of their opponents.

Despite his not being pleased with the Westminster diocese's upsetting insolence, the Nigerian leader chose to exercise restraint. He was looking forward to the Anglican Consultative Council (ACC) meeting just around the corner. The ACC was scheduled to meet on September 16, 2002, two months after the diocese's unlawful step, and Akinola saw the forum as a good opportunity to deal with the dirty thumb the Canadian church was sticking into the Communion's nose.

Though Archbishop of Canterbury George Carey, who was also president of the Council, could afford to be nonchalant since he was on his way out, he utilized the occasion to wax prophetic in his parting message. His address was a blunt dressing down, a serious tongue lashing, particularly of Bishop Michael Ingham, regarding what he had done. Still, Carey was a man schooled in the art of diplomacy, so he spoke of the action as a matter prompting the "greatest worry." But he also said he must call "a spade a spade," saying that he would be "failing in his duty if [he] recoiled from pointing out the assumption that silence is the safer option." He added, "An erosion of [the] Communion through the adoption of local options [is] reaching crisis proportions today." In simple, clear and unequivocal terms, the Anglican Church leader laid bare his worry to the gathering, stressing that, "my concern is that our Communion is being steadily undermined by diocese and individual bishops taking unilateral action, usually (but not always) in matters to do with sexuality."

Carey warned of a church steadily being driven "towards serious fragmentation," with "the real possibility of two (or, more likely, many more) Anglican bodies emerging." He added, "This erosion of [the] Communion through the adoption of local options has been going on for some thirty years," and the situation had reached a "crisis proportion today."

Regarding Westminster, Carey was charitable in his censure. Difficult as the situation was, he expressed respect for "the sincerity of Bishop Ingham and his diocesan synod," and their belief that "they are acting in the best interests of all." But he made it clear he thought that what they had done was patently wrong:

> Michael [Ingham] and his synod, and other bishops and dioceses in similar situations in North America seem to be making such decisions without regard to the rest of us and against the clear statements of Lambeth '98.

Despite Carey's status as Canterbury's outgoing archbishop, he stoked the fire where it was the fiercest. He spoke the mind of the majority at the gathering, and the "ACC members gave their President a standing ovation." Never could there have been a grander way for him to bow out.

Nine months later, Archbishop Akinola was to render a similar judgement in a comparable situation. By then, Rowan Williams had formally been enthroned as the 104th archbishop of Canterbury, having been installed in February 2003. Three months after his enthronement, the primates had had their first meeting with the new archbishop in Gramado, Southern Brazil. Though five of the 38 primates were unable to attend, it was still a productive meeting, issuing a "Pastoral Letter from the Primates" to all bishops, clergy, and church members in the worldwide Anglican Communion.

It began with exploration of "Our Work Together," which focused on forging a strong theological bond among members of the church, with common standards of theological education. Another important challenge was the problem of HIV/AIDS, and they resolved to build on progress already recorded. Furthermore, the leaders desired to rekindle the bond of fellowship within, through a program of renewal—"Our Shared Communion in Christ."

All 38 provinces of the Church were reminded that they "are irrevocably called into a special relationship of fellowship with one another." The primates, therefore, were enjoined to ensure that "in each province there is a sincere desire to understand how the Gospel is to be applied in our generation." This was followed with another injunction, the requirement "to work and pray that the communion between our churches is sustained and deepened; and to seek from God 'a right judgment in all things' (as the Collect of Pentecost enshrined)."

As expected, the letter moved to human sexuality. The primates declared that "the question of public rites for the blessing of same sex unions is still potentially a cause of divisive controversy" within the Church. The archbishop of Canterbury had, however, spoken on the matter. The Anglican leaders had agreed with the Archbishop of Canterbury on the matter and reiterated that he had indeed captured their minds when he said, "It is through liturgy that we express what we believe, and that there is no theological consensus about same sex unions." Furthermore, they noted that they "as a body cannot support the authorization of such rites." The declaration provoked no dissents, nor were there reports of individuals or groups who grumbled about it. From all indications, the Gramado meeting of the primates went well. It began without a hitch and ended in like manner.

There was, however, a strange "coincidence." The openly-gay Jeffrey John was announced by the Church of England as the diocese of Reading's bishop nominee while the Primates were meeting in Gramado. Indeed, the date of John's announcement, May 20, 2003, was the date the primates had chosen to come together "in a spirit of common prayer and worship, listening for the voice of God as revealed in the Holy Scriptures." Was someone out to play a cruel joke on the primates? Some coincidences can be stranger than fiction. Stranger still was the man at the center of both events—the archbishop of Canterbury. He was leading his colleagues in Brazil in prayers, yet he was also making an announcement in London that negated all the tenets contained in the declaration made at the meeting! Thus, two conflicting roles were performed by Archbishop Williams that day.

The "Pastoral Letter" had reaffirmed the Communion's stand rejecting the authorization of the same-sex rites and ordination of homosexuals, so Akinola was at a loss over why the authorities of Church of England would allow such an affront to occur. Though everybody returned to their respective provinces and picked up their daily chores, the dust raised by John's appointment had begun spreading round the Communion. Through the rest of May and June, John's nomination remained a hotly debated concern within the Church.

Akinola saw no reason for the fuss and confusion. The decisions reached by Church leaders were clear and indisputable. Consequently, he made his stand public in an article titled "Why I Object to Homosexuality," which appeared in *Church Times* on July 4, 2003. He argued that "when scripture says something is wrong and some people say that it is right, such people make God a liar." He disagreed vehemently with the notion that homosexuality was "God-given." Bluntly, he called it "an acquired aberration," (emphasis that of the archbishop). Furthermore, he insisted that the "issue is such an important one, such a defining one, because it has become a chronic aberration, which is being defended and promoted in the church of God." He warned that it had the "potential [of] splitting the Communion."

Akinola echoed Carey's sentiments, but he was not Carey. He didn't share the milieu and background that shaped the latter, and he didn't know how vile the homosexuals' campaign could be. At the same time, he had no awareness concerning the extent and depth of their transnational connections. The Nigerian primate was a novice who had not in any way or form been involved with or exposed to fighting international conspiracies. He was a pastor devoted to building congregations, who, in the course of his long clerical career, had risen to become a reputable church leader of national and international prominence. He possessed strength of character as a person of honor, integrity, and uprightness. He was steadfast in his calling. Yet, as good as possession of those attributes may be, they do not guarantee the capacity to survive in the murky water of politics, whether at the local or international level. Truth can be bitter, change can be hard, and to stand for both in public life is tough. Akinola's gospel-protection activism naturally put him on a firing line.

Coincidentally, the drama that surrounded John's appointment ended dramatically two days after *Church Times* published Akinola's article. The surprising withdrawal occurred on Sunday, July 6, 2003. It probably didn't have anything to do with Akinola. But with the article, he had set up an important marker regarding his principles and conviction.

Added to this was the Lagos meeting that he had with the John Chew six days later on July 12, 2003, where plans for resuscitating of the Global South were agreed upon.[3] And then there was the proposed trouble-shooting mission to America, where he was to lead a gathering of the "Worldwide Anglican Mainstream Leaders." The July 23, 2003, undertaking was to persuade the American church's General Convention to withhold its planned confirmation of the openly-gay priest Gene Robinson, to avert confrontation with the Communion. Akinola had no prepared formula or organized scheme to confront the challenges thrust upon him. However, he had accepted the responsibility, and there was no turning back for him. Even with the small step he had taken already, he had stirred a tumultuous wind, one whose impact he could scarcely imagine.

---

3. "Minutes Notes (Archbishop Peter Akinola & Bishop John Chew)."

7

The Last-Ditch Attempt

America, 2003

Archbishop Akinola arrived at Fairfax, Virginia, in the United States of America, on July 23, 2003, for a prearranged conference to persuade the American General Convention not to confirm the openly gay, divorced father of two, and practicing homosexual Gene Robinson as a bishop. The event came barely seventeen days after the archbishop of Canterbury laid to rest the scandalous appointment of Jeffrey John as a bishop in England. Six other archbishops had joined Akinola, plus fifteen bishops from the United States. The laity was represented as well, coming from Canada and around the globe. It was truly, as labelled, a "Gathering of Worldwide Anglican Mainstream Leaders."[1]

Archbishop Akinola was entrusted with the responsibility of presiding over the meeting of leaders representing "a majority of the world's 75 million Anglicans."[2] With him were the Most Rev. Drexel Gomez (archbishop and primate of the West Indies), Archbishops Emmanuel Kolini (primate of Rwanda), Bernard Malango (primate of Central Africa), Gregory Venables (primate of the Southern Cone), Yong Ping Chung (primate of South East Asia), and Peter Jensen of Sydney. Again, the church leaders' objective in the United States was to present a united front to dissuade the Episcopal Church in the United States from confirming the openly gay priest Gene Robinson as a bishop. His nomination had already passed in New Hampshire and was generating quite a furor in the Communion, but his confirmation was cruising to an unfettered victory at the national level. Still, the "Worldwide Anglican Mainstream Leaders" had converged at Fairfax to make a last-ditch effort to stop this travesty.

---

1. "Statement from the Gathering of Worldwide Anglican Mainstream Leaders on the Eve of General Convention," obtained from the private papers of Archbishop Peter Akinola.

2. "Statement from the Gathering of Worldwide Anglican Mainstream Leaders on the Eve of General Convention."

Without doubt, they underestimated the capacity for intransigence among those pushing the gay agenda in the American Church. In hindsight, the archbishops were simplistic in the extreme with their assumptions. Their episcopal stature and pedigree, perhaps, gave them an unrealistic sense of their power and influence. Apparently, many of them were not students of the game involved in advancing social causes.

Their one-day meeting ended with the usual communique filled with the ecclesial version of talking tough. In the widely-circulated media release, they said (1) that they had gathered "on the eve of the General Convention of the Episcopal Church out of profound love for the church"; (2) that they had "a deep concern for the constitutional crisis" that was imminent; (3) that they were particularly concerned over "proposed actions by the General Convention to confirm a non-celibate homosexual as a bishop of this Communion, or to approve the creation of liturgies for the blessing of relationships outside marriage"; (4) that these actions "would shatter the church"; (5) that these missteps would mean (a) separating the church from historic Christian faith and teaching; (b) alienating the church from the fellowship and accountability of the worldwide Anglican family; and, (c) confusing the witness of the church to the love and joy of Christian marriage.

They declared that American Episcopal persistence on this matter would "precipitate a dramatic alignment of the Church." Already, the American bishops at the Fairfax meeting had stated their resolve "to respond as faithful members of the Anglican Communion," which had spoken through a two-thirds majority vote at Lambeth.

The Fairfax gathering came and went. The primates had their say, promising to respond appropriately "to the actions of the General Convention" should they proceed with Robinson's confirmation. Nevertheless, the General Convention went ahead and confirmed Gene Robinson. The American church and Robinson achieved what the Church of England and Jeffery John couldn't accomplish, and so scorned the "Worldwide Anglican Mainstream Leaders." But it meant nothing to them. Metaphorically, not only was the elephant dragged into the room this time around; it was made to sit with pomp and pageantry in the so-called circle of men of revered order.

For the American church, rebellion didn't start with either Gene Robinson or the homosexual issue. Revolt had long been an integral part of her life, a kind of bug stuck in her heart.

According to the Most Rev. Moses Tay, bishop of Singapore and archbishop of Southeast Asia, the Mainstream Leaders meeting was an exercise in futility. He wasn't a feeble man. He had a reputation for being a powerhouse of convictions in his own right. Though he had his reservations over their attempt to persuade the Episcopal Church, he was still of one mind with them, but he was more enthusiastic about concrete action. His tiny frame belied a sturdy and solid character with stallion principles. He could confront a mob without budging.

Tay inherited the Anglican province of Southeast Asia in 1996 and became the first archbishop of the 210-year-old church. He didn't take to priesthood as a matter of occupational convenience. He was born into a devout Christian home. But he didn't become a priest when the time was ripe for him to choose a career. He opted for the life-saving profession of medicine, taking a degree from the University of Singapore in 1962. Then, for eight years, he worked in neighboring Malaysia, before returning home to Singapore to work in the Ministry of Health. Tay was one of only about 98,000 Anglicans within Singapore's estimated population of 23.8 million. He was one of the very few passionate about promoting Christianity in the multi-religious country. He obtained his bachelor of divinity (with honors) through external studies from London University in 1971. The following year, he completed his master of medicine in internal medicine at the University of Singapore. Tay remained at his job of tending to the sick, serving as the medical superintendent of Alexandra Hospital. Then, in 1982, he rose to become the director of Tan Tock Seng Hospital.

Meanwhile, in 1978, he was ordained as a non-stipendiary priest. Four years later, at the height of his medical practice, serving as the administrator of the Tock Seng Hospital, he was elected as the bishop of Singapore, seventh in the line of episcopal succession at the see. In 1996, the province of South East Asia, comprising the dioceses of West Malaysia, Singapore, Kuching, and Sabah, attained autocephaly, that is, became a self-governing church. The archbishop of Canterbury, Dr George Carey, installed Tay on February 2, 1996, as its first archbishop.

Tay was to take a swipe at that same Carey. Tay was one of the few Anglican Church leaders with early foresight concerning the contemptuous attitude of the American Episcopal Church. Back in 1999, he had taken a principled stand against members of the Communion who were flagrantly scornful of the decision reached by the collective body. For that reason, he decided not to attend a meeting of the Anglican Consultative Council called by Carey. The meeting was scheduled for Scotland, the territory of Richard Holloway, primus of the Scottish Episcopal Church and a leading promoter of rebellion against the Church. Tay took serious exception to the chosen venue. He felt that so dignifying that church was tantamount to treating dissent with kid gloves. It would add insult to injury and could add to the "increasing number of Bishops and Primates who are deliberately going against the Lambeth Resolutions on Biblical Authority and Morality."[3] Tay copied his letter to Carey to a wide range of concerned primates, bishops and other relevant groups within the Communion.

His church was among the first to have taken a principled stand on the issue. In this connection, he reminded the archbishop of Canterbury that the Southeast Asia House of Bishops had endorsed the 1997 Kuala Lumpur Statement of the Communion. The Southeast Asia bishops had pledged to "support and be in communion with that part of the Anglican Communion which accepts and endorses the principles aforesaid and not otherwise." There was no ground for them to rescind the decision. Instead, their recent House of Bishops meeting had added more bite to the provision

3. "Bishop of Singapore Slams Other Provinces for 'Departing from the Faith.'"

by stipulating further "that those who have gone against the Lambeth position on Biblical Authority and Morality are deemed to have departed from the faith."

Poor Carey! At that moment, his was an uneasy head wearing the crown. Facing him was a dilemma. Tay insisted there was no justification for a tardy response to concerns raised by a group of primates, bishops, and other concerned people who met in Singapore in April 1999. Refreshing Carey's memory about the meeting, he said, "Six of us wrote to you and Frank Griswold (the Episcopal Church Presiding Bishop) with the hope that you and the Primates will deal decisively with the deliberate deviations from the faith." Though the Canterbury archbishop dignified them with a reply, the rejoinder left them bewildered, failing to address the issues at hand. Tay faulted him for his dithering and for characterizing their request "for action as nothing more than exacerbating tensions." Tay disliked Carey's double-dealing, for he had demanded from them a "moratorium on correspondence," and he had shown no evidence of a willingness to enforce a "similar moratorium on Bishops and Dioceses going against Lambeth's position on Biblical Authority and Morality."

Tay felt the Communion direly needed fearless, bold, and decisive executive and moral leadership: "We need to face up to the deep divisions within our Communion because of the continuing deviation from the 'faith once delivered to the saints.'" He added, "We cannot value unity above truth, which is intolerant of error." Otherwise, he emphatically stated, the Communion would be putting forward a "façade of unity [which] is no more than proverbial invisible clothes worn by the King."

Apparently, Tay was not motivated by ill feeling against Carey. Nor did it appear the Southeast Asian leader's intention was to deprecate or ridicule his Canterbury counterpart. Tay had written with the annoyance of a man tired of seeing things continue to go wrong and weary of Carey's simply turning a blind eye. He implored Carey to "look at what is happening in ECUSA after the Lambeth"; to look "at the horrendous and heretical statement by the Primus of Scotland"; to look "at the patronising and racist statements boldly made against African and Asian bishops." Enough was enough, he ended sternly.

Four years had elapsed since Tay's strongly worded letter to Carey. Tay had closed the letter of September 1999 exhorting his fellow Anglican leaders to act decisively. He urged them to "also protest and de-recognise the Dioceses and Provinces that have departed from the faith."

If things had happened the way the Southeast Asian leader had urged, events at the October 2003 meeting of the primates would have been different. The thirty-eight primates from all provinces of the Church had gathered again at the behest of the archbishop of Canterbury. This time, Carey was out, and the Most Rev. Rowan Williams was in as global head of the Church. He was also the meeting's convener. For two days, October 15–16, 2003, the primates gathered at the Lambeth Palace. Archbishop Akinola and his group of "Worldwide Anglican Mainstream Leaders" were in attendance. The primates' meeting at Lambeth came nearly three months after their final effort at stopping the General Convention of the Episcopal Church in America from confirming Robonson's election.

Moses Tay, however, was absent. This time, Tay's absence wasn't the result of boycott, as in 1999. He had retired. Replacing him was the Most Rev. Datuk Yong Ping Chung, who was also bishop of Sabah. But nothing had changed regarding the issues that led to Tay's indignation. Furthermore, the South East Asia House of Bishops remained collectively disturbed by the Communion's leadership in 1999. Critical observers would not have failed to notice the widening gulf between leaders of the Communion on the subjects of homosexual marriage and ordination.

Archbishop Akinola and his colleagues brought to the meeting their experience from the July meeting in America. In fact, the Lambeth primates' meeting was convened against the backdrop of US Episcopalians' provocative actions. First to be placed on the table was the "controversial decisions by the Diocese of New Westminster to authorize a Public Rite of Blessing for those in committed same sex relationships." Second was the issue of the 74th General Convention of the American Episcopal Church's "election of a priest in a committed same sex relationship to the office and work of a Bishop."[4] There was no dispute that the actions of the two provinces constituted rebellion. The primates were unequivocal in their stand: "These actions threaten the unity of our Communion," they asserted. They left no room for doubt as they insisted, "As Primates of our Communion seeking to exercise the 'enhanced responsibility' entrusted to us by successive Lambeth Conferences, we re-affirm our common understanding of the centrality of Scripture in faith." Indeed, they declared,

> We also re-affirm the resolutions made by the bishops of the Anglican Communion gathered at the Lambeth Conference in 1998 on issues of human sexuality as having moral force and commanding the respect of the Communion as its present position on these issues.

The primates had not gathered in London to sit as a commission of enquiry to find facts proving the wrongdoing of the two Anglican provinces. They were already proven beyond all reasonable doubt. Under honest leadership, the Episcopal Church in the United States of America and its Siamese twin, the Anglican Church of Canada, already would have been censured.

Instead, the primates returned to their familiar empty rhetoric: "We must make clear that [the] recent actions in New Westminster and in the Episcopal Church (USA) do not express the mind of the Communion as a whole." Further, they reminded the Americans and Canadians that their "decisions jeopardize our sacramental fellowship with each other."

Where did the rebuke and warning leave Frank Griswold, presiding bishop of the American Episcopal Church? It's likely he received these words with amusement,

4. [i] Primates Statement October 16, 2003, [ii] Commission's Mandate October 29, 2003 Paragraph 2 from the private papers and collections of Archbishop Peter Akinola.

chuckling within himself at the naiveté of his colleagues. They were crassly ignorant of the American church; they saw but could not comprehend because they were merely looking at the surface. Even as presiding bishop, Griswold had his limitations. He faced severe hurdles that he dared not cross, but he had successfully been playing his ecclesiastical cards, an effort that demanded astute organizational leadership.

Surprisingly, for instance, his name was conspicuously missing among the 1998 signatories of the "Pastoral Letter to Anglican Gays and Lesbians"—despite the fact that America was at the forefront of the rebellion and had the highest number of signatories. Likewise, he wasn't included among the nine primates who most prominently supported the revolt: Archbishops Glauco Soares de Lima of Brazil, Michael Peers of Canada, Khotso Makhulu of Central Africa, Robin Eames of Ireland, Ellison L. Pogo of Melanesia, and John Paterson of New Zealand; plus Richard Holloway of Scotland, South Africa's Njongokulu Ndungane, and Rowan Williams of Wales. Yet it would be gullible to suggest Griswold was out of step with his rebellious American body. Similarly, it would be foolhardy to exonerate him from the June 2003 plot that resulted in Robinson's confirmation.

He was elected as head of the American Church a year before the 1998 Lambeth Conference, where he served on the standing committee. Griswold had become the presiding bishop of ECUSA at the age of 60, hardly an age to experiment with activism. Furthermore, his trajectory in the ministry was not that of a crusading or politically-conscious type. He was ordained in 1963 at age 26 and settled comfortably into his calling, performing grinding church work for the first 24 years of his priestly service. This took him to three parishes in Pennsylvania. He didn't cast the image of a heckler, whether on the upbeat or the downbeat side of the whirlwind gathering momentum around him. He seemed content minding his own business—his ministering and shepherding work.

Then, in 1987, he became bishop of Chicago, but still didn't come across as the revolutionary type. In any case, the diocese itself was no place to be insensitive to a plurality of views. The social and cultural milieu of the area drew strength from ethnic diversity. Besides being one of the twelve largest congregations in the Episcopal Church, the level of its multicultural and multi-national diversity also made it the most ethnically rich of the dioceses. The diocese was more diverse than the Episcopal Church itself. From Hispanics to Koreans to Africans, the diocese was a melting pot of races. It included as many as eight African-American congregations, four Hispanic congregations, and another four congregations providing Spanish services. For ten years, Griswold served the diocese, a season with no earth-shaking incidents. He devoted his time to pursuing his core interests, landing him on national and international committees on liturgy, worship, and ecumenism. He loved the Anglo-Catholic tradition and interfaith dialogue, explaining his membership in the Fellowship of the Society of St. John the Evangelist and his service on the board of the Elijah Interfaith Institute. None of this embroiled him in controversy.

But that changed. He was presiding bishop at the election of an openly gay bishop in defiance of the agreed-upon position at the 1998 Lambeth Conference. He knew the undercurrents and overtones concerning human sexuality in the Communion. As events kept unfolding and cascading, two inescapable truths were becoming clear about Griswold: (1) His hands must have been tied, for he and the office had been compromised; (2) He'd ascended a church whose soul had long been possessed and was terribly haunted by ghosts from its past. Griswold could not do anything: he had neither the power nor the will to confront the powers behind his throne.

Consequently, in reaction to the scolding the American church received from his colleagues, he mounted a spirited defence of Robinson's confirmation. He emphasized the "constitutional framework" within which the election had taken place, but the primates didn't consider his argument tenable. Griswold was told the truth about the feebleness of his leadership:

> In most of our provinces, the election of Canon Gene Robinson would not have been possible since his chosen lifestyle would give rise to a canonical impediment to his consecration as a bishop.

And so, a stern warning: "If his consecration proceeds," Griswold was notified, "the future of the Communion will be put in jeopardy." The American presiding bishop said nothing.

Proverbially, whatever applies to the goose must equally apply to the gander. The two North American churches were partners in the gross misconduct against the decision of the Communion. Neither was exonerated in any way. Instead, there was joint culpability beyond any doubt. Consequently, the primates concluded that "similar considerations apply to the situation pertaining in the Diocese of New Westminster."

The primates decided to focus on these issues with the aim of settling them. The first issue was their "concern for those who in all conscience feel bound to dissent from the teaching and practice of their province on such matters." The primates called for "adequate provision of episcopal oversight" for the dissenting groups. Archbishop Rowan Williams was mandated to implement this decision. The second issue was the need to respect the "autonomy and territorial integrity of dioceses and provinces." Respecting territorial jurisdiction by not crossing boundaries used to be a tradition in the Anglican Church until the dispute started creating realignment of groups sharing common beliefs across borders. Third, the primates called on Archbishop Williams to establish proactively, in accordance with another of the 1998 Lambeth Conference resolutions, "a commission to consider his role in maintaining communion *within* and *between* provinces when grave difficulties arise." In other words, Canterbury was being asked to examine its duty regarding enforcement of moral and ethical discipline within the Communion in periods of stress.

The crisis portended a house divided against itself. But the majority of church leaders at the gathering still clung to hope that the situation might be salvaged. They were placing hope in the ad hoc commission recommended to help rescue the Communion. Perhaps motivated by a sense of urgency, they pleaded fervently with the archbishop of Canterbury "that such a commission complete its work within twelve months."

A clear warning was issued to the American Episcopal Church, with the primates saying the "ministry of this one bishop will not be recognised by most of the Anglican world." Put simply, only birds of the same feather should look forward to flocking together in the Anglican nest. Gene Robinson would be a pariah in the purple club.

A week before the primates' meeting in Lambeth, the "Plano Conference" had been held in America. It was organised by the American Anglican Council (AAC) in conjunction with Christ Church of Plano, Texas. The October 7–9, 2003, conference met under the theme, "A Place to Stand: Declaring, Preparing." The conference was very well attended, with 2,200 participants representing every corner of the nation, including 95 of the 110 dioceses comprising the Episcopal Church. On board were 40 bishops, 729 priests, 43 deacons, 91 seminary students, and 1,219 lay members from Episcopal churches across the length and breadth of America.[5] They sought to ensure that "mainstream Anglicans in the Episcopal Church are mobilized" and to "find a way to remain within the Anglican family."[6] It was a rallying point for the group to reiterate their solidarity with the majority in the worldwide Anglican Communion. Loud was the chorus of their voice in unison. Deafeningly, they proclaimed in the "Statement of Faith" issued after the conference, "As we have said all along, we're not leaving." As far as they were concerned, "It is the Episcopal Church that has departed from the historic teachings of the Christian church and separated itself from the Anglican Communion."

The Plano Conference claimed a number of striking achievements. The number of priests attending was "equivalent to roughly 10 percent of all active clergy in ECUSA." Furthermore, the Plano Conference was said to have had a bigger turnout than that of the "ECUSA deputies and bishops who attended [the] General Convention." Enthusiastically, the Plano Conference declared,

> When teachings and practices contrary to Scripture and to orthodox Anglican perspectives are permitted within the Church—or even authorized by conventions or synods—we, in obedience to God, will disassociate ourselves from those specific teachings and practices and will resist them in every way possible.

Fortunately, the Plano Conference and the American Anglican Council that spearheaded its convening were not alone in raising a discordant voice. One of the earliest declarations of opposition was from a group of nineteen American bishops, headed by the bishop of the diocese of Pittsburgh, Robert Duncan. This was in August immediately after the General Convention had given Robinson its consent vote. Though they were twice in number compared to their counterparts in England who

5. Mason, "Latest AAC Update on Plano, TX Meeting."
6. https://americananglican.org/about-us/.

campaigned against the appointment of Jeffrey John, they were simply ignored by the leaders of the Episcopal Church. But they didn't give up. New mail arrived daily at the headquarters of the Episcopal Church. The critics would simply not be placated; day after day they increased in number and variety.

Archbishop Williams spoke on the matter in a BBC interview on October 18, 2003. He agonized that "undoubtedly, there is a huge crisis looming."[7] When asked whether he believed Robinson should have been made a bishop, he crisply answered "No, I don't, because I believe that on a major issue of this kind, the Church has to make a decision together." Williams explained, in effect, that there were a "large number—the very, very, large number—of Anglican provinces who feel that, quite simply, a decision has been made which commits them or involves them in some way and yet in which they have had no part at all."

The archbishop apparently believed that the American decision was a way to arm-twist a large majority of the Anglican leaders. The unstated inference was that to avert the crisis, Robinson's election had to be reversed. Now that the man in whom unmatched power and influence in the Anglican Church resided had added his voice to that of the Anglican primates and the group meeting in Plano—all speaking of stern and serious repercussions for further transgression—eyes turned to the American church. Would it heed the voices of reason? Would the consecration of Gene Robinson proceed? Or would it be withheld to save the unity of the Anglican Church?

7. Archbishop of Canterbury BBC Radio Interview, October 18, 2003, in Woodliff, "Rediscovering Christian Orthodoxy in Episcopal Anglicanism."

8

Tearing the Communion's Fabric

America, 2003

O n November 2, 2003, Canon Gene Robinson was consecrated the bishop of New Hampshire. Any impact the opinion of the archbishop of Canterbury, the Most Rev. Dr. Rowan Williams, had on the decision was negligible. The bishops, clergy, and congregations promising reactions were snubbed. Flamboyantly and with uncustomary pomp and pageantry, Gene Robinson was enthroned. The Episcopal Church was determined to make his consecration an eloquently colorful ceremony— a public statement not just for local consumption; an international audience must have been intended.

Rather than holding it in a church auditorium, the venue shifted to a grandiose location. The Elections and Transitions Committee chose the Whittemore Centre, which didn't come cheap. The $30 million facility, erected in Durham in 1995, was owned by the University of New Hampshire. Built as an ice hockey arena, it was now used for a range of events, including tradeshows, concerts, and the type of consecration it was now to host. In its original state, the facility could accommodate 6,500 spectators for hockey games, but for events like a concert, the space could seat as many as 7,500. Gene Robinson's consecration only half filled the facility, the guests numbering about 3,000 (compared to the 2,200 faithful Episcopalians who had gathered at the Christ Church of Plano in Texas).

No effort was spared to give the event massive hype. The media corps was a large invited contingent numbering about 300 journalists. The choir was 200-strong. Security was tight, and uninvited guests were excluded. Yet Robinson apparently didn't feel so safe and secure. He arrived at the venue with a bulging robe, covering a bulletproof vest. Apart from Bishop Barbara Harris, the first woman to be ordained bishop in the Anglican Communion, no one else knew of Robinson's secret. He had jokingly showed the bulletproof vest to the bishop consecrated in 1989, perhaps as a kind of rekindling of a kindred spirit with her.

Arguably, Robinson would not match the courage of Harris, an African-American woman. Besides Harris's being the first American female to be elected bishop, she was also the first African-American woman to reach the episcopate. Her election had attracted death threats and obscene messages. Fears for her safety and security had reportedly led to her being urged to wear a bulletproof vest to her consecration. Harris stoutly refused. Instead, a contingent of the Boston police was assigned to the venue of her consecration. Their job was to ensure that nothing negative occurred during the ceremony. Of course, nothing unusual happened.

Fortification of the Whittemore Centre with watertight security still apparently didn't give Robinson a feeling of safety. But if he trembled inwardly, he still managed to put on a façade, a public show as self-assured and confident. Robinson also capitalized on his family's display of moral backing. In addition to his parents, his sister also attended the event. Equally conspicuous was Boo, his divorced wife, and one of his daughters. However, cleverly played down to nearly a position of obscurity was his gay partner, Mark Andrew. If Andrew attended the ceremony, it was difficult to spot him from the crowd. He kept a low profile, withdrawing from the public. He was neither beside nor behind his partner celebrating his success with him.

From the American church's episcopal circle, Robinson pulled the expected crowd of bishops known for supporting his aberrant lifestyle. Leading six others as the joint-consecrating bishops of Gene Robinson was the Episcopal Church presiding bishop, Frank Griswold, and his predecessor, Edmond Browning. Naturally, Otis Charles, a bishop who came out as gay after his retirement, was there. Charles was elected the eighth bishop of Utah and enjoyed all the privileges attached to episcopal office for 18 years. Within the House of Bishops, he earned respect, heading some important committees. In 1985 he became dean of the Episcopal Divinity School, an office of influence in shaping the minds of future priests.

Charles married at age of 25 in 1951. His 42 years of marriage were blessed with five children. In 1993, he retired from the episcopacy at age 67. Odd was the transfiguration that happened to him in old age. Charles' retirement was celebrated with his publicly coming out as gay. It was a record-breaking event. He was the first Christian bishop to do so. Perhaps, he was also the first bishop and father of five to divorce his wife of over four decades in preference for a male partner. Charles was later to marry Dr. Felipe Sanchez-Paris, with one version of the story stating the "two had five marriages between them."[1] Hardly would such a man fail to be counted on occasions where birds of the same feather were flocking together.

In a similar vein, Bishop George Walker Jr. could not resist joining in the event. Also present were the trio of Joe Burnett, Edward Jones, and Thomas Ely, who had been a friend in need and indeed. (He was the bishop of the Vermont Episcopalian, David Lewis, who had accused Robinson of misconduct but had quickly recanted.) Of course, Bishop of New Hampshire Douglas Theuner was the star of the day. The mentor and

1. "A Timeline of Defining Actions," www.americananglican.org.

godfather of Gene Robinson was there to behold the fruit of his labor. From Canada, Michael Ingham, the bishop of New Westminster, flew in to show solidarity. He was the lone outsider who spiced up the event with a paltry international appearance.

Robinson's consecration was intended to be an extravaganza. Part of the effort was inflating attendance figures to create an aura of high solemnity for the event and provoke acceptance of its product. The presence of 48 bishops was proudly proclaimed, but these numbered less than half of the 110 total in America. Be that as it may, Robinson had his day. The Episcopal Church too had its way.

However, many were the "what next?" questions arising from the defiant step. What next should be expected from the archbishop of Canterbury and his fellow primates in the Communion whose views had been defied? What next would follow from the Global South, which had stated its determination to not compromise? What next for opposition groups within the Episcopal Church that had vowed never to succumb to the revision of Scripture? The overall question was what next for the Communion as it confronted clashing opinions and inflexibility on the part of all combatants within its fold? How could the Anglican Church proceed in the face of the apocalypse into which the gay crisis was plunging it?

9

Disgust Across, Within, and Outside

Nigeria, 2003

Swift was the reaction from the Global South primates. Archbishop Peter Akinola authored a strongly worded statement on behalf of the group. The group's pronouncement was issued the very day of Robinson's installation before the event's conclusion. It was as if Akinola were watching a livestream of the New Hampshire event from Nigeria. "We are appalled," Akinola said bluntly in the statement.[1] Indignation mixed with horror as he expressed the dismay of the Global South primates that "the Episcopal Church USA (ECUSA) ignored the heartfelt plea of the Communion not to proceed with the scheduled consecration of Canon Gene Robinson." The question of what would follow was not left hanging:

> The overwhelming majority of the Primates of the *Global South* cannot and
> will not recognise the office or ministry of Canon Gene Robinson as a bishop.

It was impossible to excuse the American church leader for his weak leadership. Griswold's pliant nature troubled his Nigerian counterpart. Akinola was miffed that the whole lot of them, the primates of the Anglican Communion, were physically present when the decision was made at Lambeth. They had agreed unanimously. Griswold had raised no objection. With his consent, he was not just a party to the resolution but was bound by it. And the effect was spelled out: Consecrating an openly homosexual bishop would precipitate "detrimental consequences for the unity of the Communion." To permit Gene Robinson's consecration, Griswold had acted inappropriately, and doubly so as the chief consecrator. He had abused the trust and betrayed the confidence of his colleagues. He had exposed himself and his leadership to personal ridicule.

---

1. Akinola, "We are Appalled," from the private papers and collections of Archbishop Peter Akinola.

Of course, Griswold was not the only person deserving rebuke over the American church's improper conduct. Guilty by association were all "those bishops who have taken part in the consecration which has now divided the Church," Akinola asserted on behalf of the Global South leaders. The attendant implications were grave and grievous, and, indeed, the Global South had decided to employ its biting teeth, declaring that a "state of impaired communion now exists both within a significant part of ECUSA and between ECUSA and most of the provinces within the Communion."

Impunity tends to be a recipe for chaos and unmitigated disasters. The Nigerian church leader was emphatic that the "ECUSA is [to be] held responsible for this division." It had made clear its unwillingness to show remorse for "violating the clear and consistent teaching of the Bible." Akinola believed that not only had the American church become a sore to the Anglican Communion, but that it had rubbed salt into the injury through an imperious, scant regard for "the common teaching, common practice, and common witness within the one Anglican Communion." Akinola concluded that the ECUSA had torn "the fabric of the Communion at its deepest level."

Catastrophes are products of unchecked excess. It seemed that the uncontrollable immoderations of the Episcopal Church had begun to push the Anglican Communion to a dead end. Nevertheless, and even in spite of the belligerent tone of the Global South's letter, there was a clamor for a serious détente, a search for peaceful resolution of the crisis. And Akinola concurred, as evidenced by the entreaties he made to Archbishop of Canterbury Rowan Williams to intervene in the lingering crisis in order to save the Communion.

The Global South leader urged the Anglican Church head to "urgently" establish a mechanism that would "guarantee 'adequate provision of episcopal oversight' for parishes and clergy" not in agreement with the perfidious step of the Episcopal Church. He urged the same action for the Canadian church, where the diocese of New Westminster had unilaterally introduced the blessing of same-sex unions. Providing safe haven for the minority groups in both countries' churches, those who opposed the action of their national leadership, had been a subject on which the primates themselves had spoken and taken a stand.

The leadership of the two churches were merely looking in another direction, pretending the issue did not exist. On the other hand, rapid and grinding were the lawsuits against many of the churches and congregations wanting to step away from the pro-homosexual group. Akinola solicited intervention by the Archbishop of Canterbury, pleading with him to use his influence to push back against those who had initiated the "law suits that further tear the fabric of our common life" and ask them "to withdraw their destructive worldly actions."

He compared the lawsuits to the willful actions of the two North American churches that disobeyed the decisions of the Church and violated Scripture. All the while, he made it clear that the Global South would be resolute under his watch: "We will do everything that is necessary to uphold historic Anglicanism and advance our common faith, life, mission and ministry."

The response that followed Akinola's salvo showed the "time of rhetoric was over." Some provinces declared a state of "impaired or broken communion with all or part of ECUSA."[2] Yet the American church leaders were unfazed by what they took to be a morally confused and inconsequential initiative on the part of Global South leaders. The church was so intoxicated by its contemptuous path that nothing seemed to deter it from its adversarial and destructive ways. In fact, less than a week after the Global South's statement, the American church doubled down on its error.

On Saturday, November 8, 2003, an American newspaper hit the street with the headline, "Episcopal priest who opposed gay bishop ousted." As the story went, the reverend in question, Donald Wilson, had had the audacity to challenge the authority of the New Hampshire diocese's leadership over the homosexuality issue. Wilson was interim priest of the Church of the Redeemer in the diocese, having replaced the incumbent rector upon the latter's retirement in April 2003. Though small, with a congregation of roughly 60 members, the church had opposed the consecration of Gene Robinson. Wilson had written to the New Hampshire Bishop Douglas Theuner conveying the stand of his congregation, which happened to coincide with his personal scriptural conviction. He maintained that because of his "greater loyalty to our Lord," he could not assure loyalty to Robinson. The bishop, Theuner, deemed the letter as an insult. He would brook no dissent regarding homosexuality nor countenance such "hostility" toward his protégé. So Wilson was summarily "removed from his church."[3]

Theuner did what he could to deny the action was based on the priest's convictions regarding homosexuality. Instead, Wilson supposedly was fired for "responding in an 'insubordinate way' to a request to meet with Bishop Douglas Theuner." All through the saga, Theuner avoided the press. Rather, he used one of his advisers, the Rev. Hays Junkin, as a spokesman. Some of the press got inquisitive about the timing of the punishment. They wondered why it had to occur barely a week after Robinson's consecration. Junkin made a spirited effort at inventing an ingenious explanation. But journalists saw beyond the smokescreen.

Of course, the truth of the matter was that Wilson had boldly told Theuner that he could not pledge his obedience to Robinson and that submitting to Robinson's authority would contravene his "greater loyalty to our Lord." As a priest in New Hampshire, Wilson was supposed to be part of the elected gay bishop's episcopate. But he and his church belonged to the minority group for which the Anglican primates had requested episcopal oversight, given their unwillingness to violate their consciences.

From Theuner's perspective, this scriptural, vocal minority was like a cancerous lump that had to be removed before metastasizing into malignant tumour, and he

2. Woodliff, "Rediscovering Christian Orthodoxy in Episcopal Anglicanism."

3. "Episcopal Priest Who Opposed Gay Bishop Ousted," http://lubbockonline.com/stories/110803/rel_110803091.shtml#.VglsZ30YGz8.

was there like a surgeon to excise it. If for eighteen years the godfather had shielded his godson, how could he now allow a "misguided" priest to frustrate the labor of the well-laid-out scheme? Theuner was determined to pass a clean slate on to Robinson whatever the cost. He was resolute to protect his ward. The sack of Donald Wilson the week following the consecration marked the beginning of the systematic war of attrition to eliminate every known and imagined opponent in the diocese. Yet it was a losing battle. Day after day, the antagonisms grew, the opposition expanding, becoming bigger, larger, stronger, and sturdier. Furthermore, an international coalition was also coalescing into a formidable group.

Just four days after Wilson was shown the way out of the New Hampshire diocese, the archbishop of Central Africa, Bernard Malango, wrote a "no-holds-barred" letter to his Episcopal Church counterpart, Presiding Bishop Frank Griswold. Malango could not understand his American colleague's failure to provide effective leadership. He wrote, "In charity and heartbreak, I call on you to repent. Until that time, you have broken our fellowship." He underlined the disagreement with an emphasis: "We are not one." The reason he proffered was simple: "We do not share the same faith and Gospel." He concluded, "You should resign and let someone else lead, someone who shares the faith of the Communion—the faith of the church catholic."

This was not the last of such intensely worded indictments received by the offending parties, for they had opened the gateway to a sea of condemnation.[4] The mail brought a daily flood of reactions, and the media took note as the controversy boiled over in various church meetings. One commentator observed, "We are facing an issue that touches the very core of the Gospel. It is not trivial, and it will not go away." The prediction proved to be accurate.

The next clash came with the archbishop of Uganda, the Most Rev. Livingstone Nkoyoyo, which almost raised an earthquake. Griswold made the mistake of attempting to play a divide-and-conquer game with the Global South primates, attempting to woo Nkoyoyo to the side of the Episcopal Church. He had sent an official delegation to Uganda for Nkoyoyo's enthronement as the country's archbishop and sought to win over the new Ugandan church leader. Nkoyoyo resisted the temptation; perhaps "snubbed it" would be more apt. Griswold said that if Nkoyoyo could endorse the Episcopal Church's action, the church would reciprocate with "aid and assistance to the people who live in desperate conditions in camps in Gulu." Gulu was a horrid, poor, ravaged, and degraded community in Uganda, one the Americans had ignored for years despite a plea for assistance. Through the delegation that attended his enthronement, Nkoyoyo sent back a biting reply: "The gospel of Jesus Christ is not for sale."

Desperate as the situation in Gulu was, Nkoyoyo considered the offer a gratuitous insult. Apart from shunning the offer, he told the American church leader some blunt truths. He said that "even among the poorest of us who have no money," we have

4. "The Washington Times of December 2 & 3, 2003 on the reactions of other World Churches," in Woodliff, "Rediscovering Christian Orthodoxy in Episcopal Anglicanism."

pride. He explained that he was not a mercenary and didn't come from a culture where the gospel had been turned to a piece of merchandise. He added, "If your hearts remain hardened to what the Bible clearly teaches, and your ears remain deaf to the cries of other Christians, genuine love demands that we do not pretend that everything is normal." Light and darkness do not associate, and Nkoyoyo didn't see light coming from the American darkness. He slammed the door shut in the face of the wealthy Americans, declaring that the Ugandan church would neither "share fellowship nor even receive desperately needed resources" from sources who had lost credibility. The episode occurred in December 2003, less than a month after the American church set the Anglican Communion on fire with the Gene Robinson trouble.

The fire was smoldering and spreading everywhere. Robinson was the world's first openly homosexual bishop, and the Christian world didn't appear ready to welcome him and his perversion with an affectionate embrace. In fact, serious concerns were surfacing in the top-level ecclesiastical organs of the Christian faith throughout the world.

The Roman Catholic Church openly expressed its apprehensions on December 2, 2003. Incidentally, before that, the Roman Catholic Church and the Anglican Communion were involved in exploratory "top level talks" regarding how to reconcile "theological issues which divide the two churches." The talks had come a long way, sustained for nearly 33 years, and had resulted in their setting up the "Anglican-Roman International Commission (ARIC)." In addition to collapsing the extensive talks, the Gene Robinson trouble also led to Griswold's resignation from his co-chairmanship.

Additionally, several orthodox churches including the Russian, Armenian, Syrian, Coptic, and Ethiopian churches suspended ties with the Episcopal Church. In its public statement, the Russian Orthodox Church took exception both to Gene Robinson's consecration and to "those who consecrated him": "We shall not be able to cooperate with these people not only in the theological dialogue, but also in the humanitarian and religious and public spheres." Robinson's consecration, to them, was "profoundly anti-Christian and blasphemous." In the same way that countries pursuing dangerous and extremist ideologies become pariah states in the community of nations, the Episcopal Church was finding itself shunned by decent and upright religious bodies. The church was becoming like a leper.

If the church had been less headstrong in its rebellion, it would have known that the action it was taking conflicted with the mood of Christendom. Members of the American National Clergy Council, for example, boycotted Robinson's consecration. The Council claimed a substantial collection of church leaders in America, representing 5,000 Catholic, evangelical, Orthodox, and Protestant churches. The executive committee of the Council had issued a prompt public statement to denounce Robinson's consecration the same day, November 3, 2003, that Archbishop Akinola did so on behalf of the Global South. The Council observed that Robinson's consecration by some bishops within the Episcopal Church broke "with universal Christian moral teaching." Practically, the Episcopal Church had closed "their doors to Christians who remain faithful to church and biblical traditions." Consequently, the Council resolved to severe "fellowship on any level with the radical bishops and members of the Episcopal Church who condoned and participated in the supremely immoral act."

Faced with imminent implosion within and explosion from without, the Episcopal Church in the United States could not say that 2003 ended favorably. The self-inflicted problems were as much a burden for the church as they were for the worldwide Anglican Communion, and the trouble washed over into 2004. As early as January 20, the combatants were back to the trenches, as conservative Episcopalians reconvened in Plano.

Unlike the October 2003 conference held before Robinson's consecration, a meeting during which it looked like they were gauging their chances, searching for a "a place to stand," as the theme of their meeting suggested, they were very definite this time around. They resolved to move forward in the defence of their faith. They decided on action, birthing the Network of Anglican Communion Dioceses and Parishes, shortened to Anglican Communion Network (ACN). The ACN wasn't intended to be a tea club, a cheerleader, or a support club. It was to be a "united biblically-based missionary movement."[5] Further resolved was that the organization would remain strong in the defence of its objectives. They vowed that their long-term goal would be "bringing 'true and legitimate' expression of Anglicanism to North America." Though it originated in a season of oppressiveness within the local church, the ACN exuded a strong will to stand in the tough time ahead.

Fortunately, The Rt. Rev. Robert Duncan—bishop of Pittsburgh and the person around whom leadership of the embryonic organization revolved—was an honest and truthful crusading minister. He was given neither to deception nor to self-seeking egoism. He was self-effacing and guileless.

Interestingly, Duncan and Gene Robinson had much in common. They were born a year apart, Robinson a year older than Duncan (1947 and 1948 respectively). Like Robinson, Duncan had childhood troubles. An abusive mother had raised him, and he was subjected to horrid treatment including beatings. The mother herself was a victim of mental illness. Duncan miraculously survived early life with its traumatizing tragedies.

Bordentown, New Jersey, where he grew up, was a small community. Everybody essentially knew each other. In these troubling times, Duncan found strength in the church—the Bordentown Christ Episcopal Church. There he found refuge, the opportunity and freedom to pray and meditate. God responded to his inner pleas, and Duncan emerged with a dazzling mind, much as Robinson emerged from his infantile difficulties shining brilliantly.

5. Smith, "Bishop Duncan Retiring from Anglican Post"; "Dissenting Episcopal Bishop Pittsburgh Bishop Robert Duncan on CNN."

At 22, Duncan graduated from college with an A.B., *cum laude*. Amazingly, the duo—Duncan and Robinson—were classmates at the General Episcopal Theological Seminary in New York. They obtained their masters of divinity at the same time and were ordained the same year, 1973. Robinson was 26 and Duncan 25 years of age. They both became canons to the ordinary, and both came under the influence of powerful episcopal figures. While the bishop of New Hampshire, Douglas Theuner, adopted Robinson as his protégé, the then-bishop of Pittsburgh, Alden M. Hathaway, mentored Duncan. Robinson served 18 years with his mentor while Duncan served five years under Hathaway. Both succeeded their mentors. But that's where the similarities ended and the differences began.

Duncan's ministerial career was seemingly broader and richer. Significant as well was that while Theuner was obsessed to see Robinson succeed him, Alden Hathaway didn't have such ambition.

In 1992, Hathaway appointed Duncan a canon to the ordinary. Oddly, when the initial process for selecting Hathaway's replacement began in 1997, Duncan was not given a thought. Yet he was the diocese's bishop coadjutor, the engine room that had been assisting the bishop in the smooth administration of the diocese. Hathaway, a theologically conservative church leader, neither manipulated nor influenced the selection process, even if he favored Duncan to be his successor. On the floor of the diocesan convention, Duncan's name made a surprising appearance. The man initially passed over became the hottest candidate. It appeared his time had come. Duncan's nomination sailed through, and on September 13, 1997, his consecration as bishop of Pittsburgh finally took place.

Duncan was one of the American bishops at the 1998 Lambeth Conference. As expected, he distanced himself from his colleagues. He wasn't part of the dissenting group who wrote the letter of appeasement to gays and lesbians. Instead, he worked with a committee which created the Network for Anglicans in Mission and Evangelism.

Duncan's opposition to Robinson's consecration stemmed from principles. The beginning and end of his disagreement centered on the authority of Scripture. To Duncan, the Bible was inviolable: "In my experience I learned the one person I could trust was Jesus Christ and the only testament that was reliable was what was in Scripture." In his childhood trying times, he had found succor in the church and the solace of the Word, his best comfort.

Faith and courage that stemmed from the Scripture sustained him. From the adversity had grown gallantry and daringness, culminating in an indomitable spirit. Duncan could be as steadfast as he was uncompromisingly forthright in his convictions. He remained firm in his principle that Robinson's consecration ran "directly contrary to Scripture." "It's heresy," he charged.[6] Ironclad was his resolve to stand

6. "Anglican Church in North America: Reaching North America with the Transforming Love of Jesus Christ—The Most Reverend Robert W. Duncan"; "Who is Doing the Dividing?"; "Dissenting Episcopal Bishop Pittsburgh Bishop Robert Duncan on CNN"; and Virtue, "The Mind and Mission of

against the perversion. Plainly and plaintively, he said, "I cannot let the Church, of all bodies, challenge the notion that you can't trust the plain meaning of Scripture."

Duncan's uncompromising stance exposed him to charges of being a conservative, fundamentalist, extremist, and fanatic, but this never moved him. For thirty years, he had been part of the American church system. His insider knowledge gave him the advantage of knowing what would take outsiders ages of laborious study to learn about the American church. He knew full well that "revisionism within the Episcopal Church has been going on for decades."

Physicists talk of the law of gravity, that whatever goes up must come down. Duncan saw the parallel with Gene Robinson's consecration. For a long time, a group within the American church had perverted the Scripture with impunity. The voices of the minority had not always been gagged, but often these people suffered oppression and repression. But a new dynamic was emerging, and even if Duncan had been acting alone, he would still have been a formidable opponent, for he had a remarkable pedigree as an overcomer and survivalist.

Providentially, the ACN represented a substantial coalition of forces. Under its canopy were bishops from twelve Episcopal Church dioceses, along with other faithful Episcopalians. Additionally, its formation was said to have the blessing of the archbishop of Canterbury, Dr. Rowan Williams, who apparently first suggested its establishment. The final concept was however attributed to a "gathering of Anglican Mainstream Leaders attended by four Primates in London in November 2003." Further inspiring the group was the fact that the majority of provinces in the Anglican Communion were getting tired of the Episcopal Church's impunity. They found its stance repulsive, its actions putting a serious strain on the cherished fellowship that used to be the hallmark of the Anglican Communion. Consequently, many of the provinces had tired of rhetoric and were looking toward practical actions.

The ACN was fortunate to have had its birth under such circumstances, for it was able to attain legitimacy within a short time. Twenty-one provinces declared either impaired or broken communion with ECUSA. More than half of the 38 provinces had either ostracized or severed ties with the American church. Fourteen primates in the worldwide Anglican Communion have recognized the ACN as "the legitimate Anglican presence in North America." The group was welcomed as if it were a long sought child in the hands of a parent with the problem of infertility, so it was quick to acquire a measure of self-assurance and confidence.

Anyone familiar with the history of the pro-homosexual groups in the American church would have probably laughed at ACN's expressed sanguinity. The expression "give up" was not in the vocabulary of the homosexuality advocates. However, the ACN underlined boldly, too, that it did not intend to quit the Episcopal Church, but would stay within the fold. It also pledged it would act "in good faith and within the Constitution of ECUSA." How feasible was that? Did the ACN have a superior

---

Anglican Archbishop Robert Duncan."

counteroffensive to match the entrenched homosexual activists within the church? Was it not being simplistic for the ACN to assume it could reverse the direction that gay and lesbian ideologues had been rowing the Episcopal Church's boat? There was no sure answer to these questions.

What clearly manifested at the time was that the ship of the Anglican Communion was sinking, and speedily too! Since the Gene Robinson trouble, the different groups of stakeholders that had emerged had been going in opposing directions, all of them inflexibly holding to their positions and digging into their trenches further and further. Warnings of imminent danger to the Communion had been consistent. The sad development was that rather than abating, the troublesome winds and storms blasting at the Communion's sail raged on. Yet the archbishop of Canterbury held the sail and the compass to navigate the sinking ship out of the troubled waters. He alone had the ace, and became the binocular for all eyes. The choice before him was narrow: either to save the one Communion he inherited or watch it sink.

10

Lambeth Commission to the Rescue

London, 2004

Archbishop Williams did not sit idly by, waiting for too long. He seized the initiative provided by the Anglican primates at their October 2003 meeting in Lambeth by setting up the commission recommended to him. Its goal was to find an amicable solution to the lingering crisis tearing up the Communion. Archbishop Williams formally inaugurated the Commission in February 2004, and the candidate he picked to head the important commission was Archbishop Robin Eames, primate of all Ireland. In the secular world, Eames would have faced serious credibility problems. There would have been questions about his ability to guarantee impartiality, justice, and fairness. Eames was one of the nine primates who had signed the 1998 dissenting "Pastoral Statement to Lesbian and Gay Anglicans."

There appeared to be a conflict of interest on Eames's part. But the ecclesiastical world is far different from the secular world. Church politics and church ways of doing things have their peculiar approach, style, and method—and particularly in terms of values on which notions like uprightness, reputation, and integrity are built. Be that as it may, no one was worthier in the Communion to be entrusted with the enormous responsibility at hand. His pedigree and experience made him more than eminently qualified, for he was a troubleshooting veteran for the Anglican Communion.

He was the head of the archbishop of Canterbury's commission on "Communion and Women in the Episcopate." His handling of that contentious issue, which ravaged the Communion from 1988 to 1989, etched his name in the Communion's book of respectable leaders. Eames, at 57 years of age, was barely two years in the archiepiscopacy when he was given the challenging assignment. Two years later, he was drafted again to work on the Inter-Anglican Theological and Doctrinal Commission. Eames was an inexhaustible reservoir of academic and clerical knowledge.

The son of a Methodist minister, he graduated from the Methodist College in Belfast. He enrolled for a divinity course at Trinity College, Dublin, but having found it "intellectually unsatisfying," he dropped the idea. Next, he explored law, graduating with an LL.B. in upper class second division with honors in 1960. But somehow, Eames found a way of reconnecting to his father's vocation. He pursued tirelessly the daunting academic steps to earn his doctorate in ecclesiastical law and history. If divinity was "intellectually unsatisfying," the same could not be said of ecclesiastical law. In 1963, he obtained his Ph.D., found his way to the priesthood, and was appointed as curate assistant at the Bangor Parish Church.

Like every young person of his age, time, and environment, he dabbled briefly in politics. He was a member of the Young Unionists during his undergraduate days. Also, he was said to have briefly flirted with Freemasonry. The Freemasons were regarded a secret society and barred from priesthood. A serious controversy was to confront Eames regarding his membership and exit from the group. While the Church of Ireland maintained that "he resigned while a curate," a published press interview with the grand secretary of the Freemasons in Ireland by the *Sunday Business Post* undermined that story. Though the grand secretary acknowledged, "Archbishop Eames resigned from his lodges," the real issue was about the precise time he renounced his membership. "He was a member of more than one lodge," and his final exit was "about the time he was appointed a primate," the grand secretary claimed.

Yet Eames successfully overcame the Freemasonry controversy. He became the youngest bishop elected in the history of his diocese, the cross-border diocese of Derry and Raphoe, in 1975. He was 38 years old and barely a dozen years into his priestly calling. A year before his golden birthday, Eames became the leader of his country's church, the archbishop of Armagh and primate of all Ireland. Apart from the dents that were footnotes to his background, his prominence in the Anglican Communion was preeminent, due in large measure to his work at disentangling the worldwide church from challenging theological and doctrinal problems.

In fairness to Eames, the same doubts about potential of conflict of interest equally applied to his colleagues on the Commission from the West Indies and Central Africa. Archbishops Drexel Gomez and Bernard Malango both expressed strong opinions on the homosexual issue openly. Also, they were very active in the Global South, which had maintained an unbending stand on the subject. The remaining fifteen members of the Commission were a balanced group of male and female church leaders, lawyers, and theologians.[1] From Canada was Rev. Canon Alyson Barnett-Cowan, director of faith, worship, and ministry. Barnett-Cowan was head of the Canadian church ecumenical desk, overseeing, among other matters, issues of diversity and dialogue on sexuality. Bishop David Beetge, the dean of the Church of the Province of Southern Africa, was an experienced clergyman, working with a very diverse constituency and running an extensive AIDS/HIV ministry.

Professor Norman Doe, an expert in canon law and international Anglicanism, was director of the Centre for Law and Religion at Cardiff University in Wales. Bishop

---

1. "The Lambeth Commission of Communion—The Windsor Report 2004."

Mark Dyer, a former Roman Catholic monk, had renounced the monastic life in 1969. Two years later, the Episcopal Diocese of Bethlehem received him as a priest, and he was consecrated bishop of the diocese in 1982. After his retirement, he became professor of theology and director of spiritual formation at the American Virginia Theological Seminary in Alexandria, Virginia, where he was also director in charge of the faculty. Dyer was a strong advocate of women's ordination and opposed the enactment of sodomy laws when Virginia attempted to enact a prohibitive law against the vice.

Archbishop Josiah Iduwo-Fearon, archbishop of Kaduna in the Anglican Church of Nigeria, was known for maintaining a strong stand on the issue that the Commission was set to investigate. Rev. Dorothy Lau was one of five women appointed to the eighteen-member Commission. She was director of the Hong Kong Sheng Kung Hui Welfare Council, which had an accomplished record of running over 380 social welfare programs and schools in the diocese. Dr. Esther Mombo, the academic dean of St Paul's United Theological Seminary at Limuru, Kenya, was a "feminist theologian" who had played active role in AIDS/HIV ministry with women and had also been a guest speaker on sexuality at the primates' meetings. Rubie Nottage, chancellor of the West Indies, was a canon lawyer and in the top hierarchy by virtue of her position working with Archbishop Gomez. Dr. Jenny Te Paa was the principal of the College of Saint John the Evangelist, Auckland, New Zealand. A self-identified "liberal," she was, at the time, a doctoral student at Graduate Theological Union, Berkley, California, in the United States of America.

Archbishop Barry Morgan, the primate of Wales, was a moderate, with no known position on the dividing issue. His inclination was the preservation of Anglican diversity. Bishop John Paterson, the primate of Aotearoa, New Zealand, and Polynesia, maintained the same neutrality. This should be expected, as he was chairman of the Anglican Consultative Council. He had refrained from condemning Gene Robinson. Paterson had had the onerous responsibility of mediating between factions in his own province because his country, New Zealand, was yet to arrive at a position concerning gay clergy.

The same reticence applied to Bishop James Terom, moderator of the Church of North India. In spite of being associated with African bishops, he had withheld public comments on the matters of homosexuality and the church. However, Thomas Wright, the new bishop of Durham in the Church of England, contrasted with Terom in a big way. He came into the Commission with a reputation as respected theologian and historian. Wright had served on the Anglican Communion's Inter-Anglican Theological and Doctrinal Commission. His unique selling point was his famed intellectual precocity. He evidenced no constraints in expressing his views boldly, even on the most controversial theological subjects. He had independence of mind and could fearlessly break ranks with orthodox or traditional views, which he had done several times. Wright was the type that abhorred a herd mentality.

Rev. Canon John Rees found his way to the Commission as its legal consultant. Rees's position as the Anglican Consultative Council's legal adviser would stand the Commission in good stead, benefitting it with a wealth of experience. Then, there was the Rev. Canon Gregory Cameron, secretary to the Commission. Cameron came with two advantages. In the first place, he was the director of ecumenical affairs and studies in the Anglican Communion, a new, relatively high position. On the other hand, he was a former chaplain to Archbishop Rowan Williams when the latter was archbishop of Wales. It's not clear whether his appointment was due to the need for an efficient secretary or simply the desire of his boss to ensure that a person of trust and loyalty was assigned to the task.

Then there was Ms. Anne McGavin,[2] whose appointment to the Commission led to a curious twist. A lawyer, she became the first female chancellor in the Scottish Episcopal Church in 1991. Her duties covered advising the primate of the church on all aspects of church law. McGavin also scored another first. She was the first Scot to earn a master of laws degree in canon law. She must have come under the tutelage of Norman Doe, professor of canon law and international Anglicanism and director of the Centre for Law and Religion at Cardiff University, Wales. McGavin spoke of her gains from the "first Canon Law degree to be awarded to anyone in Scotland since the Reformation." It afforded her opportunity to learn "everything from the ornaments in the church to how different ecclesiastical systems deal with naughty priests,'" she said. Intriguing to her also was "how the different provinces of the Anglican communion deal with things." The puzzling development, however, was McGavin's resignation from the Commission after the first meeting for "personal reasons."

McGavin's withdrawal from the Commission was well-managed. It raised no dust and was kept out of public view. The Commission, thus, began life without needless controversy. Neither was its progress hampered by a crisis of confidence. It even managed to build some sort of trust. Even among groups vocally opposed to the unilateral actions of the Canadian and American churches, there seemed to be faith in the Commission. No group raised objections regarding the Commission's composition, even if the composition and leadership of the Commission tilted toward the West. Of the eighteen members, ten were from the West, seven from the Global South, which incidentally accounted for more than two-thirds of the membership of the Anglican Communion.[3] The Commission's two most significant positions—the chair and the secretary's position—went to the West. All members were personal appointees of Archbishop Rowan Williams.

The archbishop also exclusively decided the Commission's terms of service. Its primary mandate was to look at the "legal and theological implication flowing from the decisions of the Episcopal Church (USA) to appoint a priest in a committed same

2. "Advocate Makes History Again with a Masterly Performance."

3. "Commission Appointed by Archbishop of Canterbury Rowan Williams: A Preliminary Analysis by Progressive Episcopalians of Pittsburgh," http://progressiveepiscopalians.com.

sex relationship as one of its bishops." A corollary matter for examination was the decision "of the Diocese of New Westminster to authorise services for use in connection with same sex unions."

The directive also involved examining "specifically the canonical understanding of communion, impaired and broken communion, and the ways in which provinces of the Anglican Communion may relate to one another in situations where ecclesiastical authorities of one province feel unable to maintain the fullness of communion with another part of the Anglican Communion." In this connection, the Archbishop asked the Commission to suggest means of "episcopal oversight for those Anglicans within a particular jurisdiction, where full communion within a province is under threat." They were required to take account of "the highest degree of communion that may be possible in the circumstances, both within and between the churches of the Anglican Communion."

Another mandate of the Commission raised the inescapable question of how the archbishop could exercise moral authority in periods of crisis such as the situation at hand. The Commission was tasked to make recommendations on the "exceptional circumstances and conditions under which it would be appropriate for the Archbishop of Canterbury to exercise an extraordinary ministry of episcope with regard to the internal affairs of a province other than his own." In other words, the Commission was to come up with the best way for the archbishop of Canterbury to intervene in "the internal affairs of a province other than his own for the sake of maintaining communion with the said province and between the said province and the rest of the Anglican Communion."

When Archbishop Williams inaugurated the Commission in February 2004, he gave them a seven-month deadline of September 30, 2004, to submit their report. This gave him temporary relief, for all eyes turned to the Commission. Many thought the group could lead the Communion out of the cauldron with the crisis resolved. Even cynics were ready to give the Commission a chance, hopeful that even if it could not find a permanent cure for the malaise afflicting the Communion, at least it could save the floundering Anglican Communion ship from sinking.

The Lambeth Commission concluded its assignment in October 2004 with a report to the archbishop of Canterbury. The report, dubbed the "Windsor Report," took on a life of its own, becoming reference material on the Anglican Communion's crisis. The panel had worked under the strictest, self-imposed confidentiality, and this helped safeguard its work from exposure to harmful speculations. In addition, the decision shielded the members of the Commission from avoidable pressure.

For nine months, keen interest had mounted in expectation of what the Commission had to say. The Eames squad had been thrown into the furnace to douse a burning fire and did the work to the best of its ability. As was bound to happen, it faced difficulties. The members were not unanimous on the subject given them to investigate. There was not one among them without "opinions [which] have been shared openly." Nevertheless, to their credit, the divergence did not prevent them from presenting a report as a team. There was no minority report; nor did a group break away to denounce the others as traitors. They had beaten down the ideological dividing wall and succeeded in hammering out a common position, though they'd been given very little chance of overcoming their differences.

Their report was a solution to a problem, but it also noted something of a problem for their solution. They recognized the issue and noted a caveat—that no meaningful benefits would attend their recommendations if "realistic and visionary ways cannot be agreed to meet the level of disagreements." They understood that division had festered like a cancer that had eaten deep into the organs of the Church. Painfully, the Commission had to admit that even during the course of its work, the problem remained profound. It showed no abatement, and the culprits were unwilling to embrace repentance. Thus, the Commission was forced to stick to the reality that strong "voices and declarations have portrayed a Communion in crisis." Serious divisions had appeared. The splits were far reaching at "several levels of Anglican life." Discord existed at every turn, "between provinces, between dioceses, and between individual Anglican clergy and laity."

The Eames Commission sounded less than sanguine regarding the likelihood of the Church resolving its dispute through compromise. Opinions had become so sharply divided within the Communion, the Commission stated, that the odds of warring parties' embracing reconciliation were near zero. Leaders and groups were dug into positions, and their stands had taken on an inflexible cast.

The hardline positions seemed to revolve around a number of key problems that the Anglican Church had not found meaningful ways to address. First, and most important, was a question "about the nature of authority in the Anglican Communion." Second was the issue of "inter-relationship of the traditional 'Instrument of the Unity.'" This, essentially, referenced the relative authority of the archbishop of Canterbury, the primates, the Anglican Consultative Council, and the pronouncements of the Lambeth Council. Third was the fundamental issue of "the ways in which the Holy Scripture is interpreted by Anglicans." Fourth, and of no less significance, was the manner of exercising "the historic autonomy enshrined in Anglican provinces." Fifth were "issues of justice."

First among those fundamental issues addressed by the Lambeth Commission was the question of how the Church should interpret the Holy Scripture. It declared that the Anglican Communion was a scripturally-based Church. The Commission's clarification was significant. The categorical statement addressed one contentious issue at the heart of the crisis. Though it followed the usual pattern of convoluted ecclesiastical writings, nonetheless, the Commission's logic behind the declaration was self-explanatory.

Setting the tone in the preamble to the report, the Commission stated, "God has unveiled, in Jesus Christ, his glorious plan for the rescue of the created order."

Amplifying the exposition further, the "glorious plan" was defined as the "created order" in its entirety, apart from "all that defaces, corrupts and destroys it." Accordingly, the Eames Commission submitted that whether the issue be "unity of the church" or the "communion of all its members," nothing, and absolutely nothing, undermines their being "rooted in the Trinitarian life and purposes of God."

Putting the twin issue—unity and communion—in its right perspective, the Commission wanted it to be understood that they were not ends in themselves. "They are designed not for their own sake," the report averred. They had a purpose, which was "to serve and signify God's mission to the world." Life in the Anglican Communion, given this background, could not but be erected on two essential pillars—shared gift and advancement of God's mission. The two remain mutually inclusive as they equally, jointly reinforce the life of the Church.

The Lambeth Commission didn't want a misunderstanding concerning this issue of mutual existence within the Communion. It had been a major theme of the third Anglican Conference, held in Toronto, Canada, in 1963. Addressing "Anglican life in communion," they declared that "mutual interdependence and responsibility in the Body of Christ" constituted the foundation of life in the Communion. It subsequently laid out "Ten Principles of Partnership" to govern relationships in the Anglican Church. (This was through a "Mission Issues and Strategy Advisory Group.")

Topmost among the ten identified parameters was the principle of "mutuality." The "mutuality" norm connoted a "deep sense of open and joint responsibility." It emphasised the duty of being "open to one another as friends" and demanded that provinces deal with each other "on the basis of commitment, mutual trust, confession and forgiveness, keeping one another informed of all plans programmes and submitting ourselves to mutual accountability and correction." Regarding the question of decision making within the Communion, the "mutuality" section enjoined "sharing power" among the constituent organs.

> For example, major decisions affecting partners (in the South), should not be taken without their participation in the decision whether by their presence when it is made or by prior consultation.

There was also an "integrity" section. By the group's conception, "integrity" meant upholding truthfulness "at all levels". This meant being "real and honest," with a pattern of "listening to each other and being willing to repent and change when we have been in error."

Perhaps it was no accident that "transparency" followed "integrity." Transparency has always been a major issue in public affairs. It had no less remained a burden in the church. The Anglican Communion's "Ten Principles of Partnership" insisted that being truthfully open should not be considered foreign to managing the affairs of the Church. Rather, the Church should hold onto it as a core value. "Transparency" implied maintaining "openness and honesty with one another." Within the Communion, therefore, "information needs to be fully shared with one another." It meant every structure of the Church had an obligation to give and take from the others "information about all of our relationships."

Incidentally, these ten principles to catalyze common existence in the Anglican Communion predated the 2003 crisis by exactly 40 years! The rules had no expiration date. Because there had been no recall by the Lambeth Commission, they continued being valid as a benchmark for measuring relations within the Communion.

Inexplicably, the Lambeth Commission did not elaborate on the principles in its report. Eames and his team avoided applying the "Ten Principles of Partnership" to the behavior of the two North American churches who had ignited the crisis engulfing the Communion. Interestingly, the Commission resorted to drawing a parallel between the homosexuality campaign and another significant issue that also represented a revolutionary change in the life of the Communion, the ordination of women. From when the idea began until the final stage of its adoption in the Anglican Church, women's ordination to priesthood and the episcopate was a highly contentious subject.

The debate was sparked in 1944 with the ordination of Florence Li Tim-Oi. Venerated by the two North American churches, Florence Li was a flamboyant star, who arose from an odd place in Anglican history. She was Chinese, born in Hong Kong in 1907, and witnessed the ordination of a fellow woman, Lucy Vincent, in Hong Kong in 1931. In what amounted to an "altar call," the preacher exhorted other women at the ordination to consider volunteering themselves to God and the ministry. Florence Li was inspired, and she spent seven years pursuing that dream, including study at Canton Union Theological College. She returned to Hong Kong in 1938, worked for two years in Kowloon, and was later sent by Bishop Ronald Hall to assist refugees in Macau. Everything then happened not by her will, but seemingly by God's design for her life.

She returned six months later to Hong Kong and was ordained a deaconess by Bishop Hall on May 22, 1941. Then the Japanese occupation of Hong Kong and some other parts of China created new circumstances for her. Despite the neutrality of Macau, Anglican priests were finding it difficult to get to the town; indeed, there was no resident Anglican priest in the town. Hall arrived at an ad hoc solution, authorizing Florence Li to fill the vacuum. He gave her permission to give the sacraments to the Anglicans in those extenuating circumstances. Hall's explanation to Archbishop of Canterbury William Temple expressed his constraints demurely:

> I'm not an advocate for the ordination of women. I am, however, determined that no prejudices should prevent the congregations committed to my care [from] having the sacraments of the Church.[4]

Hall decided to boost Florence Li's status in 1944, ordaining her as a priest. She thus had the official and legal right to administer the sacraments. Sympathetic as

4. https://en.wikipedia.org/wiki/Florence_Li_Tim-Oi.

Canterbury Archbishop Temple was to Hall's predicament, he still took a very strong stand against the decision. In fact, it wasn't until thirty years later that the Anglican Church ratified the ordination of women throughout the Communion. (This was after the 1968 Lambeth Conference, at which the diocese of Hong Kong and Macao formally brought the issue to the floor.)

At the 1968 Lambeth Conference, no conclusive answer followed discussion by the Anglican leaders. They felt that "the theological arguments presented for and against the ordination of women to the priesthood are inconclusive." Accordingly, they passed a declaration, Resolution 34, expressing the mind of the Church on the subject. It declared, "Before any regional or national church or province [makes] a final decision to ordain women to the priesthood they should consider carefully the advice of the Anglican Consultative Council (ACC)." In deference to that decision, the bishop of Hong Kong and Macao had to wait another two years before opportunity presented itself for the matter to be placed at the doorstep of the ACC.

The ACC was just undergoing its birth then in 1970. Its maiden meeting in Limuru, Kenya, accordingly, became a theater of sorts, with hot debates and contentious questions about the propriety of ordaining women. Opinions were sharply divided. Eventually, the matter went to vote. The female ordination advocates won the day with a slight majority of 24 to 22.[5] The victory, however, was not absolute. The Council gave the bishop of Hong Kong and Macao a condition to fulfill. He had to go back home and secure "the approval of his Synod." Once he succeeded in achieving this, he was assured that "his action would be acceptable to the Council."

The Lambeth Commission made a cogent allusion to Hong Kong as an example: "What needs to be noted is that Hong Kong did not understand itself to be so autonomous." It didn't feel that it could "proceed without bringing the matter to the Anglican Consultative Council as requested by the Lambeth Conference 1968." Furthermore, the diocese only took action "with the cooperation of the Instruments of Unity." Also, after the diocese of Hong Kong and Macau had set the precedent, by the time of the 1978 Lambeth Conference, a number of countries had followed suit—Canada, the United States, and New Zealand. Eight additional provinces had also agreed to women's ordination in principle.

Still, the subject had to return to the Lambeth Conference, but the debate that ensued was less acrimonious. It was at the 1978 Lambeth Conference that the subject was finally laid to rest with a vote of 316 for, 37 against, and 17 abstentions. Overwhelming were those in support of women's ordination. Consequently, the Conference passed a resolution to give effect to the majority decision—Resolution 21. The declaration, entitled Women in the Priesthood, affirmed the majority's decision, but with a slight clarification. This was sub-section 3a of the resolution, where "the autonomy of each of its member Churches" included "the legal right of each Church to make its own decision about the appropriateness of admitting women to Holy Orders."

5. "Resolution 1—The Ordination or Consecration of Women to the Episcopate."

The Anglican Church leaders, taking into consideration the volatility of the subject, further highlighted the need to bear in mind that the action of a province "has consequences for the Anglican Communion as whole." They urged "a commitment to the preservation of unity within and between all member Churches of the Anglican Communion." Explosive as the issue of female ordination was, the lesson to be derived was that the mature and rule-abiding nature of the diocese of Hong Kong and Macau did not threaten to implode the Anglican Church.

In sharp contrast was a development from the American Episcopal Church that took the matter a notch higher in 1985. The General Convention of the church had indicated its intention "not to withhold consent to the election of a bishop on the grounds of gender." As far as they were concerned, the ordination of female priests was a forgone conclusion. To them, the most important matter was seeing women become bishops. The then-American presiding bishop knew the decision was an explosive one. It wasn't as domestic as it looked, because it was bound to have a natural spillover effect throughout the Anglican Communion. The presiding bishop decided to act prudently and cautiously. He decided to take his fellow primates in the Communion along.

Incidentally, the Communion had just decided to institute a routine meeting among the primates, and the 1985 meeting was their first. It was providential that the maiden gathering of the primates was scheduled for Toronto, Canada, the city and country that hosted the first Anglican Gathering in 1963, which led to production of the "Ten Principles of Partnership." When their American colleague brought up the issue of women's ordination to the bishopric, the archbishop of Canterbury and his fellow primates referred the matter for further consultation, examination, and evaluation. The primate of Australia, John Grindrod, and a committee were appointed to work on the issue. Their mandate was to provide the 1988 Lambeth Conference with a way to move forward on the question. Grindrod's committee did the work well.

The 1988 report of the Grindrod committee was entitled "Listening as a Mark of Communion." Grindrod and members of his committee must have learnt from the past, taking wisdom from the issue of women's ordination and the way it was resolved. Now the issue was bishops, and for this they suggested two principles: The first was a vigorous plea for restraint, trusting that "the moral authority inherent in a gathering of all the bishops of the Communion would find a response at the provincial level." Second, they urged that when a province considered it compelling to ordain women into the episcopate, it must be ready to convince the Communion of the necessity of its action. What Grindrod's committee was saying therefore was that the practice of ordaining women into the episcopate must be justified on a case by case basis, e.g., by showing "compelling doctrinal reasons," "experience of women in the priesthood," "demands of mission in the region," and, where it became evident, the "overwhelming support of the dioceses."

Votes on the issue were straightforward. Those in favor of the proposal out-numbered those objecting, with 423 for, 28 against, and 10 abstaining. The victory occasioned 1988 Lambeth Resolution I, enjoining each province to "respect the decision." Similarly, provinces embracing the idea were requested to consider the "attitude of other provinces." A clarification was made, however, to the effect that the Communion's call for mutual tolerance and acceptance of the practice did not entail "acceptance of the principles involved." The result, therefore, was that those provinces overwhelmingly in favor of the idea should still strive to maintain "the highest possible communion with the provinces which differ."

The minority who were defeated over the issue didn't have any animosity toward the majority. They nursed no bitterness over the verdict. They didn't overreact by willfully attempting to undermine the majority's decision. They accepted their conquest with grace. Choosing to be proactive, the Communion established the Commission on Women in the Anglican Episcopate—the "Eames Commission"—to ensure that the decision didn't tear down the Communion. Evidently, the Commission had virtually nothing to do; there was hardly any group to mollify or assuage. They were tasked to issue a situation report in 1998, after ten years of service, but there was little to report in terms of conflict resolution, for nothing eventful or startling had occurred (except for a little dustup at the end, when Eames expressed sympathy for those opposed to female bishops).

The Eames Commission was pleased to observe that "decision-making on serious and contentious issues has been, and can be, carried out without division." They also wanted doubts erased about the organs of the Church—the Instruments of Unity—that possessed the inherent constitutional powers to make decisions for the Church. They listed the four institutions, namely the archbishop of Canterbury, the Lambeth Conference, the Anglican Consultative Council, and the primates' meeting, adding that autonomy of provinces was therefore not sacrosanct. It was limited by "Anglican interdependence," especially "on matters of deep theological concern to the whole Communion."

From the history on which the 2004 Commission based its opinion, there were cases to show how the four Instruments had exercised power in making decisions for the Communion. In sharp contrast, the Lambeth Commission lamented, "the precedent . . . set by this procedure has not, unfortunately, been followed in the matters currently before the Communion." The consequence manifested itself vividly to them. In a mournful tone, the Commission reflected, "This, we conclude, lies at the heart of the problem we currently face."

The Lambeth Commission unearthed various early warning signs presaging the disagreement. Much of what the Eames team discovered has already been explained. But it did trace the genesis of conflict to "experimentation with blessings of same-sex relationships [that] had begun as early as 1973 within North America." The in-house rebellion was a ticking time bomb because "no part of the church can ignore its life in communion with the rest." As the Commission asserted, "What is done in one place can, and does affect all." In addition, the North American churches were found to have flagrantly and willfully violated the Communion's processes and procedures. Their deeds were undertaken with calculated insouciance. By March 2003, the two churches, particularly the American Episcopal Church, had pushed the revolt to such a height that it created a moral burden for them within the global Anglican Communion. The Lambeth Commission cited some of the facts relating to that conclusion.

On March 18, 2003, the Theology Committee of the House of Bishops of the American church had presented a theological report on human sexuality to the House. The report affirmed that "sexual discipline and holiness of life must be very serious considerations for bishops, Standing Committees, and Commissions on Ministry as they discern and exhibit 'a wholesome example to all people.'" Three key propositions were also clarified in the report. The first was that dioceses "discern and raise up fit persons for the ministry of word and sacrament." The second called on "bishops and Standing Committees to be respectful of the ways in which decisions made in one Diocese have ramifications on others." Third was a reminder "that ordination is for the whole Church." Contrary to all the provisions, the synod of the American Episcopal Church at its General Convention in 2003 decided to approve the election of a gay bishop. The Commission noted that the revolt was in spite of a warning by the Anglican Church primates that such actions would "tear the fabric of our Communion at its deepest level."

The American and Canadian churches acted perfidiously. Painfully, the Commission observed that even "after this Commission had already been set up, the General Synod of the Anglican Church of Canada passed a resolution affirming 'the integrity and sanctity of committed adult same-sex relationships.'" Never had there been a time in the Church's history that such scant regard was paid to the global integrity of the Communion. The Lambeth Commission showed that many provinces deplored the condescending attitude of their North American colleagues. They found their haughtiness too contemptuous to accept. The Commission's fact finding revealed that "some eighteen of the thirty-eight provinces of the Anglican Communion, or their primates on their behalf, have issued statements which indicate, in its variety of ways, their basic belief that the developments in North America are 'contrary to biblical teaching and as such unacceptable.'" The Anglican Church, as it were, became deeply divided, and consequently the dangerous haemorrhaging to which it had been subjected continued.

On the other hand, the Lambeth Commission seemed committed to not be one-sided in its conclusion. From its introductory pages, the Commission presented alternative views. A comment on 1998 Lambeth Resolution 1.10, for instance, acknowledged, "There has been some controversy about the way in which this resolution was arrived at and voted upon." But they immediately dismissed the specious claim. Instead, they stated unequivocally that the "primates unanimously upheld the resolution as the standard of Anglican teaching on the matter in their statement of October 16, 2003." The Commission maintained that the two churches, the Episcopal Church in the United States of America and its Canadian counterpart, acted willfully to defy the rules of the Communion forbidding their actions.

Even if the Commission was willing to grant churches the right of pursuing innovations and novelties, the boundaries of their contemplated actions were limited to "matters on which the Church has not so far made up its mind." Their freedom did not extend to taking "actions which are explicitly against the current teaching of the Anglican Communion as a whole, and/or of individual provinces." On this, the Commission spoke bluntly: "No province, diocese or parish has the right to introduce a novelty which goes against such teaching."

But the violation had already occurred. So what did the Commission believe the Communion should do? Interesting were the recommendations of the Commission. The suggestions covered over 59 paragraphs and occupied a whole section in the report. In "Our Future Life Together," the various proposals began with examination of the "Instruments of Unity" in the Communion. Here the Commission focused on problems associated with the decision-making organs in the Church and "the nature of authority in the Anglican Communion." The way these organs were treated struck the Commission as the first fundamental problem, which led in turn to the crisis engulfing the Communion. It observed that "the views of the Instruments of Unity have been ignored or sidelined by sections of the Communion." These organs were so contemptuously and shabbily treated as to negate their significance in providing law and order within the Communion. Accordingly, the Commission "concluded that there needs to be a clearer understanding" regarding how provinces should respond "to the decisions of these Instruments."

They also discovered that a clear line of authority was missing in the Communion, so they suggested that the "Primates Meeting [become] known as the Primates' Conference (which in a way would make it a kind of 'Lambeth Standing Committee')." In addition, they canvassed a similar elevation in standing for the archbishop of Canterbury, suggesting that he "should not be regarded as a figure-head." The Communion should instead "look to the holder of this office to speak directly to any provincial situation on behalf of the Communion." Such interventions should "not be viewed as outside interference."

Furthermore, the archbishop of Canterbury should be free to invite "whomsoever he believes appropriate" to the Lambeth Conference and the primates' meeting. Perhaps as a check on the way the archbishop makes important decisions, the establishment of a "Council of Advice" was recommended, a body made up of people with suitable knowledge of "the life of the Communion, and of the theological, ecclesiological and canonical" matters applicable to any situation.

Next, the Commission endorsed development of a "common Anglican Covenant," urging the primates to consider the pledge's "adoption by the churches of the

Communion." The Covenant would make "explicit and forceful the loyalty and bonds of affection which govern the relationships between the churches of the Communion." To this end, parameters were recommended to make the Covenant effective: it should deal with the common identity of relationships within the Communion; the extent or level of autonomy within the Communion must be determined; protocols for the management of communion affairs, including disputes, must be delineated.

The Commission believed the need for such a Covenant to be "overwhelming." Indeed, the "Anglican Communion cannot again afford, in every sense, the crippling prospect of [another] repeated worldwide inter-Anglican conflict." For all intents and purposes, the Covenant was envisaged to be a regulation, an "international obligation [binding] a church [from] changing its mind about the covenantal commitments" in a unilateral manner.

In its "General Findings," the Lambeth Commission had no complimentary words for the American Episcopal Church or the Anglican Church of Canada. Their verdict was damning, charging that "they have not attached sufficient importance to the impact of their decisions on other parts of the Communion." The Commission was pushed to express four "regrets": (1) That "the Episcopal Church (USA) proceed-ed with the consecration of Gene Robinson" (2) That "the 74th General Convention of the Episcopal Church (USA) . . . [engaged in] celebrating and blessing same-sex unions"; (3) That "the Diocese of New Westminster approved the use of public Rites for the Blessing of same-sex unions"; and (4) That "the General Synod of the Anglican Church of Canada issued a statement affirming the integrity and sanctity of commit-ted same-sex relationship."

The Commission then moved to the other warring group. Not spared were the "number of primates and provinces [that] have declared themselves in impaired or broken communion with the Episcopal Church (USA) or the Diocese of New Westminster." The complaint of the Commission related to appeals for "calm" by the archbishop of Canterbury, a similar entreaty from the primates themselves, and an appeal from the Commission, who had urged all parties to allow a grace period un-til the Commission completed its work. Nevertheless, the confrontations continued unabated. It noted that "a number of primates and other bishops have taken it upon themselves to intervene in the affairs of other provinces of the Communion." All these actions, the Commission found regrettable.

Then, in a section titled "On elections to the Episcopate," they shifted focus to the central issue: an unwholesome candidate that the Communion had opposed. Of the thirteen paragraphs dealing with this issue, none spoke with the forthrightness or candor with which the Commission had spoken up to this stage. It looked as if the Commission had suddenly lost its appetite for honest and frank appraisal. The Lambeth Commission was no longer searching for the truth but, rather, desperately struggling with the truth.

It required no genius to see the tough battle that had emerged within the Commission and the consequent attempt at twisting the obvious. The Commission started employing rationalizations, excuses, apologies, and illogical justifications in order to avoid calling a spade a spade. On the one hand, for example, it noted that, "A bishop is more than simply the chief pastor to a local church," for "they represent the universal to the local, and the local to the universal." Furthermore, "the Communion has also made its collective position clear on the issue of ordaining those who are involved in same gender unions." Yet, bizarre was the inference it drew immediately thereafter:

> We do not believe that those involved in the election of a bishop to the See
> of New Hampshire and the consent to the election are entirely or exclusively
> blameworthy in relation to this.

Eames and his team tried desperately to forge a justification, but it could not stand the test of elementary logic. The argument they put forward was embarrassing, that "not everyone involved in the processes will necessarily have been fully acquainted with the contents of the resolutions we have quoted." Was there a bishop to be found in the Anglican Communion at that time without knowledge of the raging controversy about homosexuality in the Church? And if that were possible, what about the primate or the archbishop of such a province, not to mention its House of Bishops? The Lambeth Commission wounded the truth where the injury was most conspicuous.

The Commission wasn't as generous to Gene Robinson. He was given no soft landing. The Commission upheld a sanction already imposed by the Archbishop of Canterbury, denying Robinson recognition. He would remain excluded from the Communion and its activities until the Council of Advice (when it became functional) or the primates' meeting reviewed his pariah status.

With regard to the Episcopal Church, the real leprous hand, the Commission "debated long and hard." Its conclusion was that "the Episcopal Church be invited to express its regret." The panel gave two reasons for its recommendation. The first was that "the proper constraints of the bonds of affection were breached in the events surrounding the election and consecration" of Robinson. Second were the "consequences which followed." The Commission also concluded that should "the desire of the Episcopal Church (USA) [be] to remain within the Communion," the condition of remaining should be "its willingness to repent." To demonstrate its willingness to abide by the decision of the Communion, the Commission stated, the Episcopal Church should "effect a moratorium on the election and consecration of anyone in [a] same-sex relationship." The ban was to remain in force until the Anglican Church arrived at a new consensus on the subject.

Regarding the Canadian church and its offending Diocese of New Westminster, the Commission found no reason to exculpate either from complicity. The Commission traced the roots of the malfeasance to 1998, the year of Lambeth Resolution 1.10. The diocese had taken preliminary steps through a synodical resolution on the blessing of same-sex unions. But the step remained local as "there is no record of any formal attempt to consult the wider province." Neither was the diocese prepared "to delay [the] processes to allow such consultation to take place." The bishop of the diocese, Michael Ingham, decided to act despite his knowledge of the position of the Communion on the issue. It was an arbitrary decision on his part, premeditated and calculated. Ingham lacked the *locus standi* to erect the aberrant canon. The Commission emphatically undercut the notion of

> unqualified freedom on the part of any bishop or diocese to authorise liturgical texts if they are likely to be inconsistent with the norms of liturgical and doctrinal usage extant in the province's *Book of Common Prayer* or other provincially authorised texts.

Both the ordination of homosexual priests and public rites for the blessing of same-sex unions violated the stand of the Church and breached the Christian faith on which it stood.

The Commission arrived at a multi-point recommendation: a "moratorium on all such rites"; a call for "regret" (the ecclesiastical word for repentance and penitence) on the part of "bishops who have authorised such rites in the United States and Canada"; failing that, the need that "such bishops [should] consider [withdrawing] from representative functions in the Anglican Communion"; and readiness in the provinces "to take responsibility for endeavouring to ensure commitment on the part of their bishops." In other words, provinces must be ready to provide effective and accountable leadership on ecclesiastical matters in their countries.

For the American and Canadian provinces, the Commission was probably coming with the proverbial medicine after death. The national leadership of the two churches had been compromised. Their prejudices were not hidden. The problems engulfing these churches were not just about Scripture and biblical authority but also a lust for power. Power had shifted so fundamentally that a deep polarization had occurred in the American and Canadian churches.

The churches had developed into two extreme groups. On one side were the powerful cliques in control, and on the other were the alienated minorities struggling for space to exist. The situation bred a large, oppressive, power-wielding, terrorizing group tormenting the minority, who were victims at the periphery of power. The evidence was clear that leadership of both the Episcopal Church and the Anglican Church of Canada were not neutral. They had lost the vital ingredients of fairness and justice that must accompany effective leadership. More or less, they had become the executive arm of the tyrannical homosexual wings within their churches.

On this point, the Lambeth Commission erred again. It tried to whitewash the blatant abuse of power, the unhidden attempt at crushing those questioning the revisionist agenda. The victims, however, made their voice known to the Commission.

They cried out about "the hurt and alienation" being perpetrated on them. The Commission was to recognize their plight in its report.

The result was that first, the Commission asked "the church or province in question to recognise first that dissenting groups in their midst are like themselves." The second entreaty was to urge the "home bishops" and the "intervening bishops" to work tirelessly to rebuild trust which had been lost. Furthermore, "a conditional and temporary provision of delegated pastoral oversight" for the dissenters was suggested. The Commission submitted that the oversight must offer "a credible degree of security" and assurance to the minority groups. Besides protecting them, it must ensure that they were "not at the mercy of a potentially hostile leadership." The Commission offered ideas regarding who could be considered competent to be saddled with pastoral oversight. They were "retired bishops from within the province in question" or "bishops from other provinces in the Communion." The Commission seemed to be angling for a win-win solution, a kind of no-victor/no-vanquished compromise in its handling of the Communion's crisis.

Perhaps that desire informed the report's conclusion. Reserved for last was the controversial matter of "parallel jurisdictions." Though the Commission found extenuating circumstances to justify the election, consent, and consecration of Gene Robinson as a bishop, it didn't offer a warm rationale for "parallel jurisdictions." Rather, the tone was harsh, employing innuendo and sarcasm. It began, "We call upon those bishops who believe it is their conscientious duty to intervene in provinces, dioceses and parishes other than own," and then it got worse.

Eames and his team felt that those provinces that had engaged in such "parallel jurisdictions" needed "to express regret for the consequence of their actions" and "to affirm their desire to remain in the Communion." The third and final recommendation was that they too should "effect a moratorium on any further action" because "what is good for the goose is also good for the gander."

But this was not the counsel of justice and fairness. For in addition to chastising the bishops who had intervened in the other provinces, the panel called upon these archbishops and bishops "to seek an accommodation with the bishops of the dioceses whose parishes they have taken into their own care." How fair was it to ask that the two to reconcile without resolution of the grievance that had sharply divided them in the first place?

The Commission's bias was palpable. For instance, they faulted "those diocesan bishops of the Episcopal Church (USA) who have refused to countenance the proposals set out by their House of Bishops to reconsider their own stance on this matter." The Commission continued, "If they refuse to do so . . . in our view, they will be making a profoundly dismissive statement about their adherence to the polity of their own church." But the commissioners avoided the corollary question of what should happen to those bishops within the same church who continued to flout the decision of the Instruments of Unity of the Communion, thus perpetuating the crisis. Justice is about coming to equity court with clean hands, not one but both hands, not one hand visibly clean while the other is both soiled and hidden.

Granted, the body was not established as a "truth commission." But there was no way for it to run from the truth. The undeniable truth about the Anglican Communion crisis was that it was not primarily about differences in theology and doctrine. After all, by the admission of the Commission itself, the Church had dealt with similar contentious subjects—in particular the ordination of women—without rancor. Respect and restraint tailored by wise counsel seemed to prevail on those occasions. Respect for process and procedure resulted in amicably agreeing to disagree. No side assumed an arrogant posture, nor was there a mentality of master and servant in the Communion. There was no desperate effort on the part of a group to foist a narrow agenda on the majority. The Communion was healthy, nurtured by a spirit of collective decision making. Disagreements were resolved by mutual consent while the atmosphere was full of trust and respect. As such, the Communion fared well as a global organization. The Anglican Church was a stable and progressive global Church.

Crises arise when mindsets clash with truth. To grapple with truth is to have the ability to admit truth to oneself, accept it, and receive it from others, even if the truth is blunt, bitter, and uncomfortable. Coming to terms with truth resolves crises; telling it fearlessly is the hallmark of just individuals. There were blunt, bitter, and uncomfortable truths the Lambeth Commission unearthed. The truth was that the Anglican crisis—involving a chain of misfeasance, perfidy, disobedience, actions, and reactions—stemmed from a single cause: "naughty priests," as Anne McGavin, the only member to decline service on the Commission, would describe them. Not only were there "naughty priests" in North American and United Kingdom churches; there were also "naughty bishops" and "naughty primates," who had begun to join the fold. At all levels, the "naughty" groups were growing significantly in number. They were also acquiring tremendous power to shape the policy of national churches through penetration of their polities.

The Lambeth Commission was not about "naughty priests," "naughty bishops," or "naughty primates." Least of its concerns was what the Communion should do with them. The Lambeth Commission was to find facts, and it did find the facts. It toed the path of sounding "politically correct," wanting no victor, no vanquished in its verdict, preferring a balanced judgement or equal apportionment of blames. Eames and his colleagues held the justice pendulum down and kept it from swinging either right or left. But the facts the Commission uncovered were self-evident truths, realities with which all the key players were familiar.

When the Commission expressed serious concern over the possibility of the Communion not resolving the crisis, it unwittingly questioned the value of its own work. The nagging worry it voiced was the "real danger that we (the Communion) will not choose to walk together." Walking apart had only one meaning: that parties might prefer to go their separate ways! This was a grave fear for the Commission to express. But were they wrong?

Not at all. As stated in their report, nothing seemed to have changed concerning the crisis. Before and during the Commission's work, the contempt and rebellion did not lessen. Rather, the revolt seemed to have become a norm in the life of the Anglican Communion. What then was the possibility of the Communion overcoming the crisis? The Lambeth Commission wasn't sure. However, it had answers about the limited options facing the Church.

Bluntly, its position was that the worldwide Anglican Communion must decide whether "to walk together" or "to walk apart." The Commission believed the Communion had little or no room to maneuver from this inevitability. There was no middle ground. By the Commission's account, the tight rope had already been stretched to the breaking point. The Communion must confront the truth facing it with courage and boldness. Running away from the truth would only continue to hold the Church hostage to unending torment and pressure. The Lambeth Commission implied in its report that though the Anglican Church might not have reached its terminus yet, it was not at the best juncture and it was difficult to look forward to a promising time. The overall conclusion was that the global Church was in a precarious situation and that time was ticking away for the Communion.

1 1

Equal Actions and Opposite Reactions

America, 2004

Western countries pride themselves on respect for the rule of law. Arbitrariness or fraud, whether on the part of citizens, organizations, leaders, or government officials, tends to be frowned upon as anathema. A cherished social norm is that the laws apply equally to all. A corollary to this precious democratic principle is that courts and other juridical authorities must be respected. Liberty and expression of dissent are valued highly, but acting contemptuously of the courts or any other properly constituted authority is rarely permitted. No country in the West is without laws and sanctions against such offenses.

Were the American and Canadian churches to have perpetrated their condescension in the secular world, it would have attracted a serious reprimand. When the Lambeth Commission was instituted, the directive across the Communion to all parties was to maintain the *status quo ante bellum*. Everybody was expected, in other words, to do nothing contemptuous toward the Commission's work or to undertake actions that patently ridiculed the panel. In light of that expectation, the bishop of the Episcopal Church diocese of Washington, the Rt. Rev. John Chane, would have been a sure candidate for a contempt trial.

Barely two months after the Lambeth Commission was constituted, Saturday, May 29, 2004, Chane, rekindled the fire that the Communion had empanelled the Lambeth Commission to douse. As a *Washington Post* headline put it, "Episcopal Bishop to Bless Gay Priest's Union in Md."[1] The sizzling story was that "Bishop John Bryson Chane, head of the Episcopal Diocese of Washington, plans to formally bless the long-time relationship of a gay Episcopal priest and his partner next month at a ceremony in Maryland." The announcement was startling. Nothing like that had happened in the diocese. Chane was not only contemplating a forbidden action, but also engaging in an act of brazen contempt against the Communion. In fact, he had

1. Murphy, "Episcopal Bishop to Bless Gay Priest's Union in Md."

developed a new liturgy for blessing same-sex unions, which was to be premiered at the service.

He acted intentionally, and he had constituted a committee within the Washington diocese to write the same-sex union liturgy. The committee was headed jointly by Rev. Michael Hopkins and Rev. Susan Blue. Hopkins, a priest in the diocese, was the president of Integrity USA, a radical gay and lesbian group within the Episcopal Church. To boot, he was also the gay priest in question, to be joined in wedlock with his partner John Clinton Bradley. Chane would be using the new liturgy that Hopkins had helped to write. By his account, Chane would be "celebrating the life of a friend." He alone determined his personal law "because he believes covenant relationships, in which two people have committed themselves to spending their lives together, 'are holy and deserve to be blessed.'"

Chane was elected bishop of the Washington diocese on June 1, 2002. He was not a popular candidate, and it took a second ballot to elect him. Chane didn't have the privilege of attending the 1998 Lambeth Conference, and so was not involved in the rebellious "Pastoral Letter to Gay and Lesbian Anglicans." Equally, he was not at the Whittemore Centre for the consecration of Gene Robinson. But Chane found advancing the gay cause enticing. He latched onto it and pushed it forward. Though his diocese was aware of his support for the gay movement, he still got their bishopric. Once installed, he brought liberal clergy to his staff, including retired Massachusetts Suffragan Bishop Barbara Harris. He supported same-sex marriage and closed his eyes to gay weddings performed in the diocese. The planned blessing of Hopkins and his partner by Chane was not a surprise. The Washington diocese was already a rascal in disobedience, with notoriety accruing to its leader. He loved showmanship and media attention. If he had been lacking in those two qualities, the Washington see would have probably passed him over.

The diocese was an important and strategic one. It served as home of the National Cathedral and the National House of Prayer. Though it receives no money from the government, the cathedral is a national monument.[2] Also, it plays a dual role. It is the official seat of the presiding bishop of the Episcopal Church as well as that of the bishop of the Diocese of Washington. It would be absurd to have a bishop at odds with his or her presiding bishop share a common seat without a major conflict arising. Besides, Washington is the heartbeat of America. It is the center where power, politics, and position meet to shape the destiny of the country. Key institutions of the state, as well as representatives of significant private sector bodies, are located in Washington. The National Cathedral is part of that setup. Apart from being a house of worship, the cathedral is also an avenue to shape, define, and address America's "pressing moral and social issues of the day." The cathedral has played host to social and political activism. It's the place where the African-American civil rights leader Martin Luther King delivered his last Sunday service sermon in 1968. Annually, it is estimated that

2. Meyer, "Mysteries of the Washington National Cathedral."

the cathedral hosts between 700,000 and 800,000 visitors. It stands to influence and interact with the power brokers in America.

It worked well for the gay and lesbian clergy to have the cathedral on their side as this afforded national prominence to their agenda. In addition to importation of homosexuals into the life of the church, the result was a strategic effort to ensure that homosexuals dominated the clergy and church leadership. The relationship between the Episcopal Church and Chane was symbiotic. The church had upfront in Washington a reliable official in tune with its agenda; he had in the church a platform to advance his personal goals.

Bishop Chane made no pretence about his Washington ambition. On arrival, he had stated his desire, which was to "engage the secular and political leadership of the District of Columbia, the Congress of the United States and those who hold the highest elected and appointed offices of this nation." In this, he did himself proud. He bestrode Washington like an ambitious statesman, and Washington gave him fame in national politics in return. The national and international issues he addressed conferred enormous standing on him. *Washingtonian Magazine* found Chane to be one of the 150 most influential leaders in the District of Columbia. And the *London Telegraph* adjudged him one of the 50 most prominent leaders in the Anglican Communion. The recipient of a variety of awards, he was an American folk hero celebrated for speaking openly and boldly on popular causes.

But in his primary area of responsibility, Bishop Chane was a woeful failure. He was a disastrous church leader. He came to Washington, made a name for himself, and used the Washington diocese to achieve his aim. But as a church leader, his record was dismal. As The *Washington Post* put it in 2010, "Bishop to retire after lacklustre tenure."[3] Every part of the Chane's balance sheet was in the red, a crying deficit. The growing and vibrant church he inherited took a negative turn during his tenure. Chane failed the church, and accordingly, the church failed under Chane. Church growth was zero, a fact he had to admit: "Parochial reports filed by the parishes of our diocese for the most part tell a story of no real measurable growth in membership within the last 12 years." Furthermore, he admitted, "Financial giving has been stagnant . . . The budget that supports the missionary work of the diocese to its congregations, schools and our mission outreach beyond our borders has been stagnant as well." He added, "There has been no strong upward trend in pledged giving to the diocese by our congregations." Chane brought the diocese to near bankruptcy. Everything was run almost aground. Successful as he was in the secular world of politics and international diplomacy, he could not deliver shepherd's care to his congregations.

The plight of his diocese was underscored by the dynamic growth of a variety of congregations throughout the area, including McLean Bible Church in Northern Virginia; Covenant Life Church in Gaithersburg, Maryland; Jericho City of Praise in Landover, Maryland; and National Community Church in Washington. A remarkable

3. Duin, "Bishop to Retire After Lackluster Tenure."

feature common to the thriving churches was that "all are evangelical and conservative." They contrasted sharply with "the Washington Diocese [that] has become known for its support of the District's decision to legalize same-sex marriage and for allowing such ceremonies in its sanctuaries." Chane was aware of the toll his action was taking on the churches under him. Yet, rather than save the diocese from disintegration by renouncing the divisive liturgy and approval for blessings of same-sex marriage, he preferred to oversee the slow, deathward decline of the diocese. Chane's attitude was neither strange nor baffling. It was consistent with the familiar stubborn, rebellious, and destructive conduct that had become engrained among most top leaders in the Episcopal Church.

The same was true of Bishop Jon Bruno of the Diocese of Los Angeles, who demonstrated similar arrogance just days after Chane's blessing of a same-sex union. Bruno was familiar with the costliness of defying legitimate authority. He was an ex-police officer. As a law enforcement official, he wouldn't have countermanded his superior's instruction. Nor would he have ventured to defy a court. Yet on May 16, 2004, Bruno willfully disobeyed the same-sex celebration restriction order of the Anglican Church, thus marking the essential difference between the Bruno the former police officer and Bruno the bishop of Los Angeles.

Bruno obtained his license in criminology from California State University, Long Beach, in 1972, and he decided to follow up with a bachelor's degree in physical education from the same university in 1974. Apart from working with the city of Burbank police, he also tried his hand at professional football, signing a contract with the Denver Broncos. An injury however cut his career short. It was during this period that he found his way to the priesthood. In 1977, he attended Virginia Theological Seminary for his theological education, earning the master of divinity degree. The following year, 1978, the bishop of the diocese of Los Angeles, Robert Claflin Rusack, ordained him as a priest.

Bruno began his new vocation with flying colors. He brought to the job such passion that it seemed he had missed his road in the earlier professions of crime busting and ball tossing. He was full of energy and boundless in his thirst to advance the work of the church. Within three years, he had established a commendable reputation for his work in building church facilities and new congregations, such as St. Matthews Church in 1980. The Los Angeles diocese might have had other competent hands, but Bruno's indefatigability distinguished him as one of the most dedicated clergy the diocese had. Alongside Bishop Borsch, his energy found expression in many innovative projects, such as Cathedral Centre, which was built as a base for youth and family advocacy, and projects for reducing gang violence and promoting equality for immigrants. As provost of the Cathedral Centre of St. Paul, Los Angeles, he gave Christianity practical meaning. Bruno saw through to a successful end a project meeting the housing needs of the poor. Through the Nehemiah West Housing Corporation, of which he was the vice chair, low and moderate income families were provided with about 300 housing units for purchase. Ordinarily, for such a committed priest, exemplifying impressive devotion to care of his congregations, the sky was the limit. And so it was for Bruno.

He was elected bishop coadjutor of the diocese on November 13, 1999. That made him heir apparent to the Los Angeles diocese's bishopric. In 2000, he moved a notch higher as he was elected deputy to the Episcopal Church's General Convention. He was not a newcomer to the affairs of the church at the national level. He had assisted with operations and security services at the national conventions of the church for several years.

On February 1, 2002, Bruno formally assumed the bishopric of the Diocese of Los Angeles. But then, Bruno became of the exact opposite of everything he once was, as power apparently became a corrupting influence. Canons, doctrines, teachings, and Scriptures ceased to have any respectable meaning to him. This was the situation on May 16, 2004, when he decided to bless a same-sex union in violation of the moratorium decreed by the worldwide Anglican Church leaders.

In the same St. Paul's Cathedral, Los Angeles, where he had once served as provost, Bruno presided over the blessing of Rev. Malcolm Boyd and Mark Thompson. He was well aware that both were gay men. Boyd and Thompson had been in a same-sex relationship for twenty years and were in the church to celebrate the two decades of their togetherness with the blessing. Bruno recognized that such a union was contrary to the Anglican Communion's teaching and position. He wasn't ignorant of how the issue had polarized the Church. Above all, he couldn't claim to be oblivious to the purpose for which the Lambeth Commission had been set up—to stem the crisis into which the very action he was repeating had thrown the Communion.

Yet he couldn't care less. Though Bruno wouldn't as a uniformed officer of the state have risked trampling on American law so contemptuously, he had no such scruples when it came to the Church's authority. Bruno's behavior was reprehensible, with no justification or excuse for his audacious defiance. Another rookie bishop might have attempted to plead mitigating or extenuating circumstances barely two years into the episcopate, but Bruno's experience of 26 years in the priesthood, three of which he had understudied his predecessor as a bishop coadjutor, negated any plea of innocence that might be entered on his behalf. Besides, at 60 years of age, he was far beyond the impetuosity of youth. He had supposedly reached the stage of contemplative discernment.

Nevertheless, Bruno went ahead with his reckless action. He knew he had nothing to worry about, as no repercussion would follow, for the Episcopal Church had shown a lack of effective and disciplined leadership. The veneration that ought to accompany the episcopate as well as the dignity that should inhere in the office and its holder had all been eroded. The holiness that used to be a distinguishing mark of bishops had been sold in a market of cultural conformity. So much had broken down—rules, regulations, canons, Scripture, ethos, and morals—that in the life of the church, nothing seemed sacred any longer. It seemed everyone had turned into a law unto himself or herself in the American church.

Sad to say, in May of 2004, it looked as though holes had been torn in the sail of the Lambeth Commission as it journeyed out on its reconciliation mission. It was in May that the bishop of the Washington diocese, John Chane, announced his intention to bless same-sex unions with his new liturgy. Bruno's blessing of Malcolm Boyd and Mark Thompson occurred in May. That same May witnessed the Anglican Church of Canada's holding its General Synod, with same-sex issues featuring prominently on the agenda. The Canadian church was as defiant as its American counterpart, and it too faced a groundswell of opposition, particularly directed at the unilateral action of the diocese of New Westminster to authorize the same-sex blessing. The split was deep: 41 bishops of the church had attended the 1998 Lambeth Conference; of this number, 17 had joined the dissenting group in signing the letter to gay and lesbian Anglicans while 24 had preferred to go along with the majority in the Anglican Communion. But the minority had an advantage: The Canadian archbishop and primate, Michael Peers, was an incurable homosexuality backer. Like Frank Griswold, his American colleague, Michael Peers was part of every process undertaken by the primates, including the October 2003 unanimous decision that culminated in the Lambeth Commission and the directive asking everyone not to take prejudicial steps until the Commission had completed its work.

Peers did not return home to be faithful to or bear true witness to the decision reached with his colleagues. He acted to the contrary, writing an assuring letter instead to homosexuals, promising that "Canadian gays and lesbians will continue to be welcomed and received . . . and to have their contributions to our common life honoured." But now he would face the Canadian church's General Synod in May 2004. Convening every three years, it was the highest governing body of the church and was statutorily open to all bishops, elected clergy, and lay people from the 30 dioceses of the church.

One inevitable topic was same-sex unions, with everyone aware that the New Westminster diocese's bishop, Michael Ingham, had blazed the trail by conducting the first same-sex union in the Canadian church. (The solemnization took place in the basement of St. Margaret's Cedar Cottage Church, Vancouver). Since then, ten more dioceses had followed the path of New Westminster. Yet it would be erroneous to say the entire Canadian church had "gone gay." Nineteen of the thirty dioceses decided to remain straight, inflexible, and stoutly committed to the teaching of the Anglican Communion. Nineteen out of thirty is more than half, so the majority were against the homosexual advocacy pushed by the minority.

Victims of political manipulation are familiar in the secular world, but it was more surprising to see them in the Canadian church. The majority of Canadian Anglicans resisting homosexuality in their church became a helpless and hapless minority. The strong and well-positioned minority took control, trouncing and pummelling their majority opponents. In broad daylight, the Lambeth Commission's injunction was violated. Motion A134 was placed before the synod, and it sailed through with ease. With its passage, the synod resolved to "affirm the integrity and sanctity of committed adult same-sex relationships." Plainly, the resolution amounted to a slap against the two principal organs of the Communion—the archbishop of Canterbury and the primates—who had requested all parties to stop further actions until the Lambeth Commission concluded its work. And then there was a second resolution, in which the Anglican Church of Canada haughtily proclaimed it would

> continue intentionally involving gay and lesbian persons . . . to prepare resources for the church to use in addressing issues relating to human sexuality including the blessing of same-sex unions.

The real goal of the church was to accommodate "the changing definition of marriage in society" (emphasis mine). In others words, the desire of the church was to see marriage cease existing in the God-ordained form and nature. With what did the ACC want to replace the old hallowed institution? It was with a new age of amoral, narcissistic, counter-cultural, sexual permissiveness. Not many understood the precariousness of the situation the Anglican Communion was experiencing, thanks to some Anglican Church leaders in the West obsessed with promoting the homosexual agenda in the Communion. Many were not able to understand the grave danger facing the world's oldest institution—marriage—in the hands of the counter-culture revisionists determined to destroy it at all costs. Even the greater percentage of Anglicans worldwide did not realize the depth of the Church's culpability and vulnerability as it provided the route to smuggle a vile, aberrant behavior into Christendom.

Archbishop Akinola wasn't fooled, however. Lambeth Commission or no Lambeth Commission, he wasn't tricked. He had serious doubts about the American and Canadian churches, for they had not shown themselves to be churches of principle or integrity. With the little he had seen of them and from them, he was convinced that their words were not their bonds.

In April 2004, Archbishop Akinola was in the United States of America for a two-day visit. The Atlanta trip afforded a meeting with Bishop Robert Duncan, Canons David Anderson, Martyn Minns, Ellis Burst, and Dr. Gordon Okunsanya.[4] The group was very small, and not much was expected from the meeting compared with the one held nine months earlier with 60 in attendance.[5]

The archbishop had the benefit of firsthand information on the three fingers of rebellion. Regarding the United Kingdom, for instance, he was briefed about how the

4. Akinola, "Minutes of Meeting of Archbishop Akinola with Bishop Robert Duncan, Canon David Anderson, Dr. Gordon Okunsanya, Canon Martyn Minns and Canon Ellis Brust," from the private papers and collections of Archbishop Peter Akinola.

5. Akinola, "Meeting at Truro Church" July 22–23, 2003 between Archbishop Peter Akinola and Bishop Bob Duncan, Martyn Minns, Vinay Samuel and 60 other participants, from the private papers and collections of Archbishop Peter Akinola.

archbishop of Canterbury met December 1, 2003, "with a number of Primates and bishops from ECUSA." He had learned also that those "strongly in favour of [Jeffrey John's] appointment were astonished, disappointed, very angry." But based on a dispatch from the United Kingdom concerning John's aborted bishopric quest, it seemed a gay bishop was "just a matter of time."

From Canada, the news coming in was not encouraging either. It had a pessimistic note. Emerging were omens that even if the "the issue of blessings of same-sex unions [was] concluded," it might not resolve the problem already growing in the church. Beyond the earlier unilateral decision, the church suddenly seemed to have caught the fancy of incubating innovations. New inventions kept emerging in one direction and were "being imposed on the dioceses." Though people were challenging the revisions, their capacity to effectively contain or resist the impositions was limited.

In America, rebellion had become magnified in the life of the church. Revolt, no less, continued to spring up like thriving daffodils. Gravely, the American team observed that "this has been going on for years." The report painted a gloomy picture of how self-destructive ways had become a standard way of life in the church. In contrast with their Canadian counterparts, not all the American clergy had been slumbering over the years. A few had the boldness to challenge the brazen revisionism. Determined as the small number were, they had been incapacitated one way or the other. They felt "helpless and powerless," especially against the power abuse and intimidation to which the American church leaders were subjecting them.

The 2003 meeting with Akinola had represented a turning point for them. They had a resurgence of hope: "With the support of the worldwide Communion, we have a way forward." Bolstering their confidence was the revived, animated spirit of the Global South to stand firm in redeeming the situation. The American group gave a clear assurance. They wanted it known that the Episcopal Church had lost integrity. Character and honor were no longer virtues it cared about. Time proved that the church had taken a wrong course. Its soul was lost, and it could not be trusted. The chorus at that meeting was that it was time for practical action!

The archbishop's Atlanta meeting of April 2–3, 2004, was therefore a kind of follow-up to the first meeting. It was an opportunity for a small party of church leaders to examine developments since that last assembly. Archbishop Akinola had assured the first gathering of the British, Canadian, and American church leaders of the Global South's readiness to support them: "We will stand by you every inch of the way." But, bluntly, he told them, "You must make up your mind and take your decision." They were like commanders locked up in a situation room weighing options in strategic maneuvers. Each had a significant connection with the unfolding developments.

The bishop of Pittsburgh, the Rt. Rev. Robert Duncan, was a familiar name already. He was the public face of the Anglican Communion Network (ACN). Canon Martyn Minns was rector of the Truro Church, the church that hosted the groundbreaking conference of July 2003. Canon David Anderson was of the American

Anglican Council (AAC) while Canon Ellis Brust represented the Anglican Mission in America (AMiA). Dr. Gordon Okunsanya was the Nigerian chaplain in America. Akinola's primary concern at the meeting was provision of pastoral care and episcopal oversight for Nigerian Anglicans in the United States.

Nigeria had declared a state of "impaired" communion with the Episcopal Church. Both the Nigerian House of Bishops and the Synod Committee of the church, the two highest governing bodies, had given Akinola the mandate to find ways of providing pastoral care for Nigerian Anglicans in the United States. Based on insight coming from the Nigerian chaplain, Gordon Okunsanya, Nigerians with whom he had been having contact preferred "a Nigerian or CAPA (Council of Anglican Primates in Africa) Convocation." Without doubt, they would want the Convocation to be in partnership with the Anglican Communion Network. Nigerian Anglicans hold to the purity of the Bible. The call for a place to stand in expressing their faith was unsurprising. Beyond the conveyed wish to protect the integrity of their faith through association with the Network, they wanted a sense of security. Accordingly, they stated "strongly [the] desire to have a bishop of their own."

Akinola understood the implications of the Nigerian church having a bishop in America. Quixotic as he was, he was a rules-keeping man at the same time. Rarely would he radically trample on existing procedures. Given the implications of the idea, he considered it a tall dream. Archbishop Akinola could not unilaterally decide the matter. He did not believe that his office as the Nigerian primate conferred on him the power to do so. On the one hand, the decision and approval belonged to the Nigerian House of Bishops. There were also other organs within the Communion that must be consulted. As a matter of collegial respect, he must work with his colleagues in the Council of Anglican Primates in Africa. The archbishop of Canterbury would have to be accorded the same gesture of consultation. Whatever the shortcomings of the Episcopal Church, the church itself must receive the courtesy of being informed of the matter as well. Akinola elaborated painstakingly the process involved in the action that the Nigerian Anglicans were demanding. As displeased as he was with the developments in America, he was not going to take law into his own hands either. He was resolved that their meeting was no place to arrive at a decision on an issue of that magnitude and with such sensitivity. They agreed and moved on to the next issue.

The Anglican Communion Network (ACN) had come to life about four months earlier. Atop their agenda was its status. Canon Anderson assured them that the process to give the Network a legal backing was almost completed. He reiterated that they were not going back in their resolve to stand against the Episcopal Church's foolishness.

He gave a bird's eye view of the support base for the organization, telling them that not all bishops opposing the consecration of Gene Robinson could be counted on to be loyal and helpful. While some bishops were willing to join with the ACN to protect Scripture, others didn't want to antagonize those in error. Those in the latter group, he asserted before the gathering, "will never join the network."

Anderson was finding a particular issue disturbing—the growing "hostility suffered by many Network clergy and congregations in hostile dioceses." The pro-gay bishops were becoming terror machines obsessed with running over any clergy standing in their way, threatening their vocation and ministry. They employed a variety of oppressive tactics, determined to "crush" the opposition, and they seemed to enjoy the backing of the Episcopal Church. The leadership of the church was mute and blind to the oppression; its attitude conveyed a tacit and explicit approval of the illegalities.

The Diocese of Washington was a case in point. The rites that the diocese developed went "beyond even that which was authorised by General Convention" of the Episcopal Church. The ocean of absurdities the church was swimming in had been made wider. Anderson's summation of developments in the American church showed that now, there was nothing profane which would not be accommodated in the House of God. Irreverence and irreligiosity had become objects of worship. The church seemed to be on the journey of taking America away from the guiding spirit and soul that had led her to power, fame, and prosperity in the world, a path emptying the motto "In God We Trust" of all meaning.

The archbishop wondered, "How widespread is the revisionist agenda?" America was not his territory and country, and developments related to the crisis were not always conveyed to him. Heading the Nigerian church and the extended Global South gave him no consular services privilege. Anderson set the number of rebellious ECUSA dioceses at 12 to 20 out of 120. But the figure was misleading. The pro-homosexuality group knew where power resided in the church, and so they were able to control the critical organs of decision making. Network members realized the limit of their power and the seriousness of the odds confronting them. Carefully, they weighed their options. They were realistic about not engaging in false pride or braggadocio by attempting to challenge the leadership of the Episcopal Church. It would be a foolish blunder. They would not win a contest of supremacy with them. The result would leave them bruised and cowed into submission. If they were to be clever, they had to develop survival strategies and maneuvering options that would prove practical and realistic.

The Network members knew their colleagues in the Episcopal Church inside and out, a group whose leadership was soulless, without compassion or compunction. So the Network members were willing to make concessions, perhaps reaching some kind of agreement on constitutional accommodation and mutual coexistence. They believed that such an agreement could spare Network members the ordeal of lengthy and expensive court cases. They were sure vile attacks were coming, and they resolved to request that their members concede on many grounds if it got to the point of vengeful litigation. Whatever agreement was required to achieve amicable settlement, they had told those on their side to embrace it readily, even if it meant the forfeiture of property as well as assets of their dioceses. For their part, they were keenly looking forward to the institution of "delegated episcopal pastoral oversight," as the primates had agreed.

The other side was not so gracious. They were not in the least willing to accept the peace offer. Publicly, they had demonstrated their loathing for the harmonious effort; an official statement by the church had made that obvious. But there would be no going back, even if the ground on which they were standing shifted. The Network would remain firm, solid, immovable.

As uncertain as the atmosphere tended to be in those early days, there were some positive, encouraging stories to tell. The intransigence of the American church resulted in cracks leading toward implosion as "12–15 congregations in the US" had come "under the jurisdictions of various non-ECUSA bishops." The Communion's tradition of respecting the territorial integrity of national churches had started crumbling. A number of countries had taken the initiative of establishing offshore partnerships on American soil, including Malawi, Zambia, Uganda, Bolivia, and Caledonia. Apart from that, the number of those willing to work in concert toward upholding the Anglican tradition and maintaining the sanctity of God's Word was expanding at a phenomenal rate.

Still, there were negative developments as well. One was the increasing use of draconian and coercive measures by the Episcopal Church's leadership, notwithstanding the olive branch being extended to them. The targets of these frequently malicious attacks were bishops and, by extension, the clergy of their congregations. The weapons varied. No means or approaches were considered out of bounds—whatever would instil fear in both the clergy and the bishops. Subtle and direct, covert and overt, from blackmail to intimidation to coercion, none of the tools was counted immoral, as long as the aim of bending or exacting compliance from people was achieved. The end justified the means.

Archbishop Akinola was flabbergasted at this abuse of individual liberty, freedom, and dignity in a country boasting a democratic culture. Under assault were people's freedom of conscience, thought, and expression. Nowhere in Africa would mouths have refrained from wagging about such intolerable and unconscionable use of blackmail, fear, coercion, and intimidation to effect compliance. Worse, it was happening not in the secular society, but in the House of God. Though he was 60 years old at the time, the archbishop had not slipped into the forgetfulness that age tends to visit on the elderly. He recalled fully what he had said a year earlier when the larger group had met in Truro. He reiterated the same pledge: "We will support you."

However, there was a "but" to that statement this time around: "You must decide what you want to do," he told them frankly. Personally, he didn't think the American group had much choice or room to maneuver. Their options were very limited. There seemed to be no middle way for them to negotiate. It was a matter of either/or, either stand by what they considered to be right and pure or be dragged into muck and dirt.

"Either you support the faith once delivered to the saints or you are a friend of the revisionists," he said to them brusquely. "The ball is in your court."

Twelve days after the Atlanta meeting, Archbishop Akinola was in Nairobi, Kenya to preside over the Global South primates' meeting.[6] The April 15–16 gathering developed from an earlier "Global South Primates Working Committee" meeting held in the same place February 17, during which the archbishop was mandated to convene the full primates meeting in April. As the primates gathered, there were two major issues for them to tackle. The number one topic was the Lambeth Commission. The second was the third South-South Encounter. In terms of weight, the second item was peripheral, more or less. It wouldn't require lengthy discussion or court a lengthy debate. Indeed, it didn't take the primates long to resolve to convene the third South-South Encounter. They believed the assembly had become inevitable, and Egypt was unanimously chosen to host it. A theme was also adopted: "One, Holy, Catholic and Apostolic Church."

Then focus shifted to the major issue: the Lambeth Commission. It was a hot subject. Several misgivings were aired about the panel. Some were irked by its composition, insisting that the Global South "had been cheated." Some felt establishment of the Commission should have been preceded by an unconditional ultimatum of "no further action by ECUSA." They were troubled that the American church had continued to exhibit intransigence, initiating violation after violation in mockery of the Communion. Accordingly, their position was that "the Commission has lost its relevance" and was essentially dead on arrival. They would have preferred a hardline stance against the Episcopal Church for its continued rebellion against the Communion. There were also moderate voices, those still appealing for restraint. Their argument followed the African proverb of not throwing away the baby with the bath water. In other words, they pled against wholesale rejection of the Commission. They urged that the panel be allowed to do its work, giving it the benefit of the doubt. Back and forth they went.

A greater percentage of the primates, however, felt that the archbishop of Canterbury had not acted with propriety regarding the matter. The critics considered inappropriate Archbishop Williams' approach of unilaterally selecting members of the Lambeth Commission. The primates had no knowledge about criteria used or the distribution ratio employed among the constituent parts of the Communion. The way the archbishop went about selecting commissioners instilled no confidence regarding the outcome of the Commission's work. Instead, they saw his approach as a deft political move to "divide and rule" them. They believed the appointees' loyalty would most likely be to Canterbury and its archbishop, their sole appointing authority, rather than to their provinces or primates. It seemed that even if a member chose to be honest and fair, doing so would be a tightrope walk in view of the likely pull of conflicting loyalties.

6. Akinola, "Notes of Meeting of Working Committee of Global South Primates" and "Statement of the Global South Primates," from the private papers and collections of Archbishop Peter Akinola.

Another worry among the primates was the absence of prior discussion regarding "terms of reference" for the Commission. The primates felt seriously undermined and demoralized that their collective input, which would have provided the Commission with a better guide regarding the focus of its investigation, was undervalued. Again, Archbishop Williams' decision to determine by himself the Commission's objectives eroded their confidence in the procedure. Stern and grave were the reservations they expressed. Ye opinions were not uniform in terms of umbrage. Many were more than mild in tone. Others called for an assertive stance in expressing the Global South's displeasure.

This group was convinced the system was rigged. They wanted the Global South to forestall Canterbury's self-serving result by withholding its "presence and participation . . . at all levels of Communion activities . . . until the ECUSA discipline is resolved appropriately." For this group—and it represented more than a fair share of the Global South primates—the archbishop of Canterbury could not be exculpated. They were strident in their claim that the "real problem is with Canterbury." Consequently, Archbishop Akinola was mandated to write Canterbury. He was told to convey their decision that they "would not attend the next ACC Standing Committee [meeting] where ECUSA is present." Furthermore, he was requested to send copies of the letter to "all members of the ACC Standing Committee and [the] Primates, including Frank Griswold."

However, in spite of the hard feelings expressed about how the archbishop of Canterbury had gone about constituting the Lambeth Commission, the primates still bent over backwards to express support for the panel.

In closing, the Global South came up with five points, which they agreed would constitute their memorandum to the Commission. The first was an unequivocal statement that "the Commission should include in its report a specific call to ECUSA to repent." The repentance would involve "revoking and rescinding their decision and action regarding the election and consecration of Gene Robinson as a Bishop in the Church of God." Secondly, they suggested that "should ECUSA fail to comply within three months, the Archbishop of Canterbury and the Primates should then take appropriate disciplinary action." The discipline they deemed appropriate included "expulsion of ECUSA from the fellowship and membership of the Anglican Communion."

Thirdly, they proposed that "recognition and full Episcopal and pastoral oversight should be given by the Archbishop of Canterbury and the Primates to those dioceses, parishes and laity within ECUSA who continue to uphold the historic faith and order of the Anglican Communion." Fourthly, with respect to the diocese of New Westminster in the Anglican Church of Canada, the primates advised that "similar measures should be applied to the Bishop and Synod . . . for their unilateral approval and implementation of rites for the blessing of same-sex union." Finally, the primates noted how the Communion could prevent crises of a similar nature in the future. They urged "the Commission to give urgent consideration to the renewal of mutual accountability and the harmonization of constitution and canon of the various Provinces in the Communion."

The memorandum closed with the Global South leaders' indicating that they had spoken with one mind. They believed the suggestions offered were "essential to preserve our Communion in true unity." Though the pattern of not being taken seriously had been established, nevertheless, they were prepared to once more exhibit magnanimity. But it would be naïve to assume their points would be granted. Should the usual contempt repeat itself, they warned of serious repercussions. Such disdain, they warned, would catapult the Communion into "tragic realignment."

12

Africa Comes of Age

Nigeria, 2004

Archbishop Peter Akinola has said, "Africa and African leaders can seemingly appear poor and beggarly, derided, despised, and degraded by their American and European counterparts, but in terms of spirituality, God has not created Christians in Africa as imitation of any race." The fact many Africans had their earliest contact with Christianity through white missionaries does not diminish the divine creation of Africans as equal to any other humans. Archbishop Akinola has never accepted the notion of racial superiority. Color is a pigmentation adaption of people to nature. It is an identity, not a mark of preeminence. Also invalid is the notion of superior intelligence among some races. Differences in the quality of national progress are due to the way societies have enhanced, nurtured, and developed the minds of their people over time.

Unfortunately, Africa has never succeeded in overcoming the poverty of mind in its peoples. Shackled by years of predatory colonialism, bound to a neo-imperialistic yoke, the African mind is enslaved through its own submissive will. Numerous problems may beset the continent, but Africa is not a lost cause. Several times, the continent has missed opportunities. Still, the fate of the continent is not a forgone conclusion. The reality is that the salvation of the continent does not lie outside Africa. Neither does its development depend upon the hands of other peoples or regions. It will take Africans to develop Africa. Assistance, support, aid, development (whether multilateral or bilateral)—whatever you might call it—will not uplift Africa. These cannot substitute for genuine investment of effort by Africans in the African cause, undertaking deliberate action in the task of redeeming the continent from perennial retardation of progress and the perpetual bondage of backwardness.

From the day of his election as primate of the Church of Nigeria in 2000, Archbishop Akinola had envisioned a broad focus on challenging Africa's underdevelopment. The Nigerian church was big, with over 17 million members, the largest in the worldwide Anglican Communion. Size, at times, does not represent advantage, but in this instance there was benefit. The Nigerian church has achieved a frontline status in the worldwide Anglican Communion. As Nigeria is a country too big to be ignored in the world, the Church of Nigeria is too vital to be neglected in the global affairs of the Anglican Communion. For every one Anglican in the rest of the world, there are four Nigerian Anglicans.[1] And with this comes the burden of leadership.

Archbishop Akinola was determined to build on this legacy, to use the Nigerian church's strength purposefully, to harness its strategic position to foster better global inter-Anglican relations. In Africa, the Nigerian Anglican church has been and remains an essential force in the development of the continent. Even with its limited resources, through various missions, it has provided assistance to different African countries. When the Anglican Church struggled to gain a foothold in any part of Africa, the Church of Nigeria, within the constraints of resources, always provided a shoulder to lean on.

Immediately after his enthronement, Archbishop Akinola organized a vision-setting exercise for Nigerian Anglican Church leaders, the cardinal objective of which was to set the agenda for his tenure, including enhancement of Nigeria's global inter-Anglican relations. His desire was to see Nigeria take a more active interest in the affairs of such bodies as the Anglican Consultative Council, the Lambeth Conference, the Anglican South-South Encounter, and the Conference of Anglican Provinces of Africa.

For instance, a key element of the vision document was a plan for every Nigerian bishop to attend the once-in-a-decade Lambeth Conference (eight years away), but not through the usual beggarly approach. An estimated cost of the trip had been worked out for each bishop, who was then expected to make monthly contributions to the purse. This would free them from eleventh-hour pressure to go cap in hand soliciting travel funds. In the main, however, Africa was the archbishop's focus.

The Standing Committee of the Nigerian church, on September 13, 2000, formally endorsed the idea. "The Church of Nigeria," the vision document read, "should have links with, and strengthen relations with, the Anglican churches in Africa."[2] At the Standing Committee's meeting of March 15, 2001, in Port Harcourt, River State (Nigeria's oil capital), preliminary reports showed that a positive step had been taken to further the objective agreed upon months earlier. An African primates' meeting was scheduled for August 2001. There was, however, another major development, perhaps a bigger landmark: as Archbishop Akinola informed the gathering, the "African Bishops Forum had also been initiated."[3]

1. Various publications from the Church of Nigeria and the Anglican Communion Office agree regarding the size of the Church of Nigeria and its being the biggest and fastest growing national church globally in the Communion. Seventeen million was the figure frequently quoted in 2000, when Archbishop Akinola became primate of the Church of Nigeria.

2. Church of Nigeria, "Minutes of the Standing Committee Meeting," from the Archives of the National Headquarters of the Church of Nigeria (Anglican Communion), Abuja, FCT, Nigeria.

3. "Minutes of the Standing Committee Meeting."

The African Bishops Forum was a novel idea. Such a gathering had never occurred in the history of Anglican Church in Africa. The vision behind it was strong, the desire to see it through to fruition sturdy. Delegates at the Standing Committee meeting were told that a 2004 date had been fixed for convening the first ever African Bishops Forum, almost three years away, with Nigeria as the meeting site.

Right on time (October 26–November 1, 2004), Anglican Church leaders from the different parts of Africa convened in Lagos for their first continental gathering. However, a number of changes had occurred in the Anglican Communion during the three intervening years. The Most Rev. George Carey had been succeeded by Dr. Rowan Williams as archbishop of Canterbury. At the time the African Bishops Forum was conceived, none of the three-fingers of rebellion in the Anglican Communion had yet demonstrated its worst behavior. Furthermore, in 2001, there was nothing like the Lambeth Commission, but by 2004, the Commission had become one of the most important and widely discussed subjects in the Communion. New expressions like "impaired" and "broken communion" had found their way into the global Anglican Church's lexicon. All this set the background for the Church of Nigeria's attempt at strengthening its global inter-Anglican relations.

Archbishop Akinola had become chairman of the Global South, as well as chairman of the Conference of the Anglican Provinces in Africa (CAPA).[4] The positions were of towering influence. He was speaking not only for Africa but for the entire Global South, and thus was in a position to rally an overwhelming two-thirds of Anglicans worldwide behind him, a power enhanced by his boldness, courage, and principle. Enigmatic characters are puzzling, and Archbishop Akinola had emerged on center stage of the Anglican Church maelstrom as a baffling personality. He was not, however, a man troubled by how people viewed him, whether rightly or wrongly. One thing he was not apt to do was to try to be "politically correct" to please people.

Akinola was a man entrusted with a task. Irrespective of the cost, he would see it through. For that reason, the years 2001 to 2004 saw him working relentlessly to make the First African Anglican Bishops Conference become a reality. He brought along the CAPA secretariat in Kenya as the engine of the Conference's design team. In Nigeria, a Local Organising Committee (LOC) was constituted.[5]

At the head of the LOC was the Rt. Rev. Dr. Peter Adebiyi, bishop of the Lagos West diocese. He doubled as chairman of the Church of Nigeria's Committee on Anglican Global Relations. Adebiyi wasn't new to taking on innovative or challenging duties. Nor did he lack knowledge about organizing a major international forum. His thirty-three-year priestly career had seen him knotting different threads of missionary, social, and national work into a fine tapestry. He served as episcopal secretary to

---

4. "Mission Makes the Church," in Gbesan and Enilolobo, *In The World But Not of The World*; see also Council of Anglican Provinces of Africa, http://www.capa-hq.org/; http://www.capa-hq.org/index.php/about-us/background.

5. "Minutes of the Standing Committee Meeting."

the bishops of the Church of Nigeria as well as being a member of the country's Code of Conduct Bureau and a participant at the National Political Reform Conference, representing the Christian community of the southwest geopolitical zone of Nigeria. Adebiyi threw the support of his diocese behind the conference, and provided the venue, the Archbishop Vining Memorial Cathedral Church.[7]

Adebiyi's unstinting commitment to the task was a relief to Archbishop Akinola. The former's effective coordination of logistics connected with the Conference freed the archbishop to devote time to other explosive events, both at home and internationally. The venue was perfect. The Archbishop Vining Memorial Cathedral Church was in Nigeria's former capital, Lagos, which retained its effervescence as the nation's economic heartbeat. It was just five kilometres away from the Murtala Muhammed International Airport. Flights from all parts of Africa were guaranteed. There were also hotels of different sizes within the Ikeja business district. And of course, Lagos retains its status as the media capital of Nigeria. The event could therefore be guaranteed its fair share of media coverage.

Funding generally proved to be an obstacle, but not this time. Archbishop Akinola urged a self-reliant church. He had promised his colleagues Nigeria would host the conference, knowing that it would be a problem. But he was determined not to go begging. Neither was he ready to accept Greek gifts, whether from governments or any other source. Western nations were excluded from his assistance list. Their philanthropy would have amounted to poisonous largesse. Yet he had assured the delegates they only needed their air tickets. The remaining logistics and accommodations were guaranteed. Nigeria would provide them.

Getting the funds was not easy, but it wasn't unattainable. The diocese of Lagos West was a generous host. So were the dioceses of Abuja, Ibadan, and Aba, which showed enthusiastic support. By the time the Standing Committee of the Church of Nigeria met, September 15–19, 2004, to receive a formal update about the Conference, all arrangements had been concluded. The weeklong conference would begin October 26 and end November 1, 2004. Expected were 270 bishops from Africa along with their wives. Guests anticipated from other countries included the Archbishop of Canterbury, Dr. Rowan Williams, who had received an official invitation.

The Archbishop Vining Memorial Cathedral Church bubbled into life with the first African Anglican Bishops Conference, just a week after the Lambeth Commission placed its Windsor Report into the hands of the Archbishop of Canterbury. Now the Lagos meeting shifted the attention of Anglicans all over the world to what had been dubbed the "Africa comes of age" conference. Nigeria's President Olusegun Obasanjo was in Lagos to be part of the gathering.[6]

The conference was not timed deliberately to coincide with release of the Windsor Report.[7] Part of the reason for meeting was Archbishop Akinola's desire to fos-

6. "Obasanjo Chides Same Sex Marriage, Homosexuality."

7. "A Statement from the Primates gathered at the first African Anglican Bishops Conference held

ter inter-Anglican relations. This had attracted favorable reaction from his fellow Nigerian church leaders. The idea predated all events in the Communion that gave rise to the Lambeth Commission. Another impetus was the desire to convene African spiritual leaders to discuss how best Africa could embark on a self-discovery journey. Archbishop Akinola considered African church leaders absolutely necessary for the positive shaping of the continent; spiritual reawakening must take center stage. Particularly upsetting to him was the fact that Africa sometimes seemed resigned to the poverty and want scandalously ravaging its peoples. As he put it,

> Africa had always been a blessed continent. Africans cannot be in denial that Africans originate and are responsible for the continent's modern day African problems. The solutions to the problems are here in Africa and in the hands of Africans and nowhere else.

There were 43 countries in Africa in 2004, the year of the first African Anglican Bishops Conference. None lacked human and/or natural resources. Properly harnessed, the resources of Africa as a whole could set the region on the path of progress. However, as vast as the continent's resources were, equally monumental were her missed opportunities, including the odd variety of self-liming constraints curtailing her development. One was the slow growth of democratic governance—the lack of genuinely representative governments and the ballot box charades that accompanied most of the authoritarian regimes. Although autocratic regimes had declined, shrinking drastically from "a peak of 36 countries in 1989 to only 5 in 2004," there was a serious problem with political instability crippling many emerging African societies.[8] Exacerbating the problem was the high rate of inter-ethnic conflicts and wars. The result was the deepening developmental challenges confronting many African countries. Feuds, bitterness, and violence inhibited meaningful human development, whether in the short, medium or long term in Africa.

These factors complicated the pursuit of security, education, health, basic social services, investments in infrastructure, communications, information technology, and a justice system—indeed, every component of the goods and services needed to make development thrive. Ruefully, Archbishop Akinola observed:

> The failure of development in Africa mirrors the disaster of human failing. It shows leadership failure rather than resource constraints. Africa's rich endowments seemed to have been cropped largely by predatory leaders lacking in vision, competence, honesty, patriotism and exemplary conduct. Many were pirates that brazenly abused the trust of the people.

The Anglican Church in Africa is spread across twelve provinces in four regions of East, West, Central, and Southern parts of the continent. From the biggest country

---

in Lagos, Nigeria, October 2004," from the private papers and collections of Archbishop Peter Akinola.

8. http://www.systemicpeace.org/vlibrary/ConflictTrendsAfrica2006MGMarshall.pdf.

in Africa, Nigeria in West Africa, to tiny Mauritius, the small island republic in the Indian Ocean, the Church had made significant contributions. Though much that had been done in the past, Akinola believed new vistas could be created in the lives of Africa's peoples and countries. The archbishop's opinion was that "the Church cannot be preaching an ideal and living a different life." That would be a lie, a deceitful existence. If the Church was counseling African leaders to be self-reliant, the Church must show the way. The Church in Africa must regain its prophetic voice. It must revive its missionary zeal to be a catalyst for change. The Church must be a bull in working for "the transformation of our continent!"

The Lagos conference brought a renaissance to the African church. But times had changed, and the challenges facing Africa were different from those of the missionary years. In their various complexities, the problems were political, economic, social, health related, technological, and security related. Collectively, the bishops agreed on the need for a reawakening and the need to work assiduously to revive the African Church as a mission-based church. To start the revival, they agreed on a common front—"to fight against poverty, HIV/AIDS, malaria and other health concerns, corruption, conflicts and human rights." The gathering emerged with a new resolve, a fresh effervescence of spirit underpinned by a strong will. Determinedly, there was resolution that the time had come for the African mission of "from everywhere to everywhere."

Lagos injected a new valor in the bishops. They were no longer content to watch African development from the periphery. They resolved that the time was ripe for Church leaders to "engage in dialogue with our political leaders to identify the opportunities and strategies for maximising Africa's vast but grossly misappropriated resources." Africans are known for being good in talks and less skilled in practical actions. But for the African Anglican leaders at that Lagos meeting, this was a turning point. They shared a common notion that their coming together marked a historical rebirth for Africa. They declared that, "The Church must take active interest in working for the political maturity of Africa."

Maturity is not about age; it is acting in an enlightened, educated, and informed way. It is about behaving responsibly. Maturity involves making rational decisions instead of making poor, arbitrary, and irrational judgments. Wisdom, prudence, and restraint demonstrate maturity as opposed to the impulsiveness, indiscretion, and intemperance that are hallmarks of immaturity. A mature Africa, the bishops stated, should witness the "empowerment of women, youth, children and other disadvantaged groups." In the same vein, a mature Africa must be able to uphold its own "through relevant education and the gate-keeping of cherished values now under attack."

The African Anglican Church leaders were in Lagos to make a statement—and not just about their African identity but their Anglican heritage as well. In their "Anglican Self-Evaluation," they subjected that heritage to candid and bold review. The

African Church leaders told the world a new light shone, a sun had risen to proclaim that "Africa comes of age!"

It would have been surprising for Anglican bishops to gather for a week without discussing homosexuality and addressing the Windsor Report, which had just been released. Indeed, the first African Anglican Bishops Conference became a testing ground of sorts, the place to gauge likely reaction to the report. Prior to the Lagos Conference, the Africans constituted only a part of the larger Global South platform. The Lagos Conference, however, had identified the African Anglicans as a distinct group. Behind the 270 bishops were lined up all the Anglican Churches in Africa, whose membership numbered about 30 million, almost half of the worldwide Anglican population.[9] Africa had ten times more Anglicans than Canada and the United States together. Plus, the church in Africa was still growing, unlike the Anglican churches in Western nations. Naturally, the principled stand of the African leaders, coupled with their meeting at that time, could not have failed to incite international anxiety. Indeed, the apprehension had begun long before the conference's opening day.

One early controversy surrounding the Lagos assembly was whether the archbishop of Canterbury, Dr. Rowan Williams, was going to attend. At a pre-conference meeting with the media in Nigeria, Archbishop Akinola was candid. He told journalists that "whether or not he [the archbishop of Canterbury] attends, the conference will go on."[10] He confirmed that a formal invitation had been extended to Williams as the head of the worldwide Anglican Communion. It would have been a serious blunder if the organizers had neglected to do so for a pan-African Anglican gathering of such magnitude. But Archbishop Williams withheld his presence from the conference. He may have had good reasons for keeping away from the biggest Anglican gathering on the African continent, but there was no clear alibi.

In the West, Archbishop Akinola and the conference became objects of smear campaigns. One month before the conference, the Scottish newspaper *Scotland on Sunday*, in typical, biased, Western media fashion, published a dangerous, speculative story about the conference. The story's aim, apparently, was to denounce Akinola and cast serious aspersions on the conference, misrepresenting its intentions. It dishonestly declared, "More than 30 million African Anglicans are set to form a breakaway church." Surely, the newspaper knew its story was fabricated and false. According to the article, the purported breakaway was "prompted by a backlash against liberal attitudes to gays and lesbians in the west." Of course, respect for truth and honesty are standard ethical norms in journalistic practice, but when it came to covering gay issues, lesbianism, and related aberrations, journalistic ethics go out the window. The Sunday, September 5, 2004, edition of *Scotland on Sunday* reflected a calculated plot to defame Akinola and the African Bishops Conference:

9. Grundy, "Mugabe Fuels 'Reformation' Against Gays."
10. Otufodunrin, "Lagos: Williams Absent at African Bishops Conference."

> Nigerian clerics, who are led by the fearfully homophobic Archbishop Peter Akinola, say they are linking up with Evangelicals who not only support Mugabe, but also President George W. Bush and the Republican Party in the US, Ben Mkapa in Tanzania and Sam Nujoma in Namibia, to wipe clean the 'evil stain' of homosexuality from the face of Africa.

It was a devious story, a concocted lie, and a dirty smear. Perhaps, the presumption was that the propaganda would effectively discourage attendance at the conference by putting a question mark on its credibility. Disingenuously, the story was dressed with a screaming headline: "Mugabe fuels 'Reformation' against gays." At the time, the paths of Akinola and Zimbabwean President Robert Mugabe had never crossed! As expected, every country in Africa was defamed as "uncivilised" because they all, "with the exception of South Africa, shun gay people."

Notably, one world leader that *Scotland on Sunday* had not demonized for expressing anti-gay feelings was Nigerian President Olusegun Obasanjo. Until the Lagos African Anglican Bishops Conference, neither the government of which he was its head nor any of its top-ranking functionaries had made public comments about the homosexuality issue. Archbishop Akinola was the only internationally known Nigerian voice then. President Obasanjo was, however, not a man to miss the good opportunity of a public forum to offer sound bites and grab newspapers' headlines. He was legendary for being acerbic when opportunity arose. Incidentally, by accident of nature, Obasanjo compared favorably with the biting bluntness of Presidents George W. Bush of America, Sam Nujoma of Namibia, and Robert Mugabe of Zimbabwe, whom *Scotland on Sunday* had lumped together as gay haters.

At the opening of the first African Bishops Conference, Obasanjo was unequivocal in his denunciation of homosexuality. Before the packed hall, he had told them in explicit terms that the aberration was "un-Biblical, unnatural and definitely un-African.[11] He threw Nigeria's support behind those opposing the abnormal act and "praised the African bishops for their principled stand against the totally unacceptable tendency towards same-sex marriages and homosexual practices." Obasanjo condemned the practice, but, perhaps because his language was mellow compared with that of some others, he was excused from the scorn of the gay community.

Contrarily, Robert Mugabe, the once upon a time "termless" Methuselah leader of Zimbabwe, had caused a stir when he described homosexuals as "worse than dogs and pigs." The statement had literally ended an international book fair that his country was hosting. Two Nobel Prize winners in literature, Wole Soyinka of Nigeria and Nadine Gordimer of South Africa, had quietly packed their bags and deserted the event without fanfare. Mugabe attempted to clarify his statement by explaining that his analogy was not about people but about the act of same-sex mating, which "not even dogs and pigs would do." As expected, his attempt at clarification failed to mollify

---

11. "Obasanjo Chides Same Sex Marriage, Homosexuality."

the angered homosexuals, and who determined the Zimbabwean president must be brought to public ridicule wherever he went.

The job of executing the sentence, at least on British soil, found a willing hand in Peter Tatchell, the British gay anarchist. Tatchell organized a protest of the so-called "LGBT rights in Zimbabwe" in 1995 outside the Zimbabwe High Commission in London. Two years later, he became more audacious. During a conference marking "Africa at 40" at Central Hall, Westminster, London, Tatchell broke the police security cordon by disguising himself as a TV camera operator. He secured a false television interview with the Zimbabwean leader, and, after toying with him with innocuous questions, he told him he was gay. Was he expecting the "gay hater" to react violently to his taunt, which he would use as an opportunity to create a scandalous scene at the gathering of the distinguished international political leaders? Somehow, Mugabe put himself under a strict control. Fortunately, too, the aides of the grandmaster of Zimbabwean politics were nearby. They summoned the Special Branch of the UK Police who ensured the ejection of Tatchell from the hall.

Two years later, Tatchell and three members of his gay movement, Outrage, attempted a citizen's arrest of Mugabe on October 30, 1999. They accosted Mugabe's car in an open London street forced the door open, grabbed him, and began to pull him out of the car. Quickly, the police waded in. Tatchell and his group were subsequently arrested. However, charges of criminal damage, assault, and breach of the peace were dropped the same day that their trial opened.

On March 5, 2001, Tatchell took his "gay inquisition" to Brussels, the Belgian capital. Again, he attempted a citizen's arrest. This time around, he paid dearly for the foolhardiness. Mugabe's bodyguards knocked him unconscious. He woke up with a serious injury. He did however receive a coveted prize for his bravado. Worldwide, he captured news headlines as an instant hero.

Fortunately, the Lagos gathering of the African bishops was spared a repeat of the Mugabe "Africa at 40" experience in London. Participants were not looking over their shoulders as they openly spoke their minds. They could speak valiantly and express their views sincerely, vibrantly, and candidly. Ahead of President Obasanjo's opening remarks, during which he too denounced homosexuality, Archbishop Akinola had spoken as the chief host to welcome all the guests. He was as forthright as ever in his views. He reiterated that his position on homosexuality was irreversible. The message he gave was not the kind homosexuals loved to hear: he damned their permissiveness in accommodating weakness of the flesh.

In due season, Tatchell and Akinola were to be pitched in combat. Akinola became one of his implacable enemies, another of his targets. But Akinola was unfazed by the prospect. He used the first African Anglican bishops' Lagos conference to underscore that homosexuality remained to him an abomination because of its contradiction to the Bible and African values, and the Western countries attempting it were walking blindly on the shores of theological drift and orthodox Bible teachings.[12]

He told his fellow African church leaders in a burdened tone:

> The theology of the West was haemorrhaging deplorably from the desperate effort to twist the Word and corrupt God.

Akinola believed it was time for Africa to steer clear of Western theology's toxic influence and abandon the tradition of "theological training of African clergy in Western institutions." Rather, it was time they developed their own "well-resourced, highly rated and contextually relevant theological institutions that can engage intelligently with our peculiar challenges from an African perspective." He made it clear that Africa and North America had little chance of relating together as long their core theological differences persisted.

The impact of the conference was magnified by the presence of selected international guests: secretary of the Global South, Archbishop John Chew; bishop of the Pittsburgh diocese, Bob Duncan, leader of the Anglican Communion Network (ACN) in the USA; Canon Martyn Minns of the Truro Church; Canon Ellis Brust of the Anglican Mission in America (AMiA); and Rev. Canon Oge Beauvoir. Archbishop Akinola had kept the promise made in Atlanta assuring Duncan and the ACN of the Global South's support. Nothing had changed from what Duncan told the African bishops at the conference. The ACN remained committed to not going astray within America. With his personal convictions receiving a new boost of strength from the Lagos gathering, Duncan reassured the African bishops that in the arid American desert of spirituality, "10 dioceses, 1,000 parishes, and 1,200 clergy across the Unites States" were still "orthodox and faithful Anglicans." He wanted the bishops to know that

> There are tens of thousands for whom I speak, who are at one with you in Africa . . . for whom our North American Primates do not speak.

If the conference had ended after the round of the rousing speeches, it would have finished befittingly, a clear success with insightful outcomes. The meeting dealt with the participants' many perspectives, and those attending were able to take home reports on a wide range of subjects. Among these was Canon Herman Browne, who had been sent to represent the head of the Anglican Communion at the conference. No doubt, he would have passed along word that the Church in Africa had come of age!

Again, ten days before the conference, the archbishop of Canterbury had received the Windsor Report and commended it for discussion throughout the Communion. If he had honored the Lagos African Anglican Bishops' Conference with his presence,

---

12. "A Statement from the Primates gathered at the first African Anglican Bishops Conference held in Lagos, Nigeria, October 2004"; "African Anglican Bishops' Joint Statement Responds to Windsor Report: 'Homosexuality is clearly un-Biblical, unnatural and definitely un-African.'"

he could have set the tone for discussion in the worldwide Communion. It would have afforded a chance too to discern the mind of the most populous section of the Communion and its leaders. But he frittered away those unique opportunities. The Lagos assembly exhibited the divergent opinions of African church leaders that the Windsor Report was bound to elicit.

On the Windsor Report alone, two separate statements emerged from the conference. The primates, on their own, apart from the general communique, issued a ten-paragraph statement. Unimpassioned in tone, the church leaders had generous words for the "hard work of the Commission and the dedicated servant-leadership offered by the Most Reverend Robin Eames." They said the *"Windsor Report* offers a way forward," but they expressed a very small reservation—that the report's potential must be "marked with God's grace" (ecclesiastical shorthand for demanding honesty in the report's implementation).

With an uncommon outspokenness, the African bishops said "the Windsor Report correctly points out that the Episcopal Church USA and the Diocese of New Westminster have pushed the Anglican Communion to the breaking point." The primates were incisive in their observation that the two churches "did not listen to the clear voices of the Communion." They also seconded the Commission's view that the American Episcopal Church and the Canadian Anglican Church had damned and rejected every wise counsel. On this basis, they announced, "We call on the Episcopal Church USA and the Anglican Church of Canada to take seriously the need for 're-pentance, forgiveness and reconciliation' (Windsor Report [134])."

The general communique of the conference joined in the primates' demand for a visible, "genuine change of hearts and mind." The African Anglican Church leaders insisted that, without honest repentance, they would presume these wayward bodies to "have chosen to 'walk alone,'" meaning to have departed from the Anglican Communion. They believed that to continue with the way they had chosen would indicate they had decided to "follow another religion."

A third area of agreement with the Windsor Report was endorsement of the Lambeth Commission's call "for a moratorium on the election and consecration of any candidate to the episcopate who is living in same gender union and the use of rites for the blessing of same-sex unions." This was the issue at the heart of the impasse between the pro- and anti-homosexual groups in the Church. Once more, the African Anglican bishops appealed passionately to the two provinces—America and Canada—to respect and honor Lambeth Resolution 1.10. They reiterated their stand that continued defiance of the majority "would indicate that they, the Episcopal Church in the United States of America and Anglican Church of Canada, have chosen to 'walk alone.'"

The African leaders did, however, take exception to the Commission's lament over the "great pain that has been inflicted" on the two churches by the anti-homosexual groups opposed to their doctrinal inventions. The Commission complained that such groups had violated the global position of the Communion and that some provinces were inappropriately extending their jurisdictions to American soil. Flatly, the bishops at the African Anglican Conference disagreed. They considered it inconceivable that Eames and his members could rank the action and reaction as being of equal weight. The Commission's argument, to them, was patently incorrect, injurious, and illogical. They considered the conclusion seriously defective, with "moral equivalence drawn between those who initiated the crisis" and those "in the *Global South* who have responded to cries for help from beleaguered friends." They asserted in one voice: "To call on us to express regret and reassert our commitment to the Communion is offensive."

The primates recalled their previous early warning signals to the American Episcopal Church and its Canadian counterpart. They insisted that if those churches had listened and not been contemptuous toward the majority, they would not have "torn the fabric of our Communion at its deepest level," and "our action would not have been necessary." The African leaders denied any culpability, insisting that they were compelled to react as they did in response to the deviant behavior of the "naughty" North American churches. The disagreement notwithstanding, the African bishops praised the Commission for recognizing that "extraordinary episcopal care is needed for congregations alienated from their diocesan bishops."

They made two requests in this direction. The first was a suggestion regarding how to ensure the effectiveness of the proposed care. They believed the person wearing the shoe, so to speak, was in the best position to know where it pinched the most. Put simply, the "adequacy of that care should be determined by those who receive it." Secondly, the African church leaders stressed that there must be convincing evidence that the "delegated episcopal oversight" was effective.

The primates' views and comments on the Windsor Report ran into ten paragraphs, discussing sixteen serious issues. There were commendations and knocks, areas of agreement and disagreement over the Lambeth Commission's work. No other region or province had embarked on a critical examination of the report or offered an official opinion, as had the leaders of Anglicans in Africa.

By their action, the African leaders had raised the bar on discussion of the report in the Communion. However, the salient question was the extent to which the views of African primates would carry weight in the Communion. They recognized the odds. Nevertheless, Lagos, to them, was a springboard, the beginning of a new process. They did not expect immediate or automatic results. Their centuries-old experience within the Communion taught them it would take time to change. They were, nonetheless, assured that something different had happened in Lagos.

In this respect, one recommendation of the Lambeth Commission had left them enamoured. The Commission had called "for restructuring the various Instruments of Unity" in the Communion, the structures employed in worldwide governance of the

Church. Wholeheartedly, they endorsed the recommendation. Enthusiastically, they declared that the move "would strengthen our common life."

Though Africa had the largest population in the Anglican Communion, the reverse had always been the case in terms of the continent's representation in major governing organs of the Church. The African primates welcomed the suggestion that the Anglican Church should work to ensure that "voices of the majority in the Anglican Communion are adequately represented in those various instruments." They put to rest the insinuation of *Scotland on Sunday* and its ilk that they were a breakaway group. "We are committed to the future of the Anglican Communion," the primates stated. But the unconditional ground of their dedication was "truthfulness to the Gospel of Jesus Christ."

13

Leadership for an African Renaissance

Kenya, 2003

For four years (beginning September 24, 2003), Archbishop Peter Akinola led CAPA, the Council of Anglican Provinces in Africa. In this role, he succeeded the Most Rev. Robert Okine, archbishop and primate of the Province of West Africa. Okine was an eminent church leader, who was finishing 39 years of meritorious clerical service, both at home in Ghana as well as throughout the West Africa province. He was the pioneer bishop of the diocese of Koforidua-Ho, in his native Ghana. Okine's episcopate began during an inauspicious period of social and economic turbulence in his home country, a period marked by serious hardships. Like a Christian soldier, he marched into the episcopate with an indomitable spirit.

Okine was a courageous leader with a deep sense of mission. He laid a good foundation for his diocese. Keen on evangelism and spiritual growth, he was also devoted to practical intervention programs yielding direct benefits to the people.

He became the seventh archbishop and primate of the Church of the Province of West Africa in 1993. The remarkable service he rendered to the province led to his being honored as an emeritus archbishop. With this distinguished record, he was a natural pick for the leadership of CAPA, an organization founded in 1979.

CAPA originated from the desire of African primates for "a coordinating body that would help in bringing the Anglican Communion together in Africa."[1] The idea had emerged at a gathering in Chilema, Malawi, the aim being to provide a platform for "articulating issues affecting the Church in Africa." CAPA also was designed to foster "beneficial relationships between [the primates] and with the wider Anglican Communion." Similarly, they looked to CAPA to "provide a forum for the Church in Africa to share experiences, consult and support each other," and "confer about common responsibilities to the African continent." Considering their strength and their distribution over thirteen provinces in Africa—Nigeria, West Africa, Sudan, Kenya,

---

1. http://www.capa-hq.org/; http://www.capa-hq.org/index.php/about-us/background.

Uganda, Tanzania, Congo, Rwanda, Burundi, Central Africa, Southern Africa, Indian Oceans, and Egypt—CAPA was expected to open new possibilities for "collaboration and joint projects."

CAPA's founding primates nursed big ideas. They imagined CAPA would "maintain and develop relationships between the Anglican Church in Africa and partners as well as other denominations, national and regional councils." They saw it as the next round in Africa's de-colonialization struggles, which had birth a number of independent African nations. Both developments were met with ecstatic celebrations. But after the birth came a long spell of stunted growth. As countries, many of the emergent African independent nations began teetering toward collapse and failure. CAPA met a similar fate. None of the lofty dreams successfully translated into a purposeful mission. The problem, aptly summarized in one of the organization's official publications, was that, CAPA "since its formation [did] not [have] a strategic plan to guide its activities."

Consequently, Archbishop Akinola inherited a weakened CAPA in 2003. There were no funds, nor did a functional secretariat exist.[2] In addition, the organization was "experiencing a leadership crisis."[3] But Archbishop Akinola's assumption of leadership brought CAPA fresh vitality. With it, the moribund CAPA roared into life for the first time in the nearly two and a half decades. The revival began with the strong Lagos conference for African Anglican Church leaders. Akinola believed that the Anglican Church in Africa needed to be transformed into a change agent imbued with redemptive power. Not only would that benefit the church on the continent; it would also help in uplifting its various nations. Akinola's major concern at that early stage of revitalizing CAPA, however, was to rejuvenate it from its "bottle-fed organization" status, nurtured with the imported baby formula of charity from the Western nations. From his perspective, CAPA had become so dependent that weaning it would be a serious struggle.

CAPA's reliance on external assistance had reduced it to the point of helplessness. The small number of programs it had succeeded in undertaking in the past had been with and through foreign assistance. Typical were the 1987 pre-Lambeth conference for bishops and a continental communications workshop. The two were held with the generosity of the Western nations. Compounding CAPA's problem was its ineffective secretariat, a mere local administrative office. Remove the donors' support, and the secretariat had small chance of survival. In fact, since its establishment in 1994, external donors had always been responsible for more than 80 percent of its budget. Inescapably and inexorably, CAPA was tied to the apron strings of the West. Archbishop Akinola found the situation bothersome:

2. Interview with the Most Revd. Peter J. Akinola conducted various times in Abuja and Abeokuta, Nigeria between 2006 and 2007.

3. http://www.capa-hq.org/; http://www.capa-hq.org/index.php/about-us/background.

The over-dependence seriously compromised CAPA's independence, integrity and freedom to be innovative and inventive in its goals and mission. In every manner that it ought not to have been, CAPA was hamstrung and susceptible to serious manipulation.

For a greater part of its life, therefore, CAPA was merely CAPA in name. It was like many African organizations, good on paper but poor in action—without identity, esteem, dignity, and character to support its claim of being an African organization and the rallying point for the Anglican Church in Africa. Akinola believed it was shameful for an organization which was supposed to be the mouthpiece of Africa to exist as a lackey of foreign powers:

> For centuries, we walked on the crutches of colonialism; for the greater part of our independence years, Africa felt no shame being wheeled about in the imperialistic wheelchair. For how long would we remain dependent? I felt it was time for us to get up and walk.

The archbishop was convinced that Africa had to go through a renaissance. There must be a historical rebirth in Africa and for Africa:

> No matter how tottering our first steps may be, we simply have to get up, stand up, rise up, and take the determined walk forward! We may rise and fall at the beginning. Walk, nevertheless, we must.

He was convinced, nevertheless, that the beleaguered organization's long endurance meant that "CAPA has come to stay." The challenge now was for the organization to undertake "a radical departure from the past."

As expected, the archbishop threw himself into the job enthusiastically. Three days before Christmas in 2003, he was in Nairobi, Kenya, barely three months in office as the elected leader of CAPA. He had convened a meeting of CAPA's Management Board as well as its Standing and Finance Committees. It was the first time all the members of these key executive organs saddled with the management of CAPA came together at one meeting. Previously, lack of funds would have made such a gathering impossible. Archbishop Akinola used the opportunity to unveil his vision for the organization and outline goals for "the period of our four-year tenure."

The primary goal was to overcome CAPA's overdependence on external support. He told his colleagues unequivocally that the situation was unhealthy. They must reverse it. The Anglican Church in Africa must own CAPA in every sense of the word: "We must make a radical departure from the past."[4] "We must own CAPA," he stressed.

Before the meeting, he considered how to raise funds for the organization. The first step was for the primates to meet. The heads of the Anglican Church in Africa

---

4. Akinola, "Mission Makes the Church," in Gbesan and Enilolobo, *In The World But Not of The World.*

had to have a consultation among themselves without further delay. He proposed Nairobi, Kenya, for the summit, providing two potential dates—February 22–24, 2004, or March 17–20, 2004. The maiden meeting was to serve two ends. The first was to provide an avenue for the primates to hear the vision and mission of the new management team. The second goal was for the meeting to serve as a springboard, imbuing the leaders with a sense of collective ownership of CAPA that had been missing in the past. By sharing the vision and mission with the leaders as well as helping them own CAPA, Archbishop Akinola hoped to make the primates accept responsibility for co-financing the organization.

Part of the lesson Akinola thought his colleagues should begin to learn was how to underwrite some of their own expenses, particularly their traveling costs for CAPA meetings. The organization, on the other hand, would finance the accommodations and local transportation costs. By his calculation, CAPA would incur an estimated cost of about US$12,000 each time the primates were brought together, a cost it could not afford. CAPA had no such money in its account. Nevertheless, he was sure that once they mustered the will, they were bound to find a way. There were challenges in this direction, however. Whatever optimism the new leadership had, it must be met with the complementary willingness from followers. From the highest to the lowest level of church leadership in Africa, there must be genuine interest in the work of CAPA.

Yet CAPA's potential at any given point in time far outweighed its problems. Its difficulties seemed essentially human, natural byproducts of wrong attitudes and mindsets. If CAPA was to undergo any meaningful renaissance, therefore, the mentality of its leaders had to change. Archbishop Akinola acknowledged that change would not come easily. But it had started well because church leaders agreed on virtually all major issues during their initial meeting.

Archbishop Akinola realized that if rapid progress were to be recorded, the mobilization of his colleagues must top the agenda. He had pledged not to wait for events to happen but to dictate the pace at which actions would unfold. To put the actions in high gear, he resolved to visit his fellow primates in their respective provinces along with his deputy. The two parties—the visitors and their hosts—would examine the new vision of CAPA with a view to learning from each other's perspectives. Akinola was enthusiastic about the impetus these exchanges would give to CAPA's revitalization as a collective voice.

He also used the visits to make face-to-face appeals to his fellow primates on the urgent need to reappraise the annual bishops' training program. He proposed that the training become biennial rather than annual, and regionally-based instead of tied to one central location. This would mean that instead of one country hosting it, with all the planning, logistics, and funding becoming unnecessarily complicated, four independent training events would be held—in the West, East, Central, and Southern African regions. The proposed arrangement would reduce the difficulty associated with organizing the training annually. The regional proposal also ensured that both the name and the image of CAPA would be in the public mind all year, with the four training events spaced out on the calendar. Eventually, the talks were over and the actions began.

Before Akinola assumed the chairmanship, a number of intervention programs had been held to sensitize church leaders to the scourge of Acquired Immune Deficiency Syndrome (AIDS). AIDS had become a pandemic in Africa as well as globally. In 2001, the Boksburg AIDS Conference was held in South Africa, the first attempt toward drawing the attention of Anglican Church leaders to the devastation the disease was causing in the continent. The initial effort led to the establishment of an HIV/AIDS Coordinating Office in CAPA's Nairobi, Kenya, office. Then, in 2003, when Archbishop Akinola took over, another HIV/AIDS conference was scheduled, which brought all the provinces together in Mukono, Uganda.[5] Simultaneously, a Communications Office was established in CAPA's office at Nairobi, Kenya, designed to facilitate the coordination of information, education, and communication about HIV/AIDS within the church. Akinola found the response of the provinces and the results from the practical steps taken very encouraging. However, he was inclined toward taking an even more proactive approach to the HIV/AIDS problem and the communication program in terms of funding. Again, he didn't like being tied to the apron strings of donors, so he was determined to find sustainable funding sources that would strengthen the work of the two units in the CAPA office.

In any case, the gospel of reliance and the mantra of unity had become the two resounding themes that the archbishop travelled with, and he never tired of pressing them on his colleagues at every occasion that presented itself. Early in 2004, he had met with his fellow primates and told them all:

> The reality was that the dioceses and provinces would have to brace up towards increasing their financial contributions to the organisation . . . It remained the chief way to sustain CAPA.[6]

Archbishop Akinola proposed that the primates consider a new assessment formula to help CAPA grow financially and stabilize. He didn't wait to see whether his idea would gain acceptance, but pressed ahead in canvassing also for an increase in the assessment being paid by the provinces. He also insisted the time had come for CAPA to start thinking of capital investments. His idea was for CAPA to go into commercial investment.

His projection to his colleagues was that with a capital investment of about US$1.5 million in commercial property, CAPA would benefit tremendously in returns. The property could also provide office and staff residential space. He suggested that if all churches in the African continent devoted one Sunday a year to CAPA, to

5. "Pomp and Colour Marks the Launch of the Strategic Plan."

6. Akinola, "Unity: The Basis for Africa's Emergence," in Gbesan and Enilolobo, *In The World But Not of The World*.

pray and assist its work by making all collections realized that day available to it, the step would go a long way in building the organization's financial capacity. Averse as he was to donations and other Greek gifts, Akinola still believed that nothing was wrong with CAPA's accepting support and assistance to supplement its independent sources of income. But CAPA must be selective, rejecting tainted donations, whether from Africa or from outside the continent.

Akinola also raised the possibility of CAPA securing loans from banks to execute projects with the potential of cost recovery and earning returns on investments. He had done it before for his diocese in Nigeria, and it had been rewarding. The only requirement for the risky venture was prudent financial management and administration of the project on which the investment was made. Though the Nigerian primate had experience managing projects established with loans back home in Nigeria, it was debatable whether his Nigerian knowledge would suffice in a place like Nairobi, Kenya. On matters of this nature, however, Akinola's quixotic nature quite often received nourishment from his boundless enthusiasm for wanting to break new ground and leap forward in a new direction.

Along with his relentless activism for the financial independence of CAPA, Archbishop Akinola equally raised a strong voice for the protection of Africa's theological purity. Indefensible to him was the theological drift of the West, which had become noxious and polluting: "The time is auspicious for CAPA to tackle boldly the contamination of the theological thoughts in Africa with toxic and irrelevant ideas." Consequently, he proposed that CAPA should establish the African Anglican Theological Doctrinal Commission, whose principal purpose would be the creation of theological centers for priests and lay workers. These centers would be dedicated to the education of priests and other church workers alike, from the basic degree to post graduate levels. Archbishop Akinola didn't mince words: "It's with a view of reducing our dependence on the Western institutions that are proving very unhelpful to the Church in Africa."

Training African priests and workers to appreciate African perspectives was just one side of the coin; the other was the need to work on improved collaboration between Anglican churches in Africa, not excluding the dioceses. Inter-African Anglican Church relations, he argued, were the way Anglican churches could build their common African identity. He believed that the Anglican churches in Africa owed each other support and care. He sought to improve CAPA's capability to become that wheel of unity, bringing forward a range of activities that could connect the churches, e.g., matching dioceses up with each other for prayers; organizing exchange visits; and sharing human capital and other material resources to help build the capacities of the churches, individually and collectively. In this, he showed such infectious enthusiasm that he convinced the churches to support his ideas.

His optimism was hinged on the belief that, given the right leadership, the secretariat could be functional in some areas. He was strong, for instance, in his conviction that it was unjustifiable for CAPA not to be respected within its host community as an international organization. He also insisted that there be synergy between the Anglican Church of Kenya and the CAPA secretariat. Nothing, the archbishop believed, justified the existence of CAPA in Nairobi if the secretariat and the host lacked a close and collaborative relationship: "If Africans are to own CAPA, where that idea gets practical demonstration, first and foremost, is Kenya." The value of that partnership must be obvious, with local parishes and individual Christians in the country well aware of CAPA, and thus motivated to provide support for it and the charitable ventures it brought to their country: Then "we can truly say, in every perspective that charity has meaningfully begun at home," he enthused.

Akinola also insisted that the secretariat, with little effort, could facilitate links among the dioceses. The archbishop was correct in his outlook that if life were breathed into CAPA, the possibility of its roaring into life was high and that with committed leadership, the organization could be jumpedstarted on a transformation process.

The month was not over when again, in April 2004, he returned to Kenya for another round of meetings and conferences. The first was the mission and evangelism meeting. The discussion, held April 12–15, attracted over thirty participants from all the CAPA provinces and the diocese of Egypt. Near the end of that meeting, he took time off to host the CAPA primates on another round of consultation. Barely had he said farewell to the mission and evangelism participants before he began hosting of an enlarged meeting of the Global South primates on April 16.

CAPA was no longer a laidback organization. In June 2004, the secretariat was moved temporarily to Dar-es-Salaam, Tanzania, where training for African bishops was stepped up, with about twenty Bishops attending. Just as the Dar-es-Salaam assignment was winding down, the secretariat was on its toes, looking ahead to the big one—the October, Lagos, historic, first African Anglican Bishops Conference—during which Africa came of age.

As 2005 dawned, the Global South primates only managed to celebrate the New Year at home before they were brought back January 27–28 to the Kenyan capital, Nairobi, for another round of consultation. Six months later, CAPA's HIV/AIDS Board of Management found its way to Johannesburg, South Africa, for a crucial meeting, which was also a prelude to another two-day conference in Dar-es-Salaam, Tanzania, scheduled for September 19–21. The theme of the Tanzaian conference was "Making Poverty History in Africa." The summit examined extensively the scourge of poverty in Africa within the context of the overall economic development challenges facing the continent. The meeting enabled the sharing of insights between the CAPA primates and some of the organizations collaborating with them in the UK. Rising from the meeting, the primates pledged, among other things, their preparedness to continue offering moral leadership in the fight against poverty, diseases, and social injustice in their countries as well as on the continent of Africa in general.

CAPA ended the year playing a leading role in the organization of the Global South's third South-South Encounter, which brought together primates, bishops, clergy, and laity from all parts of the Global South to Cairo.[7] It was from that historic city that a trumpet—the *Third Trumpet*—sounded. The proclamations were serious. They centred on theological, ecclesiastical, ecclesial, and global issues. The old, indeed, had begun to give way to the new in the Anglican Communion. Africa said it had come of age, and Global South, with nearly two-thirds of the global Church's membership, was canvassing opinions with wide ranging implications for the Communion. The impact didn't begin to manifest itself until a later point in the life of the Communion, but CAPA as an organization could look back with pride on its performance that year. The two years of Akinola's leadership dramatically outshone CAPA's previous twenty-four years' experience. Officials at the secretariat found the advances and progress exhilarating, and after three years, it said so in an official publication:

> CAPA's activities have expanded particularly in the last three years . . . with its newly acquired capacity to respond to the challenges facing Africa today. The new position is owed to a change in leadership, which has enabled CAPA to attain its own identity.

Since 2001, CAPA had been intervening in the problem of HIV/AIDS in Africa. In August 2006, it stepped up attention to the scourge through convening an "HIV/AIDS, TB and Malaria Strategic Planning Meeting" in Nairobi, Kenya.[8] The meeting brought together the program's board members, provincial coordinators, and their partners. February 2007 marked the official launch of the multi-stakeholder group comprising CAPA primates, the program's board members, provincial coordinators, program partners, NGOs, church leaders, and members of the diplomatic community. CAPA's concern was about not only HIV/AIDS but also about TB and malaria, which were among leading causes of death in Africa. They were worried that minor gains made in the past on the continent were being seriously eroded. TB and malaria, which were once under control, were beginning to reemerge, along with the danger that resurgence of these diseases could undermine the work at controlling HIV/AIDS.

At the strategic planning meeting, Archbishop Akinola spoke emphatically about the need for innovative and holistic approaches to contain the unprecedented challenges the triple epidemics were posing:

> This explains the rationale behind CAPA's development and launching of a five-year—2007–2011—integrated strategic plan for HIV/AIDS, TB and Malaria.

Archbishop Akinola was optimistic, stating confidently that:

---

7. Akinola, "A Return to the Alexandrian School," in Gbesan and Enilolobo, *In The World But Not of The World*.

8. "Pomp and Colour Marks the Launch of the Strategic Plan."

> CAPA may not have all the money required to meet the activities but we can be resourceful, making the best out of our ingenuity to be innovative and inventive.

He proposed two routes for the organization. The first was a link between communication departments in the national churches and CAPA's Health Office, allowing economies of scale, whereby they would complement each other and facilitate optimal diffusion of information and education throughout the continent. Second, the CAPA secretariat should develop an effective monitoring and evaluation strategy, with periodic assessment requiring a good database and reliable documentation. He believed the two preliminary steps were within the ability of the CAPA secretariat to achieve. Fortunately, the secretariat agreed, seeing an opportunity in the archbishop's roadmap; though growth had been slow, recent progress was encouraging.

The irony was that, in the midst of this progress and advancement, some critics within and outside Africa started a campaign to fault the Anglican Church in Africa for misplaced priorities. Akinola was criticized for not paying sufficient attention to the major problems of Africa like HIV/AIDS, TB, malaria, and poverty while he was busy pursuing "shadows" of homosexuality. Was that true or a cheap smear campaign? The answer was in the legacy he left behind at CAPA.

Just about the time CAPA was celebrating its impressive debut into maturity, Archbishop Akinola had to relinquish leadership at the close of his four-year tenure. At the 10th Council Meeting in Mauritius, Seychelles, on October 2, 2007, he addressed his colleagues for the last time as the chairman.

There was much to reflect on from those four years: the successes, the challenges, the breakthroughs, and the inventions. One particular issue stood out, one dear to his heart—the challenge of making CAPA a self-reliant and sustainable organization. His determination was to see CAPA weaned from being a "bottle-feeding organization." As consummate as his efforts were, paradoxically, Akinola was departing office with a heavy heart. Four months before the end of his tenure, June 2007, the final report from the treasurer showed an outstanding debt of US$112,448 owed to CAPA by the provinces.[9] Apart from the dioceses of Egypt and Rwanda, which had paid fully their arrears as well as their assessments for that year, many of the other provinces were chronic debtors. Of the US$49,850 to have been paid for that year, only US$16,743 was received—a serious shortfall. By the time of the Council meeting, only six provinces had paid their subscriptions, leaving CAPA with a debt overhang of US$145,555. The huge amount comprised US$112,448 in arrears plus the US$33,107 balance yet to be paid from the 2007 assessment. Akinola wasn't happy about the state of affairs, all the more since they had resolved at the first African Anglican Bishops Conference in Lagos that Africa had come of age. Depressing as the situation was, once again, he roused his colleagues to the task ahead, reminding them:

9. Akinola, "Gospel of Christ vs Gospel of Sexuality," in Gbesan and Enilolobo, *In The World But Not of The World.*

> We need to become self-reliant, just as the Church has been self-governing
> and self-propagating . . . Our drive must be for economic self-empowerment
> . . . [and] . . . a new orientation and thinking, and a culture of extending the
> frontier of our investment and economic activities.

Akinola provided exemplary leadership for his colleagues. The Nigerian church
also backed him up. As a practical demonstration of the ideals the Nigerian primate
was preaching, the Nigerian church voluntarily increased its subscription to CAPA
from US$5,000 yearly to US$17,000. The increase represented more than a 300 percent jump. Justifying the Nigerian church's phenomenal increase in its annual contributions, Archbishop Akinola said, "We did that to encourage others; that we shouldn't
be going cap in hands begging for funds from tainted sources." The dream, however,
was for a bigger picture to emerge beyond Nigeria, because to him every Anglican
Church in Africa must have pride, principle, and honor. It was the lesson that African
churches and their leaders must learn. It was not in their interest to take their independence for granted or resort to pawning their reputation.

> Otherwise, we shall be continually tempted by those outside our borders who
> dangle money in return for our silence on controversial issues, such as has
> occurred recently in the Anglican Communion.

Understandable was Akinola's passion for every Anglican province in Africa to
become respectable. Africa couldn't advertise publicly that it had come of age and
still allow itself to be taken for granted. He disliked the notion that Africans were like
cheap commodities ready to be picked from the shelf at a discounted price. It had always been the point of friction between him and some of his colleagues. Some simply
refused to be convinced that they were not inferior to their Western counterparts.
Particularly contentious was Akinola's frequent argument with them that they could
do without the so-called aid and financial assistance. His efforts to draw some of those
extremely weak church leaders to the reasonability of his position had been unsuccessful. Even in his valedictory address he was not about to give up. He remained as
dogged as ever:

> The resources they needed for their ministry, for their missions, were already
> there at their doorsteps; that what they needed was just to open their eyes,
> recognise those Godly gifts, tap and develop them.

Maybe in another era and in a different century, Akinola would have been more
appreciated for his vision and pan-African ideals. He would have been celebrated for
his statesman qualities, given another context and region. He wanted a new life for
the Church in Africa, and when he had the opportunity, he exemplified the ideas he
was preaching. The type of change he wanted, however, was not the type that was
rapidly occurring in Africa. He wanted a revolution of the mind, a drastic change in
the way Africans think and relate with reality. "Regretfully, Africa is yet to overcome

this hurdle of mental slavery and poverty of ideas," he observed painfully. The greatest challenge to him, however, was apathy. Africa must loosen itself from the yokes of voluntary and involuntary servitude;

> No people, country or nation remaining in perpetual bondage, whether self-willed or imposed, and especially of mental nature, can ever develop, or change its circumstance from bad to good, or from poor to better.

Akinola was succeeded by the Most Rev. Ian Ernest, archbishop and primate of Indian Oceans. The four years he had led CAPA (2003–2007) had further added to Akinola's standing in international church leadership. At home in Nigeria, besides being primate of the Church of Nigeria, he was the public face of all Christians in the country as president of the Christian Association of Nigeria (CAN). Within the Anglican Communion, he spoke for the most populous singular bloc, CAPA. Within the global Anglican Communion, no other voice was as influential as his, representing over two-thirds of Anglicans in the world as members of the Global South. From Nigeria and across the span of Africa to Latin America, Asia, Europe, and America, no individual had started to attract world attention so powerfully in the sphere of religion at the dawn of the twenty-first century as this relatively unknown Nigerian archbishop. He was becoming a rallying point in some sections of the West as Anglicans began to turn to him for leadership.

Akinola's early reticence confused many, causing him to be taken for granted. When he emerged on the international scene and started to break his silence, his new outspokenness led to the convulsion of many groups. The irony was that he attracted intense feelings from both sides. Those who loved him loved him with devotion while those who hated him hated with equal passion. Beginning from the dawn of the twenty-first century, however, he had arrived prominently on the international scene, and the defining issue of his global leadership, the homosexuality question, was flying dangerously in the world's third largest church, the Anglican Church.

14

Birth of the Homosexuality Campaign

Germany, 1867

I n his book *Queer Science: The Use and Abuse of Research into Homosexuality,* Simon LeVay rightly indicates that "America was not the birthplace of gay-rights movement."[1] Though America has a large national ego and an incurable tendency to claim any idea or discovery—good or bad—it was a latecomer to the gay rights campaign, joining the bandwagon 58 years after the death of Karl Heinrich Ulrichs, the pioneer of the modern gay rights movement. Ulrichs had become a sort of cult hero among homosexuals, even in America.

Ulrichs was born in Aurich, Hanover, part of today's Germany, on August 25, 1825. From his recollection, he loved to dress like and play with girls during his childhood. Ulrichs didn't appear to come from a poor family though the extent of his family's wealth is not certain. If his background denied him a silver spoon, he was not deprived of the basic comforts of life. The family could afford riding lessons, and it was in the course of his horse-tending lesson that he got "involved in a brief affair" with his male riding instructor at age 14.[2] Nobody knew about the pedophile relationship. Ulrichs told no one. Nor was the German culture and law permissive toward this social aberration. Laws regulating conduct like that were, indeed, stiff, with stringent enforcement. He kept his secret guarded. He did not break the news of his homosexual tendency to his family and friends until the age of 37, five years after he had been dismissed from his job as official legal adviser to the district court of Hildesheim in the Kingdom of Hanover in 1857. The dismissal followed revelation of his homosexuality.

Ulrichs had graduated in law and theology from Gottingen University at 21. He possessed a brilliant mind, and the two years after his graduation in 1846, he studied history at the Berlin University, producing a dissertation that he wrote in Latin on the

1. LeVay, "Queer Science—The Use Abuse of Research into Homosexuality."
2. https://wikipedia.org/w/index.php?title=Karl_Heinrich_Ulrichs&oldid=661394356.

Peace of Westphalia (a series of peace treaties signed between May and October 1648; while they failed to restore peace throughout Europe, they did provide the foundation for national self-determination). Ulrichs spent time exploring the subject of war and peace from an academic perspective, and strife was to become a major theme of his life after he let his family and friends in on the peculiarity of his sexual orientation.

He devoted time to writing and advocating for society's understanding of "urning," his term for homosexuality. Initially employing a pseudonym, he finally came out boldly, owning the views he expressed in many of his articles. He wrote tirelessly, producing no fewer than twelve books in both German and Latin within a decade and a half. He not only studied law; he practised it and respected a law-and-order society. On his 42nd birthday, he began the campaign to get homosexuality laws repealed, addressing the Congress of German Jurists the next day, on August 29, 1867. He was a solitary voice both in the chamber and in public, and his petition interested no one. So the jurists shut him up.

Twelve years after he began his appeal to the Congress of German Jurists, a period that also saw him travel round the country with persistent encounters with the law, Ulrichs decided on a self-imposed exile to Italy. His ceaseless efforts may have contributed to his failing health. But not all was bleak for his pioneering endeavors. Two years after Ulrichs launched his futile, desperate bid to find listening ears in the Congress of German Jurists, the Hungarian writer Karl-Maria Kerthbeny coined the term "homosexual." In the meantime, Ulrichs' exile to Italy afforded him opportunity to find peace with himself. He needed rejuvenation for his failing health. After initial travel round the country, he eventually settled in Naples with Marquis Niccolo Persichetti, a landowner, as his benefactor. He didn't live long after that. Forty-six days before his 70th birthday in 1895, he passed away in Italy.

Ulrichs' ultimate contribution to the homosexual movement was his program of struggle. He brought an intellectual approach to engaging society on the matter of sexual maladjustment. Ulrichs didn't employ the nihilistic or narcissistic template of the contemporary, anarchic gay struggle. At no time did he suggest supplanting society's basic institutions of marriage and family life. Instead, he argued for a rational approach to viewing and resolving the problem. Drawing on his military studies for a metaphor, he argued that society cannot, and should not, wage "war" against gays. Rather, society would need to live in "peace" with them. "The Urning [or homosexual] too, is a person," he argued. He said they had "inalienable rights" and that "sexual orientation is a right established by nature." He contented:

> Legislators have no rights to veto nature, no right to persecute nature in the course of its work, no right to torture living creatures who are subject to those drives nature gave them.

On the other hand, Ulrichs also didn't propose a world where homosexuals were handed a *carte blanche* licence. With the same forcefulness that he had admonished legislators to be considerate of homosexuals, he added, "To be sure, legislators do have the right to make laws to contain certain expressions of the Uranian [or homosexual] drive."

Ulrichs never supported rebellion. He was emphatic that homosexuals must be submissive to the law, insisting that was the only way for them to live in "peace." "Just as lawmakers are empowered to legislate the behaviour of all citizens," he contended, the behaviour of homosexuals should be regulated. Ulrichs identified three distinct types of behavior that homosexuals should be denied: first, "seduction of male minors"; second, the "violation of civil rights (by force, threat, abuse of unconscious people, etc.);" third, "public indecency." Some of Ulrichs' ideas found their way into the modern gay and lesbian rights movement, but not the spirit of his balanced perspective on mutual coexistence between homosexuals and the rest of society.

One man who picked up Ulrichs' pioneering thread was the Jewish physician and sexologist Magnus Hirschfeld. Hirschfeld was forty-three years younger than Ulrichs. The son of a doctor, he studied medicine in Strasbourg, Munich, Heidelberg, and Berlin from 1888 to 1892, when he earned his doctoral degree. Upon completion of his studies, he toured the United States for eight months and eventually moved his practice to Berlin, the German capital, in 1896. He arrived in the city seventeen years after Ulrichs' departure on his voluntary exile to Italy.

Hirschfeld didn't take up residence in Berlin by accident. The city had a significant gay subculture, as did many large cities at the time. Hirschfeld found everything he wanted in Berlin. There was opportunity to learn, to discover, and to understand the seedy and sordid side of gay and lesbian life. Within the first year, he published a pamphlet on homosexuality. His eight-year stay gave him what he needed to write an engaging book, whose title translated into English as *Berlin's Third Sex*.

If there had been any change since Ulrichs' time, it had to do with the rate that gay and lesbian culture was developing. Hirschfeld was struck by the "countless stable lesbian and gay relationships" rapidly emerging.[3] Nevertheless, homosexuality was "far less visible than we are accustomed to today." Important as well, the German law forbidding homosexual practice was still stringent. Paragraph 175 of the country's Penal Code, inherited from Prussia, imposed six-month imprisonment for the felonious act. German police enforced the law through "surveillance, entrapment, and by the use of informers." The result was imprisonment of no fewer than 500 men annually. Notwithstanding the clampdown, continuing growth of the homosexual subculture was not impeded. The practice developed into a lucrative commercial trade: male prostitution. For the new generation of male prostitutes, "blackmail was the whole point and purpose of the trade." A book, which investigated the phenomenon of male prostitution in Berlin in 1906, made the shocking discovery that "countless men were driven to suicide by blackmail" over the threat of disclosure.

---

3. LeVay, "Queer Science—The Use Abuse of Research into Homosexuality."

Hirschfeld didn't wait to complete his study on homosexuality before he launched his gay-rights crusade. His objective was to pressure the German government to reverse its anti-gay policy. Deriving strength from his publication *Sappho and Socrates*, authored a year after his arrival in the German capital, he began the advocacy that became his life-long cause. Unlike Ulrichs, a one-man crusading army, he founded the *Wissenschaftlich-humanitares Komitee* (Whk or "Scientific-humanitarian Committee") along with three associates. This 1897 group is regarded as the world's first gay-rights organization.

The Whk sprang into action immediately, submitting a petition to both chambers of the German legislative assembly. It had enlisted the support of a substantial number of German elites—"about two hundred jurists, professors of medicine, and others" who signed their appeal. The petition to the Bundesrat and the Reichstag had both familiar and fresh lines of entreaty. It offered the usual argument, that same-sex relationships were just as normal as heterosexual ones. In this connection, they claimed that "scientific research, especially carried out over the last twenty years in German, English and French-speaking countries . . . has without exception confirmed . . . that this phenomenon has been uniformly encountered in all countries." But the data was old, predating Ulrich's death by two years. It was all a matter of wishful projection.

They further claimed that "the lifting of similar penalties in France, Italy, Holland and numerous other countries has not led to decline in public morals or to any other unfavourable consequences." Again, this was disinformation, and the lawmakers rejected it, hurling the petition back in the face of Whk. But Hirschfeld and his cohorts pressed the cause for over thirty years, endlessly presenting the petition to the legislators. With each new presentation, their list of endorsers increased to "a total of over three thousand people," including Richard Kraft-Ebing, Albert Einstein, Thomas and Heinrich Mann, and Rainer Maria Rilke among others. These were men and women of intellectual influence in German life, but the big names failed to persuade the legislators to remove the anti-homosexual law from the penal code.

Hirschfeld was a persistent, persevering, and prodigious researcher, and he came to be known as the "Einstein of sex." In this, German society was not commending him. Rather, this was deprecation for his unorthodox views and findings.

The criticism and antagonisms from professional colleagues did not, however, stop Hirschfeld from continuing with his ideals. He established the *Institut für Sexualwissenschaft* (Institute for Sexual Research), which opened July 6, 1919. It crystallised everything about his life and work, and it featured a Museum of Sex. Unluckily for him, the hostility against him had risen to a new height by the time Nazis assumed power in Germany, and they torched his property on May 6, 1933. Gone were the books; gone were the entire archives of the *Institut*. At least he was spared the spectacle, for he was out of the country at the time.

Hirschfeld and the Whk had become the most influential gay-rights activist organization, with an extensive mix of communication channels to propagate the organization's view—pamphlets, books, lectures, conferences, and later films. No means of communication appealed to Hirschfeld more than the public lectures, of which "he must have given thousands." His happiest times were "when addressing large groups" whether of students or workers or of society's elites, and it was while he was on one of these speaking tours that the Nazis destroyed his institute. The eighteen-month trip had taken him to the United States and many countries in Asia. Receiving the news of the arson mid-trip, he never returned to Germany. After meandering through Athens and Vienna, and taking the opportunity in Zurich to work on a travelogue, he settled in Paris.

Hirschfeld refused to give in to mental, emotional, psychological, and physiological defeat. He still found the energy to research, write, and continue his campaign. He even contemplated a French successor to his burned Berlin institute. But on his 67th birthday, two years after his arrival in Paris, he suffered a fatal heart attack at home, his life span three years shorter that than of his pioneering predecessor, Ulrichs.

Hirschfeld remained for long a prophet without honor in his own home. His life and work, however, became a springboard for gay activism in the United States. Curiously, he didn't win his first convert on American soil. Nor did his impact come from his many speaking engagements in the country. Also, very improbable, he met the man who turned out to be his American disciple when the man came to Germany as a soldier and there became fascinated with the work of Hirschfeld's Whk. The pupil returned home a believer; Hirschfeld's Whk won him over and the transformation was permanent. America was never to be the same again.

The man, Harry Gerber, was born "Henry Joseph Dittmar" in 1892, the same year Hirschfeld earned his doctorate. Gerber immigrated to the United States at age 21, and upon arrival, he took the new name Harry Gerber. His middle name of Joseph had spelling dispute, as some spelled it "Josef."

Four years after taking up residence in the United States, he had his first run-in with the law and was committed to a mental institution for a brief term. His offence was homosexuality. While incarcerated, he was confronted with an unpleasant choice: being treated as an "enemy alien" or enlisting in the United States Army, then at war with Germany. Enlisting in the army appeared to him to be the lesser of two evils. During his three years of service, he was a printer and proofreader with the Allied Army of Occupation in the German territory of Coblenz, and his homosexuality accompanied him to the war front.

Frequently, he traveled to Berlin, whose thriving gay subculture fascinated him. He learned about Magnus Hirschfeld and was attracted to the work of the emerging Scientific-Humanitarian Committee. Naturally, he was for reform of the German anti-homosexual law, especially the repeal of Paragraph 175 that precluded sex between men. Although there was practically no way for Gerber to get involved in the highly volatile politics of the country, he made his little contribution by subscribing to at least one homosexual magazine. He was not convinced by all of what Hirschfeld had to say, but he was hooked to the notion that homosexual men were naturally effeminate.

Gerber might have served on the fringe of active combat in Germany, but he returned home with an array of coveted war spoils—Hirschfeld's activist spirit and awareness of literature's value for shaping public opinion. Back home in America, he was bubbling with ideas, bristling with the desire to reincarnate the heroic work of Hirschfeld and the Whk. He longed to have an American version of Whk, with himself in the driver's seat. Yet between Hirschfeld and Gerber there was a vast difference. Gerber had neither the educational background nor the social standing of the late physician and sexologist. He was a lowly blue-collar worker, who succeeded only in landing a post office job after his military service. He was, however, a man of strong convictions and courage, one who refused to be held down by the lack of social and economic standing. And so he founded an organization in America similar to Hirschfeld's Scientific-Humanitarian Committee.

He didn't have to shop for a willing partner. He got an African-American clergyman named John T. Graves interested, and he was able to enlist four others, bringing to five the number of pioneering members of the organization, which he named the Society for Human Rights (SHR) in imitation of Hirschfeld's Scientific-Humanitarian Committee. To give the organization legal standing, he applied for its registration as a nonprofit group in the state of Illinois, 29 years after Karl Ulrichs' death (when Gerber was three).

He never met Ulrichs. Neither was it likely that he read Ulrichs' thoughts on homosexuality. Yet Gerber's aims for the embryonic organization bore striking similarity to Ulrichs' thoughts. The SHR was "to promote and protect the interests of people who by reasons of mental and physical abnormalities are abused and hindered in the legal pursuit of happiness which is guaranteed them by the Declaration of Independence." Another goal was "to combat the public prejudices against them." Further, there would be "dissemination of factors [concerning homosexuality] according to modern science among intellectuals of mature age." In a manner reminiscent of Ulrichs, the American gay activist declared, "The Society stands only for law and order." Additionally, "It is in harmony with any and all general laws insofar as they protect the rights of others." Again, echoing Ulrichs, the SHR "does in no manner recommend any acts in violation of present laws, nor advocate any manner inimical to the public welfare."

On December 10, 1924, the SHR received the legal nod it requested. With the registration, Gerber gave the United States its first documented homosexual organization. He followed up with the first known American gay publication, *Friendship and Freedom*. His optimism however soon gave way to pessimism, for the newsletter was faced with low patronage. Few of the targeted readers were willing to receive the newsletter and risk infringement of the law. The likelihood of its being classified as obscene material by postal inspectors was high. Thus, *Friendship and Freedom* was short-lived, lasting only two issues.

But it wasn't the publication alone that was fleeting. Without intending it, the name chosen by Gerber for the maiden American gay periodical, *Friendship and Freedom*, was rich with irony. The friendship that Gerber presumed did not materialize while the freedom sought became a mirage. Gerber and Graves, being secretary and president respectively of the fledgling SHR, made a decision that hastened Gerber's loss of faith in his own cause. The two had resolved to exclude bisexuals from the organization. Unknown to them, SHR vice president Al Weininger was married with two children at the time, and his new lifestyle caused his wife unbearable discomfort. She took her case to a social worker, complaining about SHR and its "degenerates." This was in the summer of 1925, barely a year after it became a legal entity.

The police interrogated Gerber and the others. Along with Graves, Weininger, and another member of the SHR, he was arrested. Even before his day in court, the media had conducted their own trial, reporting, "Strange Sex Cult Exposed." Gerber went through an expensive legal defense. Eventually, the charges were dismissed, but his life savings had been wiped out. Compared to Gerber's drawn-out prosecution, however, Weninger's was short in terms of both time and fine. He was assessed only a paltry $10 for "disorderly conduct," but he also lost his post office job, terminated for "conduct unbecoming a postal worker." The case, succeeded in breaking up the "strange sex cult"; SHR was destroyed. Gerber became disillusioned, embittered that his plight did not enlist the interest of wealthy gays in Chicago. None came to his aid.

Yet he felt his mission was to advance the common good, and he remained committed to the homosexual cause. For more than thirty years, he wrote on homosexual issues. He built a large archive of correspondence with important New York gay men from the 1950s, discussing extensively strategies for organizing and meeting the needs of gay men. Although Gerber lived to the age of 80, dying in his home on December 31, 1972, he didn't get credit on the pioneers roll of honor for giving America her first enduring gay rights organization. Nevertheless, it would be a disservice to disassociate him from the founding of the first gay rights organisation to survive in America—the Mattachine Society.

If the name, Mattachine Society, sounded bizarre for an organization begging understanding from a reluctant society, the life and times of the man behind it, Harry Hay Jr., was even weirder. Everything about Hay was a matter of ceaseless revolt, of endless fights with society. Hardly was there any institution of society with which he had no conflict—parents, religion, education, marriage, family, culture, and government. Hay traced his personal failings in life to shortcomings of the social structures behind his nature and nurture.

Between him and his father, there was no love lost. The first thing that Hay Jr. despised was the family's religion. He repudiated Catholicism, in which he and his siblings were raised. Their father had converted to the religion on marrying their Catholic mother. Hay Sr. was a stickler for discipline, refusing to spare the rod, lest his son be spoiled. Neither did he shield his boy from hard work. Hay Sr. had acquired a

30-acre citrus farm after an industrial accident forced him into an early retirement, and he saw no reason why his son should not work on the family's agricultural estate.

To Hay Jr., his father's discipline seemed like tyranny. He loathed him so much that he preferred the exact opposite of everything his father stood for or expected from him. Accordingly, his father would beat him. A potential root cause of their disagreement was the embarrassment the son caused his father. As Hay Jr. recalled, his father "disliked him for having effeminate traits." In the end, Hay Jr.'s construction of reality took roots in the logic of self-righteousness, convinced that his father was wrong.

> If my father could be wrong, then the teacher could be wrong. And if the teacher could be wrong, then the priest could be wrong. And if the priest could be wrong, then maybe even God could be wrong.[4]

But he apparently never turned the same reasoning over in his mind. If others could be wrong, he too could be wrong!

Hay Jr. did not long enjoy childhood innocence. At age 9, he took part in a sexual activity with a 12-year-old neighbor boy and continued engaging in homosexual activity during his adolescence, on at least one occasion allegedly with an adult who attempted to keep Hay silent about the encounter. A voracious reader, his choice of literature reflected his homosexual tendency. One book from his early adventure in the public library was Edward Carpenter's *The Intermediate Sex*. At 21, it clarified for him that he was gay.

Hay Jr. graduated from high school at age 19, the aberrations notwithstanding. Initially, he wanted to study paleontology, but the elder Hay would not hear of his son majoring in such an esoteric subject. Rather, he wanted him to study law, to be in a choice profession. So Hay Sr., as a man of means and connections, secured for his son a job at a friend's legal office.

Hay Jr. snubbed his father's preference. In Los Angeles, he began searching for casual, anonymous one-time sex partners. He succeeded in finding a companion, one who happened to be a former lover of one of Harry Gerber's SHR compatriots. Through him, he learned about the Society. Hay Jr. didn't act immediately. He kept the information for later use. This was around the time he took a course in international relations at Stanford University. Along with international relations, he decided also to take courses in English, history, and political science. Philandering, however, remained his notorious habit. His university days were therefore full of escapades.

Hay Jr. was a familiar sight at the gay scene in both Los Angeles and San Francisco. His time was full of wild parties "where men danced with men, women danced with women, and people cross-dressed." Alcohol was also consumed beyond reasonable limits. His permissiveness and weakness of the flesh were limitless and much of his behavior illegal. He dated at will and engaged in romantic trysts. His stay at

4. https://en.wikipedia.org/wiki/Harry_Hay.

Stanford was brief. University education ended for him in 1932, the second year he was enrolled as a student. He contracted a severe sinus infection, and after recuperating at his cousin's Nevada ranch, he turned his back on university education.

When he was 29, Hay Jr. formally announced what was public knowledge, or, at least, widely suspected. He came out as gay. Although no reported cases of violence greeted his admission, it prompted some backlash. Some of his colleagues, including those who were gay, withdrew from the circle of his friendship. They maintained a clear distance from him. Some were never to be seen in his company again.

At one point, Hay Jr. thought he could straighten himself out. He wanted to make a U-turn and leave the fast lane in which he had been driving. In 1937, Hay Sr. had a stroke and was paralyzed. The incapacitated old man left management of family affairs to his errant son. That same year, Hay Jr. had gone in search of psychiatric help. He was subjected to Jungian analysis, a form of clinical psychology which was prominent then. The result was that Hay Jr. was advised to find himself "boyish girl."

By this time, as well, he had become a staunch communist. He drew his most trusted confidants from the inner circle of fellow ideologues. Ironically, the party had always deprecated homosexuality as another evidence of "bourgeoisie decadence." To Hay Jr., his father, teacher, priest, and God, all could be wrong, but apparently not his communist soulmates.

In 1938, without elaborate ceremony, he married a fellow party member, Anna Platky. Lamentably, neither his reach for psychiatrist treatment nor the marriage cured him. Before their first anniversary, Hay Jr. returned to gay prowling. He sought out different men for sexual encounters on a weekly basis. The new bride was initially unsuspecting, but by 1940, Hay was a having series of affairs with men in the city, and was also was deeply involved in a long-term homosexual relationship with an architect, William Alexander. The affair lasted for seven months. At the height of the romantic relationship, Hay Jr. contemplated leaving his wife for his gay lover. Somehow, he managed to stay with the marriage a little longer. The couple even adopted two daughters, Hannah Margaret, in September 1943, and Kate Neall, two years later. Nonetheless, it was obvious that Hay Jr.'s heart was not with Anna.

In addition to his amorous dealings with Alexander, he was involved in the research of American sexologist Alfred Kinsey. For two reasons, Kinsey's study could not but be of interest to Hay Jr. First, it had to do with sex. Second was the weird, controversial method employed by the researcher.

Kinsey published the outcome of his research in twin reports, five years apart. The first, *Sexual Behavior in the Human Male*, was published in 1948, while the second, *Sexual Behavior in the Human Female*, was released in 1953. The reports appeared innocent on the surface, but less agreeable were Kinsey's research methods. The detachment that a researcher was expected to bring to his investigation didn't apply to Kinsey, who was a bisexual. The agreement between the respected scholar and his wife was strange. Both could sleep with other people of their choice and could still come back to meet as husband and wife. He exercised his licence to the fullest. Kinsey slept with other men, including his students. His research, therefore, included participation in sexual activity.

Sometimes he used his coworkers as tools in the experiment. No method was too offensive, and no approach was too obscene. Kinsey encouraged his subjects to "engage in a wide range of sexual activity, to the extent that they felt comfortable."[5] From the attic of his home, he filmed the scenes. In the end, the study exposed humanity's vile culture. Science was stripped of its ethical standards. Kinsey's study didn't stop at adults; it included exploring "pre-adolescent orgasms." He claimed to have made "observations of orgasms in over three-hundred children between the ages of five months and fourteen years." The knowledge was, however, not from the children themselves. Rather, the data came from "adults' childhood memories, or from parent or teacher observation." He even interviewed "nine men who had sexual experiences with children, and who told him about the children's responses and reactions."

The horror of children becoming guinea pigs in a debauched experiment raised little ire then. However, the ghosts of Kinsey's unscrupulousness came to haunt him later when society realized the horror of celebrating pedophilia. Unfortunately, he was dead by then, and the opportunity to bring him to justice was long gone.

However, his impact was to enlarge the range of sexual activity acceptable to society in the 1960s and 1970s, culminating in the so-called "sexual revolution." The sexual revolution rebelled against society's traditional norms of conducting relationships within the bounds of social decency and morality. It began a new age of hedonistic celebration of sex outside the home, contraception, public nudity, premarital sex, abortion, and of course homosexuality. These social and cultural aberrations were promoted as fair, right, and acceptable. For a man like Hay Jr., this was not only his desired world but also the kind of society he felt the duty to foster.

The *Kinsey Report* influenced and inspired him greatly. He took part in the study, though the extent of his participation remains a matter of speculation. The report influenced him to think about launching a homosexual activist group. Incidentally, 1948 was a presidential election year. He was rooting for the Progressive Party presidential candidate, Henry A. Wallace, and at a social gathering, he floated the idea of gays' supporting the presidential ambition of Wallace under the banner, "bachelors for Wallace." From those he sounded out, there were whispers of agreement, and within a short time, he had formulated aims to guide the emergence of the group, which he dubbed "The Call."

Three years earlier, Hay Jr. had been diagnosed with hypoglycaemia, a health condition with symptoms that included clumsiness, trouble talking, confusion, loss of consciousness, and seizures. Hay Jr.'s disorder was complicated by his intense mental anxiety and repeated nightmares that extended to sleepwalking. Luckily, his condition had tremendously improved by 1948. Hay Jr. couldn't, however, believe what

5. https://en.wikipedia.org/wiki/Alfred_Kinsey.

happened the night in 1948 when he had gone home thrilled that his idea of forming a homosexual activist group was warmly welcomed. No, he had not sleepwalked that night, nor was he laboring under a hallucination. Yet, he had woken up to a harsh reality. Not a single individual showed interest in the idea they had all agreed on the previous night. Hay Jr. was alone, deserted, but he refused to give in to disappointment.

For two years, he polished and re-polished the idea. He thought of different names for it and improved it in divergent ways. It occurred to him to call it an "international . . . fraternal order." Also, he thought of casting it as "a service and welfare organization devoted to the protection and improvement of Society's Androgynous Minority." A possible name he considered for the organization was Bachelors Anonymous, analogous to Alcoholics Anonymous, an organization devoted to helping in the rehabilitation of alcoholics. All the thoughts of Hay Jr. remained ideas on paper.

Then he met the American fashion designer Rudi Gernreich in July 1950.[6] Gernreich was gay, and they soon entered into a relationship. The bond extended to Gernreich's sharing Hay Jr.'s leftist ideas. Hay Jr. succeeded in securing for himself not only a gay partner but also a supporter of his cause, who backed him financially. Consequently, on November 11, 1950, five gay men congregated in Los Angeles. Present were Hay Jr., his new partner Gernreich, along with three other friends, Dale Jennings, Bob Hull, and Chuck Rowland. The purpose of their meeting was protecting the interest of gays through an association. The first name that occurred to them was Society of Fools.

The group soon realized how ludicrous their choice of name was, and five months later, they changed it. The new name was a product of one of their early members, not among the original five who conceived the association. James Gruber joined them in April 1951, and he gets credit for the new name—Mattachine Society. Instantaneously, Hay Jr. fell in love with it, and it was adopted. The fledgling Mattachine Society occupied the central point in Hay Jr.'s life. In April 1951, he returned home enthusiastically to tell Anna about the developments. Four months later, their thirteen-year marriage collapsed.

Hay Jr. moved out of their home. Seemingly, the marriage had been like a kind of prison for him. As he described it, his situation was like "living in an exile world." Now he had the liberty to fly, roam, and soar like an eagle. The world was at his feet. But while he had come to think that his father, teacher, priest, and even God could be wrong, he got to learn that his wild imaginations could be wrong as well. A key sequence of events began when Gernreich ended their relationship in 1952, the same year Hay's marriage to Anna dissolved. Gernreich was a fashion designer, a top flier in an industry witnessing rapid expansion at the time. He may have considered it wise not to mix business with pleasure. A year before dumping Hay Jr., he had been arrested and convicted in a case of police homosexual entrapment. Shrewdly, he had kept his homosexuality a matter of public guesses, and he realized Hay Jr. was a "politically

6. https://en.wikipedia.org/wiki/Rudi_Gernreich.

exposed risk," constantly under the attention of the Federal Bureau of Investigation (FBI). Gernreich didn't need the adverse publicity. So he took his leave of Hay Jr., yet he remained gay and indeed picked a new partner, Oreste Pucciani, then-future chairman of the French department at the University of California, Los Angeles. Both, however, kept their relationship private.

Nevertheless, Hay Jr. did well with the Mattachine Society, on which he concentrated. And that same year, he entered into a new relationship with a Danish hat maker named Jorn Kamgren, the affair lasting for 11 years. All through that period, the Mattachine Society remained his top priority, and he ended his membership of the Communist Party. Of course, the Party had not changed its denunciation of the gay sexual preference as reflecting the decadent bourgeoisie! Given the choice between ideological purity and indulgence of his hedonistic weakness, it seemed that Hay Jr. would rather put up with his weakness than sacrifice for the cause of the party.

The fourfold goals of the Mattachine Society were not significantly different from those of Henry Gerber's Society for Human Rights. The first and paramount aim was to "unify homosexuals." Second was to "educate homosexuals and heterosexuals toward an ethical homosexual culture." Third was a program of action that would "provide leadership to the whole mass of social variants." Finally, the Mattachine Society aimed to "assist gays who are victimized daily as a result of oppression." Absent, however, was a strategic plan regarding how the organization or its leaders intended to achieve these objectives.

The organization's structure was a hybrid, deriving partly from the Communist Party hierarchical arrangement and fraternal brotherhoods like Freemasonry. The organizational structure was designed in layered horizontal and vertical cells and orders. Common to every one of those structures were oaths of secrecy. At the top were the founding members of the organization. To the outside world, they remained faceless and anonymous, like mafia leaders.

Overzealousness by government law enforcement agencies can help groups agitating for one cause or another to gain public visibility. When such opportunities are exploited cleverly, the organizations and their causes can be catapulted to the national and international limelight, attaining some form of legitimacy in their struggles. And this is what happened to the Mattachine Society cause. In February 1952, one of its founding members, Dale Jennings, was arrested in a Los Angeles park for lewd behavior and was arraigned in court. Men of Jennings' status and standing in society often simply pled guilty to their charge and paid their fine quietly. They usually would want to avoid the public scandal that media attention to their trial would bring. It was not so, however, with Jennings and the rest of the "Fifth Order," as the top leadership of the Mattachine Society was called. They saw good opportunity arising from the case to attack police "entrapment."

Jennings faced the trial. Shrewdly, concealing their identities, the group began publicising the case through a front organization called Citizens Committee to Outlaw

Entrapment. Jennings made the case sensational, admitting for the first time that he was a homosexual. Flatly, however, he denied committing any wrong, and he played on the public's tendency to side with the oppressed. This was especially effective when the alleged oppressor happened to be the government. Jennings's case whipped up public sentiments, and the jury was deadlocked, with eleven in favor of acquittal and only one voting for conviction. The judge was left with no other choice than to dismiss the charges. Jennings' discharge was a big moral victory for the society. Similarly, its financial support and people pledging volunteer support increased. By May 1953, the membership of the organization had grown rapidly, hitting over 2,000. On average, as many as 100 new people were welcomed at every meeting of the organization's discussion group.

Yet the bigger an organization grows, the more internal conflicts it can expect. Within a short time, cracks began to appear. People came in with different ideological persuasions, and questions arose about the organization's political outlook. Though Hay Jr. had resigned his membership in the Communist Party, the connection remained in some minds, and most felt there should be a clear divide between the society and the Communist Party. So Hay Jr. surrendered his leadership position, bowing to sentiment that the Mattachine Society must "have a more open, democratic structure."

By the time of the group's convention in 1953, Hay Jr.'s Mattachine Society was gone. Born was a new pacifist organization with new leadership. The men of the Fifth Order who had lived behind masks revealed their identities publicly, and they had to step down. As its official policy, the Mattachine Society adopted a non-confrontational principle. Paradoxically, the choice of name of the Mattachine Society had been informed by the fond attraction of Hay Jr. and his fellow founding members to the story of the "mask-wearing 'Mattaccino," who delighted in "speaking the truth to the king when nobody else would."

Whatever truth the American Mattachine Society was to speak from that time onward was to be within the realm of loyalty and respect for the United States and her laws, the society pledged. The new Mattachine Society promised to be different from the old order. Hay Jr. was seriously disappointed by the turn of events, but there was nothing he could do. Pitifully, he suffered emotional breakdown. Nevertheless, he could console himself that his efforts were not in vain, for gay rights activism was on the rise.

Up to a point, however, the Mattachine Society operated as a monolithic, single-tier, national organization with its headquarters, first, being in Los Angeles. Around 1956, the control center of its operations shifted to San Francisco, from where the organization expanded to other parts of America, with new and growing chapters in New York, Washington, D.C., Chicago, and a few other cities. In 1961, a serious internal disagreement arose, resulting in the disbanding of the national organization and the emergence of autonomous branches. While the national chapter in San Francisco retained the name Mattachine Society, others employed variants of the name—the Mattachine Society of New York, Inc.; the Mattachine Society of Washington; and the Mattachine Society of the Niagara Frontier, among others. A major result of the proliferation of chapters was an increase in mentoring provided to younger gays. In this connection, the Mattachine Society of Washington provided support for the East Coast Homophile Organizations, and the Mattachine Midwest provided a shoulder on which the North American Conference of Homophile Organizations could lean.

By the dawn of the '60s, the Mattachine Society had developed an image as the foremost American gay rights organization. It provided the practically unchallenged center of gravity around which the cause revolved in the country. Throughout the United States, no other organization enjoyed the public visibility and strong voice that the Mattachine Society had on gay rights.

Harry Hay Jr. didn't give America its first gay organization, but it was through him that the country recorded its first surviving effort at organizing members of the group into a political force. The Stonewall riots of 1969, however, changed everything—dramatically and irreversibly.

15

The Whole World Must Go Gay

America, 1972

The Stonewall riot of 1969 in New York marked a radical turning point in the history of gay activism in the United States.[1] None of the emerging gay groups within the homophile movement, the popular appellation for gay rights activism then, would have been unhappy with the way the events turned out.[2] Some did not wholly agree, however, with the methods activists used, as they expressed later. But the spontaneous events had caught everyone by surprise—the government, the police, the general public, and gay groups themselves, including the Daughters of Bilitis (DOB).[3] The upheaval, which attracted national attention, occurred fourteen years after the DOB was founded, and the issues that provoked the riot were the same that informed the group's formation.

The DOB was the first American, organized lesbian group, the first to press openly for the rights of lesbians in the United States. In 1950, Del Martin, whose maiden name was Dorothy Louise Taliaferro (hence, the acronym 'Del'), met Phyllis Ann Lyon in Seattle.[4] Both were on the staff of a magazine. Del, the elder by three years, was married. She and James Martin, her husband of four years, had a daughter, Kendra Mon. The workplace friendship of the 29-year-old Del and the younger Phyllis turned to dating, and they became lovers in 1952. They entered into a partnership in 1953 and moved to San Francisco together. Del divorced her husband but decided to retain his name. The three years of their association showed the couple the depth of society's rejection of their way of life. They wanted to do those things people in love do

1. https://en.wikipedia.org/wiki/AfricanAmerican_Civil_Rights_Movement_%281954%E2%80%9368%29.

2. LeVay, "Queer Science—The Use Abuse of Research into Homosexuality."

3. https://en.wikipedia.org/w/index.php?title=Daughters_of_Bilitis&printable=yes.

4. https://en.wikipedia.org/w/index.php?title=Del_Martin_and_Phyllis_Lyon&printable=yes.

in public, but they couldn't because they were barred. Those things were only allowed in the privacy of their room.

Through a chance encounter, they met a gay couple to whom they expressed their frustrations. They asked the couple if they knew of other lesbian couples with whom they could associate. Through them, they met several lesbian couples. One of the couples came up with the idea that they establish a social club. In October 1955, four lesbian couples met to create a social forum for interaction. Though they had a clear idea of what led to their association, they lacked any clue as to where it would lead them. Regularly, however, they met, and it provided them a much-needed social life. They had a place to dance without fear of harassment by the police or discomforting quizzical gazes from family and friends.

They were also concerned with the bigger questions of how to "educate other women about lesbians" and how they could encourage women in their position to "reduce their self-loathing brought on by the socially repressive times." They realized the need to organize regular meetings. Martin was elected as the group's president, but there was a problem: they didn't know what to name themselves. At their second meeting, the idea of Daughters of Bilitis (DOB) suggested itself. Bilitis was the name of a fictional lesbian created by the French poet Pierre Louÿs in his 1894 work *The Songs of Bilitis and the Daughters*. Behind their choice was an interest in evoking "association with other American social associations such as the Daughters of the American Revolution."

Though the DOB didn't set out to be a radical or confrontational outfit, it was determined to correct deep-seated prejudice. It chose to operate and work discretely, with members telling outsiders, "We belong to a poetry club."

There was no doubt that the DOB drew significant influence from the Mattachine Society, as its male counterpart. The two organizations were the first homosexual rights campaigners in the United States. As with the Mattachine Society, events sometimes forced the DOB to redefine its outlook and re-strategize its approach. Though it lacked the luck of a high-profile event like the prosecution of Jennings to catapult it into public eye, the DOB still managed to experience rapid growth. Five years after its founding, it had spread to Chicago, New York, New Orleans, San Diego, Los Angeles, Detroit, Denver, Cleveland, and Philadelphia. By any standard, this was phenomenal. It also established a newsletter.

Phyllis edited the newsletter, *The Ladder*, which began in 1956. Then Martin took over from 1960 to 1962. The newsletter achieved modest success. It had 500 subscribers, though that might be a conservative figure because far more women read it but didn't put their names on its subscription list for fear of reprisal. However, the newsletter was a useful instrument. It provided the DOB with an effective means to advertise its ideals. On the inside cover of every issue, the organization repeated its goal—"A Woman's Organization for the purpose of Promoting the Integration of the Homosexual into Society." Its strategy involved the:

education of lesbians, education of the public, participation in research projects, and investigation of the penal code as it pertains to the homosexual. Their best way therefore was non-violence. Their underlying desire was social acceptance; convince the public "to accept the Lesbian homosexual into society."

By 1960, the DOB had succeeded in popularizing its views. It had become so successful that it planned its first convention. The maiden gathering in San Francisco was productive and fruitful, with about 200 in attendance. It culminated in the decision of DOB to gather biennially. The police were there to see "if any of the DOB members were wearing men's clothes." Del Martin brought them in with a churlish grin. They were free to satisfy their curiosity. None of the women had dressed in an embarrassing manner. They all wore prim outfits with stockings and heels to match.

Ironically, the police caused no stir at the conference compared to one of their invited speakers. Two attorneys had debated about the legality and morality of gay bars. The debate went well. Then the American Civil Liberties Union made a presentation. That still did not ruffle any feathers. Next, was an Episcopal priest, and he was the one who rocked the gathering with a bombshell. Point-blank, he told the audience that lesbianism was a sin. Not a whisper escaped from the hall. A pin-drop silence followed the speech. "They listened politely," testified the accounts given of the incident.

Del and Phyllis, however, took a mental note of where to take the next battle. Though the DOB lacked the numerical strength of the Mattachine Society and were females, they realised, "If we ever hope to win our battle, we must fight." They fought from 1961 to 1964, seizing opportunities when they presented themselves and confronting challenges when they threatened as obstacles. Fortune however came DOB's way in 1963, when a single, anonymous donor made a financial behest of $100,000 to the organization. The largesse was spread over a five-year period. The patron, who was unknown, consistently "wrote $3,000 checks to different DOB members, who in turn signed them over to the organization."

Though DOB was still young, Del and Phyllis believed that their founders' job should end. They believed that by 1964, they had done enough mentoring and nurturing of the organization: "We felt that if the organization had any validity at all it couldn't be based on two people, it had to be able to stand and grow on its own. And it was never going to do it if we didn't move out." They stayed on for four years more, and then took their exit from the DOB. It was the end of an era but not the climax of the struggle, as the duo headed in a new direction.

The Episcopal priest who had spoken at their 1960 maiden conference highlighted an important area of engagement. Del and Phyllis saw an opportunity in the Council on Religion and the Homosexual (CRH), which they helped found. The CRH was an initiative of the Rev. Ted McIlvenna, who worked for the Glide Urban Center, a private Methodist foundation in San Francisco, where he had been concerned with issues confronting homosexuals. Along with Del and Phyllis, the Glide Memorial Methodist Church, where he was one of the pastors, convened an initial meeting that led to the Mill Valley Conference. The conference, held May 31–June 2, 1964, brought sixteen Methodist, Episcopal, United Church of Christ, and Lutheran clergymen together with thirteen leaders of the homosexual community. The outcome of that conference was formation of the CRH, which was incorporated in December of that year. Central to the organization's objectives was

> education of religious communities about gay and lesbian issues as well as enlisting religious leaders to advocate for homosexual concerns.

The CRH marked the beginning of the involvement of the church in the politics of homosexuality in the United States.

Indeed, the new organization had no reservation regarding its involvement. It was the first American group to use the word "homosexual" in its name. The duo of Del and Phyllis, however, couldn't lead the DOB to join the new organization formally. The DOB charter precluded it from joining any other separate organization.

The DOB itself was in transition; after all, the '60s were changing times. Younger members of the organization were opting for a more radical, if not revolutionary, approach compared to the style of the older members. Managing the growing tension became a problem. Many chapters were finding the parent organization's powers stifling, especially its prohibition of making important local decisions without approval of the national group. This disillusionment prompted the exodus of members, particularly younger ones. By its 1968 convention, the hemorrhaging DOB was comatose, seriously gasping for breath. That year's convention attracted fewer than two dozen participants. Though the DOB managed to survive until another convention, the 1970 biennial gathering was to be its last. The DOB was disbanded.

Between those two conventions was the Stonewall riot of 1969 in New York, which no one had anticipated. Mafia money had bought a previously rundown restaurant and bar in the city and brought it back to life through the Genovese family, a family almost "unmatched in terms of power" in the organized crime world of New York. They refurbished the Stonewall Inn, and recreated it as lucrative business, an entertainment facility. It became the rendezvous for gays, who were its main clientele. It was the only club where gays could dance. Stonewall Inn needed no other business niche to build its fortune, and it became known as a gay club.

Not all business of the club was legal. The bar didn't allow prostitution, but sales of drugs and other "cash transactions" thrived under its roof. Also, despite its not having a liquor license, alcohol sale was a flourishing trade. Police were aware of the illegal transactions. Regularly, the police stopped by. Irritating as the incursions were, the owners and their clients had conditioned themselves to tolerate the unwanted guests. But a raid on Saturday, June 28, 1969, at 1:20 a.m., proved to be different.

The police arrived in the usual manner. Uncommon however was the reception they met. Everything went awry from the beginning. No longer were those arrested submissive and hapless. The Stonewall Inn patrons encountered on that day showed uncharacteristic defiance. For hours, a melee ensued. The battle was fierce, but the combatants were undaunted, refusing to give up. The riot continued into a second day, with "street battling again until 4:00 a.m." "When police captured demonstrators, whom the majority of witnesses described as 'sissies' or 'swishes,'" the irrepressible crowd would surge forward "to recapture them." Their intention was to render the police impotent to make any arrest. From that single event, the gays and lesbians stumbled on a new discovery: fear was a cyst that courage could rupture. That night, gay rights activism broke down the wall of fear. A new dawn and shout emerged: "Gay Power!"[5]

Throughout America, the Stonewall Inn riots gave homosexuals a new revolutionary zeal. Many spillover effects developed from them. Swiftly and spontaneously, groups began to emerge, cashing in on the electrifying moment. A gay couple unconnected with the event, Craig Rodwell and his partner Fred Sargeant, saw the crisis as an opportunity to begin a nationwide campaign to rid gay clubs of incessant police raids. Swinging into action the morning after the first day's riot, they flooded the streets with a mass leaflet screaming, "Get the Mafia and the Cops out of Gay Bars." More than 5,000 copies of the leaflet pilloried the authorities. Also, they called for "gays to own their own establishments." Homosexuals were no longer in a defensive position. Not only had weapons and tactics changed, the campaign itself had taken a new turn. Gays and lesbians were on the offensive. Openly, demands were made that the authorities "investigate the 'intolerable situation.'"

From the Stonewall cinders burst a fresh fire. The enthusiasm precipitated a revolutionary zeal in the homosexual campaign in America, occasioning the birth of the Gay Liberation Front (GLF), which was explicit with its strategic approach, one that differed from those of its predecessors, the Mattachine Society and the Daughters of Billitis. The previous homophile groups had avoided trouble. They hid behind innocuous names that did not directly portray their mission. That wasn't the case, however, with GLF. The radical nature of the organization was explicitly stated. Likewise, too, it wanted no one to misunderstand the community of people it was serving—the gays—and hence, boldly, it employed the word "gay" as a major part of its public name. Also provocative was its use of the expression "liberation front," which was commonly associated with terrorists and guerrilla warfare groups. Unfortunately, GLF lived up to its name, and within a short time, "the rise of militancy became apparent" in the American gay rights struggle.

Unfortunately for them, the GLF leaders were to become victims of their new mindset. Pompous with their newfound power, they believed they "could work to restructure American society." They sought to piggyback on the phenomena of racial and anti-war demonstrations, along with groups like the Black Panthers and other radical New Left causes. If the GLF leaders lacked strategies of their own, they were

5. See also American Psychological Association, "History of Lesbian, Gay, & Bisexual Social Movements," http://www.apa.org/pl/lgbt/resources/history.aspx.

not reluctant to borrow tactics from the other groups. Brashly, the GLF many times latched on to strategies some of these organizations employed in their wars against society. Quicker than they could imagine, however, GLF leaders ran the organization aground. The GLF died faster than the early gay organizations it had been rebuking for being "too mild." Four months after its formation, it became history.

What accounted for the early death of the GLF? The major cause was internal disagreement over operational methods. At a meeting in late December of 1969, the differences had become so acute that some members walked out. The group that boycotted the meeting didn't return to the fold. Then a new group emerged from the dying GLF—the Gay Activist Alliance (GAA).

Unlike GLF, with its tendency to be almost anarchic, the GAA decided its style would take the form of refined advocacy, promising to be "more orderly." However, as subtle it might seem, the GAA was categorical that it would not abandon the radical advocacy gay rights in America: "We as liberated homosexual activists demand the freedom for expression of our dignity and value as human beings," they proclaimed in the preamble to their constitution. And the focus of their work was politics, pressure, and public opinion.

They evolved a scheme. The plot was based on a "developed and perfected confrontational tactic called zap." The chief method of zap was employing an ingenious line of attack involving ambushing people. The group would trap a politician at a public event and then "force him or her to acknowledge gay and lesbian rights." At any public event of note, where a politician was bound to make an appearance, the organization ensured that "GAA members made up the majority of the audience." They would then harass him or her to the point of no choice but to publicly acknowledge gay rights.

Comic as zap might look when compared to past gay militant approaches, still, it wasn't a civil or civilized weapon. But it worked. Gay and lesbians issues were brought to the public sphere faster. Brazenly, they sought opponents for public exchanges. The result was that politicians and other public figures who had hitherto expressed their views candidly without any fear of molestation started becoming jittery. Zap changed the game in favor of homosexuals, giving them protection. They were practically impossible to assault, intimidate, or arrest in the public glare without causing a serious embarrassment.

The '70s thus became a frontier-expanding decade for gay rights activism in America. "Gay Power!" became both a mantra and a war cry. The rapid growth rate of gay groups in America had not been matched in the country's history.

Two years after the Stonewall riots, "every major American city" had gay rights groups. "People who had felt oppressed now felt empowered." Gay activism amassed clout throughout the length and breadth of American society within that short period. Identifiable were voices and faces of the struggle, and people were making historical connections to prove their point. Though the "raids on gay bars had not stopped after the Stonewall riots," gays and lesbians were no longer intimidated.

Swelling with their acquired confidence, they began exporting the aberrant life-style to other countries, beginning with Canada, Australia, and Western Europe, following the template they developed for the "homosexualization of America." The once cacophonous, inchoate, and incoherent disparate groups emerged with a national voice, operating as a cohesive and coordinated Pan-American homosexual movement. All over America, gay groups mushroomed exponentially. Before the Stonewall riots, according to reports, there were only "fifty to sixty gay groups in the country." A year after the incident, the total figure had risen to nearly 1,500. Then, a year later, conservative estimates said, "to the extent that a count could be made," the groups were in the "region of twenty-five hundred." Building on this proliferation, activists midwifed the National Coalition of Gay Organizations.

By 1965, four years before the Stonewall riots, "picketing" of institutions and organizations had been adopted as one weapon of their campaign. At one time or the other, some of the highest American political offices and institutions were targeted, including the White House, the State Department, and a dozen other federal establishments. These efforts peaked around 1965 and 1966. Two newspapers were launched—*Come Out!* and *Gay Power*—both emerging within a six-week period. By 1970, "Gay Pride" marches began. Introduced as commemorative annual events to propagate the homosexuality ideal, they surfaced first in Los Angeles and Chicago and soon spread to Boston, Dallas, and Milwaukee.

The hard and focused work of the gay groups was beginning to pay off. In fact, they had begun to push for the extension of their hold on the American political system. To this end, gay men and lesbians formed a common front in 1977. The aim was to identify political organizations sympathetic to their cause and penetrate them, beginning at the local or grassroots level, where the choice of candidates for elective political offices could be influenced.

However, two major hurdles still stood out, both concerning a shift in public attitude. First was the issue of how to overcome the scientific classification of homosexuality as a disorder. The second was its labelling by the Church as a sin. The two matters—scientific and spiritual rejection of homosexuality—were of critical importance. In fact, the struggle to "de-classify and de-iniquitize" homosexuality dated back to the '50s and '60s.

The claim that homosexuality correlated with a mental disorder happened to be America's peculiar creation. Such a claim did not surface in the public discussion of same-sex attraction in Germany, the United Kingdom, or Canada. In their pioneering studies or during their lifelong campaigns on gay rights, neither Karl Ulrichs, Magnus Hirschfeld, Sigmund Freud, Adolf Brand, nor Leontine Sagan suggested a direct or indirect relationship between homosexuality and mental disorder. The "large-scale study of homosexuality" that was said to have prepared the ground for the classification in the United States showed no concrete evidence of the relationship. The scientific opinion that could most plausibly be linked to that assertion came from Albert Ellis, an American psychologist regarded as the second most influential psychotherapist in the world.

Ellis had written a book entitled *Homosexuality: Its Causes and Cure* in 1965, concluding that it was a "pathology and therefore a condition to be cured."[6] The year before, Ellis had been a guest of the East Coast Homophile Organizations (ECHO), where he stirred the hornets' nest with his presentation and jabbing comments. Matter-of-factly, he had thrown a rib-cracking punch by saying, "The exclusive homosexual is a psychopath." Naturally, his audience had not taken kindly to this comment, and one of his listeners retorted, "Any homosexual who would come to you for treatment, Dr. Ellis, would *have* to be a psychopath!" From the crowd rose a hilarious supporting applause.

The historical context for this exchange was set, in part, in the 1950s, a period characterized as the McCarthy era. Obsessed with safeguarding America at all costs, the government sought to rid every vital American institution of "anarchists, communists, and other people deemed un-American." To rout out the subversive elements, the government utilized congressional committees, which combed "for communists in the U.S. government, the U.S. Army, and other government-funded agencies and institutions." The committees ended up raising more issues than resolutions. Loud were the voices of protestation against Congress's action in connection with several cases of victimization, persecution, oppression, and the like, including some allegedly directed toward homosexuals.

In 1950, a Senate committee chaired by Clyde R. Hoey addressed the allegations of victimization, persecution, and the like levelled against previous government activities. It concluded that "those who engage in overt acts of perversion lack the emotional stability of normal persons." The committee agreed with government intelligence agencies that "sex perverts in Government constitute security risks." Consequently, the US State Department decided to get rid of homosexuals in the agency "on the theory that they were susceptible to blackmail."

Firings and closed job opportunities followed. Within three years, "1,700 federal job applications were denied" to those suspected of being homosexuals. On the same basis, "4,380 people were discharged from the military, and 420 fired from their government jobs." Incidentally, the Mattachine Society was founded around this time, and the bulk of its founders were communists. Those were dangerous times to wear those two labels—communist and homosexual—a period when the Federal Bureau of Investigation (FBI) and the police maintained surveillance through "monitoring of homosexuals, keeping their lists, their favoured establishments, and friends."[7]

6. https://en.wikipedia.org/w/index.php?title=Albert_Ellis&printable=yes.

7. https://en.wikipedia.org/w/index.php?title=Crittenden_Report&printable=yes; https://en.wikipedia.org/w/index.php?title=Lavender_scare&printable=yes; and https://en.wikipedia.org/w/

One of the government's targets was Frank Kameny, classified as a "security risk." On the staff of U.S. Army Map Service, he was fired for being suspected as a homosexual. Endlessly, he struggled to regain his lost job through the courts but to no avail. Annoyed and frustrated, he joined the Mattachine Society and spent his time establishing the Washington, D.C., chapter. Over time, Kameny concluded that the issue involved was far deeper than government policy. What was being questioned was the rational and psychological balance of the homosexual, casting serious aspersions on the mental health of gays and lesbians.

Kameny began to draw the attention of homosexual mental health professionals to the issue at meetings of Mattachine and DOB. He would tease and provoke them, calling his compatriots "abnormal" people.

Back in 1952, the American Psychiatric Association (APA) had classified homosexuality in the *Diagnostic and Statistical Manual* (DSM) as a mental disorder. An important assertion made to justify the claim concerned the homosexual's "supposed pathological hidden fear of the opposite sex," which was grounded in "traumatic parent-child relationships." The problem with the declarations was that they lacked scientifically convincing evidence, and some suspected they were influenced by the politics that characterized America in the '50s and '60s. It raised questions of objectivity and truthfulness.

One factor in the classification may have been Executive Order 10450, issued on April 27, 1953, by President Dwight Eisenhower. It revoked a previous executive order issued by President Harry Truman in 1947. The new order was far reaching, in that it authorized "heads of federal agencies and the Office of Personnel Management, supported by the Federal Bureau of Investigation (FBI)," to investigate federal employees and "determine whether they posed security risks." Though homosexuality was not mentioned specifically, the group of risks identified included "sexual perversion" and those "personal habits [which] are such that they might be subject to blackmail." In effect, one of the outcomes was "banning gay men and lesbians from working for any agency of the federal government." The de facto ban was based on the belief homosexuality represented a "sexual perversion" and the sufferer constituted a risk to state security. The DSM classification lent further credence to the government's position.

Two events were to reshape public opinion. The first was a study by Evelyn Hooker.[8] One of her students in an introductory psychology class in 1944 had fired her curiosity on homosexuality. She earned the student's trust to the extent that he confided in her he was gay, as were most of his friends. She related with him well and extended her sociable attitude to his same-sex friends, whom she concluded were intelligent people. Through their friendship, she met the American writer Christopher Isherwood and poet Stephen Spender, both gay. Then, one day, her student asked,

---

index.php?title=Clyde_R._Hoey&printable=yes.

8. https://en.wikipedia.org/w/index.php?title=Evelyn_Hooker&printable=yes.

Why not conduct research on homosexuals to determine whether homosexuality was some sort of disease or disorder and not relevant to a person's psychological makeup?

Hooker was intrigued by the challenge. The years of her troubled childhood flooded back to her memory, for she had suffered acute social rejection through those difficult times. In her professional life, too, she was not spared discrimination; she had had to work as a lowly maid for a family of landed gentry. As tough as the journey was, she always mustered the psychological strength to keep afloat in the stormy oceans of life. Unfortunately, the professional and private life of Evelyn Gentry—her maiden name—took a different course for the next twenty years after her student prompted her homosexual research.

She married Edward Hooker, a professor of English at UCLA. By stroke of coincidence, Christopher Isherwood became a neighbor. He was the gay writer she met through her friend and student. Hooker might be interested in studying homosexuality, but she wasn't sympathetic to living below the morally acceptable boundary. She disliked the partnership of the elderly gay Christopher Isherwood with a much younger Don Bachardy. Firmly and sternly, she declared her house out of bounds to the two gay neighbors. In the meantime, she put her study in gear. She had begun collecting her data in 1954, taking advantage of close relationship with her homosexual friends, but the study lacked scientific rigor.

Hooker turned to the National Institute of Mental Health (NIMH) for assistance, and her funded research employed a sample of thirty heterosexual men and thirty homosexual men. They were paired, based on "equivalent IQ (Intelligence Quotient), age, and education." To eliminate bias, she ensured "that none of the men from either group have previously been seen for psychological help, in disciplinary barracks in the Armed Services, in prison, showed evidence of considerable disturbance, or were in therapy." For her "exclusively homosexual" group, she "contacted the Mattachine Society to find a large portion of homosexual men."

A major limitation which she confessed was the "greater difficulty finding heterosexual men for the study." The interviews on which the interpretation of her data was based were conducted at her home "to protect the participants' anonymity." Working for a year, she came up with sixty unmarked psychological profiles. To avoid possible personal bias, she submitted her work to three experts for interpretation, all respectable professionals in the field of psychology. They used different methods, with one taking six months for his analysis and another performing his exercise twice to ensure a satisfactory level of accuracy.

In the end, the trio arrived at the same conclusion. Their verdict was that "both groups were highly similar in their psychological make-up." Hooker's study ran for two years, beginning in 1954 and ending in 1956.

In 1956, when she finished her research, she was the toast of the American Psychological Association at its convention in Chicago. She took the podium to present her findings, contending that "homosexuality is not a mental disorder, as there was no detectable difference between homosexual and heterosexual men in terms of mental adjustment." It was a bombshell. This was not the belief of government. The view also contradicted the existing stand of the association. Hooker's argument was that the error had arisen from narrow sampling of "homosexual men with a history of treatment for mental illness." Even before Hooker's report, a fact not known to many Americans was that a government committee had clarified the same cloudy issue of perception about homosexuality within government circles.

Known as the Crittenden Report and released in 1957, the report was at the behest of the United States Navy Board of Inquiry.[9] The focus of the committee's work was direct and explicit—to undertake a "revision of policies, procedures and directives dealing with homosexuals." The conclusion of the committee in plain and unequivocal language was that there was "no sound basis for the belief that homosexuals posed a security risk." In justifying its position, the committee pointed to the fact that "no intelligence agency, as far as can be learned, adduced any factual data . . . with which to support these opinions." Though submitted on March 15, 1957, the Crittenden Report was safely hidden in a drawer and was gathering dust until 1976. By that time, the homosexual rights movement had acquired a militancy that enabled it to overpower the American Psychiatric Association and forced the association to delete homosexuality's "mental disorder" classification from its book.

Hooker, in the meantime, benefited from government's tardiness in that it opened for her a fresh window of professional opportunity and fame. She became an instant success, a celebrity sought as a national and international speaker. In 1961, apart from the fact that the report led to further support of her work by the NIMH, the institution invited her to "produce a report on what the institution should do about homosexual men." Hooker recommended "decriminalization of homosexuality." In addition, she advocated "the provision of similar rights to both homosexual and heterosexual people." She submitted her report in 1969, shortly after Richard Nixon's election as president. The politics of the time stalled any consideration of the report, but the hold would prove temporary.

Hooker's report found its way to the press in 1970, and the American gay rights movement seized upon it as a vital assault weapon, and their first target was the American Psychiatric Association. They pounced on the APA for its DSM classification of homosexuality as a "mental disorder."

Every cause has its public faces and its people-behind-the-scene—and Frank Kameny occupied both categories eminently. He never forgave the government for booting him out of his job for being a gay. Kameny was resentful, a bomb looking for an

9. Crittenden Report, https://en.wikipedia.org/w/index.php?title=Crittenden_Report&printable=yes.

opportunity to explode, inflicting injury on the government. He was the brain behind picketing of the White House and other government agencies in Washington, D.C. He was also an early proponent of the militarizing the gay struggle. Whenever there was any opportunity to confront government, he lined up to be counted. No American better matched the anarchist character of the London gay rights campaigner Paul Tatchell than him.

He was, at the same time, a frontline general and a foot soldier in the fight; he was at home both in the trenches and in the halls. Fortunately, for him, he had a female counterpart, Barbara Gittings. She matched him in every way except that she didn't work for the government and had not been dismissed by it for being a lesbian. But she supported militarization of the struggle. Indeed, she was side by side with Kameny in picketing the White House and other federal establishments. In many of the gay movement's defiant acts of the period, Gittings was a commanding figure. She was a member of the Daughters of Bilitis, the president of its New York chapter. Less agreeable to her was the pacifist style of its founders. She preferred a more radical, combative approach.

She took over editorship of the organization's newsletter, *The Ladder*, from Del Martin. Gittings turned the informational journal into revolutionary propaganda media. She introduced a personal column called "Living Propaganda." The objective was to encourage women to "come out" to their friends and family members about their lesbianism. Her association with Frank Kameny, whom she found to be a soul mate, demonstrated her thinking and attitude in the struggle. Constantly, she used the latter's articles to urge "political action," and she began aligning DOB with other social and political clubs of gays and lesbians. This did not go over well with DOB leaders, who disliked Kameny, whom Gittings' used extensively in the magazine. So she was terminated as editor of the newspaper in 1966. But following the 1969 Stonewall riots, Kameny and Gittings read the omens accurately, that militancy in the gay struggle was inevitable.

The timing of the leakage of Evelyn Hooker's report in 1970 must have been plotted. The American Psychiatric Association was scheduled to have its convention in May of that year in Los Angeles. Around the same time, the Gay Liberation Front of Los Angeles was to meet, and they decided to zap the APA convention, using the strategy developed by the Gay Activists Alliance.

Conference attendees were unaware what was afoot. The GLF had, however, ensured that its members were planted in strategic positions throughout the hall. Then, as customary with such scientific gatherings, a member was given the nod to make his presentation. Coincidentally, the theme of the conference was "behavior modification." In exploring the subject, he had relied on a film to demonstrate how what he called "electroshock therapy" could be applied to decrease same-sex attraction. From the crowd, a lone voice embarrassingly interrupted the presentation with a shout of "Torture!" followed by another cry, "Barbarism!" Before the packed hall figured out what was happening, others shouted those words, drowning out everything else, shocking the presenter. The microphone was seized, and a mob of protesters overran the stage. With microphone in hand, a protester proclaimed that "medical professionals who prescribed such therapy for their homosexual patients were complicit in torturing them."

Disturbed by the rude and uncivilized interruption of their conference, twenty of the psychiatrists stormed out of the hall, but there was no forum for rational appeal there. The GLF had declared war on the conference with a resolute will to zap the American Psychiatric Association. Their mission was to ambush the delegates and all the public figures at the conference and cow them into submission until they acknowledge gay rights. Those wise enough to dash for a quick exit were lucky. Those remaining in the hall were given a message to take away to their other colleagues, that "homosexuals were not mentally ill."

The following year, in 1971, the APA conference was zapped again. The convention, held in Washington, chose the wrong place to convene. It was Kameny's territory. Pushing himself onto to the podium, he seized the microphone and poured loud invectives on psychiatrists who diagnosed homosexuality as a mental disorder.

The APA decided therefore that its 1972 annual conference should be devoted to the subject, choosing a noncommittal theme, "Psychiatry: Friend or Foe to Homosexuals: A Dialogue." Kameny and Gittings loved the choice. Eagerly, the two were looking forward to the D-day. Theirs was an unquenchable thirst to hit the government hard and to ridicule it, including those perceived to be its collaborators, including the APA.

Participants approached the meeting with caution, but they weren't prepared for the comedic melodrama that ensued. Proceedings were going smoothly when a man jumped on the stage. He was dressed comically in a tuxedo with a wig to match and a mask. The ill-fitting costume contrasted sharply with the impeccable dress of the men and women in the hall. After finding his way to the stage, he took over a seat left by members of the association who had previously spoken. Another man on the right side (Kameny) and a woman on the left (Gittings) flanked the mystery man, and the three sat imperiously, watching the audience below them intensely.

Kameny then took the microphone and introduced the speaker, a "Dr H. Anonymous," whose voice was muffled because the mic had been tampered with to disguise it. He began with the words, "I am a homosexual," followed with, "I am a psychiatrist" and then spoke of "the lives of the many gay psychiatrists among the American Psychiatric Association." To help audience members believe the claim, "Dr. Anonymous" described in vivid details how they "had to hide their sexuality from their colleagues for fear of discrimination." Worse for them, they couldn't even relate to their "fellow homosexuals owing to the disdain in which the psychiatric profession was held among the gay community."

He challenged his colleagues in two areas. First, to find "ways in which gay psychiatrists could subtly and 'creatively' challenge prejudice in their profession without disclosing their sexuality"; second, to "help gay patients adjust to a society that considered their sexual preferences a sign of psychopathology." There was no report that anyone staged a walkout. (The identity of the mystery "Dr. Anonymous" became known later—34-year-old John Fryer, a gay psychiatrist.)

A report widely fed to the public was that the APA "voted 13–10 to remove homosexuality from its *DSM-II* (the official list of psychiatric disorders)" in 1973. An additional resolution followed—to urge "an end to all private and public discrimination against homosexuals." There was serious contention, however, about how the decisions were reached. The public was said to have been fed half-truths regarding what transpired behind the closed doors over the matter, according to a well-placed insider, Dr. Jeffrey Satinover, a former fellow in psychiatry and child psychiatry at Yale University. Satinover was so moved by the dishonesty of the events that he felt compelled to share the truth of what had really happened in a book, *Homosexuality and the Politics of Truth*.[10]

He reported, "When the committee met formally to consider the issue in 1973, the outcome had already been arranged behind closed doors." Satinover was a psychiatrist and not an activist; otherwise, he would have known that APA committee members like him faced a *coup de theatre*: "No new data was introduced, and objectors were given only fifteen minutes to present a rebuttal." Satinover lamented the "series of political manoeuvres, lies and outright flim-flams" employed. The result, he noted painfully, was that those "who did not go along with the political definition were soon silenced at our professional meetings." Science was over, and politics was the game.

Dr. Charles Socarides (an expert in clinical psychiatry at Albert Einstein College of Medicine and Montefiore Medical Centre in New York, and also a former president of the National Association for Research and Therapy of Homosexuality) was another insider who found the shift objectionable. Socarides was part of a vocal minority within psychiatry that saw dangers ahead in an America condoning hedonism. *Homosexuality: A Freedom Gone Too Far!* was both the title of his book and the pivot on which he stood.[11]

From the blowback to his book, one would think it wasn't homosexuality that had gone too far, but rather Socarides! "Our lectures were cancelled inside academe," and our "research papers [were] turned down in the learned journals." Helplessly, he watched as "worse things followed in the culture at large." Television and the motion picture industry began to promote "homosexuality as a legitimate lifestyle." Publishers started turning down books "objecting to the gay revolution." Even schools were not spared. Gays and lesbians had started to shape the content and teaching of sex education, as well as determining the makeup of college faculty committees.

10. https://en.wikipedia.org/wiki/Jeffrey_Satinover.
11. https://en.wikipedia.org/wiki/Charles_W._Socarides.

By 1996, Socarides was mourning the rapid changes in an article for *The Journal of Human Sexuality.* The rate that America had gone gay was unbelievable. In less than half a century, gays and lesbians were no longer asking for tolerance and acceptance from society. Rather, they were now out to subdue and dominate the world in which they were a fractional part. Twentieth-century America had caved in and given way to a sweeping moral collapse.

To achieve that aim, the homosexual movement didn't just work harder, it worked smarter. From 1972, gay activists had begun making steady and aggressive inroads into national politics. The first incursion was into the Democratic Party. Gay issues and gay delegates were featured for the first time in 1972 at the Democratic National Convention. Then they moved to consolidate their gains.

They formed an umbrella organization called the National Coalition of Gay Organizations, which published the *Gay Platform,* a sort of gay manifesto. Both the declaration and the organization resulted from a national convention in Chicago, hence the platform's alternate title, the "Chicago Declaration." It contained a 17-point demand, nine of the requests directed to the federal government and eight to state governments.[12]

It called on the authorities to amend "all federal Civil Rights Acts, other legislation and government controls to prohibit discrimination in employment, housing, public accommodations and public services." It also sought "issuance by the President of an executive order prohibiting discrimination in the federal civil service because of sexual orientation, in hiring and promoting; and prohibiting discriminations against homosexuals in security clearances." (Of course, Frank Kameny, with his history, was particularly keen on these demands.) They went on to urge "federal encouragement and support for sex education courses, prepared and taught by gay women and men, presenting homosexuality as a valid, healthy preference and lifestyle as a viable alternative to heterosexuality."

They also called for the repeal "of all state laws prohibiting private sexual acts involving consenting persons; equalization for homosexuals and heterosexuals for the enforcement of all laws"; the repeal of "all state laws prohibiting solicitation for private voluntary sexual liaisons; and laws prohibiting prostitution, both male and female;" and, most alarming, the repeal "of all laws governing the age of sexual consent." In other words, government must licence hedonism and close its eyes to the self-indulgent debauchery of the small minority who lacked the strength of character to exercise self-control.

It went on to endorse the repeal "of all legislative provisions that restrict the sex or number of persons entering into a marriage unit" and "the extension of legal benefits to all persons who cohabit regardless of sex or numbers." In other words, the homosexuals wanted to legalize all forms of polyamory, including one man relating with many men, one woman to many women, one man to many women, or one woman

12. "The 1972 Gay Rights Platform Platform."

to many men, as the case may be. There was every reason, therefore, to agonize along with Socarides, who sounded the warning as early as possible over *Homosexuality: A Freedom Too Far!*

Almost invisible to the majority was the deliberate manipulation of their minds. America was not up against an external enemy, which would have raised their guard. The homosexual movement had cashed in on the innocence and simple-mindedness of the American people, using one of the vilest weapons for corrupting the mind: propaganda. Adolf Hitler's *Mein Kampf* was exhumed from its resting place. Exported to the United States, it became their handy manual. From it, they developed a six-point strategy of accomplishing a radical change in "America's perception of homosexual behaviour."

The overall strategies were short, easy to learn and memorize, and uncomplicated to deliver. Every activist was expected to be familiar with the instructional manual. The general thrust was to "talk about gays and gayness loudly and [as] often as possible." Secondly, in all situations, they must "portray gays as victims," and never as "aggressive challengers"; they were always to be presented as objects of persecution. The third strategy concerned the necessity of drawing sympathy to "gay homosexual protectors" by making their actions look and sound like "a just cause." The fourth was to "make gays look good"; the fifth, on the other hand, was "to make victimizers look bad," to demonize them. The last directed activists to "solicit for funds," to get "corporate America and the foundations to financially support the homosexual cause."

In less than 25 years, the American gay rights movement had recorded a huge success. The accomplishments were phenomenal, never recorded in the worldwide history of the gay rights campaign. American was no longer the same. The goal of a "radical shift in public attitudes toward homosexual behaviour" was achieved. Hardly was there any portion of American life and society left untouched. There was infiltration everywhere, from government to business, from educational to scientific, cultural, military, judicial, media, and creative organizations. They had succeeded in making homosexuality a populist agenda that dominated the public space.

Gays and lesbians were no longer talking about living cooperatively in society. They had a new goal—to "reinvent human nature, [and] reinvent themselves." There was also a vision of a bigger and grander scheme. From Dennis Altman's *Homosexualisation of America,* which was considered an authoritative account of how the American success was achieved, came the unfolding of the larger plan for the entire world. The United States was no longer to be the sole target of the hedonistic culture. The long-term objective would be "to make the whole world gay."

The new age had bred narcissistic men and women driven by triumphalism. There was, however, the attendant problem of church and religion. People hold on to them as strong points of protection. Unless the homosexual movement destroyed these last two standing shields of society, the probability of their achieving their aim was zero. In fact, Magnus Hirschfeld and his *Wissenschaftlich-humanitares Komitee* learned this bitter truth. Hirschfeld had disregarded the "traditional Christian injunctions against homosexuality" in his work, and church leaders had little trouble prevailing over his arguments. They simply supplied the parliament with biblical texts containing prohibitions of homosexuality. The matter ended abruptly, partly owing to this response. But the American gay rights movement was wiser than its German counterpart. It didn't treat the church as an unimportant institution. Indeed, it saw the church as a key organ of the society that must be penetrated and perverted.

As far back as 1964, the American Council on Religion and the Homosexual (CRH) had been formed.[13] Still, the church remained the apparent biggest obstacle to mainstreaming homosexuality in the American life. The desire for votes and money that made American politics vulnerable to the gay rights assault had little impact on the church at first. The confrontation and defiance that checkmated the police were of no effect on the church either. Zapping too was ineffective, though the American Psychiatric Association was forced through it to delist homosexuality as a mental disorder. God's pronouncement about homosexuality in the Scriptures was clear, unequivocal, and immutable. In fact, of the four churches—Methodist, Episcopal, United Church of Christ, and Lutheran—whose sixteen clergy had gathered with thirteen leaders of the homosexual community to form the CRH, none had officially changed its stance on homosexuality by 1972.

Of course, spirited efforts were made to create defiance within religious circles. In 1968, for instance, four years after the launch of the CRH, a Pentecostal minister, Troy Perry, tried to establish "the first openly homosexual denomination." But his efforts didn't amount to much as his Metropolitan Community Church failed to become a significant Christian denomination. Ten years after the so-called first homosexual denomination, the American church was still tightly shut to the homosexual movement, and the door to the priestly order was still tightly closed against it. Though there were seven gays and lesbians in elective positions nationally at the time, gay clergy numbered only two. The duo, Anne Holmes of the United Church of Christ and Ellen Barrett of the Episcopal Church of the United States, shared the same ordination year of 1977. In time, a severe crisis was to arise in connection with the two ordinations, particularly in the Episcopal Church, which experienced implosion.

Having charted its course, the homosexual movement didn't relent. Changing the church was pursued with the same fanatical obsession with which the movement attempted to damage other institutions. Numerous gay advocacy groups began to spring up in some of the major American denominations. In the Lutheran Church, for example, Lutherans Concerned was born. The United Methodists had Affirmation. In the case of the Episcopal Church, it was Integrity. In the Catholic Church, the covert organization was Dignity. And then there was Kinship, which was Seventh Day Adventist.

---

13. https://en.wikipedia.org/w/index.php?title=Council_on_Religion_and_the_Homosexual &printable=yes.

Dr. Louie Crew was the point man for the Episcopal campaign. In 1974, he chose the Grace Cathedral in San Francisco to begin the infiltration of the church. He went to the church asking to be connected with fellow gay Episcopalians, knowing full well the church had no such directory to hand to him.[14]

San Francisco had built the image of being a perfect place for the job at hand, the place where irrepressible Bishop James Pike found indulgence for his ceaseless defamatory attacks on Christian theology. Pike was a shining sun in the America's religious firmament of the '60s as Rev. Martin Luther King Jr. was for the civil rights movement, but he ended as one of the period's tragic heroes. His impressive education and scholastic brain only brought him an acute identity crisis. At 33, after a number of leading jobs, he settled finally for priesthood, where, within a short time, he ruffled feathers. Three times—in 1964, 1965, and 1966—the church contemplated sanctioning him. Pike's maverick nature and iconoclastic achievements in social causes intimidated his colleagues.

In time, he helped relieve the church of its deep embarrassment by voluntarily abdicating his episcopate in 1966. Twenty years of his ministry were not helpful to the life of the Episcopal Church. Gone was the authority the church exercised over its officials. Broken was the control that the church exercised over doctrinal, canonical, spiritual, and moral matters. With Pike, the leadership and institutional integrity of the Episcopal Church evaporated. The church's critical governing institutions—the presiding bishop and the House of Bishops—lost control. Over the years, other sundry developments combined with the Pike affair to make the church rudderless, leaderless, and predisposed to wanton abuse from many quarters. The Episcopal Church in the United States of America tragically became a church of "anything goes." Any mention of San Francisco could not but raise ghosts of Pike.

Then there was the shocking behavior of the double-faced bishop Otis Charles, who waited to exploit all the prerogatives of his office before seeking refuge in San Francisco for his post-episcopate, gay hara-kiri, the same San Francisco where Harry Hay's same-sex peccadilloes found robust expression, home of the Mattachine Society. When Del Martin deserted her husband and child in favor of her young lesbian partner Phyllis Lyon, the nest to incubate and hatch the relationship was none other than San Francisco. The first successful national convention of the Daughters of Bilitis took place there. Moreover, San Francisco was the birthplace of the Council on Religion and the Homosexual (CRH). So, it was no accident that Crew undertook his work in San Francisco.

At first, Integrity USA revolved around Crew. Then, it morphed into a pressure group consisting of his few cohorts. After that, it grew into a network, building alliances at all levels of the church. Finally, Integrity USA emerged as a power bloc within the church, with collaborators such as the Rt. Rev. John Spong, bishop of Newark, who

14. https://en.wikipedia.org/w/index.php?title=Louie_Crew&oldid=684019043.

helped open the door wide for Crew to have unimpeded access to the heart and soul of the church.

If Crew was an incurable maverick, Bishop John Spong was a headstrong eccentric. Spong and Crew were a powerful duo, one a priest-king, the other a doting zealot; one the ego, the other the alter ego. Spong and Crew were products of the same generation, the former having a five-year edge over his comrade-in-arms (Spong was born in 1931, Crew in 1936). Beyond age, however, Spong had an advantage. He was a priest, an ordained minister of God. Spong had donned the collar when he was 24 years of age, and, from 1955, when he took on the vocational calling, to 1979, when he became the bishop of Newark diocese, he had a string of pastoral appointments in various parishes. He was, in many ways, a carbon copy of Bishop James Pike—and even worse in that he was constantly stirring controversies with his heretical views and his ridicule of the church.[15]

Spong and Crew's symbiotic relationship resembled that of Frank Kameny and Barbara Gittings. Spong had no regard for the rule of law, nor respect for authority. In utter contravention of the canon, doctrine, and directive of the Episcopal Church and the larger Anglican Communion worldwide, he ordained the first Episcopal gay priest on December 16, 1989. The 34-year old Robert Williams, raised a Southern Baptist, founded the Texas branch of Integrity USA. (Both Crew's movement to the Newark diocese and the ordination of Williams occurred in 1989.) A major part of the scandal surrounding Williams' ordination, however, was his sordid life; he wasn't shy about publicly flaunting his homosexuality. Spong used Williams to found The Oasis, an outreach for the homosexuals within the Episcopal Church. The patron and the protégé eventually fell out in an irreconcilable split. Subsequently, Williams died of AIDS, but The Oasis survived. And their work, whereby Integrity USA and The Oasis joined to overturn the Episcopal Church's long-standing position on homosexuality, brought on the crisis they desired.

Beginning in the '80s and pursued intensely for 20 years, a variety of theological sources were used to justify homosexuality. But activists' goal remained a utopian dream; they kept encountering serious obstacles from the resolute opposing group within the church. The result was that the gay issue divided the church. Not even political manipulations at the highest level of the church succeeded in silencing the anti-gay Episcopalians. The pockets of resistance had always remained active.

The gay movement had not anticipated such strenuous opposition from within the Episcopal Church. It had assumed the church to be a walkover. As with the APA, plots were hatched to counteract churches that rigidly adhered to the Scriptures. The American Episcopal Church was not counted as one of those scripture-based churches; it was considered to be a "more liberal" church with "Scriptural and theological vulnerability."

15. http://en.wikipedia.org/w/index.php?title=John_Shelby_Spong &oldid=673261444; Stannard, "Hero or Heretic, Spong Won't Be Forgotten"; Hirsley, "Episcopalians Approve Guidelines That Conflict On Homosexuality."

So they were confident in a subtle approach to influence it "toward a pro-gay position." Whatever judgement or knowledge the plan was based on, it fell short.

The entire Episcopal Church in the United States of America did not go gay, and even if it had, it would be naïve to assume that this would force the rest of the Anglican Communion to go gay, especially considering that the issues in question concerned God's Word—not politics, police, science, or a professional group's classification. The undiluted Word of God remained the core issue. Without doubt, the gay struggle in America did emerge from obscurity into the heart of the nation and the public agenda. The Episcopal Church, however, did not constitute the global Anglican Communion, especially in an era when imperialism was no longer in fashion. And, indeed, the indications were strong that those who would not go gay in the Anglican Communion would maintain their stand—fearlessly, confidently, and resolutely.

16

Nigeria Will Not Go Gay

Nigeria, 2004

W ithin a day, the Church of Nigeria made a decision that was an obvious reply to its American counterpart's illusion that it could force every part of the
Communion to go gay. Usually, the Standing Committee of the Church, its highest
governing organ, met twice a year. The committee had perfected a methodical system
of working. It set up various committees whose responsibilities included preparing
position papers. The appropriate committee in charge of a particular subject or issue
would examine matters, consider the developments, and then present a report suggesting a range of options.

At the March 12, 2004, meeting held in Ilesha, in the southwestern part of Nigeria, the Committee on Global Anglican Relations brought a list of issues for consideration of the national leaders of the church.[1] A number of the issues centred specifically
on the type of relationship the CON should maintain with churches that were violating the Scriptures as well as disobeying the position of the Communion on the issue
of human sexuality. The position paper examined the view that the Church of Nigeria
and those parts within it which were "in link with the over-liberal ECUSA dioceses
should relinquish such links." Furthermore, the Committee on Global Anglican Relations stated that the national leaders of the church should direct concerned "diocesan
bishops" to "take immediate action." In addition, the committee urged the church
leaders to direct the "Primate to write retired Bishops to desist from recommend-
ing priests for overseas scholarships." Put simply, the Committee on Global Anglican
Relations wanted the Nigerian church to sever links with churches violating the scripture, ensure that its house was in order, and maintain discipline across every level of
its collective membership.

---

1. "Minutes of the Standing Committee Meeting," from the Archives of the National Headquarters
of the Church of Nigeria (Anglican Communion), Abuja, FCT, Nigeria.

Once a committee made its presentation at the plenary session of the meeting, the usual style was for the Nigerian church leader to call for discussions before decisions were made. Archbishop Akinola had hardly finished placing the report on the floor of the house when a hand shot up from the hall; it belonged to the Very Revd. Yinka Omololu, provost of The Cathedral Church of Christ, Marina, Lagos.[2]

"Yes, Very Revd. Yinka Omololu?" Archbishop Akinola called out quizzically.

Omololu replied that he would like to make a motion.

"What's your motion all about?" the archbishop inquired.

Responding in a clear voice, he said the general thrust of his motion was for the CON to take a definite stand on the revisionist tendencies and defiance of some of its colleague churches in the Communion.

Omololu was not a frivolous man. Slim, athletic, and bespectacled, he was as staunch as his straight physique and he stood firm on the Bible. Discipline was not foreign to him. By vocation, Omololu was a soldier and a doctor by training. He later settled to work as a fisher of men. After qualifying as a medical doctor, he had joined the Nigerian Navy, where he rose to become chief of naval medical services. An eighteen-year medical career along with the comfort of a top military position didn't dim his desire to preach the Word and work for God. He was ordained in 1984, and rose to become the sixth provost of the oldest cathedral in Nigeria.

As he rose to his full height, he gave the archbishop a soldierly stare and waited for his green light to continue. Somebody had to second the motion, so Archbishop Akinola asked if anyone in the hall wanted to support Omololu's proposal. If no one showed interest, then the motion was as good as dead on arrival. From the hall, another hand rose into the air. A white cassock eased itself into the air, followed by the voice of Ven. F. C. Chukwuka from Jalingo Diocese. Incidentally, neither of the two, Omololu, the proponent, nor Chukwuka, the seconder of the motion, was a member of the Global Anglican Relations Committee.

Three other interrelated steps were required before the process reached its culmination. The archbishop had to ask first if any counter-motion existed. In other words, was there anyone feeling otherwise about the propriety of the motion? No hand went up. No voice was heard. Finally, he asked Omololu for his motion. Enunciating every word, he spoke boldly into the microphone for everybody to hear:

> I move that the Church of Nigeria (Anglican Communion) should remain in communion with Anglican Dioceses that take a similar stand as our Communion on human sexuality, that is, being biblically-based. Where a Diocese differs with our stand and what the Bible teaches on homosexuality, we should make necessary arrangements to provide spiritual cover for our members in such Dioceses.

Done, Omololu took his seat.

2. Fafowora, *The Cathedral Church of Christ Marina, Lagos (1867–2007)*.

The archbishop called for the required vote on the motion. It was a voice vote.

"Those in agreement with the motion say 'yes,'" he requested.

The hall was rocked with a thunderous "yes."

Those against the proposal should say no. There was not a single faint "nay."

This, then, was the position of the Church of Nigeria as the archbishop read out the motion verbatim again. A rider accompanied the motion, to the effect that:

> The Primate and the Secretariat are given the end of March to put necessary modalities in place to execute the decision of the Standing Committee.

The two major decisions of the March 2004 meeting of the CON were certainly revolutionary. Yet those conclusions sounded and looked laughable. What powers and influence did the Nigerian church or its leaders have that could match that of their American counterparts? Did they have resources to stand up to the churches of the West that were the culprits? What experience and exposure or pedigree in pursuing social causes did they have, whether at home or in the world at large, that they could draw strength from in fulfilling their mission? Simple as the two decisions sounded, in practical terms, their implications were severe.

Apart from redefining relations with dioceses considered turncoats, the Nigerian church's decision to provide a "spiritual cover" for their members in those places where there had been perversion of the Holy Bible could not but be provocative. The Anglican Communion had a traditional policy guiding that type of decision. Provinces were not supposed to cross boundaries without first obtaining the consent of the host provinces. However, the times were not ordinary, and the issues involved were not conventional. Indeed, the Nigeria church's decision was like David coming against Goliath—without doubt, facing three giants (America, Canada, and Britain)—who would stop at nothing to enforce their decision across the Communion. How possible was it for a minion like the Nigerian church with no experience in international politics to take on this challenge? The fact was that Nigerian church leaders not only wanted action; they also desired it promptly. They had met in March and had ordered that the Nigerian primate ensure by "the end of March to put necessary modalities" in place to execute the decisions.

Though it was a CON decision, only one person was the face of this action in the international arena. The person was Archbishop Akinola, whose position was not enviable at the time. He was placed in a very vulnerable situation, expected to do the bidding of the CON, that is, to take on the American church. A lot of people did not realize the vicious but surreptitious work of the gay movement, which was proving to be an octopus, an all-crushing, sturdy machine with massive powers and connections across the world. Metaphorically, the decision of the Nigerian church was like hanging a cat in the mouth of a hyena; or, to use a biblical analogy, like throwing another Daniel into the lion's den. To take on the American church was tantamount to challenging the entire American gay machine, which had placed a target on the backs of those who adhere rigidly to an authoritarian belief structure (i.e. an orthodox religion), that condemns homosexuality . . . our primary objective regarding die-hard homohaters of this sort is to cow and silence them.[3]

But it didn't appear in the least that Archbishop Akinola was frightened by the threat of the gay movement to "cow and silence" opponents. He was ready to carry on with the cause as he presided over the meeting of the Global South primates in Nairobi, Kenya, ten months after the Nigerian vote.[4] It was obvious that the two-day meeting held January 27–28, 2005, could not end without addressing the homosexual issue. First, however, there were a number of miscellaneous matters, which included setting the date for their third South-South Encounter in Egypt for October 25–31.

The primates then moved to the central point of their agenda—the report of the Lambeth Commission, the Windsor Report. If they had any division regarding the recommendations, the areas of disagreement would be few and minor. They were beginning to sound like a broken record repeating the same old message of how the American Episcopal Church and its Canadian neighbor had "torn the fabric of our Communion." They added that "to date, there have been no concrete steps taken towards repentance and reconciliation."

At the Kenya meeting, the tone changed. This time around, they went beyond talking tough to setting deadlines for a positive response to their resolutions. This was extraordinary for the Global South leaders. Even when their Western counterparts were riding them like camels, they had still maintained a peaceful demeanor, but that was changing, as they stated:

> Failing any substantial change in direction within the next three months (i.e. by May 31st 2005) the Global South Primates and the others who share our convictions would confirm that they have chosen to "walk alone" and follow another religion.

They were specific about the form and manner in which the change in direction must occur. The two North American churches must "move beyond informal expression of regret for the effect of their actions" and show clearly a "genuine change of heart and mind." One had to wonder whether these Global South Anglicans were serious? Were they being realistic? How feasible were their propositions?

How could anyone believe the American and Canadian churches would comply with the request? In fact, the primates had the evidence in their hands, but they either glossed over it or decided to ignore it. The Lambeth Commission's chairman, the Most Rev. Robert Eames, in his preface to the Windsor Report had laid bare the contemptuous manner with which the commission was treated by the two North American

3. Woodliff, "Rediscovering Christian Orthodoxy in Episcopal Anglicanism."

4. Global South Primates, "A Statement from Global South Primates Meeting in Nairobi, January 27th/28th, 2005," from the Private Papers and Collection of Archbishop Peter Akinola.

churches.[5] He drew attention to the fact that both the archbishop of Canterbury and the primates had counselled all parties to the crisis to maintain the status quo during the commission's work period. And the chairman recalled that it was exactly during this period that the General Synod of the Canadian Church decided to affirm "the integrity and sanctity of committed adult same-sex relationships." As for the Americans, their bishops continued to take actions defying the instruction of the Communion; for instance, Bishops John Chane and Jon Bruno of the Washington and Los Angeles dioceses respectively chose to bless formally long-time same-sex relationships.[6]

At the same time, the man at the center of the crisis, Gene Robinson, was not repentant. He continued to make incendiary speeches. In a *Washington Times* interview of October 10, 2004, Robinson's utterances were deliberately provocative and profane. "The Bible has been 'hijacked by the religious right,'" he told his interviewer. "It's time we take it back," he remonstrated, continuing brazenly, "I keep on saying to gay and lesbian people: Let's reclaim this book. It is our story." And he boasted, "Even if anything happened to me, there are gay and lesbian people everywhere waiting to be elected."[7]

On January 13, 2005, the American House of Bishops met in Salt Lake City, Utah, and the Windsor Report was on the table.[8] The bishops were sharply divided on the matter, some of them supporting the call for repentance as the report recommended. They came out with "A Statement of Acceptance and Submission," agreeing on the necessity of "renouncing the actions that have been so injurious to our common life" and accepting the requirement "that in the future they [The Episcopal Church] will only act in ways that are 'fully compatible with the interests, standards, unity and order of the Anglican Communion.'" The group was certainly being contrite, and their appeal was rational. Unfortunately, these conciliatory bishops were in the minority, though they enjoyed the support of the Global South primates, who had called on the majority to join them "in declaring full communion with these bishops."

The Episcopal Church presiding bishop, Frank Griswold, didn't delay a moment in letting his Global South colleagues know that they must be acting under an illusion to assume repentance on part of the American church. In an interview with *Religion and Ethics Weekly*, he was frank in his deprecation. He told them it was futile to ask the Episcopal Church to mend its ways. To him, the Bible "is an unfolding reality and is not simply fixed or circumscribed at a particular moment or by the pages of Scripture itself."[9] In other words, nothing is wrong if the "Holy Spirit has inspired and led to

5. "The Lambeth Commission of Communion—The Windsor Report 2004."

6. Murphy, "Episcopal Bishop to Bless Gay Priest's Union in Md."; https://en.wikipedia.org/w/index.php?title=J._Jon_Bruno&printable=yes.

7. http://en.wikipedia.org/wiki/Gene_Robinson.

8. American Anglican Council, "A Timeline of Defining Actions"; Woodliff, "Rediscovering Christian Orthodoxy in Episcopal Anglicanism."

9. http://en.wikipedia.org/w/index.php?title=Frank_Griswold&oldid=593526410.

new understanding and appreciations." So, there was a standoff, with the Episcopal Church insisting that its own version of the Bible could be edited and re-edited at will, while the Global South primates maintained that "faithfulness to the Holy Scriptures" should be a condition for reconciliation of the crisis.

One clear rule of engagement in conflict is to never give an ultimatum that cannot be followed up by decisive action. The Episcopal Church was a veteran in psychological warfare. It had fought numerous battles both within its domestic environment and internationally. At hand were the internet, social media, and other potent tools of the modern information age. At its disposal were allies, including Canada, England, Scotland, Ireland, and South Africa. Hovering above all, was the vile, malevolent, and omnipresent octopus—the gay movement. What could a group like the Global South boast of? Was it their number, the strength of being the biggest bloc in the Communion? No, in modern warfare, demographic size has ceased to count. The deciding factors are technology, skill, and resources. Nevertheless, history has shown that the best army can lose the most elementary war. Other factors may undermine well-constructed plans.

As should be expected, the Episcopal Church replied with the usual defiance. Its leaders snubbed their Global South colleagues, calling their supposed bluff contemptuously. Nevertheless, Archbishop Akinola was not one to betray a trust. Once he had pledged himself to a position, he remained inflexible. Of course, he had no shortage of critics. Equally determined was the homosexual movement, which did not believe in concession. There was no going back until they had their way—that the worldwide Anglican Church must go gay.

So Akinola came to be viewed as an enemy of gays worldwide, one to be "cowed and silenced," but he refused to be intimidated. He was unfazed and untroubled. Boldly and courageously, he stood firm against all the odds. As he explained,

> I was ready, I was prepared, and I was not perturbed in any way because the battle was for the Lord who declared homosexuality a sin to fight. Whatever the desperation to obscure the Word, the bible does not tell lie. As in the beginning, homosexuality is, shall, and will remain what it is—a sin. It is a sin without prejudice to colour, language, region and religion, gender and age.

17

No Middle Ground Could Be Found

England 2005

B efore the Anglican Communion primates meeting set for Dromantine, Northern Ireland, in February 2005, to discuss the Lambeth Commission's Windsor Report, the gay movement had declared war on Archbishop Akinola. Every homosexual group in America, Canada, Scotland, and England had him on their sworn-enemy list. The gay groups knew what to do, to employ the strategy developed from Adolf Hitler's *Mein Kampf*.

The lesbian and gay movement in Britain was the first to throw down the gauntlet. They launched a vile campaign to see him declared *persona non grata* in Britain, thus denying him entry into the country.[1] The media was drawn into the campaign, and Archbishop Akinola was denigrated, disparaged, and demonized globally. Every opportunity and every means to taint, stigmatize, and stereotype him was exploited in the campaign of calumny. Among the printable names, he was called a "homophobe," "homo-hater," and "homo-maniac."

In their attempts to have him declared *persona non grata* to their country, they cited "his open criticism and condemnation of the ordination of gays as priests and a bishop of the Anglican Communion." Their argument was that his view was "promoting hatred towards homosexuals." The secretary of the movement, Rev. Richard Kirker, alleged that there were "many examples of language used" by him inciting disaffection against homosexuals. However, he didn't provide a single example of those inflammatory words. Kirker nevertheless maintained strongly that Akinola was a "serious danger" to the existence of British gays and lesbians.

He raised the fear of public peace being breached the moment Akinola set foot on British soil. He added that a revolt against homosexuals was bound to follow. Of course, the lesbian and gay movement in Britain was not without its own public image problem. It remained a "fundamentalist movement" in some media circles. Politically,

1. https://en.wikipedia.org/w/index.php?title=Peter_Tatchell&oldid=675719387.

however, it had some good fortune, enjoying "a number of backers within the Labour Party. It could count on their clout in advancing its cause. The British Home Office, however, cleverly avoided being dragged into the controversy. It declined banning Archbishop Akinola from entering Britain, as was done to the American Nation of Islam leader Louis Farrakhan a year earlier. Farrakhan had intended to visit Britain but was barred from the country, an action that generated international uproar.

An African proverb counsels that it is better to be forearmed if you have been forewarned, and the archbishop began taking serious precautions on his international travels. He adopted the style of travelling incognito to hostile countries. Even if he could not guarantee his safety from shocking and embarrassing attacks, at least he could minimize the damage by taking reasonable precautions to reduce the risk of exposure. Akinola was not over-playing his fears or becoming paranoid. He had every reason to be triple-cautious to avoid being bitten once.

Two months before the campaign against Akinola started, an innocent Ugandan priest had paid the price for not being circumspect while opposing homosexuality. The unsuspecting priest was made the target of a xenophobic attack in London. He was "rough-handled and almost beaten in a street by those who were sympathetic to the gay movement and who regard any priest from Africa as against them." That type of lawless, anarchist attack was no longer anathema in the streets of London. The emerging trend elevated thuggery so that it no longer offended national sensibility. Akinola could imagine the sensation it would create if he were stripped in public and dragged about in the streets of London to a chorus of "homophobe," "homo-hater," and "homo-maniac." If jeering had happened to Carey as the Archbishop of Canterbury and Mugabe as head of state of a sovereign country, surely he would not be spared a rough ordeal.

The command to "cow and silence" Akinola foreshadowed the meeting of the Anglican primates in February 2005. As stated previously, the purpose of their gathering was to consider the Windsor Report. Interestingly, the meeting was not spared its own drama. The American Episcopal Church came to Dromantine in full force.[2] The church flew in with all its pranks and theatrics. Coincidentally, the opposing forces were ready too, prepared to meet wits for wits.

The Dromantine Retreat and Conference Centre, the venue of the meeting, was not designed for media exploitation. It was a 19th-century Italian-styled mansion. Situated in a quiet, unobstructed hilltop at Newry in Northern Ireland, it was home to a Catholic Seminary. The center was Spartan, without any worldly or ostentatious contamination. Its meeting rooms were sparsely furnished. In this modest setting, the primates were to gather for their discussions. The intention of Canterbury in choosing the location was to keep the primates away from distraction to the extent possible. Also, strictly controlled to the venue were human and vehicular traffic to ensure that those who had no business with the meeting did not interfere. Nevertheless, it was

2. Conger, "Behind the Scenes at the Primates Meeting: Part 2"; Boyer, "A Church Asunder."

alleged that a number of "American and British church activists took rooms in Newry and kept in contact with the primates," namely the "Rev. Canon David Anderson, president of the AAC; the Rev. Canon Bill Atwood, general secretary of Ekklesia; Bishop Robert Duncan of Pittsburgh and moderator of the Anglican Communion Network; and, Diane Knippers, president of the IRD." Of course, all these were men known for opposing the homosexualisation of the American church. They were also the people to whom the Global South had given active support, working with them as partners.

In the meeting, Akinola's two colleagues from the Global South were the Most Rev. Henry Orombi of Uganda and his Argentinian counterpart, Archbishop Gregory Venables. The pro-gay activists charged that anti-gay forces were breaching protocols to "gain access to the Primates" and "passing notes to the Primates." The Rev. George Conger in a *Church of England Newspaper* article said that "traffic to Dromantine was busy throughout [that] week as [the] conservative activists would take [the] Primates off-campus from the centre to dine and strategize." The impression being sown was simple. It was that the primates were being guided by their American and British colleagues like robots being manipulated to a programmed end.

However, contrary to the grossly inaccurate and misleading newspaper report, the real drama was playing out at the center of the meeting between the primates. As usual, the meeting included Eucharistic worship, and it was in this service that the first hint of trouble was manifested. The three Global South primates bluntly refused to share communion with their American counterparts. They predicated their action on the "broken communion" they had declared with the church. Indeed, even if no other primates at the meeting followed suit, the three of them were resolved on the action. When the time came, however, several other primates also "refused to attend the Eucharist with the [American] church's Primate, Presiding Bishop Frank Griswold."

Cold shoulders from the primates weren't Griswold's major headache at the time. His chief worry was a disconcerting "document alleging various abuses of conservative Episcopal clergy and congregations" circulating among his colleagues. He was disturbed by the report. Surreptitiously, the damaging account had found its way to every primates table. It was impossible for any of his colleagues to miss the impeaching document. The big-lettered title of the report was winking at them from every part of the room.

Griswold couldn't contain his rage. He was livid. But the harm was done already. There was no way he could recall the embarrassing document, and he could think of one and only one source for the indicting document—"the American activists." But what could they have written that was not common knowledge to the Anglican leaders at the meeting? Nevertheless, letting the primates have an authentic story of the way the anti-gay priests in America were being persecuted had left Griswold disconcerted.

The anger was not directed only at his American colleagues, whom he accused of disservice to the American church, but extended also to those of his colleagues he considered their collaborators. Whatever Griswold was anticipating in Dromantine, his interview with the online publication *Beliefnet*, after the meeting showed the extent to which he was surprised and taken aback, miffed at the impeaching "pieces of paper." He'd confronted his colleagues: "Why are these people, down the road, in constant communication with various of you?" "Who is determining our agenda?" He had bellowed out.

Despite Griswold's histrionics, the primates reported a sombre, purposeful, and productive meeting. They said the "meeting was characterised by generosity of spirit, and a readiness to respect one another's integrity." Thirty-five of them, Anglican leaders from all parts of the world, attended the five-day parley from February 20–25, 2005. The three who were absent were the primates of Burundi (who suffered a family death) and Hong Kong (the result of health problems), and the moderator of the United Church of North India (owing to unavoidable circumstances).

Ostensibly, the single most important agenda item was the 2004 Lambeth Commission's Windsor Report. The Commission had done its work, found the facts, and had presented its findings, including its recommendations to the archbishop of Canterbury, who now had brought it before the primates for their consideration and decision. At that point, nothing was more important to the Anglican Communion worldwide. Extensively and exhaustively, the primates debated the report: "We reflected for many hours." The chair of the Commission, Archbishop Robins Eames, opened the discussion with a presentation of the general framework. He was followed by Primus Bruce Cameron of Scottish Episcopal Church, who had replaced Archbishop Peter Kwong as chair of the Reception Reference Group. The Reception Reference Group had prepared another document from responses to the Windsor Report. They had invited contributions and opinions from across the Communion, and they had received an overwhelming 322 communications. They took time to painstakingly examine every reaction and add copious comments on each of the points considered. Ultimately, they presented "a careful analysis of the 322 responses" to the primates. The majority opinion contained "a high measure of general support for the recommendations of the *Windsor Report*." Those that raised issues merely expressed "concerns in relation to matters of detail."

From the hallowed chambers where the Anglican leaders had rubbed minds and shared thoughts, conclusions coincided with the general feelings reported by the Communion. The primates lamented that the "position overwhelmingly adopted by the bishops of the Anglican Communion has been seriously undermined by the recent developments in North America." But, as in Resolution 1.10 of the 1998 Lambeth Conference, they expressed once more the commitment of the Anglican Church to "continue, unreservedly, to be committed to pastoral support and care of homosexual people." Nevertheless, the primates categorically dismissed any compromise on the perfidies of the two North American churches. They were decisive with their expectation, and they wondered "whether the North American churches are willing to accept the same teaching on matters of sexual morality as is generally accepted in the Communion." And it seemed the Communion was willing to wield the stick this time around. Given the contemptuous behavior of the two churches, and in the face of their continued recalcitrance, the primates called on

> the Episcopal Church (USA) and the Anglican Church of Canada to voluntarily withdraw their members from the Anglican Consultative Council for the period leading to the next Lambeth Conference.

The Lambeth Conference was not scheduled until 2008, and till then the two churches had opportunity to make amends. The leaders expected them to consult with their respective governing organs toward addressing issues noted in the Windsor Report if they wanted to continue as part of the worldwide church.

Decisive as the Communion's leaders were, they still showed magnanimity toward the two recalcitrant churches. Consequently, they directed the Anglican Consultative Council (ACC) to meet about five months later to "organise a hearing at its meeting in Nottingham, England, in June 2005." They wanted the body to hear representatives of the two rebelling churches, considering the reasons behind their actions. But they weren't ready to back away from "reaffirming that the 1998 Lambeth Conference Resolution 1.10 [remained] as the position of the Anglican Communion."

They insisted that whatever decisions the ACC arrived at during the June meeting must be within the bounds of the "resolutions not only at Lambeth Conference in 1998, but earlier Conferences as well." There would be no equivocation regarding "groups in serious theological dispute with their diocesan bishop, or dioceses in dispute with their Provinces." And they placed the matter at the doorstep of the archbishop of Canterbury, requesting him to "appoint, as a matter of urgency, a panel of reference to supervise the adequacy of pastoral provisions made by any churches for such members." In the meantime, the primates pledged among themselves "neither to encourage nor to initiate cross-boundary interventions."

The elegantly crafted Dromantine decisions of the primates should have imbued new spirits in the American Episcopal Church and its Canadian counterpart. Deplorably, the words beautifully assembled at Dromantine turned out to be empty rhetoric. They added up to another missed opportunity. Peace was nowhere in sight.

Evidently, the American Episcopal Church was not in Dramantine with the intention of abandoning its ostrich position. Its Presiding Bishop Frank Griswold was hardly back to his seat when he fired the first salvo. Without recourse to diplomatic finesse, he upbraided his colleagues, exhibiting America's haughtiness and pride in talking down to people: "I think the regret we can offer wholeheartedly and as a unified body is regret for the consequences our actions have had in other contexts." He clarified that the expression of regret did "not mean that we necessarily regret the action itself." Griswold made it clear that he had no apology for taking part in the consecration of Gene Robinson. Neither he nor the other bishops involved "regret having done so."[3]

There was nothing brave or spectacular in the statement or action of Griswold. He was merely parroting the voice of his masters. Already, the most influential groups and personalities within the Episcopal Church had denounced the Windsor Report. The American presiding bishop dared not antagonise them. Integrity USA, the prominent gay movement within the Episcopal Church, and its maverick founder, Louie Crew, were among the intimidators.

Crew had moved into the top hierarchy of the church to have a seat on its Executive Council. The Executive Council represented one of the church's topmost decision-making organs. Crew denounced the six months labor offered by Eames and his committee with scathing remarks: "The *Windsor Report* is a monstrous interference in the life of the Episcopal Church." "It has made a crisis where there was no crisis." And he berated the primates who had sat to consider "the Windsor Report [that] stoops to isolate Gene Robinson and to shame those who participated in or even approved his consecration."[4]

Crew echoed the sentiments of the eccentric bishop of Washington John Chane, who was another inveterate gay advocate. Chane felt that "failure to accept him [referring to Gene Robinson] is to . . . question the very presence and role of the Holy Spirit in the ordination/consecration process of all ordained and consecrated persons in the Episcopal Church."

Crew and Chane, however, were not the only Episcopal Church "war mongers." The bishop assistant in the Diocese of Los Angeles, Sergio Carranza, for instance, saw no reason "to placate some arrogant Primates of the Anglican Communion who want to humiliate, excoriate, and severely punish the Episcopal Church for its sin of embracing all of God's children." "Since when does the Church of Jesus Christ have to apologize for its prophetic acts?" "The Primates meeting," he decried, had become "an idol," and since "idols demand human sacrifices, they want blood." Carranza wondered if the Episcopal Church should offer "our brothers and sisters as a propitiatory sacrifice?" An obstinate 3 percent of the 78-million-strong global Communion was ready for collision with the rest of the Communion. The bishop of Virginia, Peter

---

3. A lot of material was generated by the Anglican Communion Institute on the action and reaction of the American church, including the following: "The Anglican Communion: Where Are We Now and Where Are We Headed? A Brief Analysis"; "The Anglican Way: The Significance of the Episcopal Office for the Communion of the Church"; "Which Way Ahead?" by Ephraim Radner; "Fruits of Repentance" by Andrew Goddard; "Come Up Higher: A Response to the Report of the Special Commission on the Episcopal Church and the Anglican Communion" by Ephraim Radner; "The Corrupted Church: A Comment on the Pragmatism of To Set Our Hope On Christ" by Ephraim Radner; "An Open Letter to the House of Bishops of the Episcopal Church USA," by Donald Armstrong, Ephraim Radner, Christopher Seitz, and Philip Turner; "Anglican Christianity—For Consideration by the Bishops of the Episcopal Church" by Phillip Turner, Ephraim Radner & Donald Armstrong, http://www.anglicancommunioninstitute.com/.

4. "TEC Leaders In Their Own Words," www.americananglican.com.

Lee, offered his take on the situation: "If you must make a choice between heresy and schism, always choose heresy."

The American Episcopal Church had become an *enfant terrible* to the Anglican Communion. The problematic church was choking its worldwide compatriots to near suffocation, confronting the global church with testy situations. In March 2005, its House of Bishops met and took a stand against the primates' demand for a moratorium on election and consecration of anyone in a same-sex relationship. Rather than limiting the temporary suspension to people in same-sex relationships, the House of Bishops clamped a general ban on consecration of all candidates to the position of bishop until the church's General Convention in 2006. In a follow-up Executive Council meeting, it dismissed the demand that the church send its representatives to the ACC meeting to give reasons for its actions. The council decided that the church would instead "send their delegation to the June ACC meeting for observation but not for official participation."

Nevertheless, Griswold simultaneously commissioned a group of Episcopal theologians to prepare the church's official position ahead of that same ACC meeting. Just days before the ACC gathering, the commissioned report was released. The 130-page report, made public on June 21, 2005, was titled "To Set Our Hope On Christ (TSOH)." Fluid and coated with sacchariny humility, TSOH veered away from the familiar rancorous belligerency of the American church. The tone and language was subtle and restrained. However, the American church still had a viewpoint that it was desperate to sell. It wanted a church accepted on its own terms and conditions.

The report's first claim was that fallibility was intrinsic to human nature. TSOH, as a platform, projected that view. It proposed that "we could be wrong," that the church could not be excluded from the ranks of generally fallible creatures. This was done to create room to argue the church's cause within the "somewhat hostile and sceptical Communion" in which it had found itself. They sought to establish that in sorting out "what is true and good," differences of opinion should be expected. Repeatedly, the document alluded to the notion that there should be "give and take of identity-groups, cultures and epochs" in the search for truth. With regard to Scripture, they spoke of "'contested and contesting biblical interpretations,' 'rival accounts' and 'countering positions within Scripture and the Christian tradition.'" For them, Scripture was a "forum where God and humanity engage one another, seeking truth in the process of resolving difficulties."

They went to say, "No one culture, no one period of history, has a monopoly of insight into the truth of Gospel." Indeed, in matters concerning the Gospel, "It is essential for the fullest apprehension of truth that context is in dialogue with context." "Sometimes," as they pontificated sanctimoniously, "the lived experience of a particular community enables Christian truth to be perceived afresh for the whole community." And they had supposedly made the vital discovery of the Episcopal

Church's new Christian truth—"how a person living in a same sex gender union may be considered eligible to lead the flock of Christ."

The writing group of TSOH was one-sided, dominated by "those who favoured the decisions of GC 2003 that precipitated the crisis." Excluded were all those who opposed the church's radical gay agenda. The oppression of conservatives was "quite open and brazen," with traditionalists being excluded from "the councils of TEC." The church's topmost decision-making body, the Executive Council, reflected the extent of the homosexuals' growth in both number and influence, for "7 of their 38 members are lesbigay." And the remaining 31 members would not have occupied their positions if they had not been gay sympathizers. Increasingly, too, at other levels of administration, anti-gay church members were considered no longer fit for "appointments to diocesan, provincial and national committees." Nor were they considered fit to be "voted by diocesan or national conventions onto decision-making councils."

The repression was not limited to the domestic front. Anyone known for not supporting the gay agenda became a target for demonization and character assassination. When those in the anti-gay group, for example, "are appointed to Communion committees or councils, they are subjected from within TEC to howls, protests and negative campaigns, engaged in not simply by individuals, but by bishops and diocesan representatives." The church's obsession was to coerce support for its gay agenda without caring about the cost. From intent to content, therefore, TSOH mutilated the truth. It was another propaganda stunt. By the time the document was released, every critical decision-making arm of the church had already been infiltrated by the gay movement. In fact, the American House of Bishops had declared "that the alienation between TEC's leadership and the Anglican Communion . . . has become unbridgeable." The matter of gay inclusion was "non-negotiable." With the words, "no going back," Presiding Bishop Griswold had ruled out any possibility of budging or reconsidering the decision.

The ACC was not fooled when it met in June 2005 to consider the defense of the American church and its Canadian counterpart.[5] The TSOH position paper ignited no excitement among members of the gathering. Impressive as its rhetoric was, sophisticated as was its sophistry, it was simply a remix of the same old, worn out tunes. Stubbornly confronting it was Lambeth Resolution 1.10., the 1998 human sexuality decision. Consequently, the ACC didn't beat about bush. It insisted that the Communion's teaching on human sexuality be adhered to. The members saw through the ploy of the American church and TSOH. As a result, the ACC was resolute in standing with the primates. The Episcopal Church and its Canadian compatriot were requested to withdraw their representatives from the body until the 2008 Lambeth Conference. Though the word "suspended" was familiar in the secular world, the decision to ask the two churches to step aside for a time was almost novel in the history of the global Anglican Church.

5. Anglican Consultative Council, "Resolutions ACC—11."

It would be naïve to think that the unparalleled chastening made the two church-es toe the line of contrition. No, they continued defiantly with their mischief. In quick response, the leadership of the American church wrote a pastoral letter to its churches and congregations. The leaders wanted to downplay the blows the church was receiv-ing from all sides of the Communion. By its tone and content, the letter was designed to boost the morale and confidence of the ordinary members. It spoke of "how the holy Spirit is acting in our different contexts" and assured the congregations of the church's new status globally. They had become a "Prophetic witness" amid a "new Pentecost." The transformation of the American church into this spiritual role would not be without a price. But it was worth it, since

> they must neither accept constraints—from Scripture, tradition, or the world-wide church—nor apologise for breaching constraints and acting contrary to Christian love.

The Episcopal Church in the United of States of America could not pass a test of modesty. Only a creature with a large ego could talk the way the leadership of the church had talked, saying that they owed no one an apology, not even God, because not even the "constraints" of Scripture could stop them from their chosen path. Those words were not empty, for on a daily basis, the church dramatized its rebellion for the world to see. Every day, it also made clear the only way for the Communion to end the crisis. The path was for the vast majority of the Anglicans worldwide to accept homosexuality; they must go gay.

The American and Canadian churches were not just neighbors, but they seemed to suffer the same oversized self-impression. And on the Canadian church side, the embattled New Westminster bishop Michael Ingham did not help matters. He moved quickly from being impolitic to displaying bombastic ego, making unpolished and tactless statements and ending heretically. Ingham picked on the Global South lead-ers as targets of his insults. "The next battle," he said scornfully, "will move beyond sexuality." Where would it be heading? Ingham predicted happily that they would next "focus on the exclusivity of Christianity and the need to recognise Jesus as a way, but not as the only way."

If the North American churches had taught the Anglican Communion any les-son, it was not to take them and their words for granted. Their propensity for adven-turous exuberance was unlimited. Unfortunately, conceit sometimes blinded them. They could be myopic. They failed to realize that the Africa, Asia, Latin America, and Indian Ocean nations they were coming up against were no longer colonial territories. Neither were their leaders errand boys of yesteryear. At the head of the Global South churches, now, was a new generation of leaders. They might not be rascally rambunc-tious, but docility was not one of their weaknesses. They could bark and they could bite; their teeth were sharp and strong. The North American churches got it all wrong. In dealing with the Global South leaders, they were using the wrong algebra. And as they rigidly continued with their disobedience, the Global South leaders equally stood their ground. No middle ground could be found between the two sides as each held tightly to their diametrically opposed positions. No solution was in sight as the Anglican Communion's crisis continued to spiral.

18

A Double-Faced Canterbury

England, 2005

After the botched attempt at getting the openly gay Jeffrey John into the episcopate, a relative calm prevailed in Canterbury. But underneath was the problem of how to contain the raging controversy surrounding the refusal of the North
American churches to abide by the majority decision on homosexuality. The matter
continued to tear the church apart. Strangely, it was at this time also that the United
Kingdom stoked the smoldering fire. On November 18, 2004, the British government
had enacted a new law endorsing homosexuality. The legislation, Civil Partnerships
Act, gave same-sex couples "essentially the same rights and responsibilities as civil
marriage." Its implementation was delayed, however, for another year, with December
5, 2005, set as its take-off date.[1]

Coincidentally, the law was passed almost back-to-back with the archbishop
of Canterbury's receipt of the Windsor Report in October 2004 from the Lambeth
Commission. The law didn't begin to generate international attention until 2005 when
its actual implementation commenced. Candidly, it was an inauspicious time for the
Church of England to get entangled with such a hotly divisive issue already tearing
the Communion apart. In all fairness, the Church of England could plead not guilty to
charges of gross misfeasance on the issue. At the same time, it would be wrong to free
the seat of global Anglicanism of complicity regarding this development on British
soil. The balance of guilt was such that though the Church of England didn't lobby for
the same-sex civil partnership law, it waged no battle against it either. Nor did it seek
opinions from the rest of the Communion on such a sensitive issue. The law was not
a product of sudden legislative effort. It took years to bring it to life. Importantly, the
law was of cross-national significance, with implications for the crisis raging in the
Anglican Communion.

---

1. See Civil Partnership in the United Kingdom https://en.wikipedia.org/wiki/Civil_partnership_
in_the_United_Kingdom.

As stated, the Church of England could pretend it had nothing to do with the law and deceptively get away with that claim. Behind the civil partnerships law was Lord Lester of Herne Hill. Those pushing for the law were lucky to have such a respectable, reputable, and dignified lawmaker as its advocate. His forte was building strongholds for human rights and justice, making him one of the most renowned consciences in British society at the time. His greatest gift was legislative advocacy, which he used as an instrument for socially re-engineering society. He was a methodical, meticulous man who understood the power of objective and evidence-based argument to sway political opinion—not a run-of-the-mill politician depending on demagogic skill.

Accordingly, he established the Odysseus Trust, a think tank and legislative support organization centred on promoting good governance, plural democratic values, public accountability, human rights, and fundamental freedoms. On the morning of January 25, 2002, Lester had arrived at the House of Lords determined to swing the United Kingdom on another revolutionary path. He had presented a legislative proposal about "unmarried couples living in a mutually supportive relationship to make provision for their joint protection within a coherent legal framework." Lester's 25-minute speech introducing the proposed bill laid the basis for the proposed law and its essential framework, which had taken over eight months to prepare.

However, the Odysseus Trust, and by extension Lester, were not sole owners of the idea. There was "collaboration with Stonewall" as an organization, and "especially its wise director, Angela Mason." Both drew effusive praise from him.

"Stonewall" was a British gay rights activist group, founded in 1989, seventeen years after the American gay Stonewall riots. The British group had begun with a small band of people who felt offended by the law denying "'promotion' of homosexuality in schools, as well as stigmatising lesbian, gay and bi people."[2] Their resolve was to see to the end of Section 28 of the British Local Government Act, the offending provisions. They wanted it expunged from the statute book.

Despite sharing the name of a gay riotous event in the United States, the British Stonewall group veered away from being confrontational or militaristic. Unlike the American Gay Liberation Force, Stonewall had not stoned the wall of any institutions implementing the aggravating law, nor had it zapped state officials responsible for its enactment. Its strategy was to campaign, lobby, and win legislative support for enactment of a law to achieve its aim. At the same time, it worked to achieve equalization of consent age and lifting of the ban on homosexuals serving in the military. Its desire, which had brought it in contact with the Odysseus Trust and its benefactor, Lester, was to secure civil partnerships for same-sex couples. As deeply involved as Stonewall was in the struggle, it tactically avoided being at its forefront, leaving that to Lester and the Odysseus Trust.

Lester, a three-decade veteran in parliamentary activism, was not insensitive to public mood in advancing contentious, radical legislative reforms. He packaged

2. "Our mission—Stonewall," http://www.stonewall.org.uk.

cleverly the Civil Partnership Bill he was proposing, giving it an omnibus flavor. He began with an outline of the social background for the proposed law, highlighting the defectiveness of the existing English law that "gives full effect to the bond between couples if they are lawfully married, but not if they are unmarried." The supposed anomaly to which he drew attention was that "whether people living together are of the same sex or of both sexes, the law treats them much less favourably than married couples," "even if they have close and long-standing relationships." The main point, which he underlined, was that "cohabiting partners, unlike married ones, do not enjoy a standard set of legal rights and responsibilities."

Lester appealed to the changing social dynamics of the United Kingdom. Family life had been witnessing tremendous changes. Marriages were at their lowest ebb since 1917. The UK's divorce was the highest in the European Union. Contrastingly, cohabitation had been growing in leaps over the years. A quarter of British children were being born into cohabiting households. A survey of British citizens reportedly indicated that more than two-thirds of them expressed their belief "that it is acceptable for a couple to live together without being married." Among homosexuals and heterosexuals, more and more people were preferring cohabitation. There were "heterosexual couples choosing not to marry." Equally, quite a number were "choosing to cohabit before they eventually do marry." There was also "an increase in the number of homosexual men and women who wish to secure public and legal recognition of their partnerships." Lester got to the heart of his submission: "Their wish should surely be respected."

He was optimistic about the nation's potential gains. His legal framework would provide "essential protection for partners in the face of adverse circumstances, such as ill health, domestic violence or death." They could share a home with the additional advantage that partnership "agreements will be binding except in cases of financial or other hardship." The partnership, like marriage, could be dissolved either by "mutual consent or by court order."

As polished as the bill was, skeptical questions were raised about it. Some believed it was a "threat to marriage." Lester disagreed: "The Bill may well actually promote marriage." Equally, attention was raised about another omission of the bill: "matters affecting the interests of children arising from civil partnerships or their break-up." Lester was a bit tongue-tied on that. He didn't deny the highlighted weakness. However, he mustered a defense, saying the omission was necessary "both to avoid unnecessary controversy and complexity." The presumption was that other legislation better dealt with the interests of children, including such matters as adoption and custody. Lester wanted it known that the "Bill does not attempt to tackle every problem." His conviction, nevertheless, was that "it tackles many of them." On that basis, he drummed up the support of his fellow lawmakers: "The time is over-ripe for legislation to create a legally recognised civil partnership system."

Despite the brilliant efforts of Lester, the bill still ran into obstacles on its first journey in the House. Naturally, there were those supporting the bill. Equally, it had its share of opponents. Each group dwelled eloquently on the merits and demerits of the proposed law. The two sides deployed passionate and articulate arguments to justify their positions. The United Kingdom was a country where catchphrases like injustice, discrimination, legal and institutional oppression, and suppression had been woven into the story of homosexuals. The persecution lore was a popular note in the emerging culture of the country. Supporters drew extensively from a variety of anecdotal accounts portraying the discrimination to justify their case. Opponents, in turn, raised "three important social issues" indicating, in their estimation, how injurious the law would be to British life.

The first harmful effect was that the law was built on a false premise concerning those who were cohabiting and preferring not to get married. In the face of complaints that the partners were not recognized as a unit, that they could suffer from too few protections, and that they might not be shielded from poverty as single parents, the reality was that "the protections that such people seek are readily available to them," for they had the option of availing themselves of "a form of civil registration at a register office." The argument of the bill's opponents was that it was improper to "give heterosexuals who choose not to take on the responsibilities of marriage the privileges of those who do marry." Rather than promote the well-being of society, they said, the bill would do the exact opposite. Marriage, they maintained, remained a critical institution of the society. Matrimony allowed individuals to exhibit publicly declared commitment, with a link between present and future generations. Marriage also was the "environment where shared values and support are best transmitted." Any effort at undermining the institution was like sticking a knife into the heart of the British society. Antagonists of the bill insisted that this was the intent of the Civil Partnerships Law, an impropriety the people should not encourage.

Then, there was the issue of children, "little mentioned in the Bill." Children were the products that "marriage has at its very heart." But, "in the proposed civil partnership, children are mentioned only in terms of property." The bill made children to be material possessions protected merely from "non-molestation, inheritance and intervention orders." This failed to express adequately the premium that English law and culture put on children. Children were at the heart of British life, values, and society to the point that, "If the marriage fails, they are the first and proper concern." Regrettably, the Civil Partnerships Law had none of that core national ethos as its primary interest.

Even the claims of bill proponents regarding cohabiting couples were not spared from contention. Particularly controversial was the general claim that cohabiting couples had no options. Opponents criticized that position as a hoax, a misleading claim, for couples "can still gain the majority of benefits included in the Bill by instructing a solicitor or by going through the courts." In other words, British society had already provided mechanisms to meet the so-called deficiencies that the Bill said it was out to eliminate. Options exist, for example, to "set up a cohabitation arrangement," or "they can write a will," besides other opportunities available.

In spite of their strong objection, opponents of the bill could not hide their admiration for the manner in which it presented homosexual partnerships. They were impressed with the way the relationships "were movingly described" and how Lester attempted to justify the law by resting it on the "two underlying principles of freedom of association and equality." The opponents were, however, not cowed. They believed the central issue had to do with the fact that "the Bill relates to a surprisingly small group of people" in British society, and it amounted to immoral arm-twisting. While those opposing the bill were open to state sanction of a "homosexual lifestyle lived within the context of a single committed relationship and recognised as such," they still wanted the distinction to be made unequivocally that "this is not 'marriage.'" They insisted on the dissimilarity being underscored because it concerned the fact that "God gave us that wonderful sacrament as the building-block for society." Marriage, they argued, was "ordained for the procreation of children and nurturing them" and as "a remedy against sin." And central to its beneficial value was that it assisted the development of "mutual society, help and comfort that one ought to have in the other, both in prosperity and in adversity."

Notwithstanding the profound criticisms, there was applause in the House of Lords at the declaration that "much in the Bill is good." The overriding question became whether the United Kingdom needed the bill at that particular point in time. By coincidence, the government had just initiated a cross-departmental review of the implications of granting rights and benefits to cohabiting couples. The House was confronted with a dilemma. Should it proceed? "Would it be better for the House to wait and hear the Government's proposals?" The impasse was not easy to resolve.

Eventually, the bill was delayed.

Two years later, the bill returned to the Lords.[3] This time around, the government's heart and might was solidly behind it. In November 2003, the queen's speech indicated a likelihood of reviving the bill, hinting about the possibility of sending it back again to the House of Lords by March 2004. As a prelude, and important part of the process, a number of consultations were planned with different interest groups. The Women and Equality Unit of the Directorate of Trade and Industry had begun the coordination of public discussions starting in June 2003, five months before the queen's message. The key issue requiring a sampling of public opinion was the desirability of "same-sex interdependent, stable relationships that are intended to be permanent." Evidently, this was another word for marriage. The Civil Partnerships Bill had changed focus from the one Lester proposed earlier. The government had redefined the intent, object, and target of the law as well as its beneficiaries. Now, the law was principally for and about same-sex couples. The government was confident about

3. House of Lords Proceedings, "House of Lords, Business of the House: Debates, 'Civil Partnerships Bill [HL].'"

a positive legislative outcome. It felt optimistic about the "informed and constructive debate in the public sphere over the question of recognition of same-sex couples." Public opinion was on its side.

The Church of England, in the meantime, had also reacted to the proposed law. It greeted the idea with caution. Its statement reiterated that though the Church "attaches high importance to the promotion of social justice and the safeguarding of human rights," its "approach to ethical issues is founded on Holy Scripture, interpreted in the light of Tradition and Reason."[4] It explained that the application of "Tradition and Reason" in no way vitiates its teaching, which has always been "that marriage—that is, faithful, committed, permanent and legally sanctioned relationships between a man and a woman—is central to the stability and health of human society." Furthermore, it reiterated that it had no reason to change its stand that marriage "continues to provide the best context for the raising of children." Accordingly, the Church of England was categorical in its desire that government "do nothing to devalue or undermine marriage and the family." Though it recognized "the importance of using the law of the land to promote justice and human rights," the church called for the government's recognition of the "distinctive place of marriage in the law of our country and the need to preserve it."

The church affirmed the need to uphold the rights of "individuals within same sex relationships in relation to such matters as protection from domestic violence, the registration of a death and inheritance matters including tenancy succession." At the same time, it stated, "We note that the consultation document states at para 1.3 that it is a matter of public record that the Government has no plans to introduce same-sex marriage." It hoped government would keep it at that. The church made its official response public on September 30, 2003. The draft bill was not presented to the House until April 2004, an interval of almost seven months, allowing the government to clean and weed unnecessary clutters out from the bill.

The bill that got to the House of Lords was a "product of two years' serious and intensive work by the Government." Its strength was that it "places civil partnership firmly in the civil sphere of our national life." The Lords were cheerily told that government had succeeded in finding "a secular solution to the disadvantages which same-sex couples face in the way they are treated" by English laws. And the government guaranteed that the new law "does not undermine or weaken the importance of marriage." The central point of the law was that it enabled same-sex couples to "gain legal recognition" and "organise their lives together." The termination of the union or relationship was permissible only on the death of a partner, dissolution or annulment." Irrespective of the gender, two people over 16 years of age could register as civil partners. Parental consent was an automatic requirement for those less than 18

---

4. Civil Partnership–Church of England Response to DTI Consultation Document, https://www.churchofengland.org/media/45595/civil.pdf; Civil Partnerships, https://www.churchofengland.org/our-views/marriage,-family-and-sexuality-issues/civil-partnerships.aspx.

years old. As in the law forbidding bigamy, no one in an existing civil partnership or marriage could contract another one. In addition, people with certain degrees of blood relationship were prohibited from entering into a partnership. They included "siblings, parents and children."

Civil partnership was to be a strictly secular process. Same-sex couples would have an initial waiting period of at least fifteen days before they could become partners, allowing for necessary checks regarding their eligibility. Then, at an agreed time and place decided by the couple and the local authority, the couple would sign the civil partnership document before a civil partnership registrar. Two witnesses were required. Religious premises were, however, out of bounds for registration of a civil partnership. Ceremonies were not deemed important aspects of the process. Local authorities were free, however, to explore ceremonial options if the couple so desired.

Then there was the complex issue of children in same-sex families. Even before the law, there were "already same-sex couples in the UK . . . raising children together." The "provisions relating to children will apply to the rights of children of these families in the same way as to children of a marriage," and the legislation addressed "child support, social security and tax credits so as to enable same-sex partners receive similar treatment as opposite-sex couples." In spite of the broad rights that would be granted to homosexuals, the government continued to maintain that it was not legalizing same-sex marriage but merely treating "same-sex couples with fairness and dignity."

Government is seldom the place to find the truth. Nor is politics a place where honesty habitually dwells. A free society, however, offers opportunity to learn when government is less than truthful and politics are tainted by dishonesty. When the House of Lords took hold of the proposed bill, better packaged as it was, and approved it, the matter was far from settled in society. For one thing, despite overwhelming votes of 248 to 27, the Church had two contrasting official positions on the law. The first strongly reaffirmed "that marriage warrants a unique place in the law" of the British society. The other traveled from an opposite direction, supporting "the creation of new legal rights" for "people whose relationships are not based on marriage." Still, the church apparently wasn't bothered by its differing positions despite the unambiguous pronouncement of the worldwide Communion on the issue.

Of paramount interest to the bishop of Oxford, Rt. Rev. Richard Harries, for instance, was the prohibition of a religious civil partnership ceremony. He saw this as one inadequacy of the bill. Emphatically, the provisions "statutorily prevent registration taking place in any premises designed or mainly used for religious purposes." The bishop attacked the provision for two reasons. First, it infringed on "the proper freedom of religious authorities to control such premises." He contended that the decision ought to have been left "for those authorities and not for the state," for government ought not to interfere with religious authorities' power to "decide whether or not their premises should be available to be used for registration purposes." He was willing to accommodate this provision if it were of "overriding national interest." But it wasn't, he said. And he was displeased that it would "deny some couples the possibility of a religious celebration," especially when a church was within a "close proximity to a civil registration," and the couple desired "a commitment with a religious dimension."

He thought occasions might arise when same-sex partners "may want to have a civil registration in a church hall," and then, after the secular ceremony, move to a religious ceremony in the church proper. Bishop Harries, however, quickly noted, "Of course, that is not allowed in the Church of England and some other Christian denominations," but he was sure that "there may very well be religious bodies which would not only permit but welcome such a development." Passionate he was that it was wrong to exclude the ceremonies from "proximity to a church hall."

The second part of his disagreement with the law was like the first. He complained that the civil partnership procedure lacked religious flavor. The way government designed the ceremony made it bland, insipid, lacking color, and uninspiring. He complained that "there is no specified wording," no "vow," "oath," or "covenant" to each other as in marriage between people of the opposite sex. They were simply to sign on a plain paper. The bishop wanted that changed. He used as reference point the Anglican prayer book, which during solemnization of marriage made the couple exchange a vow of "for better for worse, for richer for poorer, in sickness and in health." He wanted a replica of that vow, which would be "not only a written statement that such a partnership now exists, but some verbal understanding that this is a commitment of two human beings to one another through all the vicissitudes of human existence."

The vow's wording would be the only difference between marriage and civil partnership, according to Bishop Harries' perspective. To him, "marriage in both its civil and religious form" has always been "a commitment of two people to one another to the exclusion of all others." He stressed he "would also like to see some reflection of that when two people are committing themselves to enter into and register their civil partnership." What was the bishop proposing other than marriage? Yet the public stands of the Church of England and the British government rested on the same claim that "government has no plans to introduce same-sex marriage."

In contrast to the tedium of the bill's advocates in the House and the doublespeak of Church of England bishops on the matter, a strong, daring, and opposing voice stood up in the House—Baroness O'Cathain. She didn't mind to be different from the herd. Neither was she worried that she was almost a lone voice in the hallowed chamber. Brutally frank, she told her colleagues, "I realise that I am probably in a very small minority of noble Lords who are going to oppose the Bill."[5] She saw through the subterfuge and the government's ploy to deliberately create misconceptions in the public mind. "The public will struggle," she warned, with the fact that those who "say that they are opposed to same-sex marriage . . . at the same time bring forward

5. House of Lords Proceedings, "House of Lords, Business of the House: Debates, 'Civil Partnerships Bill [HL].'"

this Bill." She found no extenuating circumstances to excuse the way government had acted in bad faith.

She cut through the butter of lies like a hot knife. "This is a gay marriage Bill," she contended, dismissing official pretence to the contrary. Hitting the nail on the head further, she insisted, "The Government may call it civil partnership but in reality it is a form of marriage for same-sex couples." Three times she repeated the incontestable fact that "this Bill creates gay marriage," as if to exorcise the falsehood of pretending otherwise from her colleagues. She went on to observe that they all knew the vast majority of citizens did not want same-sex marriage. "Only gay rights groups want gay marriage."

Methodically, she sawed through the log of lies. She disproved the notion that the union being proposed for same-sex couples was civil. She drew attention to the bishop of Oxford's speech, noting it was but the tip of what was to come in the future. Every aspect of the civil partnership was modeled after marriage. The similarities were not accidents. Government had made the admission itself that "significant rights and responsibilities" were addressed in the bill to bring civil partnerships in line with married couples. Fiercely, she told her colleagues that it would be dishonest not to admit the truth. The baroness referred to the "House of Commons Hansard on 20 October 2003, cols. 491–92," which gave similar indication. She also referenced the "Explanatory Notes to the Civil Partnerships Bill in Paragraph 703," which made clear that, "The procedures for civil partnership registration . . . are modelled on the proposed procedures for civil marriages."

Sternly, she told her colleagues to quit the play on words. No one was deceived. The public was not as gullible as they thought. She drew attention to "*The Guardian* on 30 June," that deprecatingly called the civil partnership "legal marriage in all but name." Similarly, the legal journal *Lawyer* said, "by achieving the same result under a different name, the Government has so far managed to avoid a public backlash." Even "the Labour Party's own website regards this as a form of marriage," she said. "So, let there be no mistake—this is a gay marriage Bill in all but name."

Though Baroness O'Cathain had her say, democracy had its way. The bill proceeded to the committee stage in the House on April 22, 2004. It advanced to the Grand Committee level without any major impediments, aside from a number of amendments suggested here and there. When it got to the report stage two months later, on June 24, 2004, Baroness O'Cathain, again, made a spirited effort to correct the one-sided nature of the Bill. In concert with the bishop of Winchester and others, she sponsored a series of amendments. One of them was to "extend the benefits of the Bill to family members who have lived together on a long-term basis," as in the example of "two sisters or any two close relations who have lived together for 12 years." She contended that the law should accommodate partnerships, and not be restricted to same-sex partners.

The amendments managed to scale through by a 148–30 margin. From the House of Lords, the Civil Partnerships Bill found its way to the Commons in September 2004 with the amendments proposed. A large majority at the Commons turned down the amendments. The Bill returned to the Lords. By rule of practice, the option before the Lords was to pass the Bill in its original form. They did on November 17, 2004. The following day, the Civil Partnership Bill received the Royal Assent proclaiming it an act of parliament.

Opponents accepted their defeat gallantly. Seldom are honors distributed evenly when democracy is the rule of the game. The majority who believed in civil partnerships won the contest.

The success of the civil partnership law, however, confronted the Church of England with a serious dilemma. In British life and government, the Church occupies a strategic position. Therefore, it owes the British crown certain secular responsibilities. Institutionally, the Church is part of the British political and governing system. It is heavily represented in the House of Lords, the highest legislative arm of the British two-chamber parliament. Only a very few of its bishops do not sit automatically in the revered House.

In addition to its secular responsibilities to the British crown, it has spiritual duties and obligations to the Anglican Communion worldwide, being the international administrative and spiritual headquarters of the world's third largest Christian denomination. As a result, its action and inaction, errors of omission and acts of deliberate commission are bound to have implications in the Communion. It is on this score that its double-faced behavior in relation to the civil partnership law became unsettling.

Every level of the Church of England, from its individual bishops to the collegiate House of Bishops, and extending to its highest ecclesiastical organ, the Archbishop's Council, was aware of the position of the Anglican Communion on human sexuality. Indeed, the Church as the seat of the archbishop of Canterbury, stood at the center of all issues related to the crisis over homosexuality. Every major decision on the issue—from the 1998 Lambeth Conference to the last 2005 ACC meeting—was made on the British soil. This made the Church of England's hypocrisy galling, the two-faced pretence of its "being here and being there" at the same time. In light of events before the Civil Partnership Bill and developments related to it, the side on which the Church of England stood was not in dispute, notwithstanding its hypocritical deceit.

The Archbishop's Council's response to the Consultation Document on the Civil Partnership Bill, for instance, had talked of the Church's commitment to Christian marriage and ethics. Yet it had contradicted itself by endorsing "conferring some new rights on adults who wish to share important parts of their lives with each other." What the bishop of Oxford, the Rt. Rev. Richard Harries, said on the floor of the House during the Civil Partnership Bill's debate had only reiterated the official position of the Church. Furthermore, on July 25, 2005, seven months before enactment of the law, the House of Bishops issued a "Pastoral Statement on Civil Partnerships."[6] The timing of the statement made its intent suspicious.

For, inexplicably, it was released shortly after the ACC's meeting in Nottingham, England, the meeting where the American and Canadian churches were suspended from the Communion's activities until the 2008 Lambeth Conference. Could the Pastoral Statement, therefore, be a somewhat veiled message to the embattled two churches not to worry, that it's not over yet? How could Church of England become so insensitive to the feelings of the majority of the Anglican Church regarding the two North American churches?

The Church of England's approach was to attempt making a politically correct statement out of what the American and Canadian churches said blatantly. It was a master craft of double standards, the typical British diplomacy. The bishops' official response to the government's civil partnership proposal was their insistence that "sex properly belongs within marriage." Their categorical definition of marriage was that it must be "a faithful, committed, permanent and legally sanctioned relationship between a man and a woman."

Conversely, incredible was the new position they were staking out in the Pastoral Statement. "The House of Bishops does not regard entering into a civil partnership as intrinsically incompatible with holy orders," they said emphatically. There was a proviso, however. The condition applied to the clergy solely. They maintained that a priest must be "willing to give assurances to his or her bishop that the relationship is consistent with the standards for the clergy set out in *Issues in Human Sexuality.*" What were those standards that *Issues in Human Sexuality* prescribed for clergy not in marriage? The bishops kept silent on them. Presumably, they were referring to the regulation about sexual abstinence, which was the Church's position for those who could not embrace the institution of marriage. The Pastoral Statement, however, excluded lay gay and lesbian members of the Church from the abstinence rule imposed on the priests. The Bishops justified the exclusion on the grounds that

> the Church did not want to exclude the fellowship of those [with] gay or lesbian orientation who, in conscience, were unable to accept that a life of sexual abstinence was required of them and instead chose to enter into a faithful, committed relationship.

Lay civil partners, the bishops directed priests, shouldn't be asked "to give assurances about the nature of their relationship before being admitted to baptism, confirmation and communion." The Church of England's bishops knew they were playing games. They were slipping the ball into the net from the wrong end. The Church had just gone the way of its American and Canadian counterparts. They were endorsing homosexuality. Was it an act of cleverness or scented hypocrisy when the bishops

---

6. "House of Bishops Issues Pastoral Statement on Civil Partnerships," https://www.churchofengland.org/mediacentre/news/2005/07/pr5605.aspx.

entered a *nota bene* at the end of the Pastoral Statement that "the Church's teaching on sexual ethics remains unchanged"?

Archbishop Akinola's straightforward answer was that the Church of England was being dishonest. The Pastoral Statement of the British House of Bishops on the civil partnership law took him aback. He was surprised at how the Church failed to see the weak moral ground on which its decision on the issue had thrown it. Akinola saw a Church buffeted by contradiction of values. Here was a Church submitting itself to the dictates of the democratic process at the secular level. And here was the same Church, in an act of self-defeating incongruity, repudiating a similarly valid democratic decision in the spiritual sphere. Lambeth Conference Resolution 1.10 on human sexuality was democratically adopted in 1998 at a conference convened by the archbishop of Canterbury. Anglicans worldwide spoke. Nothing had changed or vitiated that stand. Archbishop Akinola's view was,

> For Church of England and its House of Bishops, particularly with the Archbishop of Canterbury as its Metropolitan and chairman, to employ guile in denouncing the collective stand of the Communion through the guise of hiding under a national law was, simply, an act of hypocrisy.

The archbishop's view on the Pastoral Statement of the House of Bishops was made public in August 2005.[7] Though he expressed satisfaction about "the reaffirmation of the Church's historic teaching on both marriage and sexual intimacy," he was distressed "that these words are not matched by corresponding actions." Akinola and Baroness O'Cathain would have made a good pair if they had the privilege of being in the House of Lords together. Both saw the civil partnership as nothing short of "gay marriage." He called it "same-sex marriage in everything but name." He was particularly dismissive of the idea that the bishops would accommodate clergy "who register that there will be no sexual intimacy" between them and their partners. "Totally unworkable . . . deception . . . and ridicule," Akinola observed. "How on earth can this be honoured?"

Akinola's second apprehension concerned the Church's instruction to its priests to ask nothing of lay, same-sex, registered civil partners "before they are admitted to baptism, confirmation and communion." He felt the directive "dishonours the sacraments of the Church." He was distressed that neither the Church of England bishops nor any leader in the Anglican Communion could claim ignorance about implications of the steps the Church of England had taken. The actions of the Church amounted to a "deliberate change in the doctrine of the Anglican Communion." The bishops were well aware of the decisions made regarding the North American churches. The situation disheartened him:

7. Akinola, "A Statement On The Church Of England's Response To Civil Partnerships By The Primate of All Nigeria," The Church of Nigeria (Anglican Communion), Abuja, Nigeria.

I found it awfully disturbing, especially, in the light of the great affection and respect possessed for the historic role that the Church of England has played in our lives, that the Church would take deliberate steps to ignore the teaching of the Bible. And could be doing so with brazen impunity.

"It is not a path that we can follow," Akinola wrote in the statement, reiterating the point to underscore it.

Akinola was utterly disappointed with the Church of England. He was at a loss about how the Church could deliberately stoke "further division at a time when we are still struggling with fragmentation and disunity within the Communion." The carefree attitude wounded him deeply. It looked as if evil forces were at work to reverse the historic roles of the Church of England in the life of the Communion. Serious was the note of concern ringing in his head. "Generations of church men had worked hard to build the Communion," he reflected in the public statement. "Many lost their lives in the course of propagating the Gospel and building missions abroad," he recalled. Sullenly, he remarked,

> It's an irony of history that another generation was working as hard, as well, to wreck the erected legacy.

Justice is also about equal treatment of offenders. So an ultimatum, similar to the one given to the two North American renegades, was issued to the Church of England

> to renounce their statement and declare their unqualified commitment to the historic faith, teaching and practice of the Church.

The demand included a cost for noncompliance: "Failure to do [so] will only add to our current crisis." What could a group or province within the Communion, however, do to the Church of England, the ubiquitous symbol of authority and center of power in the Anglican Church worldwide? Still, Archbishop Akinola was confident that "no church is beyond discipline."

19

Attempt to Divide and Rule

Egypt, 2005

The Nigerian church leader might truly have believed in the possibility of bringing the errant Church of England to "discipline" for its offense of narrow-mindedness, but practically, that seemed like an illusion. The center of power in the Anglican Church revolved around one church—the Church of England. Its archbishop held the commanding authority over the affairs of the Communion. Canterbury was also indivisible from British grand power. To confront such a gigantic structure was to challenge imperial might. Neither Archbishop Akinola nor the Church of Nigeria could boast of such awesome powers. At that time, however, the two men at the helms of affairs—of stronger Canterbury and the weaker Nigerian church—had one thing in common. Both had courage of convictions. They were men of very strong character.

Archbishop Akinola was clear-eyed about the conspiracy of Canterbury—and that included Archbishop Williams—regarding the events unfolding within the Communion. Canterbury and its occupant could not be absolved of bias in the Anglican crisis. The reticence of the archbishop disguised poorly his loud body language of one-sidedness. All the powers he needed to keep the game within the rules of play were with him. He was the custodian of the laws. Yet, he kept encouraging violation of rules by closing his eyes to the atrocities.

The suspension of the two North American churches until the 2008 Lambeth Conference appeared to Akinola to be part of a plot to create a deliberate delay. He couldn't find any justification for Canterbury's dilly-dallying or foot-dragging over the excellent work the Lambeth Commission had done. He understood that the only ones standing to gain from the delay were the gays. By 2008, they would have mustered a good deal of power, strength, capacity, and possibly a wider global reach, bolstered by the intimidation of a number of national governments, especially those in developing countries, to pass gay-approving laws like the Civil Partnerships Act. The argument would have then developed at Lambeth that conditions across the world had made it ripe for the Communion to review its stand on human sexuality. The diligent, Scripture-obfuscating work of the gay-supporting theologians would have matured. And it would be foolhardy to count on the archbishop of Canterbury, for he would preemptively deliver a *coup de grace*!

On September 14, 2005, the Church of Nigeria took a decisive step against the subterranean maneuvers of the North American churches and the Church of England.[1] The action was undertaken less than a month after the public statement of Archbishop Akinola warning the Church of England of dire consequences for reversing the Communion's teaching on human sexuality. The Nigerian church radically redefined its existence within the Anglican Communion. Formerly, allegiance to the See of Canterbury was the mark of bond with the Communion. That September synod showed it wasn't Archbishop Akinola alone who was dissatisfied with the antics of the American, Canadian, and British churches. Scarcely were there any Nigerian church leaders not exasperated with their Western colleagues' contemptuous behavior. The matter, thus, reached its peak at the General Synod, which was the highest legislative organ of the Church of Nigeria. A unanimous decision was reached to effect a fundamental change in the constitution of the Church. The process of altering the law governing the affairs of the Church was not easy, for the procedure had to follow an orderly, guided course.

First, the synod would constitute a committee. The committee would collate the amendments being proposed when there happened to be more than one. The committee would then assemble reactions from the dioceses. These steps were taken. Subsequently, three amendments were brought before the synod by the Justice Oguntade Constitutional Amendment Committee. Top on the list was one on "the relationship of the Church of Nigeria with churches that are Bible-based." The second dealt with the restructuring of the membership of the Provincial Synod. Last was one that related to the "establishment of Chapelry overseas."

According to procedure, a member of the synod had to move formally their adoption before the General Synod, and if accepted, they would be incorporated into the Church's constitution. The Hon. Justice Ekundayo Kolawole, chancellor of the Ilesa Diocese, moved that those amendments be accepted. The Ven. David Ekwueme supported him. Once validly placed before the assembly, a minimum vote of two-thirds of the members was required for the change to take place. The first amendment had proposed deletion of three subsections in Chapter I of the Church of Nigeria's constitution and their replacement with three new ones. By wide acclamation, the amendments were passed. A major modification was, therefore, effected in the constitution of the church as follows:

> "The Church of Nigeria" or "This Church" shall be in full communion with
> all Anglican Churches, Dioceses and Provinces that hold and maintain the

---

1. Minutes of the General Synod, September 12, 2005, held at Anambra State, Nigeria.

Historic Faith, Doctrine, Sacrament and Discipline of the one Holy, Catholic, and Apostolic Church as the Lord has commanded in His holy word and as the same are received as taught in the Book of Common Prayer and the ordinal of 1662 and in the Thirty-Nine Article of Religion.

The change was a fundamental alteration. Palpable was its radical implication. The Nigerian Church was distancing itself from its hard-nosed Western colleagues. Categorical also was its stand to sever relationship with any church that decided to trample on the Bible or the teachings of the Communion.

Reaction to the decision of the Nigerian church by the hawks in the gay movement was understandable. All sorts of daggers were drawn on the church. Ironically, little attention seemed to be paid to another part of the amendments that contained a more serious implication for relations between the Nigerian Church and the global Anglican Communion. In Chapter IX Section 39 (c) of the constitution, a new clause had been added that empowered the primate of the Church of Nigeria

to create convocations, chaplaincies of like-minded faithful outside Nigeria and to appoint persons within or outside Nigeria to administer them and the Primate shall give Episcopal Oversight.

One of the basic laws of motion in physics is that action and reaction are equal and opposite. The Nigerian church had gone exactly opposite to the direction of its American, Canadian, and British counterparts. Intriguing however was the last part of the amendment empowering its primate "to create convocations, chaplaincies of like-minded faithful outside Nigeria." This was more revolutionary than the radical decision of altering its constitution. It meant the church could become an umbrella for dissenting Anglicans in the American, Canadian, and British churches. Did Nigeria have the capability to see the idea through? Only one man held the key, and that was Archbishop Akinola, the primate and head of the Church of Nigeria.

Exactly forty days after the monumental Nigerian decision, the archbishop was in Egypt. Akinola's trip was for the Third Global South-South Encounter. The Egypt Encounter came eight years after the previous one. The second Encounter was hosted by Kuala Lumpur, Malaysia. From the situation developing, the Third Global South-South Encounter was bound to be of interest, not just within the Global South but to countries outside the bloc too. The last time the group met in Kuala Lumpur was on the eve of the Lambeth Conference and its outcome, the *Second Trumpet,* had serious impact on both the proceeding and the major resolution reached, the decision on human sexuality. At the Egypt Encounter, 103 delegates from twenty provinces of the Communion had converged on the land of the Pharaohs. They were there from October 25–30, 2005. The assembly, its location, and the theme selected for discussion were symbolic and indicative.[2]

2. "Third Trumpet: Communique from 3rd South to South Encounter" and "Delegates and Guests List at the 3rd South to South Encounter," from the personal papers of Archbishop Peter Akinola.

Turnout for this meeting was larger than that of the previous one. Egypt's Ain El Sukhna city, the venue of the Encounter, which was by the Red Sea, conveyed a sense of biblical, historical reawakening. It echoed that part of Bible history when God called his people to cross into a new land and be "a light to the nations" of the world. From the explicit and implicit thoughts and actions of the leaders, the Global South primates' journey to Egypt was a renaissance of sorts. The theme of the Encounter, "One, Holy, Catholic and Apostolic Church: Being a Faithful Church for such a Time as This," spoke volumes. Every key word of the theme—One, Holy, Catholic, Apostolic, and Faithful Church—touched on the root of the Communion's crisis. The doctrinal difference was also at the core of their disagreement with their Western counterparts.

One week later, the retreat ended. The Global South leaders reflected on the purpose of the coming to the Red Sea, to "seek the face of God, to hear His Word afresh and to be renewed by His spirit." They wanted an "encounter," which is why they had not termed their assembly a conference. From the Red Sea, they issued the *Third Trumpet*. The communique was comprehensive and extensive. Copious, it dealt with every major issue of concern to their common existence. The *Third Trumpet* addressed 19 sub-themes in its 45 paragraphs. It's appropriate to call the views of the leaders the "Red Sea Declaration." They touched on very broad subjects, ranging from poverty to illiteracy to HIV/AIDS, drought, and natural disasters like earthquakes and hurricanes. However, unmistakable was the central point of their interest. In the first part of the *Trumpet*, they expressed their chief concern:

> Apart from the world conditions, our own Anglican Communion, sadly, continues to be weakened by unchecked revisionist teaching and practices.

No Global South leader was at the Encounter without a prior individual position or viewpoint on the boiling issue dividing the Communion. Nigeria, for instance, arrived at the retreat after a fresh adjustment to its constitution.[3] The Church of the Province of South East Asia remained inflexible on its stand that both the culprits and their accomplices must recant or remain pariahs from the Communion. The Southern Cone had already taken the battle to American soil. Justifying the action, the province said it was forced to intervene rather than watching from the sidelines and agonizing over the American church's continued persecution of opponents of their illegal action. Their pragmatic step had enabled the embattled churches and their leaders to have the episcopal oversight they needed. The same opportunity was extended to the Diocese of Recife of the Anglican Episcopal Church of Brazil, whose primate had continued to persecute opponents for rejecting his pro-gay stand. Uganda, Tanzania, Kenya, and Rwanda all equally indicated inflexible stands against the unilateral rewriting of the Communion's majority decision on human sexuality. Further irksome to the Global

---

3. Minutes of the General Synod, September 12, 2005, held at Anambra State, Nigeria.

South leaders was the outcome of the ACC's Nottingham meeting that had continued to witness the North American churches' displaying arrogance.

The Egypt Encounter marked the boiling point as well as a turning point for the Anglican crisis.

The first major resolution of the leaders was formation of the Council of Anglican Provinces of the Americas and the Caribbean (CAPAC). Parallel to the Council of Anglican Provinces in Africa (CAPA) that Archbishop Akinola was leading, CAPAC's objective was to bring together Anglican provinces in the Americas and Caribbean. The two organizations were similar in work, outlook, and structure. CAPAC would extend to the region a platform of sustaining the "historic formularies of Anglican faith." Embedded in its mission was also the task of providing an avenue for interaction and partnership among the churches. The implication of the resolution might not be obvious unless carefully scrutinized. It appeared a subtle move on the part of the Global South leaders to curtail the prodigious influence of the Western churches, particularly the United States, on their Global South counterparts. Addiction to the charity of the West had only made them weak, vulnerable, and susceptible to manipulation, which would be exploited to corrupt their faith and doctrine.

Following the first resolution, the *Trumpet* blew loud and strident on the crisis bedevilling the Communion. Categorically, the leaders deplored "the current crisis provoked by North American intransigence." Once more, they demanded the "innovating provinces/dioceses conform to the historic teaching." The alternative would be that "the offending provinces will, by their actions, be choosing to walk apart." There was nothing new to this threat. Owing to the way the expression had been so overused, it had virtually lost its punch. Yet the threat seemed to have teeth this time around. "The Global South calls for the errant provinces to be disciplined," they echoed.

Simultaneously, they proposed the adoption of an Anglican Covenant. The Covenant, they believed, constituted an inviolable way to resolve the Communion's protracted crisis. They insisted that a Covenant "rooted in historic faith and formularies . . . provides a biblical foundation for our life, ministry and mission as a Communion." They expected the bond between them to be strengthened by the Covenant because they would "be mutually accountable, thereby providing an authentic fellowship within the Communion." The Global South leaders pledged to "go forward as those entrusted 'with the faith once delivered.'"

Amazingly, the first reaction came from the most unusual of all places and quarters. It was from Archbishop Njongonkulu Ndungane, primate of the Anglican Church of Southern Africa. He had no welcoming word for the communique, but rather venom. The criticism was as hostile as the mind behind it. Was the reaction surprising or expected? It would depend on one's ability to read correctly underlying or driving motives. For reasons best known to him, Archbishop Ndungane had withheld his personal attendance at the Encounter.[4] But Southern Africa still sent an official delegation to the retreat in Egypt.[5] The three-member delegation included the Rt. Rev Dr. J. T. Seoka, Ven. Keith De Vos, and Canon Maureen Sithole.

Since the end of the 1998 Lambeth Conference, Ndungane had not had a warm relationship with the Global South despite his being one of its leaders. He headed a Lambeth Conference committee that examined the human sexuality issue, the one which had favored adoption of gay and lesbian ordination.[6] Overwhelmingly, the majority threw out the recommendation. After the Conference, Ndungane broke ranks with his colleagues. The Southern African primate was one of the two primates in Africa who signed the so-called 1998 pastoral letter to the gays and lesbians. The Global South had no fewer than twenty primates within its fold, and only two, Ndungane and Archbishop Khotso Makhulu, the bishop of Botswana and primate of Central Africa, tailed along with the Western church leaders.

Until the underlying reason revealed itself, Ndungane's revolt against the stand of Global South colleagues could have passed as a mark of strength, suggesting he was upholding a principled stand or defending a conviction, even if unpopular. Or perhaps he found himself in an unfortunate situation like that of the American Presiding Bishop Frank Griswold, where his hands were tied. But, unlike Griswold, Ndugane didn't suffer the trajectory of a disobedient church plus an entrenched gay group that had compromised the church's leadership, making its leader a figurehead. There was no evidence that his Southern African bishops appiled pressure on him to take the stand he had maintained on the Communion's crisis over homosexuality. As a group, the Southern African bishops were not homosexuality champions. Admittedly, there were those with sympathy for the aberrant lifestyle. Indeed, out of the thirty-one bishops that attended the 1998 Lambeth Conference from Southern Africa, including Ndungane, only eight signed the infamous pastoral letter. That left an overwhelming twenty-three other bishops not in support of homosexuality. Looming large, however, like a huge shadow was Ndungane's predecessor—Archbishop Desmond Tutu.[13]

The former Southern Africa archbishop was an avatar. He had a commanding presence in the life of the Southern African church. Two years before the 1998 Lambeth Conference, Tutu had retired from his leadership of the church in Southern Africa paving the way for Ndungane as his successor. Tutu reminded one of those iconic and enigmatic American church leaders, but he was black and a victim of apartheid. Religion and politics seemed not to have a dividing line between them with him. Any headcount of church leaders in Southern Africa was bound to have Tutu on top of

4. Akinola, "A Message to Archbishop Ndungane," from archive and personal papers of Archbishop Peter Akinola.

5. "Delegates and Guests List at the 3rd South to South Encounter," from the archive and personal papers of Archbishop Peter Akinola.

6. http://www.anglicancommunion.org/resources/document-library/lambeth-conference/2008/section-h-human-sexuality?author=Lambeth+Conference&year=2008 retrieved.

the veneration list. He was the ubiquitous father of the church, especially during the political struggle against apartheid.

The politics of protest nurtured Tutu; they defined his leadership in both South Africa and the world. Initially, his ambition was to train as a physician. Owing to poverty, the desire failed to materialize, and instead he pursued his father's profession of teaching. For a while, he remained in the profession, but in protest, he resigned his appointment following passage of the Bantu Education Act. The unjust law had limited the educational prospects of South African blacks. This affronted Tutu's sense of justice. So he moved on to train at St. Peter's Theology College in Rosettenville, South Africa. Twenty-nine years old at the time, he was ordained as an Anglican minister in 1960. Two years later, he began his climb to world fame with further education, receiving his bachelor's and master's degrees at the King's College, London. While there, he served as part-time curate at the St. Albans Cathedral. The gay priest Jeffery John, rejected as a bishop, was posted to the same church as its dean forty-two years later.

Tutu had much courage and, perhaps, the luck to emerge at a time his audacity had a big foe to fight with a great impact. From 1967 to 1972, in his early career with the church in South Africa, he was at the front of the attack on the obnoxious apartheid regime. He might not have been in the trenches or throwing his fists fiercely in the air or organizing boycotts, but his constant fiery speeches decried the "circumstances of the African population." The cassock, the trademark of his vocation, probably bought him a sort of immunity. Christianity had anointed him as a messenger of God, and it seemed the South African apartheid regime was unwilling to incur God's further damnation by touching His anointed. Furthermore, Tutu's philosophy of nonviolence endeared him to major countries of the West. He was not afraid to take unpopular stands, though they tended to make him a prophet without honor in own home. Not only did he fault the apartheid system, but he levelled "harsh criticism" against "the violent tactics of some of the anti-apartheid groups such as the African National Congress," where the bulk of the South Africa's freedom fighters congregated.

The turning point came in 1976 with the Soweto riots.[7] Like the Stonewall riots in America that radically redefined the homosexual battle, the violence that erupted in Soweto altered irrevocably the struggle against apartheid. The government had made the Afrikaans language the compulsory medium of instruction in black schools, and this prompted the uprising. Tutu seized the opportunity and campaigned vigorously for an "economic boycott of South Africa." By this time, he was the bishop of Lesotho, and then he moved auspiciously higher to become secretary-general of the South African Council of Churches, a position he held for two years, 1976–1978. That broader platform gave him immeasurable opportunities. Tutu spoke now for all the churches in South Africa. The boost bolstered his international image. Except for a brief period of incarceration in 1980 after a protest march, and the revocation of his passport twice, the South African apartheid regime knew the limit to its harassment of Tutu.

7. http://www.sahistory.org.za/topic/june-16-soweto-youth-uprising.

He mastered the weak points of the obnoxious regime, relentlessly punching the regime hardest where it was most vulnerable. Vigorously, he incited global opinion against the government. Often, he compared the regime and the situation in South Africa to the despicable condition brought on by Nazis and communists. Tutu's finest hour came on October 16, 1984, when he was awarded the Nobel Peace Prize. His name was strengthened by further honors that started coming his way from different parts of the world.

Back at home, in 1985, he was appointed bishop of Johannesburg. A year later, he rose to the peak of his episcopal career, becoming the first black leader of the South African church. Amassing more influence, for almost a decade, he served as president of the All Africa Conference of Churches. Even after the end of apartheid and his leadership of the South African church, Tutu found public causes for which to fight. He headed the South African Truth and Reconciliation Commission established in 1999. In a similar vein, he was elected to the board of directors of the International Criminal Court's Trust Fund for Victims in 2003.

Furthermore, the United Nations named him to its advisory panel on genocide in 2006. Earlier, in 2000, the Desmond Tutu Peace Foundation was launched, and two years later he established the same organization in America—the Desmond Tutu Peace Foundation USA. Incidentally, America would have been a welcoming place for him if he had decided to make the country his home. Tutu received all the head-swelling honors that any individual could get from America. Of his approximately one hundred honors and awards across the world over a thirty-year period (1978–2008), the most from a single country (38) came from America. He was the toast of institutions and groups of various kinds, including homosexual organizations.

Tutu was a great world personality of African origin. Yet, great people are not without their character flaws. Writ large in his inspiring accomplishments was that he was a man of the world, who served the world, and was not of the Word. At the outbreak of the controversy over homosexuality in the Anglican Communion, it was not surprising where he pitched his tent. He was one of the first former leaders of the Church globally to openly comment on Gene Robinson's consecration. Tutu saw nothing wrong in the aberration committed by the American church. To him, "All belong . . . Gay, lesbian, so-called straight . . . All."

Tutu wasn't at the 1998 Lambeth Conference. He had been out of office for more than six years when the disagreement began. Of course, from his vantage point, he knew that the Communion's stand reflected the majority opinion. For over a decade, he was part of the international leadership of the Anglican Church, and he knew the way major decisions were made. Allegedly, Tutu was once considered for the Communion's topmost ecclesiastical position, the revered seat of the archbishop of Canterbury. He missed it narrowly in 1990. George Carey edged him out just as Rowan Williams displaced Michael Nazir-Ali as Carey's successor. Beyond this, however, was the fact that Tutu's prominence extended beyond the Anglican Communion's narrow world. His role at the World Council of Churches further added to his reputation as an international church leader. Again, it is a truism that prominence, fame, or reputation does not mean the individual is infallible.

His support for gay and lesbian ordination was certainly an attempt at pleasing his American friends. Of apparently little consequence to him was the deliberate scriptural violation and moral aberration the perversion involved. Not only was the Bible being undermined; distressing as well was the contempt with which he held the views of Anglican Church leaders. Tutu would rather see his African colleagues be politically correct than maintain the sanctity of the Bible. Publicly, he upbraided the principled stand, lamenting that "in the face of some of the most horrendous problems facing Africa, we concentrate on 'what do I do in bed with whom.'" It was a kick in the groin for those he caricatured as religious zealots.

Tutu was a gallant solider of the anti-apartheid struggle, never apologizing for his efforts. He loathed the obnoxious minority rule with passion, and with the same breadth of zealotry crusaded for a government of majority rule. But what yardstick was he now using to justify a parallel vicious minority enforcing their will over the majority? There was a contradiction between the Tutu who saw minority enslavement of the majority under apartheid as unjust, and the other Tutu who chastised the majority for rejecting the oppressive coercion of the minority. The two Tutus simply didn't match.

Nevertheless, the archbishop emeritus exercised a powerful influence over the South African church. He had said publicly and with confidence that, "In our Church here in South Africa, [sexual orientation] doesn't make a difference." Tutu spoke with authority, notwithstanding the fact that 23 South African bishops at the Lambeth Conference declined to associate with the pro-gay agenda. Perhaps to compensate, he added, "We believe that they should remain celibate." But was Jeffrey John or Gene Robinson celibate? Yet Tutu was unmoved: "We don't see what the fuss is about."[8]

Events were to prove him wrong because a later "fuss" developed. Ironically, the man who raised the "fuss" was his successor and trusted ally, Ndungane. Prior to an astonishing expression of regret over the gay issue, he had given the impression of being one of the staunchest defenders of the aberrant life style. Though he stood in the minority with his predecessor and with only a few others in the entire South African church, Ndungane was still not a bootlicking or cringing office seeker.

He was a hero of the anti-apartheid struggle. A decade younger than Tutu, he was born in 1941 while Tutu's birth date was 1931. As a 19-year-old radical, he was already an undergraduate at the University of Cape Town with the trait that characterized most every progressive South African youth of his time—idealism. He also had audacity, another attribute of many of the young radicals. As expected, Ndungane didn't stand by watching the vile apartheid regime. In March 1960, as a University of Cape Town student, he joined others in the anti-Pass Law protest. The 1952 law—the

8. Bates, "A Match Made in Heaven."

Natives (Abolition of Passes and Co-ordination of Documents) Act—turned South Africans to foreigners in their own home.[9] Every black South African age 16 and above was required "to carry a "pass book" at all times within white areas. Failure to do so would lead to arrest and imprisonment. Ndungane not only joined in the protest but also was unrelenting in his involvement with other anti-apartheid activities.

Predictably, he was arrested. And unlike Desmond Tutu, he was sent to Robben Island along with many other political prisoners. For Ndungane, the three-year incarceration offered an environment for meditation, and it was during this period that he decided to seek ordination. He found favor with the archbishop of Cape Town, the Most Rev. Robert Selby Taylor, who guided him from 1971 to 1975, when he was ordained. In one of the few ways his path followed that of Desmond Tutu, he enrolled at King's College London. Like him, he earned both his bachelor of divinity and master of theology degrees there.

After sundry clerical responsibilities, he was elected to the episcopate in 1991. He was elected the archbishop of Cape Town and metropolitan of the Anglican Church of Southern Africa in 1996, as Tutu's successor. In a step identical to his predecessor, Ndungane founded the Africa Monitor, a private, non-profit, and pan-Africa organization. Its goal was to monitor "the fulfilment of the promises of both the aid-giving and aid-receiving countries." Noticeably, in the same fashion as Tutu, Ndungane didn't spare his colleagues from the Global South. Constantly, he berated them for their resolute stand against their Western counterparts on the gay issue.

This was what brought him and Archbishop Akinola into collision immediately after the conclusion of Egypt's Global South Encounter and the issuance of the *Third Trumpet,* its official communique. The media exchange between Archbishops Akinola and Ndungane probably marked the only time when the Nigerian church leader engaged a fellow African archbishop in hot public exchange.

Ndungane fired the first salvo. At the conclusion of the Encounter, the Global South leaders, apart from the official communique, had released "a letter that was sharply critical of Williams (the Archbishop of Canterbury)." The Anglican Church leader had attended the Cairo conference where he also addressed the participants. Publicly, Ndungane had denounced Akinola's letter to Williams on behalf of the Global South. Short of calling the letter a fraud, he alleged that his "delegate at the meeting, Bishop Johannes Seoka had found himself excluded from meetings, including those at which the letter was discussed." For reasons best known to him, Ndungane refused to demand an explanation from the archbishop. Nor did he query the secretariat of the Global South regarding the matter. Instead, he used the *Church Times* of Britain to pour out his umbrage.

The message he gave to the public showed the side of the matter on which he stood. The tone was that of an undisguised smear campaign. It was a calculated attempt to bring the Global South leadership to disrepute and to denounce the integrity

9. https://en.wikipedia.org/wiki/Pass_laws.

of his Nigerian colleague. Archbishop Akinola was disheartened. The message and not the messenger was what depressed him. He was displeased with the contents and the channel selected for the communication. The most distressing aspect, however, was that he found out about the offensive publication through another British media outlet that wanted his reaction to the diatribe. Frequently, Ndungane had chided fellow Global South primates that they were expending too much energy on "the less important issue of homosexuality." His refrain parroted the constant Western propaganda message that developing countries were wasting time on unnecessary issues instead of concentrating attention on serious challenges facing them like "peace, hunger, sharia and HIV/AIDS." This was a mantra Desmond Tutu was equally fond of employing.

Archbishop Akinola' rebuttal to Ndungane's public claims was prompt. He wove the refutation with a fine silk of gentle rebuke. In the rebuttal that he published on November 18, 2005, "Brother Ndungane, you got it all wrong," he admonished in one pithy sentence.[10] He accused his South African compatriot of feeding the public with "unfortunate presuppositions" and of engaging in "an attempt to cause a division amongst the African and *Global South* leaders." He added, "These leaders can no longer be pulled by the nose." Akinola wondered why Ndungane, who fought for majority rule in his country, decided to accept the "arrogance of a few flagrantly disregarding the stand of the entire Anglican Communion." "Should there not be a protest against such disrespect?" he questioned. "Should we keep quiet because they say we are 'poor' and do not have the capacity to challenge the 'affluent' West?"

Akinola suspected the root of Ndungane's malice, the motive for his "unguarded and scathing criticism." Feeling sorry for him, he believed Ndungane was overcome by the "latent feeling of hurt since the Lambeth Conference Committee on Human Sexuality." The South African church leader chaired the committee that had worked on the issue. Unfortunately, against their expectations, their recommendation "was overwhelmingly overruled." Since then his bitterness had not healed. Nor had he succeeded in managing his indignation against his colleagues.

For reasons only he could fathom, Ndungane decided to single out his Nigerian counterpart for personal attack in the tirade. He hit him below the belt, disparaging his leadership of the Nigerian church. He ridiculed Akinola, portraying him as an ineffectual, ineffective, and inefficient leader. He told the Nigerian church leader to heal himself first before attempting to cure others; Akinola should cure his Nigerian church first of its problems before venturing to lead the struggle of addressing the Communion's ills.

Akinola told Ndungane politely that he was not "informed on issues concerning Nigeria." Obviously, Ndungane lacked personal knowledge of his Nigerian colleague. Akinola was not a "media buff" or someone with a lust for publicity. "That you have not heard any fuss from me in the foreign media," he wrote in the reply, "does not

10. Akinola, "A Message to Archbishop Ndungane," from the archive and personal papers of Archbishop Peter Akinola.

mean the Church . . . I lead is doing nothing." The truth was that within the short time of his leadership, the Nigerian church had accomplished a lot, both at home and abroad. Akinola was hurt that his colleague could choose to disparage him in the foreign media without any valid reason or just cause. Closing his response to Ndungane as civilly as he could, Akinola wrote: "I ask you dear brother to face issues and not fall into the temptation of 'casting stones.'"

In the courteous ending of his rejoinder, Akinola had exhorted Ndungane to act decorously, fairly, and honestly. To overlook the vitriolic attack would have done a severe moral wrong to Akinola and the other Global South leaders. As he put it,

> Remote was the possibility that I wanted to pick a fight with a fellow brother, colleague and Archbishop. The tirades were vented in public and I owed it a duty to correct it publicly too.

On December 1, 2005, a dramatic event was to occur, just twelve days after the conflict surfaced between Ndungane and Akinola. The South African Constitutional Court had delivered a landmark judgement, ruling that it was "unconstitutional for the state to deny same-sex couples the ability to marry."[11] The court directed parliament to rectify the situation within one year. The Constitutional Court's judgement was a watershed in the South African homosexual community's quest to have equal treatment with their heterosexual counterparts.

The genesis of the case was the country's post-apartheid constitution. Both the Interim Constitution of April 27, 1994, and the final one ratified three years later on February 4, 1997, forbade "discrimination on the basis of sex, gender or *sexual orientation*." It was a unique South African invention as no other country in the world had such a provision in its law, that is, the use of the specific phrase "sexual orientation." It armed South African gays and lesbians with the weapon to begin a series of court cases in different areas where they desired advantage. Incrementally, they began to establish a foothold in society. The Constitutional Court's decision became the hallmark. The government responded to the verdict with the promulgation of the Civil Union Act on November 30, 2006.

The South African Civil Union Act was no different from the United Kingdom's civil partnership law; it was all about same-sex marriage except in name. It paralleled the country's Marriage Act, which applied only to opposite-sex marriages. Now, a replica of it was available for homosexuals. With passage of the new civil union law, South Africa, indeed, had achieved a feat. She was the fifth country in the world to legalize same-sex marriage. In Africa, she was the odd one out, even as of January 2016. Within the Anglican Communion and the Global South, she had the unenviable position of being only the second country outside Europe to permit same-sex marriage.

The biggest irony was that the celebrated accomplishment didn't elate Archbishop Ndungane. He was depressed by the development. Unbelievable was his coming out

11. https://en.wikipedia.org/wiki/Minister_of_Home_Affairs_v_Fourie.

publicly to denounce the law. Ndungane's *volte-face* was incredible. Here was a previous critic of his Global South colleagues on homosexuality now objecting to legalized same-sex partnerships on his country's soil. Inconceivable also was his return to the position of the Anglican Church that he had maligned so many times. Could he have suffered temporary amnesia that he was one of the eight primates who signed the 1998 perfidious Pastoral Letter to the Anglican Gays and Lesbians during the Lambeth Conference? With his new light of awareness, Ndungane began singing the same tune as his Global South colleagues.

> As far as we are concerned as a church, our understanding of marriage is between a man and a woman. And as a church, and the Anglican Church in particular, we have said no to same-sex unions.[12]

The South African archbishop swallowed his pride. He was not embarrassed to recant publicly the position that he had once defended vigorously. It was a sort of parting of ways with his predecessor, Archbishop Desmond Tutu. A veteran soldier of public causes, the archbishop emeritus of Cape Town remained adamant. He exploited every opportunity to engage in remonstration on the subject. At a forum, for instance, Tutu paraded his theology of rebellion saying he would "never worship a 'homophobic God.'" If it should come to that, he "would rather go to hell."

Tutu's view was an unpopular one both within South African society and the Southern African Church. South Africans in great numbers deplored the gay marriage law. Indeed, the predominant public attitude was not in support of homosexuality. Three years after the country had permitted gay marriage, this still was the case. A 2008 survey showed that "84% of South Africans said homosexual sexual behaviour is always wrong." The overwhelming majority contrasted sharply with the minute "8% who said that it is not wrong at all." Repeated half a decade after legalization of same-sex unions, people's opinion remained unchanged. More than half of South Africans (61%) "said society should not accept homosexuality." As admired as Desmond Tutu was in South Africa, a solid majority of the population differed with the Nobel Peace Prize winner on this issue.

Even in his immediate constituency, the church, his influence was limited on this matter. The Anglican Church of Southern Africa extends beyond South Africa. South Africa might be its hub, the most populous nation, with three to four million Anglicans, and twenty-one out of the twenty-eight dioceses making up the province. Still, it is just one country. Mozambique, with two dioceses, is part of the province. There are also Angola, Lesotho, Namibia, Swaziland, and Saint Helena, each with a diocese. Incidentally, all eight bishops from this region who signed the 1998 pro-gay and lesbian letter during the Lambeth Conference were from the nation of South Africa. None was from any of these other geographical dioceses. Furthermore, only the government of South Africa had passed the gay marriage law.

12. "Archbishop Njongonkulu of Cape Town Declares Same-Sex Marriages Unchristian."

Despite the uninformed outside commentators, and the naïve external opportunists wanting to cash in on the popularity of an individual, the Southern African Anglican Church was wise enough to guard its internal cohesion from disruption. The Church, to external observers, was "the most liberal Anglican province in Africa," the yardstick constructed mainly based on the issues of women's ordination and homosexuality. The country was rated as "the only African Anglican province that ordains women to the episcopate."

Prudently, however, the Southern African church maintained its delicate stand by stating it had "no official position" on "the ordination of homosexuals." Understandably, however, the Western media peddled the falsehood that "some dioceses have ordained openly gay and lesbian priests." The wholly untrue propaganda was a bid to delude the world, convincing it that the aberrant behavior was not peculiar to the Western churches.

Possibly that was the reason Desmond Tutu's daughter put distance between herself and South Africa—indeed, Africa—when she decided to follow in her father's vocation. Mpho Tutu was a bold lady, a chip off Desmond Tutu's old block.[13] Power and authority rarely overawed her. Tutu remembered that his daughter's strength of character had been engrained from childhood. She had a natural inquisitiveness and precocity, and was an extrovert fond of pestering her father with her childish curiosity. Desmond's method of buying his peace from her was to bully her with a command to "shut up! You talk too much!" Rather than being contrite, she would fire back, "*You* talk too much too," and would add, "You talk all alone in church."

Her traits led to social activism, which she undertook later on in life. She began devoting her time to running after-school and summer programs for children from poor and single-parent homes. Later, she opted for ordination. Mpho enrolled at the College of the Transfiguration, an Anglican provincial seminary in South Africa. This was around the time of the 1998 Lambeth Conference, which foreclosed ordination of gays and lesbians in the Anglican Church. While in school, she had an opportunity to develop a pastoral care program, and the Episcopal Evangelical Education Society in the United States provided her the grant for it.

After one year at her South African seminary, she moved to the United States. There, she enrolled at the Episcopal Divinity School in Cambridge, Massachusetts, for a three-year master of divinity program. The Episcopal Divinity School was a center for revolt. It offered refuge to two of the Philadelphia Eleven—women who were ordained to the priesthood before it was allowed by the Episcopal Church—providing them faculty appointments and full priestly duties, including celebration of the Eucharist, which the Church leadership had forbidden. Indeed, the school rewarded every act of deviant behavior, from homosexuality to heresy.

Mpho completed her theological education and on June 7, 2003, was ordained as a deacon at age 39 at Christ Church Cathedral in Springfield, Massachusetts. She didn't

13. Scaife, "Desmond Tutu's Daughter Follows in Father's Footsteps."

leave the Episcopal Divinity School without taking the school's influence with her as accompanying baggage. She had begun work in the ministry as a married woman with a daughter, her husband, Joe Burris, a sportswriter for the Boston Globe. Joe and Mpho added another daughter, and in the meantime, Mpho became not only a full priest but rose in status to be a reverend canon. Yet Rev. Canon Mpho Tutu's trajectory resembled that of Rev. Canon Gene Robinson. Just as Robinson divorced his wife after two children, Mpho, too, broke up with her husband. In the same way that he took to a gay partner, she also settled with her lesbian spouse, Marceline van Furth.

Mpho and Marceline developed their mutual attraction in the workplace. Mpho was the executive director of the Desmond and Leah Tutu Legacy Foundation, and Marceline was a professor of pediatric infectious diseases at the Vrije University in Amsterdam. She also occupied the Desmond Tutu Chair in Medicine at the university. Three years before the relationship became a full-blown union, reports say, Marceline secured "a €2 million (R36.62 million) donation" to the Tutu Legacy Foundation. The two women were both divorced and were said to be "long time lesbian partners." They were wed at a private ceremony in Oegstgeest, a municipal town in the Netherlands' South Holland province.[14] Their love transcended color, creed, and culture. The nuptial ties between Mpho, a South African, and Marceline, a Dutch, broke ground by crossing social, cultural, and religious barriers.

Easy as it was to get the union accomplished, one knotty problem trailed it. Mpho couldn't put the obstacle away. It was the Anglican Church's embargo on ordaining gays and lesbians as priests, a regulation still in effect twelve years later when, on December 30, 2015, Mpho entered her lesbian marriage. In other words, Mpho was ineligible to be made a priest except in a country like America that had no respect for the decision of the Communion. However, the Southern African Church was not willing to be dragged into the controversy, as it knew the consequences. Diplomatically, it employed the usual ecclesiastical language of obfuscation to explain away the dilemma.

Thabo Makgoba had succeeded Archbishop Ndungane at the forefront of Southern African Church leadership. Makgoba wasn't one disposed to sounding politically correct or bowing to political interests. He spoke the language of the majority of Southern African Church leaders; he accepted his role as their public voice. Makgoba wasn't at the 1998 Lambeth Conference, and perhaps, that helped him. It also helped him that he hadn't inherited the office from a legendary figure and thus was not susceptible to walking in his shadow, unlike his predecessor.

To date, Makgoba was the youngest South African Anglican archbishop. Still, at age 47, he wasn't a man of limited experience when he assumed office in 2007. He had received the Cross of St. Augustine, the second highest international honor for outstanding service in the Anglican Communion, from the archbishop of Canterbury.

14. Virtue, "Netherlands: Daughter of Archbishop Desmond Tutu Ties Knot with Woman Professor."

A year later, the Episcopal Divinity School in the United States, the same institution that produced Mpho Tutu, had thrown a fellowship at him. He was made a procter fellow at the institution. Yet, reading between the lines, Makgoba wasn't a man easily influenced by patronage or fawning opportunism. When asked about the deliberate perversion of the Communion's stand by Mpho, he had tactfully, though firmly, asserted the position of the Southern Africa Church. He maintained categorically that "our Province has in the past sought and reached consensus on the issues."[15] Nagged continuously by journalists to speak on the defiance, he was clear on his stand: "I wish to continue that tradition."

Journalists adept at interpreting nuanced language would not fail to detect the import of the South African church leader's statement. He helped make it further intelligible through a clarification: "There is sometimes a tendency among our fellow Anglicans in other provinces, to use African Christians as proxies in their own culture war." Makgoba preferred not to rush where caution was due. Part of his self-imposed restraint was to be careful "addressing the issues . . . in first instance, in the British and American church media." Any intelligent observer would know that the Western media were as knowledgeable about happenings in the Communion as they were motivated by overt partisanship. They were as much part of the unresolved charade as those playing the game within the Communion itself. They knew the score, for instance, because Mpho had told the press many times herself that "she was ordained in the Episcopal Church in the US." By the polity of the Church, she was "'canonically resident'" in the Diocese of Washington, DC. And she assured all, "In terms of the canon, I must have the approval of my diocesan bishop to marry, which I have." Of course, her bishop was an American. Mpho's transgression was neither a burden nor a cross for the South African Church, therefore, to bear. Her being an openly practicing lesbian brought no new challenge to the worldwide Anglican Communion.

The candor with which Archbishop Makgoba spoke in 2016 about the homosexuality issue was striking. Almost nine years in office, he underscored the foolhardiness of the Western churches in continuing to assume that the Global South could be browbeaten into submission. An African proverb says, "A small axe is not sufficient to cut down a large tree." Thus, the aberrant churches of the West could not find an axe with which to cut the Global South leaders to size. Despite their inexhaustible bag of tricks, the many contrived plots always flopped. Even in 2005, when Ndungane had picked on Akinola, the voice might have been that of the South African archbishop, but the tune definitely was not his. The question was whether the South African church leader was aware of the broader plot or just an innocent tool in the hands of those trying to subvert the Global South leaders, particularly its main man in front, Archbishop Akinola.

What gave the conspiracy away was the timing of Archbishop Ndungane's media attack on Akinola, coinciding with the latter's trip to America for a crucial conference

15. Conger, "Cape Town Archbishop Responds to Tutu Gay Wedding News."

in Pittsburgh.[16] He was to lead a gathering of fellow, anti-gay bishops and priests at that November 22, 2005, meeting where they were scheduled to consider "the way forward for a new life of Anglicanism in the United States and North America." It's not, therefore, surprising why there was a desperate move to soil his name and bring him to disrepute before the Western media. Scurrilous as the malicious publication was, however, it didn't scuttle the conference.

To the contrary, Akinola arrived to an enthusiastic hero's welcome. The venue was suffused with high expectations. Two other archbishops from the Global South were also in attendance—Archbishop Henry Orombi, the Ugandan Church primate, and his retiring counterpart from South East Asia, Archbishop Yong Ping Chung. From Canada, the moderator of the Anglican Network in Canada, David Harvey, flew in to be part of the gathering. The Brazilian bishop of Recife, Robinson Cavalcanti, whom his primate had turned into an outcast because of his anti-gay stand, was there as well. A surfeit of the principled American clergy opposed to the Episcopal Church's stand on homosexuality attended. Conspicuous by his presence was the moderator of the Anglican Communion Network and Episcopal bishop of Pittsburgh, Robert Duncan, who coordinated the conference. Also, occupying the frontline was the fiery speaker and president of Forward In Faith North America, Bishop Keith Ackerman, the bishop of Quincy Diocese under the Episcopal Church. David Anderson, president of the American Anglican Council, was also in attendance.

The conference, similarly, attracted the attention of the chairman of the Common Cause Partnership, Presiding Bishop Leonard Riches, whose church had parted ways with the Episcopal Church about 132 years earlier over disagreement on doctrinal issues. Likewise present was Pastor Rick Warren, popular author of the bestselling book *Purpose Driven Life*, Anne Graham Lotz, daughter of American evangelist Billy Graham, and scores of others, including Joni Eareckson Tada, a quadriplegic member of the Reformed Episcopal Church.

From the theme, "The way forward for a new life of Anglicanism in the United States and North America," the conference was bound to raise the temperature. Archbishop Akinola was visible and played active roles throughout the two-day meeting. The underlying tone of the momentousness gathering was set right from the beginning. Duncan addressed them pointedly: "There are three choices we must make and in which we must stand." The first, as he put it, was to choose "truth over accommodation." The second was deciding on "accountability over autonomy." The third was choosing "mission over sullen inaction." Duncan paused, and then summarized, "Whether evangelical, catholic, or charismatic we are at a new beginning for Anglicanism in this country." Could this really be true? Was he referring to the same America where gay groups had assured of the country's total "homosexualization"?

---

16. Acker, "A Hope and a Future Conference—Realizing A New Day in the West," www.forward-faith.com.

Duncan should know the difference between a sermon and social action. Indeed, he seemed to be adequately persuaded of the necessity for the actions he was proposing.

For three years, they, as a group maintaining the pro-Communion stand, had been involved in fierce engagement with the gay campaigners within the Episcopal Church. The gay supporters had been outpacing them. In spite of their courage and will, the reality was that the gays were more combative in their approach. Duncan called attention to a recent conversation: Three weeks earlier, Archbishop of Canterbury Rowan Williams had told him, "I recognise the bishops, priests, and people of the Network as full members of the Anglican Communion . . . no matter what the jurisdiction." The declaration of the Canterbury was significant, coming from Archbishop Williams, who had the power and the authority to curtail the embarrassing situation in which the North American churches had put the Communion. Previously, with no success, the primates of the council had made a similar suggestion, to appoint episcopal oversight for disagreeing groups and churches seeing homosexuality the way the rest of the Anglican Church saw it.

Archbishop Henry Orombi, primate of the Anglican Church of Uganda, spoke after Duncan, dropping a bombshell: "The time for debate and talk is over." Orombi wasn't impressed by the guile and the deceit of doing things in politically correct ways. He added, to his North American colleagues, "You will suffer for the faith."

Orombi came from a background noted for Christian suffering. He had succeeded Livingstone Nkoyoyo, the Ugandan archbishop who had thrown American Presiding Bishop Frank Griswold's filthy lucre back at his face. His predecessor attended the 1998 Lambeth Conference, and Orombi hadn't assumed office until 2004, a year after the beginning of the Gene Robinson trouble. But he had not departed from the principled stand of his forerunner. He ventured encouragement: "The suffering is for a short while," adding "Don't lose hope."

Uganda, his home country, was once witness to severely brutal and repressive regimes. In the early period of Christianity, besides the expulsion of the pioneer missionaries, Christian converts were pressed to abandon their faith on pain of torture or death, but people would rather be martyred than forsake Christ. There had been an 1885 incident, the killing of three Anglican Ugandans and the execution of the arriving party of the archbishop of the Province of Eastern Equatorial Africa, James Hannington. The repression reached its height from 1886 to 1887, a period that became known as the era of Christian "martyrs of Uganda." In more recent times, there was the execution of the Ugandan Archbishop Janani Jakaliya Luwum, the second indigenous archbishop of the country, entering office in 1974, three years after Ugandan dictator Idi Amin had assumed power in a 1971 coup d'état. Amin returned Uganda to the animal kingdom. He made life short, nasty, and brutish for anyone who dared to oppose him. Luwum spoke out against Idi Amin, and in 1977, he ordered the archbishop's execution.

Nevertheless, the Church of Uganda still stands today, with nearly 9 million members, constituting nearly 40% of the population. Orombi found meaning in the Scripture: "We need to get on with the preaching the Gospel of Jesus Christ, though it may cost us dearly." The time for indecision was over. To him, they should no longer "be held back or be distracted by the Episcopal Church USA in its endless talk or delay."

Orombi's remarks opened the floodgate for yet other penetrating views. Bishop Ackerman of Forward in Faith North America followed with a subdued address. He regretted that the American church had "failed in our accountability." Unreserved was his apology for the harm that the American church had done through its "failure to our brothers and sisters of the Anglican Communion." The gathering represented for him a "historic moment in rebirth of Anglicanism in love and obedience to Jesus Christ." The moderator of the Anglican Network in Canada, David Harvey, couldn't agree with him more. He added primly, "The talk is finished; stand firm in the Gospel and don't compromise the truth."

Bishop Robinson Cavalcanti provided a living example and a practical testimony. He had refused to "compromise the truth." Beaten hard though he was, his head remained unbowed. He was a valiant soldier who bore with fortitude "his own suffering and that of his diocese." The first reality he thought the Network members should learn was "not [to] be afraid of losing position, status, job, or license." Office, position, status, jobs, and all those ephemeral assortments of life predisposed the individual to being vulnerable and exploitable. They were tools that could be used as threats to cow submission. Addressing his American colleagues, he observed, "You are the world's strongest nation but your message of the gospel is weak," adding, "There is an urgent need to reform Anglicanism." He went on, "It may be necessary to break man's law that we may follow the law of God." "Please don't be afraid," he exhorted them. "Go and tell!"

Tell who? Would it be the Presiding Bishop Frank Griswold? Or retired bishops like John Spong, Otis Charles, and Douglas Theuner? Or the current ones typified by John Chane and Jon Bruno? Or the 76 bishops that signed the perfidious letter to Anglican gays and lesbians during the 1988 Lambeth Conference? Or people like Louie Crew of Integrity USA, the weevil eating at the stalk of the Episcopal Church?

Cavalcanti's words were a call for action. Indeed, everyone in the hall was primed for it. On that bright day of November 23, 2005, in the city of Pittsburgh, the Anglican crisis entered a new phase. The gathering of the respectable Christian faithful answered in a sombre, orderly, and peaceful manner, in contrast with what the gays and lesbians dramatically expressed in 1969 on the night of the Stonewall riots in New York. Heads were not broken nor legs crushed. There was no disturbing of public peace nor fighting with the law. With a determined expression, the leaders resolved to give unto Anglicanism what was scripturally Anglican.

Archbishop Akinola assured the Americans and Canadians, "We are with you," even as he subtly chided his colleagues:

Anglicans in this country let too many things get in their way of taking a clear stand for the Gospel. From this great nation, we have seen a weak stand for the faith.

He added, "But you have to tell us how to help you." It wasn't that Akinola didn't know how aggravating the situation had become for the faithful American church leaders and congregations defending the Bible and the stand of the Communion. Indeed, he was well aware of the provocations, including the need to "express their disappointment with the Panel of Reference appointed to hear the cases of the oppression of the orthodox Anglicans." Known as well was the Panel's infuriating, deliberate foot-dragging. At the time of their meeting in Pittsburgh, the panel "has not even heard its first case." Their attitude was nonchalant, behaving as if "urgency is not evident" in what had become a serious matter of concern. Furthermore, the Communion itself at the highest level of its ecclesiastical authority seemed to be aiding these gross acts of intimidation, denial, and deprivation. Otherwise, it would not be watching with silent unconcern.

The conference, therefore, took a stand. They resolved that the American church's "2006 General Convention was the last chance [for it] to respond with repentance in the spirit of the Windsor Report." That date would be the "last deciding moment." The Episcopal Church would have to choose either to "walk with or walk apart" from the Anglican Communion. The gathering agreed that until then, all "those within the Episcopal Church USA were to 'stay as long as you can.'" Once more, the group took the traditional approach of appealing to the North American churches to walk the path of reconciliation.

For over 40 years, however, the Episcopal Church had defied every authority of the Communion. Neither had it shown regard for the voices of reason within Christendom worldwide. Since 2003, egoistic pride had taken a turn for the worst. At every point and turn since the Gene Robinson trouble started, the American church had not hesitated to demonstrate combative arrogance. Between the Pittsburgh conference and the convening of the Episcopal Church's General Convention, however, there were seven months, a long interregnum for broken fences to be mended. The pressing question was, how possible was it within that short time to undo a mind-set that had been engrained deeply for 40 years? Unless the Pittsburgh gathering was being overly optimistic, they should have known, in the words of an African proverb, that "it is difficult to bend a dry fish without breaking it." Or as another axiom suggests, rarely does a leopard change its skin.

Even before they departed, there were ominous signs. Right before them was the media, spinning and twisting the proceedings in which they were all participants, and Archbishop Akinola was its target. Subtle but obvious was the slanderous intention of reporting about the archbishop. He was alleged to have blackmailed the delegates into making their decisions. The spurious claim was credited to Peter Boyer of *The New*

Yorker, who pictured Akinola as warning the "2500 capacity audience" that "many of you have one leg in the ECUSA and one leg in the Network."[17] "With that, my friends, comes disaster," he had told them. Then came the bogus claim that Akinola threatened them with, "While that remains, you can't have our support." He was said to have arm-twisted them by telling them, "If you want Global South to partner with you, you must let us know exactly where you stand." Boyer said Akinola had asked the American delegates, "Are you ECUSA? Or are you Network? Which one?" Of course, this was contrary to the decision reached at the meeting, which had asked "those within the Episcopal Church USA . . . 'stay as long as you can.'"

For all intents and purposes, the aim of the news report was simple. Boyer wanted readers to believe that the Nigerian primate and chair of the Global South was the one fueling the division within the American church. Every line of his story was misleading. Was the concocted story part of the grand conspiracy ahead of the critical 2006 General Convention? Or was it an isolated incident? There was no way of giving the question a precise answer. But one thing that was clear was that Akinola was amassing more enemies at every turn. The gay groups were there and would stop at nothing to demobilize their "No. 1 International Enemy." The American church had now been drawn into the fray with all eyes on the 2006 ultimatum delivered to its General Convention. A lot was to happen during that seven-month interval.

17. Boyer, "A Church Asunder."

20

A Leader Unwelcomed to the Fold

America, 2006

Finally, D-Day arrived. The Episcopal Church in the United States of America held the anticipated General Convention on June 18, 2006.[1] As expected, vital decisions emerged from the forum. But they did little to douse the fire engulfing the Communion. Rather, these were steps calculated to drive the fire into a wild inferno. The first was the election of Katherine Jefferts Schori. The ballot made history and broke records at the same time. Schori was the first female head of the American church. Internationally, she was also the first woman to be elected a primate in the worldwide Anglican Communion. The forces behind her election as the 26th presiding bishop of the American church no doubt celebrated the action. However, in the light of events that the Communion was still grappling with, no choice could have been more disastrous. This had nothing to do with her gender. The issue was about her mindset.

Between her and Frank Griswold, there was a great difference. Their outlooks and approaches were antithetical. Even if they were two sides of a bad coin, one still managed to be more tolerable than the other, and there was no dispute about who that was. Griswold was like a worm that survived by burrowing his way through the grimy mud. That could not be said of his successor. Schori was aggressive and combative. She's like a bulldozer with no qualms about removing obstacles in her path. In the secular world, Schori would have found it difficult to shake off the stigma of being a despotic, totalitarian leader. Interestingly, at the start of the conflict, of which she was now the generalissimo, she was nowhere near the frontline.

Schori was not at the pivotal 1998 Lambeth Conference.[2] At that time, she was a junior priest, just four years old in the calling. She was 40 years old and had just

---

1. McLaughlin, "The Rev. Katharine Jefferts Schori Elected to be 26th Presiding Bishop of the Episcopal Church; First Female Presiding Bishop and Primate."

2. https://en.wikipedia.org/w/index.php?title=Katharine_Jefferts_Schori&oldid=672303228.

earned her master of divinity in 1994 from the Church Divinity School of the Pacific. That same year she was ordained as a priest. Her progress in the ministry was marked by a rapid rise, and she became a bishop within seven years. Her election as the ninth bishop of the Diocese of Nevada followed the sudden death of the Rt. Rev. Stewart Clark Zabriskie, who had spent thirteen years piloting the affairs of the diocese. His own predecessor, the Rt. Rev. Wesley Frensdorff, had spent fifteen years in office before passing the baton to Zabriskie. Schori's ascent was more dramatic than theirs; within five years, she rose to the peak, gaining one of the topmost episcopal positions available both at the national and international level of the Anglican Church. All told, she rose from the lowest rung of the priestly ladder to the crowning pinnacle of international ecclesiastical fame within a twelve years!

Politics, and nothing else but politics, shaped her election at the 75th General Convention of the Episcopal Church. Discerning how the pendulum had swung in her favor was easy. At 51, Jefferts Schori was the youngest of the contestants. She was, equally, the person with the least ecclesiastical experience among nominees vying for the position. The 29-member Joint Nominating Committee chaired by Bishops Peter J. Lee of Virginia and Diane B. Pollard of New York initially proposed four candidates for election to the office. There was John Neil Alexander, the 52-year-old bishop of Atlanta, with 18 years' cumulative experience in the ordained ministry. Familiar within the church's governing hierarchy, he was one of the Episcopal Church's point-men at the June 2005 meeting of the Anglican Consultative Council. Alexander was a rich blend of academic and ministerial precocity. The former seminary professor endeared himself to the council by showing good grasp of the Episcopal Church's policies on sexuality.

Next was the 58-year-old Edwin F. Gulick, bishop of the Diocese of Kentucky with 32 years' vocational career in the priesthood. He was at the 1998 Lambeth Conference and among the seventy-six American bishops who signed the apology letter to gays and lesbians. In 2000, he also served the General Convention's Committee 22, which dealt with questions relating to human sexuality and resolution DO39 "acknowledging relationships other than marriage."

After him was Henry Nutt Parsely, the bishop of Alabama. At 57, the bulk of Parsely's life had been devoted to the ministry, where he had put in 33 years. Like Gulick, he was at the 1998 Lambeth Conference, but unlike his colleague, he refused to be part of the defiant pro-gay minority. Nevertheless, he played leading roles in various aspects of the life of the church. This included his serving as a member of the Planning Committee of the House of Bishops, the chair of the Standing Commission on Stewardship and Development, and as a member of the board of the Presiding Bishop's Fund for World Relief (later renamed Episcopal Relief and Development).

Owing to unanticipated developments, two additional names joined the original list, those of Bishops Charles Edward Jenkins and Francisco J. Duque-Gomez.[3] The

3. "Two More Bishops Nominated for Presiding Bishop."

House of Bishops, at a meeting in North Carolina on March 19, 2006, had favorably considered the bid for their inclusion. Charles Edward Jenkins, 56 years old, the third longest serving priest among the lot, had put in 29 years of service. The bishop of Louisiana, Jenkins had initially signified interest but was dropped inexplicably by the Nominating Committee. Twelve bishops revived his nomination, which he accepted. Incidentally, Jenkins was a close friend of outgoing Presiding Bishop Frank Griswold. He was the first bishop that Griswold consecrated when he assumed office.

They had a fundamental difference between them, however. Jenkins was opposed to the church's stand on homosexuality. On the other hand, he was a pacifist, preferring to stand in safe mode in the Episcopal moral and scriptural perversion crisis. Of the six-member delegation that took the case of the church to the Nottingham meeting of the Anglican Consultative Council, he was the "conservative voice." He was known for his "no" answer to every question on the homosexuality enquiry. He declined to be part of the gay and lesbian appeasement group at the 1998 Lambeth Conference. Likewise, he voted against the election of Gene Robinson as bishop of New Hampshire in 2003. Notwithstanding, he was appointed to the Presiding Bishop's Council of Advice that same year and became its president the year after. Jenkins had abiding loyalty to friendship. He was supportive of Griswold, whose leadership he eulogized. "Both Griswold and Rowan Williams have," he said, "taken actions they normally would not have taken." He didn't however give examples of such unusual actions. He held them close to his chest, not sharing them with the public to appreciate.

Francisco J. Duque-Gomez, the bishop of Columbia, was of a different mold. The second oldest of the nominees—a year behind Parsely—at 56, the Columbian was the longest-serving priest among the contenders, a veteran of 39 years in ordained ministry. He got the call in 1967, 27 years before Jefferts Schori's entry into priesthood. Both Duque-Gomez and Schori, however, rose to the episcopate the same year, 2001. Besides his doctorate in law and service as a practicing trial attorney, he was also a professor of constitution and canons. Duque-Gomez was the first non-stipendiary priest of the Diocese of Colombia, serving for twelve years with no remuneration. Effective and noticeable was his presence in church life, including serving as president of the Province IX Court of Appeal. His expertise and position made him one of the few, in the words of Scotland Church Chancellor Anne McGavin, who could "deal with naughty priests."

Added to his strength of character, Duque-Gomez wasn't easily swayed, not even by sentimental notions such as bearing allegiance to friendship. He, too, was neither a party to the election of Gene Robinson nor an endorser of his consecration. In fact, the trio of Duque-Gomez, Jenkins, and Parsely were birds of the same feather on that score. All the three opposed Robinson's admission into the revered episcopacy because of his unwholesomeness. Perhaps, Duque-Gomez was sensitive enough to discern the slimness of his chances for the Episcopal Church's topmost job. The process and the air surrounding it were heavily laden with politics. Unlike Jenkins, he wrote no letter to his diocese to apprise them of his nomination. Probably, in his wisdom, he felt it was better to leave his chances to luck.

By regulations governing the selection process, all nominees must pass through the same background checks and screenings. In February 2006, before the March clearance of Jenkins and Duque-Gomez, Bishop Stacy F. Sauls of Lexington was cleared. About the same age as Schori, Sauls was, however, years ahead of her in the ministry.[4] He had put 17 years of service into church work. A lawyer by profession, he had also been involved in the administration of the church. He had served as a member of the Episcopal Church Executive Council, the Standing Commission on World Mission, and the Budgetary Funding Task Force.

Sauls, with the six other final nominees, had to address the House of Bishops. They had to share their "views on the ministry of the Presiding Bishop in church, national and global contexts." On the same day (March 19, 2006) that Jenkins and Duque-Gomez received their nods to join the race, the candidates shared their vision with their colleagues at an evening session. Each told what it would be like to be the leader of the American church. From the outside, matters appeared to be proceeding as a sincere, Spirit-led election process should. However, away from public view, politics were at work as usual. One did not have to be a political pundit to see the direction the pendulum would most probably swing.

Certainly, the trio of Parsely, Jenkins, and Duque-Gomez were not favorites. They were opposed to the mainstream gay thinking in the church. Even Jenkins' pacifist nature was no compensation. It would be dangerous to give him the benefit of the doubt. He could betray the cause which forces within the church had deemed irreversible and to which he had maintained his opposition openly. That limited the top potential candidates to four: Bishops Alexander of Atlanta, Gulick of Kentucky, Schori of Nevada, and Sauls of Lexington. All four supported the election of Gene Robinson. None of them, however, took part in his consecration. The shape of the crisis confronting the church internationally also made some other factors important.

The new presiding bishop must be a person of strong character, who would be tough, assertive, and a tiger with full fighting spirit. No doubt, the Global South leaders' uncompromising position was a major factor in the choice of the successor to Frank Griswold. The American church had to be a step ahead of the Global South. This gave the Nevada bishop an edge. She might be the youngest with the fewest years in priestly calling, but she had the distinguishing credential: Jefferts Schori was a woman. Until that time, the worldwide Anglican Communion had no female primate.

For the American church, her election was needed for two strategic ends. The first was the catch-22 her choice would present to the Global South leaders. If they rejected her, it would buttress criticism that they were "conservatives" and an anti-progress group. It would also be a way to incite women against their leadership. Should they

---

4. Virtue, "General Convention: What Ails Bishop Stacy Sauls Ails Episcopalians."

accept her, the recognition might be used to argue they should also loosen their stance on ordaining gays and lesbians and electing them into the episcopate.

Raising the feminist issue was a strategic move on the part of the Episcopal Church. By expanding the disagreement further to another contentious subject on which the Anglican Church had no common mind globally, the American church gained an advantage. The carpet would be pulled out from under the feet of the Global South. Women's ordination was not a common practice or one favorably received in many of their own countries. The calculation was that a female leader and fellow primate would be a bitter pill to swallow for the Global South. Ingenious was the scheme because it would arm the American church with a moral claim to stake against their Global South counterparts.

The timing for such a deft, radical move appeared to be ripe. It was thirty years since the church had made women's ordination official. What a way to celebrate the triumph: by offering progressives another rallying point in their ongoing confrontation of those "conservatives" opposed to ordination of homosexuals.

Jefferts Schori was in the right place at the right time. The pool of female bishops from which to choose was extremely small. Pioneer warhorses like suffragan Bishop Barbara Harris of Massachusetts, Jane Holmes Dixon of the Diocese of Washington D.C. (who incidentally was Archbishop Akinola's classmate at Virginia Theological Seminary between 1988 and 1989), and Bishop Mary Adelia McLeod of Vermont were already settled in the retirement stable. Harris retired in 2003. McLeod and Dixon had left at almost the same time in 2002. Even among the group of second-generation female episcopal leaders, the options were seriously narrow.

Chilton Abbie Richardson Knudsen was a case in point. She was elected as the bishop of Maine in 1997. She was independent-minded, headstrong, and believed in the ordination of partnered gay and lesbian clergy, and in making them bishops. Not caring that her position contravened the official position of her diocese, she maintained openly her stand. She had voted for Gene Robinson, participated in his consecration, and presided at his investiture service. She was at the 1998 Lambeth Conference, was among the signatories of the infamous letter to the gays and lesbians, and had rooted for the blessing of same-sex unions.[5]

Among the few women occupying episcopal positions—there were about six of them, with four being suffragan bishops—only Knusden and Schori had full diocesan authority. Knusden's only problem was her limited time. She had just two more years before her retirement, which was set for 2008. By the law governing election of the presiding bishop, a candidate to the office must have a minimum of nine years remaining before the mandatory retirement age of 72.

At personal level, Jefferts Schori was a high achiever. At 20, she had finished her bachelor of science in biology from Stanford University, earned her master of science degree in oceanography at 23, and by 29 had completed her doctorate in the same

5. https://en.wikipedia.org/wiki/Chilton_R._Knudsen.

discipline from Oregon State University. Self-driven, she was always strong-minded and sought to prove herself. This was how she became a pilot in her college years. Both of her parents were pilots. Her father had thrown a challenge to her: "If she would pass the written exam for flying," which had been her long-held dream, "he would pay for flying lessons and exam." She succeeded, and two years into college, she qualified as an instrument-rated pilot. But since then, she "had not flown a great deal." Similarly, she had to knock down the wall of gender bias early in her career. As a young ocean-ographer, she had gone on an ocean cruise as the only female on board. "The captain ignored me, the only woman, for about fifteen minutes," she recalled, but she soon established herself. And as the years passed, she became smarter, sharper, and shrewder.

Interestingly, Schori's childhood and youthful fantasies had never placed her in a cassock. A career in the ministry was not one of her dream jobs. From an Irish family, Schori had taken her father's middle name—Jefferts—and was raised initially in the Roman Catholic Church. Then in 1963, her parents moved out of the church. Schori, aged 8, was transferred to the Episcopal Church while her mother converted to Eastern Orthodoxy a few years later. Once she made the decision in 1994 to become a priest, she integrated herself with the church at the national level. She served on the Special Commission on the Episcopal Church as well as that of the Anglican Communion. Also, she was involved with the House of Bishops peer coaching program; the House of Bishops' Pastoral Development, Racism, and Planning Committees; the Court for Review of a Trial of a Bishop; and the Bishops of Small Dioceses group. For two years, 2001 to 2003, she was a member of the "20/20 Strategy Group." At the 2003 General Convention, she was appointed as the secretary of the House of Bishops Ministry Committee. So Schori was not completely a dark horse, but she was not the most outstanding of the candidates in terms of pastoral experience. However, she stood out as the anointed, the preferred choice of the power-brokers in the church.

Nevertheless, the June 18, 2006, election of Jefferts Schori as the 26th presiding bishop wasn't achieved with a click of the fingers, as the "godfathers" hoped. It was far from being a cinch as 188 bishops gathered in the conclave to decide between the seven candidates. On the first ballot, Schori failed to win the election. On the second, she still didn't emerge as the choice of the majority. On the third and fourth ballots, victory was far from her. Then at 3:35 p.m., after the fifth ballot, the chair of the Committee on the Consecration of Bishops stepped to the podium. He held his breath for a moment and then announced, "On the fifth ballot, The Rt. Rev. Katharine Jefferts Schori is elected to be the 26th Presiding Bishop of the Episcopal Church." She had managed only 95 of the 188 votes cast, just over the 50 percent of those in attendance.

The House of Deputies had to confirm the election, but that seemed to be a place of strength for her. There were quite a number of back-end fixers, people like Louie Crew, members and sympathisers of Integrity USA. Crew's membership on the church's 38-member Executive Council still held, as did his position in the House of Deputies, where he had been a notable figure for four consecutive, triennial, national,

General Conventions—1994, 1997, 2000, and 2003. In much the same way that Gene Robinson's election was a matter of interest to gays and lesbians, their organizations and sympathizers within and outside the Episcopal Church felt the same about Jefferts Schori's.

As such, before her election got to the House of Deputies, the confirmation vote seemed to be a mere formality. The popular acclamation that she could not receive among her senior peers she received overwhelmingly from the broad spectrum of the church's laity and clerical representatives. There were two orders in the House, the lay and the clerical, and both endorsed Schori enthusiastically. The lay order voted 93 in support from the available 108 votes. The clergy support was no less ardent; out of their 108 delegates, 94 voted for Schori, with 10 against and an insignificant 4 divided.

Fortunately for her, no one questioned the propriety of her candidacy, the sort of thing that marred Gene Robinson's election in 2003. Schori's emergence was the high point of the Episcopal Church 75th General Convention, and the outgoing presiding bishop, Frank Griswold, was elated. He had every cause to be. At 68, he had spent the last nine years of his life in high-wire politics and games of survival. Following tradition, Griswold formally presented his successor to a broad audience—convention delegates, journalists, invited local and international dignitaries. Over 200 media members gathered at the Hyatt Regency Ballroom in Columbus, Ohio, for the introduction. The prolonged standing ovation kept Griswold and Schori on their feet for minutes at the podium.

Griswold was circumspect in his statement, a typical speech tailored to the occasion. He was, first, grateful to the House of Bishops "for the prayerful and careful way in which they set about to discern who would best serve the Church as its 26th Presiding Bishop." As for the woman stepping into his shoes, he called her "a person gifted in mind, heart, and spirit," adding, "I am fully confident that the Church and the Communion will be blessed by her ministry in the years ahead."

However, beyond the television lights and the flashing bulbs of the press photographers, Griswold was aware of the reality. He had experienced the Episcopal Church's political whirlwinds. In a kind of valedictory interview on June 11, 2006, with *The New York Times*, he was asked about his retirement plans. He answered, "I like to scythe" since "grass obeys in a way people sometimes don't."

As for Schori, when asked, "What message do you think your election sends to the wider communion?" she responded, "That God welcomes all to the table." Actually, Schori's election was not a move to promote rapprochement between the Anglican Communion and the Episcopal Church, for she was a hard-core, hardnosed, and hardy heretic, who believed "homosexual behaviour is not a sin."[6] Neither did she consider "Jesus the only way to the Father." And she believed that "revelation continues." The bishops who inspired her were the likes of John Spong and another

6. American Anglican Council, "A Timeline of Defining Actions," www.americananglican.com.

maverick, Marcus Borg.[7] She invited them frequently to speak to her clergy. Borg was a distinguished professor in religion and culture and faculty member at Oregon State University, his career spanning from 1979 until his retirement in 2007, a period that coincided with Schori's student days in the same university. In Spong and Borg, she had prominent enablers.

The Episcopal Church seemed, however, to have its own plan for its newly elected presiding bishop. Once the election was concluded, the remaining days of the General Convention, June 19–21, were devoted to legislative matters. In none of its decisions was the Episcopal Church willing to shift ground on any of the matters that had brought it into conflict with the majority of worldwide Anglicans. Perhaps in preparation for any eventual consequence, it adopted a new designation; in place of Episcopal Church in the United States of America (ECUSA), it took the name The Episcopal Church (TEC), which freed it from a geographic boundary. TEC captured the "presence of the church in 16 countries," the General Convention indicated. The reasoning was that the earlier it started projecting the image of an international religious organization, the better it would be should push come to shove.

Thereafter, defiant resolutions started coming one after the other. Contrary to the Windsor Report recommendation that the Episcopal Church should observe a moratorium on the consecration of gays and lesbians until the Communion reached a decision on the matter, the church only asked its bishops to exercise restraint. As spelled out in Resolution B033, the standing commissions and bishops were enjoined to "exercise restraint by not consenting to the consecration of any candidate to the episcopate whose manner of life presents a challenge to the wider church and will lead to further strains on the Communion." In the same breath, it followed with Resolution A161, which rejected the call that it should express "regret for consenting to 'the consecration of a bishop living openly in a same-gender relationship.'"

Furthermore, Resolution A095 on "Gay and Lesbian Affirmation" declared homosexuals' status as children of God who should enjoy all the rights enjoyed by heterosexual married couples. A subsidiary resolution, A167, proclaimed "Full and Equal Claim for All Baptized," meaning "inclusion of 'openly homosexual persons on every committee, commissions, or task forces developed for the purpose of discussing issues about sexuality." It also "requested the same by the rest of the Anglican Communion." Definitely, the new TEC was a carbon copy of the defunct Episcopal Church in the United States of America. Their grand illusion was the same, and they assumed that legitimacy could be bought through a laundered media image.

The Episcopal News Service, therefore, immediately swung into action. With the dateline reading "from Columbus," the headline crowed, "Anglican leaders reflect favorably on Jefferts Schori election." Topping the list of the Anglican leaders mentioned was Bishop Trevor Mwamba of Botswana from Central Africa. Mwamba virtually

7. Stannard, "Hero or Heretic, Spong Won't Be Forgotten"; https://en.wikipedia.org/wiki/Marcus_Borg.

parroted outgoing Presiding Bishop Griswold in reflecting positively on "what she has to contribute to the life of the Anglican Communion." Similarly, the Rev. Canon Kenneth Kearon, secretary general of the Anglican Communion, "as well as three Anglican primates" who were not named, "look forward to welcoming Jefferts Schori to future Primates meetings." While Archbishop Andrew Hutchison, the primate of the Anglican Church of Canada, expressed his "enormous respect for her and her competence," the Primate of Mexico, The Most Rev. Carlos Touche-Porter was simply "thrilled." Everything looked set for the new American presiding bishop, the set-pieces having been finely and neatly arranged.

Despite a 24-hour delay, the endorsement from a much-expected source came on the day following of Schori's election. As warm as Archbishop of Canterbury Rowan Williams' greetings were, there was an unmistakable diplomatic tone to them. Archbishop Williams said he was confident that Schori "will bring many intellectual and pastoral gifts to her new work," while alerting her that she was taking "up a deeply demanding position at a critical time." Tactfully, the archbishop identified two important challenges bound to confront her leadership: "Her election will undoubtedly have an impact on the collegial life of the Anglican Primates"; furthermore, "it also brings into focus some continuing issues in several of our ecumenical dialogues." He closed with a cliché typical of church letters: "We are continuing to pray for the General Convention of the Episcopal Church as it confronts a series of exceptionally difficult choices."

The Convention ended on June 21, 2006, giving a four-month interregnum before her assumption of office on November 4, 2006. And in this period, a potential scandal arose: the accusation was that Jefferts Schori had dressed up her curriculum vitae.

The man at the center of the allegation was David Virtue,[8] the same man who accused Gene Robinson of pornographic involvement at his consent hearing during the 2003 General Convention. Unlike Robinson's case, where his evidence was tenuous, this time around, Virtue succeeded in unearthing a scoop. He exposed incoming Presiding Bishop Jefferts Schori as doping the truth in her bid to get to the hallowed office. Virtue's exposé was published in July 2006, barely a month after the conclusion of the General Convention.

As already mentioned, part of the election process was subjecting "each nominee . . . to the same background checks and screenings." Also, a "Blue Book" containing their views before the House of Bishops was published for public consumption. With respect to Schori, a problem of inconsistency in the information fed to the public was discovered. Schori reportedly claimed to have served as a "pastoral associate and dean of the Good Samaritan School of Theology in Corvallis, Oregon, from 1994 to 2000." The six-year period was half of her entire experience in the ministry before her bid for the topmost Episcopal Church position.

In addition, she claimed to have served as a priest in charge of El Buen Samaritano in the same place and at the same time. The dispute was with her pastoral and dean

8. Virtue, "Episcopal Presiding Bishop 'Revises' Her Online Biography at Wikipedia."

position claims at the Good Samaritan School of Theology. Virtue debunked the assertions. A writer for David Virtue's website *Virtue Online*, Terry Ward, was detailed to conduct background checks on aspirants to the office. Ward discovered a scandalous discrepancy in Schori's claims. Some of her declarations contradicted the facts. Above all, "he could find no record of the existence of the Good Samaritan School of Theology."

Ward expended serious efforts "in his examination of the webpages and church newsletters of the Good Samaritan Church of Corvallis, Oregon." He found nothing. Next, he searched "the web pages of the Episcopal Church USA and the Oregon and Nevada Dioceses." They too were dead ends. Trying "the web pages of the Association of Theological Schools, which listed all accredited and affiliated institutions in the U.S. and Canada," was also futile. There was no evidence of the existence of the school in all the sources. The "Good Samaritan School of Theology" might as well have been a phantom institution. Embarrassingly, neither its "staff nor facilities" could be traced, not to mention its officials such as its dean and pastoral associates.

Ward tried one more source that he thought should be a sure bet: the city phone directories. "There is no trace of the Good Samaritan School of Theology in the city phone directories of Corvallis or Benton County, Oregon," he wrote. Following ethical journalism standards, he asked Schori for her views on the troubling issues. He requested her to supply material facts about the school: "How many students did it have?" "Who were the faculty members?" and "Where were the classes held?" He wanted to know "What was its theological orientation?" as well as what the graduates of the school had been doing.

The bombshell caught Schori by surprise during that critical post-victory, euphoric period. She however demonstrated no shortage of capacity to respond to scandals swiftly. To Ward she replied that, "The Good Samaritan School of Theology was the then-rector's term for all adult education programs."[9] The programs were "both internally and externally focused." Was there no difference between "a school of theology" and "adult education programs"? Such a distinction didn't appear to be in Schori's dictionary. She could only manage a jumble of what she defined as the curriculum of the school, including "initiation of such programs as Education for Ministry; 'popcorn theology' (movies and discussion); a weeknight meal and education offerings for all ages."

As for the faculty members, she claimed they "included clergy and academics from across western Oregon." Regarding where the classes were held, she said, they "were held at a parish in Wilsonville." Where could the alumni of the school be found? Schori was unsure. "I believe the alumni now include clergy and active lay people in several dioceses in the West." She was, however sure of her answer to a specific question—the fact that she had spent "a year as Dean of the School of Theology and Ministry for the Diocese of Oregon (1990–991)." This, still, was far short of academic leadership in a theological institution, which was the image she had painted in her

9. "New Top Episcopal Bishop Challenged on Her Resume."

profile. In Schori's exact words, "This was a more formal academic program intended to provide education for a variety of lay ministries."

Virtue caught Schori red-handed tarnishing the word integrity. But that's a word that hardly troubles the gay movement or those in their circle. Just like Robinson was resuscitated with a quick breath in 2003 through the wiping of evidence pertaining to his link with pornographic websites, the same happened to Schori. Within the shortest time, threads of reference to the once-phantom school began to grow in the American media. The once nonexistent school started to have "dozens of references to it, in USA Today, Washington Post and other major papers." The stories were also related to "the election of Schori and her reliance on that major qualification." David Virtue lacked the gay mafia power or its organizational structure. His revelation should have made sensational headlines, but it changed nothing. It produced no startling outcome. On November 4, 2006, at the Washington National Cathedral, the scandal surrounding the rise of Jefferts Schori to one of the world's episcopal heights was put aside. She was installed as the 26th presiding bishop of the American Episcopal Church.

The problem with truth, however, is that it can be a relentless hunter of those fighting against it. Schori could not shake off the fact that her rise to world fame and eminence in religious power was plagued with a false claim. The desperate attempt to employ the media to launder her image and whitewash the unethical conduct did not help either. Five years later, the truth resurfaced. Virtue was vindicated. On February 2011, Schori decided to atone for the blemish. That inaccurate portion of her official biography, which had been fed to millions around the world through *Wikipedia*, the popular international resource, was deleted. It was done with a quiet abasement. Virtue, again, latched onto the big story. He contacted the Communication Office of the Episcopal Church. "Who ordered the change?" he enquired from an official. The reply was, "An 815 staff person with the e-mail handle 'Matisse412' had effected the changes." "The edits were made per Bishop Jefferts Schori's suggestion," the official replied. He badgered the official further demanding, "Why the changes were made?"

Barefacedly, the official told him, "The information was incorrect and it was changed." "We were not about to have inaccurate info there." But, as to the identity of "who Matisse-412 is," the source retorted sharply, "I prefer not to name who that is." The important point, he emphasised, "is correcting items that are wrong." And on that dismissive note, he ended the conversation. The "offending section" that had been rewritten in Schori's public profile was the same that *Virtue Online* had identified as fraudulent.

The experience didn't, however, humble her. Power intoxicates, especially, when the world is at one's feet. After only a dozen years, her rise to the height of spiritual leadership through a competition that witnessed seniors and more experienced colleagues being trounced was stupefying. Schori was overawed with her assumed invincibility. She overrated her indomitability. The lesson she was far from learning was about power itself—that power is a double-edged sword; it cuts both ways. Nor is any human's power limitless and endless. Schori was the presiding bishop of the American Church no doubt. But her power was not infinite and boundless. No sooner than she got into office in 2006, she began to realize this fundamental truth.

Indeed, ahead of Jefferts Schori's June 2006 election, the Global South Primates' Committee had met in Singapore.[10] The gathering was not on her account. They wanted to "kill two birds with one stone" as the axiom said. They decided to honor their worthy colleague as well as use the occasion to deliberate on developments in the Communion. Bishop John Chew was to succeed retiring Archbishop Yong Ping Chung as the archbishop of the Anglican Province of South East. The installation was fixed for February 5, 2006, and the primates had decided to honor one of their own. The two events were successful and rewarding. However, they had not envisaged the emergence of Jefferts Schori as the new presiding bishop. Their focus was on how the General Convention would respond to the issues that the Communion had placed before the American Church. Consequently, they agreed to intervene at the pre-Convention stage with a sensitization program, with the aim "to encourage the faithful," and then after the Convention, "to respond to the decisions made" swiftly, promptly, and decisively.

They decided that "a meeting of the GS Primates be called as soon as the ECUSA General Convention is over." Of course, they were not blind to the American church's desire to compromise many of them through American versions of the "Greek Gifts." The corrupting of the provinces from mostly developing countries with cash and in-kind inducements was dubbed, euphemistically, "815 charm offensives," a reference to the Episcopal Church headquarters, which was situated at 815 2nd Avenue, New York City. An aggressive plan sought to buy the consent of church leaders in the Global South in exchange for support of the American church.

Archbishop Akinola had barely returned home when he had to jet out again in that same month of February to Nairobi, Kenya. He was in the East African country for a meeting of the Council of Anglican Provinces in Africa (CAPA). The meeting included two significant decisions. The first was the commissioning of a position paper—"The Road to Lambeth"—to assist the Council in making an informed decision regarding the Conference. [11] Secondly, the primates decided to make their meeting rotational. Following that Kenya meeting, from May 1–2, he was in Heathrow, London, as the Global South Primates Steering Committee had agreed in Singapore. From June 21 to 22, he was on the shuttle again to Kampala, Uganda, for the CAPA primates' meeting. This was to be their first rotational meeting in line with the CAPA primates' decision. Incidentally, this particular meeting occurred barely three days after the election of Jefferts Schori. Interestingly, the primates did not refer to the

10. Minns, Marty & Angela, "Notes from a visit for the Installation of the Right Reverend John Chew as Archbishop of the Anglican Province of South East Asia and a meeting of the Global South Primates Committee," from the papers and archive of the Archbishop Peter Akinola.

11. CAPA, "The Road to Lambeth," from the papers and archive of the Archbishop Peter Akinola.

election. Nor did they raise any of the subjects on which they had given ultimatums to the General Convention of the American Episcopal Church. The reason for their quietness became clear, however when they met in Kigali, Rwanda, on September 19, 2006. The Kigali meeting killed two birds with one stone. Both CAPA and Global South Primates met simultaneously, back-to-back, in the country.

The simultaneity of the meetings afforded Archbishop Akinola an advantage. He had the ability to change roles and positions in quick succession with no barriers of geographic space. At night, he would chair the meeting of the Council of Anglican Provinces in Africa. In the morning, he would preside over discussion of the Global South primates.

Before that meeting, the Global South Primates Steering Committee had met twice. This time, however, the Episcopal Church's General Convention had met and had reached its conclusion, and all the primates knew the outcome. Their counterparts had once again snubbed them, with their "woeful failure to repent and give up their new doctrine."[12] There was not a single smiling face at the table; these were men who had reached the end of their patience. Archbishop Akinola's opening remarks caught the prevailing mood, urging, "We must reaffirm our resolve" to "stand firm on the unique revelation and authority of the Holy Scriptures."

The archbishop believed that their strength would continue "to be severely tested in four main ways." The first test would be over the issue of money. He was sure that inadequate financial resources would continue to challenge the numerous ideas they were planning to execute, and he saw it as the chief means of potentially corrupting their integrity. Second would be employment of the usual "divide-and-rule tactics, coupled with the targeting of individuals for attack and demonization." Archbishop Akinola was at pains to observe that "we have seen the horrors but not the end." He was referring to the vile treatment that he and others had been subjected to. Their third test of will, he was sure, was bound to come from "secularist unfavourable legislations" that the Western societies had counted as a mark of progress.

There was need to fear the compulsive drive with which some Western countries were pursuing the agenda of blackmailing the entire world into accepting their cultural revisionism. This cross-border nihilism stemmed from a misconception, which Archbishop Akinola identified as the attempt "to equate faith with social action." Akinola was glad that his colleagues saw through the chicanery and had remained resolute. He was full of praise for their "steadfastness and refusal of being carried along by the agenda of the world." As moving as the opening remarks were, the primates had not come to Kigali for a sermon from the chairman's pulpit. They were there for business—to discuss together and decide together.

The "Anglican Covenant" took the lead. Archbishop Chew presented the draft that his committee had put together. At the end, he requested that the meeting ratify

12. Akinola, "Opening Remarks by Most Rev. Dr. Peter J. Akinola, Chairman, Global South Steering Committee," from the papers and archive of the Archbishop Peter Akinola.

the document. Akinola's view was that once approved, the agreed Covenant should "in turn [be offered] uncompromisingly to the Anglican Communion as the barest minimum [that] everyone who desires to be part of our Church must subscribe to and honour."[13]

There was also the Global South Economic Empowerment Consultation, whose final framework was tabled at the meeting. Discussions on the idea featured prominently, with plans drawn for further action, with Canon Martyn at the consultation's helm. Also, the Theological Education in the Global South Committee would continue to work, with the only remaining question being how the Global South would translate decisions "into positive action."

Then the CAPA primates' commissioned paper, "The Road to Lambeth," was shared with the meeting. The document was to serve as "additional resource material" complementing the position of the African Anglican Church leaders on "where we stand in relation to the Lambeth Conference." Akinola commended the report, which was influenced by "the ongoing sexuality controversy," to the Global South for study, indicating that "The Road to Lambeth" offered Global South leaders insight into the mind of the African Church leaders. Even without CAPA's "The Road to Lambeth," chances were remote that other Global South primates had a sanguine view about the crisis bedevilling their Anglican Communion. The group had long discussed the bewildering Anglican crisis.

Before them were their despairing counterparts from the Anglican Church of Canada, continually victimized by their church owing to their uncompromising opposition to its homosexuality policy. They grieved that "same-sex blessings had continued in the New Westminster Diocese with no disciplinary action taken against Michael Ingham or the diocese."[14] Indeed, rather than being censured for his treachery, Ingham had grown in stature, becoming an institution within an institution and an ecclesiastical order within an ecclesiastical order. He fixed his own canons and set their boundaries. Right in his diocese, the dean of the New Westminster Cathedral, Rev. Peter Elliot, was in an open homosexual partnership.

Elliot was like a clone of Ingham. He was lucky to find himself in the right position at the right time. He was the prolocutor for the General Synod and served as the bishop's commissary when Ingham went on sabbatical leave. Ever since the New Westminster rebellion, the perfidy had indeed become a fertilizer nourishing more revolts in the Canadian church. Joining the rebellion in speedy succession was the Niagara Diocese, which affirmed same-sex marriage. It passed its same-sex motion on the same day that the Communion was considering the Windsor Report!

13. "Global South Primates Kigali Communique, September 2006," from the papers and archive of the Archbishop Peter Akinola.

14. Anglican Network in Canada, " Presentation to the Global South Primates from the Anglican Network in Canada September 2006—A More Detailed Update," from the papers and archive of the Archbishop Peter Akinola; "Homosexuality and the Anglican Church of Canada" https://en.wikipedia.org/wiki/Homosexuality_and_the_Anglican_Church_of_Canada.

More aggravating was the fact that across Canada the demonstration of brazen contempt had become widespread, with "priests living in openly homosexual relationships," with little differentiation from America. Signs suggested that the Canadian church had reached a point of no return on matters concerning homosexuality. Actually, the church's commitment was confirmed later when "The General Synod of the Anglican Church of Canada . . . voted to affirm the integrity and sanctity of same-sex relationships." And while the pro-gay supporters advanced their cause without any restraining hand, their opponents were victims of high-handed leadership. In every possible way, the leadership ensured the victimisation, repression, intimidation, and persecution of the anti-gay group. The "Panel of Reference" that was expected to prevent such abuse was a complete let-down, even refusing to "acknowledge the Anglican Network in Canada." Bluntly, it refused to accept the "adequate episcopal oversight" that the Anglican primates had approved for the two North American churches. Yet, the Kigali meeting was coming "over a year and a half" after the Anglican leaders had made the call "for the Panel of Reference to act 'urgently!'"

The Anglican Church of Canada's intention to deliberately victimize the helpless anti-gay members in its midst was made clear by its swift and decisive action against priests and congregations it adjudged "insubordinate" to the church. A priest whose "parish voted 66% in favour of theological agreement with the majority of the Anglican Communion" was "summarily dismissed." In addition, he was "prohibited from performing Anglican ministry within the geographical territory." There was also the case of two congregations that wanted to plant churches in the diocese of New Westminster, given the stand of the latter on same-sex blessing. They could not do so because their "biblically faithful ordinands [were] not able to be ordained and licensed" by the diocese. Furthermore, the Global South primates were told, "There are many parishes and clergy in the Anglican Church of Canada who are waiting . . . for the solution that will be offered." Their situation was dire, for, astonishingly, the primate of Canada had ruled the case of same-sex marriage closed on his return from the primates' meeting in Dromantine, with the blatant statement that the Anglican Church of Canada is willing to walk away from the Anglican Communion.

It was agonizing to anti-gay Anglicans that the language and behavior of the Communion's topmost hierarchies had rekindled no hope in them. They cited the typical examples of reactions from the "many Communion officials, including Gregory Cameron and Kenneth Kearon and the Panel of Reference." Their pronouncements were not only hurtful, but also appalling for the false impression they created publicly. Though they knew the truth, the officials had continued to inflict more damage by talking from both sides of their mouth. Part of their strategy was to demonize traditionalists before the public to arouse feelings against them as traitors. "Locally, we are seen as 'schismatic,'" as those "acting unilaterally and independently of the Communion and Primates," they told the Global South primates. For four years, they had had to endure persecution at home, and Canterbury gave them no hope. Their desperation for survival within the Anglican Communion had pushed them to Kigali, where they made a strenuous appeal to the Global South leaders: "We desire to work with you," adding,

> There is one hope for the Communion, which is for the Primates to remain united . . . We need you to be clear . . . not only in Rwanda . . . [but] when you go to the next full Primates' meeting in February.

This resonated with Archbishop Akinola's opening remarks at the meeting, where he had emphasized the propriety of an "Anglican Covenant." Consequently, the Covenant that the Chew committee proposed was adopted, beginning with the preamble: "We, the Churches of the Anglican Communion, under the Lordship of Jesus Christ answerable to the Holy Spirit, in order . . . to grow together as a worldwide Communion . . . solemnly establish this Covenant . . . to which we shall adhere."

There were three main articles of faith in the body of the covenant. The first declared, "Each Church shall uphold and act in continuity and compatibly with the catholic and apostolic faith, order and tradition, and biblical moral values." The next prescribed that each member church shall "primarily through its bishops and synods ensure that biblical texts are handled canonically, faithfully, respectfully and plainly . . . on our best tradition." The third demanded that every member church commit "itself to an inter-dependent pilgrimage with other members of the Communion." Basic to the Covenant as well was the upholding of the old governing structure in the Communion. Nevertheless, there was a provision for a new order.

Accordingly, while it was conceded that "each inter-dependent/autonomous Church has the right to order and regulate its own affairs," at the same time, "each Church shall in the exercise of its inter-dependence/autonomy have regard to the common good of the Communion." When there is an "issue threatening the unity and mutual accountability of the Communion," the Covenant said that the over-riding "decision lies with the Communion's Instruments of Unity," namely "the Primates Meeting . . . the Anglican Consultative Council . . . [and the] Archbishop of Canterbury [who] should work in collegial council with the Primates of the Communion." A penalty was attached for the breach of the code: "Failing to do so, may lead to exclusion from the worldwide Communion."

Clearly, the Global South primates didn't congregate in Kigali by accident. The country, Rwanda, was a kind of metaphor. After their horrendous genocide experience in 1994, Rwandans emerged from the ghastly horrors to say, "Never Again!"[15] The Anglican leaders were mortified and said, "Never Again!" too. As the primates eloquently put it, the Rwandan carnage reminded them of "the utter depravity and inhumanity" of human nature. Within 100 days, about 1,174,000 citizens had been lost to the genocide. Every minute, seven individuals were being murdered, 400 every hour, and at the end of every day the death toll amounted to 10,000 innocent lives.

15. https://en.wikipedia.org/wiki/Rwandan_genocide.

It was a small country of about 7.3 million people, 84% of whom were Hutu, 15% Tutsi, and 1% Twa. At the end of the misery, "as many as 70% of the Tutsi and 20% of Rwanda's total population" were sent to early graves. Coming face to face with the "mass grave of 250,000 helpless victims," the primates felt a stab of heart pain. Their anguish was compounded by the reality that "during this time, Rwanda was abandoned to its fate by the world."

The lesson that struck them was about the evils that could accompany misuse of the instruments of power and government. For the Global South leaders, the tragedy reawakened a consciousness in them. They resolved "not to abandon the poor or the persecuted wherever they may be and in whatever circumstances." The abuse of power behind the Rwandan tragedy was similar to the cancer eating dangerously into the organ of their own Anglican Communion. Consequently, "there is now a growing number of congregations and dioceses in the USA and Canada who believe that their Anglican identity is at risk." So, the primates declared, "As leaders of that Communion we will work together to recognise the Anglican identity of all who receive, hold and maintain the Scriptures."

"This is an unprecedented situation in our Communion," the primates observed with a tone of anguish. A number of the congregations that had been pushed to the wall were already "receiving oversight from dioceses in the Global South," they noted. Still, the Global South dioceses continued to have "requests to provide Alternative Primatial Oversight." The Global South primates were willing to help, but also wanted to exercise caution surrounding the disconcerting situation, which had not been "helped by the slow response from the Panel of Reference." As far as they were concerned, the reason for the Panel's lethargy was obvious. Nonetheless, "they still wanted to give it a chance."

Consequently, they asked the "Global South Steering Committee to meet with the leadership of the dioceses requesting [the] Alternative Primatial Oversight." The meeting was to be "in consultation with the Archbishop of Canterbury, the Network and the 'Windsor Dioceses.'" All these were parties or stakeholders to the issues. The objective of the proposed meeting would be "to investigate [the matter] in greater detail and develop a proposal [on] the ways by which the requested Primatial Oversight can be adequately provided."

Finally, the agenda turned to the big issue of Jefferts Schori's election. Contrary to the media hype and the false claim made at the Hyatt Regency Ballroom in Columbus, Ohio, giving the impression of wide acceptance of Jefferts Schori across the Communion, the opposite was the case. As with Gene Robinson, whose bishopric was rejected by majority of the Anglican provinces worldwide, Schori's election was shunned. She was told that her leadership was unwelcome in a gathering of Anglican leaders of their calibre, hence the wording of their communique:

> At the next meeting of the Primates in February 2007, some of us will not be
> able to recognise Katharine Jefferts Schori as a Primate at the table with us.

This was not good news for the newly elected presiding bishop of the Episcopal Church, for the denunciation had come from nearly two-thirds of the Anglicans worldwide. Not everyone at the meeting was inclined to the hardline position, but all resolved that there was no going back on the "impaired communion with her as a representative of the Episcopal Church."

Schori had problems on her hands due to the reality that the Global South leaders had drawn the battle line with her by insisting that she lacked the legitimacy to "represent those dioceses and congregations who are abiding by the teaching of the Communion." Instead, the Global South primates proposed "that another bishop, chosen by these dioceses, be present at that meeting so [as to] listen to their voices." Indeed, they observed that

> The time has now come, to take initial steps towards the formation of what will be recognised as a separate ecclesiastical structure of the Anglican Communion in the USA.

Now they were prepared to take the battle to the backyard of the Episcopal Church. The Primates Steering Committee was mandated to develop a proposal to actualize the resolution in consultation with the necessary Instruments of Unity of the Communion. Though they acknowledged the "serious implications of this decision," they insisted that there was to be no going back, the action irreversible. "We would be failing in our apostolic witness if we do not make this provision for those who hold firmly to a commitment to historic Anglican faith," they stated.

The outcome of the Kigali meeting was neat, a consensus with no dissenting voice. Nobody publicly disowned the proceedings. Twenty of them attended the meeting, including the archbishop of Southern Africa. Only two Provinces were absent, Bangladesh and Philippines, but their primates still sent representatives. The turnout spoke volumes. And they were hopeful that a lot could be achieved in the six months before the meeting of the primates, that the possibility of effecting a genuine reconciliation within the Church was real.

Could the worldwide Church do this? Was it able to avert the looming implosion? Had the answers to these questions been positive, the situation with the Anglican Church would be different today.

21

The New Sheriff in Town

America, 2006

The Most Rev. Jefferts Schori's rise to power as the presiding bishop of the American Episcopal Church turned out to be unprecedented disaster for the oldest Anglican denomination outside the British Isles. It marked a sharp departure from the even-tempered administrations of the past. Despite their leadership failings, Schori's predecessors were careful to keep the sparks and flames away from the hay barn. But she seemed content to burn it down. She might defend herself as the product of a tempestuous period, for none of her forerunners was without his baggage of rebellion. From Presiding Bishop Thomas Staley to Edmond Browning and Frank Griswold, her immediate predecessor, all grappled with one form of turbulence or other. Despite their lack of moral courage to uphold discipline and dispense justice fairly and equitably, it can still be said of them that they exhibited a measure of mature leadership.

Their mellowed disposition had its value. It helped the Episcopal Church avert implosion. Indeed, their tempered manner also prompted a measure of control in the behavior of their extremist colleagues. This had extended to the gay crisis. Yes, the presiding bishops failed in their duty to contain the snowballing damage, but they didn't use their office to multiply and magnify it.

In fact, their body language sometimes had the effect of mellowing some of their militant colleagues. John Chane, the bishop of Washington Diocese, was a case in point.[1] Headstrong as he was, he amazed all with his preparedness to embrace conciliation with the parishes and congregations in dispute with him over homosexuality. Chane took the first step in brokering peace. In a behind-the-scenes move, he "reached out to the few conservative clergy and churches. A worldly man, he had vast experience in trouble-shooting in a number of volatile countries and hot spots

---

1. https://en.wikipedia.org/w/index.php?title=John_Bryson_Chane&oldid=674537453.

around the world, and he knew the value of trust and confidence in truce negotiations between fiercely opposing groups.

He started "first of all negotiating an agreement with a conservative Accokeek, Md., parish with which the diocese was embroiled in a lawsuit." The parish, like others that differed with the diocese, had repudiated his episcopal authority. Chane listened to them, which, in a way, was what the recommended "listening process" counselled by the primates of the Communion was all about. Conflict resolution was about give-and-take, negotiating compromise, reaching agreement from two differing positions. He agreed "to allow conservative bishops—such as retired Archbishop of Canterbury George Carey—to perform confirmations in his stead at theologically traditional parishes." However, he did extract his own compromise in return. Chane insisted on his "personal privilege" to extend "generous pastoral care to theological minorities." The episcopate of Chane lasted nine years, 2002 to 2011, long enough for his practiced conciliation and mediation skill to rub off on fellow die-hard homosexual advocates within the American church.

Actually, Chane was reported to have undertaken "more behind-the-scenes work" in the larger Episcopal Church. The purported goal of his diplomatic maneuver was the same as his goal in the diocese, to broker peace. He was said to have "conducted various negotiations with conservative bishops or with Anglican officials overseas." He had as his teammate the Los Angeles bishop, Jon Bruno, who reportedly complemented his efforts.[2] However, evidence suggested their motives were far from altruistic, but rather may have been a façade, at least in the case of Los Angeles Bishop Bruno, who showed no mercy to parishes under him that disagreed with his pro-gay stand.[3]

For instance, in 2004, St. James, Newport Beach, decided to leave the Diocese of Los Angeles, and Bruno brought a bitter retaliatory lawsuit, one lasting almost nine years. Exhausted after exploring all available legal avenues, the parish took the only option left for it, "to vacate the property." The congregation also decided not to seek further redress on the matter, leaving the property to the remaining members of the "congregation that wished to remain in the Episcopal Church (USA)."

A year later, while the remnant parish was still struggling to build more congregations, Bishop Bruno announced the sale of the building. The "$15 million [sale] to Legacy Partners Residential Development" was for the property "to be re-developed into 22 luxury town homes." About a month after the announcement, "representatives of the Diocese . . . changed the locks" of the church, rendering the parishioners homeless. They "could no longer access the church." Bruno enjoyed sole possession of the "proceeds of the church's sale," and the earnings sat comfortably in the accounts of his personal corporation. Nothing was "distributed to parishioners of St. James the Great

2. https://en.wikipedia.org/w/index.php?title=John_Bryson_Chane&oldid=674537453.
3. "Charges Filed Against + Bruno by Clergy and Parishioners."

to establish a new church." So the congregation decided, courageously, to continue their "worship outdoors near the vacant church."

The case exhibited the high-handedness with which the gay-supporting bishops dealt with congregations and parishes in disagreement with them. Members of the St. James parish, including a number of clergy in the diocese, filed charges against the bishop, alleging abuse of office, saying he had "repeatedly lied and misrepresented his intentions to them, and that he is attempting to sell the valuable property on which their church is located without any appraisal, and at far below its market value."

Bruno's reply was a mockery, for he was the one who had initiated the protracted court cases against them. Now, as he said, he had to sell their property "to recoup the Diocese's litigation expenses" (incurred in suing four former parishes, including the previous congregation of St. James). Bruno was looking for about "nine million dollars!" Besides their oppressive nature, the expensive lawsuits were bankrupting the church. Yet for leaders like Bruno, the court cases were still better options than agreeing to reconciliation with the churches and their fellow Episcopalians who dissented from their anti-scriptural homosexuality stand.

Unfortunately, unlike her predecessors, who chose a subtle and diplomatic approach, Presiding Bishop Jefferts Schori incautiously asserted the position of the pro-gay bishops at the national level. From the start, she made it evident that she wasn't in office for peace. Her demeanor expressed combativeness.

From the moment of her inauguration, on November 4, 2006, Schori employed a "no-nonsense" containment policy. She was determined to "nick them all"—individuals, parishes, congregations, and dioceses—who were not on the side of the gay agenda. They must be brought to their knees. But the opponents of the gay plan were equally resolute, refusing to be intimidated. Eight bishops rejected immediately her apostolic authority and "requested alternative pastoral oversight."[4] They served the dioceses of Central Florida, Dallas, Fort Worth, and of course, Pittsburgh, the diocese of Bishop Robert Duncan. Others were Quincy, San Joaquin (California), South Carolina, and Springfield (Illinois). Within the first month of her occupying the office of the presiding bishop, floods of "individual parishes also attempting to leave the Episcopal Church" began flowing to Schori's desk.

On December 17, 2006, the St. John's Episcopal Church in Petaluma, California, "took the lead in the decision to sever links with the American church," the first in the Diocese of Northern California to opt out of the Episcopal Church. St. John's Church was lucky to have taken the lead initiative, for she succeeded in leaving with her property. And on the same day, "in the Diocese of Virginia, eight parishes voted overwhelmingly to leave." They included "Truro Church in Fairfax; The Falls Church, Virginia; Church of the Apostles, Fairfax; Church of the Word, Gainesville;

---

4. see http://en.wikipedia.org/wiki/Episcopal_Church_in_the_United_States_of_America; http://en.wikipedia.org/w/index.php?tittle=Homosexuality_and_Anglicanism&oldid=604065487; http://en.wikipedia.org/wiki/Continuing_Anglican_Movement.

St Stephens, Heathsville; St Margaret's Church, Woodbridge; Potomac Falls Episcopal, Sterling, and Christ the Redeemer, Centreville." All this came barely a month into Schori's administration.

Incidentally, some of these churches' quest for alternative jurisdiction predated Schori, for example, The Falls Church in Virginia, now The Falls Church Anglican (TFCA).[5] Historical, with a commitment to biblical purity, TFCA stood like a beacon against contemporary scriptural revisionism. Two of America's founding fathers served as its vestrymen—George Washington and George Mason. TCFA "sometimes served as a hospital and sometimes as a stable" during the period of hostilities. TCFA believed in the Bible, social care, and the spirituality of the Living Word. Luckily, it had a rector matching its ideals.

The Rev. Dr. John W. Yates II was a quintessential priest. He accepted the role of shepherd for the church in 1978, and 35 years later had grown "the congregation from a few hundred to several thousand." Yates also upgraded the church property he inherited. An admirable new sanctuary complemented the existing old church. Worthy as these developments were, the real value of Yates was the man inside. Heart and soul, godly beauty synergized and radiated in him. Yates was a scriptural purist, one who could not countenance heretical perversion of the hallowed Word of God in the manner that the Episcopal Church leaders were doing.

Naturally, therefore, Yates opposed election of the gay priest Gene Robinson as a bishop, though his church wasn't the only opposing one within the Virginia region of the Episcopal Church. After endless attempts to make their objections heard, but to no avail, his church along with "some 14 Episcopal churches gathered to consider their options." The situation had continued to degenerate. Apart from being denied the "listening process," the "alternative episcopal oversight" that the entire Communion of Primates prescribed was made unavailable to them. Head and tail, they were being squeezed, but that had not stopped them from continuing negotiations with the Diocese of Virginia.

Yates was at the forefront of the negotiating team. Luckily, they succeeded in working out a kind of "protocol for peaceful departure" with the diocese. For its part, TFCA (as TFC was then known) was willing "to pay a significant sum to leave with their historic property." The congregation considered the offer reasonable. Their church "predated the TEC and the Diocese had never contributed financially to [its] upkeep." The diocese had made no investment in either the land or buildings or in any of the expansion schemes that they had undertaken. To the other churches as well, the "protocol negotiated by Yates with Bishop Lee" was reasonable and acceptable.

The result was that in December 2006, "each church . . . decided to separate from the Episcopal Church." Yates conveyed results of the votes to Bishop Lee. The votes

---

5. Fertig-Dykes, Susan & John W. Yates, "The Falls Church Anglican," submitted as input for use of Archbishop Akinola in his publication, retrieved from the Archive and papers of Archbishop Peter Akinola.

and the decisions complied with the mutually agreed upon process. Yates returned to Bishop Lee for a follow-up and was stunned by a repudiation of the agreement.

"John, I'm sorry," the bishop told him mournfully. "There's a new 'sheriff' in town." Jolting as Lee's decision was, Yates wasn't totally surprised. He had often warned his flock concerning the challenges ahead. He had always cautioned, "We may be worshipping in a corn field before long." Yates' premonition turned out to be true.

The new "sheriff" was determined to root out every nonconforming priest, parish, and diocese still within the Episcopal Church. By fiat, "any agreements made by the diocese were revoked." Presiding Bishop Schori assumed full authority and power over all matters connected with the subject. She alone decided the course matters would take, and with no negotiation. Gone was the era of compromise or amicable settlement.

From then on, the Episcopal Church "began taking to court the departing churches across the nation." There are times in a group or community's life when decisions are made innocuously without members' paying close attention to their potential future implications. Such was now the case. In the 1970s, a canon had been approved at the provincial assembly of the Episcopal Church, one that vested the national church with sweeping power. Regrettably, most of the delegates had left the assembly thinking the voting was over before that law was smuggled in. The "Dennis Canon," as the edict was known, "unilaterally declared that all property of the TEC churches belonged to the relevant diocese."

It was a law lacking the majority's approval, but unfortunately it remained the extant legislation. It served Schori as the weapon with which to badger the nonconforming churches into submission. Thus began the era when merciless litigation mounted against dissenters. The Episcopal Church had the time and money to spend, as well as the energy and vigor.

Once a parish decided to take the ill-advised step of seeking to opt out of TEC, the new "sheriff" moved in for the kill. Whether the parish was small or big, popular or innocuous, city-based or in a rural community, there was no sparing. It was either a takeover or foreclosure of the parish's property, and there was no shortage of court cases. No fewer than 57 lawsuits spread over 25 dioceses were initiated, involving embattled churches in the dioceses of Atlanta, Central Gulf Coast, Central New York, Colorado, Connecticut, East Carolina, Florida, Fort Worth, Georgia, Long Island, and Los Angeles. Diocese like Milwaukee, Nebraska, Northern California, North-west Texas, Ohio, Pennsylvania, Pittsburgh, Rio Grande, Rochester, San Diego, San Joaquin, Wisconsin, and Virginia were also victims. Massachusetts was an exception, settling out of court. If a congregation won at a lower court, the Episcopal Church moved on to the next in appellate rank.

This was what happened in the case of TEC and the Diocese of Virginia against the nine departing parishes of the diocese. The nine parishes won the first round, but TEC and the diocese appealed immediately. By this time, "both sides had already spent more than $5 million total for legal expenses associated with the suit." In the end, TFCA got wiser. They knew they were at a disadvantage, and they would only continue to waste resources. Accordingly, the church decided to walk away from "all its property, from 5 acres of land and buildings to vestments and Communion silver." Its congregation of nearly 4,000 "was displaced for a fewer than 100" who chose to return to the Episcopal Church.

Tough and trying as the crushing legal battles were, none of the embattled parishes was easy to break. Schori was not guided by prudence in the use of power. She was looking for victory. Such leaders are susceptible to paranoia; they live in a world of grand delusion. Schori was caught in a misapprehension of reality, and the cost didn't matter; the important thing was to crush the rebels.

Over time, the protracted legal battle became an embarrassment both within and outside the American church. The Anglican Communion primates made "repeated requests to suspend the litigation." She ignored the constant calls to relent, and several other dioceses joined in litigation. Schori's crusade came at no personal expense to her, because the resources she devoted to waging her war were contributions of the ordinary church members, including those she was fighting. Wondering at the cost, "in 2007, over 5,000 people signed a petition demanding TEC reveal the sources of funds, and how much money it has 'spent since 2004 on litigation.'"[6] On the heels of that petition, "five retired bishops also wrote the Executive Council requesting the same information."

Neither of the two requests did she consider worthy of a detailed answer. The grudging response was that "the church is receiving extraordinary value for the funds it does spend." Glaring however was evidence that the so-called "extraordinary value" from those expenditures was a fiction.

From 2003 onward, with the Gene Robinson trouble, the Episcopal Church began to decline drastically. In a three year span, 2003–2006, no fewer than 125 parishes and missions wanted out.[7] There were 7,220 parishes and missions in 2003 and only 7,095 in 2006. The first-year leadership of Schori brought no improvement, with a further drop to 7,055, a loss of another 40. But Schori was unfazed. In 2007 alone, TEC accrued "over a million dollars for legal fees." The next year, "TEC spent $1,970,000 on litigation." Faced with the continuously rising cost, the church was forced to tap "into $1,520,000 of [its] short-term reserves." Though the decision didn't follow sound cost-benefit analysis, it didn't seem to matter to the leadership of Episcopal Church—to commit millions of dollars in chasing out several thousand worshippers only to gain tens of thousands of dollars in return.

Incredibly, the "Executive Council [still] budgeted $600,000 for litigation in 2009." In fact, that same year they prepared for an all-out legal onslaught, setting

6. See "A Timeline of Defining Actions"; http://en.wikipedia.org/wiki/Continuing_Anglican _Movement.

7. American Anglican Council, "Episcopal Church in Decline," www.americananglican.com.

aside the "Trust Fund [tagged] #1033 and [named] The St. Ives Fund, to support non budgetary legal expenses." As expected, the pressure that piled on the purse of the church was beginning to cause a groan. The American church might not have gone bankrupt, but it was not financially buoyant either. Yet the uneconomical nature of the expenditure didn't make Schori shrink from her hard stance. After all, she owned the arch-episcopal decision-making machine. It's not only in the secular world that absolute power corrupts; it can do so also in spiritual places.

The Schori era was a horror. Priests and bishops faced nightmares of legal and administrative persecution. They would rush to the courts in the morning, only to come back in the afternoon to find letters of inhibition waiting on their tables. By one count, "at least 10 bishops and 108 priests and deacons" were "unlawfully inhibited and deposed." The standard allegation against the priests and the bishops was "abandonment of communion or renunciation of their Holy orders." Yet impeccable evidence showed that "they did neither."

But to whom could they complain? The Episcopal Church's majestic authority had decided, and so be it! It seemed immaterial whether her decision contravened the process established by the canon of the church. The leadership of the church apparently wasn't worried that, most times, its approach was a "violation of its own canons to punish the orthodox." Not only were individual priests persecuted; the net was extended to established governing structures of the so-called "enemy" churches.

A typical case involved the Diocese of San Joaquin, whose eight bishops rejected Schori's apostolic authority. Despite her knowledge that the standing committee of the diocese was constitutionally constituted, the "Presiding Bishop dissolved it and substituted it with another without warrant." However, there are occasions that persecution becomes counter-productive, for it can lead to a hardening of position.

The dissidents frequently reiterated, "We are not leaving; we would not leave!"[8] Rather, they maintained, "it's TEC that has left us!" And from the turbulence, they gathered new strength. As Rev. Dr. Yates, rector of The Falls Church Anglican, reflected, there was effervescence of hope pervading throughout the dissenting churches during those troubled days. He called it a kind of "tabernacling season," one that helped them to emerge as a "portable church . . . to be resilient . . . which strengthened us." It struck them that, as a church, "we are not about a building; we are about our faith and our body, about our relationships with each other and the Lord." And he added, "We have seen how faithful our God is."

Many ropes were dropped simultaneously into the sea to pull the American churches to safety. The deposed Bishop Duncan located a tug from the Anglican Province of the Southern Cone. Immediately, the province made him a "bishop-at-large," and so, within fifty days, his episcopate authority was fully restored. He was subsequently elected bishop of the new "Anglican Diocese of Pittsburgh." Then the

8. "The Falls Church Anglican"; "A Timeline of Defining Actions"; http://www.beliefnet.com/Faiths/Christianity/2004/02/Who-Is-Doing-The-Dividing.aspx?p=7.

nine Episcopal churches of Virginia opted for help from the Convocation of Anglicans in North America, the Nigerian initiative.[9] And like everything associated with Archbishop Akinola, this raised particularly heated controversy.

Of course, this wasn't the first such division in the American church. In 1976, because of the women's rebellion, the General Convention approved formally women's ordination.[10] The decision did not enjoy consensus, and several thousand dissenting clergy and laypeople gathered in St. Louis, Missouri, to weigh their options.[11] Convened as the Fellowship of Concerned Churchmen, the group concluded their deliberation with a statement called the "Affirmation of St. Louis," wherein they resolved "to continue in the Catholic Faith, Apostolic Order, Orthodox Worship and Evangelical Witness of the traditional Anglican Church." This was followed with a proclamation that they would do "all things necessary for the continuance of same."

It wasn't an empty boast, for from the event grew a new church with an interim name—Anglican Church in North America. Committed to seeing their mission through, the Rt. Rev. Charles D. D. Doren was named as its first bishop. He was consecrated by a retired bishop of the Episcopal Church, Rt. Rev. Albert Chambers, along with a bishop of the Philippines Independent Catholic Church. The third expected consecrator, the Rt. Rev. Mark Pae of the Anglican Church of Korea, compensated for his absence with a letter of consent. In response, Presiding Bishop John Allin closed his eyes to the incident.

Twenty years later, the same chicken came home to roost under Presiding Bishop Edmond Browning. A number of priests had found unconscionable his dovish empathy for Bishop John Spong's heresy and his abhorrent The Oasis, a gay organization supposedly within the Episcopal Church.[12] In 1997, thirty priests led by Chuck Murphy showed their disgust publicly. They released a document entitled, *The First Promise*. Without mincing words, they declared the "authority of the Episcopal Church to be 'fundamentally impaired' because they no longer upheld the 'truth of the gospel,'" hence, "the crisis in faith and leadership."

Without invitation, two archbishops, Emmanuel Kolini and Moses Tay of South East Asia, decided to take action. They "believed the time had come for Missionary Bishops to safeguard the faith in North America."[13] On January 29, 2000, at St. Andrew's Cathedral in Singapore, they consecrated Chuck Murphy and John Rodger as bishops. Six months later, The Anglican Mission in the Americas (AMiA) was launched

9. Minns, "What is CANA?" from the archive and papers of the Most Rev. Peter Akinola.

10. See https://en.wikipedia.org/w/index.php?title=Philadelphia_Eleven&oldid=677647569; https://en.wikipedia.org/w/index.php?title=Philadelphia_Eleven&printable=yes; Woo, "George Barrett; Episcopal Bishop Defied Church to Ordain 4 Women Priests."

11. https://en.wikipedia.org/wiki/Anglican_Church_in_North_America; http://en.wikipedia.org/wiki/Continuing_Anglican_Movement.

12. https://en.wikipedia.org/w/index.php?title=Oasis_Commission&oldid=600809358.

13. https://en.wikipedia.org/wiki/Emmanuel_Kolini; https://en.wikipedia.org/w/index.php?title=Moses_Tay&oldid=675231014.

officially in Amsterdam, Netherlands. The primates of Rwanda and South East Asia were to provide oversight for the new church. One of the churches to identify with the network was The St. Andrews Church of Little Rock, Arkansas. By that singular act, the congregation became the first in North America "to come under the oversight of the Global South provinces." Still, Presiding Bishop Browning neither rained fire nor brimstone on the church nor brought heavens to fall on his fellow primates.

Presiding Bishop Jefferts Schori had a different, fight-to-the-finish leadership style. She was determined to contain the "dissidents" at home and engage the "rabble-rousers" abroad. Among her targets at home was the Rev. Canon Martyn Minns. Abroad was the Nigerian archbishop, Akinola, who, with Minns, was working on the departure of the Virginia churches from the Episcopal Church. Schori was affronted by their boldness, and serious legal-cum-political battles between her and the two men ensued. Perhaps, if she had turned back into history—taking wisdom from the use of détente and her predecessor Griswold's deliberate policy preventing an implosion—she would have learned the lesson of how difficult it is to win an imperial war against people who fight with their heart.

Archbishop Akinola and Canon Minns shared the gift of undiluted courage, strong convictions, and tenacity of purpose. Incidentally, they belonged to the same generation, born ten months apart in 1943–1944. The common bond, however, was their uncompromising stand on the authority of the Bible. The two could be typecast as old-order, "conservative" priests. Minns's unrepentant faith in the Bible was in contrast with his early days, before he ventured into priestly calling.

An English-born American, he was raised in Nottingham, England. His education centred on empirical proof as the standard of scholarship. Graduating in 1964 with a bachelor of science, with honors in mathematics and statistics, from the University of Birmingham in England, he became an executive with the Mobil Corporation in New York before calling it quits after about a decade and a half, when he turned to the area of his passion—serving God. After receiving the master of divinity degree from Virginia Theological Seminary in 1978, he was ordained into priesthood in 1979, got appointed to various churches as priest, and, in 1991, became rector of the Truro Church in Fairfax, Virginia. Unquestioning in his obedience to the Scriptures, he venerated the gospel heartily, wholly, and holistically. Minns was also a forthright fighter and a brilliant administrator. He was meticulous to the point of nearly being a perfectionist. Plus, he was gifted as a remarkable communicator. He had the ability of turning words into poetry and making classics out of sermons. The Truro Church leader's qualities resonated with Akinola, and they formed a fruitful relationship.

The chances of Akinola and Minns crossing paths would have been slim, had not the American church imposed Gene Robinson's trouble on the worldwide Anglican Communion. Akinola was head of the biggest national church in the Anglican Communion and a primate. Minns was a parish priest, the shepherd of a congregation, though his Truro Church was the largest and most conspicuous in the Virginia diocese. The crisis brought them together in a meeting hosted by Truro Church on July 22–23, 2003, at the outbreak of the Robinson's crisis.[14]

Also, Minns was part of the select group that Archbishop Akinola met in Atlanta on April 2–3, 2004, and was part of the discussion during the Global South Primates Steering Committee meeting in Singapore in February 2006. At the latter meeting, the primates learned of the threats, the persecution, and the rising risks to a number of congregations and dioceses in the USA and Canada, and their call for help through "alternative primatial oversight." At none of these meetings was Minns a bench-warmer. He was an intelligent voice with great, articulated perspectives on the strategic path to tread. And like Akinola, he followed up on decisions with a single-minded tenacity. Not surprising, then, the Truro church decided to pitch its tent with CANA, on the model floated by the Nigerian church.

Actually, Minns had visited Nigeria two months after the Atlanta meeting in April 2004.[15] The "church on the move" tour was extensive. It was even broader than that of the former Canterbury Archbishop George Carey, when the latter paid his archiepiscopal visit to Nigeria at the invitation of Akinola in 2001. Minns had gone round the east, west, north, and south of the vast country. Broad, deep, and diversified was his interaction with the various segments of Nigerian Anglicans—encompassing lay people, priests, bishops, and archbishops. From local to regional sections, he encountered the feverish pace at which missions and evangelism were fuelling the Nigerian church's staggering expansion, making it the most formidable national church in the worldwide Anglican Communion.

Minns also had a one-on-one meeting with Archbishop Akinola. You don't know the true character of an individual until you get close to the person, and, indeed, the six-hour session with the Nigerian church leader gave Minns an inroad into the impressive knowledge of the man and the Nigerian church. Akinola's "frenetic pace" and his "financial management of the Nigerian church," through which "he has quadrupled the Provincial budget," led Minns to call Akinola "remarkable." He was much impressed with the "deliberate process of increasing investments and other income streams" and Akinola's goal "to continue reducing assessments so that local funds can be used for initiatives, especially church planting."

Minns, at 61, was beyond the age of a man easily tempted by candy or the "815 charm offensives" that the American church was notorious for. When the push came

14. See Notes and Minutes of the "Meeting at Truro Church" July 22–23, 2003 between Archbishop Peter Akinola and Bishop Bob Duncan, Martyn Minns, Vinay Samuel, and 60 other participants, from the personal archive of the Archbishop; "Minutes of Meeting of Archbishop Akinola with Bishop Robert Duncan, Canon David Anderson, Dr. Gordon Okunsanya, Canon Martyn Minns and Canon Ellis Brust"; Minns, Marty & Angela, " Notes from a visit for the Installation of the Right Reverend John Chew as Archbishop of the Anglican Province of South East Asia and a meeting of the Global South Primates Committee," from the papers and archive of Archbishop Peter Akinola.

15. Minns, "A Church on the Move—Notes from a Short Term Mission to the Church of Nigeria (Anglican Communion), Martyn, Angela and Rachel Minns," from the papers and archive of Archbishop Peter Akinola.

to shove and Schori was nudging disagreeing congregations overboard, it wasn't surprising that Minns and his colleagues in the Virginia diocese grabbed hold of the Nigerian church boat.

Through amendment to the Nigerian church's constitution, the Nigerian church could take the action free of any legal encumbrances. A provision of Chapter IX Section 39 of the Constitution empowered the primate "to create convocations, chaplaincies of like-minded faithful outside Nigeria."[16] Akinola was further vested with the authority "to appoint persons within or outside Nigeria to administer them." Likewise, he was given the full right of providing episcopal oversight to these missions.

Those intent on demonizing the Nigerian church leader were oblivious to the cards Akinola was carrying in his pocket that he could use to re-direct the game. When the American church unilaterally sacked the Nigerian chaplain, the Rev. Canon Gordon Okusanya, he kept his cool. Okusanya's responsibility was ministering to the Nigerian Anglicans in the United States, which included a significant pool of diverse professionals in sectors like medicine, communications, business, and finance. Akinola knew he already had a mandate from the church's national leadership to secure a home for the Nigerian Anglicans exiled by the American church, and he had no reason to hesitate—thus the formation of CANA, the Convocation of Anglicans in North America.

As expected, Akinola, CANA, and Minns all drew fierce and aggressive reactions. The pro-gay Episcopalians counted Akinola's action "a challenge and an intervention;"[17] insisting, "To think otherwise is foolish." But while the upbraiding was still going on, the Nigerian leader dispatched three teams to the United States, their mission to study and assess the various hurdles to cross in making CANA succeed.[18] They included senior Nigerian bishops like the Most Rev. M.S.C. Anikwenwa, Rt. Rev. M. Owadayo, Rt. Rev. Peter Adebiyi, Rt. Rev. E. Chukwuma, Rt. Rev. H. Ndukuba, and Rt. Rev. Ikechi Nwosu. Their reports indicated the existence of "the potentials for fruitful ministry" and became "the guiding light in further moves."

Archbishop Akinola was determined to actualize their recommendation, and by February 2006, the board of trustees for CANA was constituted. Elected as its chairman was Abraham Yisa, a lawyer and the registrar of the Nigerian church. A Nupe, Yisa was from the pro-Muslim northern part of Nigeria. But he was a man accustomed to statesmanship. With an acute legal mind, he had a knack for steering the course of preventive law rather than pursuing curative legal action. Yisa followed up on the earlier visits of Nigerian bishops to the United States, interacting with a broad

16. Minutes of the General Synod, September 12, 2005, held at Anambra State, Nigeria.

17. Gledhill, "For God's Sake."

18. Akinola, "Primates Opening Remarks at the Standing Committee Meeting held at Ibadan North Diocese"; "Primates Opening Remarks at the Standing Committee Meeting held at the St. Paul's Cathedral, Diobil, Port Harcourt, Niger Delta North Diocese"; Minutes of the Standing Committee held at the same venues, all retrieved from the archive and papers of the Most Rev. Peter Akinola.

cross section of Nigerians and Americans. He was impressed by their enthusiasm for "contributing towards the success of the project."[19] From his reading of the situation, CANA had already translated to a broader platform. By the time he reported to the larger meeting of the Standing Committee of the Church of Nigeria, Yisa was in a high gear of enthusiasm, informing the gathering that "CANA was fully incorporated in America" and "already a success."

At the Standing Committee meeting, twelve Nigerian dioceses—Awka, Lagos, Abuja, Ibadan, Kaduna, Orlu, Enugu, On the Niger, Lagos West, Niger Delta North, Ilesa, and Umuahia—rose quickly in support of the initiative.[20] They pledged to contribute N600,000 (the equivalent of US$40,000) each year for three years "to support this and other mission work."

Now CANA would need "the presence of a domestic church structure and a local bishop," that is, in America. These were issues that the Nigerian primate would have to address and report upon. In the meantime, "the CANA report was adopted by the House unanimously."

Akinola took the first step on June 28, 2006. The Nigerian House of Bishops had met to elect four new bishops, including one for its American missionary organization. Undoubtedly, the favorite to lead CANA was Canon Marty Minns. Impeccable were his credentials, records, and character, and Minns received overwhelming endorsement from the bishops as CANA's founding missionary bishop. Akinola and the Nigerian church were euphoric. Directly opposite to their own elation was the American church's bellyaching at the decision. The grumble precipitated a rash of media vilifications, cyber-attacks, and terrorism. The hostile attacks bothered neither Akinola nor the Nigerian church. They turned their backs to them, oblivious to the ill and malicious vitriol.

What mattered to Akinola was that Minns had been offered a mission and had accepted his commission to lead "the growing number of CANA congregations and clergy" in the United States. Minns' consecration, with due pomp, followed on August 20, 2006, two months after his election.[21] The "hugely celebrated event," as the *Voice of America* (VOA) described it, took place at Nigeria's newly constructed National Christian Centre in the capital city of Abuja. The former Truro Church rector shared the honor with three Nigerian colleagues who were elected into the episcopate along with him, and Minns's consecration was destined to be a turning point in Nigerian-American Anglican relations. It magnified the polarization between the leaders of the two countries' churches since the outbreak of the Gene Robinson trouble.

19. Interview with Mr. Abraham Yisa at his Abuja residence in 2007.

20. "Minutes of the Standing Committee" held at Ibadan North Diocese, February 22–25 2006 & at the St. Paul's Cathedral, Diobil, Port Harcourt, Niger Delta North Diocese September 12–16, 2006, retrieved from the archive and papers of the Most Rev. Peter Akinola.

21. Voice Of America, "Anglican Church of Nigeria Installs Bishop From America," retrieved from the archive and papers of the Most Rev. Peter Akinola.

Archbishop Akinola wasn't naïve, thinking that the fanatical pro-gay American church leaders would welcome his action. Nor was he expecting a red carpet reception for Minns. But he wasn't deterred. He recognized that the game had changed; or more appropriately, that he had technically altered the pattern of play. As the VOA put it, the "event could complicate the already simmering tensions in the Episcopal Church." He wasn't expecting the American presiding bishop to receive the initiative with open hands, but the Nigerian church leader had no apology to offer for the action taken. It was a necessity compelled by what the VOA itself had rightly described as circumstances demanding "a haven for Episcopalians alienated by the U.S. Episcopal Church."

They needed their freedom of worship to be safeguarded. This was the liberty the Episcopal Church had been denying all those not in support of its pro-gay stance. The *Voice of America* also predicted that more of the so-called "conservative parishes could leave the U.S. Episcopal Church, and form new ties with the Church of Nigeria." Akinola's reply was that the Church of Nigeria was ready to accept responsibility for ensuring that Christians who desired to be true to their faith and Anglican identity were not shackled in any way. "As the need arises, we will be meeting the challenges," he told the VOA reporter.

In fact, he was already looking beyond the instant. He had confidence in Minns' missionary zeal, confident that he was not going to be a mere contingency manager but rather a new-vistas opener. Akinola was sure CANA was bringing a fresh light, introducing a brighter prospect, and stimulating strength and faith among loyal disciples of Christ. His view of the future was sanguine: "There is no way one bishop can cope," he said. Cheerily, he continued, "We have had the first one now, and, hopefully, in another six months, one year, or so, we will have two, three, more, maybe five or 10 more."

There was no denying the fact that the archbishop's action stirred the hornet's nest, or, to put it another way, tipped over the Episcopal Church's boiling pot of soup! The audacious move added more to the centripetal and centrifugal forces sharply dividing the Communion. While Akinola and the Church of Nigeria felt reasonably justified that their action was right, the Episcopal Church was incensed with the Nigerian church's cross-boundary intervention. The American church opined that the act violated conventional practice within the Communion. Minns was, however, emphatic that "CANA is God's gift to those of us who want to serve and grow as Anglicans."[22] He observed that, regrettably, we "cannot do so, in good conscience within The Episcopal Church as it is being currently led." What they wanted was "to get on with the work of evangelism and church planting . . . see lives transformed and not simply excused . . . [and] be a church where everyone is welcome but no one leaves unchanged."

---

22. Minns, "These Are Difficult Days For Those Of Us Who Are Anglican Christians," Sermon delivered at the Installation service of Rt. Rev. Martyn Minns as the Bishop of CANA, National Christian Centre, Abuja, August 20, 2006, retrieved from the archive and papers of the Most Rev. Peter Akinola.

Invariably, the matter degenerated to another round of clashing wills. On one side was the threesome of Akinola, the Church of Nigeria, and Minns. In the opposing corner of the ring was "the new Sheriff in town," Presiding Bishop Schori, the diocesan bishops, and the Episcopal Church. It looked like a balanced game of three-on-three. However, despite the macho appearance of Archbishop Akinola, he was still prepared to bend a bit. In the letter he wrote to the archbishop of Canterbury as well as to his American counterpart, he let it be known that, "CANA is for the Communion and we are more than happy to surrender it to the Communion once the conditions that prompted our division have been overturned."[23] Of course, he ought to have known that in the dictionary of the Episcopal Church and its frontier woman, Presiding Bishop Schori, the word "compromise" had been deleted. And just as the Nigerian Church, Akinola, and Minns were determined to see their mission through, she and the leadership of the American church were equally resolute to thwart their efforts.

The two groups watched each other and made deft calculations like chess players. Akinola and CANA were set to take the battle to the home ground of the American Church with a planned installation of Minns on May 5, 2007, in the United States. Presiding Bishop Schori and her coterie of devotees in the Executive Council of the Episcopal Church were also waiting for Akinola at the Anglican Communion primates meeting scheduled for Dar es Salaam, Tanzania, on February 15, 2007.

Warming up on the sideline was the hired "David Mark" or Davis Mac-Iyalla, the so-called Nigerian gay rights activist, procured to be Akinola's nemesis.[24] Davis Mac-Iyalla didn't roll out from the Episcopal Church's production line. He was a product of Changing Attitude, the British gay organization. Iyalla was born in 1972 at Port Harcourt, the oil-rich Nigerian city. Oddly, there was no account of his parentage in his well-publicized online profiles. Nor was there any thread to his educational background. But, as his profile in many online sources would have it believed, "He came out to himself at the age of 14."

Iyalla discovered he was gay around 1986. But "his disinterest in dating females was not made apparent to others around him" until 17 years later. He broke the silence "after two events." The first was Gene Robinson's ordination as the bishop of New Hampshire. Second, was the death of his mentor, the Nigerian Anglican Bishop Iyobee Ugede of Otukpo Diocese. By then, he was 31 years old. Robinson was elected on June 7, 2003, and by July 2003, Iyalla had been "fired from his job as the principal of a local Anglican children's school" in Otukpo, which was owned by the Otukpo Diocese. He attributed his termination "to his being gay."

23. Akinola, Letter to The Rt. Rev. Katharine Jefferts Schori dated 2nd May, 2007, and Letter to Dr. Rowan Williams, the Archbishop of Canterbury dated Sunday, May 6th 2007, both from the from the archive and papers of the Most Rev. Peter Akinola. See the online version at http://peterakinola.blogspot.com.ng/2007/05/letter-to-archbishop-of-canterbury.html.

24. https://en.wikipedia.org/wiki/Davis_Mac-Iyalla.

After that, he "became an activist and started work with Changing Attitude." Prior to that, he and the organization were unknown entities in Nigeria. From that point on, however, he became an idolized activist, especially through the gay, online media.[25] He was adored as "one of the stiffest domestic opponents of [anti-gay] legislation [and a] Nigerian LGBT rights advocate."

Iyalla's story was an embellished, clumsy, composite picture of Karl Ulrichs, who had discovered his gay orientation at age 14 as well.[26] Ulrichs hid the fact to himself; so did Iyalla, who treated his homosexuality as a treasured personal secret. The German environment and law of the time was intolerant of homosexuality; as was also the case in Nigeria. Ulrichs finally came out when he was 32. Iyalla did so at 31. The pioneer gay activist was dismissed from his job because of his homosexuality; over a century later, Iyalla suffered the same fate. Following his firing, Ulrichs took to advancing gay rights. So did Iyalla. As much as the painters of Iyalla's portrait attempted to draw a nice picture of him, many of the lines connecting the painting to the real man were smudges and smears of thick falsehood and awful imitation that ended up making the picture a horrible counterfeit.

The fact of the case was that Iyalla was a thief, and not a petty one at that. Apart from stealing money, he was a thief of identity as well. As part of hoodwinking his hirers, he had claimed the Otukpo Diocese made him a Knight in 2002.[27] Records showed the claim to be a lie. Although Otukpo Diocese conferred the title in 2002, Iyalla wasn't one of the eight recipients. The list of the honorees for that year was Ochilgu P. S. Adoba, Chief Godwin Obiakor, Hon. Moses Onuminya, and Engr. A. Ugochukwu. The remaining were Prince Pius Anozie, Simeon Anikwe, Fidelis Onwungis, and Jesse Nwogwu. No name resembled or was spelled like Davis Iyalla. Indeed, the president of the Council of Knights in the diocese, Sir Godwin Obiakor, rebutted Iyalla's claims. Obiakor's public disclaimer on December 28, 2005, prompted a report the director of communications of the Church of Nigeria sent to warn the international community against the activities of "one fraudster and trickster calling himself Iyalla."

A Nigeria Police crime report of November 30, 2005, removed doubts about Iyalla's felonious character.[28] According to the police, "at 13:00 hours on 30/11/05"

---

25. Changing Attitude featured many articles on the subject, including, "Nigerians Criticise Akinola," October 17, 2005; "Anglican Gay Group Threatens Legal Action against Church of Nigeria," September 1, 2006; "No Claims from the Public that Mac Iyalla Was Asking for Money . . . Changing Attitude England," http://www.changingattitude.org/.

26. https://en.wikipedia.org/wiki/Davis_Mac-Iyalla.

27. Documents evidencing the falsehood of his claim included: "Letter of Council of Knights, Diocese of Oturkpo entitled 'Disclaimer" and signed by Sir. Chief Godwin Obiakor, President Council of Knights, Otukpo Diocese," "Disclaimer by Church of Nigeria, Press Release by Church of Nigeria on 28th December 2005 and signed by Rev. Canon Tunde Popoola," obtained from the Church of Nigeria headquarters at Abuja.

28. Regarding the criminal case, see "Extracts from the Crime Diary Sno. 307 IMO. Time 13.00 Claims on 30/11/05 signed and stamped by Mr. P. Onyejekure, Divisional Police Officer, Nigeria Police Oturkpo."

three men were at the Otukpo Police Station to lodge a complaint. The trio were "Ven. D. O. Mojie (M), Rev. M. Agbor (M) and Sir J. Norogwu (M)," who had brought a written complaint. They alleged "that sometime in the month of August 2005, it was discovered that one Davis Mark Iyalla (M) of Otukpo who by then was an acting Principal at St. John Anglican Secondary School, Otukpo, misappropriated the sum of N1,332,340.00 from the school fees." The report went on to say that "he converted the money to his account . . . at Bank of the North, Otukpo Branch." In addition, "he withdrew same amount and absconded from office Principal of the school (sic)." The police accepted the complaint and "referred [it] to DCD while PC Nixon Clement is detailed for more investigation." The Divisional Police Officer for Otukpo, Mr. P Onyejekure, authenticated and signed the police extract. Iyalla betrayed the trust reposed in him. And like every common criminal, he took to his heels, his guilt pursuing him. He was not heard of until his reappearance as a gay rights activist!

It was to this felon that the American church rolled out a red carpet of honor. He arrived to a hero's welcome with a tour arranged for him to speak to "55 churches in 20 cities, including Pittsburgh, Cleveland, Washington, D.C., and New York."[29] The visit suffered an initial hitch, for there was difficulty in "getting a visa to allow him in." But the constraint was overcome soon. The "founder of Changing Attitude Nigeria," as he was called, told the audience that he brought "a Nigerian point of view that so far has been silent." He wanted the people to know that "it is a lie for Akinola and others to claim that there are no homosexual people in Nigeria."

The venerated Iyalla was brought face-to-face with the Executive Council of the Episcopal Church, one of its topmost decision-making organs. The meeting had to break to welcome and celebrate him.[30] Presiding Bishop Schori took time to give the visiting star respectable treatment. Besides the discussion with the American church's highest decision making body, time was also set aside for him to meet "with [the] Council's International Concerns (INC) and National Concerns (NAC) committees," two important committees, perhaps crucial to delivering the "815 charm offensive."

It was hard to overlook the Executive Council's meeting location—Newark. It was no coincidence since the city was retired Bishop John Spong's territory. It was also Louie Crew's home. Crew was still sitting tightly in his positions of influence with Newark's diocesan affairs as well as on the 38-member Executive Council of the American Church, where he wasn't without his Midas touch. Six times, six elections, and six occasions consecutively—1994, 1997, 2000, 2003, 2006, and 2009—the diocese had put him forward as a deputy to the General Convention. Nothing had changed the character of the diocese as the hotbed of gay rebellion within the American church.

29. Carlson, "Who Is Davis Mac-Iyalla And Why Is He Here?"; Brachear, "Message to Episcopalians"; Polgreen and Goodstein, "At Axis of Episcopal Split, an Anti-Gay Nigerian."

30. "Davis Mac-Iyalla in Diocese of Newark: Nigerian Activist Tells his Story," http://telling-secrets.blogspot.com.ng/2007/06/davis-mac-iyalla-in-diocese-of-newark.html.

Newark expressed everything that the three words defiant, disobedient, and derailed could mean. American church leaders didn't give Iyalla a free lunch for nothing. The meeting with the Council's INC and NAC committees was no accident. They had a strategic purpose and mission.

Meanwhile, Iyalla returned to London, where he had been living the life of a celebrated, though fraudulent, star. Another series of lengthy speaking engagements were organized for him in London, the first with "the General Synod of the Church of England." From there he moved to York to talk to the Changing Attitude of York group, then back to the General Synod of Church of England, where he met with the bishops and members of the Synod. Overall, Iyalla was a smart fellow. He saw through the desperation of his sponsors and conned them effortlessly. For their part, they wanted a caricature in their own image, and he allowed himself to be cloned.

A good con man, Iyalla was celebrated as "the center of a growing movement of gays and lesbians in Nigeria." Within a short period of time, the Changing Attitude group he pioneered in Nigeria had become supposedly a formidable organization with strong numerical strength matching or surpassing that of similar groups in England and America. Compared to the 600 members of which its parent organization in England could boast, or the 2,500 members that the parallel American Episcopal Church gay group Integrity USA claimed, Changing Attitude Nigeria claimed between 2,500 and 3,000 members.[31]

Of course, statistics are easy causalities of lies and falsehoods because they will not talk, and Iyalla used them to propagate fictions. The figure of 2,500–3,000 gays and lesbians in Nigeria was most dishonest, for there had been no such count. And if Iyalla returned to live in Nigeria, he would be in hiding as a fugitive. Iyalla was an allegorical "white snake in black skin." He was a mercenary raised for a particular purpose. The goal was to fight the Nigerian church leader, though they had never met.

But Iyalla helped to draw the battle line for Dar es Salam, Tanzania, where the meeting of all Anglican primates was to occur, including those of the Global South who had refused to sit at the same table as Schori. On the way to the looming battle, however, Akinola had a surprising boost in international image. He was named by the *Time Magazine* as one of the 100 most influential citizens in the world.[32] The Nigerian church leader was hardly a media savvy personality. He would rather dissociate himself from the media-manipulative skill of his Western colleagues. The influential American magazine, however, had begun what it called "The Time 100," selecting "the 100 men and women whose power, talent or moral example is transforming our world." Akinola made the magazine's honored list in 2006 (and again in 2007).

He was selected in 2006 based on his "leading the worldwide revolt of evangelical Anglicans against the ordination of gay bishops in the U.S. by the Episcopal Church." The metaphor that captured his profile was succinct—"The Strength of a Lion," which

31. Virtue, "Changing Attitude Spins Disinformation on Homosexuality to Anglican Communion."
32. Van Biema, "Peter Akinola."

was the title of the short article, written by Rick Warren, author of the popular book *The Purpose Driven Life*. [33] Warren warned against committing a serious error of judgement by attempting "to caricature his ministry with that one issue." That "would severely underestimate his importance." Akinola, he said, "personifies the epochal change in the Christian church," i.e., "the leadership, influence, growth and center of gravity in Christianity is moving from the northern hemisphere to the southern." He continued, "When he speaks, far more than just Anglicans pay attention," adding, "Akinola has the strength of a lion." His strength of character was "useful in confronting Third World fundamentalism and First World relativism." Of course, he had been vilified as a "homophobe," "homo-hater," and "homo-maniac," but Warren compared him to the world-respected South African leader, Nelson Mandela:

> I believe, he, like Mandela, is a man of peace and his leadership is a model for Christians around the world.

Time's recognition was not pleasing to same-sex flag-wavers within the Anglican Communion, for Akinola was now confirmed as a force to be reckoned with. Furthermore, the Nigerian media that had largely been out of the Anglican gay fray began to be drawn to the crisis. Opinion pieces and articles started appearing. A major Nigerian tabloid, *The Punch*, devoted its editorial to the subject, examining the "Antigay pressures in Anglican Church," and there was no doubt about the side on which the newspaper stood:

> As a church man who has displayed an exemplary act of courage in reminding the West of the authenticity of the Gospel, Akinola is a statesman whose influence might help in social change.[34]

Hammering the nail home, the newspaper highlighted his intervention "against any revisionist or so-called progressive interpretation, which, in particular is the accommodation of same-sex unions in places of worship, a timely warning for the church and the society."

Nothing makes a man the prophetic voice for his generation other than his calling attention to their evil ways. Auspicious, timely, and supportive was the *Time*'s recognition, which created space for him in the international sphere and gave his voice a stronger stature worldwide than that of those vilifying him. The positive development upset the homosexual groups. It was like a fly dropping into their teacup. The gay strategy had always been to demonize their opponents, paint them as wicked, evil, and inhumane in order to dominate them. There was now a sort of counter-balance from the same Western world. But it didn't take long before another hashtag was added to

33. Warren, "Archbishop Peter Akinola—The Strength of a Lion."

34. "Anti-Gay Pressures in Anglican Church"; Ojo, "Akinola Named Among 100 Influential People on Earth"; Sagay "From Carpenter to Primate."

the archbishop's story.[35] The rumor was dropped into the gossip mill that his motive for standing against the West was to wrest power from Canterbury. Akinola wanted to create a parallel Communion by establishing "the Canterbury of the Global South," or so the viral gossip went.

A Western reporter confronted him with the allegation: "The impression in the West has been that of a man determined to wrest the leadership of the Anglican Church from Canterbury." Archbishop Akinola gave the journalist a response reserved for someone ignorant, and indeed, the news man was ill-informed. Akinola wasn't embarrassed by the lie, for he had heard far more ludicrous fabrications than this. Furthermore, in 2006, he was four years away from ending his tenure, and he was salivating over taking his leave from the stage, even considering early retirement. He had discussed this with nobody but had prayerfully kept asking God for guidance. On several occasions he had said that his stand on the Communion's crisis was predicated on two mutually reinforcing points. The first was the authority of the Scripture, while the second concerned respect for the integrity of collective decisions. He was not going to be part of any group consenting to the validation of wrongs. Therefore, Akinola stated,

> I keep on saying you do not have to go through Canterbury to get to Christ, or to be a Christian. Equity must be the cornerstone of relationship within the Communion. It is the best way to stave off confusion in the Communion.

The rumoured ambition went up and down the Communion and was brought to the attention of Bishop Martyn Minns. Veiled insinuation was even made that Minns himself was part of the plot, and, therefore, he was a "traitor" to his white kin. Minns wasn't intimidated. He debunked the falsehood, saying, "Archbishop Akinola was motivated by a conviction that the Anglican Communion must change its colonial-era leadership structure and mentality," adding, "He doesn't want to be the man; he just no longer wants to be the boy; he wants to be treated as an equal leader, with equal respect." Of course, he ought to have known that logic and reason wouldn't impact the prevailing mentality among the trio of the Episcopal Church, the Anglican Church of Canada, and the Church of England. They were possessed of a common fanatical obsession to see homosexuality imposed on the Communion at any cost. Though contemptuous, offensive, and indifferent to a large section of the Communion, they could not be bothered.

As the clock was ticking toward the crucial Dar es Salam meeting of the Anglican primates, the omens were showing that the assembly would be far from agreeable. None of the parties had mellowed its hard stance. However, Akinola had gained in stature and status internationally. His stand had acquired more standing in the public square and in the hearts of those who believed in the purity of the Bible. Covertly and overtly, too, the other side—notably, the American Episcopal Church and the Church

35. Gledhill, "For God's Sake."

of England—was strengthening its hand in the homosexuality-at-all-cost campaign within the Anglican Church. Whose way did the pendulum tilt or in whose favor would the matter finally be resolved? The battleground was Dar es Salam, Tanzania, where everyone was ready with his or her game plan.

22

The Last Straw

Dar Es Salam, 2007

Outwardly, the impending February 2007 meeting of Anglican primates from all over the world in Dar es Salam, Tanzania, evinced the image of a conclave of collegial spiritual leaders. But that façade was a farce. Ahead of the meeting, each group had perfected its scheme to outsmart the other. The archbishop of Canterbury, Dr. Rowan Williams, acted first. Williams was aware of the decision of the Anglican Consultative Council (ACC) at Nottingham, England, suspending the two North American churches till the 2008 Lambeth Conference in view of their perfidy against the stand of the Communion. What the archbishop did was to cleverly pull the rug from under his colleagues' feet. Without prior consultation with them, he extended an invitation to the meeting to America's Presiding Bishop Jefferts Schori.[1]

Of course, he was aware of the stand of the Global South's primates regarding Schori's primacy. But he had devised an ingenious scheme to backstab them. Shrewdly, he extended similar invitations to three additional bishops from the American Episcopal Church. Widely publicized, the purpose of the American invitees was to "address an extra-curricular session of the meeting of Anglican Primates in Tanzania," which would "not be part of the Primates' meeting itself." Rather, the primates' meeting would "go into recess in order to hear the presentations from the three bishops." After that, they would "reconvene at the close of the hearing." Categorically underscored was the fact that "the American bishops are guests of Archbishop Williams." They were "not of the collegial gathering, the spokesman said."

Archbishop Williams justified his decision with a cover ploy, which he communicated to his colleagues in a letter dated December 18, 2006. He told them of his "proposing to invite two or three contributors from that province." The aim was to have a session with them before the rest of their "formal business, in which the situation [within The Episcopal Church] may be reviewed." Consequently, the Rt. Rev.

1. Conger, "Three U.S. Bishops Invited to Primates' Meeting."

C. Christopher Epting, the presiding bishop's deputy for ecumenical and inter-faith relations, had been invited. Also, there was the deposed bishop of Pittsburgh, the new moderator of the Anglican Communion Network, the Rt. Rev. Robert Duncan. Completing the trio was the bishop of Western Louisiana, the Rt. Rev. D. Bruce. Bruce was president of the Presiding Bishop's Council of Advice. The three men were to provide different perspectives on the crisis in the church.

What new or fresh standpoints, however, were they going to provide that had not been over-repeated in the course of affairs? Why would the archbishop choose the collective forum of the primates' meeting for his private discussion toward understanding the divided opinion within the American church?

Archbishop Akinola was not impressed. In early January 2007, he had written a letter to Williams suggesting that the latter had deliberately twisted the facts in order to find an excuse for his autocratic decision.[2] The January letter was not the first correspondence the two exchanged on the subject. Akinola reminded Archbishop Williams about the communications "on a number of occasions on behalf of the Global South Steering Committee regarding the meeting." From their two different positions, each had nursed no illusions about the significance of the impending meeting. Dar es Salam was really going to "be an important and difficult encounter." Akinola expressed this view, and it appeared that Archbishop Williams had the same notion too.

Archbishop Williams' decision was not reassuring. Akinola's view was that "the recent letter seems to add to the difficulty" rather than reducing the tense atmosphere in the Communion, which he found to be insufferable. Akinola was convinced that Williams had not made the decision in good faith. He had allowed politics to cloud his thinking and permitted a self-serving motive to undermine the selflessness demanded by his office. Williams was aware of the Kigali decisions of the Global South primates, but he decided to ignore them. Their entreaties had no meaning to him. Instead of upholding the Windsor Report's resolution that asked bishops holding theological views at odds with those of the Communion to "withdraw themselves from representative functions in the Anglican Communion," he chose to disregard the resolution. He not only invited the American presiding bishop to the meeting but also was "insisting that she [be] present" in all of its deliberations. Williams' argument was that Schori was a "duly elected Primate of the Episcopal Church" and the Primates needed "to hear her perspective."

Akinola believed this was "problematic" and the argument a barren one. He reminded Williams that Presiding Bishop Frank Griswold, at Dromantine, Ireland, had "made it very clear that as Primate he had no authority to speak on behalf of his province except [to stand] by what his General Convention declares." And the General Convention had made its irrefutable stand known. Unequivocally, they had declared

2. Akinola, "Letter to the Global South Steering Committee," January 26, 2007, with attachment of letters from Archbishop Peter Akinola to the archbishop of Canterbury, from the archive and papers of the Archbishop Peter Akinola.

that "they have chosen to walk apart." Akinola felt that the archbishop's action was inappropriate and unfortunate. Williams ought not to be seen approbating and reprobating at the same time.

Akinola contended, "Bishop Schori's presence among us as a 'Primate' is certain to be a source of confusion and distraction." Besides, "a decision of that significance should be made by the Primates collectively." So he said, "I urge you to reconsider."

There was a second sore issue—Williams had altered the meeting's membership. He had done this to favor himself and the Church of England. In the past, he had represented both at the meeting; he would preside as the chairman of the meeting and represent the Church of England as its primate as well. This time, he had extended an invitation to the primates meeting to the archbishop of York, John Sentamu. Akinola found this "very troubling." Indeed, he was shocked by the action because it contradicted Williams' earlier assurance in correspondence. Akinola called Williams' attention to the letter that he wrote to him on June 9, 2006, one in which the archbishop of Canterbury had allayed the fears of his colleague, promising that "there will, of course, be a full discussion of the proposal." Solemnly, he had pledged that "no one has authority to impose anything."

Apparently, Akinola had read the letter naively. Williams had undertaken a turnaround that miffed Akinola, who noted caustically, "It seems that you are moving inadvertently from your role of 'primus inter pares' into a supreme executive.'" He questioned the argument put forward by Williams concerning the burden one would face with the "responsibility of chairing the meeting and representing the interest of your own province." Akinola believed Williams' argument was self-serving. Combining the two positions in the past had not seemed to present him with a problem, but now, all of a sudden, it had become a herculean task. Akinola found the explanation to be double-faced. This was because the archbishop of Canterbury was not the only primate confronted with "multiple and confronting responsibilities." Akinola was, for example, "the Bishop of the Diocese of Abuja, Primate of All Nigeria, President of Christian Association of Nigeria, Chairman of the Council of Anglican Provinces in Africa and Chairman of the Global South." Yet at the primates meeting, there was no conflict of role or position concerning his leading the Nigerian province as its primate. In any case, Akinola believed that "decisions that are of such long-lasting significance . . . must not be made and imposed on us by fiat."

Akinola should have saved himself the headache. He would not have agonized over Williams' action if he had read the latter's letter carefully. Williams knew where he was going. He had outsmarted Akinola. Deliberately and nicely, he had fed Akinola with *hors d' oeuvre*. He had given him a mouth-watering appetizer prepared for trusting people like him. And there had been a precursor to this tricky behaviour.

As far back as November 18, 2006, Akinola had written to Williams about their primates meeting in Dar es Salam. He had requested "that the proposed agenda be [made] available to all of the Primates." This, he believed, would give them "sufficient time to permit our contributions to its final form." Williams' response of November 30, 2006, had assured that "it would be available shortly." After "shortly" had come and gone, Akinola wrote a reminder to Williams on December 18, 2006, and was assured that "it was almost ready." One month later, they still had "received no such agenda." Ironically, Williams had gone swiftly ahead to invite and announce publicly the hearing with the US delegation as a major part of the meeting. Akinola lamented the move: "I am at a loss on how to interpret this," for the action had placed them "all in an impossible situation."

Moreover, there was the issue of the 2008 Lambeth Conference. Akinola had equally raised the subject as one of the issues that should be discussed in their primates' agenda. Craftily, Williams evaded the subject, dodging another issue that Akinola felt should be non-negotiable on their meeting's agenda, namely the crisis that he believed was stretching the Anglican Church to the breaking point. The Nigerian leader attributed the persistence of the crisis to two problems: The first was the "crisis of doctrine" while the second related to the "crisis of leadership." Underlying the two, as far as Akinola was concerned, was "the failure of the 'Instruments' of the Communion to exercise discipline."

The result was the division threatening "the viability of the Anglican Communion as a united Christian body under a common foundation of faith." Akinola insisted that unless those critical issues were tabled, "there can be no more worthier or important topics for discussion at our meeting in Dar es Salam." Williams waved aside the concerns expressed by the Nigerian leader. He dismissed the issues as trivialities and told Akinola that the Communion need not "become entirely paralysed by our struggles to resolve the challenges posed by decisions in North America."

Archbishop Akinola didn't keep the exchange to himself. On January 26, 2007, he wrote to all his colleagues in the Global South to alert them to the developments. Earlier, on January 24, 2007, he, along with Archbishop John Chew, secretary of the Global South Steering Committee, and Bishop Mouneer Anis of Egypt, the treasurer, had met in London. The letter to all the Global South primates followed two days after the meeting. Apart from briefing them on the questionable decisions of Williams, a number of fresh issues had developed, which these Global South leaders felt strongly should be included in the agenda of their Dar es Salam meeting.

One was the "alternative primatial oversight" question. The letter reminded the Global South primates of the requests "from a number of congregations and dioceses in The Episcopal Church." Akinola's view was that they needed to make a decision on the matter. Supporting that perspective was their Kigali resolution, which stated "that the time has now come . . . towards the formation of what will be recognized as a separate ecclesiastical structure of the Anglican Communion in the USA." He also recalled the meeting they had in Northern Virginia in November 2006. That meeting gave birth to a number of developments, including the broadening of the coalition, which led to a "gathering of bishops in Camp Allen."

The Camp Allen meeting brought together "the Anglican Communion Network" and the "Windsor bishops" with leading Bishops Bob Duncan and Don Wimberly, who were tasked with sketching a roadmap for their journey. Also, the Anglican Communion Institute (ACI) proposed an interim arrangement pending the outcome of the Communion Covenant. Archbishop Akinola happened to favor that plan as well, contending,

> I believe it would be premature and highly disruptive to attempt to create a new Province until the Covenant process has produced a clear conclusion.

However, he believed it was "essential that a structure be established." The essence would be to provide a shoulder to lean on for the churches and congregations "under increasingly militant threats of litigation from those presently in control of The Episcopal Church." He suggested a "college of bishops and dioceses." The "college," he maintained, could pool members of the Anglican Communion Network dioceses, the "Windsor" dioceses (those who accepted the 1998 Lambeth 1.10 resolution), bishops of CANA, bishops of AMiA, and bishops elected to serve in the USA providing oversight to congregations currently under the provinces/dioceses in Bolivia, Peru, Uganda, Kenya, Tanzania, and Central Africa.

Bishops of other "continuing" Anglican bodies that were a part of the Common Cause could be considered for future incorporation. Broad was his conceptualization of the "college of bishops and dioceses." Accordingly, he believed it was necessary to develop a leadership structure for the proposed body. He called for a two-part process. The first was for the college of bishops to "nominate three candidates to serve as Moderator," and second, to choose one. The moderator, "for the time being," would cover the responsibilities undertaken by the Episcopal Church's presiding bishop, including acting as chief consecrator for dioceses within the college. Logically, he would be welcome at all primates' meetings. He would be accorded the right to speak for and represent the dioceses and affiliated parishes of the college. To protect and secure the college, Akinola believed that the primates would have to work with the other Instruments of the Communion.

They would need to ensure that "any diocese or church that affiliates with this emerging entity is free to do so without fear of litigation or punitive action." Equally, they would have to ensure that "all such actions presently underway cease immediately." He was very explicit—"All arrangements are provisional." As far as he was concerned, the proposed actions "will need to be redefined when TEC (that is, the American Episcopal Church) determines its response to the Covenant." Their reply would present two options, an either-or decision, which would be applicable to both the Episcopal Church and the Global South. The choice would be either "a single undifferentiated jurisdictional structure within the Communion," or "a more permanent reordering and creation of a new Communion Province." After expressing these ideas, Akinola told his colleagues, "I would welcome your thoughts about this proposal."

Three days before the global Anglican primates meeting began, the Global South leaders shared their thoughts with him. They had converged in Dar es Salam ahead of the larger meeting.[3] Actually, their gathering went beyond the ordinary rubbing of minds. It could be dubbed a strategy planning session. In attendance were Archbishops Akinola, John Chew, and Mouneer Anis, just elected into the arch-episcopate position. The regulars were present too: Archbishops Benjamin Nzimbi, Drexel Gomez, Emmanuel Kolini, Gregory Venables and Henry Orombi. There were also new additions in the group: Archbishops Bernard Ntahoturi of Burundi, Fidèle Dirokpa Balufuga of the Democratic Republic of the Congo, Justice Ofei Akrofi, Church of the Province of West Africa, and Bishop Nathaniel Garang Anyieth of South Sudan. Item by item, the leaders considered the issues on which Archbishop Akinola had solicited their opinions. Regarding the agenda for the primates meeting, they "agreed that the draft was received too late." They were disappointed with it because "it marginalised the most important issues [that should] be shared with ABp Rowan Williams." As a consequence, they resolved to have a "closed door meeting with him."

Apparently, the Global South primates wanted the Canterbury archbishop to reconsider his decision on the issues that he had omitted from their agenda but which were of primary interest to them. They decided to push for inclusion of "the Windsor and Anglican Covenant up front in the agenda." They were so passionate about the issue that they "agreed that the first order of business" would be to see that the Windsor process was addressed squarely. The primates wanted to ensure that no maneuvers toward sidetracking the issue succeeded. One of their tactics would be to raise at the very beginning of their meeting the "actions of the American Episcopal Church." This, naturally, would put focus on the decision reached at their 2006 General Convention. This would make obvious the American church's repudiation of the primates' decision to establish a process of "listening to all the parties involved." Ultimately, this would lead to the Global South leaders' demanding that a decision had to be made "on the status of TEC in the Communion."

Even among themselves, the Global South leaders knew that the decision they were gunning for was not going to be an easy one. The Anglican Communion likely would resist taking decisive action against TEC. But they were prepared for the hurdles. Their strategy was for Archbishop Venables to lead the discussion on TEC's case. Archbishop Gomez would follow with facts highlighting "TEC's failure to meet requirements of the Windsor Report." After that, all the Global South primates would state their individual positions, with the same conclusions. They would indict TEC for not complying with the Windsor report. Once a *prima facie* case had been established for TEC's culpability, and to avoid a drawn-out debate, Archbishop Mouneer would propose the establishment of a small committee of primates to deliberate and propose necessary actions for the body of primates to approve.

3. "Global South Primates Meeting—Executive Summary of the Minutes of Meeting," Dar es Salam, Tanzania, from the archive and papers of Archbishop Peter Akinola.

The arrangement sounded foolproof like plots always do in theory. But realistically, the archbishop of Canterbury held the aces and controlled the game dexterously. One advantage was his chairmanship of the Primates Standing Committee as the archbishop of Canterbury. Also, he could exercise control over the Joint Standing Committee, which was created from the Primates Standing Committee and the Anglican Consultative Council. The archbishop therefore had tight grips on the levers controlling the Communion, besides his occupying its driver's seat. This rendered the decision-making organs of the Communion vulnerable to manipulation. The attendant effect was compromising the Anglican Church itself many times.

The Global South leaders believed there was need to change the status quo so decision making would be more dynamic in the Communion. As an example, besides Archbishop Williams, who was chairman of the Primates Standing Committee, the only other member of note on that committee was Archbishop Malango. The effect was that the Committee often lacked "the proper quorum to make valid decisions." They decided to urge reform of the Committee at the meeting. The demand would be placed immediately as the meeting began. The first necessary change was to have representation on the Committee through democratic means. As such, they would "call for elections at the beginning of the Primates meeting rather than at the end." If that suggestion was not taken, the position of the Global South leaders would be that there should be no Joint Standing Committee any more.

However, they would still agree to the existence of "the ACC Standing Committee." But they would press for modifications to its constitution and operational modalities. Part of the reform of the ACC would be to make it to be forthwith "without the Primates." At the same time, they would demand amendment of the ACC's constitution. Their position was that since the Anglican Covenant had not only "spelt out the terms of our faith but also our order," the ACC's constitution should also be understood in that light. Beyond all of this, the primates would insist that they meet regularly and not simply at the pleasure of the archbishop of Canterbury, and that they would undertake a review regarding "how appointments are made" in the Communion.

They also took a decisive stand on Alternative Primatial Oversight (APO). Representatives from the two North American churches were at the meeting with the same story of persecution and denial of the right to exist by their countries' church leadership. For more than three years, Akinola and a majority of the primates at the meeting had travelled through the same route of attending to the crisis together. At hardly any of their meetings did they fail to address the matter, taxing the patience of even the most tolerant among them. But on this occasion, the primates still preferred following a course of restraint. They would rather see themselves derided as weak and cowardly than act vainly and precipitously.

So they decided that "The *Global South* will write to ABp Williams." As in all of the previous meetings, the Rt. Rev. Robert Duncan, bishop of Pittsburgh and the new moderator of the Anglican Communion Network, was present. Duncan, like the Global South leaders, was also killing two birds with one stone. The archbishop of Canterbury had invited him to Dar es Salam along with the two other American bishops. Both parties apparently discussed the proposed meeting because the Global South leaders assured him that they would support "his requests at the Primates Meeting." But they wanted him to understand that "no outcomes can be guaranteed." "Regardless of the outcome," he told them, "he would stay on with the flock." The absolute devotion of the American church leader impressed Archbishop Orombi.

Actually, the fiery Ugandan primate, Orombi, was one of the earliest Global South leaders to have concluded that the time for talk with the American church was over. Brusquely, he had told people like Duncan and others in his camp, "You will suffer for the faith." For him, "martyrdom" was not an unfamiliar notion. He had survived repressive, despotic, and brutal regimes in Uganda. Orombi was practical and pragmatic. He believed it was self-deception to assume that the crisis would resolve itself automatically. And he didn't think their opponents could weaken the resolve of the Global South leaders by dragging things out for a long time: "The younger Primates will maintain the same stand even after the older ones retiree." Orombi and Duncan drew thunderous applause from their colleagues for their assertions.

On the other hand, the representatives of the Canadian church were not as sanguine as their American counterparts about the Global South leaders' approach to resolving the problem. The four-man delegation of Charlie Masters, David Short, Cheryl Chang, and Stephen Leung were unambiguous in the propositions they had brought for the consideration of the leaders. The "Panel of Reference" had failed them, so they shared the frustration of their American colleagues. But in their case, they would like to see immediate intervention from the Global South. They wanted authorization of "a Canadian bishop to have a jurisdiction over the dissenting parishes." With a local bishop providing them oversight, at least, the stifling environment under which they were being made to survive would be relaxed a bit.

Fortunately, they had secured a willing local bishop; "retired Bp Don Harvey is ready to perform this role." From their experience, too, the Canadian church equally believed the big stick needed to be wielded. The Global South leaders had just to "apply the Windsor requirements to the Church of Canada," they insisted. The church had been as pig-headed on the same-sex ordination and blessing issue as its American brethren. Canada had not been shy about being a clone or carbon copy of everything that America was. In the estimation of the four Canadian, anti-gay leaders, the situation demanded that the Global South primates extend to the "Canadian dissenting churches the same provisions as their American ones."

Though the Canadians were told that the "*Global South* empathizes with their predicament," which was expressed passionately at the meeting, they still heard the response, "We cannot act decisively"—that they could not act until "the Canadian General Synod has expressed its official position as requested by the Windsor Report." The primates were of the opinion that the Canadian situation was different from the

American one in the sense that the "TEC issue is resolved." The General Convention of the Episcopal Church had spoken; that was not the case with Canada, and the Canadian General Synod was not due to meet until June 2007.

So this would be the second time the Global South primates declined to act preemptively in support of the Canadian church. They reserved further decision till the outcome of the global Anglican leaders meeting, but the Canadian group didn't depart emptyhanded. They received the assurance of the Global South primates that they would not renege on their promise to "work with them all the way." For both sides, that day of reckoning didn't seem to be far off, for the much talked about summit of the global Anglican leaders was just two days away!

On one point, the leaders neither delayed nor set conditions. They reached a firm conclusion, to reassemble and undertake "reassessment of the situation in the Communion after the Primates Meeting." Nevertheless, the overall picture emerging from the primates gathering was still one of ambivalence over how they should deal with the crisis. Why would they be decisive on some issues only to be caught foot-dragging on others? Why did they talk tough in some settings and became apologetic in others? On one issue, however, they seemed to have made up their minds. The Lambeth Conference was a year away, and the opinion emerging was that many of the Global South provinces would not attend the Conference.

There was a proviso, however. The condition was that Canterbury would address "the basic issues spelled out in 'The Road to Lambeth,'" a condition they resolved "to forward . . . to ABp Williams." Agreed further was that all the members of the Steering Committee should sign the letter, and that there be a "request [for] a closed door meeting with him (that is Archbishop Williams) before the Primates Meeting officially commences," a meeting which would have the ingredients of a classical drama.

In the 139-year history of the decennial gathering, it had never happened that a substantial part of the Communion would threaten to withdraw participation from the Lambeth Conference. "Deadly serious" was the only term that could aptly describe the impending disaster. A lot was therefore attached to the Dar es Salam meeting. Would it result in salvaging the Communion? Would it produce the desired miraculous truce? The meeting of the Global South primates ended on February 13, 2007. On February 15, 2007, that of the Anglican primates worldwide began. From then until the meeting ended, all eyes were locked on Dar es Salam, the Tanzanian capital.

During the previous forty-eight hours, scant attention was paid to the over two-thirds of the Anglican Church's primates who had converged on the city. It was no longer so. From the airport to the city, Tanzania started to feel that something big was happening. The Anglican primates began streaming in at the Julius Nyerere International Airport from different parts of the world, and there was an air of excitement. The primates met last in Dromantine, Newry, a quiet sub-urban town in Northern Ireland. That February 2005 gathering was far from being a sweetly spiritual assembly, but rather an epic drama, full of spice, spikes, and countless seasonings. The heroes, not surprisingly, were the primates supporting the gay cause. Their opponents were smeared and demonized as villains. Ecstatically, the Dromantine party regrouped and reassembled, converging in the action spot of the moment: Dar es Salam.

Before the primates meeting got underway, Dar es Salam had become a bedlam, swarming with a medley of characters. The nomadic gay rights attacking force had arrived in full force, with a multitude of groups and with media of all types from different parts of the world ready to pounce. Not missing were the interlopers, the busybodies, the snoops, the mercenaries, an assortment of needless interferers put together to blather, meddle, and natter at the meeting, harassing its participants. There were, of course, officials and priests, who, though not part of the meeting, served as support staff for the primates in their entourages. Then, there were the primates themselves, the archbishops.

The muckraking in Dromantine was extended to Dar es Salam. Akinola was the man in the bull's eye—what he did and did not do; with whom he met or refused to meet; where he went or failed to go; the hand he shook and the one he failed to shake; why he did one thing and neglected doing the other were all issues for copious reporting and subjects for differing interpretations. The massive coverage given to the Nigerian primate almost overshadowed news of the real purpose for which the Anglican Church leaders gathered in Dar es Salam, the city whose name meant "the residence of peace." The city's appellation was literally reversed by the gay rights armada that invaded Dar es Salam. They were not wishing Archbishop Akinola peace of mind. He was still their "No.1 International Enemy." Every opportunity was taken to haunt and hunt him.

From the commencement of the primates meeting, Akinola endured almost round-the-clock surveillance, and soon the gay group within the Church of England, Inclusive Church, launched the assault. Its first blog, on February 18, 2007, read, "Sunday: Akinola Missed Out."[4] As a major brain behind Inclusive Church and the first casualty of Akinola's principled stand against same-sex ordination in the Anglican Church, Jeffrey John, the openly-gay British priest denied election to the episcopate, must have had a hearty laugh over the hit on his implacable foe. Inclusive Church chose to make big news of Akinola's absence from a church service to begin the primates meeting in Zanzibar. The gay group took a swipe at Akinola for absenting himself from the service.

Accurately, it reported that "all of the primates went on the trip, with the exception of dissenting bishop Peter Akinola." Akinola's colleagues who chose to attend were not spared the scorns of the gay group as well: "The other so-called Global South primates, attended the service, but appeared to not receive communion." On the other hand, the gay group, which expressed disdain for the Global South leaders, lavished adulation on the Archbishop of Canterbury, saying, for instance, "Rowan's sermon

4. https://en.m.wikipedia.org/wiki/Inclusive_Church; Gunn, "Akinola Missed Out."

was brilliant." His genius was reflected in the topic he chose: "Rowan also talked about the slave trade—and its end," Inclusive Church reported.

Williams had been brilliant in the choice of theme, for the meeting had coincided with the 200th anniversary of the abolition of slave trade in the United Kingdom. Ironically, Tanzania had had no direct connection with the ending of the trade, which occurred in the early 19th century. Indeed, the eradication of the slave trade did not result in the closing of the Zanzibar slave market. The market (in what is now Tanzania) was in operation another ninety years before it was shut down finally. Archbishop Williams, however, had his purpose of deliberately shifting attention to the place and the event. They supplied him with metaphors to relate the past with the present, an excellent medium to address the same-sex issue tearing the Anglican Church apart.

Inclusive Church triumphantly reported, "Rowan said, this evil was accepted, but light gradually dawned," adding that he "wondered what else we might need to learn." Wasn't the implication obvious? The striking parallel was that acceptance of discrimination against gays was in the same league as acceptance of the slave trade in years past. The publication lamented painfully that "Peter Akinola missed all this." "He stayed behind in Dar es Salaam presumably working with conservative leaders on his next move."

Truly, Akinola missed the program. The key reason was that Akinola stood by his promise that some of them would not recognize American Presiding Bishop Jefferts Schori, much less share Eucharist with her. Ironically, another British medium did offer a fairer and more accurate account of the event as well as other developments that transpired at the primates meeting. The *Guardian's* religious affairs and royals correspondent, Stephen Bates, did his job as professionally as any journalist should.[5] He looked behind the scene for scoops, sniffed a lot of the underlying intrigues, and sifted through the seamy maneuvers. The detachment helped him knit together the different pieces of the story into a wholesome account. Bates' story, published with the headline "Anglicans head for deadlock in talks to stave off schism," appeared on February 20, 2007, the second day after the primates meeting ended. Bates' interpretation of events at the closed-door meeting was dead-on accurate because the worldwide Anglican Communion only managed to avoid the tail end of the last straw.

A week before the conference, probably coincidental with the period that the Global South primates themselves were meeting in Dar es Salam, a working party was also busy preparing a report for the primates meeting. According to Bates, the team, "headed by Dr. Williams," was to give a "much more favourable assessment of the Episcopal Church." Their impression was therefore obvious, that the once strong opposition was weakening, and that the "815 charm offensive," desperately deployed to buy influence among the Global South leaders, was having a positive effect.[6] Unfortunately, some dry throats that needed wetting were succumbing to drinking from the

5. Bates, "Anglicans Head for Deadlock in Talks to Stave off Schism."

6. http://accurmudgeon.blogspot.com.ng/2014/06/animal-farm-at-815-second-avenue.html.

open hands, while others who could not get over their slavish mentality had remained as good pawns. Still, Akinola was confident that when the time arrived, the tail would wag the dog.

Thus, the preambles and sideshows were not of substance to him. They were not in Dar es Salam for plays and concerts. They were there to make decisions over the continued disobedience of the American and Canadian churches. As their meeting progressed, the antics and intrigues were unfolding like scenes from a prepared script. Archbishop Akinola wasn't fooled. When he thought the chicanery had gone on too far, he sought permission to contribute his opinion. It was a bombshell. "Instead of a clear call for repentance," he said stony-faced, "we have been offered warms words of sentimentality on behalf of those who have shown no godly sorrow for their action." He wasn't expecting his North American colleagues to be contrite. There had been several opportunities in the past, but they were too blinded by ego and arrogance to see the reality.

Akinola had the last straw in his hands. After all the meandering around the truth and gerrymandering around facts, he was convinced that, finally, all of them had reached the destination. He had been waiting for this moment. For him, it was the perfect time to seize the tiger by the tail and give it the rough shake of its life. In characteristic ecclesiastical manner and language, the official communique had been prepared. As usual, the primates were expected to endorse it as representing their collective decisions. But as he looked at the bland paper, he was indifferent. Unknown to them, they had just handed him the last straw to break the proverbial camel's back. He pushed the paper aside. He declined to have his name behind the disagreeable document. No, he would not sign the communique, he told his colleagues. The *Guardian* writer, Bates, captured the scene accurately when he wrote that the consequence of Akinola's action resulted in "Archbishop Williams looking discomfited." The Nigerian leader had caught his Canterbury counterpart off guard!

Apparently, the worldwide Anglican leader did not factor this development into his perfected scheme. Quickly, mediators arose to intervene to ease the developing scandalous situation. Akinola was the target of the appeal. He was prevailed upon to allow reconciliation. He was naturally amenable to conciliation, but he insisted that the pact would not come at the expense of truth. If men of God could not uphold truth, morality, and justice, then vain were their voices as the conscience of society, he told his colleagues.

As a result, the issues in contention were addressed in ways agreeable to the two sides. Archbishop Williams admitted, according to Bates, that this was the "cost of getting Archbishop Akinola to join the other primates in signing the unanimous communique." One tradeoff was the reiteration of Lambeth Resolution 1.10 as the standard teaching of the Anglican Church, with reiteration that the Church "cannot advise the legitimising or blessing of same-sex unions."[7] The primates also reasserted

7. Anglican Church News Service, "Primates' Meeting Communique (Tanzania)—The

that the Communion "as a body cannot support the authorisation of such rites" and that the "response of the Episcopal Church . . . has not persuaded the meeting." In view of this, the primates insisted that "the House of Bishops of The Episcopal Church make an unequivocal covenant that the bishops will not authorise any Rite of Blessing for same-sex unions in their dioceses or through General Convention," and that "a candidate for episcopal orders living in same-sex union shall not receive the necessary consent." There was, however, a proviso attached to the last resolution. The condition would prevail "*unless* (emphasis from source) some new consensus on these matters emerges across the Communion."

Dar es Salam was thus a *quid pro quo* in a way. Once more, the American church was walking away with another lifeline. The primates, however, demanded a categorical answer from America's House of Bishops to be "conveyed to the Primates by the Presiding Bishop by 30 September 2007." Who was fooling whom? Akinola decided to play along not because he was naïve, for he harbored no doubt about the unlikelihood of the American church changing its ways till eternity or God's Kingdom come. And the same went for their Canadian brethren. Only an incurable optimist would expect an about face. Deftly and pleasurably, the Church of England seemed to be delighting in its duplicitous role, and compounding the Anglican problem was the haughty nature of the archbishop of Canterbury. Wisdom dictates that one acts prudently and sincerely in relating with colleagues. A wise man does not treat a colleague like a fool.

Akinola knew by his agreeing to sign the communique, he had given yet more leeway to the imperious gay pushers in the church. Akinola's consolation, however, was that the concessions were forcibly extracted.

The primates had agreed that the American church would establish a "Pastoral Council." The five-member council would work with the Episcopal Church to see that it took proper steps to conform to the decisions reached by the primates. The Pastoral Council would "take whatever reasonable action is needed to give effect to this scheme and report to the Primates." There was also the issue of "A Pastoral Scheme" for "those of who have sought the oversight of other jurisdictions." The meeting upheld that the bishops involved took "those actions which they believe necessary to sustain full communion with the Anglican Communion." Consequently, they applauded the decision of the American presiding bishop in agreeing to the resolution "to appoint a Primatial Vicar."

Anybody reading the communique would believe the conclusions were fair and equitable; that they had found middle ground for the two parties to work toward amicable settlement of the crisis. But the handwriting was already on the wall. The potential for peace was bleak. All the while, the gay rights campaigners did not stop the intimidation and harassment in Dar es Salam, powered by American and British funding. In this environment, special guards protected the primates, and Akinola typically remained the main target.

Communique of the Primates' Meeting in Dar es Salam."

It wasn't surprising the Nigerian anti-Akinola campaigner Davis Mac-Iyalla was one of the agitators sent to Tanzania for the primates' meeting. Iyalla rode in as hand luggage of Changing Attitude, the British gay organization which had mobilized in full force for the event. Their mission was obvious—to intimidate Archbishop Akinola. Though Akinola was doubly careful with his personal safety and security, he was still unlucky to be in the crosshairs of Changing Attitude.

On Thursday, February 15, 2007, a pre-meeting press briefing had been organized as part of the meeting. With the afternoon media chat over, Akinola, in the company of Bishop Martyn Minns, his wife, and Canon Chris Sugden from Anglican Mainstream, were finding their way through the hotel's lobby. As they edged forward on their way toward the exit, a young man came strutting towards them. He had enough room to his right and left if he had intended to pass, but he walked straight at them and stopped just short of a head-on collision with the archbishop. Akinola and his party were forced to a stop, puzzled at whom they were facing.

Coincidentally, it was the gay organization Changing Attitude that provided on its webpage the eyewitness accounts of what transpired. According to the report, "Davis went straight to the Archbishop to introduce himself and Caro." But "the Archbishop didn't immediately recognise Davis." He "asked Davis if they had met before." Davis lied. "Yes," he replied, and embellished the lie by adding that "they had met several times." The archbishop could still not remember having met him. Davis quickly assembled a cocktail of lies. He told Akinola they had met when the archbishop "came to inaugurate the Province of Jos." Spinning the story further, Iyalla told "the Archbishop the story of the late Bishop Ugede." He recounted how "they had met at the bishop's funeral." He also remembered that "he had spent the night at his (that is, Akinola's) house following Bishop Ugede's death in Abuja." Desperate as Iyalla tried, he could not help Akinola out of his "amnesia."

After Iyalla's much ado had achieved nothing, a gush of insight flooded the archbishop's brain! "Peter Akinola then remembered who Davis was," and he "asked him what he was doing in Tanzania." Iyalla, again, lied. "Davis explained that he has come to greet him and other Primates." That probably prompted Akinola to guess his mission and purpose, and at that point he "thanked him." He wanted to continue on his way, but Iyalla refused to be dismissed. "The Archbishop jokingly asked Davis if he had been officially invited to the meeting" to which Davis replied that "no, he is not a Primate." Hovering by Iyalla's side was Colin Coward of Changing Attitude, England, who interrupted the conversation, telling the Nigerian church leader that he, too, "had met Archbishop Akinola at the Anglican Consultative Council meeting in Nottingham." Actually, Coward didn't buy the numerous gay stereotypes of Akinola as a "bigot," "homophile," "fanatic," and "gay hater." Rather, his perception of Akinola was that of a man who was warm, open, and personable, and they "exchanged handshakes and greetings." And so ended the amusing confrontation in the lobby.

Later, with the clarity of time and further light on the issues surrounding the misguided young man, Archbishop Akinola was still in defence of the Nigerian youth, saying Iyalla was not a model and standard to judge people of his generation in the country. He acknowledged that morals and ethos might have waned in Nigeria, but the debasement of Davis was the result of an infection from and assimilation to an entirely different culture. Archbishop Akinola disliked the vile use made of Iyalla, yet he bore no malice to the young man. His view was that it wasn't the young man who deserved reproach. Rather, his fall into the cesspit of indecent and irresponsible behavior was largely the fault of those who had led him astray. They exploited his weakness and preyed on his gullibility. Instead of helping to bring him back to the path of rectitude by reforming and rehabilitating his waywardness, they chose to exploit his weakness for their selfish and political ends. They had no care, concern, or compassion for him or his future, nor did they have stirring to save the world from the narcissistic sexual aberration.

And so, after what was planned as an epic encounter, Iyalla took his leave of Akinola, and Akinola said nothing. He felt serious pity for Iyalla and people like him, who had turned themselves to miscreants, "area boys" for the West. If the West intended to exploit "African sons and daughters" in an effort to get "Africa to adopt forcefully the aberrant homosexuality culture," Akinola said, "Africa, evidently, is in serious danger."

Akinola could not but see a grave hazard ahead. Colonialism had wreaked its havoc. It had left the continent weak, prostrate, and unstable. Similarly devastating would be the consequences of homosexuality. It would leave Africa worse rather than make it better. Countries of Africa would hardly be able to contain the harmful repercussions that arose from the unnatural and perverse culture. The magnitude of the resultant costs, in terms of health alone, would be calamitous. Africa could hardly afford to add another disaster to the host of development challenges facing the continent by opening its door to a permissive and indulgent lifestyle.

So many things happened in Dar es Salam that redefined Archbishop Akinola's perspective on the crisis rocking the Anglican Communion. One was the manner in which Iyalla was used without any feeling or sense of guilt about what would become of him later. It demonstrated the mindless obsession of the homosexuality advocates to force their perspective on the world at all costs. The central question in his mind was, "Why the grim determination to foist a dangerous counterculture on the world?" It would push the world down a perilous, unprecedented path.

The Nigerian church leader was sad that the Anglican Communion had been chosen as the international speedway to test drive the legitimacy of the aberrant lifestyle in the spiritual arena. That was the reason why he had said nothing in reply to the Canterbury archbishop, the Most Rev. Williams' side remark to him in Dar es Salam. Pithy as the statement was, it was fully loaded. Akinola was convinced that Williams meant every word in his declaration. Williams seemed to have an inkling as to how the crisis would end. Akinola's attitude, however, was that time would tell. But he was sure that from Dar es Salam onwards, the time for the crisis to reach its denouement was near. The time was at hand, and for the two of them—he and Williams—the time would herald a decisive moment.

23

Enough of the Agonizing Journey

Mauritius, 2007

Predictably, American Presiding Bishop Jefferts Schori returned home from Dar es Salam with no intention of offering an olive branch to the dissenting churches and clergy in her domain. She didn't go to Tanzania, in the first instance, in search for peace. The typical American mind-set accompanied her to the meeting. She flew back with her natural pugnacious nature. It's practically impossible that Schori would have steered the American church to a new path. So, on Tuesday, March 20, 2007, precisely a month after the Dar es Salam trip, the American House of Bishops met to consider the church's response to the Anglican Communion primates' demand.[1] The reply was the typical American response. Belligerent and hawkish, the bishops posted a conceited and arrogant message to Anglican leaders all over the world: "The Episcopal Church remains a part of the councils of the Anglican Communion." Whatever anyone in disagreement chooses to do, the person is at liberty to do so, implied the impertinence.

With regard to "the proposed Pastoral Scheme of the Dar es Salaam Communiqué of February 19, 2007," the bishops answered the primates bluntly, "We are unable to accept the proposed Pastoral Scheme," for they viewed the proposal as "injurious to The Episcopal Church." Consequently, they asked that "the Executive Council decline to participate in it." At the same meeting, a message was dispatched to the archbishop of Canterbury and the Primates Standing Committee: "We believe that there is an urgent need for us to meet face to face with the Archbishop of Canterbury and members of the Primates' Standing Committee."

The request was ironic. After all, the reason the archbishop of Canterbury gave for inviting the presiding bishop and the three bishops from the United States to Dar es Salam was for them to share their perspectives. They had gone and supposedly had

---

1. "TEC House of Bishops Rejects Primates' Proposed Pastoral Scheme"; "To the Archbishop of Canterbury and the members of the Primates' Standing Committee"; "A Statement from the House of Bishops—March 20, 2007."

the jaw-jaw at Dar es Salam, only to return home and summon the head of the Angli-can Church "at the earliest possible opportunity." Presiding Bishop Schori was to work out a suitable date with the archbishop. America was in a generous mood. Archbishop Williams was assured that the visit would be at their expense. The invitation was not only meant for the archbishop, but also extended to members of the Primates' Stand-ing Committee.

Whatever outcome the American church desired from its packaged tour for the top-ranking Anglican Church leaders, it didn't include reconciliation with the major-ity in the Communion. In June, the Executive Council of the church had met in a follow-up to the House of Bishops' meeting and "rejected the requests contained in the Dar es Salaam Communiqué." Thrown overboard were all the decisions of the Anglican primates. With respect to the "Pastoral Scheme," the council shifted respon-sibility to the General Convention of the church. It insisted that only the General Convention "can respond to those requests." But with characteristic belligerence, the Council questioned "the authority of the Primates to impose demands on member churches which violate their Constitutions and Canons."

Subsequently, it issued a serious warning to those "dioceses that changed their constitutions," saying they must realize that "to bypass the Church's Constitution and Canons" would make "their actions are 'null and void.'" Like the House of Bishops, the Executive Council, ruled out any live-and-let-live policy for all those disagreeing with their stand on homosexuality.

The Episcopal Church leaders, indeed, understood the game they were playing. For three months after this June meeting of the Executive Council, another meeting of the House of Bishops (HOB) was convened. This time around, the HOB, officially responded to the global Anglican primates' Tanzania communique. The September 30 deadline given by the primates for the American church to normalize its relationship with the rest of the Communion was just days away. The American bishops were less aggressive and impertinent on the issue, pledging "not to authorize public same-sex blessings," but the statement was a smokescreen because they "claimed that resolu-tion B033 pertains to non-celibate gays and lesbians." The resolution was supposed to order bishops to stop consecrating candidates into the episcopate whose manner of life was straining the peace of the Communion. Indeed, there was evidence that the bishops had no desire to place "a moratorium on same-sex blessings," nor put a stop to the election of "future non-celibate homosexual bishops."

It's worth noticing the ways in which they hedged their actions, with a time-buy-ing strategy. They averred that their decision would be "subject to change at the next General Convention in 2009." In other words, the ratification of their decision had to wait for two years! Meanwhile, the same leaders didn't see the moral contradiction or offense to the wider Communion as they "called for the Bishop of New Hampshire's full participation at the next Lambeth Conference." Definitely, nothing had changed.

Notorious as the attitude of the Episcopal Church was, it was still inconceivable that it would practice open effrontery on the eve of its hosting the Anglican Church world leader. The visit of the Canterbury archbishop, the Most Rev. Dr. Rowan Williams, began barely two weeks after the church had talked down to the entire Communion. Surprisingly, if the archbishop was aware of the aspersion cast on the integrity of his colleagues, he made nothing of it. Indeed, he treated the American Church to a warm pastoral visit, as he brought not just Canterbury but also the entire Anglican Church to America. The entourage was huge, more than requested by the Americans, with delegations representing the Primates Standing Committee (PSC) and the ACC, as well as officials of Lambeth Palace. So an army of sorts descended on the country. The American Church was prepared for it, rolling out the red carpet for their guests as they had done for Davis Mac-Iyalla. And instead of the earlier three days budgeted for the visit, the tour had to be extended to five days.

From September 20 through 25, 2007, Williams, with his retinue of officials and aides, was exposed to the ambience of perfect hospitality.[2] The archbishop began with fact-finding, learning from the presiding bishop and members of the House of Bishops, spending ten hours over two days with them. As reported, he was concerned with "understanding where we as Bishops of the Church are," and also to "understand better the life of the Episcopal Church." The members of the ACC also had a broad interaction with the bishops. Though they had already heard much from the Episcopal Church, the new interface "enabled the members of the ACC . . . to reflect on what they have heard from us." Another rare opportunity was the chance "to ask some further questions," and the ACC took full advantage.

Consequently, on all sides, from all angles, and among all the parties, the visit was gratifying. The archbishop came, he saw, and he interacted. He investigated the issues and interrogated the bishops, and was satisfied by the results, as were the two high-ranking committees of the Communion. What the Lambeth Commission had failed to learn in its six months' work, the Canterbury archbishop and the committees learned within hours. The amity that the primates meeting had failed to produce was achieved by the visit.

The ACC came out of America sounding optimistic. What had eluded the Communion for the past several months took them only a trip to the US to achieve. They were better informed and educated and had a healthier knowledge of the Episcopal Church's situation. The trip shone new lights on the previously cloudy areas, and Presiding Bishop Schori had every reason to be excited with the outcome. She deemed the meeting a "notable one in the life of the House of Bishops and an important one for the Episcopal Church."

2. http://anglicanmainstream.org/agenda-released-for-new-orleans-meeting/; "40 Days of Discernment—Updated Timeline of Defining Actions," http://www.wearestandrews.com/resources/40-days-of-discernment.aspx?ArticleId=221.

The problem, however, is that falsehood has never defeated truth, and the church had truth to confront on September 30, the deadline of the primates. A decision was due, publicly, to the entire Communion, and not to its select guests alone. The Episcopal Church had to openly confirm or deny its stand before the Anglican primates. It was either to accept reconciliation or force "rupture between the American Church and the Anglican Communion." There were no other options or middle course.

Presiding Bishop Schori and all of her colleagues in the House of Bishops were aware of the implications of their failure to honor the primates' request. Their august guests, including Archbishop Williams, understood the burden as well. What help did Williams' stately American visit provide to ease the Anglican Communion's crisis? There was no meaningful or tangible result. Except for personal interest, nothing justified Williams' visit to the United States, where his neglect of the dissenting churches and clergy was indefensible. And as hospitable as Americans could be, the idea of giving a free lunch was simply not part of the American life. Williams was needed for a purpose in the same way that Iyalla was procured for an end. The Episcopal Church did not intend to fulfill even the smallest of the Anglican primates' conditions. Williams' visit was designed to provide the America Episcopal Church front and rearguard protection.

Subsequently, when controversy broke out regarding whether the primates had "authority to expel The Episcopal Church from the Anglican Communion," the division in opinions was sharp. Fierce was the argument on both sides, between the "Ays" and the "Nays." The final say, however, rested with one man, the archbishop of Canterbury. He had the ultimate authority. Through the Windsor Report, the Lambeth Commission had spoken unequivocally; the language used was simple, clear, and straightforward—failure to repent meant a decision to "walk apart." In its simple meaning, it indicated expulsion from the Communion for those who had chosen to depart from its teaching. Furthermore, the Dar es Salam communique was equally emphatic, that the Episcopal Church would choose to "walk apart" from the Communion if it continued with its unilateral decision.

Nevertheless, Archbishop Williams' visit to the United States had changed the equation. He'd refused to act, and he'd pocketed those hands that could have restrained the misguided churches. Decisions whose meanings were straightforward earlier were being twisted to suit narrow interest. As an example, suddenly, so-called "sources within the Communion's hierarchy" were being quoted as saying, "It was incorrect to view the Dar es Salaam communique as an ultimatum." The "sources" interpreted the primates' decision to mean that the American church merely had to make "certain clarifications." Concluding, the "sources" emphasised, "It would be a 'serious misreading of the situation' to say that the Episcopal Church faced expulsion from the Primates if it failed again to respond."

The global Anglican leaders had given the American church a September 30, 2007, deadline to comply with their demands or face disciplinary action. The

Episcopal Church did nothing. Not a whimper was heard from Canterbury or the archbishop until a few days after the expiration of the deadline. Then, in October 2007, the Joint Standing Committee of the primates and the ACC released reports of their joint American tour. They gave the Episcopal Church a clean bill of health! The church had "clarified all outstanding questions" and "given the necessary assurance sought of them," they said.

The report raised questions of integrity. The document was disowned publicly from one of the least anticipated places. Archbishop Mouneer Anis, a member of the committee, openly disclaimed the document.[3] Anis was a member of the JSC as well as treasurer of the Global South Primates Committee. The report didn't go down well with him, and he shredded it openly, even though, within the Global South fold, the presiding bishop of Egypt and Jerusalem was seen as a modest and restrained person. But like the rest of the members of the Global South, he was still uncompromising on the demand that the American church renounce its gay stand and respect the decision of the majority of Anglicans worldwide. Where he differed a bit, however, was that, contrary to others who had lost hope in the possibility of the Communion's crisis being resolved, Anis was still optimistic. His hopeful nature was the motivation for continuing as a member of the JSC and participating in the committee's activities.

He was at the meeting where the report was discussed, and he was left seriously distressed at what had transpired. Ruefully, reflecting on the experience, he said, "By the time I finished the meetings of the JSC, I realized that I lost many of the hopes which I had before the meeting." Several friends had attempted to dissuade him from attending the meeting, but he had rejected the pressure, because "I don't believe in withdrawal." At the end of the day, his friends had been right. Anis was wrong. "My hopes diminished," as he put it despondently in his public reaction.

Anis was distraught with the duplicity involved in the entire process of the meeting. So beaten was his confidence that he lamented, "I cannot see any desire to follow things through as decided before." Glumly and gloomily, he was glued to his seat watching their previous efforts and decisions thrown overboard. Anis was taken aback by the closed-door manipulation that took place, and he asked rhetorically, "What action did we take or recommend in the JSC meeting?" "The answer is nothing," he answered. He was dismayed that "the very people who caused the current crisis are invited to Lambeth Conference."

Anis was upset that leadership inaction had widened "the gap and distrust between the two sides within the Communion." The latest development, that is, the JSC meeting, made him even angrier, for they ignored justice. He gave two examples. One was the fact that "very little time was given to discussing the important issues"; second was the way that the important "issues were pushed to the last day of the meeting." Anis had "expected that the very issues that are tearing the Communion apart would be

---

3. "Bishop Mouneer Anis Reflections on the Joint Standing Committee (JSC) 29/02/08–04/03/08."

given more time and priority." But no, that was not the case! Compounding the offense was the deliberate manner with which the work of the committee was tele-guided.

Episcopal Church Presiding Bishop Jefferts Schori sat stonily and woodenly throughout the meeting, using her physical presence to intimidate, as Anis observed. Roving flintily, her eyes in effect cast a spell that "inhibited other members from speaking freely." According to Anis, the fear of Schori "was clear from the comments of some other members outside the meetings." These were views that could have been expressed officially. Anis, who had nursed hope of light coming at the end of the tunnel someday, suddenly became despondent as he considered the future.

The American church had responded to his criticism in the familiar way, providing a sponsored trip to the United States to enable Anis to hear the American bishops' "perspectives." But he must have had a bitter struggle with himself in the effort to be a polite guest. He endured the drone of the rationalizations and justifications, which were hogwash to him. He had come with his opinion formed and his "perspectives" on the problem already determined. It was his own "perspectives" that he wanted his hosts to hear. Their "perspectives" represented those of a minority while his were of the majority, and he sought to let them know this: "Your actions have resulted in one of the most difficult disputes in the Communion in our generation," he told his hosts without condescension. The African church leader understood that his American counterparts chose to see their scriptural disagreements "not as core doctrinal issues." But he wanted them to understand that they did not have monopoly of wisdom or intellect: "Many like me see the opposite," and there had been many "undesired consequences and reactions" as a result of their intransigence.

Though Anis thought his American trip could have a positive influence, he was forced to conclude, "For the first time in centuries, the fabric of our Communion is torn," adding, "Our energies have been drained and our resources are lost." Indeed, "it is difficult for both of us to continue like this." He observed, "One church cannot say to the rest of churches 'I know the whole truth, you don't.'" He had come to America not for the hamburgers and the delicacies that they wanted to feed him, a guest in the supposed land of democracy, but in hopes he might help to pull the land of freedom back from its misguided misadventures. But to no avail.

Like Anis, Archbishop Akinola hadn't gone to the meeting in Dar es Salam to trade off his convictions and principled position on the crisis. Interestingly, Akinola and Schori were similarly inflexible. Their obstinacies expressed themselves from opposite directions. The American presiding bishop enjoyed her preemptive strike while her Nigerian counterpart delighted in his proactive engagement. It would be foolhardy to say Akinola trusted the American church. He knew they were not going to honor the Dar es Salam proposal. The American church was also not naïve, thinking that Akinola would give up with his crusade. The game then became one of trying to out-maneuver each other. Akinola knew he had a joker in his hand—the concession he had extracted at the primates meeting in Dar es Salam over the Convocation of

Anglicans in North America (CANA). He was sure he would use it at an appropriate time in a strategic counter-move.

Consequently, when the American House of Bishops insulted the primates by throwing their demands back at them, Akinola was watching. He had already decided what his response would be, that he would keep a date with America on May 5, 2007. Or rather that America had a date to keep with him on that day. That day, on American soil, CANA would be inaugurated and Bishop Martyn Minns installed as its first missionary bishop. The Standing Committee of the Church of Nigeria had already endorsed the decision as far back as 2006 when Minns was elected and consecrated as a bishop of the Nigerian church. Perhaps the American church leaders forgot about that event, or in their characteristic imperious manner, scoffed at the idea as a fantasy. For Akinola, however, the time was ripe to follow up with the decision since the issues that gave rise to the resolution had not changed.

The first problem to arise had nothing to do with the arrangements for Minns' installation but rather with the hostile environment for his enthronement. Presiding Bishop Schori took umbrage at the planned event. Before its scheduled date, Saturday, May 5, a kind of press war began between her and her Nigerian counterpart. Schori instigated the media battle. On April 30, 2007, she had written Akinola expressing a strong objection to the latter's invasion of her territory with his intention to install Minns. Although the letter was addressed to the Nigerian primate, he never got it. Instead, she published it at the Episcopal News Service website. To ensure that the letter achieved maximum effect, she also leaked it to the press.

Schori was angry with her Nigerian counterpart for disrespecting the Communion's conventional practice. His acceptance of "an invitation to episcopal ministry here (that is, the United States) without any notice or prior invitation" offended her. Such a step, she continued, "was not in keeping with 'the ancient practice in most of the church'"— that "Bishops minister only within their own jurisdictions." Furthermore, Schori said he was doing harm to her church and to the Anglican Communion as a whole.

In its coverage, the *Washington Times* quoted Schori generously, including her claim, "Such action would not help the efforts of reconciliation that are taking place in the Episcopal Church and in the Anglican Communion as a whole." The implicit message was that while the Episcopal Church was busy mending its broken fences, Akinola's action was meddlesome, stoking discord in the American church and the larger Communion. This also was the perspective of Reuters, the international newswire, which cast the story to make Akinola the offender: "An African archbishop's defiant intervention in the U.S. Episcopal Church has sent new shock waves through a global Anglican Church."[4] Schori, it was reported, was grieved that "such action would display to the world division and disunity." And still, Akinola was yet to lay hands on the letter!

4. Conlon, "Anglican Church Turmoil Over Gay Issues Deepens."

But, eventually, his attention was drawn to it. On May 2, 2007, three days before the planned installation, Akinola replied formally. Schori's insincerity didn't impress him, but he refrained from lambasting her lack of discretion. Akinola did observe that it was "ostensibly written to me" yet, he had not read it before it was posted publicly. He reminded her, "You will also recall from our meeting in Dar es Salam that there was specific discussion about CANA and recognition—expressed in the Communique itself." And nothing had changed to warrant reconsidering the situation that had precipitated the birth of CANA.

Akinola pledged to Schori the sincerity and nobility of his intention. Now the ball was in the Episcopal Church's court. And so he spelled out the conditions: If the "Episcopal Church will reconsider its actions the compelling drive for such measures [will] no longer be necessary." Akinola assured her that he remained committed to his earlier promise made to her predecessor. He had given the guarantee to "Presiding Bishop Frank Griswold that the Church of Nigeria would be the first to restore communion on the day that your Province abandons its current unbiblical agenda." But "until then, we have no other choice," he wrote with finality.

Bishop Minns' installation was held as scheduled in Woodbridge, Virginia.[5] The event had also drawn the ire of Rowan Williams. Like the American presiding bishop, he had written a letter objecting to the plan, and like Schori, Williams didn't give the Nigerian primate the benefit of receiving the missive before he circulated it in the media. The archbishop's spokespersons "publicised the letter and its general content" and ensured delay of its delivery to Akinola "until after the ceremony."

Of course, they sought to paint the Nigerian church leader as ambitious and schismatic. Still, the letter would not have changed anything had Akinola received it before the ceremony. Though the event was over, Akinola yet extended the courtesy of a reply to the archbishop of Canterbury. Writing on May 6, 2007, a day after Minns' installation, he was straightforward in his rejoinder, and he enclosed a copy of the letter he'd written to Presiding Bishop Schori. He reminded the Canterbury archbishop of the tortuous journey the Communion had taken since the crisis started, and how the Nigerian church had voluntarily and repeatedly exhibited restraint over time. He drew Williams' attention to "the decisions, actions, defiance and continuing intransigence of The Episcopal Church which are at the heart of our crisis."

He recalled how, as leaders, they had "spent enormous amounts of time [and] travelled huge distances." Fresh in his memory were the meetings of "Lambeth Palace in 2003, Dromantine 2005, Nottingham 2006 and Dar es Salaam 2007." Four times they had met "to no avail." He also noted the great risks and colossal financial "resources [invested] in [the] endless meetings" as well as the "numerous proposals [and] various task forces" the Communion had set up to resolve the crisis. Sad to say, "the division has only deepened," he told Williams. Frustrating as the situation had been, the Nigerian church had always ensured level-headed control over its reaction.

5. "IRD Supports CANA—All Orthodox Anglicans on Eve of Bishop Martyn Minns' Installation."

"We delayed the election of our first CANA bishop until after General Convention 2006," he explained to the archbishop. They had given "The Episcopal Church every opportunity to embrace the recommendations of the Windsor report," but this was "to no avail." Akinola wanted Williams to know that Nigeria and its church leaders had been thoughtful, responsible, and understanding. For instance, he recalled, at "the last meeting of the Church of Nigeria House of Bishops we deferred a decision regarding the election of additional suffragans for CANA." They did this "out of respect for the Dar es Salaam process." With no equivocation, he told Williams they had received "no such respect from the House of Bishops of The Episcopal Church."

Akinola considered the March 20 decision of the American bishops as "both insulting and condescending." The implication to him was "very clear that they have no intention of listening to the voice of the rest of the Communion." Akinola reminded Williams that "the Church of Nigeria established CANA as a way for Nigerian congregations and other alienated Anglicans in North America to stay in the Communion." Contrary to the Canterbury's insinuation, it's "not something that brings any advantage to us—neither financial nor political." However, they would not go back on it because there was "no other choice if we are to remain faithful to the gospel mandate." He ended reiterating the point made to Schori, that "although CANA is an initiative of the Church of Nigeria—and therefore a bona fide branch of the Communion—we have no desire to cling to it."

Williams neither acknowledged nor responded to Akinola's letter. He had already decided his next line of action.

Powerful as Canterbury was, however, the archbishop understood the limitation of his legal authority. He could neither stop the investiture nor prohibit the existence of CANA. He could, nevertheless, taint the image of its head and create a legitimacy problem for the budding organization. Williams moved shrewdly. The fortnight after receiving Akinola's letter, he unveiled his countermove. An important news item was released from the Anglican Communion Office. It concerned invitations to the decennial, 2008 Lambeth Conference.[6] He enjoyed sole prerogative over the choice of its attendees. He explained that due to "current tensions in the Communion," there "are a small number of bishops to whom invitations are not at this stage being extended." The implication was that the action was temporary "whilst Dr. Williams takes further advice." But his criterion for determining invitees was loaded, insisting that "each participant recognises and honours the task before us," leading to the exclusion of those who could be "seen as fundamentally compromising the efforts towards a credible and cohesive resolution" of the Anglican crisis.

Then Williams retreated quickly, hiding under the shell of official anonymity. His public face, Canon Kenneth Kearon, the secretary general of the Anglican Communion Office, gave the list of the precluded bishops to the press. He delineated "three

6. Minns, "A letter from Bishop Martyn Minns," May 23, 2007, from the archive and papers of Peter Akinola.

separate categories of bishops for whom invitations were being presently withheld." The first was "Bishop Gene Robinson of New Hampshire," the second, "CANA and AMiA bishops," and the third, "the Rt. Rev'd Nolbert Kunonga, the Anglican Bishop of Harare." If the reasons for the first two exclusions were self-explanatory, the last was of a different sort.

Kunonga was an embarrassment to the Anglican Church, both at home in Zimbabwe as well in the larger Communion internationally.[7] Cheeky and unbending, he couldn't care less about world opinion. He saw nothing wrong in Mugabe's gross violation of human rights, and he shunned all entreaties to break with the ironman of Zimbabwe. His case had left a sour taste in the mouth of Canterbury, and he was being spat out by the international headquarters of the Anglican Church. Indicidentally, none of the three—CANA, AmiA, and Kunonga—attracted many media headlines compared to the exclusion of Gene Robinson, who had prompted the crisis.

Left with no choice, Bishop Minns joined the media fray. His peace had been shattered by "various media inquiries." Of course, it was obvious that he would not have supported the Canterbury decision. And he did issue a rejoinder to that effect. He called attention to a number of critical points in his reply, saying that "the carefully nuanced statement from the Archbishop of Canterbury together with supposed specifics from a spokesman gives maximum flexibility for future developments." In other words, the matter was not closed as far as he could read the statement. Nevertheless, he was cynical about the sincerity and motive of the archbishop of Canterbury. Part of the reason was that as of the time the Lambeth list was released, the invitation from the Episcopal Church that later culminated in Dr. Williams' September trip to America was already lying on his table.

In his reply of May 23, 2007, Minns told the archbishop he had not addressed the real issue by excluding him. He was only running away from it: "The crisis in the Anglican Communion," Minns offered, "is not about a few individual bishops but about a worldwide Communion." He didn't see how "simply by excluding one or two individuals," he would cure the "defiant and unrepentant actions of the Episcopal Church since 2003." Rather than undertaking a salvage operation, it seemed to him that Canterbury preferred to dig the hole deeper. Minns considered the step taken as "short-sighted," wrong, and misinformed. "One thing is clear," he intoned, "a great deal can and will happen before next July." The Lambeth Conference was scheduled for July 2008, a year from the announcement, and Minns' prophecy was spot on; a "great deal" did happen during those intervening months.

Minns was a Nigerian bishop, and it ought to have been clear to the Canterbury archbishop that Akinola was not the type of leader to abandon or betray his colleagues or cause. Williams should have known he couldn't pick on Minns without having Akinola join the fray, and the Nigerian primate's reaction was predictable: Unstintingly, Akinola warned his Canterbury counterpart of the potential consequences of

---

7. https://en.wikipedia.org/wiki/Nolbert_Kunonga.

his action.[8] He was unambiguous in stating that withholding an invitation from Minns would "be viewed as withholding invitation from the entire House of Bishops of the Nigerian Church." He saw the action as bizarre, unheard of in the history of the Communion, one that "will be firmly resisted."

Akinola was not known for giving idle threats. He was unflinching when it concerned principled decisions. On the other hand, almost legendary was the survivalist trait of Archbishop Williams. Until now, in all matters concerning the Communion crisis, he had succeeded in having his way. He had firmly held the apparatus governing the global church in his hands. Among the two, who would back down at the end of the day? Would it be Williams or was it going to be Akinola?

Williams was strategically placed to influence the course he wanted events to take. He had delayed his trip to America for nearly six months to ensure that it took place about five days before the deadline the primates had given to the American church to either walk together with the rest of the Communion or walk apart from it. The other sequence of events—the rushed judgement of JSC/ACC, including Anis' visit to America—happened on the eve of Akinola's departure as chairman of the Council of Anglican Provinces of Africa (CAPA). Akinola stepped down as the CAPA chairman that same September 2007, the very day that the primates had set as deadline for the American church. Replacing him at a meeting of the organization in Mauritius, October 3–5, 2007, was the host bishop of Mauritius and archbishop of the Indian Ocean, Ian Ernest,[9] who just twenty months earlier was elected leader of the Anglican Church in the island countries of Madagascar, Mauritius, and the Seychelles, which made up the Province of the Indian Ocean.

However, Archbishop Ernest was not a newcomer to the Anglican Church. He became a priest in 1985. At 52, he was an eclectic personality. His education was multicultural in the same way that it was multi-disciplinary. He had attended schools in India, Mauritius, and United Kingdom, and of course, the US. His subjects of specialization ranged from marketing and commerce to communications and counseling to theology and pastoral care, and that became his vocation. Ernest's past recommended him for the task ahead, and his impact was obvious on the Mauritius Diocesan Board, the Provincial Synod, and the Rotary Club. His broadmindedness also served his work in national interfaith, ecumenical, and spiritual movements. Ernest gained deep respect for his generosity of spirit toward religious and social issues that were of keen interest to him.

Akinola was proud of his successor. Ernest, to him, was a well-meaning church leader, full of promise. Vibrant was his enormous capacity. Akinola was impressed with his "brimming ideas, the inflexibility in faith, the energetic ministry, and the

8. "A Most Agonizing Journey," a paper commissioned by Akinola on the position of CAPA regarding the 2008 Lambeth Commission.

9. https://en.wikipedia.org/wiki/Ian_Ernest; https://en.wikipedia.org/wiki/Church_of_the_Province_of_the_Indian_Ocean.

unwavering purpose-driven mission." He was delighted to pass CAPA to him, a group that had been renewed and was no longer an ineffective, "bottle-fed organization." Akinola's faith in Ernest was that of "a worthy successor." He was optimistic that his leadership would give the most populous bloc in the worldwide Anglican Church the required voice and visibility. Still, there was the question of how he would be able to reconcile and manage the conflicting loyalties and interests confronting him.

Ernest became the bishop of Mauritius in July 2001, the 15th successor to the episcopate leadership of the church, so he wasn't at the 1998 Lambeth Conference when the decision on human sexuality was made. He also didn't become an archbishop until 2006, a time when all the primates had virtually become exhausted and fatigued with the countless unproductive meetings they had held over the issue. Archbishop Williams, however, appointed him in 2003 as a member of the 2008 Lambeth Conference planning committee. The conference had not only stirred controversy, but had attracted serious reactions from the Anglican African Church leaders whose interest he was charged with championing.

In what would appear to be the first test of his leadership, Ernest had to preside over issues related to the 2008 Lambeth Conference. The CAPA meeting had a full house.[10] Nine of the primates attended personally while four sent representatives. Though Archbishop Mouneer Anis was absent physically, he was still able to maintain a loud presence, having forwarded his American notes from the parley he had with the Episcopal Church. There was nothing new in the points talked about or the emotional undercurrents surrounding the issues discussed. And that was what their official communique revealed at the end of the meeting: "We have spent the last ten years in a series of meetings, issuing numerous communiques, setting deadlines."

Judging the decade as a monumental waste, they regretted the obvious, that "we have made little progress." They felt let down again by the latest JSC report, which "was without credibility" and which was "compromised by numerous conflicts of interest." They could read the report's "determined effort to find a way for full inclusion of The Episcopal Church," pained that only an ignoramus would not see the strenuous attempt made to fool them. The African Anglican Church leaders had reached the end of their tolerance, and they urged Archbishop Williams to "postpone current plans for the Lambeth Conference." While regretting that the action might be seen as costly, the alternative, they believed, would even be costlier. Apart from possibility of a "divided conference," chances of "several provinces unable to participate" were also high. If this should happen, they foresaw a disastrous end ahead. "It would bring an end to the Communion as we know it," they warned.

Yet, as ominous as the position of the CAPA leaders looked, they still bent backwards to identify possible ways to avert the disaster. Their suggested postponement would "allow the current tensions to subside." The interim period, they contended,

10. "The Communique—CAPA Primates' Meeting in Mauritius," from the archive and papers of the Most Rev. Peter Akinola.

should be used to achieve the "reconciliation that must be done." They also urged "that those invited to Lambeth Conference [should] have already endorsed the Covenant." With this, they believed attendees "can come together as witness to our common faith." At the end, however, they kept the door open for reconciliation and expressed the need for the global primates to meet again. To them, "meeting together is essential." In the first instance, it would enable, "review [of] the actual response made by The Episcopal Church." They could honestly place "their words and their actions" side by side and weigh the two against each other.

The other agenda item would be to "finalize the Covenant proposal." The CAPA leaders were of the opinion that it was high time that the Communion "set a timetable for ratification by individual provinces." Clearing these hurdles, they affirmed, would "provide an opportunity for us to reunite the Communion." They had hopes that with charity on both sides, the Anglican Church worldwide could regain "our common heritage." For them and the Church, the combination of their ideas and the willingness on the part of the Communion leadership suggested "a way forward." Based on this, they sent a special appeal to Archbishop Williams to "call a special session of the Primates Meeting."

With the conclusion of the meeting, Ernest had his first challenging assignment. As the new man, he was catapulted into the maelstrom that Akinola had to endure in the past as the public face of the African Anglican leaders to the world. Though it took a while in coming on his part, he, too, expressed disgust about how vested interests within the Communion were crippling prospects for reconciliation.

24

Who Blinks First?

London, 2007

The Most Rev. Rowan Williams was the wrong archbishop to come to Canterbury at this troubled time. Yet in every area concerning scholarship, academic brilliance, and fertile intelligence, he was one of the prima donnas of the world, even beyond the Anglican Church. His achievements were stellar, and any parent would have loved to have him as a child. He gave his parents no trouble. Rupert Shortt portrayed Williams in his biography, *Rowan's Rule,* as a "prodigiously clever, studious and pious" child.[1] It's not an overstatement or embellishment. From childhood, he had begun to show a rare, potential gift to influence, a skill to get his way with others, including elders even as old as his parents.[2] The endowment couldn't have been derived from learning or as a product of deliberate cultivation; it could only have been an innate, natural gift, a blessing not so generously distributed among human beings in the world.

He was born on June 14, 1950, into a Welsh family in Swansea and was reared in a "Christian household," where, he recalls, "the name of Christ was familiar to me from my earliest childhood." He didn't come from an Anglican family, but he was the chief instrument for bringing his parents into the Anglican fold.

They were initially Nonconformists, and to be so categorized in British society of his parents' time was to carry a burden, with some limitations. The term Nonconformist denoted "any English subject belonging to a non-Anglican church" or anyone professing "non-Christian religion," and could extend to any person who advocated religious liberty.[3] Discrimination against Nonconformists lasted until the late 19th century. The Nonconformists were denied a range of opportunities in the public sphere, including "access to public office, civil service careers, or degrees at university."

1. Pepinster, "Rowan's Rule, By Rupert Shortt."
2. http://en.wikipedia.org/wiki/Rowan_Williams.
3. https://en.wikipedia.org/wiki/Nonconformist.

They were "referred to as suffering from civil disabilities." As Nonconformists, Williams' parents had rejected "the Book of Common Prayer and the Catholic strand of the Church of England," and it was in this context that Williams spent the first eleven years of his life.

He began his early primary education at Dynevor School, Swansea, the place of his birth. When we was 11, the family moved to Oystermouth, a suburb stretching from the northwest to the southeast in the district of Mumbles, Swansea, and there Williams demonstrated his precocity. He discovered the Anglican Church of All Saints, Oystermouth, surrendered himself to the embrace of the church, and also persuaded his parents to forsake their Nonconformist stand. As he reflects, "We became Anglicans and I've never been sorry about that." (Incidentally, with Rowan's flower unfurling, so to speak, it would have been a real hardship if his parents had allowed their stubbornness to get in the way of their wonderful son's climbing socially in the society, for it opened fresh vistas for him.)

His "faith was nurtured by a wonderful pastor and a wonderful congregation," he recollected, and, despite the fact he was still in his teenage years, he was already way ahead of many his age in ability to discern constructively. He recalled vividly two moments that signified both a beginning and a turning point for him, occasions when he felt, to use his exact words, "I met the living God. Not just words or rituals, but the living God."

The first encounter was not within the Anglican setting, but rather at a Russian Orthodox service. The curate in his Oystermouth parish had invited him to the service, thinking it would interest him. The service conducted by an elderly priest was celebrated in the Russian Orthodox liturgy, and Williams was awestruck: "I felt I had seen glory and praise for the first time . . . I felt I had seen and heard people who were behaving as if God were real. The service imbued him with a sense of the "absolute objectivity and majesty and beauty of God." He kept thinking, "If people worshipped God like this, I felt God must be a great deal more real." At that point, at age 14, Williams felt an emptiness in the depth of his being, and he knew he had "a long journey to make into that reality."

The "second experience" was three years later when he was 17. Williams had cultivated the habit of dividing his Saturday evening services attendance between his Anglican church and the Baptist church in Swansea. It seemed that the Anglican Church was leaving him with a void, and he found the Baptists offering "very direct and challenging mission services." Furthermore, he recalled, "That is where I learnt most of my choruses . . . where I learnt how to sing Blessed Assurance with love and delight, and heard very blunt evangelistic preaching." Plus, there were opportunities for social interactions, since often, the girls from the grammar school were there on Saturdays.

On that particular Saturday in 1967, one of the young ladies had invited him to her chapel to listen to a guest preacher, sure that Williams would love to listen to him. His name was Richard Wurmbrand.[4] He and his wife Sabina had just formed an organization known as Jesus to the Communist World, later renamed Voice of the Martyrs. It was an inter-denominational organization with initial focus on persecuted Christians in Communist countries. Over time, they expanded its scope to include persecuted believers in other places, especially in the Muslim world.

Born on March 24, 1909, Richard Wurmbrand, a Romanian Christian minister, was of Jewish descent. At 29, he became a Christian through an encounter with a Romanian Christian carpenter who shared the gospel with him and his wife, whom he had married on October 26, 1936, barely two years earlier. They both joined the Anglican Church's Ministry among Jewish People (CMJ UK), and after ten years of living their new faith, Wurmbrand began publicly proclaiming the incompatibility of Communism with Christianity. He could have just as well challenged the devil to a duel.

He was the youngest of four boys, and audacity marked him from his childhood. When he was 9, he lost his father, and when he was 15, the Wurmbrands moved from Istanbul to Romania. In due season, Wurmbrand was sent to Moscow to study Marxism, but clandestinely, he returned home a year later. He went through series of arrests and releases before seeking refuge away from Romania. His worst experience came in 1944 during the Soviet Union's occupation, which laid the groundwork for a communist regime in Romania.

Wurmbrand defied all threats to his personal safety, engaging in vigorous evangelism, targeting his Romanian compatriots as well as the Red Army soldiers with the gospel. First, working underground, he was forced to come into the open when the government decided to control churches. On his way to church on February 29, 1948, he was arrested and subjected to the worst kind of inhumane treatment.

He was moved from prison to prison, and spent three years in a solitary confinement, a dungeon twelve feet underground with no light or windows. To add to the psychological torture, the guards muted all sounds of living movement. They attached felt to the soles of their shoes whenever they had to establish contact with him. But Wurmbrand was determined to live through the hell. So, he devised a survival mechanism. During the day, he would sleep. At night, he would lie awake and compose and deliver sermons to imaginary audiences. When he was released, he could "recall more than 350 of those [sermons], a selection of which he included in his book *With God in Solitary Confinement.*

Wurmbrand wasn't sure which pain was the most difficult to bear—the psychological or the physical. As for the latter, brutal beatings left permanent scars, and in none of his more than eighteen books, including the bestseller *Tortured for Christ*, could he find the right words to capture the pains he suffered. Despite this, he was not bitter toward his tormenters; to his persecutors he gave forgiveness. He saw in them what their perverted minds could not see. He didn't look at them "as they are, but as

4. https://en.wikipedia.org/wiki/Richard_Wurmbrand.

they will be." He idealized new creatures from the horrifying beings. "I could also see in our persecutors . . . a future Apostle Paul," he wrote. His dream in confinement was to see Romania turned to a land of flourishing ministry.

Twenty-five years after they had been forced out, Richard and Sabina Wurmbrand returned home in 1990. They had paid a heavy price, but the reward was fulfilling, as he began his longed-for, unfettered preaching, joining forces with local ministers from every denomination to spread the gospel.

Williams' baptism actually occurred on that Saturday evening as he listened to Wurmbrand. The account of the man touched him profoundly. "It was the first time I had met a Christian martyr," he pointed out. In his subconscious, Williams was transposing himself into Wurmbrand, seeing himself in the man and vice versa. Though Wurmbrand and Williams were separated by 41 years, with the former old enough to be the latter's father, the feeling that came upon Williams was startling. He was measuring himself against Wurmbrand, feeling that "my own life looks very hollow by comparison." His life, person, and worldview were transfigured: "I found myself that evening kneeling at prayer in tears and feeling that I've been taken somewhere new," to a place of self-awakening, setting his life's trajectory.

In his travels, Wurmbrand had been invited to testify before the United States Internal Security Subcommittee in Washington, D.C. There, he'd taken off his shirt before TV cameras to show the public the ugly scars of his torture, and there were gasps within and outside the United States. But Wurmbrand's words alone provided enough stimuli for Williams: "I had to change, I had to grow," he kept musing to himself. Wurmbrand was the catalyst, the agent that sparked a spirit of heroism, a readiness for martyrdom: "I had to let that reality become more real for me."

Eight years after his encounter with Wurmbrand, Rowan Williams arrived at the doorstep of history. Smoothly, he climbed to the height of academia. At 25, in 1975, Williams obtained his DPhil from Wadham College, Oxford, having earlier studied at Christ's College, Cambridge. Theology was his special interest, with focus, not surprisingly, on the two areas that nurtured his worldview—Eastern Orthodox religious practice and the Christian martyrs or "confessors of faith" as he called them. Indeed, his doctoral thesis explored the unity of the two subjects.

Williams had picked the life of Vladimir Nicolaevich Lossky to study.[5] The son of a professor of philosophy, Lossky was a celebrated Orthodox Christian theologian. Born six years ahead of Wurmbrand on June 8, 1903, in Göttingen, Germany, his circumstances of birth and social status were more advantageous. Unlike his Romanian counterpart, the Russian was not a raw-hewn, street-pounding preacher (or an imprisoned one delivering sermons to a nonexistent audience at night). His was a war of the mind, analyzing the Word, enjoying the wall of protection provided by an urbane world. Nonetheless, the Russian theologian had his own sufferings. Wurmbrand experienced his in a direct and firsthand manner; Lossky's were more vicarious. He

5. https://en.wikipedia.org/wiki/Nikolay_Lossky.

had watched, in disgusted incredulity, the Soviet trial of Metropolitan Benjamin of St. Petersburg's Orthodox Church. When the horrifying execution followed, the scene kept replaying itself in his young mind like a horrible video. For Lossky, the incident was his defining moment, marking his baptism into religious activism.

At about the same age that Williams enrolled at Christ's College, Cambridge, the young Russian found his way to Petrograd University in 1920. After two years of schooling, his education was disrupted. He and his father had to emigrate, but he was able to continue his education, spending four years, 1922 to 1926, at Prague, and then studying at the Sorbonne, Paris, in 1927, specializing on medieval philosophy. The first decade and half of his post-education career is hard to trace; the records of his activities are difficult to uncover. But the last sixteen years of his life were spent in Paris, where he was a member of the Centre National de Recherche Scientifique and served as the first dean of the St. Dionysus Institute in Paris, teaching dogmatic theology and church history. He continued to teach until his death in 1958, though he changed jobs in 1953 to teach for the diocese of the patriarchate of Moscow, on "rue Pétel" in Paris.

Lossky defended and argued the supremacy of the Eastern Orthodox religion, maintaining that "the Orthodox tradition maintained the mystical dimension of theology in a more integrated way than those of the Catholic and Reformed traditions." Williams found the life and doctrine of this Russian theologian appealing, a complement to Wurmbrand's. Lossky was more a man of brain, Wurmbrand a man of brawn. While the latter was a trench-fighter, the former, in comparison, was a war strategist. Wurmbrand might have filled Williams' childhood heroism scrapbook, but he didn't provide the conception of the archetypal church leader for modern times. The world had undergone dramatic changes. Political ideologies that made men like Wurmbrand and Lossky suffer for their faith were fading away, along with the Iron Curtain. For Williams, the political, social, and cultural milieu that nurtured him was not only different from that of Wurmbrand and Lossky, but it was also undergoing change.

Williams grew up in an environment of free speech; he was a product of a society where the road to eminence was through intellectual power, reasoning, and persuasion, all elements of competitive politics. Fortunate for him, those were his greatest strengths. His DPhil prepared him well, and his age (25) favored him. Plus he'd chosen the ideological platform on which he wanted to stand, but he didn't make this as apparent as his parents had made their Nonconformist belief. Yet Williams displayed the stereotypical emblem of radicalism, of the typical Communist or Marxist. To be a comrade was to sport a fashionable beard, not something popular for a gentleman priest, but rather a trademark of rebellion.

Nevertheless, the first decade of his working life, from 1975 to 1985, appeared to have been an apolitical period dedicated to advancing his career as a theologian. The initial two years were spent lecturing at the College of the Resurrection in Mirfield, Yorkshire. In 1977, he moved to Westscott House, Cambridge. Preceding this was his ordination as a deacon at the Ely Cathedral, after which, a year later, he became a priest.

The priesthood was an inner urge that Williams seemed he just had to fulfill. At the same time, there was a raging battle between his spirit of nonconformism and a feeling of superiority. For three years, he shunned curacy, a subordinate position as assistant to a senior priest in a parish. His appointment as a lecturer in divinity at the University of Cambridge, however, overcame his reluctance. Westcott House offered limited opportunities in that it served the Church of England, whereas the University of Cambridge surely afforded a better position, prestige, and prospect. Though both were located in Cambridge, there was no denying which of the two institutions was the path for him to follow if he were to be reckoned with internationally.

On joining the faculty of Cambridge, therefore, he undertook his curacy at St. Georges, Chesterton, from 1980 to 1983. It was as if the fulfilment of that obligatory canon was necessary to advancing his career, and the year after, 1984, he became the dean and chaplain of Clare College, the second oldest of Cambridge's thirty-one colleges. Then, two years later, Oxford University appointed him as Lady Margaret Professor of Divinity. Williams was no longer a promising scholar but a confirmed top-class intellectual at 36. Young, prodigious, his youthful precocity had been utilized to earn a place of distinction in the academic hall of fame. With his professorial chair, he was automatically the residentiary canon of Christ Church, the university's chapel.

From then on, developments were like icing on the cake. In 1989, he was awarded the doctor of divinity, and the British Academy elected him fellow in 1990. At 40, Williams could look back and have some satisfaction at the trajectory of his life. Within a decade and a half, he had gotten to the height of his professional calling and become a theologian of international standing, honored as such in the media. Williams was also a renowned poet, an accomplished wordsmith gifted with turning sentences into rhythmic melody. He was able to deliver pungent soundbites and convey spicy quotations to print and broadcast outlets, enhancing his status within the church and in the larger society. But, of course, success and fame can be spiritually dangerous. Unmanaged or managed improperly, they can induce conceit, breed arrogance and a feeling of haughtiness.

It was 1985, and Williams no longer felt the need to subdue his impulses on the political front. His radical instincts could no longer be stilled. Openly and forcefully, he started expressing himself on social issues and causes of the day. Fortunately for him, the university environment usually provided a safe haven for those championing dissent in society. It's part of the tradition of academic freedom, which a university, as a marketplace of ideas and a forum for the clash of educated views, is supposed to nurture, cherish, and uphold. Williams used his freedom in an almost unfettered way.

As the chaplain of Clare College, Cambridge, he joined others in the march to support the anti-nuclear campaign. But the person he was, Williams wanted to stand above the shoulders of others to put his stamp on how things were done, and this led to his arrest in 1985, as he stood out from the crowd of protesters at Lakenheath. The protest, organized by the Committee for Nuclear Disarmament at the American air base in Suffolk, had recorded no major incident—except in the case of Williams. Throughout the protest, as if guiding the steps of the protesters with an accompanying marching song, he busied himself singing psalms repeatedly. For doing this, the police arrested him, and the college immediately paid his fine. It would appear that once Williams had decided upon the particular course his life should take, he neither wavered nor relented, and, as a corollary, he exhibited a sort of narrow-mindedness that often characterized radicals with an egoistic notion of having a superior, enlightened worldview.

Consequently, from the time he began his social crusades until the time of his becoming the archbishop of Canterbury, he threw punches at any issue that did not conform to his conception of what society should be. Williams wanted no ambiguity about his socio-political and ideological leaning. He was a member of the left-wing, Anglo-Catholic, Jubilee Group. Together with Father Kenneth, the head of the Group, he authored a number of publications, including *Essays Catholic and Radical,* a collection of articles to celebrate the 150th anniversary of the Assize Sermon. If Williams had missed the Assize Sermon's commemoration, it would have dented his social crusader's credibility and credentials.

The Assize Sermon was an immortal oration,[6] one which revolutionized British society and served as a wake-up call for the nation, and John Keble, whom Williams much admired, was its preacher. Coincidentally, Keble and Williams had a few things in common. Both were poets, Oxford professors, and priests. On the other hand, a vast gulf existed between their worldviews. Keble lived to be 74, 50 years of which he spent in his priestly calling, contented with remaining a village priest serving a small parish in Hursley near Winchester. Perhaps the most notable difference was the older man's manner as he thoughtfully addressed social reform within the context of godliness and righteousness.

Keble didn't draw attention to himself, but his thoughts magnificently did. On July 14, 1833, he had been invited as a preacher to mark the opening of the new legal year for the civil and criminal courts. Apart from honoring the invitation, Keble seized the imagination of his audience and captured the attention of the whole nation, rousing everybody from slumber with his sermon, "National Apostasy." He hit his fellow Britons hard, rebuking them for turning away from God, "for regarding the Church as a mere institution of society." Rather, the church should be "the prophetic voice of God, commissioned by Him to warn and instruct the people." The impressive address galvanized the country into action, and it became known as the famous "Assize Sermon." It reawakened a dying British society and "profoundly influenced the religious thinking, practice, and worship of large portions of Christendom."

Subsequently, commemoration of the Assize Sermon became an annual event, a reminder of the enduring legacy of John Keble, the poet, the priest, the social reformer, the conscience of the society, and the apostle of church renewal. Williams could lay

6. http://justus.anglican.org/resources/bio/123.html.

claim to two of the pedigrees held by his fellow Oxford compatriot; both of them were poets and priests. But, certainly, as far as historical eminence was concerned, Williams was nowhere near the mark of John Keble, for the latter had left a huge imprint on Christendom. Keble was 41 when he shook the nation with his sermon.

He was born in 1792, ordained in 1816, and, in 1833, his landmark sermon came in the seventeenth year of his priesthood. As for Williams, the important role he played in the 1983 commemoration of the 150th anniversary of the Assize Sermon came when he was 33, in his fifteenth year of priesthood. Certainly, he had built for himself a name, fame, and public visibility; he was respected as a brilliant, liberal, progressive, and fearless crusader, and had taken a stand on some key national and international issues. Still, he wasn't close to attaining the mark of historical eminence enjoyed by his heroes—Richard Wurmbrand, the Christian martyr; Vladimir Lossky, the Eastern Orthodox star; and John Keble, the charismatic reformer of the English Church. Nevertheless, time was on his side because Williams was not yet near 40 years of age.

Around the time he turned 40, in 1990, two significant events took place in his life, the first in 1989 while the second was in 1991. Both incidents were indicative and suggestive of Williams' action and inaction later as the archbishop of Canterbury. In 1989, Williams was invited to deliver the 10th Michael Harding Memorial Address organized by the Lesbian and Gay Christian Movement. By this time, a lot had happened to put gay and lesbian issues on the public agenda in Britain, but Williams' involvement had been fuzzy. With the 1989 lecture, that would change.

The matter was within his intellectual wheelhouse, where he could boast of versatility and competence, and so he made his entry into the fray, regal and loud. He took on the church, questioning the logic of its position, faulting it for moral inconsistency. He also charged it with failure to interpret scripture intelligently. He argued that it was tantamount to hypocrisy to deny homosexuality "in a church that accepts the legitimacy of contraception." He contended that "the absolute condemnation of same-sex relations of intimacy must rely either on an abstract fundamentalist deployment of a number of very ambiguous biblical texts, or on a problematic and non-scriptural theory about natural complementarity, applied narrowly and crudely to physical differentiation without regard to psychological structures." Put simply, those against homosexuality were either reading the Bible wrongly, imposing meaning on what is not precisely stated, or suffering from poor understanding of the nature of human creation, or both.

Williams was like all academics whose tool of trade is to shroud straightforward ideas in convoluted garb, but he was quick to realize the limit of rhetoric, no matter how elegant it was. He was not in the classroom; this was real life. So he took a step as a "practical consequence of the views he expressed." In 1996, he founded the Institute for the Study of Christianity and Sexuality, later called the Centre for the Study of

Christianity and Sexuality. And, from that day forward, Williams neither looked nor turned back as an apostle and guardian of the gay agenda.

Now in his forties, he was soon blessed with appointment as the bishop of Monmouth, a diocese on the border of Wales. Though a few found this troubling, many saw it as well deserved. Some thought the election smacked of a scheme. Maybe they were right, and perhaps they were wrong. Either way, he couldn't be moved from his avowed support for gays and lesbians.

His episcopacy commenced with simultaneous intensification of his backing for gays and lesbians through overt public acts, such as writing the foreword to a major gay and lesbian publication: *The Other Way?* The book was a collection of articles by fourteen Anglican priests and lay members who were all gays and lesbians. Williams' prologue came in the form of a mild attack on the position of the church, which, this time, he made in a straightforward way without the academic long-winded logic. "These reflections and recollections," he wrote, "will make clear the cost and integrity involved in living as a gay or lesbian person struggling to be loyal to the Christian tradition and the Christian community." In a soft-sell manner, Williams asked, "Can this seriousness be received as a *gift* in our Church?" (The editor of the book was Rev. Colin Coward, director of Changing Attitude, the gay organization that later used Davis Mac-Iyalla in its mercenary attack against Archbishop Akinola.)

It appeared that the interest of the gay organizations was to use Williams as a rallying point, for there were a quite number of them—groups like Lesbian Matters, the Evangelical Fellowship for "evangelical homosexuals," the Quaker Lesbian and Gay Fellowship, the Christian Science Lesbian and Gay Group, the Lesbian and Gay Anglicans in the Dioceses of Southwark and London, and the Lesbian and Gay Christian Movement (LGCM), which had invited Williams to deliver the address through which he had climbed to prominence within the gay fold. Established in 1976, a year after Williams obtained his DPhil, the organization met twice yearly. Williams had been a fairly regular speaker at their meetings, as were other personalities such as the headstrong, pro-gay, American bishop of Newark, the Rt. Rev. John Spong, and his Californian counterpart Bill Swing. Perhaps this was the forum that brought Williams and Spong into contact. And maybe it was connected with Williams' rise in the spiritual leadership of the Anglican Communion.

In 1997, after exercising episcopal authority in Monmouth for six years, opportunity opened for Williams to return to London and become again part of mainstream life in the British capital. He was proposed as the bishop of Southwark. Transferring to the diocese would have placed him directly under the Province of Canterbury, a position such that even if he was not under total control of the archbishop of Canterbury, at least he might have influence over him one way or the other. Coincidentally, the then-archbishop of Canterbury, the Most Rev. George Carey, was not averse to having Williams.

Southwark Diocese covered South London and East Surrey, leaving out the area of London north of the River Thames to the Diocese of London. The challenge, however, was that Southwark Diocese was one of the breeding grounds for the amorphous Lesbian and Gay Anglicans Group trying desperately to draw attention to itself. Carey reasoned that it was not prudent to have a provocateur in such a sensitive place, for he didn't want to have fire under his roof. Notwithstanding, he was willing to have Williams in the Southwark Diocese, provided he would abide by one condition. Carey told Williams to distance himself from his writings that were sympathetic to gay rights.

Poor Carey! He had considered the issue from the narrow perspective of the interest of the church. He wasn't looking at its political implications from Williams' perspective. The Lambeth Conference was knocking at the door a year away, and all the gay groups were marshalling strength to put the gay agenda through at the Conference. So it would be unthinkable for one of those seen as its champions to renounce his involvement publicly. Besides, there were only two years until the retirement of the archbishop of Wales, Alwyn Rice Jones, and the odds favored Williams as a successor. Again, to turn around midway at sea would be foolishness on his part.

There was more benefit in sticking with the group he was in than in allowing Carey to taint him as a turncoat. As archbishop of Wales, he would be one of the Communion's thirty-eight primates, a global leader. And with that position was the probability of becoming the archbishop of Canterbury. The gay groups constituted his surest support, and it was better to have them rooting for him than hooting at him. Consequently, he threw Carey's condition back at his face.

As it turned out, he was, as expected, in attendance at the 1998 Lambeth Conference, and, predictably, he was one of the signatories to the perfidious pastoral letter to lesbian and gay Anglicans that denounced the majority's decision. Then, in due course, Williams became the archbishop of Wales in 1999, putting him in the advantageous position of leading the Communion as a primate. Finally, in July 2002, eleven years of his debut as a bishop, and with three years as an archbishop, he reached the highest position of preeminence in the worldwide Anglican Communion. Succeeding George Carey on February 27, 2003, he was enthroned as the 104th archbishop of Canterbury. He was 53.

Williams' rise from obscurity in Wales to world's center stage, where his name opened doors in the highest corridors of government across nations of the world, was an historical accomplishment. As a boy, man, professor, social crusader, theologian, theological activist, bishop, archbishop, and ultimately head of the worldwide Anglican Church, he was remarkable. He also possessed transcendent self-assurance, and it served him well. At 11, Williams won his parents over from being Nonconformists. By 17, he had determined the course of his life. He marked his 25th birthday with a doctorate. Next at 34, he had become the dean of Cambridge's second oldest college. Then at 36, Williams was a professor. His 41st birthday witnessed his election as a bishop. Eight years later at 49, history further beckoned him as he was made the head of the Welsh national church, becoming its archbishop and primate. Then, just three years after his 50th birthday, he topped the achievements as the first Welshman and the first outsider from the English Church to become the Archbishop of Canterbury.

Ironically, a key ingredient of his success—confidence in his ability—turned out to be the very source of his downfall. He'd come to the office of archbishop of Canterbury with baggage, including the suspicion he was a candidate of the gay movement, the product of a scheme that took him, initially, to the position of bishop of Monmouth. The cynics and skeptics didn't keep quiet. Rife was the allegation that he owed his office to Changing Attitude, the British equivalent of the American Integrity USA, the prominent and dominant American gay rights group within the Episcopal Church. Even if the accusation lacked substance, Williams didn't help matters, for Changing attitude was "conspicuously acknowledged during the colourful enthronement of the Archbishop," one source observed.[7]

If there was any doubt beforehand, Williams' conduct of archbishopric affairs at Canterbury settled the matter. He knew the mind of the Communion, before, during, and after his enthronement. As the Instrument of Unity, the person, the office, the embodiment, and custodian of every aspect of life of the Anglican Church globally, he was bound to uphold everything the Communion stood for. Yet from the dawn of his tenure, every step he took ran contrary to what was expected of him. Williams was not a victim of innocent errors. Rather, he was the author of his own wilful acts of commission, and he alone was to blame for the first crisis of his tenure.

Three months after assuming office, Williams dragged the elephant into the room with his appointment of the openly gay Jeffrey John as a bishop. It was a contemptuous action taken brazenly. Morally, too, it was a faulty decision. John was one of the originators of "Affirming Catholicism," for which Williams was patron. On a two-count charge of deliberately perpetuating a wrong and of acting with nepotism, Williams would be hard pressed to defend himself.

Williams had bounced into the life of the Communion with his own peculiar brand of leadership, and it wasn't a style the institution was accustomed to. None of his 103 predecessors had exhibited it. He was so confident of his ability that he took his colleagues for granted. When the crisis broke out, Williams, as the new archbishop of Canterbury, convened a meeting of the Communion primates at Lambeth to find a way forward. They agreed on the Lambeth Commission, and they gave him free rein to handle the situation. Singlehandedly, he assembled and appointed members of the Commission, who then suggested actions to be taken six months after the fact-finding exercise. He assembled the primates to consider the recommendations, and they also came up with a set of resolutions.

Yet, from 2004, when the decisions were made, he deliberately chose inaction. The Anglican Consultative Council also made several decisions, but Williams delayed any concrete action, pretending that the crisis was difficult to resolve. Groups

7. Asaju, *In Defence of Christian Orthodoxy.*

like Council for Anglican Provinces in Africa and Global South shouted themselves hoarse, but Canterbury was heedless. The new Anglican Covenant followed with Williams' consent, but like the Windsor Report, he rendered it moribund as he hid behind his official façade.

A lot, indeed, had been written about Williams' archbishopric years at Canterbury, particularly Rupert Shortt's *Rowan's Rule,* a post-Canterbury biographical account of his life and times. He portrayed Williams as "an intellectual giant who towers over almost all his predecessors as Archbishop of Canterbury," and also "a complex and controversial figure."[8] Others suggested that "the difficulty for a cleric like Williams is that the Church today requires guile of a kind." The implication was that he wasn't a cunning leader. Some sympathized, suggesting that he was a victim of a world inclined "to judge people in public life, even if they aren't politicians, as if they should behave like them."[9]

To quite a few others, he was "too high-handed and, well, too holy to be that successful an archbishop." To be high-handed was to be autocratic, and Shortt counted this an insult: rather, in Shortt's words, "Williams doesn't like being bullied, but is susceptible to pressure." Unfortunately, in Shortt's view, this gave "the well-organised conservative factions the assurance that, in the words of their would-be leader, Peter Akinola, archbishop of Nigeria, 'he'll do what we tell him.'" (Shortt, of course, was Rowan Williams' student, and he made it clear "that he himself is on the liberal side of the argument.")

Williams would have done better to remain a classroom hero rather than parachute himself into the life of the Communion and throw the worldwide Anglican Church into a big crisis of leadership. He tried to mix the sheltered life of college idealism with the practical demands of leadership in a big, complex, dynamic global organization. It didn't work, but rather than make the necessary adjustments when the truth confronted him, he ignored reality. In his words and deeds, actions and inaction, and from the beginning to the end of his tenure, Williams as archbishop of Canterbury and head of the global Anglican Communion would rather see the Communion break up than swallow his pride. Nevertheless, the tragic truth was cleverly and successfully hidden from the public with well-oiled media spin. Thus, it was fortuitous that Peter Akinola made and preserved the minutes of the crucial meeting between him and Rowan Williams.

Back to the February 15, 2007, worldwide Anglican primates meeting in Dar es Salam, Tanzania during which the serious impasse had developed between Akinola and Williams. At the root of the standoff was the covert manner with which the meeting's communique was being manipulated, and also the hypocritical manner that Williams used in addressing the intransigence of the American and Canadian churches.

8. Pepinster, "Rowan's Rule, By Rupert Shortt"; Bates, "God's Squad."

9. Pepinster, "Rowan's Rule, By Rupert Shortt"; Gledhill, "Rowan Williams 'Hated' Being Archbishop of Canterbury."

To recount the standoff, Akinola was successfully placated in the end to sign the communique. But also significant was the fact that Williams had said something specifically to the Nigerian archbishop to which the latter made no reply at the time. Williams was not a man carefree or imprecise with his choice of words. Certainly not during the emotionally charged atmosphere characterizing the Dar es Salam meeting would he have allowed artlessness to hinder his communication. But here was what seemed to be his gaffe. Mockingly, he had challenged Akinola: "We shall see who blinks first!" Akinola chose at the time a studied silence in response to Williams's inflammatory dare.

Loaded into that statement were the game and gambit, the subterfuge and the stratagem that had characterized Williams' approach to managing the Communion's crisis. Indeed, the tactics had served him well in deceiving his colleagues and fooling the public about the intractability of the crisis. And all along, he was aided by well-orchestrated media spin and massive propaganda to oil the deception.

Akinola had long suspected that the archbishop did not intend to use Canterbury to provide trustworthy leadership to the Anglican Church. He had seen through the chicanery, and he was bothered by its potential consequences for the Church. This was why he had always drawn the archbishop's attention to the fact that it served no useful purpose for Williams to twist their decisions whenever the primates made a decision. Akinola had grown up with the Yoruba proverb, *"kan gun kan gun, a kan gun sibi kan,"* meaning simply, "Whatever the guile, smartness, deceit and pretence, it will come to an end one day."

Surprisingly, it was Williams himself who opened the door for the truth to emerge. He had invited Akinola for a private, one-on-one meeting.[10] The closed-door encounter was slated for the Holiday Inn near Heathrow Airport, London, on September 16, 2007, seven months after the altercations between the two in Dar es Salaam.

Akinola found his way to the meeting directly from Nnewi, a town in the eastern part of Nigeria, where he had presided over a statutory assembly of the Standing Committee of the Church of Nigeria. Only the two of them were in the room, and no note taking was allowed. From the setting, it appeared the two were poised for an unrestrained, heart-to-heart talk, which would have been in the best interest of the worldwide church. The coming together of the two leaders to talk together, to work out common ground, to foster a unanimous agreement would have been the most helpful antidote toward mitigating the crisis tearing the Anglican Church apart. Imaginative as Canterbury's media spinners and political strategists were, Archbishop Williams knew that a counter, formidable group existed with Akinola at the center.

Once secluded behind closed doors, Williams fired the first questions after Akinola had said the opening prayer. Williams was direct, wanting to know the Nigerian leader's

---

10. Akinola, "Notes of a private & confidential conversation between The Most Rev'd Rowan Williams, Archbishop of Canterbury, and The Most Rev'd Peter J. Akinola, Primate of All Nigeria," from the archive and personal papers of Archbishop Peter Akinola.

"expectations regarding [his] forthcoming visit to TEC House of Bishops." Akinola replied that the document "A Most Agonizing Journey" had already articulated his views. Nothing had happened since then to change or diminish his position. Since the "Anglican Communion leadership over the past ten years has been devoted to resolving the crisis with ECUSA," and yet there was "no evidence of any change," Akinola was emphatic that he did not "have optimism for the outcome" of Williams' visit to America. Williams did not dispute Akinola's position. He, however, expressed worry about the division within the American church, and he said it was his desire to "save the middle and ensure that they remain part of the Communion." In his estimation, the American church had been polarized along three lines. First, "there are approximately 30% on the extreme left." The second group had "30% that are on the extreme right," and then there was "the 30% in the middle." He was anxious to ensure that the 30% sitting on the fence was "saved" and that they remained in the Communion.

Williams admitted honestly to Akinola that "the current presiding bishop [Schori] is no part of the middle," and he assured Akinola that he would "inform TEC that it cannot be business as usual." It seemed, then, that Williams had woken up to the imperative to take pragmatic action. This echoed something he'd said a year earlier, exactly six months preceding the volatile Dar es Salam meeting. In an interview with a Dutch newspaper, published on August 24, 2006, under the headline, "Anglican Head: US Church has 'Pushed the Boundary,'" Williams was quoted as admitting that the American church had "pushed the boundaries" because it "has made a decision that is not the decision of the wider body of Christ."

At the one-on-one Heathrow meeting, he added, "No more playing games with words or deception," and, "There must be a change even if it is costly." Waxing scriptural, he observed, "All bear the cross to claim the benefits of the resurrection." Hearing this, the Nigerian leader was ambivalent in his feelings. He neither believed nor disbelieved the truthfulness of what his host was saying, his promise of acting decisively with the rebellious churches.

The summary notes don't indicate Akinola's response to his host's declarations. But we do read his direct, follow-up question: "+PJA asked whether +RW would be calling a Primates' Meeting to evaluate the adequacy of the response of TEC." Williams evaded the question. He kept silent. Then, he suggested that the primates might not be willing to participate in such a meeting. To bolster his claim, he said that "at least 12 primates have indicated great reluctance because of [their] nightmare experience in Dar es Salam." He also raised the problem of financial cost, but Akinola refused to be put off by the objections. Even if he could not guarantee the safety and security of the primates from harassment by gay activists, with he himself being a prime target, he pledged that the Global South "will help pay for a portion of the cost [of the meeting] if it is held in the Global South." As the report notes, "There was no comment from +RW."

Akinola pressed ahead, maintaining that "since [the] Primates initiated the Windsor process" and "requested response from TEC," he believed it was appropriate that they should have opportunity to "evaluate [the] adequacy of [the] response." Williams wasn't ready to be cornered, saying only that "the Primates' Meeting is still open." Akinola had to leave it at that since he could not badger him on the point without offending meeting etiquette. In any case, Williams, as the archbishop of Canterbury, held the ace. He reserved the power to convene the meeting or not. Anything and everything about the primates' meeting was his prerogative. Therefore, Akinola let go of the subject.

Still, there remained an element of camaraderie, with which the two began the meeting, and so they continued. Williams raised the issue of CANA, saying that he "would have to defend" both Akinola and CANA at the proposed meeting with TEC, given that the Episcopal Church was alleging that CANA and "similar actions by other GS Primates [were acts of] defiance." Of course, this issue had been thoroughly addressed already. Schori and Akinola had exchanged letters on the matter with explanations offered on both sides.[11] Furthermore, Williams and Akinola had treated the topic in earlier correspondence. They both knew his stand, but Akinola reiterated his position: "We are willing to turn CANA over to the Communion once the conditions that prompted its formation have been reversed."

Akinola drew Williams' attention to what appeared to him to be an inconsistency. He wondered what had been done with respect to "the Church of England and TEC, both [of which] took similar actions in establishing Convocations in Europe." No eyebrows were raised from any quarters, he reminded Williams. Now, that the Global South resorted to doing the same thing, objections were being raised by the churches in the West. Again, "no response by +RW," the notes reported.

Williams was however blunt in his response to Akinola when the latter asked for the postponement of the Lambeth Conference. "No," he replied sharply. He was not prepared to delay it and was not going to consider suspension. He gave three reasons: The first was that "approximately 50%" of those expected had already responded. Secondly, he had to "honour those who have worked so hard preparing over the past year." Thirdly, and perhaps most importantly, he wasn't convinced that a delay of twelve to twenty-four months would make any real difference to the situation.

Akinola disagreed with his host. He insisted that the period of the delay would afford opportunity for the Communion to finalize and agree on the Anglican Covenant, which, in his estimation, offered the most practical way forward. But he was wasting his time, for Williams' mind was made up. He had two non-negotiables—remaining "committed to the Lambeth Conference" and "ensuring that ECUSA is not lost to the Communion." So Akinola asked, "How can two walk together if they are not agreed?" and "How can we engage in prayer and discernment in an atmosphere filled with disdain and distrust?"

11. See http://peterakinola.blogspot.com.ng/2007/05/letter-to-archbishop-of-canterbury.html.

Williams was unruffled. With cultivated calmness, he answered with a coldness laced with indifferent candor: "That is how our life is at the moment."

Akinola then raised the possibility of several Global South primates' boycotting the Conference. After all, the Global South constituted the majority in the Communion, about two-thirds of its size. Perhaps Akinola had forgotten that the same warning was already contained in the document "A Most Agonizing Journey" that he had sent to Williams. The archbishop seemed to have a prepared answer: "+RW responded that he would be saddened," but it wouldn't make him abandon the Conference. He told Akinola that boycott "is not without precedence," adding nonchalantly, "Absences have happened before."

In the long history of the Lambeth Conference, the meeting had been postponed twice. The first was the fifth Lambeth Conference under Archbishop Randall Davidson, when instead of holding it in 1918, they waited until 1920. The second delay came during the tenure of Geoffrey Fisher as archbishop of Canterbury. Fisher's predecessor, Archbishop Cosmo Gordon Lang, had convened the seventh Lambeth in 1930 with the lot falling naturally on Fisher to organize the next decennial edition in 1940. World War II, however, disrupted arrangements, and it wasn't until 1948, eight years later, that the eighth Lambeth Conference was convened. None of the 349 bishops from around the world stayed back when it eventually took place. Indeed, in these two cases, the circumstances leading to the postponement did not match those facing Williams. Disagreement over doctrinal issues played no role in the earlier cases, nor did they involve the prospect of mass boycott. Yet Williams was unruffled. He seemed ready to countenance any cost, the consequences be damned.

Continuing, Akinola suggested that the "GS absence would indicate that the Communion is broken." Williams disagreed, calling it "regrettable" while maintaining it would "not have any long-term significance." And so they'd hit a dead end: "No agreement," the entry candidly observed. Concluding, they moved on to a less disagreeable subject. Akinola urged the archbishop to take a second look at the case of Bishop Orama (who was alleged to have said some very harsh things about homosexuals). Williams was pleased that his Nigerian colleague intervened, and he promised to reconsider the case.

Surprisingly, the archbishop of Canterbury gave his guest a fixed look of sincere expression and put aside his pride, something unlikely in a public forum: "+RW offered his regrets about his humiliation of +PJA at Dar es Salaam," the notes reported. He added, "Situation was hard and remains so." What else could Akinola do in that situation other than to accept the expression of regret? Hence, "+PJA accepted the apology." That was the way the notes captured it.

Williams said the closing prayer and the two departed. Akinola made the notes when his memory of the discussion was still fresh: He wrote in the preamble, "These notes are based on the next day recollections of Archbishop Akinola" (that is, September 17, 2007).

Despite his show of contrition, Williams reverted to type. The evidence suggested he didn't have the promised frank talk with the American church leaders. With a fiat, the American church was cleared of any transgression. The Joint Standing Committee of Primates and the Anglican Consultative Council also absolved it of any guilt. The recriminations were acerbic and strident; the report was denounced a fraud publicly. But if the situation embarrassed the archbishop and left him scandalized, his reaction didn't show it. He never asked that the report be retrieved. Nor did he call his fellow primates to a meeting, to the forum which Akinola and the Global South leaders believed was imperative for all of them to decide if the American church's response was adequate.

Clearly, Williams was avoiding the primates meeting. He would not have succeeded in passing the nonsense through them. And so, at 57, he faced his "midlife crisis." He had been over-confident of his ability and so had boxed himself into a corner. The gay movement looked up to him as the man to achieve the impossible feat in the Anglican Church. On the other hand, his fellow primates who numbered in the majority objected to him and to the little minority in league with him for their willingness to lord decisions over them. But the Anglican Church did not give way. So he was confronted with a serious dilemma. Which of the two competing forces should he disappoint? Should it be his gay supporters or the resolute fellow Anglican leaders?

Neither of the two options was attractive to him. And so it was that the man who came with a soaring ego into office left it with his aura badly shattered. Williams might have been a brilliant theologian, but his education in practical leadership, particularly in managing dire conflicts, was evidently limited. Rather than surrender, he beat a retreat into the protective cocoon of inaction. If he could not bend the Anglican Communion to legitimize homosexuality, at least it was within his power to erect a protective shield around its proponents. This he struggled to do all through his tenure. Through deliberate acts of conspiracy, complicity, and collusion, Williams pushed the Anglican Church to a dangerous precipice. Archbishop Akinola had warned him of this, and events proved him right.

25

Enough of Chaos and Compromise

Kenya, 2007

Between Archbishop Peter Akinola and Canterbury Archbishop Rowan Williams, it was not so much a matter of love lost as one of ten times bitten and a hundredfold shy. The areas of unresolved disagreement between the two at their private meeting were what divided them. Akinola didn't expect Williams to act justly and equitably, so he wasn't surprised by the gift he presented to the Communion from America. Like all of his other colleagues in the leadership of the Communion, Akinola knew where the partisan interest of the Canterbury archbishop lay. To expect an overnight change was expecting a modern day miracle. His partisanship was putting the future of the Anglican Church in jeopardy, and virtually all were tired of the rigmarole. Even before their Heathrow meeting, the deplorable situation had reached a climax. Several warnings had been served on Williams that the state of affairs could not continue indefinitely. While Williams may not have brought the Communion to the boiling point, he had dragged it to the crossroads. Archbishop Akinola thought the time was ripe to search for a way out of the caldron, for there was no point in their sitting idly and continuing to agonize.

Akinola had his ideas, but he felt he had to talk with others. Thus, three months after the meeting with Williams, and following no positive developments from Lambeth Palace, he convened a consultative meeting in Nairobi, Kenya.[1] Twelve of them gathered around the table on that mid-December 2007 morning. Present were the

---

1. The following papers, minutes of meetings, notes, and letters regarding GAFON were retrieved from the personal papers and archive of Archbishop Peter Akinola: letter to Archbishop Mouneer Anis on GAFCON (exact date not indicated); Follow-up letter on the Nairobi Consultation, copies of which were sent to meeting's participants (exact date not indicated); "Letter from Archbishop Peter J. Akinola to the Global South Primates" (exact date not stated); Letter to Bishop Suheil (exact date not stated); Itinerary and agenda during visit to Jerusalem between January 11 & 15, 2008; "Transcript of Archbishop Akinola's presentation to Bishop Dawani"; and "Notes towards a communique from Archbishop Akinola and Dawani By gathering."

regulars, trusted allies, compatriots like Archbishops Emmanuel Kolini, the primate of Rwanda; Benjamin Nzimbi of Kenya; Henry Orombi, the Ugandan primate; as well as America's Rt. Revs. Robert Duncan, Martyn Minns, and Bill Atwood. From the United Kingdom, was Canon Dr. Chris Sugden, executive secretary of the Anglican Mainstream. There were some fresh faces at the table though they were not new to the struggles within the Anglican Church.

The Most Rev. Peter Jensen, the archbishop of Sydney, Australia, was also present.[2] Jensen was not an outsider to the deep-seated Anglican rift. He was one of the "Worldwide Anglican Mainstream Leaders" who had gathered in Fairfax in 2003 during that last ditch effort to stop the General Convention from ratifying openly-gay Gene Robinson's election as the bishop of New Hampshire. Since then, Jensen had maintained a principled stand along with his colleagues around the table, not surprising since his life had revolved around character molding and formation. Aside from a two-year study of law and work as an articled clerk after college, his entire life had been devoted to teaching. He began as a primary school teacher and then moved to Moore Theological College in the late 1960s, where he won the Hey Sharp Prize for leading the class in the licentiate of theology. Apart from his master of arts degree from Sydney University, he had also completed a bachelor of divinity degree from the University of London and a doctor of philosophy (DPhil) from the University of Oxford. From 1970 on, when he was ordained as a priest, the greater part of his career was in the academia. Eventually, he became the principal of Moore Theological College, serving from 1985 until 2001, when he was made a bishop. The first year of the twenty-first century seemed to be his year of glory, as on 5 June 2001, Jensen became the eleventh archbishop of Sydney. Besides enjoying educational attainments, the archbishop of Sydney was also a formidable, gifted preacher and a strong personality.

Jensen was a man who would not surrender his strongly held view on the tyranny of vile public opinion. Dogged in his opposition to same-sex marriage, he continually and publicly deplored the aberrant lifestyle any time the opportunity presented itself. Consistently and forthrightly, he maintained that same-sex marriage could not be "for the moral good." Likewise, he disdained the notion of same-sex "marriage equality." Drawing his parishioners to the standpoint of the Bible, he took umbrage at the notion that the state could create family aside from or in conflict with the traditional perspective that God had enshrined in the Scripture. He said the state had no business imposing the "idea that a family can be founded on the sexual union of two men or two women as a valid alternative to that of a man and a woman." He refused to bat an eye when the gay movement attacked him for touching one of these sore points. Rather than retract the statement, he went on to bring up the shorter lifespan of homosexuals compared to heterosexuals as more evidence for his point.

---

2. Jensen, "Archbishop Jensen on the Conference"; Steele, "Dr Peter Jensen on the Future of the Anglican Communion."

Boldly, in an interview program, he "questioned whether the health and longevity of gay men was as good as that of 'the ordinary, so-called heterosexual man.'" That's one item homosexuals never liked to hear. But Jensen's position had been informed by real life experience with two, close, openly-gay friends. Despite his abhorrence of that way of life, it didn't negate friendship with those predisposed to this sexual orientation. He had lost these two friends to HIV/AIDS in the 1980s.

Gay marriage advocates tried to make minced meat of him for his public stands, but Jensen refused to budge or be intimidated. Instead, as often as they hit the ball to his court, he returned it to them neatly. Constantly, he argued "forcefully that gay marriage was an impossibility." "Marriage," he contented, "requires a sexual consummation." Jensen didn't see why people should deny "that is what men and women do." When pressed to define what he meant by "consummation," he retorted, "How do two men have sexual union?" Refusing to let go until his opponents saw the illogicality of their reasoning, he said, "You have joined a couple of people together at a spot where they shouldn't be joined together, really."[3]

Jensen wasn't at the 1998 Lambeth Conference. If he had been, it was clear on which side he would have voted in the human sexuality debate. Since becoming the archbishop of Sydney, he was as consistent in his view as he was vocal in his public utterances damning homosexuality. His opposition before, during, and after the Nairobi consultative meeting was steadfast. He was even willing to take roles that were more visible on the anti-gay issue.

In contrast was the elderly and senior Rt. Rev. Donald Harvey, a retired Canadian bishop. Harvey was the archetypical "old soldier that never dies." He was five years older than Jensen, who was born in 1943. Harvey was also six years ahead of the younger man in priestly vocation. Ordained in 1964, the relatively junior Jensen trailed behind in 1970. Incidentally, both had been teachers. After his university education, the Canadian served briefly as a schoolteacher. But the bulk of his working life, spanning nearly thirty years, was spent in ministering and teaching the gospel. Besides serving in various parishes in Newfoundland and Labrador, he was for a six-year period a lecturer in English language and literature at the Memorial University of Newfoundland as well as the university's chaplain. He also did some teaching in pastoral theology at Queen's College, St. John's, Newfoundland.

It's interesting to compare him with Archbishop Rowan Williams. Both shared an interest in the work and life of John Keble. The two possessed creative minds with flair for poetry. But that's where their similarities ended. Harvey's interest in Keble stemmed from a scholarly and theological point of view. It was different from the social action perspective that was Williams' entry-point to the iconoclastic preacher. Twenty-three years of engaging in parish work left Harvey wanting to retool through post-graduate study. This had led to a master of arts in 1987, with his dissertation focusing on the life and poetry of the Reverend John Keble. Harvey didn't just study

3. Snow, "Exit Jensen, Enigma and True Believer."

Keble, but was a student of his theological school as well. He viewed the Church as greater than an ordinary vessel that society could use as an instrument of convenience.

On his elevation to the episcopate in 1993, Harvey kept to his theological ideals with an undiluted passion. He was one of the forty-one bishops from Canada who attended the 1998 Lambeth Conference. Unsurprisingly, he was among the twenty-four majority bishops who refused to be part of the minority seventeen dissidents who promised to overturn the Communion's decision on human sexuality. When Bishop Michael Ingham, the bishop of New Westminster, made the unilateral decision to bless same-sex unions in the diocese in 2002, it affronted him. Harvey retired in 2004 at the mandatory age of 70. Nevertheless, this did not mark the expiration of his interest in revisionism of the Bible within the Canadian church. A month before the meeting, in November 2007, he relinquished his ministry in the Anglican Church of Canada. This was in line with the canon of the church. He refused, however, to watch from the sidelines, gaping at the impasse. Cheerily, the Anglican Church of the Southern Cone, under Archbishop Gregory Venables, welcomed Harvey. Having him was a blessing and morale booster to the Canadian Anglicans who were being persecuted for dissenting from the pro-gay stand of the top hierarchy of their church. Harvey became a bishop of the Southern Cone as a volunteer. As the moderator bishop, his duty was to offer episcopal oversight to a number of Canadian Anglican parishes that could no longer stand the polluting doctrinal influence of the Anglican Church of Canada. This was how he found his way to the table.

Next was the Most Rev. Nicholas Okoh, a Nigerian archbishop.[4] Like the Church of England, with two archbishops (the archbishop of York and the archbishop of Canterbury, who is primate of All England), Nigeria had multiple archbishops, with Okoh as one of the ten. Concurrently, he was the bishop of the Asaba Diocese, an area in the oil-rich Niger Delta, as well as the archbishop of Bendel, overseeing substantial territory.

Okoh was to succeed Akinola as the head of the Nigerian church, and it was obvious that the Nigerian primate was grooming his younger colleague the way that his own predecessor, the late Most Rev. Abiodun Adetiloye, had prepared him, without giving Akinola any hint of the planned succession. Okoh, who was 52 years-old then, had grown from severe childhood poverty to become one of the leaders of the Nigerian church. A son of two peasant farmers, he seemed to have been blessed with a warrior instinct. As he fought against early life deprivations, he also participated in the Nigerian Civil War that ended in 1970. He was almost a victim of post-war traumatic effect. Luckily, he escaped any serious damage. He almost lost his faith in Christianity during the war but was able to regain it when he read the Bible from Genesis to Revelation in 1971. That singular act marked a turning point, with his conversion in 1971 and subsequent confirmation in 1975.

4. "The Most Revd. Nicholas Dikeriehi Orogodo Okoh," https://anglican-nig.org/the-primate/; https://en.wikipedia.org/wiki/Nicholas_Okoh.

For a brief period between 1975 and 1976, he served as a freelance minister and evangelist as he moved toward seminary, the Immanuel College, Ibadan, where he undertook pastoral studies from 1976 to 1979. Then, he completed undergraduate and postgraduate degrees at the University of Ibadan in 1982 and 1985 respectively. Progressively, he moved higher up in the two vocations of his life, the priesthood and the military. He was ordained a deacon in 1979, became a priest in 1980, a canon in 1987, an archdeacon in 1991, a consecrated bishop in May 2001, and an elected archbishop in 2005. Matching that systematic rise in the priesthood was his equal advancement in the Nigerian Army. He was commissioned a lieutenant in 1982, rose to the position of a captain in 1986, promoted to major in 1991, and elevated as a lieutenant colonel in 1996. Twenty-five years as a priest and a greater period in the military had ingrained in Okoh the virtue of personal and professional loyalty. He showed loyalty to the Scripture as a priest and loyalty to the country as a gentleman officer of the Nigerian Army. It was his background of unquestionable loyalty, of which he was not particularly aware at the time, which brought Okoh to the table with some of the notable international leaders of the Anglican Church.

There was also the Most Rev. Donald Mtetemela.[5] Strictly speaking, Mtetemela couldn't be described as a new face around that table since he'd been the archbishop of Tanzania since 1998 and a member of the Council of Anglican Provinces in Africa as well as of the Global South primates. He was not only at the 1998 Lambeth Conference, but also, from the beginning of the crisis, he had vocally objected to the pro-homosexuality policies of the Episcopal Church of the United States and the Anglican Church of Canada. Mtetemela was a rugged priest and a dogged fighter. The greater part of his thirty-six years in ministry prior to the Nairobi meeting had seen him engaging in quiet but zealous evangelism and church planting in his country. Minimal attention from the media had helped him escape the radar of the Western churches. Yet Mtetemela was as formidable as any of the Anglican global leaders gathered in the room or outside it. Resolutely, he was opposed to any form of revisionism regarding the Bible, and he wouldn't shrink from being combative against anyone sullying the integrity of the Anglican Communion through perversion of the Church's teaching. Unassuming as his nature and image were, it was a mistake to presume him to be a lily-livered fighter in the Anglican crisis.

The same self-effacing nature characterized Canon. Dr. Vinay Samuel,[6] director of the Oxford Centre for Religion and Public Life (OCRPL). Samuel, an Indian and an ordained Anglican priest, was also the founder and past executive director of the Oxford Centre of Mission Studies (OCMS). His area of interest was the academic investigation of missions. Internationally, he was a respected missiologist and theologian,

5. https://en.wikipedia.org/wiki/Donald_Mtetemela.

6. Notes and minutes of the "Meeting at Truro Church" July 22–23, 2003 between Archbishop Peter Akinola and Bishop Bob Duncan, Martyn Minns, Vinay Samuel and 60 other participants, from the personal archive of Archbishop Akinola.

a crosscutting work blending theoretical and practical theology that helped in the understanding of how to synergize mission, culture, and strategy. People like Samuel are best left to work in the laboratory of ideas, thinking and provoking thoughts. In fact, he started out as executive director of the International Fellowship of Evangelical Mission Theologians, which had OCMS at its research and study center. The OCMS also served as a training center for mission practitioners from the Global South. Samuel's presence at the Nairobi meeting brought a unique perspective to the discussion.

The dozen men and Akinola gathered around the table for an engaging discussion. Detailed, thorough, and exhaustive was their deliberation while the outcome of their conversation was predictable. Everybody at the table felt the same way about the intractability of the Communion's crisis. Akinola, however, held his views to himself temporarily, preferring to draw from the wisdom of his colleagues. Jensen spoke first. He saw no redeeming features in the attitude of the two churches. He believed that there would be no end to the boondoggle to which the Communion had been subjected. The blunt reaction of Kolini was that further talks were useless. Mtetemela felt the two churches had exhausted the patience of everybody. Nzimbi's position was that decisive action must be taken to end the continued pampering of those subjecting the Communion to ridicule. Though new, Okoh equally felt that it was time for action. The unending guile had tired Orombi. Attwood's feelings were that he had seen enough of the con game to know that it would never stop. Duncan had worn the shoe and experienced the pains of being at the epicenter of the crisis. Harvey's view was that the Canadian church's affliction was no less chronic than that of its American counterpart. Minns believed it was time to act in self-defence. Samuel's fear was for the future of the Anglican Church. Above all, Sugden saw no bright lights coming from the dark clouds casting a spell over Canterbury and continuing to be spread to the Communion.

They arrived at a unanimous decision. Everyone was tired and frustrated about the depressing situation. Somberly, they looked at the tortuous road they had taken. "We have had countless meetings, issued numerous counsels and communiques to no avail," they recalled. It had become obvious to them that Archbishop Williams did not intend to give a second thought to his decisions that were further aggravating tension within the Communion. They had to deal with Williams' foreclosure of their "repeated request to meet together as Primates to discern a way forward." Instead, he had gone ahead to handpick "facilitators and a sub-group of primates."

Provocative all the more was his "Advent letter." He had made emphatically clear in the letter the unlikelihood of disciplinary action being taken against the American church, a position that stood alongside the questionable obstinacy of his other decision, to bar the bishops opposing the pro-gay stand of the American church from the Lambeth Conference. To the men in the gathering, several of the archbishop of Canterbury's latest actions further deepened the frictions from his numerous previous insulting decisions. He put the final period on his condescending attitude. It amounted to pushing them to the limit.

As a result, they agreed that the time had come "to chart the future for the orthodox within the Global Anglican community." Enough of the "chaos and compromise," they resolved. It was at this point that they stopped for the day and retired to their rooms at the Hilton Nairobi. Later, his Nigerian colleague Archbishop Nicholas Okoh joined Akinola in his room. Their conversation drifted from subject to subject initially. Later, it strayed to a review of their meeting earlier in the day. The frustrations, agonies, depression, and annoyance shared by all around the table over the way the Communion's crisis was being disastrously managed was brought back again. Then Okoh, in something akin to a burst of divine inspiration, looked at his boss and said: "Perhaps what they are telling us is to have the Global Anglican Future Conference." Akinola repeated the phrase—"Global Anglican Future Conference."

"Yes," Okoh replied, "GAFCON" for short.

The Nigerian primate was fascinated. He was intrigued. He was charmed by the name, "Global Anglican Future Conference" and the acronym "GAFCON." They were a cinch! They captured the goal and essence of what they needed to do.

The following morning when they reconvened, there was no belaboring the point any further. The meeting accepted and adopted the idea—especially in the light of the "pastoral responsibility," which they believed they owed "to our bishops and wives and people." They felt there was a compelling need to bring them "together around the central and unchanging tenets of the Anglican confession of faith." Collectively, they began examining the modalities for the Conference.

GAFCON, they agreed, would be a medium for the "gospel of power and transformation." It should serve as an avenue "to inform and inspire invited leaders." Importantly, the platform should be a means for them, together, "to shape the future, reform the church and transform persons, communities and societies." They stressed that paramount to the coming together must be the inseparability of their faith and the core of their belief—"the gospel of our Lord Jesus Christ." An "invitation [was to] be extended to bishops and their wives, senior clergy and laity, including the next generation of young leaders" in the Anglican Communion. They chose June, a month before the Lambeth Conference, to converge for the Conference, with Jerusalem as its venue. This, certainly, was a *coup d'arret*, a counter attack intended to take advantage of the Williams' preemptive attack.

It is difficult to find in living memory a time when the situation reached such a disturbing climax within the Anglican Communion. Though in 1997, the Global South had held the second Encounter ahead of the 1998 Lambeth Conference, the situation obtaining was totally different. There was no widespread atmosphere of dissatisfaction within the Communion prior to the conference while participation did not extend beyond the Global South. This time around, the global Anglican community seemed like a Communion divided into two. GAFCON went beyond a regional grouping because it was intended to be broader and wider with participation expected from all groups and regions in the Communion. In terms of focus, from GAFCON's projected outlook, the Conference was intended to go beyond addressing the gay issue. It was to mark a revolutionary step forward in defence of the faith, the gospel, and, importantly, their cherished Anglican heritage.

Right there and then, the men began to sort the diverse operational and logistical challenges into different categories. The first major task centred on planning and coordination of the Conference. They wanted a venue that was most convenient for the Conference. A place that readily suggested itself was Israel, their preference being somewhere outside the city proper if they could get a suitable venue. They wanted a pilgrimage-like atmosphere for the event. In order words, their desire was deep spiritual content for the Conference, to make it like a "pilgrimage to the Holy Land" that would help participants "reestablish our Biblical roots." The key elements considered, the men divided themselves into groups as tasks were apportioned.

Archbishops Akinola and Jensen and Canon Sugden were given the responsibility of undertaking a preliminary visit to Jerusalem between January 11 and 16, 2008. They were to meet with Bishop Suheil Dawani, the bishop in charge of the Holy City. But before then, on Christmas Eve 2007, Jensen was to break the news of the Conference. They agreed to have the list of "names of attendees by March 1, 2008." This brought their Kenya meeting to an end as they resolved to meet next in Heathrow, London, from March 11 to 13, 2008.

Apparently, Akinola and the duo of Archbishops Mouneer Anis and John Crew had disagreed on an idea that Akinola had brought before the twelve men for discussion. Akinola, Anis, and Crew constituted the "Three Musketeers," the three most important functionaries in the life of the Global South. They held the positions of chairman, treasurer, and secretary respectively. On October 20–21, 2007, the Global South primates had made a trip to China stemming from an invitation extended by the State Administration for Religious Affairs of the People's Republic of China. Unanimously, the primates agreed to honor the request. Their stand was that the tour would serve "as an encouragement to the church in China."[7] Many may not know that the Communist country has a long history with Christianity. The encounter dated back to the seventh century during the Tang dynasty. Mainland China had early missionary contact with different Anglican agencies. Jostling and competing were British agencies, American Church Mission, the Church of England in Canada, and the Chinese Church itself, which had its reserved area. Despite that early beginning, however, the Church didn't make much progress in China. Christianity failed to flourish there. The Global South primates considered the invitation, therefore, an opportunity to "introduce the Chinese government to non-Western Christianity" and to take advantage of

---

7. "Anglicans Set to Renew Links with Chinese Christians as Archbishops Pay Mission Exploratory Visit."

the country's turnaround from isolationism to becoming more "open" and establishing more contact with the outside world.

Nine Global South primates, including Anis and Chew, formed the touring party. During the trip, Akinola had sampled the opinion of his two closest colleagues in the leadership of the Global South on the propriety of having their own alternative gathering to the Lambeth Conference. Anis was ambivalent regarding the idea. He was neither for nor against it. Though distressed with the "new theological direction of the North American churches and the lack of discipline" in the Communion, and also of the opinion that it's "important that the orthodox Anglicans should meet and discuss the challenges before us," still, he had strong reservations about the "timing and the venue of such a meeting."[8]

Anis seemed to have misconstrued Akinola's idea. He perceived it as being deeper and farther beyond the ordinary deliberation of like-minded leaders of the Communion that the latter had in mind. His view was that "any discussion of a structured network for orthodox Anglicans with statements of faith, constitution and organisational structure needs proper preparation." Clearly, he was assuming the idea was a step toward establishing a schismatic organization, a kind of breakaway faction from the Anglican Communion. Akinola disabused him. The idea, he explained, was to have a forum for the orthodox bishops who would not go the Lambeth Conference to come together, share views, and draw inspiration from their collective wisdom on the way forward as to how to rescue the Communion from the intractable crisis plaguing it.

The three men—Akinola, Anis, and Chew—didn't resolve the matter in China, as evidenced by an exchange of letters between them. Anis still expressed his reservation in his missive. Once more, Akinola disabused his colleague about the wrong notion he was holding concerning the Conference.[9] Akinola was emphatic that his idea was far away from having a parallel organization. "We are not at that point yet," he stressed. Indeed, he reiterated that the divergent ideas held by many of them on the way to resolve the crisis should illustrate that "we need to meet in June."

Addressing the issue of "timing," Akinola didn't think it right that the conference should be held immediately before or after the Lambeth Conference. Anis had suggested that they hold the Conference after the Lambeth Conference. "I think it would rather be too impetuous," Akinola had pointed out. "Our meeting must not be in reaction to Lambeth," he indicated. Rather, he said, their goals should focus on how "to set the agenda of the gospel first," followed by how to "provide the spiritual care" to the bishops in need of encouragement, which, he was sure, the conference they were considering would achieve.

---

8. Letter to Archbishop Mouneer Anis on GAFCON (exact date not indicated); Follow-up letter on the Nairobi Consultation (exact date not indicated); "Letter from Archbishop Peter J. Akinola to the Global South Primates" (exact date not stated).

9. Letter to Archbishop Mouneer Anis on GAFCON (exact date not indicated).

Anis wasn't at the Nairobi meeting. However, his views were adequately present-ed.[10] Indeed, Anis had sent copies of the letter he wrote Akinola to the other primates in the Global South. Nonetheless, since the Kenyan meeting had reached a consensus that the Conference should proceed, Akinola made this known to him through a let-ter, copies of which he made available to other primates. The Global South chair em-barked on a further step: another letter to all the Global South primates.[11] Essentially, the correspondence was to inform them about the reasons, motives, goals, date, and venue of GAFCON.

Archbishop John Chew had expressed similar ill feelings about the conference as Anis's, especially on the question of "timing." In the letter to his Global South col-leagues conveying the idea of the Conference, Akinola openly acknowledged Chew's position. However, he stated the decision of the Nairobi meeting, which was not to delay or postpone the Conference. On top of this, Akinola also wrote The Most Rev. Suheil Dawani, the archbishop of Jerusalem. Dawani was reported to have been critical of the Conference occurring in his territory. It's odd that a man whose daily existence was surrounded by turmoil, and whose life, career, and rise to the top were governed by dramatic happenings would be afraid of storms. But he was new in the episcopate, barely eight months in office at the time, making his cautious stance understandable.

Dawani was the fourteenth Anglican bishop in Jerusalem.[12] He emerged on April 15, 2007, after a dramatic election process. He was not the favored candidate of his predecessor, the Rt. Rev. Bishop Riah Abu-Assal of Nazareth, who, according to the constitution of the diocese, had to retire at age 68. Two years before retirement, a coadjutor bishop must be elected to facilitate a smooth and orderly succession, and enable a time of learning for both predecessor and successor. Unfortunately, Dawani didn't have the support of his predecessor, whose favorite candidate was Canon Kamal Farah, whom he endorsed publicly. Eventually, there were three candidates—Abu-As-sal's favored candidate, Farah; Suheil Dawani; and Rev. Fayeq Hadad. The first round of voting was tough, with no clear winner emerging. It went to second round with Canons Farah and Dawani left to compete. In a dramatic surprise, Dawani floored Farah with a sizeable vote of 47 to 34.

Once elected, the drama continued as he lived in the tense atmosphere that char-acterized daily life in Jerusalem. The Episcopal Diocese of Jerusalem constituted one of the smaller denominations in the Middle East. It had only 7,000 Anglicans, but it covered Israel, Palestine, Jordan, Syria, and Lebanon.[13] Notwithstanding its small size, the church was active, "with 35 service institutions, 29 parishes, 1500 employees, 200 hospital beds and 6000 students." All these were distributed throughout the five

10. Minutes of meetings, notes, and letters regarding GAFON.

11. "Letter from Archbishop Peter J. Akinola to the Global South Primates."

12. The Most Revd Suheil Dawani http://j-diocese.org/index.php?lang=en&page=1299404835564; https://en.wikipedia.org/wiki/Suheil_Dawani.

13. http://www.j-diocese.org/.

countries, including Gaza. Apart from the overall leadership of the churches under his episcopate, Dawani was also chairman of the thirty-five institutions providing education and healthcare services. Coupled with this was his having to walk a tightrope in the multicultural, multi-faith and multiethnic environment constantly under tension and in a perpetual state of anxiety and unrest.

Born in Nablus, West Bank, in 1951, ordained as a priest in 1977, his thirty-one years of priesthood had resulted in his being prominent in many ecumenical and interfaith organizations. For instance, he joined with other Jerusalem churches in organizing six summer camps for Muslim and Christian children. At the Communion level, he was also working with the archbishop of Canterbury on Anglican and interfaith issues. And Dawani was one of the thirteen recognized Heads of Churches in Israel. By nature and inclination, he was a moderate. He sued for peace and preached reconciliation, with a strong disposition toward promoting the Church as a mediating Body, especially in his home environment, a region prone to violence and persistent conflict. It's therefore understandable that he was anxious about GAFCON's convening in Jerusalem.

Akinola's letter to him was merely to provide information about the intention of the Nairobi group to convene the conference in Jerusalem.[14] Once more, he honestly admitted the position of Mouneer Anis to Dawani, but reiterated the decision of the group to go ahead. Evidently, the planning committee had been working behind the scenes, even beyond the concerns of those with anxieties over the Conference. As yet, no specific dates were fixed for the conference, but now, in the letter to Dawani, the Nigerian church leader was quite specific, proposing June 15–22, 2008. Then he informed his Jerusalem counterpart of the planned visit the "leadership team" of the conference would be making to Jerusalem, January 11–15, 2008, to brief him on other arrangements.

Poor Archbishop Dawani! By the time he hosted Archbishops Akinola and Jensen at the scheduled talks, he was already pushed into a tight corner.[15] Akinola and Jensen had arrived on Tuesday, January 15, 2008, as planned. That same evening, they called on their host at the bishop's house. Dawani harbored concerns, but he succeeded to a reasonable extent in hiding his distress with affability when he met the two men. The conference notification and its timing had unsettled him. He was caught unaware, cornered because of the "little time to respond." The announcement, to him, was made "at a difficult time of the year, the Christmas Eve." He considered it a gravely inopportune time to have such a huge issue dumped on him. Jensen was full

14. Akinola, "Letter to Bishop Suheil," from the personal papers and archive of Archbishop Peter Akinola.

15. Akinola, "Itinerary and agenda during visit to Jerusalem between January 11 & 15, 2008"; "Transcript of Archbishop Akinola's presentation to Bishop Dawani"; "Notes towards a communique from Archbishop Akinola and Dawani By gathering"; Draft Report of Working Party on Conference Delivery; "Draft Agenda," Theological Resource Team Meeting , Lagos, January 28–30, from personal papers and archive of Archbishop Peter Akinola.

of apologies, explaining that the announcement had to be rushed because the "news of the meeting had begun to leak and the need to release authentic information was pressing." Both men assured him of their personal esteem for him as well as that of the general leadership of GAFCON.

The trio settled down to a conference to learn "at first hand what the concerns of the Bishop are." Akinola and Jensen desired to explore ways through which they could mutually "consider what he has asked of them, [and] what can be done to ameliorate" Dawani's concerns. Whatever Dawani's concerns were, one area they wanted their host to be reassured was that they were strictly committed to "guard against any ill consequences" for him and the church in his home city. They wanted him to be at ease, "in particular, [that] it is no wish of those organising the Conference to increase tensions around or within the local Church." Nor were they coming to Jerusalem "to decrease [the church's] standing within the community." Patiently listening, Dawani was still reluctant to let go of his "reservations about the venue." In particular, he was afraid that the conference "would demonstrate a division in the church to heads of local Christian churches, to the inter-faith partners, and could be misused by the political parties."

On the other hand, he recognized that coming to the "Holy Land reflects the grief of many in the Communion over the events of the last five years." He, too, shared "the desire to seek the Lord's will by gathering together." But he made it clear that he "would prefer the Bishops to attend the Lambeth Conference." At the end, serious as Dawani's concerns were regarding the "wisdom of the Conference at this time and in this place," he conceded that "the Holy Land ought to be the venue." He assured them that he would go along with them. He promised he would be "willing to meet the Leadership team on their arrival, pray with them, and to do all he can to welcome them as fellow-Anglicans to Jerusalem."

That was pleasing to the duo. Appreciative of their host's kind consideration, they urged him not to entertain any fear. "The presence of Anglicans from all over the world in Jerusalem is capable of enriching not diminishing the local church," they told him in a confident tone. As they parted, they assured him they would work with "his people and all the Anglicans in Jerusalem as far as possible."

Meeting Dawani was, however, not the sole reason for the duo's visit to Israel. Their second day had a loaded itinerary of arranging the logistics for the conference. Over breakfast, they met with Robin Aldridge, head of the Church's Ministry to the Jews, which represented the oldest Anglican presence in Jerusalem. From there, they conferred with the deputy director at the Ministry of Tourism, Rafael Ben Hur. There-after, they paid a courtesy visit to the Papal Nuncio before undertaking an excursion to the holy sites. They came back to assess available hotels and facilities, agreeing on the one they considered suitable. The challenge was that the hotel was booked for the period they desired, so they had to alter the dates.

Similar predicaments confronted them with connecting flights from different parts of the world to Israel. Most would arrive either late in the morning or in the afternoon, meaning that arrival of many delegates would be delayed. Compounding the travel logistics was the Sabbath. By the custom of the Jewish people, all activities are suspended during its observance, so the ideal time for the conference would be the weekdays. The last part of their visit was taken up by discussion with a travel agency on travel and visa arrangements, particularly for the African delegates. By the allocated number of delegates from different regions, Africa had the lion's share with 65%, with countries of Anglo descent accounting for 12%, while the Indian subcontinent had the least, at 6.7%. For Akinola and Jensen, from their experience of the preliminary tour, the conference had a good outlook—so far, so good.

Added to this, by the end of January, GAFCON's Theological Resource Team had worked out the draft program for the conference.[16] At the Lagos summit, January 28–30, 2008, the team worked feverishly to have a "summary theological document for GAFCON." Nigerian Archbishop Okoh led the discussion on "finalizing agenda, identifying expectations and outcomes," including "mapping Anglican identity today" against the background of "challenges, components, convictions and concerns." Ashley Null followed with exploration of the "Anglican Reformation and its relevance for us today," while Vinay Samuel brought in his expertise in wrapping up the session. Stephen Noll worked on the issue of "Anglican orthodoxy," while Chris Sugden provided background material on "gospel and culture." Mike Ovey examined "secularism and the church," with Joel Obetia honing in on "Anglican worship."

For two days, they discussed intensely and brainstormed extensively, producing the road map and program for GAFCON. The committee agreed that every theme would have four connected workshops with lead speakers. The lead speakers would be people endowed with the requisite knowledge, depth, exposure, and capacity for quality discussions. There were also to be other programs on the side, one for wives and another for musicians and worship leaders. The men at the Lagos gathering could pat themselves on the back at the end of the two days, happy that GAFCON's program was ready—at least on paper. The only outstanding part was the Leadership Team's ratification. The focus, therefore, shifted to Oxford, where top leaders of the team were scheduled to meet in March.

Ahead of the March meeting in England was the gathering of the Global South Primates Steering Committee. Differences of opinion had seemingly developed among them ever since the GAFCON initiative began. Known to have reservations concerning the conference were Archbishops Mouneer Anis and John Chew, most especially concerning its timing. Of course, Archbishops Akinola, Venables, and Kolini were not only strong proponents of the idea but were its leading lights. The five

---

16. "Draft Report of Working Party on Conference Delivery" and "Draft Agenda" from the Theological Resource Team Meeting, Lagos, January 28–30, 2008, from personal papers and archive of Archbishop Peter Akinola.

of them—the pro and those with reservations—had converged in Oxford, and it was clear the assembly was a fence-mending one. For two days, March 13–15, 2008, they secluded themselves "for some heart to heart conversations," as they admitted.[17] One fear was that GAFCON might weaken or overshadow the Global South. The communique issued after the meeting confirmed the concern. And this made what happened next instructive.

In an honest acknowledgment, the assembly admitted that "initiatives and challenges have emerged which could lead to further fragmentation and disintegration of the Communion." Shunning hypocrisy, they admitted that such a development would not augur well for the Church, "which is already in the nadir of collegial trust and confidence." The reservation of Anis and Chew about the "inappropriate timing" of GAFCON apparently could not be kept away from the communique. The point was restated. The instructive aspect of the meeting, however, was that, divided as the primates were, they sat together to "share frankly and converse in collegial accountability." There was no doubt that the group had entered the meeting at odds with each other on the GAFCON issue, but succeeded in striking a mutual understanding in the end.

It was obvious that the continued relevance of the Global South in the face of the emergence of GAFCON was paramount to one side of the table. But to the credit of the leaders, they were able to quickly and amicably resolve their differences. Trust and confidence was restored, allowing respect for each side's point of view. "We were able to focus in unity on the original spirit, vision and vocation of the Global South in the Anglican Communion," they announced enthusiastically. GAFCON or no GAFCON, collectively they agreed not to let go of their Global South bond, for it was a relationship that "had developed and deepened since the fateful event of November 2003." So said the statement. As such, they chose not to allow minor differences to disrupt the bond of unity existing between them.

Ultimately, the discussion turned to GAFCON, which had emerged as the latest major development within the Communion. Expecting Akinola and other primates supporting the initiative to back down was an illusion. The walk to Golgotha had taken them a long time but finally, they had reached the juncture where there was no turning back. Through their "conversations together and clarifications made," they led their colleagues to "understand and appreciate the principled reasons for participation in GAFCON (June 2008)." They stressed that GAFCON and the Lambeth Conference had "different perspectives." The two were neither synonyms nor antonyms to each other. Each had a life of its own, with separate identity and focus. And they urged their fellow GAFCON participants "to bear in mind the under-girding and wider framework of the united vocation and mission of the Global South for the life and witness of the wider Anglican Communion."

17. "Statement from the Global South Primates Steering Committee, London," March 13–15, 2008, from the papers and archive of Archbishop Peter Akinola.

The pro-GAFCON primates, however, were willing to explore further conciliation on the matter. The three of them on the side of GAFCON and the two with reservations agreed unanimously, as evidenced by the communique, that "the primatial leadership of the GAFCON recognises and supports the significance of the Windsor-Covenant process." They warned that "the initiative and need for GAFCON critically serves to remind us that the 'torn fabric at the deepest level of the Anglican Communion is still a living reality.'" The primates' differences didn't stand in the way of their collectively agreeing that neither GAFCON nor Lambeth symbolized the end to the gloom plaguing the Church. They emphasized that "unless the primary reason for the current crisis and division in the Communion is properly addressed, the common life of the Communion cannot be expected to continue normally."

On several occasions, Akinola had expressed same sentiments to Canterbury's Archbishop Williams—the same position he had conveyed to America's Presiding Bishop Schori when they exchanged letters on the CANA issue. To him, the communique was repeating the obvious. Overall, the March 2008 meeting of the five Global South primates ended amicably. They had arrived at the room divided. But they had talked together, reasoned together, and together had resolved the knotty issues confronting them. None stuck to his gun. Across the table, they shared wise counsel and tolerance. They agreed to disagree at certain points and then settled for compromises and negotiated settlement. No one side gloried in victory while the other sulked in defeat. With charity across the table, they allowed the bigger interest of the Communion to prevail. There was spirit of give and take at the meeting. Those believing in GAFCON didn't let go. They affirmed it as nonnegotiable. Yet they conceded to the pro-Lambeth Conference group the right to exercise their freedom of choice.

Worldwide, the two dates—June and July of 2008—raised serious anxiety within the Anglican Communion. The two coming events—GAFCON and the Lambeth Conference—were big and ominous. It had never happened like this in the past, having two gatherings of Anglicans throughout the world back to back. Still, there were those who felt the Anglican Church could derive benefits from the anomalous situation. Some thought that the Communion might be spurred to a new beginning. The five primates were sanguine in their communique: "We are persuaded that after GAFCON (June 2008) and Lambeth Conference, the primary and urgent task is to move the global Anglican Communion substantially and effectively forward." In the meantime, they agreed to convene the 4th Global South Encounter. Even if they did not all share the aspiration of GAFCON, somehow the infectious spirit of radical change in the air was beginning to catch on among them. Consequently, they decided that the 4th Encounter would be different from all the previous ones. They concluded that it would "have a broadened representation." Incidentally, this was the design of GAFCON too!

26

Still, No Reprieve

Canada, 2007

Surprisingly, through the period of the desperate attempts by Archbishops Mouneer Anis and John Chew to pacify their exasperated Global South colleagues, Canterbury maintained a graveyard dead silence. No clue could be found suggesting Archbishop Rowan Williams tried to reclaim the confidence of his colleagues, whether privately or publicly. The unfortunate irony was that Canada and America continued their assault on the anti-gay groups in their respective countries. They kept tightening the noose around the disagreeing churches, clergy, and members. They extended no reprieve to them. Sadly, again, Canterbury merely looked sideways, refusing to take any official step to halt the belligerency. One consequence was that, preceding the Global South Primates Steering Meeting in London, in February 2008, ten Canadian parishes that were tired of the oppression decided to leave the Anglican Church of Canada.[1] Top on that list was St. John's (Shaughnessy) Anglican Church, Vancouver, the largest Anglican Church in Canada's denomination. The congregation "overwhelmingly voted (97.7%) to break fellowship" with the national church "and their diocesan bishop Michael Ingham, over the issue of homosexuality." They sought refuge from the Anglican Province of the Southern Cone under Archbishop Gregory Venables. Fifteen other parishes made a similar move owing to St. John's bold lead. Every diocese from which these congregations were departing resorted to the usual punitive legal action against them.

Incomprehensibly, the same Canadian church leadership that had wielded the big stick to forestall the purported illegal desertion looked the other way when Synods of the Ottawa, Montreal, and Niagara Dioceses adopted "motions to bless same sex marriages." Boldly and courageously, in November 2007, the embattled churches and

---

1. Anglican Network in Canada, "Global Realignment: A Canadian Chronology," www.anglican-network.ca; Anglican Network in Canada (2007) "Global Realignment—Legal Implications for Clergy and Parishes," www.anglicannetwork.ca.

groups, rather than resort to bemoaning their plight, formed themselves into Anglican Network in Canada (ANiC). ANiC assured "Adequate Episcopal Oversight and Communion connection to biblically faithful Canadian Anglicans in 'serious theological dispute' with their bishop, diocese, or the ACC." Recall that the Global South primates had denied them support in light of the legal technicality that the appropriate organ of their church had yet to make a categorical pronouncement as requested by the Communion. Now, out of their own volition, the beleaguered groups decided that rather than continuing to submit to the oppression, they would act decisively. One clarification they made was that the ANiC did not intend to expend unnecessary energy and resources on legal tussles. "We have no intention of suing the ACC," they said point-blank. Nevertheless, ardently they declared, "We will vigorously defend our members."

In the meantime, they worked hard to amass a legal team of volunteers as well as "a legal fund in the amount of $1 million." Nevertheless, their first option remained a peaceful resolution. They asked their members to continue to "pray for an act of grace and generosity by the Anglican Church of Canada." In pursuing the peace process, they requested "the ACC to grant a 90 day period of grace, during which we ask that no bishops take hostile actions against the parishes." The interregnum, they urged, should be used for "discussing the crisis and their options." The ANiC had apparently learned from the experience of their American colleagues. Frankly, they told the churches concerned to "remember, at the end of the day" that they could be "called to leave the property behind." Indeed, by March 2008 the predicted actions commenced. A series of simultaneous malicious court cases was launched against the departing parishes.

Parallel to the nasty events unfolding in Canada, the same unrelenting, horrid assault was being perpetrated in America. That same month of March, the House of Bishops decided to depose two bishops. As expected, the duo belonged to the homosexuality-opposing camp. The first was the Rt. Rev. William J. Cox.[2] In the secular world, Cox's case would have provoked jurisprudential debate. It was a case of witch hunt, a serious *mala fide*, that is, a trial masterminded by malice, hatred, and sheer wickedness. Cox, who was the retired bishop suffragan of Maryland, at 86, like his contemporary Rt. Rev. Donald Harvey of Canada, had cut short his retirement to join the fray rocking the Communion. He was opposed to implanting homosexuality into the life of the American church. In April 2005, Christ Church in Overland Park, Kansas, had voted to depart from the American Episcopal Church. They were willing to strike a bargain and agreement with the Diocese of Kansas. For ten years, the church was prepared to pay the sum of $1 million annually as part of the separation agreement in order to be allowed to retain the church's property. The severance pay, it was also believed, would buy the church's clergy their freedom of canonical obedience to the Episcopal Church.

2. Waring, "Retired Bishop William Cox to be Tried by Ecclesiastical Court."

Amid this legal process, Christ Church's clergy decided to affiliate with the Province of Uganda. This was the basis, in June 2005, upon which Cox, at the instance of the primate of Uganda, the Most Rev. Henry Orombi, ordained two priests and a deacon. The ordination and service of confirmation that followed a month later were held at Christ Church in Kansas. Cox's previous two service posts as bishop suffragan were in Maryland, from 1972 to 1980, and in Oklahoma, where he was the assistant bishop from 1980 to 1988. Naturally, Cox had stirred the hornets nest, prompting a swift reaction to his audacity. An allied force confronted the old man to do battle with him. The bishop of Kansas, where the two services were held, and the bishop of Oklahoma, from where he retired, teamed up to put Cox in the box of the accused. And so charges of violating the canons of the church were filed before Presiding Bishop Frank Griswold

Nothing short of such high-handedness should have been expected from the bishop of Kansas, the Rt. Rev. Dean Wolfe. Wolfe's episcopate began in Kansas on January 1, 2004, a year before Cox committed the alleged offence.[3] Wolfe was not at the 1998 Lambeth Conference, nor did he take part in the election of Gene Robinson or the consecration of the openly gay bishop. But he had ingratiated himself with the national leadership of the church. He was vice president of the House of Bishops, chair of its Planning Committee, its delegate to the World Council of Churches, a member of the Presiding Bishop's Council of Advice and of the Joint Committee for Planning and Arrangements for General Convention, including the Pastoral Development Committee. To have such an affront happening in his jurisdiction and for him to keep quiet about it was to jeopardize the opportunities surrounding him. It would be difficult for him to escape culpability, to avoid being considered guilty by association.

Then there was the bishop of Oklahoma, the Rt. Rev. Robert Moody, who was at the 1998 Lambeth Conference.[4] He signed the promise of a new dawn for Anglican gays and lesbians. Once a coadjutor bishop, a position to which he was elected on September 19, 1987, he succeeded his predecessor, the Rt. Rev. Gerald McAllister, in 1989. Both men believed Cox's action was provocative and insolent and warranted his being dragged before Frank Griswold. Perhaps, the unspoken factor that incensed them all the more was the destination of the departing church—the Church of Uganda!

Griswold forwarded the charges to the committee that was supposed to handle them, the "Title IV [disciplinary] Review Committee." The committee succeeded in establishing a prima facie case against Cox, and so he was tried. Griswold, however, had departed, leaving the case in the drawer. His successor, Presiding Bishop Jefferts Schori, didn't expend energy in exhuming the case. A range of punishments could be meted out to Cox. He could have been reprimanded verbally, or, in an extreme judgment, he could have been removed permanently from the ordained ministry. Given the circumstance and leadership with which the American church had found itself,

3. http://www.episcopal-ks.org/bishop/About-Bishop-Dean-E-Wolfe.php.
4. https://en.wikipedia.org/wiki/Episcopal_Diocese_of_Oklahoma.

Cox was deposed predictably. The severity of the punishment spurred allegations by those who saw the penalty as vindictive to say that the trial was not about justice but malice. The House of Bishops was challenged to make public how such a decision could have been reached in the light of the evidence that "the canonical requirement of a majority of those eligible to vote was not met." There was also a scandal arising from the baffling overnight disappearance of cases against two members of the panel.

The two persons accused were Rt. Rev. Charles E. Bennison, Jr., bishop of Pennsylvania, and his Connecticut counterpart, the Rt. Rev. Andrew Smith. Bennison was accused of "withholding financial and legal information" by a group of clergy and lay members in his diocese. On the other hand, Smith was accused of "improperly removing the rector and vestry of St. John's, Bristol." Charges were subsequently preferred against them. Miraculously, the two cases disappeared overnight! The House of Bishops claimed ignorance of them.

A further irony was that Smith was selected to be a member of the trial court in Bishop Cox's case. Though the octogenarian Cox's last act of chivalry seemed to have caused him serious public humiliation, his greatest solace would be a sense of eternal fulfillment that he answered with pride and confidence the call of his conscience and faith. Furthermore, he could also be strengthened in knowing the machination to bring him to ridicule changed nothing regarding the infamy the Episcopal Church had brought to itself. In fact, two years before Cox's humiliation, the religion and ethics editor of the *San Diego Union Tribune,* Sandi Dolbee, had fittingly described the situation in the Episcopal Church as, "A house divided carries on."[5] True to the depiction, Cox's deposition didn't change the reality that even within its own home, things continued to fall apart for the Episcopal Church.

The debacles kept increasing in scope and dimension. Further embarrassment came to the church over the case of the second man put on the firing line after Cox, the Rt. Rev. John-David Schofield, who fought till the end of his life.[6] He refused to submit or be subdued by the tyrannical and oppressive forces that had conquered the American church. He not only damned the travesty but equally braved his numerous trials and ordeals. It would have been pure luck if he had escaped the charade perpetrated to bring his downfall. Schofield was one of America's delegates to the 1998 Lambeth Conference. He was elected bishop of the Episcopal Diocese of San Joaquin in 1988. Schofield maintained a clear distance from his colleagues at the Conference. He shunned their pro-gay pandering, refusing to be part of their perfidious letter.

Back home, he opposed the election of the openly gay Gene Robinson as a bishop. Amid the boiling controversy over the gay issue in the Episcopal Church, Schofield took another action, a decisive one. He supported the view of the majority in his diocese during the diocesan convention on December 8, 2007. The delegates had voted to leave the Episcopal Church to establish a brand new Anglican Diocese

5. Dolbee, "A House Divided Carries On."

6. https://en.wikipedia.org/wiki/John-David_Schofield.

of San Joaquin.[7] They weren't merely changing the name. They wanted to be part of the majority of worldwide Anglicans. Those differing, the minority few clergy and laity who preferred to continue with the old Episcopal Diocese of San Joaquin, were left to remain on their own. The separation was not amicable. Litigations had ensued. Nationally, Schofield's diocese had always been regarded as a radical bishopric. With his tough character, Schofield complemented the diocese and vice versa. Both the congregation and their shepherd were never afraid to stand alone on matters of scriptural purity. When others within the Episcopal Church succumbed to the ordination of women as a *fait accompli*, the Diocese of San Joaquin was at the lead of those that refused to bow to the popular culture. The two other dioceses on the same path were the Dioceses of Quincy and Fort Worth.

Thus, understandably, it was only a matter of time before Schofield and Schori become entangled in a dartboard game. The day arrived on January 11, 2008.[8] Schofield was suspended, or as was fashionable in the ecclesial language, inhibited by Presiding Bishop Schori. His duties and office as bishop were taken away from him. In a surprising and valiant heroic reaction, Schofield pushed back at Schori. He resigned. He vacated his membership in the American House of Bishops on March 1, 2008. He was not without his alternative plans, of course. The former bishop of the Episcopal Diocese of San Joaquin now became bishop of the Anglican Diocese of San Joaquin, declaring that all former documents and actions remained valid. Schori could not bear the insouciance. Coincidentally, Schofield's deposition occurred a day before the London meeting of the Global South Primates Steering Committee, on March 12, 2008, where mitigating the crisis within the Communion was the prime subject. Though arrogated to the House of Bishops, the invisible hand behind Schofield's ouster was clear. Schori had maintained that "the Episcopal Church will continue in the Diocese of San Joaquin, albeit with new leadership."

That new leadership emerged with the resurrection of the retired Bishop of North Carolina, Jerry Lamb, to take Schofield's place. A special diocesan convention was convened on March 29, 2008, which ratified Lamb's election. With the gracious approval of the Executive Council of the Episcopal Church, $700,000 in financial assistance was provided "to help defray the expenses associated with reorganization in San Joaquin." There was an addendum to the windfall that "other dioceses facing similar challenges" would be beneficiaries too.

Seven months later, the real motive of the onslaught against Schofield emerged at the regular convention of the San Joaquin diocese. In October 2008, the hidden lie became an open truth. The diocese endorsed creation of the "equality commission." The work of the commission was to uphold and protect the marginalized communities within the diocese. Under it were women, several ethnic groups, and undoubtedly,

7. https://en.wikipedia.org/wiki/Anglican_Diocese_of_San_Joaquin_(ACNA).

8. Ackerman, "San Joaquin: Bishop John David Schofield Dies"; Matson, "A Man Of Joy, Courage and Prayer: Bishop John David Schofield RIP."

lesbians and gays! That same month, on October 17, 2008, the standing committee extracted the pound of flesh it had been eager to take. The sixteen deacons and thirty-six priests who had opted to realign with the Southern Cone were tried summarily. Their collective offence was abandonment of duty. Consequent to that, Lamb took the expected action, as the fifty-two clergy were dismissed summarily.

Schofield died at 75. He triumphed over his ordeals like a champion warhorse. Both in life and in ministry, he was enigmatic and paradoxical. He confused his critics and excited his admirers. He revealed the solution to the Anglican Communion's crisis. He symbolized the way and the truth regarding the gay crisis in the Anglican Church. Inherent in him was the normal baggage of human weaknesses and fallibilities, which he carried in his life journey. Yet, Schofield's was an instructive life. Part of his inscrutable life almost became an albatross, a subject nearly exposing him to public scandal.

Schofield was suspected of being a homosexual. In their usual style of exposing people in high places through "outing" (a veiled word for blackmail to coerce them to share in the group's identity), Schofield was attacked. An internet article on November 22, 2006, titled "Schofield's Closet" drew attention to this part of his life.[9] The objective of the story was evident. The writer had attacked the respected bishop scathingly, insinuating that, "Many a time, I have asked folks to urge these other gay bishops to 'out themselves.'" Schofield was painted in an unflattering picture, ridiculed as a "self-loathing person who attacks gay men and lesbians!" "This Schofield thing has finally reached the point where I just can't stand it anymore!" the writer cried with spite. Then the sting was released with venom: "Bishop Schofield is a recovering homosexual."

Still, the writer had provided the information that Schofield was "committed to celibacy." Perhaps, yes, there was truth to the claim. On the other hand, it may have been merely a smear campaign. The exact nature of Schofield's sexual orientation remained a matter of imagination and guesswork. He died with his secret. Yet it wouldn't have mattered if truly he did battle same-sex attraction. His life was instructive. Schofield like every human being was not spared his own personal woes. "He was tormented with physical ailments akin to Job," Fr. Matson Dale, who was very familiar with him, revealed.

Furthermore, he carried his cross with a rugged forbearance. Sorrow didn't cripple him; tribulation didn't drive him into a self-destructive path. He once bared his mind to Dale about how "Satan attacked him through his sister until she died and then Satan came after him." The vicissitudes, notwithstanding, he remained a stallion with stellar, stable, and steadfast commitment to his priestly calling. He didn't ask the church to change for him. Wholly, he submitted to the church. He didn't feel the Bible should be tinkered with to accommodate his weakness. He surrendered to the purity of the Word. Sacrosanct to him were the Holy Orders while the Sacrament of Holy Matrimony was indivisible and irreducible to him till his end.

9. Fox, "Schofield's Closet."

Schofield believed in being upright and acting on his convictions. This nearly cost him confirmation as bishop of San Joaquin by the General Convention of the American church. This same pristine value led to his taking a principled stand against Bishop Walter Righter, the right-hand man of the maverick bishop, the Rt. Rev. John Spong, who, in 1990, had ordained the openly gay Barry Stopfel into the diaconate. Schofield's principled stand on the case was that no Convention had sole authority to alter that which was decreed by the Holy Orders and the Sacrament of Holy Matrimony.

What Righter did was wrong, and Schofield had no inhibition in participating in his trial. But from every account of his life, if Schofield felt same-sex attraction, he didn't submit to the flesh. He fought that battle to the end. He denied the flaws that enslaved him and endangered his sacred vow. He exercised control over his weakness, or "brokenness" in ecclesial language. His Spartan discipline gave him courage to speak harsh truth to his fellow citizens. He died conquering death and became bigger in death despite the attempt to tarnish his reputation. Friends mourned the loss of a man whose epitaph was inscribed in gold. He was remembered as a "leader in virtually every organization or movement that has sought to preserve the received Faith." Also, he was a man "larger than life"; a "man of joy and courage"; and, above all, "the last of the princely Bishops."

In 2008, when Schori descended on Schofield, the latter survived all the machinations of the former. None of the weapons she fashioned against him prospered. Schofield was not intimidated, nor did he buckle under the onslaught. Furthermore, if his so-called "outing" as gay had any impact at all, it was negligible. Contrary to expectations, his public image was neither eroded nor corroded. Desirable as it is that leaders in public life be held to public scrutiny, contrived and disingenuous plots to tarnish reputation do no good. It helped that Schofield was a man of strong character. He swallowed the hurt and snubbed the cheap blackmail. Unwaveringly, he "took seriously to his vows as a Successor of the Apostles and a Defender of the Faith once delivered to the Apostles."

Schofield was around to witness GAFCON and its counterpart, the Lambeth Conference, and their outcomes. Despite the onset of ill health, his fighting spirit endured. He soldiered on to be part of those who took the Communion in a new direction after the June Jerusalem GAFCON and the July Lambeth London conference. On the road to the two events, he had been as eager as any leader of the Anglican worldwide Communion, looking forward to these events. The crisis had reached its peak with the two men up front—Nigerian Archbishop Peter Akinola, head of the GAFCON Leadership Team, and Canterbury Archbishop Rowan Williams, convener of the Lambeth Conference—having the answer in their hands. What's going to happen? They were two men positioned to determine the direction in which the worldwide church would go.

27

The Revolutionary Step Forward

Jerusalem, 2008

Not all began well for the Global Anglican Future Conference (GAFCON). But in the end, everything became a thrilling success. The initial hitch was with the Nigerian primate and chair of the GAFCON Leadership Team, Archbishop Peter Akinola himself. The weeklong event was scheduled for June 22–29, 2008, and Akinola, along with his fellow GAFCON leaders, had agreed to arrive four days early for a pre-conference meeting.[1] On June 18, 2008, the team arrived in Israel. Travelling together, they headed to Jordan for the pre-conference summit. The irony was that, though Islamic, Jordan was also significant in Christian history. The country derived its name from the Jordan River, the place where John the Baptist baptized Jesus, and many Christian priests in the Arab countries have a Jordanian background. Nevertheless, in the Middle East, where life is constantly on edge and suspicions among closely proximate nations and people are rife, officials treat both human and vehicular traffic going in and out of their respective territories with utmost scrutiny. Border security often employs extreme measures and procedures.

At one point or another, a traveler might be unlucky enough to encounter a rude, uncivil, provocative, and hostile border official. Well-traveled as he was, Archbishop Akinola had encountered border officials of various temperaments and manners. As far as the Middle East was concerned, he knew the terrain as an accustomed visitor. Some two months earlier, he was in the region to meet with Archbishop Suheil Dawani. Additionally, he had had the responsibility of organizing pilgrimages to Jerusalem for hundreds of Christians during his tenure as chair of the Abuja Christian Pilgrims Welfare Board. Nevertheless, his experience at the Jordanian border on that June 18 was incomparable in insult and indignity for a man of his position.

---

1. Interview with the Most Revd. Peter J. Akinola conducted in his Hilltop home in Abeokuta, Ogun state, Nigeria, in 2008.

He and his traveling party had gone successfully through the immigration post at the Israeli section of the border.[2] From there, they had moved to the Jordanian end, expecting to repeat the process of formal clearance. Before leaving Nigeria, Akinola had ensured that he and those in his team had obtained the required transit visa from Israel to Jordan, and he himself was traveling with a diplomatic passport. By international convention and practice, diplomatic passports confer upon their holders some privileges. They are seen as state officials or representatives of their countries on foreign soil, to be treated with extended courtesy and respect. In this instance, Akinola and his colleagues were merely transiting for a couple of days' stay in Amman before heading back to Jerusalem for the official commencement of GAFCON.

Customs had already cleared their luggage, and they were loaded into their awaiting bus. Delaying them was the return of their passports and other traveling documents by the immigration officials. Suddenly, from the noisy activities in the reception hall, a voice rang out:

"Who is Peter Akinola?" It was a sort of summon rather a question.

Responding, the archbishop followed the escort to an office where he was deposited before a stern looking official. Akinola knew something was wrong immediately. The man sitting before him seemed to be doing his best to conceal the embarrassment written all over him. Of course, Akinola was in his clerical robe. Those two explicit instruments of identity—his religious wear and the diplomatic passport—were impressive, and the official was clearly uncomfortable. He gave the archbishop a thorough visual appraisal and ended with an insulting question.

"Are you Peter Akinola?" he asked.

"Yes, please," the archbishop answered.

A moment of silence extended as if he were wracking his brain to find the next question. After that intervening period, he seemed to get it finally.

"What is your mother's name?" he demanded.

Then it began to dawn on the archbishop that this wasn't a funny development. He wasn't finding it funny either. But still, he kept the anger welling up in him under strict control, and he answered the question. Twice the length of time it had taken him to pose his second question was what it took for him to ask the third—"What is your educational qualification?"

In all of his travels around the world—and they had been numerous—Akinola felt he had not been subjected to this kind of humiliating treatment, not even once! He decided that silence was the best answer. The official couldn't have dared to be this cheeky on his own. He surmised immediately that he was being used, a mere pawn. Akinola decided he was not going to submit to the charade any longer. So he maintained perfect silence. From all indications, it seemed the official was looking forward to this type of reaction from him. It looked as though he was baiting the Nigerian archbishop, stalking him, deliberately provoking him.

2. "How I Was Denied Entry into Jordan."

He went out to join others in the hall. Three hours elapsed! Nothing happened. Others had had their passports and other traveling documents returned to them. Only his was still in custody. After a seemingly interminable period, with its looking as if nothing was going to happen, Akinola became exasperated. He searched out the official. He was in the same office, sitting without any care in the world. Coolly and putting his rage under control, the Nigerian church leader firmly and distinctly told him, "If you do not want me in your country, return my passport to me, please!" The man didn't do so immediately. Another thirty minutes passed. He then disappeared for a brief moment. Akinola felt he had caught him by surprise. He probably wasn't expecting him to be traveling with a diplomatic passport. That had implications as well as consequences that required some damage control. Whoever he had contacted upstairs must have sanctioned his action because as soon as he reappeared, he returned the passport. There was no apology, no regret, nothing whatsoever.

Later, on his return home, Akinola, narrating the ugly incident to the media, said he "did not bow to pressure to report the matter officially to the Federal Government because that would have caused a diplomatic row." The archbishop was as not as tutored as his Western counterparts in the underhanded intrigues that often characterized international politics. Otherwise, he would have known that he had just been shown a sample of international conspiracy. His embarrassment could raise dust internationally in the media, but to expect a diplomatic tussle over it was a remote possibility. Nigeria did not have diplomatic relations with the Hashemite Kingdom of Jordan, and Jordan did not have diplomatic representation in Nigeria.[3] Overseeing Jordan's affairs as its accredited representative in Nigeria was the Democratic Republic of Algeria. Had the Nigerian Foreign Affairs Ministry summoned the Algerian ambassador (representing the Jordanian government) to lodge a complaint, the effect would have been negligible.

To put the matter in context, Jordan was like a puppet of the West. The country was pro-West, and her relationship with the United Kingdom and the United States made Jordan a virtual satellite of the two countries. The Jordanian royal family's ties with Britain were close, almost to the level of consanguinity. British blood flowed in King Abdullah as his mother, Princess Muna, was British by birth. His wife, Queen Noor, maintained a permanent country house in Berkshire. Besides, the British provided training and other services to the Jordanian armed forces. Consequently, this was a matter of the UK telling her surrogate what to do. The same with the United States, with which Jordan's relationship was beyond cordiality. The US upheld a favorable policy toward the Arab country. Jordan maintained an embassy in Washington, DC, and the United States reciprocated with an embassy in Amman. With this linkage between Jordan and nations in which the Anglican Church leadership was hostile toward the archbishop, it was good that Akinola did not dignify the provocation with a strong response.

3. http://www.guidepacker.com/Africa/Nigeria/Embassy-Visa/Embassy-of-Jordan-in-Nigeria.

In any event, the case ended as what it was—an attempt at destabilizing Akinola. Disturbed but not subverted in any way, he was continuing with his plan. For as soon as he had his passport back, the party headed back in the direction from which they had come—Israel. The two countries closed their land border at night, which meant the party would have been forced to pass the night in their chartered vehicles had they not turned back. Fortunately, although they had no hotel reservations, things worked out. Akinola recalled that, luckily, "a call was placed to one or two sources, and God came with a huge blessing as accommodation was secured for everybody."

GAFCON turned out to be the greatest compensation. It erased the disgrace and brought an immeasurable grace to the revolutionary step toward rescuing the Communion from the threatening spiritual eclipse.

Unlike the initial hitch that Akinola and the advance team experienced, things went smoothly for the delegates from nineteen provinces constituting half of the worldwide Anglican Church. They had flown in from twenty-five different countries, and the group included seven primates, 291 Bishops, and over a thousand clergy, lay people, and their spouses, totaling "1,184 pilgrims." Gathering such a broad-based and diverse mixture of leaders, clergy, and lay people for consultation and spiritual rejuvenation was novel in the modern history of the Anglican Communion. From the halls, voices reverberated in extensive and exhaustive deliberations. There was no fear, no threat, no molestation, no intimidation, no bullying, and no shadowing at the doorway, in the lobby, or in the hall. Interlopers had no chance to invade the venue in an attempt to zap innocent participants. Stalking, hurling of abuse, and calling of participants' names were completely absent. The atmosphere was sober, sombre, and spiritual. Frankly and honestly, the people exchanged ideas the whole week, June 22–29, 2008. They talked about their Anglican identity, their spiritual heritage and calling. At the end, they rose with dual clarion calls—the first in "the GAFCON statement" and the other in the "Jerusalem Declaration."[4]

A rattling idea like GAFCON, within the context of the raging gay crisis within the Anglican Communion, was bound to elicit its fair share of conjectures and insinuations, particularly from the Western media, with most trying to guess the intent and motive of the GAFCON Leadership Team. The favorite speculation was that GAFCON was an attempt to create a breakaway faction from the Communion and make Akinola the leader of that splinter group. GAFCON's "Jerusalem Statement" set the record straight. Unequivocally, the leaders and members of GAFCON declared,

> We cherish our Anglican heritage and the Anglican Communion and have no intention of departing from it.

---

4. See GAFCON, "Statement on Global Anglican Future," issued in Jerusalem in Feast of St. Peter and St. Paul, June 29, 2008; GAFCON, "The Jerusalem Declaration," issued in Jerusalem on June 29, 2008, from the papers and archive of the Most Rev. Peter Akinola.

However, the participants resolved that the time had come for the "divided and distracted" Anglican Church to move on. Consequently, they asserted that "GAFCON is not just a *moment* in time, but a *movement* in the Spirit." In other words, GAFCON was not intended as an ephemeral necessity but a compelling inevitability. They had come to Jerusalem to look beyond the frustrations of the past and kick off a rebirth.

As far as the GAFCON delegates were concerned, the crisis within the Communion "cannot simply be patched." They believed that a "major realignment" had become inevitable. Three steps were highlighted in their envisaged realignment. The first was the "launch of the GAFCON as a Fellowship of Confessing Anglicans." The second was to "encourage GAFCON Primates to form a Council." And the third was enactment of "the Jerusalem Declaration" to define the "basis of the Fellowship."

Diverse and multicultural as the delegates were, they had no differences making decisions and charting the direction of their spiritual journey. A major one was establishment of the Fellowship of Confessing Anglicans (FCA), which the delegates stated would be a "fellowship of confessing Anglicans for the benefit of the Church and the furtherance of its mission." The FCA would serve as a "fellowship of *Anglicans,* including provinces, dioceses, churches, missionary jurisdictions, para-church organisations and individual Anglican Christians." The core objective would be "to reform, heal and revitalise the Anglican Communion and expand its mission to the world."

Looking at its membership and objectives, cynics might be justified in suspecting GAFCON leaders of having a hidden agenda. The FCA represented a radical step forward and had the potential to complicate further the already sharp division within the Communion. Evidently, the leaders were not unaware of the accusation's plausibility. "Our fellowship is not breaking away from the Anglican Communion," they reiterated in response. Nonetheless, they were not shy in owning up to the FCA goal—to bring together "many other faithful Anglicans throughout the world" in order for them to share the "doctrinal foundation of Anglicanism." Without any doubt, they were saying that those of them who wanted to walk together should have the means to do so, as those who had chosen to walk apart had means to travel their chosen path. What FCA suggested, therefore, was that after the years of ceaseless and empty talks, Jerusalem heralded, in a defining moment, "We intend to remain *faithful* to this standard."

It could no longer be denied that the Anglican house was divided and at odds with itself. The Church had become polarized in its core doctrine and belief as it had never been before. Worse was how the revered office of the archbishop of Canterbury had lost its pristine reverence. Never in the history of the Communion had internal dissension reached this dimension. The GAFCON delegates contended, "While acknowledging the nature of Canterbury as an historic *see*, we do not accept that Anglican identity is determined necessarily through recognition by the Archbishop of Canterbury." Serious, very serious, gravely serious was the lamentable situation facing the Communion.

The severity of the matter could be seen from the fact that the people who spoke in Jerusalem represented more than 50 million Anglicans worldwide, the vast majority of the membership of the Church. Instructive also was the fact they had a consensus. No primate dissociated himself or denied agreement with the statement. No allegation of impropriety was raised against the conference's leadership. On the other hand, the leaders of nearly two-thirds of the Anglican Church (from the six continents of the world) had left Jerusalem with a very strong common resolve that "a major realignment has occurred and will continue to unfold."

The days to come didn't bring hope that the cataclysms enveloping the Communion would abate. Indeed, the GAFCON participants and leadership had departed Jerusalem making another strong statement in a 14-point resolution called "The Jerusalem Declaration." "The Jerusalem Declaration" set out and embodied the principles that were forthwith to govern actions and relationships, first among GAFCON members, and second, between them and other members of the Communion. The declaration was akin to an ecclesiastical "charter."

Many of the points it contained were a rehash of the "tenets of orthodoxy" that they had expressed several times. Though no mention was made of the word "homosexuality," the implication was obvious with their declaration that for "bishops, priests and deacons . . . we uphold the classic Anglican Ordinal as an authoritative standard of clerical orders." In a similar vein, they reaffirmed "God's creation of humankind as male and female and the unchangeable standard of Christian marriage between one man and one woman as the proper place for sexual intimacy and the basis of the family." Furthermore, they were unequivocal that they rejected "the authority of those churches and leaders who have denied the orthodox faith in word or deed." The leaders' declaration ended with "The Road Ahead." Herein, they stated their resolve to weather the storm and confront the unsavory events in the life of the Communion.

Could they contain the unpleasant developments within the Communion in the light of how deep the entrenched powers within and outside the Communion had become? Would they succeed in their attempt? The answer was to be found in the developments occurring next.

Of course, there were attempts to destroy GAFCON, which was seen as a kind of *enfant terrible* in some quarters. Indeed, some primates in the Global South did not welcome GAFCON. For instance, Archbishops Mouneer Anis and John Chew had expressed reservations about the inappropriate "timing" of the conference. Others were less open, choosing to communicate their opposition quietly and discretely. A number were, however, very antagonistic. Those in this group were virulent in their public denunciation of the idea, branding it as further evidence of the adversarial arrogance of, particularly, the African Anglican Church leaders. Thus, the battle raged both within[5] and outside to confront the subterranean schemes and direct plots to undermine the survival of GAFCON.

5. Akinola, "Letter to Archbishop Mouneer Anis on GAFCON" (exact date not indicated); "Letter

Wisely and realistically, the GAFCON leaders had been sensible enough not to expect the road to be smooth or easy following the revolutionary step they had taken. They knew they could not expect a drastic change overnight in the Communion's situation simply because they had come to Jerusalem and produced a declaration. They avoided over-confidence and a false sense of optimism. At the same time, they were sure that Jerusalem had signposted a new, bold, brave, and purposeful beginning—for them and for the Communion. They realized that they would need to take many steps to consolidate the "development of this fellowship" that Jerusalem began.[6] They knew they needed to address urgently the division within the Global South. They felt that as minor as the differences were portending to be, they could not take the rift for granted, and they were not willing to accept the crack's widening any further. Even if they were still far from striking a mutual agreement about the necessity of GAFCON, they had to prevent the house from being divided against itself.

Consequently, the first gathering of the GAFCON primates was a sort of rapprochement meeting to foster a better understanding of those with mixed feelings. In Jerusalem, the leaders had encouraged the sharing of understanding and goodwill with their colleagues who had reservations about the conference. The necessity for this was hung on the need to spread the ideals and goals of GAFCON and ensure "participation beyond those who have come to Jerusalem." They wanted everybody willing "to walk together" to be encouraged by the spirit of vision and mission of GAFCON. Specifically, mention was made of soliciting the "cooperation of the *Global South* and the Council of Anglican Provinces in Africa." The two organizations were seen as of practical necessity in the task ahead.

From this perspective, it made sense that the leadership of GAFCON was mandated to see every crack mended because the Global South and CAPA constituted the two big groups at the heart of GAFCON. Any dissension or disagreement between the two bodies and GAFCON would truly divide the house. Accordingly, the primates, especially those in leadership of the Global South, sitting side-by-side with people like Akinola with "triple identity" (status in all the three organizations), ironed out their differences and succeeded in arriving at a compromised solution. The only unfortunate development was with the Council of Anglican Provinces in Africa (CAPA). Since the change in its leadership, the vibrancy with which the body previously spoke and conducted its affairs seemed to have died out. The London meeting ended,

from Archbishop Peter J. Akinola to the Global South Primates" (exact date not stated), all from the papers and archive of the Most Rev. Peter Akinola.

6. GAFCON, "Primates Council Meeting" Minutes of Meeting held at the Marriott Hotel, Heathrow, London, Wednesday 20th & Thursday 21st August 2008; "Communique from the GAFCON/FCA Primates Council Meeting" held in London, April 16, 2009; "Notes on Meeting of the GAFCON Primates Council," held on Tuesday, October 13, 2009, through Thursday October 15, 2009, at Renaissance Hotel, Heathrow, London; all retrieved from the collection and archive of Archbishop Peter Akinola; "Communique from the Primates Council of GAFCON/FCA," April 5–10, 2010, at Bermuda; "Nairobi Communique and Commitment—GAFCON 2013: The Nairobi Communique."

therefore, on a note of "win some and lose some," but still with the GAFCON team taking steps to consolidate the revolutionary march they had begun. The result was their establishment of the Primates' Council, parallel to the Anglican Communion's Primates Meeting, which was regarded as one of the Instruments of Unity, that is, a global decision-making organ in the Anglican Church.

It's difficult to pinpoint which feelings the primates were trying to encourage concerning establishment of the Primates' Council. The idea of a Primates' Council prompted the usual Pavlovian response of the Anglican Church to situations that warrant concrete, immediate, and cogent decisions. Avoiding timely and crucial decisions when situations were urgent and circumstances dire seems to have become a notorious norm in the life of the Anglican life. The Church appears to take delight in bureaucratic escapism. Consequently, the Primates' Meeting was as ineffectual as it was toothless, consistently demonstrating extreme impotence. On the other hand, at the sub-group level, the Global South Primates' Steering Committee, though active in a way, had the problem that its decisions were neither binding nor often accorded respect at the global Anglican level. And CAPA fared no better. Along with its Global South counterpart, it was rarely listened to.

However, it appeared that the new GAFCON Primates' Council desired to make a difference because its birth was accompanied with established, laid-down rules and regulations concerning the process and procedure for decision making. The resolution reached at the Jerusalem conference was that only those primates present at the London meeting should "form the initial Council of the GAFCON movement." This preliminary group was given the task to further undertake "enlargement of the Council." What that meant practically was that, contrary to the situation in the Communion, where being the national leader of an Anglican Church was an automatic qualification for membership to the Primates' Meeting, it was not so with the GAFCON Primates' Council.

Simultaneously, the Council was mandated to ensure that it organized and expanded the Fellowship of Confessing Anglicans (FCA). Furthermore, the GAFCON Primates' Council was expected to be radically different in nature from its counterparts. A major requirement was that it had to be proactive and purposeful. Topping the immediate goals set for it was to work expeditiously to "authenticate and recognise confessing Anglican jurisdictions, clergy and congregations." Similarly, it had the mandate of working to "encourage all Anglicans to promote the gospel and defend the faith."

GAFCON leaders had the destinations to which they were heading in mind. They were also equipped with the roadmap to lead them to the terminus. In the "Jerusalem Declaration," the conference had praised "the courageous actions of those Primates and provinces who had offered orthodox oversight to churches who had suffered under false leadership, especially in North and South America." They saw the oversight as a "positive response to pastoral necessities and mission opportunities."

Unapologetically, they affirmed that the possibility of their relenting was remote. "Such actions will continue," they pronounced flatly. They vowed not to stop as long as the action was deemed "to be necessary." This could not have been reassuring to the American and Canadian churches. Rather, it was audaciously unsettling. "We believe this is a critical moment when the Primates' Council will need to put in place structures to lead and support the church," they declared boldly.

In Jerusalem, a vital decision had been made. "The federation currently known as Common Cause Partnership" was "to be recognised by the Primates' Council." The directive was handed down to the Primates' Council to work towards implementing the goal. At that first meeting, they decided to implement the directive. With no qualms, the primates stated, "We believe the time is now ripe for the formation of a province in North America."[7]

Could the breaking of the American and Canadian churches into two along doctrinal lines be as simple as the GAFCON leaders were making it, with two distinct bodies remaining under the same Anglican Communion roof? The step was like going into the lion's den and provoking it. But the GAFCON leaders not only sounded determined but stated their resolve unequivocally. Somehow, like a Togolese proverb says, "When all men say you are a dog, it is time not just to bark but to bite." Jerusalem seemed to have changed everything—about GAFCON, its leaders, and the fighting spirit. It looked now that the sleeping dog had not only been awaked but was on all fours and ready to bite.

However, the primates ought to have known better. When the Provinces of Southern Cone and Uganda decided to accept defecting churches and dioceses into their fold, the American Episcopal Church split not a few hairs. The departing clergy had their careers broken just as the churches and congregations found themselves hounded with malicious litigation. Nigeria's attempt at convoking CANA on American soil did not attract less venom.[8] America shook hell loose to fight Nigeria and the clergy involved. How then could the Episcopal Church willingly surrender to sharing ecclesiastical power within its territory? The possibility of its happening under Presiding Bishop Jefferts Schori, the new "sheriff in town," without prompting an acrimonious response was remote.

Yet the reality was that whether the American presiding bishop liked it or not, there was new water with new fishes birthing. The old had given way to the new, and under the new dispensation, it was not about her likes, feelings, or sentiments. The issue was the Anglican Communion and what was in the interest of the worldwide Church. The question that kept nagging then was how the GAFCON leaders were

7. American Anglican Council, "A Timeline of Defining Actions."

8. Akinola, Letter to The Rt. Rev. Katharine Jefferts Schori dated May 2, 2007, and Letter to Dr. Rowan Williams, the Archbishop of Canterbury dated May 6, 2007, both retrieved from the from the archive and papers of the Most Rev. Peter Akinola. See the online version at http://peterakinola. blogspot.com.ng/2007/05/letter-to-archbishop-of-canterbury.html.

going to carry out their decision. Could they break the jinx? Was the era of being a toothless bulldog over?

Archbishop Akinola was at the center of GAFCON; he was a pillar and prime mover as well. The leadership of the GAFCON Primates' Council revolved around him. Remote was the possibility of America, Canada, or the homosexual movement bullying, frightening, or intimidating him. He had become a veteran in the Anglican Church struggle. Akinola had confronted many challenges since the crisis began. Least of the motivations for his actions was personal ambition. But, as it was bound to happen, the motive behind GAFCON was deliberately subjected to different speculations and jaundiced interpretations. There were those who felt the effort was a deliberate counterpoise to the Lambeth Conference. Some viewed it as an attempt to evolve a breakaway faction within the Anglican Church, as a grand design to place Akinola into a headship position like that of the archbishop of Canterbury.

None of those cynics and skeptics was honest enough to identify the relationship between the protracted Anglican Church crisis and GAFCON. In the international community, the Third World countries are frequently criticized as homes of intransigent leaders. The huge paradox was that not only did the Anglican Church leaders in the West became afflicted with that disease but added their own vile touch to it. The most pathetic reality was the complicity of the office and institution vested with the power to exercise control on such matters in the Anglican Communion—Canterbury. Canterbury's leadership abdicated its duty that could have contained and curtailed the Anglican problem. When deliberate effort was not being made to sweep the problems under the carpet, the leadership would employ the twin evil of hiding under bureaucratic ineptitude.

Akinola was not known to pursue utopia. He stood firmly behind GAFCON, ready to devote everything required to make the organization achieve its aims. The two goals—"Anglican Realignment" and the formation of a province in North America—remained the uppermost agenda for GAFCON's leadership. They had publicly acknowledged them as their primary goals. Unbelievably, it didn't seem that Canterbury's Archbishop Rowan Williams had any interest in arresting the degenerated situation. He pretended not to see the persecution of anti-homosexual priests and congregations in America and Canada, a big factor that had elicited the move for "Anglican Realignment" from GAFCON.

In the Anglican conflict, Akinola and the GAFCON group had the advantage of time. The Jerusalem conference had given them a lead; they had stated their position regarding the continued failure of Archbishop Williams to address the crisis. The sad development was that Williams ignored the demands of the GAFCON group in his characteristic manner. He continued to use the advantage of office in forestalling the efforts of Akinola and the GAFCON Primates' Council. Presumably, he still believed that he could outwit them with scheming and plotting. Notwithstanding, there were those looking to the Lambeth Conference, which Williams had convened, as an avenue for him to address the floundering of the Anglican Communion, especially in light of the serious warning coming from GAFCON.

Lamentably, when the 2008 Lambeth Conference came, everything about it was theatrical. On Wednesday, July 16, 2008, the Conference opened with drama.[9] The three weeks that it lasted were characterized as a high-level soap opera, from beginning to end. The 18-day gathering of Anglican Church leaders from different parts of the world had no parallel in the history of the Communion. Never had the world's third largest Church witnessed such a large-scale global embarrassment. The 2008 Conference was the fourteenth in the 141-year history of the decennial gathering of Anglican bishops from all over the world. As related earlier, only twice in the history of the Communion had the Conference been postponed, 1918 and 1940.

Twice also in the life of the Conference, it witnessed boycotts. The maiden one was in 1868 when the bishops of the province of York protested because they didn't see the reason for calling the bishops to assemble together. Twenty years later, in 1888, similar controversy occurred. Led by J.C. Ryle and a handful of other fervent bishops, a group withdrew its participation over concerns that "the conference was institutionalizing what they believed to be an un-biblical prelacy." The 1998 protest of a few disgruntled bishops on the side of homosexuality was of no historical import. Nor could it be compared in number and weight to the 2008 boycott. The decision to skip the Lambeth Conference in 2008 by the GAFCON group was unparalleled in the history of the Communion.

Expectedly, desperate attempts were made in the media to neutralize the embarrassing effect of the boycott. The Communion had 38 provinces made up of 729 dioceses, missionary districts, and ecclesial entities at the time, plus six extra-provincial jurisdictions. Official reports by Canterbury admitted that nearly 260 dioceses boycotted the Conference—36 percent of the constituent parts of the Communion, and of course, the most populous bloc of its global membership. There were also sundry absentees, like the archbishop of Polynesia, who missed because of an unavoidable national assignment, the bishop of Salisbury, who suffered a stroke, the bishop of Pennsylvania in the USA facing litigation, and bishops from the Andaman and Nicobar Islands of North India, who traditionally did not attend the Lambeth meeting.

As Akinola had warned during the protest over exclusion of Bishop Martyn Minns, and on account of Archbishop Rowan Williams' refusal to convene the Primates' Meeting to address their grievances, over one-third of the delegates did not show up in London. Unsurprisingly, Nigeria topped the list of the ten provinces whose bishops boycotted the Conference. Out of the 214 bishops who were absent, 137 were from Nigeria. Uganda was second with thirty bishops absent. Kenya followed with twenty-five bishops. Rwanda had eight bishops absent while from Australia seven bishops decided not to participate. In the Church of England itself, the archbishop of

9. Pigott, "Lambeth diary: Anglicans in turmoil"; "Lambeth Conference" https://en.wikipedia.org/wiki/Lambeth_Conference#Fourteenth:_2008; https://en.wikipedia.org/wiki/Lambeth_Conference.

Canterbury's province, three bishops denied the Conference their appearance. From Southern Cone, Episcopal Church South East Asia, and the church in Jerusalem and the Middle East, one bishop each withheld appearance. African churches were the majority of those who shunned the Conference. Of Africa's 324 dioceses, 200 (about 61 percent) declined to honor Dr. Williams' invitation. There were, however, sympathizers of both GAFCON and Lambeth, bishops who decided to attend the two conferences. They numbered about 124, feeling no harm was done by being in Jerusalem as well as in London.

Diplomatically, Archbishop Williams played down the boycott. "We're sorry you're not here," he said in his first public comment about the boycott. Nevertheless, the impact of the absence of the protesting provinces, particularly from Africa, was too big to be ignored, for this group constituted half of the Communion's global membership. The continent's membership was as high as 40 million, half of the 80 million Anglicans worldwide. Deftly, Williams seized the opportunity to address the 670 bishops present. In pretentious meekness, he said, "The great pity is that to have those voices would have been a healing and helpful thing."

Earlier, the line had been sold to the media that that the boycott was not total, with reference made to some bishops, especially from Kenya, who defied their archbishop to attend Lambeth. The media didn't know the underlying story to the boycott, so Williams was able to shift the blame onto the bishops who were staying away. He implied that they were a difficult lot, casting them as a divisive group, in contrast with their American counterparts, who "had earned their invitations through contrition." Williams insisted that the Americans had complied at both the individual and corporate level. At the individual level, not all but "some individually expressed regret for the action widely blamed for prompting the widening rift over homosexuality in the Communion," he said. "Corporately," he enthused petulantly, "the (American) House of Bishops asked for forgiveness last year."

Obviously, his statement was a reference to the report issued after his American trip. (It's worth noting that some members of the committee purported to have issued it had voided publicly its integrity.) Deliberately, the archbishop sidetracked the subject of his refusal to convene the Primates' Meeting, which his colleagues had vociferously demanded. Economical with the truth, Williams told the Lambeth participants that "50% of the provinces (individual autonomous national Anglican Churches) or a bit more said that's probably all right." Thus he issued the American church a clean bill of health.

Archbishop Williams' ingenuity extended to the invention of a novelty to prevent the potentially explosive 2008 Lambeth summit from blowing up. This led to his altering the traditional format of the 2008 Conference radically. Against the usual manner of greeting the bishops as they arrived in Canterbury at the Cathedral Close, the archbishop and his wife employed an alternative. Most on arrival were immediately ferried to the campus of the University of Kent, the venue of the Conference. Each bishop was allocated a student room on the campus where they spent the next eighteen days together to reflect, pray, and converse.

He also adopted a style called "Indaba" to replace the usual "parliamentary" method that had always guided discussions, debate, and decision making at the Conference. "Indaba" is a South African word (and coincidentally, the country of South Africa marked the limit of his African experience and exposure). He and his wife had spent a short period working with the South African Anglican Church in 1987 during the apartheid regime. "Indaba" as a discussion tool encourages talks without making any formal or conclusive decisions. For some, its best use was lubricating "conversation without end."

To help the Canterbury archbishop, he had imported Professor Ian Douglas, a lecturer at the Episcopal Divinity School in Cambridge, Massachusetts, USA. He considered "Indaba" a better approach for the Communion to adopt, arguing it would "give every bishop the chance of being heard." Furthermore, it would eliminate the "head-to-head debates that create winners or losers." He was convinced that encouraging the parliamentary style at the Conference at that point in time would "not necessarily resolve difficult issues in the life of the church," an option which "Indaba" offered. Importantly, he was sure that the parliamentary style would have compelled a decision to be taken at the end of the deliberations, which the Anglican Church could not afford at that point in time. The result "would probably have made the divisions far worse," Douglas believed. Consequently, he would prefer that the bishops be brought together for talks and talks and talks only! Archbishop Williams not only bought the idea but adopted it enthusiastically.

At Williams' Lambeth Conference, talk was plentiful and endless. Daily, each "study group" was "limited to 40 held discussions" but "carefully skirt[ed] the contentious issue facing the Communion." The sequestered global Anglican leaders underwent a kind of two-week intensive residential refresher course. Two interwoven main themes from which the bishops were expected to benefit were how to be better leaders in mission and ways to strengthen the Communion.

Under the two broad themes, topics were broken out. The focus areas stretched from Anglican identity to evangelism, including myriad others like social justice, serving together, the environment, engaging a multi-faith world, mission, listening to God and each other, and so on. There were also practical sessions—the "workshops." The bishops were expected to hold effective conversation with each other. They were to listen, share their concerns, desires, and passions on different subjects like ministry, human sexuality, and Scripture. Evening seminars were like nightcaps to tune up the bishops and their spouses. From the concept to the contents, "Indaba" would have been a good skill improvement program for the church leaders, except for its drawbacks that became obvious.

The bishops were not factory workers learning to adapt to a new floor rule or improved technology. Neither were they bureaucrats requiring a continuous training exercise for career advancement. Nor could they be compared to students badly in need of a diploma or certificate to fit into a job market. They were leaders of the church, brought together as one of the Instruments of Unity of the Communion. They had convened to make decisions that would advance the good, wellfare, growth, and development of the Anglican Church worldwide. The whole idea of "Indaba" was an illusion, meant to give the impression that the house was not burning when everyone knew otherwise.

Desirable as building the capacity of the bishops was, there was no doubt that the once-in-ten-years' gathering of the Anglican bishops was not meant for that. Ostensibly, Williams too realized he was only avoiding the real issue. He was merely teasing a chasing shadow in a mocking walk. Known to all was that at that point in Anglican history, anywhere Anglicans gathered, the key issue was the subject tearing the house apart—homosexuality and the contemptuous behavior of the American and Canadian churches. The crisis had morphed into a Frankenstein monster, too humongous and too horrid to be ignored.

In fact, Williams and the Lambeth Design and Planning Team knew there was no way of completely avoiding the homosexuality issue. Accordingly, they had made careful preparations to accommodate the eventuality. Tactically, they had created room during the Conference to inject the knotty and naughty subject into the discussion. Cleverly, they reserved it to "only at the very end—after a two-week 'cooling-off period,'" when the bishops would have expended themselves. Craftily, a small "Indaba" team, a select group of forty members, was appointed as the people allowed to discuss the issue. Inherent in the group was the power to discuss everything about the burning issue. However, they were strictly forbidden from making any decision. Expressly and unequivocally stated to them was the fact that "there will be no vote and no resolution." Equally proscribed was the opening of their meeting to media presence. Obviously, the Williams Lambeth Conference was in a class of its own.

Perhaps it was good that the bishops who opted for GAFCON and decided to boycott the Lambeth Conference did so. Would they have suffered gladly the chic sham? Not likely, given the 18-day, psychological drudgery. For Akinola in particular, not attending the Lambeth Conference seemed a prudent choice. Though the discussion venues were made strictly off-limits to media, the rambunctious gay groups didn't stay away. While they didn't dare make a spectacle in Jerusalem, they had a field day in Kent. The venue was turned into something of a carnival.

All through the days, students from Western Michigan University in the United States deployed a community theater outside the arena. They were there to stage a play on seven biblical passages deemed hostile to homosexuality. Deliberately, they turned the passages upside down. It was not a mistake or an error but a considered act of perversion of the original biblical texts. They rendered their own corrupted and contradictory radical versions of the texts. At the closing of the curtain, they concluded their drama with loud denunciation of those who advocated biblical morality and with glamorization of the aberrant lifestyle. Universities are supposed to be centers of culture and civilization, with students expected to be worthy in learning and character to justify their membership in the community. Though their performance was not admirable, they still behaved better than Paul Tatchell and his anarchist gay organization, Outrage!

The Lambeth Conference provided the anarchist group a full range of opportunities to target, harass, intimidate, embarrass, and scandalize the Anglican leaders who didn't support homosexuality. Tatchell and his group were not the only association on the prowl.[10] The Lesbian and Gay Christian Movement also had a significant presence. Though they were confined to the outside of the conference venue, their voices rent the air with war cries. One of the popular choruses was, "Defend gays, fight Christian bigots."

Despite the fact that the Nigerian primate was nowhere near the venue, Akinola remained the reviled enemy of the gay activists. Archbishop Orombi, the Ugandan church leader, also had the bad fortune to have been added to the list of the "Christian bigots" denounced for opposing the gays. And in a surprising turn of events, the gay tantrums were also directed at Williams. Tatchell wondered aloud, if "Dr. Williams would not appease a racist or anti-Semitic bishop, why is he appeasing boastful homophobes like Archbishop Akinola of Nigeria and Archbishop Orombi of Uganda?"

Evidently, Akinola would have made a great mistake coming near the venue of the Conference. He could not have escaped the wrath of Tatchell, who was waiting for him and charging that "Archbishop Akinola has endorsed anti-gay legislation in Nigeria that would ban gay organisations, gay churches, gay safer sex education and the advocacy of human rights." In the case of Orombi, his sin was that he "excommunicated Bishop Christopher Senyonjo for ministering to the lesbian and gay community of Uganda." Williams was luckier, since he was charged with the lesser crimes of conspiracy and negligence, due to his failure to censure the two African church leaders. Tatchell considered the archbishop of Canterbury's action "a tragic betrayal of lesbian and gay rights," and his punishment would be limited to vitriolic attack. Akinola and Orambi, on the other hand, would have likely faced physical assault. Security would not have kept the men from being zapped by the gay motley crowd.

Akinola's absence also saved him from another contrived plot that would have involved a second encounter with the white mercenary Mac Davis-Iyalla. A week before the beginning of Lambeth Conference, the Nigerian turncoat had "been granted indefinite leave to remain in the UK." On one side of the University of Kent, Iyalla presented his so-called African ensemble, "gay Anglicans from churches in Africa." A cacophonous crowd, they danced to the beat of drums outside the venue, hoping "to catch the eye of media starved of access to official events." Produced by America and directed by the United Kingdom, with the rehearsal having taken place in Tanzania during the Primates' Meeting, Iyalla's script was no longer suitable for its targeted

10. "Lambeth Conference Makes No Decisions on Gays in the Church."

349

audience. It was written around a main character—Akinola—but the "villain" wasn't there to be mocked. Davis-Iyalla was ill-equipped to improvise. His script called for him to be the hero who was "disowned by his Church . . . because he was honest enough to accept his sexuality," but, again, the target was not there, and the play fell flat. Instead, he settled for throwing mud at "several of the 670 bishops in Canterbury [who] were also gay, but were simply too timid to admit it."

Incidentally, the bishop of Buckingham, Alan Wilson, had claimed in a book that "one in ten of Church of England bishops are secretly gay." Tatchell had latched onto that disclosure to threaten "to *out* some of these if they do not *out* themselves." But his public accusation that there were gay bishops—secretly and openly in the Anglican Church—was no longer news. The story was stale and gained him no newspaper coverage. The big story was the arrival of, as one newspaper described him, the man "who brought the worldwide Anglican Communion to the brink of self-destruction."[11]

Though banned officially, America's Gene Robinson continued with his contemptuous ways by showing up. The media always excited Robinson. Modesty and discretion were not in his nature as he flaunted his non-celibacy, despite being a shepherd and the father of two girls. The lurid details Robinson shared sometimes shocked decency, but he justified relating them as part of his being a more open and honest person, better than his fellow bishops whose fear had kept them in the "closet." Robinson had therefore arrived in London to maximum media coverage, which stretched from pre- to post-Lambeth Conference time. He was "determined that other Anglican bishops should not meet without a reminder of his presence."

Before Kent, his first stop was at the Southbank Centre in London. There, he was a guest at the premiere of the controversial documentary "For the Bible Tells Me So." He used the occasion to deliver his first jab at the church. Appearing with Sir Ian McKellen, the acclaimed actor and gay rights campaigner, Robinson crowed, "I'm the first elected bishop not to be invited to the conference since it began in 1867." (Actually, this was false.) As for McKellen, he was notorious for heckling the church, jeering that "the church has to grow up." He repeated his familiar line on that occasion too.

From there, Robinson departed to make his heroic arrival at Kent. He had designed his own unofficial "Indaba," and he had the media's full attention. And the students from the Western Michigan drama troupe were on hand to bolster his claim that "many of his supporters from America and many other countries" were waiting for his arrival. In the excitement, he observed, "I must be a pretty scary guy."

Finally, the eighteen days came to end. Whatever new sun that Williams and his team had expected to emerge failed to rise. The Anglican Communion remained at sunset, with its old, tired, foxy ways. Williams' highly praised "Indaba" had failed to ease the tension wracking the Communion. Sparkling, alive, and unbridgeable was the sharp division within the Church. It was evident from the word go that the intention of Archbishop Williams did not include a resolution to the divisive issues breaking

---

11. Griggs and Moreton, "Gay Bishop Defies his Lambeth Conference Ban."

the unity of the Anglican Church. Seemingly, the strategy was to buy time and avoid a difficult but necessary decision. His long-term plan was to develop a "covenant," an agreement "setting down of the basic principles of Anglicanism," one to which every province or church must agree "to be bound." To ensure compliance with the established principles, a special body—the "pastoral forum"—was to be established. Archbishop Williams wasn't shy in telling his colleagues that the implication of the "covenant" was that "their churches should be ready to sacrifice some of their independence in order to preserve the Communion."

Quite surprisingly, Williams said that "to work, the covenant would require a ban on the ordination of gay bishops and another on the public blessing of homosexual relationships in church services." And he spoke of "the liberal American and Canadian churches," stating unequivocally that unless they "accepted the need for a ban on gay bishops and blessings, 'then to say the least we are no further forward.'" Something was definitely confounding here. This was because the same Archbishop Williams had earlier given a clean bill of health to "some individuals" and the "corporate" American church at his opening speech. But in a U-turn now, he openly chastised them, saying that "the practices of certain dioceses in the American church continue to put our relations as a communion under strain," adding that the "problems won't be resolved while those practices continue."[12]

It was hard to explain how Williams now found it imperative to rescue the groups that continued to be persecuted for standing by the orthodox decision of the Communion. Not only did he break his years of self-imposed silence on the issue; he was decisive in choosing to "place them under the care of the 'pastoral commission,'" where they "would be part of the communion," the "chairman of the pastoral commission to minister to them." Though the decision was late in coming, all were impressed with the breadth of vison and thoughtfulness that the archbishop brought into resolving the protracted crisis of the Communion. Williams seemed to have become a born-again leader, given his uncharacteristic assertiveness.

A notable example was the measure to ensure that the "covenant" was respected, one involving sanctions on any of the thirty-eight provinces disobeying the rules. One condition was that failure to sign the agreement "could even mean some sort of 'diminished status'" in the Communion. He also stressed the importance of "a more general agreement about what Anglicanism is and a way of preserving it." And so Williams began to enjoy the image of a leader with recovered zeal to cure the Communion of its ills.

The archbishop provided the media cause to shift their focus from the nearly eighteen days of gay-group coverage. He got their full attention, generating a variety of analyses, articles, and opinions. Williams became the instantaneous toast of the media, basking in adulation for introducing "unprecedented discipline and 'structure' in the Anglican Communion." "Whether or not Rowan Williams' gamble pays off,"

---

12. Butt, "Lambeth Conference: Archbishop Blames Liberals for Church Rift."

wrote Robert Pigott, the BBC's religious affairs correspondent, "it seems a little bit of church history will be made at Lambeth 2008 after all."

However, for anyone familiar with the trajectory of the Anglican Communion's crisis since Williams assumed leadership of the Church, a major question arose over a matter that had dogged his leadership—sincerity. Impressive as his ideas were, suspicions surfaced that this might be an old book repackaged with a fresh cover and title and deceptively put on the shelf as a new work. For one thing, what would the new Pastoral Commission do that the past Lambeth Commission had not done? What difference was there between this new item and what the Windsor Report had originally proclaimed? What distinguished the Pastoral Commission from the Panel of Reference that never worked? And how did appointing a "chairman of the pastoral commission to minister to . . . the American traditionalists who have left the Episcopal Church because of its liberal attitude to homosexuality" differ from the agreed "Episcopal Oversight" snubbed by the American church? In any case, the Lambeth Conference did not close before it began to occur to some that Williams' approach might be an exercise in futility or a well-designed diversionary tactic by a grandmaster in subterfuge.

America's Bishop Stacy Sauls of the Lexington Diocese fired the first salvo.[13] Sauls might not have been the custodian of the collective mind of the American church leaders, but he served as the barometer of their thinking. He had moved up in the hierarchy of the national church after Presiding Bishop Schori defeated him in the race for that office. Bluntly, he made it clear that "he could not support the majority view of the Bible that homosexual practice was wrong." He had no apology to offer and couldn't care less if that would cause a strain in his relationship with other parts of the Communion. "If . . . the only way I can persuade them to stay in relationship with us is to change what I believe, I can't do that with integrity," he said nonchalantly. The bishop of Los Angeles, Jon Bruno, followed suit in the same brash manner. Haughtily, he told all those calling "for a stop [to] blessing same-sex relationships" to forget it. "For people who think that this is going to lead us to disenfranchise any gay or lesbian person, they are sadly mistaken."

In Akinola's absence, the person in Kent who took public umbrage at the conceited remarks was, surprisingly, the archbishop and primate of the Episcopal Church of Sudan, Daniel Deng Bul Yak.[14] Elected as archbishop and primate about three months before the Lambeth Conference on 20 April 2008, he was nonetheless a veteran of sorts, the 2008 Conference being his third. Deng Bul Yak was the first African church leader to voice disgust at the continued condescending way the homosexuality issue was being treated by the Communion. Behind him was the presiding bishop of Egypt and Jerusalem, Mouneer Anis. Then the church leaders from South Asia added their

13. http://stillonpatrol.typepad.com/still_on_patrol/2008/03/is-stacy-sauls.html?utm_source=StandFirm&utm_medium=post&utm_campaign=link.

14. https://en.wikipedia.org/wiki/Daniel_Deng_Bul.

opinions through a joint statement. Collectively, the South Asian leaders, the Most Revs John Gladstone of the Church of South India, Alexander Malik of Pakistan, Paul S. Sarker of the Church of Bangladesh, and the Rt. Rev. Brojen Malakar of North India, acknowledged "the biblical norms on human sexuality and urge[d] that within the Anglican Communion this may be upheld for the effective witness of the Gospel."[15] So the matter was clearly and urgently on the table, but Archbishop Williams seemed to have no answer.

The 2008 Lambeth talks did not, therefore, save the Anglican Church from collapse, and the event didn't come cheap, costing £5.2 million or US$7.56 million, overshooting its budget by £388,000 or US$564,000.[16] One item alone, "the Big Top, the huge blue tent that housed the main meeting space, cost £411,000 ($597,000)." Though the Lambeth Company had been formed as far back as 2006 to raise money and manage the expenses of the Conference, the deficit was still unavoidable. At the preliminary report to the Board of Governors of the Church Commissioners and the Archbishops' Council of the Church of England in August 2008, the Company wasn't too optimistic about raising quickly "contributions throughout the Anglican Communion to overcome the deficit." To complicate matters, some of the debts fell due within weeks or a few months after the conclusion of Lambeth. Four years later, however, substantial progress had been made. By 2012, the Company gave assurance of clearing the debt by the end of that year. It kept to that promise, and the outstanding amount of £48,000 was liquidated completely by the given date. In 2014, when a final report was presented to the Standing Committee, no red ink appeared in the Conference's book of accounts. Every debt "had been cleared."

The irony was that the Communion whose leadership worked so hard to clear its books of financial debt was unable to exert similar energy in resolving the crisis tearing it apart. The Anglican Church found it far easier and quicker to liquidate its monetary debt than to solve her doctrinal and leadership disputes. The beginning of the end in this game of wits had begun.

15. "Lambeth: South Asia Bishops Take Stand Against Homosexuality."

16. "Lambeth Conference" https://en.wikipedia.org/wiki/Lambeth_Conference#Fourteenth:_2008; "Lambeth Conference: Funding," http://www.thinkinganglicans.org.uk/archives/cat_lambeth_conference_2008.htm.

2 8

Realignment and Reformation

London, 2008

The Global Anglican Future Conference (GAFCON) leadership team tarried in the wings for the Lambeth Conference to conclude before revving into action. On August 20, 2008, seventeen days after London had bid farewell to the Lambeth delegates, the GAFCON leadership team regrouped in the same city.[1] Huddled around a table in a small conference room at the Marriot Hotel, Heathrow, were six of them—Archbishops Peter Akinola, Nigeria; Peter Jensen, Sydney; Henry Orombi, Uganda; Emmanuel Kolini, Rwanda; Gregory Venables, the Southern Cone; and Benjamin Nzimbi, Kenya. At Jerusalem, they had agreed on the road ahead. Before the Lambeth Conference, they had a preliminary meeting in London, a review session to examine the propriety of the actions so far taken. It had become obvious to all that nothing had happened at the Lambeth Conference to suggest or indicate that the Communion's leadership was willing to save the haemorrhaging Church. The men considered the time ripe for concerted action. The road that the GAFCON leadership envisaged included taking the initiative beyond that of a mere pressure group or movement. Now they felt the time was ripe for action. The metamorphosis of GAFCON into an organization had become inevitable. They had to give it form and structure. This was the objective before the London meeting.

On top of their agenda was how to "form the initial Primates Council," the highest organ for the intended body. Swiftly, the matter was resolved. Unanimously, a resolution was passed agreeing that "a Council was hereby constituted consisting of both the initial Primates and other Primates who may be admitted to it in future." A clause was inserted to the effect that membership on the Council would terminate at the retirement of the incumbent primate, and the position would go to the successor automatically. Representation on the Council was on a provincial basis. A second clause

---

1. GAFCON, "Primates Council Meeting," Minutes of Meeting held at the Marriott Hotel, Heathrow, London, August 20–21, 2008, from the collection and archive of Archbishop Peter Akinola.

354

stated that "admission of Primates is strictly by invitation." Subsequently, appointed to provide leadership for the new Council were Archbishops Akinola as the chairperson, Greg Venables as the vice chairman, and Peter Jensen as the honorary secretary. Jensen was to be assisted by Canon Prof. Daju Asaju of Nigeria. Nevertheless, the primates stated they had no intention of monopolizing GAFCON or hoarding it from collective ownership. Accordingly, the primates in attendance were mandated to "engage with their colleagues in nearby provinces to formally invite them to the Council." Uganda was to reach out to Sudan; Rwanda to Burundi, Central African and Congo; Southern Cone to the West Indies; Tanzania to South Africa; Kenya to the Indian Ocean. The Middle East and South East Asia were reserved for Nigeria. Though Nigeria was neither proximate to the Middle East nor contiguous with South East Asia, the primates of the three areas seemed to enjoy healthy respect for one another with a close working relationship as executives of the Global South.

Despite accepting the desirability of an open-door policy, it was insisted that the GAFCON Primates Council be safeguarded from corrupt and toxic ideas. Consequently, it was resolved that "those to be admitted must subscribe to the GAFCON Jerusalem Declaration." Curiously, in the embryonic stage of the GAFCON initiative, Archbishop Mouneer Anis had been the first leader to float the idea of a "structured network for orthodox Anglicans with statements of faith, constitution and organisational structure."[2] At the Marriott Hotel meeting in London, the primates simply proceeded with those features. After the Primates Council, they also created the Primates Council Advisory Board. Selected to be on the board were "experienced, eminent and gifted" individuals—bishops, clergy and laity—from the different parts of the Global Communion. Their work "will [be to] advise and carry out functions as directed by the Council." Among the high caliber Anglican Church leaders constituted into the board were Bishop Michael Nazir Ali, Archbishop Peter Jensen, Bishop Wallace Benn, Bishop A Vun, Bishop Harold Miller, Bishop Bob Duncan, and Archbishop Nicholas Okoh. The leadership of the Board tipped in favor of Bishop Wallace Benn, and he was nominated to be its chairman. All the appointments were, however, voluntary and conditional, depending upon formal acceptance by each nominee.

At the meeting, the roles, functions, and duties of every office along with the organs required to execute the envisaged myriad activities were established. The chairman calls and presides over meetings; draws up the agenda to be confirmed by the meeting; consults with other primates while undertaking his assignments; and acts as the organization's chief spokesperson. When absent, the deputy or vice performs all these functions. The secretary's primary duty is to run the secretariat, in conjunction with a team of assistants drawn from various parts of the Communion. The secretary also maintains the official website of GAFCON and issues statements on behalf of the organization after complying with due process and gaining approval of the Primates Council.

2. Akinola, letter to Archbishop Mouneer Anis on GAFCON (exact date not indicated), from the collection and archive of Archbishop Peter Akinola.

Deliberations were also concluded on the Fellowship of Confessing Anglicans (FCA). Its formal structure and organs received the primates' approval. The Fellowship had three key organs—the first, the theological arm headed by Archbishop Nicholas Okoh; the second, the body for mission under the leadership of Bishop Zac Niringiye; the third, the Empowerment Committee reserved for a North American Diocese to provide its leadership. The FCA was to conduct its affairs on a voluntary basis without paid staff or employees. The Theological Resource Group was tasked with immediately formulating "an appropriate and simple statement of *Creedal* beliefs that captures what the Christian Anglicans believe and do not believe, which should be used in the affirmations and worship of its member churches at local and grassroots levels." The publications were to be "translated into various local languages" along with other GAFCON materials.

Thereafter, the primates set about establishing the minor details that would govern GAFON's corporate affairs. This included the scheduling of its meetings. It was agreed that the GAFCON Primates Council would meet twice a year. The meetings would be preceded by a day meeting of the Advisory Board. Duration was set for the primates' meeting, with the agreement that it should not be for more than three days. Those who were not primates could also be invited in special cases to represent provinces whose primates were not members of GAFCON. No acrimony or discord attended these details. With the conclusion of the corporate guidelines, attention shifted to money. This meeting was the first time GAFCON's finances were being discussed formally since the Jerusalem event. A report was officially laid before the primates.

Considering the two—Lambeth Conference and GAFCON—there was simply no basis for comparison, especially as to which of the two had the biggest financial chest. Of course, it was evident that while there was no sparing of the almighty British pounds at the Lambeth Conference, GAFCON had to struggle frugally to pay its way. Lambeth's overall expenditure of £5.2 million was over six times as much as GAFCON's paltry £821,831. Furthermore, out of its £821,831 total expenditure, the donations received by GAFCON amounted to only £284,004 or 30 per cent of the budget. The bulk of the remaining £573,827 was made up of "contributions of provinces towards the travel and registration of their respective pilgrims that totalled 1056 at the conference." Besides, out of the £284,004 in donations, only £153,669 was spent. GAFCON therefore broke even with a credit balance of £130,334. The conference had no burden of unpaid debts or anxiety over outstanding claims.

Ordinarily, GAFCON finances ought not to fuel any public debate. After all, Lambeth's didn't. But, both within the Communion, and no less in the media, there had been spurious allegations about the sources of funding for GAFCON. The underlying intention apparently was to blackmail the leadership of GAFCON with such accusations. Among the allegations being peddled was that "some secret financiers" seeking to wrest power from the Canterbury archbishop were behind GAFCON's leadership team. It was a lie; a mischievous falsehood undermined by the fact that the "majority of the funding (52%) were from supporters of GAFCON in the United Kingdom." Contrary to the mischievous propaganda, what it meant was that right on British soil, there were many people in disagreement with the wrongly headed direction of Canterbury. A mass of people stood with "the majority of Anglicans in different parts of the globe." They were not only ready to stand out boldly but also eager to support the "reformation which GAFCON is leading in defence of faith, authority of the scripture, and priority of the gospel."

Broadly appraising the financial performance of GAFCON, the primates were happy and excited that the Conference finished with clean books. The man who worked brilliantly to achieve the feat was Hugh Pratt. Pratt received generous commendations for his excellent services from the gratified primates. A frugal and finicky fellow in his personal life, Pratt had transferred his personal attributes to his professional life, from which GAFCON was a beneficiary. The accolades aside, the primates believed there was one more step to go—an audit of the organization's financial transactions. They requested that the records be comprehensive, underlining contributions made by the various provinces, dioceses, and individuals.

Done with the appraisal of their financial records, they turned their attention to the Lambeth Conference. The primates were unanimous in their disappointment at the Lambeth Conference's outcome. In any case, only a hypocrite would expect them to be sanguine regarding its ending. The 2008 Williams Lambeth Conference was a whited sepulchre, a magnificent symphony that had no harmony. The GAFCON primates were not surprised with its result. The Communion had only continued to engage in the same unedifying waltz, dancing round in a circle. Subtle as their indictment sounded, the chastisement was unmistakably loud: "The Voice of Lambeth 2008 was seriously flawed." It was a hogwash "because it merely repeated what has been said by the Primates repeatedly."

They wondered how the outcome was different from their past several meetings—Gramada, Brazil in early 2003; Lambeth, October 2003; Dromantine, February 2005; and Dar es Salaam, February 2007—held to resolve the issue, all to no avail. The gatherings had "all proved to change nothing," they agonized. The same dismal failure had also characterised other series of dialogues held with Archbishop Rowan Williams. "No tangible fruit" attended the efforts, they observed. The Lambeth Conference was another missed opportunity that could have been used to avert the collapse threatening the Communion. Unfortunately, the archbishop betrayed that hope. The "inability of Lambeth to resolve the contentious issues that threaten the Anglican Communion" was glaring to all except the pretenders. From the painful torments, they realized that the Communion had seemingly reached the end of the road. The precipice appeared inevitable. It was time for realignment in the Anglican Church.

Indeed, their decision was to be irreversible. They resolved no going back or turning away from their stand. One of the agreed positions was that "GAFCON will maintain its current positions, activities and cross border episcopal duties." All the actions would not cease "until a viable alternative emerges," they decided. As a practical step in that direction, they concluded that the time had come for "the North American Dioceses (Common Cause Partnership) to set in motion [the] necessary machinery towards constituting themselves into a Province." They asked the partners to see to the execution of the goal "within a period of four months." As far as the Global Primates Council was concerned, the "Council would recognise the Province." Conditions were, however, attached to the goal: the first was that the GAFCON Primates Council must be "satisfied with the proposal" presented by the Common Cause Partnership; the second, that "the constituents of the proposed Province are to be forwarded to the Primates Council for consideration." Once the two conditions were fulfilled, the Council assured, they would walk and work all the way with the American group. The group could count on their "advisory and technical support," including their resolve to "facilitate the quick realisation of the objective."

From all indications, with the decision of the GAFCON Primates Council, the Anglican Communion had reached a critical juncture. Clearly, a new phase had begun in the life of the Church. The once cohesive church was dividing into two tents with conflicting outlooks and beliefs. The developments, however, didn't preclude the GAFCON primates from willingness to consider reconciliatory options.

In February 2009, for instance, Archbishop Rowan Williams had convened a meeting of the Anglican primates. The focus of the meeting was "to discuss the emergent problems in the Communion." Initially, the GAFCON primates were divided on the propriety of attending the meeting. In the end, they resolved to honor the invitation. The argument persuading their attendance of the meeting was that it could be a good forum to further make a passionate appeal to Archbishop Williams on issues vexing GAFCON. They agreed to seek an audience with the archbishop prior to the meeting, choosing an early December date for that purpose. Ideas were bandied around at the table toward articulating the issues. In the end, Archbishop Greg Venables was requested to organize the issues in a coherent manner.

Would their plea for rapprochement work this time around? They were not sure. They couldn't be certain of their efforts' being met with a positive outcome. Thus, they were leery of attaching much hope to the outcome of the exchange. Their own meeting of August 20–21, 2008, which had brought them together to review and examine the road ahead, couldn't be judged other than as successful. They were departing feeling exceedingly satisfied at having achieved their mission. Remaining was their assignment to "engage formally with their colleagues" on the realignment, which they decided to do conscientiously.

Whether he desired it or not, Archbishop Akinola was thrown again into the center of events. As chairman and spokesman for the GAFCON Primates Council, he had to wear the uneasy crown. Still, it was obvious that anything that his hands found to do, he would do it with might and all of his heart. And so far, he had refused to blink! Remote was the possibility of that happening now. Yet Archbishop Williams was a man of similarly strong will, as were the presiding bishop and the entire leadership of the American Episcopal Church. Whether in support of right or wrong causes, motivated by good or wrong reasons, the differing groups within the Communion shared the characteristic of sticking to their guns inflexibly. The casualty usually was the Church itself, the Anglican Communion.

It had become painfully clear that no force on earth could have made the American church change its aberrant policy on homosexuality. Typical of TEC's recklessness was the inflammatory reaction of the bishop of the Los Angeles diocese, the Rt. Rev. Jon Bruno, to Archbishop Williams' statement asking for a reversal of the church's position.[3] Blatantly, he told the leader of the Anglican Church worldwide that anyone contemplating reversal of the American church's homosexuality stand was "sadly mistaken." Impetuously he added, "It was a blunt truth." This flaunted obstinacy had become the norm, further exemplified by the unruliness of the bishop of the Episcopal Diocese of California, the Rt. Rev. Marc Andrus.[4] Despite being a neophyte in the episcopate, Andrus had taken his combative spirit to the 2008 Lambeth Conference.

Andrus' episcopate was fresh, barely two years old. He was chosen through a hard-fought, three-ballot election on July 22, 2006. The California diocese and other contiguous ones were not places the Episcopal Church wanted to see become hotbeds of opposition to the church's gay agenda, and Andrus was adept at keeping troublemakers in line. Seven out of his 18 years in the priesthood had been spent watching over errant school pupils as a chaplain at Episcopal High School in Alexandria, Virginia. He'd devoted another five years to parish administration as rector of Emmanuel Church in Middleburg, Virginia. Then he'd served five years as a suffragan bishop, helping in administration of the Diocese of Alabama before his February 7, 2002, election.[5] Events in California had begun to go topsy-turvy two years before his arrival, and here was a good opportunity for him to earn his loyalty badge and demonstrate his tough stance in combatting dissent from anti-establishment opponents.

On June 9, 2008, about a month and a half before the opening of the Lambeth Conference, Andus wrote to the clergy in his diocese, urging them to begin blessing "all couples, whether gay or straight, to be married in a civil ceremony." The letter followed on the ruling of the California Supreme Court declaring the right of all people to marry.[6] The California case had been a long-drawn battle, dating to 1977, and the tug of war reached its climax in February 2004. Opponents of same-sex marriage had filed five civil lawsuits in San Francisco Superior Court and another case in a Los Angeles court of similar jurisdiction. The parties included individuals and organizations opposed to same-sex marriage who wanted to stop San Francisco from issuing marriage licenses to same-sex couples. This came in response to attempts by the City

---

3. American Anglican Council, "A Timeline of Defining Actions."

4. https://en.wikipedia.org/wiki/Marc_Andrus.

5. "Bishop Andrus of California: Same Sex Marriage Guidelines."

6. https://en.wikipedia.org/wiki/Same-sex_marriage_in_California.

and County of San Francisco and some individuals to overturn the existing state law limiting marriage to opposite-sex couples only. The six cases were eventually consolidated into one, with a San Francisco Superior Court Judge, Richard Kramer, assigned to hear it. On March 14, 2005, Judge Kramer declared the law limiting marriage to opposite-sex couples unconstitutional.

Opponents of homosexual marriage, including the government, appealed the ruling. On July 10, 2006, a three-judge panel heard extended oral arguments on the case. In the subsequent judgment, the appellate court overturned the lower court's verdict by a 2-to-1 majority. Still not satisfied, defenders of the traditional form of marriage in November 2006 petitioned the Supreme Court of California to review the decision. Drawing support from the state's attorney general Bill Lockyer, the Supreme Court took up the case. In a unanimous vote in December 2006, the Supreme Court agreed to a review of all six cases. Subsequently, it heard oral arguments for and against the issue on March 4, 2008. Eleven days later, it arrived at a decision, overturning the 1977 California one-man, one-woman marriage law.

Clinging to the last straw, advocates of orthodox marriage asked for a stay of the ruling. Firmly, the court declined. On June 4, 2008, the court also issued a one-page order refusing to delay enforcement of the decision until after the November, California election. Nevertheless, ahead of the Supreme Court's ruling, defenders of orthodox marriage had found another route for their cause. A petition to put the matter on the ballot for California's electorate, the famed "Proposition 8," was initiated. Its aim, as suggested by the title, was to secure a "California Marriage Protection Act" and "limit on Marriage."

All of the twelve marriage amendments proposed previously had failed disastrously, none of them meeting the requirements to qualify for inclusion on the ballot. But Proposition 8 achieved a miracle, gathering 764,063 valid signatures to qualify for inclusion on the November 4, 2008, ballot. But the Supreme Court insisted that "the decision filed on May 15, 2008, would become final on June 16, 2008, at 5 p.m." In other words, same-sex marriage could proceed. San Francisco Mayor Gavin Newsom announced that exactly one minute past the official closing time of 5 p.m., on the court's appointed date of June 16, same-sex marriages would begin. Within a short period, there was an avalanche of same-sex marriages, resulting in approximately 4,000 marriage licenses being issued. From all over America and a few other countries—Canada, Denmark, France, Germany, the Netherlands, Switzerland, Thailand, United Kingdom, and Venezuela—homosexual couples trooped to California to seize the opportunity.

Unlike the city and county officials who were, perhaps, struggling to devise means of coping with the massive onslaught, Andrus had worked out the path his diocese would take. The June 9, 2008, letter was very explicit with his episcopal directive. Besides the order to clergy to conduct the marriages, he bade "all members of the diocese to become volunteer Deputy Marriage Commissioners," adding that he intended "to volunteer in this capacity." The step, he reminded them, was another advance along their chosen path, for "Clergy and lay leaders in the diocese have been working for the rights of LGBT people and for their full inclusion in our Church for more than forty years." And he assured his flock he would be taking "the witness of our LGBT sisters and brothers to this summer's Lambeth Conference," that is, Lambeth 2008.

Andrus' dream for his diocese: "Providing leadership at next summer's General Convention to bring our marriage practices and theology in line with our fundamental baptismal theology." In spite of the brief tenure of his episcopate, he was sure that his diocese, through "advocacy and example," would show the "way forward for The Episcopal Church so that the marriage of same-sex couples will be a part of our official marriage rites." Andrus enjoined every priest in his diocese "to encourage all couples, regardless of orientation, to follow the pattern of first being married in a secular service and then being blessed in the Episcopal Church." And he underscored the point that all measures and guidelines were temporary, merely "a process to arrive at a more studied, permanent answer for Episcopal clergy presiding at same-sex marriages in this diocese." Already, he had established "a panel of diocesan clergy to make recommendations about how to move toward equality of marriage rites for all people." The intended outcome was to have "an official diocesan policy." Regarding Proposition 8, he was opposed to "the initiative to overturn the Supreme Court ruling." In this connection, he planned to "publish advertising around June 17 celebrating the Supreme Court ruling." And an invitation would go out inviting same-sex couples to go "to our churches for pre-marital counselling and nourishment in communities of faith."

This was the grand illusion that Andrus took to the Lambeth Conference. His promise of influencing the Conference in this direction was bold, but he lacked the clout. Still, on his return home, Andrus was back to his arrogant self. In the month of August, the diocese recorded "five publicised same-sex blessings," and he continued to work against Proposition 8.

This put him at odds with the Roman Catholic Church, which came out forcefully in support of the proposition. The Roman Catholic lay fraternal organization the Knights of Columbus added their weight to the cause, contributing "more than $1.4 million" to the campaign, the largest single contribution among supporters. Furthermore, both the California Catholic Conference and the Church of Jesus Christ of Latter-day Saints (the LDS Church or, informally, the Mormon Church) issued statements publicly supporting the proposition, and their church members were urged to volunteer time and treasure to support the proposed constitutional amendment. Their efforts yielded "over $20 million, about 4% of out-of-state contributions." Other religious organizations such as the Union of Orthodox Jewish Congregations of America, the Eastern Orthodox Church, and a group of evangelical Christians led by Jim Garlow and Miles McPherson, as well as Rick Warren, pastor of Saddleback Church, all came forcefully into the open to support the proposal.

On the other hand, the Episcopal Church stood alone in its unpopular stand. On September 10, 2008, "the six Episcopal diocesan bishops in California jointly issued a statement opposing Proposition 8." Ultimately, the citizens decided with their votes. Supporters of Proposition 8 garnered 52.47% of the vote as against 47.53% by the opponents. Attempts to truncate the decision of the majority through the courts suffered a crushing defeat. On May 26, 2009, the California Supreme Court upheld the proposition. However, it certified all same-sex marriages conducted before its earlier June 2008 ruling as well as those contracted before the November 4 election.

The affair underlined the hypocrisy of the American Episcopal Church. At home, the leaders would readily submit to institutional and democratic processes. Yet internationally, they would scorn the global Anglican Church and its institutions, disparaging decisions arrived at democratically with impunity. And Presiding Bishop Jefferts Schori led the way. She displayed a kind of saucy sullenness in response to the Lambeth Conference's proposition regarding a covenant to guide relationships within the Communion. She scoffed at the idea, saying she would "'strongly discourage' any effort to consider or approve a proposed Anglican Covenant at the Episcopal Church's General Convention." The convention was scheduled for July 2009, almost eleven months after the Lambeth Conference. Rather than have the matter discussed, she would defer decision on it until 2012—a crooked ploy, anticipatory and preemptive.

The Anglican Consultative Council was to meet May 1–2, 2009, with reviewing the covenant as one of its major agenda items. After the meeting, the covenant was expected to be presented to the provinces for approval that same month, but Schori said it was "'inappropriate to make a decision that weighty' quickly." But, given the General Convention's history, the excuse could be seen for what it was, for the delegates at their meeting in 2003 didn't consider approval of the openly gay Gene Robinson as a bishop a weighty subject that should be delayed. Instead, they made it quickly. Furthermore, the presiding bishop did not see anything wrong in fast tracking another "weighty" case that she had brought against Pittsburgh's bishop, Robert Duncan. Promptly, decisively, and expeditiously, Schori dealt with the matter without batting an eye.

Actually, it would have been a miracle if Duncan had escaped Schori's victimization. Duncan was one of the leading vocal and unrepentant domestic opponents of the Episcopal Church's aberrant homosexual policy. From the beginning, he stood firmly against the church's derailment from biblical orthodoxy. However, at about the time news of GAFCON broke in December 2007, a nebulous charge was leveled against him.[7] Brought forth on January 15, 2008, the accusation held that he had "abandoned the Communion." By the rule of the Episcopal Church, "the three most senior bishops in the Episcopal Church had the option to inhibit Duncan," but the bishops who were appointed decided against taking the preliminary step. Duncan was, however,

---

7. "Duncan Deposed"; "Dissenting Episcopal Bishop Pittsburgh Bishop Robert Duncan on CNN"; "The Mind and Mission of Anglican Archbishop Robert Duncan"; https://en.wikipedia.org/wiki/Same-sex_marriage_in_California.

given two months by Presiding Bishop Schori to provide evidence exonerating him from the alleged offence. In a letter of March 14, 2008, he not only replied formally to the charges but also disproved every one of the allegations. For six months, nothing happened. Then, when the GAFCON Primates Council at its August 2008 meeting pledged its readiness to assist the American group to become a province, that is, a separate autonomous Anglican Church in America, Duncan's suspended charges were revived immediately. A meeting of TEC's House of Bishops was convened, with Duncan on the agenda. When the vote came over whether to depose him, eighty-eight bishops said he should go, thirty-five disagreed, and four abstained. Though it was alleged that the "canonical requirement of a majority of those eligible to vote was not met," the axe still fell on Duncan. On September 20, 2008, Presiding Bishop Schori communicated the House of Bishops' majority decision taken two days earlier—that Duncan was to be "deprived of the right to exercise the gifts and spirituality of God's words . . . and related secular offices held."

The Episcopal Church sent him packing abruptly. But the reaction to Duncan's expulsion was swift. In October 2008, the month following the deposition, Duncan's diocese voted overwhelmingly by 240 to 102 to sever links with the Episcopal Church. The congregations decided to realign with the Anglican Province of the Southern Cone. Fifty days later, he was elected the bishop of a new Anglican Diocese of Pittsburgh. With the GAFCON Primate Council's encouragement to the American group to become an autonomous province, the die was cast. Metaphorically, Schori broke the egg, and Duncan made it into an omelette. The former was the first to chuckle while the latter laughed last and best.

On December 1, 2008, three representatives from each of the nine Common Cause Partners began a crucial three-day meeting in Illinois.[8] Represented also was the Anglican Mission in America and Anglican Coalition in Canada led by the Rt. Rev. Charles Murphy. The mission and coalition were affiliated to the Anglican Church of Rwanda, with 140 parishes. Likewise, there was the Anglican Church of Canada with twenty-three parishes. The Canadian group had pitched their tent with the Anglican Church of the Southern Cone, having recalled veteran Canadian bishop Rt. Rev. Donald Harvey as their leader. Of course, the Convocation of Anglicans in North America (CANA) was there. This was Bishop Martyn Minns' group, affiliated with the Church of Nigeria, with all sixty parishes committed. The unaffiliated, 150-parish-strong Reformed Episcopal Church, led by the Rt. Rev. Leonard W. Riches, also showed up to be part of the gathering, as did the three missionary convocations of Kenya, Uganda, and Southern Cone. The Rt. Rev. Bill Atwood represented Kenya; Uganda had the Rt. Rev. John Guernsey representing it; and the Southern Cone commanded the widest spread and largest parishes. Affiliates of the Anglican Church of

8. Anglican Church in North America, "Our Genesis," http://anglicanchurch.net/media/acna_our_genesis_june_2009.pdf; https://en.wikipedia.org/w/index.php?title=Anglican_Church_in_North_America&oldid=675671559.

the Southern Cone spread across the dioceses of San Joaquin, Pittsburgh, Quincy, and Fort Worth. Between them, they shared as many as 163 parishes that were tired of the Episcopal Church and desired a renewal of spirit.

Neither the American Anglican Council nor Forward in Faith North America, an advocacy organization promoting orthodox Anglicanism, was left out. Nor was a sister organization, the Anglican Communion Network, an assembly of clergy, parishes, and dioceses both within and outside the American Episcopal Church. Between these nine organizations, there were as many as 86,000 to 100,000 parishioners, 800 clergy, and 30 bishops. They outweighed some provinces of the Communion in terms of membership, congregations, parishes, and number of both clergy and episcopates.

All the organizations and their leaders were in Illinois for business. From the atmosphere, the Illinois meeting seemed like an American version of the Global Anglican Future Conference. Unanimous was the revolutionary step they took forward in forming the Anglican Church in North America (ACNA). Apparently, they had come to the conference prepared and equipped, and they wasted no time in framing their "provisional constitution and nine initial canons to govern the church."

The first statement of the constitution proclaimed the ACNA's mission. Aptly and unambiguously, it stated that "the mission of the Province is to present Jesus Christ in the power of the Holy Spirit so that people everywhere will come to know Him as Lord." Next was its governing structure. They decided on three main governing bodies. The first was the Provincial Assembly. It was the biggest of the three and was made up of the dioceses/clusters/networks within the ACNA. The second was the Provincial Council. This group was smaller than the Assembly and brought together lay and clergy representatives along with the leading bishops. The third was the College of Bishops, which was no different in form from that to be found generally in the provinces of the Anglican Communion. It was an exclusive platform that would bring all ACNA bishops together. They didn't forget the past or where they were coming from. Accordingly, there was explicit definition and articulation of the responsibility of the province, and the documentation of the governance codes.

Topping the goals set for each of the provinces was the requirement to work hard "to equip each member so that they may reconcile the world to Christ." Following that was the prescribed duty to "plant new congregations and make disciples of all nations." This goal had a second aspect: The clergy were to follow the doctrine of "baptizing in the name of the Father, and of the Son and of the Holy Spirit." The third important duty was that they should teach the world "everything commanded by Jesus." ACNA's constitution defined the "fundamental agency of mission in the Province [as] the local congregation." In terms of property ownership, the statute also provided that "all church property, both real and personal, [is] owned by each member congregation."

It delegated "discipline and governance to the purview of other groups" besides the Provincial Assembly. The Provincial Assembly was to be strictly limited to its primary focus, which was mission. Nevertheless, ACNA wasn't conceived to be impervious to correction or structured to be led dictatorially. Its decision-making process allowed for flexibility and consensus-building. For instance, regarding the controversial women's ordination issue, "Article VIII limits provincial authority so that each diocese can maintain its own practice regarding this." On one point, however, it had a categorical and unequivocal stand—"All Bishops must be male and at least 35 years old." After the establishment of its principles, law, and governance codes, the organization resolved that its next step would be for the province to "seek recognition by the Anglican Communion so it can represent orthodox North American Anglicans in the councils of the church."

At the end of the official proclamation of the birth of the Anglican Church in North America, they resolved to meet next in Texas, June 22–25, 2009. There, they planned to undertake any amendments that might be necessary before adopting and ratifying the ACNA's constitution and canons. It was no surprise that before the delegates departed, reactions had begun. Angst was being raised from both sides of the Communion divide. Expectedly, GAFCON primates were swift in the public acknowledgment of ACNA as promised. "We fully support this development with our prayer and blessing," they said. To the primates, the bold step by the Anglicans in North America showed the "determination of those faithful Christians to remain authentic Anglicans." With the breathing of life into the ACNA, the crisis in the Anglican Church had now reached its climax. It was a decisive end to years of fake, phoney, pretentious lies and dubious fence-mending exercises.

The launching of GAFCON and ACNA redefined the crisis within the Anglican Communion. As such, the year 2008 remained a watershed in the history of the Anglican Church. The forces and methods of engagement were redefined. Gone was the idea of a monolithic, united Anglican Communion tied by a common bond of doctrine, canon, tradition, and belief. A divided house emerged. One group believed in homosexuality and the fallibility of the Bible and of Jesus Christ. To the opposing group, this was a heresy and blasphemy. The orthodox group considered inviolable the sanctity of marriage, the orthodoxy of the Word of God, immortality, and the eternal work of Jesus Christ, who is the Life and the Only Way to salvation and redemption. The Anglican Communion was fundamentally divided between pro- and anti-homosexuality groups.

The formal launch of the ACNA finally took place on June 21, 2009, in Texas. The man of the moment and the cynosure of the occasion was the Rt. Rev. Robert Duncan. Apart from amending and ratifying the constitution and canons of the organization, the leaders of ACNA had that same day also elected their first archbishop and primate. The cap fit the Pittsburgh bishop, the Rt. Rev. Robert Duncan, eminently. The ACNA leaders wasted no time in actualizing the decision; Duncan was installed on the fourth day of their meeting. The June 25, 2009, event was epochal. The occasion marked a renewal of Anglican history in North America. Duncan was installed at Christ Church, Plano, the same church at which, six years earlier, from October 7–9,

2003, about 2,200 of them had gathered at the conference with the theme: "A Place to Stand: Declaring, Preparing."[9] At that conference, they rang out a loud warning to their colleagues about the peril of the gay agenda within the Episcopal Church, assuring them they would neither be intimidated nor pushed out of the Anglican Communion. "We're not leaving," they said confidently. Rather, "it is the Episcopal Church that has departed from the historic teachings of the Christian church," they told their pro-gay colleagues. Unfortunately, they were looked down upon and not taken seriously at the time. But their unheeded warning turned out to be a shocking reality for the American church.

The Anglican Church in North America emerged, undoubtedly, as a formidable rival to the Episcopal Church. Duncan's entry into the arch-episcopacy was historic. Archbishop Duncan became to the Anglican Church in North America what Presiding Bishop Jefferts Schori was to The Episcopal Church, national head of a version of the Anglican Church in America. There were two captains in a ship, each with control of his or her part of the boat.

Maturity and experience were on Duncan's side. He had just celebrated his sixtieth birthday when he was entrusted with the responsibility of piloting the affairs of the North American province. His over three decades in the American church had taught him the important lessons of what needed to be done fast. In this case, ACNA needed a call to "reunite the significant portion of our Anglican Church family here in North America."

Duncan told the crowd at the installation ceremony that his intention was "to serve for five years before stepping down." He would be 65 by that time and still have another five years before the mandatory retirement age. The import of his statement was that he was going to take the pioneer's responsibility, put his wealth of experience behind the ACNA toward giving it a solid footing during its infancy. Duncan nursed no anxiety about the future of ACNA. He wasn't boasting but had confidence that God's work would be done. Nobody should doubt that fact, he guaranteed. Neither did any "sheriff" have the power to breathe on his neck, nor threaten running him out of town. Gone were those days of begging, pleading, and remonstrating. From that time on, Duncan saw nothing but action—positive and dynamic action.

Through this all, the GAFCON Primates Council could not deny being the invisible hand behind the unfolding drama. Least surprising was the fact that at their first meeting in April 2009, ACNA was one of their top topics. Of course, they welcomed the newborn baby warmly. The praises were glowing and affectionate. "The FCA Primates Council," they said cheerily, "recognises the Anglican Church in North America." They viewed their American colleagues "as genuinely Anglican." Besides their own unequivocal endorsement, they urged that other "Anglican Provinces affirm full communion with the ACNA." As far as they were concerned, the existence of ACNA as a parallel North American province was a forgone conclusion. In fact, by

9. https://americananglican.org/about-us/.

the time the Primates Council had its last meeting of the year at the Renaissance Hotel in Heathrow, London, October 13–15, 2009, evidence was clear that the only battle ACNA had to fight was its formal admission into the larger Anglican Communion.[10] The power to grant the admission resided with the archbishop of Canterbury. Had Archbishop Williams undertaken the action, ACNA would have been the Anglican Communion's thirty-ninth province.

The GAFCON/FCA group was quick to extend a solid footing to ACNA, providing a guaranteed seat as an equal partner. Indeed, Archbishop Robert Duncan took his chair as a fellow national leader of an Anglican Church at the group's meeting. At the debut meeting, he too came with reports highlighting developments in the new American province. Duncan had no fears about the future of ACNA. He was confident, sanguine, and his lofty vision for the future was as bright as ever. He repeated his earlier pledge of "planting 1000 churches in the next five years." In addition, he assured the primates that all the churches would have their "rootedness in the three streams of Anglican tradition: Evangelical, Catholic and Charismatic." This was the creed that the primates around the table had been fighting for and Duncan couldn't but receive from them "an enthusiastic response to his presentation." Individually and collectively, he had their "strong expressions of support."

After focussing on ACNA, the GAFCON Primates Council turned to the subject of the Fellowship of Confessing Anglicans (FCA), who had begun to yield startling results, recording massive expansion with many regional chapters and networks being established. It was becoming quite clear that more and more Anglicans saw the need to "share a commitment to the theological formularies of true Anglicanism." Actually, before the meeting, FCA had been elevated, popularized, and transformed into a buzzword along with GAFCON within the Anglican Communion. The primates themselves had helped FCA gain currency among Anglicans across the world. They had even changed the nomenclature of their council, making it inclusive to become the GAFCON/FCA Primates Council.

Emanating from all parts of the Communion, the progress reports tendered about FCA at the meeting were thrilling. The primates couldn't believe such strides had been made within that short time. Some of the startling good news was even coming from the United Kingdom, where the FCA was sprouting. This was the seat of Canterbury as well as the home of Anglicanism. So great was the progress that the primates felt it warranted a formal launch of FCA on British soil. The decision was approved unanimously. A date, July 6, 2009, was selected for the inauguration of FCA at the Westminster Central Hall.

Eleven men had huddled around the table, generating these momentous decisions. Archbishop Peter Akinola was at the head, as usual, presiding as chair of the Council. The five other archbishops physically present were the Most Revs. Emmanuel

10. GAFCON, "Notes on Meeting of the GAFCON Primates Council," October 13–15, 2009, at Renaissance Hotel, Heathrow, London, from the collection and archive of Archbishop Peter Akinola.

Kolini, Valentino Mokiwa, Gregory Venables, Eliud Wabukala, and Peter Jensen, the Council's secretary. Two sent apologies—the Most Rev. Justice Akrofi of Ghana and Deng Bul Yak, the archbishop of Sudan. Also represented was Henry Orombi of Uganda, who sent Prof. Stephen Noll to take his place. The old soldiers, the Rt. Revs. Martyn Minns, assistant secretary of the Council; David Anderson, the treasurer; Bill Attwood, its Ambassador; Wallace Benns, chair of the Primates Advisory Council and Bishop of Lewes in the Church of England were all there. If historians were to look for the starting point of what later came to be characterized as "Global Anglican Realignment," certainly, this was it; that day was when every one of the major redefining steps was stamped with final authority.

The resolutions were touchstones establishing their vision of a new Anglican Church. The first to emerge concerned "the latest version of the [Anglican] Covenant and the role of the Primates Meeting and the GAFCON Primates Council." Like Duncan, Nigerian Archbishop Nicholas Okoh, who was chairman of FCA's Theology Resource Group, was at the meeting to present the report of their work. "There are serious questions," he told the primates, about the covenant. One of their major discoveries was that "the Covenant produces a new instrument . . . the Joint Standing Committee." The group observed that it contradicted the Communion's constitution of 1930. Notable, also, was the fact that "the Joint Standing Committee subsumes the Primates' power." Their contention before the GAFCON primates was that it was improper to "subsume under the JSC the Primates as metropolitans responsible for the Communion."

And there was the additional problem that the "Archbishop of Canterbury referees [the JSC's] decisions." Worse, he "remains unaccountable [and] oversees the process . . . with space to act independently." But the committee couldn't place trust and confidence in him that he would use the vested power fairly, judiciously, and prudently. A convincing piece evidence was that, despite the strident calls of his colleagues for Williams to do so, the "Primates Meeting has not been called." To concentrate all the powers in the archbishop, they believed, was to give him all he required to guillotine the Primates' Meeting, which was supposed to be an important governing arm of the Communion, a veritable source of counterforce to abuse of power by the Canterbury archbishop.

Furthermore, the Theological Resource Group held that "there is canonical rationale for the Primates to make decisions as metropolitans together." They enjoined the Primates Council to take preventive actions to forestall the ploy at the Communion level to block Primates from serving as a statutory governing organ of the Communion. Indeed, "the Primates have the authority to act beyond their provinces to ensure the integrity of their faith." The Theological Resource Group added that "the GAFCON primates have been acting in the way that the Primates Meeting ought to have been allowed to act." As far as they were concerned, therefore, the deliberate attempt at not calling the Primates Meeting was only being clever by half. They observed that the Primates Meeting "has the calling to implement Lambeth 1.10," and since the situation had been allowed to reach "divergence to the point of disruption" to the Communion's life, "formal action" could shift to the "several Churches of the Anglican Communion individually." In their opinion, since the "primates ARE those provinces and national churches by representation," the coming together of the GAFCON/FCA primates, accordingly, was not only legal but also valid from the point of view of a 1930 Lambeth Resolution.

What was the lengthy explanation about the rights and constitutionality of the action of the GAFCON/FCA primates supposed to achieve? What could it change? It wasn't as if Canterbury or others pushing the Anglican Communion to the apocalypse didn't know the right approach to stave off the disgraceful disaster. Was it not obvious that the GAFCON/FCA primates had reached the end of the road? Individually and collectively, their involvement with bringing back the Communion from its path of errors had exposed them to bullying, demonization, harassment, and intimidation. But they had weathered the storms stoutly and courageously, calling the bluff of their oppressors. Their October 2009 meeting was, therefore, more of a denouement. All the decisions came with an air of finality.

The same sense of events having reached the point of no return was reflected in the formalization of FCA's structure. With Archbishop Mokiwa of Tanzania moving and Gregory Venables from the Southern Cone seconding, the Council unanimously adopted the bylaws of the Fellowship. The secretariat was constituted with Archbishop Peter Jensen appointed as the general secretary of the FCA Council and the ex officio head of the secretariat. Along with him as members of the secretariat were Bishops David Anderson and Bill Atwood plus Archbishop Nicholas Okoh and Mrs. Eva Macharia. In addition, Atwood was entrusted with the specific duty of being deputy head of the secretariat. Anderson was to be the treasurer, and Macharia would be in charge of secretarial services. All the appointments were subject to the appointees' "being or becoming a member of Fellowship of Confessing Anglicans," as stipulated in the bylaws of the organization.

As a follow-up to formalizing the structure of the FCA, the Council confirmed the appointment of an eleven-member Advisory Board. The board included Bishops Michael Nazir Ali, Wallace Benn, Chuck Murphy, Albert Vun, John Edmondson, and their Bethlehem counterpart among others. The FCA's formal structure coupled with the scope and composition of its leadership differentiated it from previous initiatives within the Anglican Communion. The only organized group like it in the Communion, but which still was in no way comparable with it, was the Global South. Though a bigger platform, the Global South was yet a limited network. Its composition was limited to Anglican Church leaders from the Southern hemisphere. Besides, it lacked the formal structure of the FCA. Nor was its membership required to openly express "commitment to the theological formularies of true Anglicanism," which was a requirement for membership in the FCA.

Then there were the two African networks, the Council of Anglican Provinces in Africa (CAPA) and the All African Bishops Conference (AABC). Though CAPA had a formal structure, its dependence on external support had continued to make it vulnerable to Western manipulation. On the other hand, the AABC was a relatively young, contemporary enterprise, a platform for African bishops to gather for discussion. Consequently, the FCA uniquely coalesced the fundamental Anglican theological perspective across diverse cultures into a single group of orthodox Anglicans. Their shared faith was rooted in a common belief regarding the undiluted Word of God and the eternity of Jesus Christ as the Lord and Savior.

By the end of that October 2009 meeting, it was obvious that the FCA had changed the complexion of efforts at rescuing the Anglican Communion from its grave errors over homosexuality. The end of the road seemed to have been reached on their part. Over were the agonizing years of headstrong homosexuality advocates in the Church taking their opponents for granted. The FCA had become a formidable counterbalance, a potent organ of redeeming the Anglican Church from its theological error. Important as well was the fact that the FCA was determined to stay steady and sturdy no matter the roughness of the road ahead. The Global Primate Council resolved that the FCA's teeth must bite when need be. The meeting resolved that whenever there was "urgent need for FCA," it must respond in a timely and expeditious manner. As a practical demonstration of the job at hand, the Council demanded that the FCA provide "oversight to the clergy and congregations alienated by their bishops and the wider church" in the UK and Ireland, from which reports of high-handedness were being received. Similarly, it directed concrete steps toward the establishment of FCA branches in the West Indies, Europe, Australia, New Zealand, and Mauritius.

After nearly a dozen years, the sequence of events showed the unfolding of a new sun, the emergence of a new spirit by the anti-gay group within the Anglican Communion. From that point on, the GAFCON Primates Council and the FCA resolved that there would be no surrender, no retreat. They would neither balk at defending the Word nor stand akimbo in helpless surrender to the perversion of Christ's Church. That was the purpose of their long struggle, the essence of the realignment and reformation in the Anglican Church. They would remain unshakably true to God, the Word, and the Faith as once delivered to the Saints.

29

Homeward, but Still Not Over

Bermuda, 2010

I t seemed that October 2009 was reserved for climaxes in the life of the Anglican Church. Another big event was the exit of Archbishop Akinola as the Nigerian primate and head of the Nigerian church. At the GAFCON Primates Council meeting in the Renaissance Hotel, Heathrow, London, October 13–15, 2009, the Nigerian church leader introduced formally his successor, Archbishop Nicholas Okoh.[1] The news jolted his colleagues from different parts of the world, for Akinola had emerged as a most formidable and frontline, 21st-century, international religious leader. Their respect for him was deep, for he was exemplary in every way: forthright, bold, courageous, devoted, reliable, and trustworthy. As relayed in several parts of this book, his leadership was a product of great fortitude and forbearance. Neither plots to subdue him nor the revisionist agenda hatched by some leading Western churches within the Communion moved him a meter. Metaphorically, Akinola dared and damned the devil and put the powers that be to shame. The outcome of his honest and determined leadership made his roles within the Anglican Church the subject of wild insinuations. Attempts were made many times to demean him and smear his altruistic motives. There were those who preferred to caricature his struggles for orthodoxy and Anglican Church integrity as serving a selfish agenda.[2] They accused him of creating the so-called "church-within-a-church" as a means to become the leader of a parallel Anglican Communion. These speculations and charges were pure fictions.

No doubt, Akinola fought hard and relentlessly, a determined and devoted warrior. Yet any honest appraisal of him was bound to exclude opportunism or power-seeking. Once he accepted responsibility, he didn't shirk it or shrink from it. As with a cult or mafia group, you don't tangle with homosexuals and avoid a fierce reprisal.

---

1. GAFCON, "Notes on Meeting of the GAFCON Primates Council," from the collection and archive of Archbishop Peter Akinola.

2. "A Gay Spirit Diary," https://joshtom.wordpress.com/.

Akinola stirred the hornets' nest, throwing a wedge between the homosexual movement and the Anglican Church, thus preventing men and women of an aberrant lifestyle from using the Church as a runway from which to launch into the world. Never
could there have been fiercer, more vile, and more unforgiving opponents than the
homosexual groups. Akinola challenged them and survived their despicable attacks
that came from all fronts—personal, political, public, and private. Now he was out
and Okoh was in as the new Nigerian primate. Okoh would be inaugurated on March
25, 2010, leaving a mere five months more for Akinola to exercise leadership at GAF-
CON/FCA and the Global South.

The five months sped by like the sun setting in a hurry. A full dozen years had
been consumed with the whole gay episode within the Anglican Communion, beginning with the 1998 Lambeth Conference that predated Akinola's leadership both
at the national and international level. Yet the powerful but destructively obstinate
minority was still undermining the decision of the majority. For a period of not less
than eight years, the greatest chunk of Akinola's engagement, as well as that of the
entire Communion's leadership, was the gay agenda. By conservative estimates, he
traveled to nearby and far-flung places for discussions, meetings, and conferences no
fewer than 200 times, but for all this, the efforts felt futile at times, as though no
positive achievement was recorded.[3] Even at his last meeting as the chair of the FCA
Primates Council, the result was still zilch. The Council had met in Bermuda, April
5–9, 2010, barely a week and a half after Akinola's formal retirement as primate of the
Church of Nigeria.[4] It was time to take a noble exit from the FCA Primates Council,
and fellow primates on the FAC Council couldn't help extolling his leadership virtues.
They found in him the commendable gifts, skills, and talents of an exceptional leader.
He received a shower of accolades, such as this one:

> We gave thanks for the visionary and sacrificial leadership of our founding
> chairman, Archbishop Peter J. Akinola, retired Primate, Church of Nigeria
> (Anglican Communion), for his courageous stand for the faith once and for
> all delivered to the saints.

Above all, they praised "his leadership both of the Church of Nigeria and also
within the wider Anglican Communion." A wise actor leaves the stage when the ovation is loudest, and now it was clear that Akinola had earned his place in history. The
battles he fought were huge, complex, and central to our collective humanity. Pivotal
was his concern over marriage, family, children, fidelity, chastity, ethos, and godliness.
Still, his prime focus was upon checkmating a very dangerous movement hell bent
on overcoming the Church of God. In spite of the tremendous odds, he refused to

3. Interview with the Most Revd. Peter J. Akinola conducted various times in Abuja and Abeokuta,
Nigeria between 2006 and 2007.

4. GAFCON, "Communique from the Primates Council of GAFCON/FCA," April 5–10, 2010,
Bermuda, from the collection and archive of Archbishop Peter Akinola.

blink, and now, his era was over. To replace him was Archbishop Gregory Venables, presiding bishop of the Southern Cone, who took over the chair of the Council of FCA Primates. Also elected were the Most Revs Emmanuel Kolini of Rwanda and Eliud Wabukala of Kenya—the two vice chairmen. Archbishop Peter Jensen of Australia retained his position as the general secretary.

The tragic reality, however, was that the exit of Archbishop Akinola did not end the gay crisis in the Anglican Church. Rather than acknowledge and address squarely the fundamental issues involved, the opposition decided to find a scapegoat to use as a diversionary tactic, and Archbishop Akinola was cast in that role, charged with promoting "schism" within the Anglican Communion for selfish reasons. Unfortunately, the propaganda was effective in some Western societies, and its proponents dug in their heels. In the end, the Communion was unwilling to change anything, leading to the principled stand of the departed Akinola.

In fact, before the new FCA chair took his seat, a very serious, fresh controversy was already brewing in the Communion. Indeed, at the transition ceremony, the FCA Primates Council observed that "the issues that divide our beloved Communion are far from being settled." They didn't see any usefulness in "the current strategy in the Anglican Communion [designed] to strengthen structures by committee and commissions." The evidence before them proved the approach "ineffective." They believed "that the current structures have lost integrity and relevance." Blunt as the primates' observations were, they made no apologies for stating them. According to an Ethiopian proverb, once reputation is lost, the kingdom is lost as well. The FCA primates believed that not only had the Anglican Communion suffered a substantial loss in reputation; the Church was in the process of losing its noble heritage as well. They warned that

> the Anglican Communion would only be able to fulfil its gospel mandate if it understands itself to be a community gathered around a confession of faith.

There was nothing new in that statement. Countless times, the same thing had been said. Nevertheless, the Anglican Communion didn't stop behaving like a leopard unwilling to change its colors. It was incomprehensible therefore that while a concrete solution was yet to be found for the Gene Robinson trouble, the same American church would make another decision plunging the Communion into fresh crisis. And, sure enough, the Episcopal Church, on December 4, 2009, decided to elect a partnered lesbian as a bishop.[5] The seventeenth woman elected into the episcopate in the American church, the Rev. Canon Mary Glasspool also became the first lesbian bishop in the entire global Anglican Communion.

The FCA Primates Council considered the action a provocation and deliberate slap at the Communion. To them, it signified that the Episcopal Church "has formally committed itself to a pattern of life which is contrary to the Scripture." They were not

5. http://bishopssuffragansearch.ladiocese.org/Candidates/glasspool.html; https://en.wikipedia.org/w/index.php?title=Mary_Glasspool&oldid=632507609.

going to deceive themselves any more. They felt that the American church's action was a further confirmation that "restraint in the Communion has come to an end." Evidence had become clear that the Anglican Church had lost its reputation and soul. The agenda of a part was being tendentiously allowed to become greater than the purpose of the whole. At that Bermuda April meeting, the FCA primates were depressingly aggrieved that the Anglican Church was deliberately being permitted to degenerate into a tottering mess. They agonized:

> Now, is the time for all orthodox biblical Anglicans, both in the USA and around the world, to demonstrate a clear and unambiguous stand for the historic faith.

But how many times had the same call been made in the past? How realistic was it to expect a change of heart from the American church or its British and Canadian cohorts? Why did the archbishop of Canterbury not take decisive decision to rescue the Communion? Could he muster the authority to discipline the erring churches, including his own? Those were the questions that had to be answered to rescue the Anglican Communion from the chaos into which it had tumbled. Some assumed that with Akinola out of the way, the conflict would abate. But in the midst of his departure came another warning that "the Communion [was] falling into deeper chaos and disintegration." The warning was contained in a letter written to Archbishop Williams by the Most Rev. Ian Ernest, archbishop and primate of Indian Ocean and chairman of the Council of Anglican Provinces in Africa (CAPA).[6]

Ernest had succeeded Archbishop Akinola in 2007 as the CAPA leader, yet, curiously, he had been consistently absent from all of the preparatory meetings of GAFCON and those held after its inception. This could not but fuel speculation about his siding with the pro-gay churches of the West, potentially becoming an instrument to destabilize the Global South. Further compounding the perception was his being seen as a lackey of the archbishop of Canterbury, in part because it was during this period that he received the Cross of St Augustine, the second highest international award in the Anglican Communion for outstanding service.[7] The award, at the exclusive discretion of the archbishop of Canterbury, was conferred in 2008. To all reasonable minds, the award smelled like a Greek gift even if Canterbury had not intended it as such, especially since its conferment occurred when the majority of African countries were planning to boycott the Lambeth Conference.

Ernest had, however, been appointed way back in 2003 by the archbishop of Canterbury as a member of the committee to organize the 2008 Lambeth Conference.[8]

---

6. "Archbishop Ian Earnest writes to the Archbishop of Canterbury," http://www.globalsouthanglican.org/index.php/blog/comments/archbishop_ian_earnest_writes_to_the_archbishop_of_canterbury.

7. https://en.wikipedia.org/wiki/Cross_of_St_Augustine; https://en.wikipedia.org/wiki/Archbishop_of_Canterbury%27s_Award_for_Outstanding_Service_to_the_Anglican_Communion.

8. http://www.anglicannews.org/news/2006/02/archbishop-ian-ernest-installed-new-primate-for-the-indian-ocean.aspx; https://en.wikipedia.org/wiki/Ian_Ernest.

He was a man of principle, not prey to herd mentality. Strong willed, he would stand by his convictions until the facts proved otherwise. Ernest's view seemed to be totally different from that of his African brothers before his letter to Canterbury. Though he was supposed to be their leader and their mouthpiece in Africa as the chair of CAPA, he took sides with the archbishop of Canterbury. He minced no words in making his stand known. It would be right to call him a "Williams' man" in a way, for he didn't hesitate to let the archbishop know that he was on his side. He never failed to indicate the pledge of loyalty when occasion presented itself. Indeed, in a letter to the archbishop, he made the open confession that "I have supported all efforts made by yourself." Against this background, Ernest's April 12, 2010, letter to Archbishop Williams was astounding.

He wrote it two days after the meeting of the FCA Primates Council, though he was neither one of the ten primates at the meeting nor a contributor to their decisions. The FCA primates had, of course, concluded that hope for "gracious restraint in the Communion has come to an end." That was the reason for their calling on all "orthodox biblical Anglicans around the world to come together." They charged every Anglican to come forward to stand for the historic faith.

Ernest's reaction was electrifying. He had never spoken in such a deprecatory manner. Why would sudden events made him "extremely distressed"? Ernest was riled by the insolence of the American church to the point that he took umbrage at the "disrespectful and high handed manner in which the TEC continues to dismiss the concerns of the rest of the Communion and to undermine the decisions taken by the Primates."

Ernest was no longer optimistic. Previously, he had "been patient and hopeful." Now, he had seen the uselessness of that approach. For years, he had shown "co-operation and listening" to Archbishop Rowan Williams. But now he was miffed that no dividend had attended his faithfulness. He had hoped that "reasoning and brotherly concern would have brought transformation," but developments that emerged had shown him he was grossly mistaken. The reality had hit hard because it was "abundantly clear to me and to my people that the Episcopal Church has no intention of honouring any of the commitments it has made whether that be in terms of 'moratoriums' or 'gracious restraint.'"

Piqued, Ernest was no longer interested in being politically correct. He was honest with himself and spoke with an unusual brutal frankness. The views he expressed were like the opinions of Akinola that tended to earn the latter denunciations and condemnations from the West. Apparently, for the Indian Ocean leader, the days of treating with kid gloves the homosexuality issue within the Anglican Communion were over. As he put it, the Episcopal Church "is to my mind hell bent on a course that is in radical disobedience to the counsels of God in Holy Scripture." And he told his friend, the Canterbury archbishop, the unsparing truth: "You have yourself been amazingly patient with TEC." He well remembered "some of us going so far as to declare broken or impaired communion with both the TEC and the Anglican Church of Canada." Similarly, he realized the honorable efforts of his colleagues in the Global South, CAPA, GAFCON, FCA, and ACNA, individually and collectively. Now, he had to admit that all had "been to no avail."

Looking at the underlying cause, it is understandable that Ernest was so riled. Presiding Bishop Schori had just poked a crude finger into her opponents' nose again. She told anyone who wanted to know "that a deliberate course has been irrevocably chosen by that church."[9] This was her church, The Episcopal Church. She was going "to proceed with the consecration of a second person living in an actively homosexual partnered relationship." Making the openly lesbian priest, the Rev. Canon Mary Glasspool, a bishop like her openly gay male counterpart, Gene Robinson, was no accident. Glasspool was raised up for confrontation in much the same way as Robinson.

A reverend, Glasspool's father was as pure and puritanical as the Anglican Church leaders now being despised as conservatives. The elderly Glasspool was opposed to women's ordination, and through his thirty-five years in the priesthood, he didn't compromise. Glasspool's respect for her father was greater than her reverence for the Bible or the global Anglican Communion. While in college, she made two choices alien to her father's convictions—her choice of vocation and her sexual orientation. Nonetheless, Glasspool, at 22 in 1976, found her way to the Episcopal Divinity School in preparation for the priesthood, and there she emerged as a lesbian. She was also becoming radicalized, though in a somewhat subdued manner.

The women who inspired Glasspool were definitely the trench fighters of that period, including one nearby, Carter Heyward, a member of the Philadelphia Eleven, women who in defiance of the House of Bishops' decision forbidding women's ordination were ordained at a joint ceremony. Heyward and another of the group, Suzanne Hiatt, were both employed as faculty with full priestly duties by the Episcopal Divinity School. Heyward was a role model to Glasspool because she had "the courage to break through the barriers." Of course, she realized this was "not without cost," and Glasspool wasn't willing to pay at the time in order to avoid her father's wrath. She guided the secret about her sexual orientation jealously away from her father. The aberrant lifestyle remained a secret from the elderly Glasspool till he died

Curiously, ten years before her father's death in 1989, she had spoken openly in support of this sexual lifestyle at the Episcopal Church's General Convention. An open hearing had been conducted on September 12, 1979, as part of a convention held in Denver, Colorado, and further deliberations had been required on the report of the Standing Commission on Human Affairs and Health, which had looked at the ordination of homosexuals. As one of five students attending the convention from the Episcopal Divinity School, she was scheduled to give a three-minute speech, which

9. Global South, "Global South Steering Committee Meeting Notes of Meeting," Changi Village Hotel, Singapore; "Global South Steering Committee Meeting Minutes," ACK Headquarters, Nairobi, Kenya, February 25–26, 2010, from the collection and archive of Archbishop Peter Akinola.

she ended with, "I trust and pray that that same love will prevent any of us from condemning others—particularly in this case, homosexuals, in our human, and full, and loving wholeness."

Among the 1,500 delegates who listened to Glasspool speak was her bishop, Paul Moore Jr., who gave her "a great big hug," asking, "Now that you've come out to 1,500 people, don't you think it's time to tell your parents?" It doesn't appear she ever did, but Glasspool was lucky to enjoy the patronage of Moore the same way Gene Robinson benefitted from the protection of Bishop Theuner.[10] Moore was an influential bishop, a defiant and deviant leader, one who had disobeyed the church to ordain Ellen Barrett despite knowing she was a lesbian. And from that January 1977 event onward, he continued his assault on the church's canons, leading to his support of Glasspool. But he was not alone in this. Glasspool also had the broad shoulder of Barbara Harris to lean on.[11]

Harris was the first female bishop in the Anglican Communion, having been elected suffragan bishop of Massachusetts in 1989. Theuner had indulged Robinson by aiding and abetting his homosexuality contrary to the church's rules and canons, and now it was Harris's turn to favor Glasspool, with the same effect. Glasspool had met her partner Becki Sander in Boston, and they had begun a relationship. Then she moved to St. Margaret's Episcopal Church in Annapolis, Maryland, where she kept secret her lesbian relationship. Through the nine and half years she spent in that church, 1992–2001, she kept her partner Becki as invisible as she could. Glasspool's leap forward, however, came in 2009, when she put herself forward to be elected as a bishop suffragan for the Episcopal Diocese of Los Angeles in Riverside, California. On December 4, 2009, the diocese's 115th Convention started the process of electing a new bishop, and the battle was tough. On the first six ballots, she failed to secure the vote required to confirm her election, but during the seventh round of voting, the tide changed, and she was elected the first openly lesbian bishop in the history of the Anglican Communion.

Just as the former Presiding Bishop Frank Griswold knew the election of Gene Robinson was transgressive, the incumbent Jefferts Schori was aware of the illegality of Glasspool's election. Nevertheless, she affirmed the election, and, on May 15, 2010, in Long Beach, California, Glasspool was consecrated. Her gender didn't make her historic, for she was the seventeenth female bishop in the Episcopal Church's history. But as the first open lesbian, Glasspool's election provided another feather to the American church's cap. But to the worldwide Anglican Church, Glasspool was another gratuitous insult.

Archbishop Ernest wrote to the archbishop of Canterbury before the date chosen for Glasspool's consecration. Did he think the archbishop would exercise discipline over the American church? That would amount to self-delusion. Ernest's plea elicited

10. "Mentor, Predecessor to Episcopal Church's First Openly Gay Bishop Dies."
11. https://en.wikipedia.org/w/index.php?title=Barbara_Harris_(bishop)&oldid=692606486.

the scorn that had been the lot of his colleagues in the past. Certainly, Presiding Bishop Schori couldn't have cared less. Schori told all opponents who were thinking that something could be done about it were wasting their time, they were engaged in wishful thinking. Nonchalantly, she said the election was "not the decision of one person, or a small group of people."[12] Rather, "it represents the mind of a majority of elected leaders in The Episcopal Church, lay, clergy, and bishops." Furthermore, she said they had "carefully considered the opinions and feelings of other members of the Anglican Communion as well as the decades-long conversations within this Church." Ernest didn't gasp out loud over the dishonest claim, but the fact that the Episcopal Church had chosen to show "disregard of the mind of the rest of the Communion" diminished him.

Schori's insouciance was what prompted Ernest to follow the path that his colleagues had trodden. He wrote a letter of protest to Archbishop Willliams. He made it plain that he was suspending "forthwith, all communication both verbal and sacramental with both the TEC and the ACC—their Primates, bishops and clergy." Ernest's only condition for rescinding his decision was a return to the *status quo ante bellum* by the two churches. So, he stated emphatically, the bond of union with the North American churches would be severed "until such time as they reverse their theological innovations, and show a commitment to abide by the decisions of the Lambeth Conference." Years ago, his colleagues in CAPA and GAFCON had taken this step, and his embargo similarly wasn't going to be a blanket ban. He said the "suspension of communion would not include those bishops and clergy who have distanced themselves from the direction of the TEC (such as the Communion Partners group)."

It might have taken him a long time, but finally Ernest was seeing the light that his colleagues had seen for years. Reality was dawning on him concerning the point of disagreement between his colleagues and Williams, that the global head of the Anglican Church was permitting "the teaching and leadership role of the Primates in matters of faith and order" to be "effectively subverted." Finally, remorseful in his tone, he was compelled to acknowledge that they had been right and he had been wrong all along. "I want to agree with them," he said tersely. As a result, he fully aligned himself with "their call for an overhaul of the structures of the Communion."

Ultimately, Ernest got to the point his colleagues had made so many times, but to which he had not attached importance in his years of gullibility. He too was now questioning the fairness and equity in the management of the Communion's affairs. "If over 80% of Anglicans live in the global south, why is this not reflected in [the] Communion structures?" he asked. The same issue he raised about "the adoption of the Anglican Covenant" and the "matter of credibility of the structures." These were all issues about which his colleagues had formerly raised questions. Circumstances change a person, and situations can alter someone's perception dramatically. Ernest became a new person as far as the crisis in the Anglican Communion was concerned.

12. American Anglican Council, "TEC Leaders In Their Own Words."

The result was that Archbishop Rowan Williams lost a friend and loyal supporter. Interestingly, Ernest's new view about the crisis in the Anglican Church coincided with that of Akinola, his predecessor in the leadership of CAPA. Ernest followed his brother Global South and GAFCON/FCA primates in enjoining Williams to "call a Primates meeting." He, too, began giving conditions regarding his continued involvement in the activities of the Communion. His participation at the primates meeting, for example, would depend on two factors—first, that they "as Primates be consulted first before the agenda is finalised," and, second, "that the Primates of TEC and the ACC are not present." The same stand earlier was what prompted the critical conflict between Akinola and Williams at the primates meeting in Tanzania. So it can be said that, after years of chummy relationship, Ernest had not only departed from the former path but, perhaps, could be on the road to his own test of who would blink first.

He was obviously challenging the power wielders in the Anglican Communion. The CAPA chair was beginning to sound tough; valor seemed to have returned to him as he addressed Archbishop Williams: "I urge you to consider seriously our request"; "failure to take prompt and decisive action at this time will only see the Communion falling into deeper chaos and disintegration." This brings to mind the African proverb, "Ears that do not listen to advice accompany the head when it is chopped off." But delayed as it might have been, it was good that Ernest permitted his own ears to listen to his inner voice. Like former Southern Africa Archbishop Njongokulu Ndungane, he ultimately encountered the truth and the truth helped to set him free.

One week after Ernest's strongly worded letter to Rowan Williams, the Global South primates converged in Singapore.[13] They were in the Asian country's capital for the Fourth Anglican South to South Encounter. In the times past, Archbishop Akinola would have received serious bashing for supposedly contriving the gathering to escalate the crisis that Glasspool's election added to the raging controversy. As leader of two organizations—CAPA and the Global South—the dual responsibilities usually exposed Akinola to blackmail or other attempts at treachery. But this time around, nothing could be pinned on him. He wasn't the leader or the voice of CAPA. Archbishop Ernest was the man of the moment, the leading light for all acts of commission and errors of omission. But Akinola still had outstanding baggage from his leadership of the Global South, issues that had to be resolved, especially the differences between GAFCON and the Global South.

Luckily, the disagreements were successfully resolved. Twice the Global South Steering Committee had met in Singapore on the road to the Encounter. The first time was on December 3, 2009, with six members present. There was only one absence recorded, that of the archbishop of the Southern Cone, Gregory Venables. Healthy as their discussions were, they had to iron out compromises on some volatile issues on which they had been sharply divided. Again, one of those knotty issues was the

13. Global South, "Global South Steering Committee Meeting Notes of Meeting," Singapore, December 3, 2009, from the collection and archive of Archbishop Peter Akinola.

relationship that should exist between GAFCON and the Global South. Archbishop Akinola was caught in between. He was the eye and the ear of both, and he wanted a diplomatic solution, forging unity instead of bickering about supremacy. He contended that the primary concern should be "to break down barriers especially with those who shared same faith." It was not hidden that Archbishop Mouneer Anis had initially expressed strong reservations about GAFCON. Up till that time, his concerns had not evaporated. He felt it might be prudent to solidify the Global South's cooperative work "before accepting leadership participation from the North." He reminded his colleagues about their earlier decision to address these issues after the Lambeth Conference. Now, with both GAFCON and the Lambeth Conference out of the way, Anis seemed troubled by the way GAFCON was evolving as a rallying point for the majority of primates as opposed to the Global South. He was unhappy that "half of GS founders [had] become GAFCON Primates Council [members while] GS Primates are yet to come together."

Archbishop Akinola allayed his fears, assuring that he didn't see anything Anis should worry about. He explained that the two initiatives shared the same foundational origin, with "GAFCON being a child of circumstances just like the GS had also evolved in the same manner." He urged, "If anything is wrong with GS and GAFCON, let's deal with it for the sake of the common good." Undoubtedly, the intense, divergent, personal feelings among the primates concerning the propriety of GAFCON had not lessened. Supporters of GAFCON like Archbishop Kolini continued to argue regarding GAFCON and the Global South that their "aims are the same but [their] methods [are] different." He maintained that they must "work together without others dividing us."

The other principal objector, Archbishop John Chew, also believed nothing should undermine the exalted position of the Global South as the most formidable bloc within the Anglican Communion. Chew wanted the group to be seen as "the more trusted body to help the majority to hold the Communion together and move it forward." The position of the South East Asian primate was understandable. He had a sentimental attachment to the Global South. But though the GS had been existence since 1993, it had been confronted with a condescending attitude by Western churches for that same length of time. It also seemed that the Western churches knew how to manipulate Global South leaders to follow their wishes until Akinola came along. Now, however, the old master-servant relationship between Western church leaders and their Global South colleagues had crumbled to an extent. The Western churches could no longer look down on their colleagues from developing countries as "boys" to be tossed up and down. Increasing was the demand of Anglican Church leaders from the South not only to be treated as equal but for the Communion also to ensure equity, fairness, and justice in the management of its affairs.

As passionate as the arguments on both sides of the divide were, the discussion was neither heated nor troubled by egoistic pride. The dialogue ended on a give-and-take note, with the adoption of a resolution to "let the 4th GS Encounter decide."

Many of the other resolutions that followed this chief one also enjoyed smooth sailing. An example concerned the fund required for hosting the 4th GS Encounter, which was set at about US$150,000. The Province of South East Asia rose quickly to the occasion. It promised a third of the needed sum, which was US$50,000. Nevertheless, that generosity didn't stop the Steering Committee from insisting that every province attending the Encounter should cultivate the spirit of self-sponsorship. The churches were urged to look inward toward raising the funds needed by their respective participants. If there were to be any outside contributions or support at all, the Steering Committee was of the opinion that such assistance, strictly speaking, must not have strings attached.

From the in-house issues, they moved to the wider Communion, considering the "Anglican Covenant." Naturally, the Covenant was a matter of abiding interest to them all. Without exception, they were all eagerly looking forward to the pact. The Covenant, a bond or treaty among Anglican churches, was to be the defining mark of Anglican identity throughout the Communion. Passage of the document, however, was being dogged by serious contentions. Archbishop Chew opened the discussion. He was concerned about its "Section 4," which their November London meeting had agreed "must remain intact." Outside the controversy dogging that section, he could report that the document was making progress substantially across the Communion. Now, as he said, it was time for the "JSC to send [it] out to all provinces."

Chew was convinced, however, that Canterbury wanted to influence the provinces on that key issue. He told his colleagues that he wasn't perturbed in any way with such an attempt. As far as he was concerned, neither Archbishop Rowan Williams nor the Anglican Communion Office's head, Kenneth Kearon, would be able to muster the power needed to achieve their goal. He was sure of the safeguards the document had in place to counter the efforts. For example, a provision in the document requested that provinces "indicate as soon as they receive the Covenant draft if they are willing to sign it." And so far as he was aware, there had been positive developments concerning the Covenant. He could confirm that Japan, Australia, the Church of England, and Ireland had all signified their support for it, notwithstanding the contentions that section 4 was raising.

Subsequently, the primates' discussion drifted to what was always an agenda item when two or three Anglican leaders gathered—the intransigence of The Episcopal Church of America and the Anglican Church of Canada. Mouneer Anis shot the arrow first. He played devil's advocate, asking a hypothetical yet practical question: "Is TEC allowed to sign, given their baggage?" Chew provided the answer: "The Working Committee has the mandate only to review Section 4, not to define who can/cannot sign or how they sign." As it were, Anis' question had upset Kolini, prompting the Rwandan church leader to observe, "If TEC signs without consequences, it will be meaningless, not a sign of repentance they are called to." Chew's response brought no comfort. Terse was his reply that "it was not the mandate of the Working Committee to discuss this."

Archbishop Akinola could not contain his aggravation any longer. Riling him was the fact that in spite of the agonizing journeys and pains to which all of them had been subjected, the Communion was still indulging the American church in its continuing blatant efforts at undermining its cohesion. He told Chew that though he was willing to concede to him that the mandate of his Committee didn't extend to considering punitive action, he could not refrain from asking him and all primates at the meeting the vexing question: "What do we do if TEC signs?" The Nigerian primate was well acquainted with the American church. He knew their antics and gambits too well. He would be a fool to trust the American church. That would be foolishness of the highest order! He let his colleagues know his unequivocal stand: "It must be clear that they cannot sign with their baggage."

Archbishop Kolini felt Akinola had not put the issue in its right perspective. He believed "it should not merely be a matter of signing." The issue must extend to the Episcopal Church's mending its ways. He insisted that the church must conform with the "spirit of Dromantine." In other words, the American church must be ready to abide by all the conditions previously stipulated. Kolini's condition was certainly outside the jurisdiction of the committee working on the Anglican Covenant, and Chew frankly told him so, stressing the impossibility of his position. Chew said, "This is the statement that GS must make, not the Working Committee." Kolini, however, still insisted that "the Covenant is not isolated but part of the whole Windsor Process." Chew judged Kolini's tack to be pointless, telling him nothing would result from it.

On the other hand, Chew suggested that a better approach would be for them to raise their concerns publicly through a statement. Back and forth the two engaged until Kolini finally agreed with Chew. After coming to terms with Chew's position, Kolini asked, "Should GS make the stand now or in April?" Again, Chew provided the answer. His reply was that "individually, GS provinces can do it even now." However, he believed that as a group, it was best done "corporately in April at the Encounter."

After his initial input, Archbishop Akinola had been mostly quiet during the deliberations, asking a question here, or making a critical observation there, or merely requesting an explanation or clarification for the benefit of all at certain points. Eventually, he interjected, "How then will the 'state of brokenness' be considered mended or restored?" Anis was the first person to answer. "Only when TEC 'completely dies out,'" he said flatly. Chew agreed that TEC needed to show evidence of "its compliance with the spirit of the process, not merely the act of signing." Anis must have dipped into his memory bank, recalling the impertinence of The Episcopal Church, which led him to voice his suspicion that TEC "may sign without intention to comply." It turned out, Chew already knew that to be the case. With some air of chagrin, Chew, a member of the Working Committee on the Covenant, hit his colleagues with the truth. Yes, he had known the truth all along but had held it back from his colleagues—the Episcopal Church had decided the aspect of the Covenant to obey and the part to reject. Demurely, he confirmed that they "only affirm Sections 1–3, not 4" of the Covenant.

Archbishop Akinola said nothing for the remainder of the meeting. Everything else appeared to him to be anticlimactic. When Chew added in a surreal manner, "When we sign, all who sign have to comply with the spirit of the process," Akinola knew Chew was engaging in wishful thinking. How feasible it is to bend the American church against it will? If it had been possible to get TEC to honor people and respect authority, the crisis in the Communion would have long been resolved. But time would tell if the leopard would change its skin.

The second meeting of the Global South Primates Steering Committee in Nairobi, Kenya, took place February 25–26, 2010. Nothing spectacular happened regarding Global South issues or the larger Communion issues. They simply fine tuned plans for the Forth Encounter, discussing, among other topics, "bringing together the GAFCON/FCA leadership with the rest of the Global South." The friction between the two groups had not been resolved. It was still simmering. Fortunately, everybody agreed that "the resolution of these differences was of the utmost importance." In this connection, Archbishop Akinola suggested an all-party assembly, bringing the "leaderships of the GAFCON/FCA together with other Global South initiatives such as EFAC to a meeting with the Primates to discern a mutually beneficial way forward." The idea appealed to all, and agreement was reached that the matter should be a top priority after their impending Encounter.

By February 26, all eyes were on Singapore for the Global South Fourth Encounter. Nineteen days before the Encounter, however, the bubbles burst. American Presiding Bishop Jefferts Schori proved right—and indeed exceeded—all apprehensions that Akinola, Kolini, Anis, and Chew had expressed at their Singapore meeting. On March 17, 2010, Schori presented an advance gift to the Global South Primates. It was a neatly packaged American speciality: the first openly Anglican Church lesbian bishop, the first in the worldwide Communion. Schori, tactically and strategically, plotted the unveiling of yet another novelty in the American church. News about Glasspool's election broke shortly before the Global South Encounter while her consecration took place twenty-one days after the Encounter on May 15, 2010.

It was a spick and span, perfect arrangement, fitting into the American church's pattern of deliberately acting in contemptuous disregard of the rest of the Communion. The last two Encounters of the Global South had coincided with similar provocative actions on the part of the American church. First was the 1997 Kuala Lumpur Encounter, where human sexuality became the major issue.[14] The 2005 Encounter became entangled in a web of controversy concerning the perfidy of the North

---

14. Adetiloye, "A Second Trumpet from the South (Trumpet II)," in Taiwo, *Joseph Abiodun Adetiloye.*

American churches on the gay issue.[15] Now, the third, and most certainly the last, Encounter to be held under Akinola's leadership got caught in another web of controversy: the election of an open lesbian as a bishop. TEC had deliberately spawned Glasspool's election as an offensive. It was no mistake. Measured and premeditated, it was an act meant to send a simple and direct message to the Global South. The American church wanted their colleagues to bury the thought that they could dictate to America or exercise control over them.

Virtually all the Global South primates ignored the American church's flippancy, with the exception of the archbishop of Indian Ocean, who was also the chair of CAPA, the Most Rev. Ian Ernest. Ernest's prompt and pointed reply has been written about in the preceding pages. The protest, conveyed through a letter written to Rowan Williams, happened a week before the opening of the Global South's Fourth Encounter. What did it achieve, however? Nothing. It merely served as an added pointer to the fact that nothing had changed in the Communion; that the ghosts of the yesteryears were yet to be buried, and that their shadows were accompanying the primates to the Fourth Encounter as they converged in Singapore.

As expected, the disturbing action of the Episcopal Church did impact the Encounter. But it didn't overshadow the overall success of the summit. From all parts of the world they had come, 130 of them cutting across twenty provinces—in Africa, the West Indies, Asia, and South America. Included also were their partners from Australia, New Zealand, and the USA. Nevertheless, the Glasspool event could not but cast a shadow, commanding unmerited attention.

The openly expressed irritation of Archbishop Ian Ernest had a saddening effect. Even those earlier inclined to believe the Communion still had opportunity to resolve the crisis were beginning to feel otherwise. Their opinions were shifting. They were thawing in their placating position, which had encouraged subtle mistrust and distrust among them, polarizing the Global South. It began to dawn on them that the more they allowed the walls of unity to crack in their fold, the greater the chance that their external adversaries would profit from the divide-and-conquer tactic they had been using against them. The consequence was that during the four days, April 19–23, 2010, Anglican Church leaders from more than two-thirds of the world turned the page from their frustrating history.

Conspicuously absent at the Encounter was the archbishop of Canterbury, Dr. Rowan Williams. His absence was significant because no gathering of any other bloc or subgroup within the Anglican Communion compared in size or status with the Global South. Archbishop Williams' greetings to the gathering came by "means of a brief video." Perhaps it's best for him to have evaded personal contact with the Global South primates, given the impertinent gift that American Presiding Bishop Schori had

---

15. Global South, "Third Trumpet: Communique from 3rd South to South Encounter"; "Delegates and Guests List at the 3rd South to South Encounter," both from the archive and personal papers of Archbishop Peter Akinola.

delivered to them on the eve of their summit. How would Williams have been able to look his colleagues in the eye and justify the American nonsense? The Global South primates would never have swallowed the slight of Schori's mindless humor. It was a mockery taken too far. Accordingly, the 4th Trumpet, that is, the official communique of their meeting was sharp, shrill and strident in tone.

Wistfully, the Global South primates recalled that for "many generations Anglicans have lived together with a shared understanding of a common faith." Their heritage included their great delight in "the Book of Common Prayer that has provided a foundation for our common life." They began noting, sadly and regrettably, that "in recent years the peace of our Communion has been deeply wounded by those who continue to claim the name Anglican but who pursue an agenda of their own," those "in opposition to historic norms of faith, teaching and practice" of the Communion. They grieved "over the life of The Episcopal Church USA (TEC) and the Anglican Church of Canada" as well as "all those churches that have rejected the Way of the Lord as expressed in Holy Scriptures." They noted, however, the peculiarity of the stubbornness of the American church, highlighted by the "election and intended consecration of Mary Glasspool." They considered the step brazen and reckless. It signified to them "yet, again, a total disregard for the mind of the Communion."

Perhaps it would have been better if they had restricted themselves to rebuking the American church. But they also asked Presiding Bishop Schori not to consecrate Glasspool. Of course, what they were suggesting was but an exercise in futility. They were merely wasting their time. What happened to all of their entreaties to the Episcopal Church in the past? Which had ever yielded any fruit? The American church apparently felt no embarrassment at being the leading threat to the "integrity of the Gospel, the Communion, and to the Church's Christian witness to the world." They did not seem bothered about the pain and dishonor that their action was inflicting on other Anglicans throughout the world. Eventually, the primates came to a resolution that seemed more practical: insisting upon the "need to review the entire Anglican Communion structure." They argued that it's undemocratic and improper for the minority to continue to hold the majority hostage. Furthermore, they bemoaned that for "over 20 years we have been distracted . . . prevented . . . from effectively fulfilling the Great Commission." They avowed that, having watched the Communion pushed into infamy, they "dare not remain silent" any longer. They were going to "respond with appropriate action," they promised.

The Fourth Trumpet from the Global South Encounter sounded the group's bugle, accompanied by the individual primates' picking up the harmonious lyrics. Singing the new tune were even the moderates of yesteryears. In a concessionary move by the archbishop of Canterbury, three Global South primates had earlier been included in some of the Communion's decision-making bodies, an accommodation rarely granted to the Global South in the past. Those holding the three positions were Archbishops Mouneer Anis of Jerusalem and the Middle East, Henry Orombi of Uganda, and Ian Ernest of the Indian Ocean. With each deciding for himself, they resolved to not "participate in meetings of the various Instruments of Communion at which representatives of The Episcopal Church USA and the Anglican Church of Canada are present." Anis, Orombi, and Ernest unequivocally stated that their "actions [were] in protest of the failure to correct the on-going crisis situation" in the Communion. It was at the Fourth Encounter that they conveyed their decision to their colleagues. An enthusiastic response greeted their decision. In unison, their colleagues patted them on the back and, with a thumb up, said in effect, "We uphold the courageous actions."

The way the events were playing out was certainly not the best way for Williams to end his career. He was the target of numerous missiles. The primates' statements were an open indictment of his leadership. For too long, Williams had not heeded the Global South's warnings about "broken and impaired Communion with The Episcopal Church USA and the Anglican Church of Canada." It was now clear that his indifference could no longer be sustained. The primates were tired of his aiding and abetting the American and Canadian churches in their "continued refusal to honour the many requests made of them by the various meetings of the Primates and through the Windsor Process."

Though smart to the point of being wily, after hiding in the shadows so long, Williams finally realized that there was no place to hide. In a damning and blunt manner, the Global South primates told him to act like a man and a leader and do the needful thing that his sacred office required. What did they want him to do? Simple! It was for him to summon the courage as "Archbishop of Canterbury to implement the recommended actions."

To be forewarned, as the saying goes, is to be forearmed. Ernest had cautioned Williams of dire consequences if he continued to encourage and lubricate perfidy against the Communion. The Fourth Trumpet of the Global South Encounter resounded the point with bigger, reverberating echoes. One point on which they now talked with full authority was the need "to reconsider their communion relationships with The Episcopal Church USA and the Anglican Church of Canada." The condition to maintaining normal relationships with the two churches would be for them to evidence "genuine repentance." The Global South wasn't interested in a face-saving gesture. They wanted "genuine repentance" from the American and Canadian rebels.

Indeed, it was as an alternative to the two errant and doctrine-corrupting churches that the Anglican Church in North America (ACNA) was conceived. Necessity conceived ACNA and inevitability midwifed it. Those who created the necessity were the ones to blame. For Global South primates, the ACNA remained the latest welcome addition to their fold in the Anglican family. They looked forward to the province becoming "partners in the Gospel." The primates admonished each of their members "to be in full communion with the clergy and people of the ACNA and the Communion Partners." Times had changed and so had dynamics of the Anglican crisis. Two representatives of the Communion Partners were at the Encounter to bear witness to the beginning of a historical epoch in the life of the Communion.

In Singapore, the past met with the present, resulting in a confluence of promising optimism. The Global South leaders succeeded in attaining one mind, a common perspective concerning the Communion's crisis. This had taken nineteen years. In the past, Global South primates had maintained a consensus against the unilateral decision of Western churches to impose homosexuality on the worldwide Communion, but they differed regarding the methods to employ in expressing their dissatisfaction. There was simply no consensus. The majority favored a strong and radical stand; a few preferred a moderate or pacifist approach; one or two would rather go with the West. This created an opportunity for Western church leaders to employ divide-and-conquer tactics to weaken them, and for some time the strategy worked.

With the Fourth Encounter, however, a new vista began to unfold. Singapore went beyond hosting a divided house. Rather, it released a new spirit with a fresh burst of energy. The Global South leaders reached a new consensus on the way forward. They agreed in unison to rescue the Anglican Communion from the grips of those determined to wreck it. This time around, Archbishop Akinola was no longer at the center of the struggle. Nor did he occupy the driver's seat. His time had come. He had to quit the stage. His tenure had ended.

Akinola had acquitted himself so well in his leadership of the Global South that his colleagues engraved his name in their golden book of honor reserved for rare, lifetime, outstanding leaders:

> We gave thanks to God for the visionary leadership of the Most Rev'd Peter
> J. Akinola recently retired Primate of the Church of Nigeria (Anglican Communion) as Chair of the Global South Primates Steering Committee for the
> past ten years.

Though Akinola's successor as the Nigerian primate, the Most Rev. Nicholas Okoh, was not due to be inaugurated until a month after the Encounter, for Akinola, the God-given task was over and it was time to move on. Opinions may differ about the impact of his leadership, but that's likely not so within the Global South, and in the broader context of the worldwide Anglican Church. Akinola was a man of immense courage. He was a forthright leader who demonstrated valor in good times and bad. Despite threats and intimidation, he neither shied away from making decisions nor betrayed the responsibilities of his office. Without him, the rampaging army of homosexuals would have overrun the worldwide Anglican Church. He was an effective speed breaker who halted the vain and desperate pursuit to make the whole world go gay.

Desperate and determined as the attempts were to colonize the Anglican Communion and make it an international gay colony, it didn't go gay. As resolute as the mindless pursuit of the narcissistic gay agenda was, Akinola refused to be intimidated.

Challenged as to who would blink first, he denied despotism a chance. On all fronts, Akinola fought—as a Nigerian, as an African, as an Anglican, as a developing nations' representative, and as a global religious leader. He gave Nigeria, Africa, and indeed every black person in the world a name and prestige in global Christian leadership.

Apart from resuscitating the Global South, he labored hard to turn it into a prophetic and potent instrument of courage. He also led the Council of Anglican Provinces in Africa (CAPA) before passing leadership to Archbishop Ian Ernest. The African Anglican Bishops Conference (AABC) was another of his innovations. Likewise, he was a driving force behind the Convocation of Anglicans in North America (CANA), the convocation for orthodox Anglicans in the United States that became an albatross around the neck of the wayward Episcopal Church. And his magnum opus, the GAFCON, redrew the landscape and redesigned the architecture of the Anglican Communion throughout the world. GAFCON remained an evergreen, 21st-century, revolutionary gift to the Anglican world, as did the Fellowship of Confessing Anglicans (FCA), determined to reform, heal, and revitalize the Anglican Communion and expand its mission to the world.

A list of people who touched history profoundly and redirected the future of humankind in the 21st century would be incomplete without the inclusion of Archbishop Peter Akinola. His role as an international church leader who halted the destruction of the church by homosexuals and their coconspirators is unparalleled. Incidentally, the war wasn't Akinola's to fight. There was no way he could have matched the vast, well-entrenched, formidable, and well-resourced gay forces and their allied coconspirators. God was the Omniscient One who fought the battle. Akinola saw himself merely a vessel. He believed God would not have him look the other way as evil destroyed the legacies of God's creation—church, Scripture, marriage, family, and children. Akinola happened to have been providentially in the right place at the right time for his divine commission. To him, the cross is always a burden, but Akinola believed he had no choice but to do his sacred duty. Submitting to God's will has always been both a requirement and a joy for people whose lives are self-sacrificing. Ideals rather than heroism are often their propelling force.

Akinola's decade of international Christian leadership startled the Anglican Church as it took worldwide Christendom by storm and surprised the gay armada. The whole world was yet to go gay as Akinola bowed out, with the Most Rev. John Chew picking up the torch of leadership of the Global South. The succession was fitting: Akinola and Chew had worked through the years as chair and secretary of the Global South, so Chew would not be navigating uncharted waters. At the same time, Archbishop Henry Orombi moved in as the vice chairman, and The Most Rev. Mouneer Anis as secretary, the position vacated by Chew. Akinola's successor in Nigeria, the Most Rev. Nicholas Okoh, was elected to step into Anis' former position as treasurer. Two ex officio members were added to the cabinet—the Rt. Rev. Albert Chama and the Most Rev. Stephen Than. The seven of them constituted the new

Global South Primates Steering Committee. On their shoulders, the future rested. For Akinola, an era had ended, and as tough as the battle was, he had refused to blink.

In 2013, three years after Akinola's retirement, GAFCON held its second international gathering of faithful Anglicans. The conference was more or less a postscript to his legacy. GAFCON 2013 was bigger, better, and boisterous. The 331 bishops, 482 clergy, and 545 members of the laity, totalling 1,358 delegates from 38 countries, gathered in Nairobi, Kenya, as representatives of tens of millions Anglicans worldwide.[16] Lamentably, nothing had changed in the perfidious attitude of the North American churches. Fifteen years after Lambeth Resolution 1.10, GAFCON leaders would "grieve that several national governments, aided by some church leaders, have claimed to redefine marriage and have turned same-sex marriage into a human rights issue."

They disagreed with identifying the aberrant lifestyle as a matter of human rights. "Human rights," they argued, "are founded on a true understanding of human nature, which is that, we are created in God's image, male and female such that a man shall leave his father and mother and be joined to his wife (Matthew 19:6; Ephesians 5:31)." They were opposed to any decision or law rewriting the core principle of marriage. They remained categorical in their stand that "any civil partnership of a sexual nature does not receive the blessing of God."

In addition, they reiterated their determination to work for redefinition of relations within the Communion. Though there had been newly emergent expressions like the Anglican Global Realignment, GAFCON, GAFCON Bishops, and more, GAFCON leaders indicated that the shifts were not going to be temporary or ephemeral. They repeated, as stated at the maiden conference, "We commit ourselves to defend essential truths of the biblical faith." Furthermore, they reiterated, "We commit ourselves to the support and defence of those who in standing for apostolic truth are marginalised or excluded from formal communion with other Anglicans in their dioceses." In demonstration of that commitment, they formally recognized the Anglican Mission in England (Amie), a canopy for those upholding authentic Anglicanism both within and outside the Church of England. In this respect, they supported and welcomed the intention of Amie to appoint a general secretary.

Formalizing Amie in England was like shifting the battle to Canterbury's backyard, the same way that Akinola had taken the fight to the courtyard of the American Episcopal Church. The GAFCON leaders also declared, "We commit ourselves to continuation of the Global Fellowship of Confessing Anglicans." Perhaps as a way of warning the homosexual hegemonists and their backers in the Communion, they reiterated for the umpteenth time that they would continue to fight for the soul of the worldwide Church, vowing,

> We shall continue to work within the Anglican Communion for its renewal and reform.

16. GAFCON, "The Nairobi Communique."

30

Back Home to Serve the People

Abeokuta, 2010

Archbishop Peter Akinola's decision was to leave Abuja the very day his successor was inaugurated. On that sunny March 25, 2010, after Archbishop Nicholas Okoh had taken his seat as the fourth primate of the Church of Nigeria, he didn't wait a minute longer in Abuja.[1] He bid the Nigerian federal capital an instant farewell. The manner of his departure was as simple as his leadership style; there were no ceremonies, no razzmatazz, and no media blitz to usher him out. The few close friends who accompanied him to the airport were the only indication the traveler was not an ordinary person. Catching the flight from Abuja to Lagos, where he passed the night, marked the beginning of his homeward journey to Abeokuta. Long before retirement, he had decided that the ancient city would be his retirement home.

Actually, if his earlier plan had materialized, the archbishop would have retired before 2010. When he celebrated his golden jubilee in 1994, he had decided to retire voluntarily when he turned 60, or 65 at the latest. The mandatory age of retirement for priests in the Anglican Church was 70. But he wanted to exit sooner. Why was he opting for early retirement? "The reason," he said, "was that by that age of 65 years, I would have spent 50 years in the North, and I thought that, at that age, it was time to go back home."

In 2000, he was 56 years old when he became primate of the Church of Nigeria. When he turned 60 in 2004, he didn't make a bid for the early retirement he had contemplated. At age 65, however, in 2009, he made the move. As for the goals he set for himself to achieve as leader of the Church of Nigeria, he could reasonably say, "So far, so good." The church was in a healthy state. It was growing rapidly and expansively, locally and internationally. The church and its leadership commanded respect all over the world. The Church of Nigeria had carved an image for itself as a

---

1. Interview with the Most Revd. Peter J. Akinola conducted at his Hilltop residence in Abeokuta, Ogun State, on July 23 & 24, 2011.

principled and forthright biblically-based church. Rich were the legacies the church had built. Additonal time in office would have been "more or less like consolidating on the achievements that had been recorded," he said. "I felt there was no point hanging there." Flatly, however, the church's Standing Committee rejected his initial bid for early retirement. Akinola felt humbled by their insistence that he should exercise patience and complete his tenure due to lapse in 2010.

However, he had been making his retirement plans all along. The problems of Nigerian youth had attracted his primary concern: "Everywhere I went, I saw young people, even as early as in the morning roaming on the streets, at the motor parks, and on the football fields." Constantly, he was struck by their purposelessness and planlessness. "I kept asking myself: Why this deplorable situation?" he said ruefully. Naturally, Akinola's duties as primate of the Church of Nigeria took him to the remotest parts of Nigeria, and he had discovered that no part of Nigeria was immune to the youth problem.

"The last straw that broke the Camel's back," he recalled, "was when I came to Abeokuta to visit my mother." Each time he undertook such a private visit, he made it a habit to worship in one of the local churches. This day, he had slipped into the church like an ordinary worshipper, and everything had gone well with the service. He was driving back home when he was confronted by the usual sight of unengaged youth: "I saw scores of young people, physically fit, able-bodied, playing football. This was on a Sunday morning, Sunday morning for that matter, playing football!"

He told his chauffeur to stop the car and park. Alighting from the car, he mingled with the youngsters in an attempt to gain as much information as he could from them. He pumped them with questions. This encounter as well as many other experiences around the country led him to realize that "the situation had changed radically in Nigeria from when life was more guided and guarded by parents." From that point on, the issue incited a passionate interest in him.

Akinola commissioned a study to determine the plight of Nigerian youth. The facts that emerged were frightening. They indicated that Nigeria might be sitting on a time bomb.[2] About 75 million or 44% of the Nigerian population fell between 0 and 14 years of age, giving the country one of the youngest and most dependent populations in the world. Exacerbating the problem was the serious challenge of massive unemployment among the youth. For instance, an average of 1.8 million youth joined the labor market annually in search of nonexistent jobs.[3] And there was the army of secondary or high school dropouts who neither had employable skills nor job opportunities. Many were taking to crime—white- and blue-collar crimes—and many were clueless regarding the future direction of their lives. Writ large on the Nigerian landscape, therefore, was the fact her youths were at a crossroads. Consequently,

2. *4 Main Initiatives of PAF.*
3. "Nigeria Population Census 1991 Analysis"; *4 Main Initiatives of PAF.*

Akinola resolved that his retirement years would be devoted to finding solutions to this deep-seated national problem.

Apart from concern for the youth, there was another area of his life which he believed he couldn't neglect. He began his priestly career humbly, climbing the ladder from the lowliest position of catechist to the highest peak of church leadership. He treasured every aspect of his progression in the ministry, the fondest part being "evangelising, preaching, and church planting." Looking back to 1968, he fondly recalled, "I had no slightest clue of ever going to be ordained as a priest, not to talk of becoming a canon or a bishop or ultimately an archbishop." His original vision was to be an evangelist, a preacher, and a church planter, an itinerant missionary proclaiming the word, planting a church, and then moving on to another station to begin all over again. He wanted to return to this calling, though in a different manner—this time through a project of evangelism extended to places yet to be touched with the gospel.

The third area of interest was more or less complementary to the second. Archbishop Akinola felt there was need for continued development of the local Anglican Church, an initiative that he called "Stand in the Gap." This third initiative fed into the last, which had to do with sustaining the unity of Anglicans in Africa. He was convinced beyond doubt that the Anglican Church in Africa and its leaders needed to forge closer ties. He knew that the desperate attempt by the West to divide them would not abate. He reasoned therefore that the closer the African Anglican leaders were to one another, the better would be their collective strength to ward off the predatory forces. He thought something like an "Anglican Unity and Self Reliance" project would assist in the promotion of solidarity and resourcefulness among the churches and their leaders in Africa. By the end of his tenure as primate of the Church of Nigeria, Archbishop Akinola wasn't, therefore, groping for direction regarding how to occupy his future. His retirement plan was all worked out. As a result, he returned to Abeokuta, to hit the ground running.

Months ahead his retirement, he had already registered the Peter Akinola Foundation (PAF), with an assemblage of distinguished Nigerians on the organization's board of trustees. The board, six in number, was made up of one female and five males, with Akinola as the board's chair. All of them had proven integrity, with outstanding personal and professional pedigrees. There was the Rt. Rev. Adebayo Akinde, pioneer bishop of the Lagos Mainland Diocese and later archbishop of the Lagos Province.[4] The bishop was a man of laudable academic and professional achievements, an excellent academic, scholar, and intellectual—a leading light in the computer profession worldwide. At 33, Akinde was ordained and thereafter worked zealously in his priestly life.

Incidentally, Akinola and Akinde were both from Abeokuta, but the two had no prior links before meeting in 1979 at an event where Akinde was struck immediately

---

4. Peter Akinola Foundation, "Board of Trustees" in *Consolidated Annual Reports 2011—2015.*

by the primate's down-to-earth nature.[5] As he recalled, "I observed some degree of impatience in him." For twenty-one years, their paths seldom crossed, but eventually they began interacting closely. Akinola found in Akinde a man who was trustworthy, reliable, and dependable, and on that basis, he thought he would be an excellent member of PAF's board of trustees.

There was also the bishop of Niger Delta North Diocese, the Rt. Rev. Ignatius Kattey, who later became archbishop of the Niger Delta Province.[6] Unlike Akinde, the archbishop had no early relationship with Akinola, becoming aware of him only in 2000. Kattey was one of the first bishops elected during Akinola's primacy. After the announcement of his election, petitions started circulating against Kattey's nomination. Though they were not acquainted, Akinola had a guiding principle in handling matters of that nature—to subject every allegation to thorough, discreet investigation to find out its veracity. The primate found not one iota of truth in the allegations, for they were frivolous. Though he dismissed them, he tarried a while to see if any more would come. Seeing that none did, he went ahead with the confirmation and subsequent enthronement of the bishop-elect. Kattey learned about the incident much later, and the due diligence that Akinola exercised to find out the truth impressed him. So he was pleased to come on board as a trustee of the foundation.

Rounding out the men in cassock on PAF's board was the Rt. Rev. Oluranti Odubogun. Odubogun once served as a general secretary of Church of Nigeria under the archbishop. He had since moved up in the church's hierarchy, becoming the bishop of Ife Diocese. He was the same polished, impeccable, and meticulous young priest brought in by the archbishop at the inception of his primacy to work on the National Endowment Fund he had established for the church. Working closely with the archbishop, Odubogun was imbued with his values and virtues. As such, Odubogun was not just a subordinate but a trusted ally. And so he was the third bishop on the board of the Peter Akinola Foundation.

Then there were three non-clerical males on the board. Leading the trio was Mr. Abraham Yisa, a lawyer, the registrar of the Church of Nigeria. Like all the others, he had deep respect for the archbishop. And the archbishop found in him the first essential ingredient that endeared him to any individual—trustworthiness. Yisa was the man Akinola had entrusted with leadership of the Church of Nigeria's missionary initiative in America, the Convocation of Anglicans in North America (CANA), which he served as trustee board chairman. His legal expertise would be of service to the new organization, lest they suffer legal difficulties.

Then, to complement Yisa's astuteness in law, Mr. Yinka Fisher was another non-clerical member who brought business management wizardry to the board. Fisher was

5. Interview with Rt. Rev. (Prof.) Adebayo Dada Akinde, Bishop of Diocese of Lagos Mainland held at his office at St. Judes Cathedral, Ebute-Metta, Lagos, on 7 June 2007.

6. Interview with the Rt. Rev. Ignatius Kattey, Bishop of Niger Delta North Diocese, Rivers State held at his office at Osun Diocese Retreat Centre, Osogbo, Osun State, September 14, 2007.

a man any organization—public or private—would be glad to have. He was an impresario in both public service and the corporate world, the quintessential professional manager and astute entrepreneur who had acquired broad experience, beginning as a junior research fellow at the Institute of Behavioural Science in the University of Ibadan. From there, he gained international experience and exposure as special assistant to the Nigerian permanent representative at the United Nations. Then Fisher became the first director and facilitator of the frontline nongovernmental organization, the Nigerian Conservation Foundation (NCF). On top of this, his skills had been put to work for companies in the environmental sector, such as Waste Management Limited and Worldwide Information and Systems Limited.

Fisher's efforts in the corporate world had seen him build and manage ICT companies, net worth service providers in banking, petroleum, estate planning, health care, politics, and public service for over thirty years. He steered Nigeria into its first ICT public-private partnership project with the implementation of an e-passport scheme both at home and in fifty Nigerian foreign missions abroad. In 2006, he was appointed a member of a presidential committee for the harmonization of a number of IT projects in Nigeria.

Two passions marked Fisher's extracurricular interest. The first was the arts, of which he was an aficionado; the second was cricket, for which he had remained a lifelong, committed enthusiast. A compulsive arts patron and major collector, he had more than 400 items in his personal collection. He also co-established the Foundation of Modern Arts and Visual Artworks, creating a database of contemporary artwork, producing documentaries on artists and collections, and publishing books on the same in Nigeria.

As for his his second love, cricket, he had remained faithful to the game from his secondary school days on through university and into his adult working life. He had served as chairman of the Nigerian Cricket Association (NCA) and the West African Cricket Conference (WACC), and he had sat on the International Cricket Council (ICC). For his meritorious contributions to the development of the game and athletics generally in Nigeria, he was inducted into the University of Lagos Sports Hall of Fame in 2005.

A lifelong member of the Anglican Church, he had played leading roles and carried out a number of important assignments for the Church in Nigeria. He was chairman of the Organizing Committee of the Consecration of Bishops in 2006 and 2007, and he chaired the committee that organized the Church's General Synod in 2008. He received the Episcopal Award for Excellence in Service from the Diocese of Lagos in 2012 and capped it with the Primatial Award from the Church of Nigeria (Anglican Communion) in 2014. Fisher was close to Archbishop Akinola, and, indeed, the archbishop loved to call him the "civilian chaplain." Not surprisingly, Fisher was involed in PAF from its conception to its birth.

Next to Fisher was Jeremy Akinola, the son of the archbishop, the third non-clerical member. A computer scientist, Jeremy represented the family on the board. After him was the only female member, Mrs. Dorcas Modupe Akinkugbe, a distinguished banker with a 39-year, fulfilling career in the industry. She began as a junior supervisor and rose steadily up the ladder to manager in a number of branches before becoming head of public sector banking for the Union Bank.[7] Born into an Anglican family, raised in the Anglican way, Mrs. Akinkugbe also married within the Anglican fold, and she was a devoted church worker, with a role in church leadership training at the Haggai Institute. She was elected treasurer of Abuja Diocese by the synod of diocese, the position that brought her into close contact with the archbishop and made her a natural member of the select team that launched the Foundation.

Archbishop Akinola put his energy into the work of PAF. His main priority was to establish a Centre for Industrial Training of Youth. The center was to equip out-of-school youths with vocational, industrial, and trade skills as a means of empowering them for sustainable livelihoods. Circumstances had compelled the archbishop to seek an audience with Nigeria's president Goodluck Jonathan. President Jonathan granted the request, and Akinola used the opportunity to brief him about the idea of the Foundation and its prospect of assisting the country in taking aimless youth off the street and helping them find ways to exercise discernment at the crossroads confronting them. Jonathan "was enthused with the idea," recalled the archbishop. There was, however, a specific reason why it was important for Akinola to meet President Jonathan: "I needed permission of the federal government to use a facility they have in Abeokuta called the Industrial Development Centre."

The Industrial Development Centre (IDC) was a type of vocational center established by the federal government of Nigeria across the country to provide hands-on training and/or industrial skills for young Nigerians who might lack the aptitude or opportunity for higher education. About twenty-one such centers existed all over Nigeria, but like everything Nigerian, the centers had become white-elephant projects—not functional, virtually all of them moribund, notwithstanding the huge resources governments committed to them over the years. President Jonathan agreed with the archbishop's request, and he referred the matter to the minister in charge of industry, Senator Jubril Martins Kuye, in whose portfolio the issue fell. After the matter had traveled up and down the bureaucratic maze, a memorandum of understanding (MOU) was finally signed between the federal government and PAF, one giving PAF fifteen years' use of the IDC facility in Abeokuta.

The greatest challenge lay with the IDC. Abandoned for a long time, the facility became absolutely decrepit, a wild forest for animals rather than the dream place envisaged for equipping young Nigerians with vocational education. Tucked about three kilometres into desolate countryside that branched off the old Lagos-to-Abeokuta

7. Interview with Akinkugbe, Modupe Dorcas, member board of trustees Peter Akinola Foundation conducted over the telephone, September 14, 2016.

highway, it was a forgotten facility, marked everywhere with evidence of neglect and decay. Every feature was crying with chronic disrepair. Electricity to the premises had been discontinued; taps were dry; all the houses were in bad shape and uninhabitable. The extent of neglect was shocking, the rot stunning. It was, surely, no place to bring anyone for learning. The placed called for massive rehabilitation.[8] Though Akinola had anticipated some forms of restoration, he had not envisaged the magnitude of the work to be done. To provide the minimum infrastructure and amenities suitable for the planned residential program, it would take millions of naira.

Akinola had benefitted from the immense goodwill of people and churches when he was retiring. Generous gifts in cash and kind were showered on him. He decided to use the cash in support of the Foundation. To put the IDC in minimal habitable condition, the financial estimate given to him ran to a colossal N18 million (the equivalent of US$120,000 at the exchange rate of N150 to US$1). Yet Akinola was ready to invest every bit of the gift with which he had been blessed, and so the Abeokuta IDC received more than a facelift. It was given a face transplant. Many of the buildings were made fit for human habitation, providing hostels and residential quarters for the trainees and the instructors. The only access road to the center was opened up to allow contact with the outside world. At the end of the massive restoration, the amount spent far exceeded the projected cost.

But Akinola was not dissuaded from the mission of launching the center. On January 29, 2012, the Peter Akinola Foundation Centre for Industrial Training of Youths, Abeokuta, admitted its first set of trainees. They were twenty-nine in number, drawn from different parts of Nigeria—twenty young men and nine young women admitted for different vocational skills. The occupations ranged from bricklaying to concrete and tile installation, carpentry and joinery, catering and hospitality, electrical installation, metal/aluminium welding and fabrication, refrigeration and air-conditioning, tailoring and fashion designing, and computer studies.

Admission was reserved for those who had dropped out of school and/or those without any form of skill training. Both tuition and accommodations were free. This was in line with the Foundation's charter as a humanitarian, charitable, and not-for-profit organization. The trainees or their sponsors, however, were expected to pay for their meals, this to ensure that they too made some kind of personal investment in their development. For their nine months in training, the program would be fully residential. Trainees were to study under master artisans and other men and women proficient in the crafts and then be presented for the federal government's trade tests at the end of their training, certifying them for employment in government or the private sector. They would also receive spiritual guidance, as well as education in family life and citizenship.

---

8. *4 Main Initiatives of PAF*; *Inroad Industrial Institute Prospectus*; Akinola, "Chairman's Address at the Passing Out Ceremony of the 1st set of Trainees of PAF's Inroad Industrial Institute."

The first set of students completed their training successfully on September 26, 2012, their eyes opened and their prospects much improved. Archbishop Akinola was pleased, for the test-run provided empirical evidence that the idea was sound. Still, the center was an expensive affair, gulping money in its daily operation. Akinola was a priest and not a business tycoon, and the financial problems were aggravated by the volatile nature of the Nigerian economy. Every projection and plan assumed to have been made with the fine-toothed comb of prudential analysis was rendered mere guesswork at the end of the day by the extreme unpredictability of government actions.

Consequently, by the end of the first year of operations, the archbishop was already feeling the heat. He had to acknowledge that the "main challenge confronting PAF was funding." At some point, he considered liquidating some of his assets to keep the project going. Whatever the challenge, he had resolved that he would not go back on the project. It was amid these difficulties that the center admitted its second stream of trainees, with the 2013 class almost doubling the pioneering figure of 29. It totalled 53—32 males and 21 females.

At the same time, it was becoming clear that the government-owned IDC property was not very serviceable. Besides the huge amount being spent on the decrepit infrastructure, they were blocked from building new structures on government property, a stricture the archbishop deemed "quite unreasonable." During that second year, his quixotic nature further manifested itself. He put before the board the idea of building their own permanent site. They agreed that "it was better for the Foundation to struggle to build its own permanent site than to keep pumping money into a borrowed location."

Actually, a permanent site was an integral part of the project's original vision. The type of facility it should be, its dimensions and architectural design had already been planned and approved by the relevant government authorities. The PAF center was to occupy a 16-acre piece of land, with its hub being the Workshop Building. The Workshop Building was to house the facilities and workshops for training in carpentry and joinery, masonry and tiling, tailoring and sewing, light auto repairs and maintenance, including electrical wheel balancing, plus a center for computer skill acquisition. The plan also projected a multipurpose hall, to seat about 500 for the center's social programs.

The hostel facilities would accommodate no fewer than 600 trainees during any one session, and each hostel was equipped with a common room and suites for the hostel masters. Apart from the central cafeteria, two additional eating rooms were provided along with a big kitchen, stores, conveniences, and offices for the catering and housekeeping managers. The chief instructors, trainers, and other administrative staff were to be fully residential. They were to be accommodated in the 4-unit 2-bedroom terraced houses, the twin 2-bedroom bungalows, or the 3-bedroom detached bungalows serving as the staff quarters. A chapel big enough to serve as a town or city worship center, along with a sports field with opportunities for a variety of sports, were part of the community's infrastructure. Once in place, the PAF's center in Abeokuta could compete favorably with any training center in any part of the world.

There was, within the Abeokuta IDC neighborhood, another government facility, the Ogun State Technology Incubation Centre. Akinola had thus considered the area suitable for him to erect the PAF's centre. In fact, he had succeeded in acquiring the requisite land in that locality. After the necessary official processes had been completed, preliminary work began on the site. He was lucky that neither serious work nor funds had been committed to the project before it ran into a setback. Akinola had acquired the land from Ogun State government in 2011, but then, following the national elections of that year, a new governor was elected in the state. For reasons best known to the new governor, he considered the PAF's allocated site inappropriate for the center's permanent location. So he directed construction to stop, and he ordered that the location be shifted to a new site.

Fortunately, the new location given to the center did come with some advantages. It brought the centre closer to the major highway serving the Ogun State capital. Thus situated along the old Abeokuta-Lagos highway, the Peter Akinola Foundation's Centre for Industrial Training of Youths gained increased visibility and accessibility. On February 1, 2013, construction work began at the site. Eighteen months later, the goal was achieved.

Now, the PAF had its own permanent site. Every structure projected was standing—the workshops, the school's multipurpose hall, the hostel blocks and adjoining conveniences, the cafeteria, the kitchen, stores and offices for the managers, the institution's chapel, staff residential quarters, and the sports arena. It was a marvel. In a country where projects would begin with fanfare only to be abandoned midway through, completing a project of that magnitude at the record time of one and a half years was a rare accomplishment. "It took a lot in terms of time, thinking, praying, and energy," the archbishop said in reflection.

At the time, the combination of the day-to-day expenses and massive capital outlay by the Foundation for building its permanent site almost choked it financially. So again, Akinola considered putting a few of his assets in the market to see the project through. A number of friends, however, came to the Foundation's rescue, including Gen. Theophilus Danjuma, the retired Nigerian Army chief, an old friend and supporter from the archbishop's days at the Abuja Diocese. Danjuma once again rose in support of his friend, and a commemorative monument stands in the center, noting the funding generosity of Danjuma and other men and women of goodwill who gave unstintingly to the Foundation.

By 2014, the center was no longer a tenant in the IDC facilities.[9] It had moved to its permanent site. Indeed, graduation exercises for the 2014 trainees were held in the new multipurpose hall while enrollment kept growing. Compared with the 53 who came in 2013, 2014 saw 81 new students. Then, in 2015, the number rose to 94,

9. Preye et al, "The Jewel."

with 63 males and 31 females.[10] The growth was not exponential, but it represented commendable numerical and geographical progression nonetheless. Akinola's dream was coming true.

Different as the trainees' backgrounds and experiences were, they ended up sharing similar testimonies of the center's value for their lives, stories of transformation and radical alteration of their worldviews. Take the case of Omoniyi Olayemi Timothy (which was his real name), who hailed from a small rural community in Ogun State.[11] Before he found his way to the center, he was, as he admits, an "idle" young man." "I didn't know anything before I came here," he declared. But passing through PAF's center changed him tremendously as he had acquired skill in refrigerator and air conditioning repair. "My plan for the future," he said, "was to set up my own business." There was also Kolo Ezra from Kutigi in the northern part of Nigeria. He was a driver with no trade or occupational skill, but he learned bricklaying and concreting and resolved to go back home to start work in these two areas.

Perhaps the most telling story was that of Ejiliwe Chidiebere Simon, who came from the Niger Delta, where the Nigerian government was struggling with youth restiveness. Many communities in the oil-rich area had suffered acutely from degradation of their environments, aggravated by criminal neglect of successive governments. Simon was the typical Niger Delta youth, with an idle hand and thus, proverbially, a devil's workshop. As he wrote in his post-training evaluation, "I don't actually have a spesific (sic) work that I am doing before." But he underwent a life-changing experience—a complete transformation. A borderline social miscreant and a confirmed deviant, he had become a much calmer, more purposeful, and goal-oriented youth. "Number one is that PAF has made me to learn a particular trade in life," he said. And "PAF has taught me punctuality." "Now, even if I sleep so late I just have to wake up by 6.00 A.M. every day; nobody needs to wake me."

After four years, there were 257 students—169 males and 88 females. Though that number might seem insignificant relative to the burgeoning figure of over 40 million unemployed youth in Nigeria, it was still a feat.[12] "Nigeria's army of unemployed youth was but a ticking time bomb to the country," the archbishop observed. "That frightening figure was nearly a fourth of Nigeria's entire population and almost [equal to the population of] six countries of West Africa put together."

He continued, "What was compounding the unemployment problem was not only that the sea of jobless youths that kept swelling year in and year out, but also the

10. Adelaja, "Coordinator's Address at the 2015 Graduation Ceremony of PAF Youth Centre for Industrial Training."

11. Peter Akinola Foundation Centre for Youth Industrial Training end of course and exiting forms for years 2012, 2013, and 2014, giving personal evaluation, benefits derived, and future plans of each trainee, Administration Department, PAF.

12. Peter Akinola Foundation, "Statistics of Graduates and Courses Undertaken 2012—2015," "Beneficiary States—Youth Industrial Training," "Examinations sat for by Graduates of Youth Industrial Training Centre," in *Consolidated Annual Reports 2011—2015*.

tragic problem of Nigeria continuing to produce graduates in areas of less productive need of the country." So, "the earlier our young people realized the profound redefinition of work and employment market facing the country, the better it would be for them to know that they've got to acquire and become proficient in trades and/or skills that could enhance their potential for self-employment." Indeed, it was not Nigeria alone but all of Africa that should benefit from his type of visionary help for youth. Thousands of young Africans who have died in the Mediterranean Sea and the Sahara Desert as they attempted to reach Europe would have been saved if an opportunity like this had been open to reorient them and give them hope of a brighter future.

Ironically, the same youth on whom he had lavished his retirement time, energy, and resources almost became the cause of his untimely death. On December 24, 2013, in broad daylight, at the entrance to his center, he was kidnapped. Akinola wasn't the first Nigerian to have been kidnapped, for abduction of people accompanied by demand for ransom had become a major crime in the country. In fact, Archbishop Ignatius Kattey, one of his colleagues on the board of PAF, had suffered a similar fate. He was abducted in front of his house in Port Harcourt, the capital of Nigeria's oil-rich Rivers state.[13] Kattey, who was the head of the Anglican Church in the Niger Delta North Diocese, vanished without any trace. For weeks, Nigerian police could not locate the bishop as the search and rescue party set up by his church also failed to make any progress.[14] Eventually, Kattey was released after he had been an unwilling guest of his abductors for weeks in a riverine area of the Rivers State. The kidnapping of his colleague distressed Akinola. On his release, Kattey had left the country quietly to recuperate from the trauma.

If Kattey was a big fish for the kidnappers' net, Akinola was a golden fish. Within minutes of his kidnapping, the event had become breaking news throughout Nigeria. The archbishop was on his way home from the center when he was abducted.[15] He had gone to present bags of rice, beef, and other items to workers at the center for a Christmas celebration. At about 2:30 p.m., he headed home. But blocking his exit to the highway, right on PAF's property, was a white car.[16] Nigerian drivers are lawless, careless, and reckless, and few have road etiquette, decency, or courtesy. Such an occurrence was therefore not unusual. Still, Akinola saw no reason for the car to block the center's exit because the highway had sufficient shoulder space before and after the school's entrance for the car to pull over if it had developed a problem.

13. "Nigerian Anglican Archbishop Ignatius Kattey Kidnapped."

14. Yafugborhi, "Police Lied About My Rescue—Archbishop Kattey."

15. Gyamfi, "Gun Men Kidnap Ex-Anglican Primate, Peter Akinola."

16. The reconstruction of events is based on interviews with the Most Rev. Peter Akinola at his Hilltop residence December 25–26, 2013, when the kidnapping incident was still fresh in his memory; Interviews with Jonah Ahmadu on the same dates and location; Gyamfi, "Kidnapping: 'My Story' by Primate Akinola."

He could see that his chauffer, Jonah, was angry with the provocation. He could predict the likely reaction of the young man, for Jonah's main challenge was anger management. Fiercely loyal and protective, he was also a responsible, reliable, and trustworthy staff member, manifesting virtues in short supply in Nigeria. From his back seat, Akinola had an idea of how Jonah might behave in such a circumstance, so he told him in Hausa (the young man was from the northern part of the country, and the two of them conversed easily in that language) not to do anything rash with the obstructing vehicle. It was good that he gave Jonah the timely warning because just then, two young men emerged from the car and walked confidently toward them. One positioned himself beside the car and signalled to him to roll down the side glass. He pointed a gun at him. Their attackers were young men, both in their twenties. The other man, on the opposite side of the car, had also brought out a rifle tucked underneath his loose, untucked shirt. He gave Akinola more than a good glimpse of the weapon and put it back in its hiding place. This was obviously big, real-time trouble, Akinola thought to himself. The car was planted deliberately to block their exit, but Jonah could drive backwards, risk a reverse back to the center. Was that possible under the circumstance? The answer was no. They would be accompanied by a volley of bullets, so they stayed put.

The one on Akinola's side demanded that he roll down the side window. He did as instructed. "Where are the dollars?" the man asked brusquely.

"Dollars?" Akinola exclaimed in genuine surprise.

(He wasn't pretending. He had no dollars.)

"I'm a village pastor. I have no dollars!" he added quickly.

He had not a single dollar on him, not even a penny, the lowest denomination of American currency. He was already thinking about the probability of being led at gunpoint to his house to be robbed of his valuables. Cases wherein people were hijacked on highways and taken to their homes to be cleaned out of their possessions were not uncommon.

Cynically, the young man retorted, "Village pastor! Village Pastor! Village Pastor indeed!" In a brusque tone, he shot out a threat, "Well, it is better for you to cooperate with us in your own interest." He paused. "If you don't, we will waste you," he said nonchalantly after the pause.

The young man spoke with a menacing arrogance. The sign of a deadly killer might not have been tattooed on his forehead, but his cold, icy tone suggested as much. Akinola wasn't willing to risk finding out if he could truly be the coldblooded killer he was purporting to be. That would be a foolish gamble. The dead is a hero only to the coffin and the undertakers.

Just then, Jonah decided to add his own complications. The other kidnapper had ordered him curtly, "Give me the key." Jonah had been reluctant and was showing evidence of defiance. Quickly, the archbishop intervened, directing him to comply. Ardently, the archbishop was praying silently that nothing would tempt Jonah to attempt any heroic deed. The robber took possession of the key and ordered Jonah to the back of the car. When he got there, he was instructed to bury himself in the legroom behind the driver's seat. The same instruction was passed on to the archbishop. Both of them squeezed themselves into those narrow spaces, not a simple matter for the former Nigerian primate, who was close to six feet tall. Clearly, the kidnappers were no respecters of anybody! Immediately, the engine roared to life. Jonah's tormentor had taken his place in the driver's seat. And zoom, the vehicle raced off.

The kidnapping ignited immediate response from Nigeria's topmost seats of political power, the presidency, and from the Ogun State government as well. While every security agency in the country was placed on red alert by the president, the Ogun State governor, Mr. Ibikunle Amosun, led the heads of key security agencies in the state to the crime scene. On the spot, they embarked on an expeditionary rescue mission. Unfortunately, it was a futile exercise. In Nigeria, criminals have a relatively high probability of success because of the head start they typically get over law enforcement agencies. The police lack such tools as closed circuit television cameras and a national database that can quickly provide information to track offenders. Though the Ogun state governor and his rescue team headed in the direction that they suspected the kidnappers would most likely have gone, their efforts turned out to be a wild goose chase. Apart from the identity and registration number of the primate's vehicle, they had no clue to guide their search. So after hours on a fruitless trail, they called off the hunt and retired to Abeokuta while security officials continued the assignment.

In a security-conscious country, the stolen vehicle would not have failed to attract attention by the reckless driving of the offenders. They were heading toward part of Ogun State that shared border with Nigeria's closest neighbor, the Benin Republic. It is a known fact that for every one official human and vehicular route to and across the border, there are tens of illegal paths used for smuggling to and from Nigeria. There was no other way for the kidnappers to go, for returning to Abeokuta would have been suicidal. So they headed toward the Benin Republic, driving at a breathtaking speed. The young kidnapper in the back keeping watch over Akinola and Jonah asked about the security of the car, and they told him there was none. (It was the absolute truth that the vehicle had no security to prevent it from being stolen.) After a while, he brought out a cell phone and dialled a number, giving whoever was at the receiving end the situation report.

Suddenly, they veered off the highway on which they were traveling. Akinola's anxiety grew as they headed into a thick forest. The ride on the dirty, earth road was bumpy. He feared that they could run out of fuel. He didn't know the distance they'd chosen to travel, but it would be better not to assume the worst not happening. And he was concerned that gas problems might be interpreted as part of the car's security system. He was determined to prevent anything untoward from happening to them, for if they were killed and buried in that bush, the possibility of their bodies ever being discovered was remote. The driver's skill in navigating the jungle indicated that he was on familiar terrain. But he didn't seem alert to the fuel gauge. So Akinola summoned the courage to tell the backseat guard, "You may need to check the fuel gauge because the vehicle can run out of fuel any time."

Akinola and Jonah's companion at the back relayed the message to the driver. He didn't stop immediately but halted the car a few minutes later. They were ordered out of the vehicle and asked to sit apart from each other, with their cotenant in the passenger's seat training his gun at them from a safe distance. Then the car was taken for refueling while the sentry kept an eagle eye watching over them. The car returned once again and their journey to the unknown destination continued.

Akinola didn't have any idea where they were or how they could reconnect with civilization. He was at a complete loss as to their location. Earlier, he and Jonah had been ordered to take off their shirts and surrender all their valuables. The archbishop had submitted everything, including his shirt, wristwatch, cell phones, socks, and shoes. Jonah received a worse humiliation. He was stripped almost naked. He had volunteered his shirt but was reluctant do without his trousers, but they insisted. The archbishop nodded to Jonah to do as he was told, so he folded the two items together and put the package with the archbishop's. Thank God that Jonah had boxers on!

Wordlessly, Akinola kept entreating God, "Lord, rescue us. I don't want to die here!" The hours had now begun to drag on, making their situation look hopeless, but then the miracle happened. It was pitch dark, for the sun had gone down since they veered into the forest. After the refueling, they drove for some time more before the car suddenly stopped. They were ordered out of the vehicle at a kind of T-junction where the road bifurcated into two parallel lines.

Akinola was ordered to move out on the road to his left. He obeyed the first part of the order but refused the second. He remained still where he was, rebuffing the command to move. He felt a cold muzzle of a gun pressing hard into the mid-section of his spine. Still, he made no effort to move. Instead, he spoke. He insisted, "I'm not moving a step if the boy is not released." He didn't know what his defiance could elicit but he was totally serious that whatever the price, he wasn't going to waver from his position. He wouldn't take a step unless he was sure that Jonah was safe and secure. For the second time, he felt the weight of the gun pressed deeper into his skin. Yet, he refused to flinch. Then came the threat. "We don't want to shed any blood tonight, so do as you're told." But, still, he held firm. "Let the boy go first, and I will follow your instructions," he told their abductors.

Then he heard, "Okay, let him go." The criminal sauntered Jonah forward with a push in the intended direction. Archbishop Akinola quickly told Jonah in Hausa to take to his heels and disappear into the bush. Like a hare escaping from a hunter, Jonah ran. He melted into the night and the bush. Then Akinola too made for the direction that their kidnappers had reserved for him. Off the kidnappers went, heading away with the car and all their valuables. Archbishop Akinola waited until after he had gained the protection of the night forest. When the lights of the departing car had disappeared, and everything had turned to total darkness, he began to yell, "Jonah, Jonah, Jonah!"

Silence greeted him. Not a squirrel moved, and not a bird chirped. Though he knew he had seen Jonah out of danger, he "was still deeply worried about him." The young man was a complete stranger to the area. Also, he didn't speak Yoruba, the native language in the area. Just like Akinola, he had no clothes or shoes on. Chances were high that he could be mistaken for a mad man, a vagrant psychotic, or another type of threatening personality. Obvioulsy, not many people would want to render assistance to a naked man on the highway. That's if he succeeded in navigating his way to the highway in the first place. Anxiety forced the archbishop to once again howl: "Jonah, Jonah, Jonah!"

Still, he heard nothing. Feverishly, he continued the silent prayer: "Lord, please rescue us. We must not die in this bush." He was like a blind man abandoned in a forest with no guide cane to navigate his way out. So he confined himself to walking down the middle of the road to avoid accidentally stepping on a trap. (Booby traps laid for game and rodents in the forest are not uncommon in areas like that.) "I was groping in the darkness without knowing where I was going," he recollected. But he kept going until he reached a T-junction with equally confusing options that made a decision difficult. He couldn't decide whether to go right or left.

"At that point," he said, "I started praying to God to send his Holy Angels to take me home." He similarly kept repeating the now-second leg of his prayer to the Almighty that he had no wish to pass the night in the forest. Unknown to him, God had heard his prayers all along. From the distance, a light flickered. It brightened as the vehicle neared. He could hear the intermittent volley of bullets accompanying the light. He was scared. But what could he do? "I raised my hands, flew them high into the air," Akinola said.

From the distance, there was another round of the gunfire. He could also pick out the faint sound of an approaching vehicle accompanying the shooting. He stopped and stood completely still. In no time the vehicle got to him. Emblazoned boldly on its bonnet was the acronym "SARS"—the State Anti-Robbery Squad. SARS was the special police squad established to fight violent crimes in the state. From the back of the open roof attached to the double-cabin vehicle scampered out a phalanx of armed security men. They didn't wait for the vehicle to stop before jumping out. Swiftly, they formed a protective ring around him. Their leader came over, faced him, scanned Akinola, and looked him over from head to toe.

"Are you the kidnapped pastor?" he asked calmly.

"Yes," the archbishop replied.

"Okay, sir, follow us."

He began, "My driver . . . ," but the police officer didn't let him finish the sentence.

"Follow me sir," he commanded respectfully.

He guided the archbishop into the backseat of their double-cabin patrol vehicle, and the police team brought him to Abeokuta. He was taken directly to the hospital where he met Jonah undergoing a medical examination as well. The archbishop paid no ransom to secure his release; nor did he sleep in the bush (his request to God answered with a yes). The nearly ten-hour ordeal didn't dissuade him from his commitment to enhancing the life of Nigerian youth.

Though scars of the ugly incident remained, he quickly put the unpleasant experience behind him. The following morning, Christmas Day of 2013, his family made a statement to the press. Akinola's son Jeremy, a member of the PAF board of trustees, said the family was extremely thankful to the "government, police, security agencies, and the generality of the people." He pledged that the archbishop would not be dissuaded from the ideal "of improving the life of our youths that is at the centrepiece of his retirement life . . . We assure Nigerian youth that his interest in advancing their cause through spiritual, social, economic empowerment and philanthropic assistance will not be diminished by this ugly incident."

It was no surprise that the incident did not alter the archbishop's commitment to helping Nigerian youth. To do otherwise would have been the surprise. Apart from working with more passion in that area, he was also zealous for progress in other aspects of the Foundation's work. In 2010, he had launched PAF's mission and evangelism project in Abuja. Its first set of partner dioceses included those of Mbamili, Damaturu, and Egba. The second set of dioceses was more in number and wider in geographical spread, covering Esan, Etchie, Ogbia, Ikwo, Ajayi Crowther, and Kontagora. Three more were added subsequently. Partnership with the Foundation included each diocese being responsible for employment of two fulltime itinerant evangelists, their training, and being empowered with motorcycles and vernacular Bibles for them to spread the gospel. The Foundation took direct responsibility for payment of their salaries. The results have been tremendous. In Egba diocese alone, eight rural communities not previously reached by evangelism were successfully reached with the gospel. The same achievement was recorded in Damaturu. Within nine months of launching the Foundation's inspired mission, close to a dozen potential worship centers were birthed in the diocese. None of the centers had fewer than fifteen worshipers while, in some instances, the emerging congregation was as large as thirty worshipers. Everywhere that PAF worked with the local diocese in this partnership, there was exhilarating success.

Akinola's drive to constantly seek improvement translated into encouraging African churches (and not just Nigerian churches) and their leadership to become self-reliant, to realize the necessity of relying on themselves and their resources. The first two provinces to benefit from this retirement venture were Kenya and Rwanda, where he met with success and was encouraged to then visit Congo, Indian Ocean, Sudan, Tanzania, Uganda, and West Africa. (In each case, he knew the leadership.) He believed there was no alternative to churches in Africa imbibing the spirit of self-reliance, particularly financial independence, lest they make themselves objects of manipulation in the hands of their affluent but decadent Western counterparts. Akinola believed that if a new course must be charted for the church in Africa, present church leaders need to work in unity and collaborate with each other to achieve that goal. Tirelessly he pursued this dream to the point that his retirement engagements amounted to a new life in service. "The amount of work I do now," he joked, "is more than when I was in fulltime employment!" "My friends," he continued, "were fond of telling me that I'm yet to retire because I have only been reassigned. This is perhaps true."

To date, neither the stolen SUV nor the kidnappers have been found. It seems unequivocally true that God listens to the archbishop in times of trouble. And in his trajectory, he seems to find himself thrown into bigger and more challenging issues, circumstances that bring out the best in him, showing his leadership gifts of boldness, resilience, decisiveness, and an indomitable spirit. This has been the mistake of his adversaries. They often take him for granted. It's easy to underrate Archbishop Akinola, for he's the type that could easily be lost in a crowd. The Nigerian archbishop is a simple, humble, and unpretentious individual. Perhaps that's why people have underestimated his strength and gambled foolishly on his perceived weakness. Yet he rarely lets obstacles turn him back once he sets his eyes on a goal. At the same time, he is wise enough to avoid the conceit that afflicts many great individuals.

He didn't arise from a socially promising background. Neither did he intend to go into the ministry. Providence brought him to that station of life. However, he remained obedient to his vocation and calling, and perhaps that was the greatest lesson of his church leadership. He was neither a political priest, nor a priest in politics, nor a priest ready to be politically correct. Akinola was known for his prophetic voice with enormous capacity for truth-telling. His voice rang out over and across cultures, creeds, and countries. He neither spared his fellow Nigerians nor his fellow Africans from difficult truth, even as he addressed the errant worldwide Anglican Church. Throughout, he was evenhanded in his criticisms.

Oftentimes the foes he fought were larger than him, but he never gave up on his convictions once he was persuaded about the rightness of his cause. Akinola's resoluteness frequently led to his demonization as a stubborn man. But, he noted,

> I fight no personal battle. But once the Lord has made a proclamation, it is the duty of every true believer, and importantly, a church leader, to defend the Word of God as revealed.

Could God have raised Akinola for such a time as this, a period that required a dogged fighter who would confront the forces of revisionism determined to create chaos and disorder through sexual permissiveness? Only God can tell.

History will not forget that, in both the wider world and the global Anglican Communion, the Nigerian church leader did the unexpected. He was at the forefront of the battle to contain a desperate effort to wreck the cherished culture of the past, a deliberate ploy to crush the nourishing order that had once held human civilization together. Akinola led a resistance battle to stymie the sexual apocalypse that a few rebellious cultural revisionists were determined to unleash on the world. Men and women who become historical figures are noted for upsetting the status quo. No matter the severity of the adversities, they don't give up. Vilified, harassed, intimidated, coerced, threatened, pilloried, and sometimes betrayed, Akinola stood against the onslaught to destroy the world's most cherished values and virtues. He maintained stoutly and steadfastly his conviction that "the Bible is an irreducible truth."

Indisputably, his tough stand defending the sanctity of the Gospel and the integrity of the Anglican Communion pitched him against the leadership of the worldwide Church. Everything possible was done to make him blink. But Akinola would neither blink nor balk. He refused to compromise the Bible and betray God. Did the Nigerian primate pursue a just cause? Time and history will tell. Was he as villainous, overly-ambitious, bigoted, old-fashioned, and retrogressive, as those in arms against him declared? Again, time and history will tell.

To that end, it is important to tell the major story of what went on behind the scenes. That is how to honor posterity: protect history from being debased by willful untruth and deliberate misrepresentation. And the safeguarding of the future should be done while events are fresh in the minds of those involved, lest history be corrupted with perjury. Truth is a treasure that everyone has the right to defend, and it is for the sake of truth and posterity that this book has been written.

3 1

Anglicans' New Leader: Justin Welby

London, 2013

In 2013, when divine hands saved Archbishop Peter Akinola from kidnappers, a comparable kind of saving occurred in Canterbury, the global headquarters of the Anglican Church. It was the end of The Most Rev. Dr. Rowan Williams' rule. It didn't come abruptly, nor did it provoke anguish. Rather, Williams, the 104th archbishop of Canterbury simply had to obey the law and step down, giving way to The Rt. Rev. Justin Portal Welby, the then-bishop of Durham, as the new global Anglican Church leader.[1]

As distinct as the two were, it was looking, at one point, as if one had coached the other. But their backgrounds were quite different. While Williams started life as a self-assured child, grew to be an adult confident of his ability, and rose to become a sanguine professional, the same could not be said of his successor. Welby was a man whose life was bound with a twine of lucky escapes at critical junctures in his earthly journey. It took sixty years for him to learn that the man whose name he bore, the one he deemed to be his father, was not his real biological parent. It would have been a big dishonor for some other people in his shoes. But for him, it was a well-managed scandal on the way to the most coveted position in the Anglican Church.

Welby's mother, Jane Portal, was a woman of noble pedigrees, whose family spread over two established genealogical trees. Jane's mother, Iris Butler (Welby's grandmother), was an upper-class woman with sound education and professional clout. She was a journalist and historian. Iris's brother, R. A. Butler (Welby's uncle), was the Lord Butler of Saffron Walden and a paragon of political and public services in Britain. He was prominent in public life in her majesty's service, moving in and out of key postings with rapid succession. From the office of chancellor of the exchequer to home secretary, deputy prime minister, and ultimately foreign secretary, Butler filled the positions with colorful impact. Their father, Sir Montagu Butler, also enjoyed the advantage of belonging to the British elite corps, serving as governor of

---

1. https://en.wikipedia.org/wiki/Justin_Welby.

the Central Provinces of British India before becoming master of Pembroke College, Cambridge. Sir Montagu himself was a product of illustrious parentage and family. He was a grandson of George Butler, who was a headmaster of Harrow School and dean of Peterborough, as well as being the grand-nephew of John Colenso, the first bishop of Natal.

Jane's father Gervas Portal came from a family of distinguished war veterans. Gervas was a half-brother to Britain's World War II air chief of staff and first viscount portal of Hungerford, Charles Portal. Noble background also marked Gervas Portal's mother, Rose Leslie Portal. Rose was a granddaughter of General Sir William Napier from his wife Caroline Amelia Fox. The family record of being warriors could be seen in the rise of three brothers to the rank of general in the Armed Forces—first Napier, then Sirs Charles and George, with the latter two respectively serving as commanders-in-chief of the British Armies in India and Cape Colony. All these gallant men took their root from one source, George Napier, who himself descended from one of the greatest thinkers in the British society, John Napier, the inventor/discoverer of logarithms. So Welby's mother Jane Portal, born in 1929, was firmly ensconced in the upper crust of the British elite.

She was recruited as a personal secretary to Winston Churchill at No. 10 Downing. A promising young woman in her early twenties, she was known for her efficiency and ability to apply the discretion her position demanded, as well as for her irresistible beauty. At No 10 she came across Anthony Montague Browne, both of them of high standing in British society. Montague, who was older at 29, was educated at Stowe and Oxford, and he followed a family tradition featuring three generations of military officers. He joined the RAF, fought in World War II, and maintained the family honor with an award for his bravery. Subsequently he joined the Foreign Office in 1946 with a posting to the British embassy in Paris. Married two years earlier, he was chosen to serve as Churchill's private secretary for foreign affairs in 1952. The year that followed his beginning of work at No 10, Montague became the father of a baby girl with his wife Noel.

Coincidentally, the girl was named Jane. By then, however, Montague had begun an affair with Jane Portal. He had a weakness for pretty women, and she was a woman of appealing looks. The duo's relationship developed beyond the platonic to the physical. Jane blamed the indiscretion on accident, "fuelled by a large amount of alcohol on both sides." Lamentably, the inapt act had occurred in the "days leading up to my very sudden marriage," Jane admitted. She was not a careless woman without knowledge of reasonable protection, but, she observed, "It appears that the precautions taken at the time didn't work." And ruefully she confessed that Justin Welby "was conceived as a result of this liaison."

Jane didn't marry Gavin Welby until April 4, 1955. By that time, she and Montague had worked together for three unbroken years, from 1952 to 1955. In fact, her wedding took place one month after she quit her job, March 1955, the same time that Churchill relinquished his post as British prime minister. Montague also returned to his Foreign Service job. With his profile still rising, he became a recipient of the Order of the British Empire award for his service on Downing Street. It was certainly no time for him to be enmeshed in a distasteful scandal. Jane and Montague had worked in the highest political office, where managing and keeping secrets had made them prize assets. The story, therefore, was that after three persistent years of trying to get Jane to marry him, Gavin Welby finally succeeded. The irony was that the young wife was without a job, and she was pregnant as well. She had no clue that she was expecting—and neither did the man responsible for putting her in this condition. Making the situation more unpleasant was the fact that she had surrendered to her proposed husband's "bullying" to "run away with him against the wishes of her parents."

Jane's two major life decisions—marriage and motherhood—proved to be problematic choices. Her husband Gavin was anything but an ideal partner to a woman of Jane's pedigree. He was a fraud in every respect where honor mattered. From birth name to date of birth to cultivated lifestyle, everything about him was a deception. His original surname was Weiler. He was 19 years senior to Jane, born in 1910, the son of a German-Jewish immigrant called Bernard, from whom he got his middle name. The family's initial wealth was lost to the First World War, and anti-German sentiment compelled the family to change its name to Welby. Trying his hand at the illegal whisky trade, he later became the New York import manager for the National Distillers Products Corporation after the US liquor prohibition ended in 1933. Gavin had become a *bon vivant*, a man desperately in need of social recognition and searching for a means of entry into the world of society's movers and shakers. He was blessed by good looks, which he used to his advantage as he sought access to the world of the affluent. However, he didn't just want to be counted among the rich in income, but wanted acceptance as a social equal of the affluent. He craved to be viewed as thinking like them, living like them, talking like them, and, therefore, a registered part of their world, a goal aided by his cultivated upper-class accent.

Among the indulgences of the rich at the time was throwing parties, wild and extravagant merrymakings. Through one of his high society parties, Gavin drew the attention of Doris Sturzenegger, the daughter of a wealthy factory owner, and they were wed in 1934, he at the age of 23 years. In less than a year, however, the marriage hit the rocks, and the two went their separate ways. Twenty-one years later, in 1955, Gavin was onto his second marriage, this one to Jane. He was 45 while Jane was still in the prime of her youth at 26. If Jane knew about her husband's first marriage, it didn't appear to have had any impact on her decision to marry him. Their union, however, failed woefully, and within three years the marriage collapsed. Gavin recovered quickly and moved rapidly to other women. Still enjoying social acceptance among the high and influential, he even dated John F. Kennedy's sister Pat among others.

Gavin turned his charms on Vanessa Redgrave, a 23-year-old actress. Head over heels in love with him, she thought nothing could stop her from tying the nuptial knot with this twice-married and twice-divorced 50-year-old. Vanessa's father, Sir Michael Redgrave, had to summon every persuasive skill in his possession to dissuade his daughter. He kept arguing that Gavin was "a rotten piece of work," and finally he persuaded his infatuated daughter to accept his wise counsel.

After the Redgrave incident, Gavin's charm faded. From then on, he couldn't get his life back on track. He took to alcohol, abusing it heavily. Living like a recluse, alone in his Kensington flat, he died of a heart attack in 1977 at age 67. Justin was 21 years old when the death of the man he presumed to be his father occurred. There was no love lost between father and son, yet while Justin Welby did not deny his father's fallibilities, he was not fond of critically appraising them either. He did grant that his father brought him up under "messy circumstances because of his alcoholism."

Justin was lucky to be spared permanent injury from the moral decadence of the adults surrounding him. He was a child unfortunately thrown between two negligent adults. He was 3 years old when the love flame between his parents burned out, and curiously, with the 1959 divorce, Gavin was granted custody of the boy. This was probably because Jane's battle with alcohol had taken a serious turn. Sadly, Gavin too hit the bottle. So Justin found himself as "the child of families with great difficulties in relationships, with substance abuse or other matters." And then there was an added difficulty—the "rumours about his paternity" that had started to fly around.

Initially, Justin wasn't bothered about the gossip. The correlation between his birth year and his parents' wedding date seemed normal. He was born on January 6, 1956, while his parents had gotten married on April 4, 1955—a nine-month interval for a "honeymoon baby." Justin was wrong. Gavin was not aware of Jane's affair with Sir Anthony Browne throughout the period of their courtship, which lasted three years, from 1952 till 1955. But Justin was the "spitting image" of Sir Anthony. Coincidentally, Sir Anthony's daughter Jane and wife Noel had come to the same conclusion—that there must be a blood connection between Justin and their father and husband.

Incidentally, too, Sir Anthony's path crossed Justin's "several times at reunions of Churchill's staff." The occasions provided further opportunities for physical, close-up assessment of father and son, and Lady Montague Browne became convinced that "her husband was Justin Welby's father." She found "the unmistakeable resemblance between the two" more than coincidental. Years later, Sir Anthony himself began teasing his wife with a humorous poke: "I'm told I have a son," adding, "You'll find out one day." But the truth would not fully emerge until several years later.

In 2012, the 56-year-old Justin was elected archbishop of Canterbury, primed to become the head of the Church of England and leader of the worldwide Anglican Church. At the time, Sir Anthony was 89 years old and living in a care home. On the other hand, Justin's mother, age 83, had made a big comeback with her life. Apart from a long career of public service as magistrate and a deputy lieutenant for Greater London, Jane had quit drinking in 1968 and married again in 1975, becoming Lady Williams of Elvel. The announcement of Justin's election raised its normal share of public curiosity about him, and, typical of the press, the Daily Telegraph of London decided to look into his background.

Somehow, luckily for the archbishop-elect, the 2012 inquiry wasn't the classic media investigation to expose lies and concealments connected with people at the top. Rather, it was something of a public relations job for the archbishop-elect. The newspaper had unearthed the story about Welby's parentage but had taken the extra step of discussing "its research with the Archbishop." On his part, Justin "decided to take a DNA test to settle the matter." Regrettably, Sir Anthony was dead by then, in 2013, when Welby decided to go through with the DNA test. Sir Anthony's second wife and widow Shelagh (he and Noel had divorced in 1970) was fortunately of help.

Sir Anthony seemed to have had weakness for calamitous office affairs. Shelagh Macklin, his second wife, had been Clementine Churchill's personal secretary. While she was working for the wife, he worked for the husband. They extended their required office closeness beyond the officialdom. Noel, Sir Anthony's wife at home, couldn't stand the sizzling affair, and she ended their marriage in 1970, making way for Shelagh. At the start of the search to discover the truth about Justin's true father, the luck was that Shelagh still "kept personal effects" of Sir Anthony, including "hairbrushes which still had some of his hair on them," providing "a DNA sample." Justin supplied mouth swabs, which were compared with the hair samples from Sir Anthony, and the test "showed a 99.9779 per cent probability that they were father and son."

The Daily Telegraph story was a win-win. It put the newspaper ahead of its competitors and it ennobled the archbishop's public image. Whatever the negative touch or dent in the story, Justin's pedigrees of blue blood from both of his parents were used as selling points in the public arena. Sir Anthony Montague Browne was a man of illustrious heritage and a worthy British figure to have fathered Welby, even if under controversial circumstances. Sir Anthony was "a decorated RAF pilot turned trusted civil servant, staff of both the Queen and Sir Winston Churchill." In comparison, Gavin Welby was "a chancer and a drinker . . . a lieutenant [who] 'promoted' himself to captain . . . and [a] twice selected Tory candidate [who] twice lost heavily." Sir Anthony represented the best dad Justin never had and Gavin the dad he had but that was never the best.

An interviewer had touched on the emotional side of Justin's life, asking him if he had been "wounded" by the series of unfortunate incidents. Words deserted him for "a very long" time, but he found solace in dignified silence. "I assume that I am," he agreed eventually when he regained his voice, "but I also assume that the grace of God is extraordinarily powerful in the healing of one's wounds." Truly evident had been the grace of God in his life. (Incidentally, the best father Justin never had, Sir Anthony, "died in 2013, days after his secret son was installed as Archbishop," and Gavin Welby, his acting father, died a year preceding his graduation in 1978.)

At 22, Justin had completed his bachelor of arts degree in history and law, graduating from Trinity College, Cambridge. (Fortunately, his great-uncle, Lord Butler of

Saffron Walden, was then a master at the institution.) He earned his master of arts degree as well, and his choice of career after graduation was in the oil industry. For eleven years, he worked in that sector, moving from one organization to another and in different regions of the world. Five of those years, he was employed by Elf Aquitaine, the French oil company based in Paris. Justin changed jobs when he was 29, the same age that his biological father, Sir Anthony, had moved from the RAF to become Churchill's private secretary for foreign affairs. In his case, Justin was appointed in 1984 as the treasurer of Enterprise Oil PLC, an oil exploration group in London, which exposed him to West African and North Sea oil projects. This experience helped him gain an understanding of the peoples, cultures, and traditions of those regions of the world.

At 39, however, Justin felt it was time to move on. His 1989 retirement from the oil industry led to a new vocation entirely, for he had sensed "a calling from God to be ordained." During his oil industry career, he had become a member of Holy Trinity Church in Brompton, London, but his decision was surprising. He wasn't raised in a Christian home, and at a point in his youth, he almost doubted the existence of God.[2] In his days at Eton College, he grappled with the reality of the Lord, though in some sense he "assumed there was a God." He recounts that, for all practical purposes, "I didn't believe . . . I wasn't interested at all."

Miraculously, a transformation came over him on the evening of October 12, 1975, during his years in Cambridge. The 19-year-old agnostic was praying with a Christian friend when he was struck by "a clear sense of something changing, the presence of something that had not been there before in my life." He was "embarrassed that this had happened to him" and pleaded with his friend, "Please don't tell anyone about this." But it was Justin himself who couldn't keep the secret, and he eventually asked to be ordained to become a priest. For reasons best known to the bishop of Kensington, John Hughes, he was turned down, with the judgement, "There is no place for you in the Church of England."

Justin wasn't dissuaded by the refusal, and he found favor with the vicar of Holy Trinity Brompton, Sandy Millar.[3] Millar whose nickname was more popular than his real name, John Alexander Kirkpatrick, was an interesting character, half quixotic and half maverick. Part of an upperclass Scottish family, he shared more than one old-boy school tie with Justin. Both had been students at Eton College and at Trinity College, Cambridge. Millar was a charismatic evangelical within the Church of England, and strong were his passions for local missions. He was neither totally aloof from nor deeply involved in the homosexuality controversy raging in the Anglican Communion. Still, he stood with the majority and had told the persecuted anti-homosexuality group within the American Episcopal Church that theirs was "a war for the very soul of the church" and that their "steadfastness in the face of a new and speciously sophisticated manifestation of evil has won you many admirers all over the world."

2. Doughty, "I Sometimes Question if God Exists."
3. https://en.wikipedia.org/wiki/Sandy_Millar.

Perhaps Millar's intention went beyond seeing Justin enrolled for priestly training. It appeared as if he wanted to mentor him. For one thing, Justin went to the same theological school attended by Millar. From 1989 to 1992, Justin studied at St John's College, Durham, where he was awarded a BA degree and a diploma in 1992. He was ordained a deacon in 1992 and subsequently became a priest in 1993. From 1992 to 1995, he held a succession of parish posts. Later, he was appointed the vicar of St Michael and All Angels, Ufton, Diocese of Coventry, where he served seven years from 1995 to 2002. And on he went from post to post through the first decade and half of his ministry, moving from parish church work to the canon residentiary of Coventry Cathedral, then becoming co-director for international ministry at the International Centre for Reconciliation, sub-dean and canon for Reconciliation Ministry, and ultimately as the dean of Liverpool in December 2007.

At 55, Justin, with 18 years' experience in his clerical career, reached a new peak. He was appointed the bishop of Durham in 2011. At that time, the man he was to succeed, Archbishop of Canterbury Rowan Williams, had only two more years in office. Justin's initial reaction to his appointment into the episcopate was to see it as "both challenging and a huge privilege." "I was astonished to be offered the role," he said, for he occupied one of the positions with defined functions to the British crown, as if providence was connecting him, as it had his father, to a distinguished role in the nation. The bishop of Durham is one of two bishops (the other is the bishop of Bath and Wells) with the duty of escorting the sovereign during a coronation. Justin occupied his seat at the House of Lords on January 12, 2012, and was made a member of the Parliamentary Commission on Banking Standards.

Justin's story became that of a stone rejected by Hughes but one that Millar helped turn into a cornerstone. Somewhere in the centers of power, the radar detected him. Within less than a year of his elevation to the bishopric, he emerged as a viable candidate for the most exalted office in the Anglican Communion: the archbishopric of Canterbury. Many didn't give him a chance. He was seen as more a pretender to the office than a real contender, especially since many believed the storms buffeting the Anglican Church precluded Williams' successor from being a person of limited experience. Indeed, bookmakers outside the Communion counted him an outright impossibility. The conviction was so strong that as of November 6, 2012, people were willing to place a bet on his poor chances of success. However, in one of the astonishing reversals of the century, he proved the bookmakers wrong. Justin confounded every doubting Thomas. The rejected stone was chosen as the successor to Williams on November 9, 2012. Justin was taken aback himself. The choice mystified him, striking him as "a joke" and "perfectly absurd." He found it so unreal "because he had only been a bishop for a short time."

Perhaps he was just being diplomatic in a politically correct manner, pretending that he was not aware of the underlying currents behind his selection. There are reasons to suspect his candidacy and election didn't just happen. In fact, it seemed to have been well conceived and methodically planned to the point that all potential obstacles were painstakingly examined and efforts were made to remove them. Interestingly—and not puzzling in any way—the Daily Telegraph story was not a happenstance. It was no masterstroke of journalistic ingenuity that the newspaper chose to launch an investigation into the family life of Justin at this time, and the paper went as far as soliciting his cooperation so that the public could be fed the truth about his parentage. This type of cooperation between the investigator and the object of investigation was rare. Indeed, critics may see the exposé as an image laundering job because no sooner than the truth was uncovered, the name and image of Sir Anthony Montague Browne began to be posted along with the profile of the archbishop.

A second development made the emergence of Justin calculated. For centuries, the pristine law of Canterbury was that "men born illegitimately were barred from becoming archbishops." However, by a curious act of providence, the law had ceased to hold, having been repealed in 1950. But the change was relatively unknown, having received relatively little publicity, most probably because the law was seldom used. Though such changes were extremely infrequent, this one never emerged as a hot subject of interest within the Church. Justin's backers were, however, experienced and educated people, up on the procedure involved in choosing the archbishop of Canterbury. They had cleverly weighed the obstacles and strategically calculated the odds against him. Not surprising therefore was the sudden interest in correcting the errors in his biological history. The power brokers won the game, and the bookmakers were embarrassed.

One last obstacle, however, remained—the British prime minister, who had the responsibility to forward the name of the person elected by the church to the queen for approval. Though rarely had any name put forward been rejected by any prime minister, it was more than doubly certain that David Cameron would give his backing to Justin Welby. Cameron was not only a sympathizer with and apologist for homosexuality; he was a leading champion of the aberrant lifestyle in office. Opposed by 130 Conservative MPs in his obsessive quest of legalizing gay marriage, he sought liaison and support from the Liberal Democrats and Labour. So he was disinclined to start a new fight at this point, and no hindrance was expected in the confirmation of Justin Welby. None indeed occurred; it was smooth sailing. In accordance with tradition and practice, Welby's announcement was made to the Privy Council of the United Kingdom. On March 21, 2013, The Most Rev. Justin Welby was enthroned as the 105th archbishop of Canterbury.

It is one thing to be elected archbishop of Canterbury but another to effectively clear up the mess into which the Anglican Church had been dragged. Unfortunately, after seven years in this role, (2013 to 2020), Archbishop Welby appeared not to have found the way to resolve the chaos left by his predecessor, The Most Rev. Dr. Rowan Williams.

Postscript

Will the Anglican Gay Crisis End?

Unfortunately, Archbishop Justin Welby was ill-equipped for the cleansing of the Anglian Communion. Yet he could not be said to have arrived in Canterbury altogether clueless. The problem was that he came into office with some confusion. Also, his methods could be clumsy. Welby's public perspective on the Anglican Communion crisis was that he wanted to effect "reconciliation" in the divided house.[1] On the other hand, he wanted the thrust of his tenure to be "mission." So he considered it imperative to break down the impasse and bring together the factions within the worldwide Church. In his thinking, as long as the Church was divided, there was no way to put it back on the path of "mission." It seemed this was his way of paying tribute to his mentor and benefactor, 74-year-old Sandy Millar, who opened the door to priesthood for him.

Welby too had cut the image of a charismatic and evangelical priest. Millar, however, as an apostle of mission and a master strategist, had testimonials to show for his exceptional passion. His "strategy for church planting throughout London" made it "possible for dying churches to have a fresh start with congregations and clergy."[2] Welby would have made Millar proud had he borrowed from his model, pouring his energy into renewing dying churches throughout the length and breadth of the Anglican Communion. The Anglican Church would have had a fresh burst of life all over the globe.

Welby's concept of mission was different, however. While still a bishop, he had expressed his notion of "mission" in an article published in the *Centre Aisle*, a newsletter owned by the Diocese of Virginia under the American Episcopal Church. Both in form and substance, the "mission" he elaborated contradicted that of his spiritual mentor. Millar's concept was wholly ecclesiastical and religious while Welby's was

1. https://en.wikipedia.org/wiki/Justin_Welby.
2. https://en.wikipedia.org/wiki/Sandy_Millar.

secular and political. In the article, "The Answer to Division in the Anglican Communion is Mission," Welby defined "mission" in terms of "regarding those with whom we disagree as fellow Christians, who may be wrong but with whom we are called to live, whose love we receive and to whom we owe such love."

Four months after the publication appeared in the American church's newsletter, Welby emerged as the top contender for the highest position in the worldwide Anglican Communion. Furthermore, he had extracurricular credentials that were sellable as well. Welby had served as a co-director of international ministry at the International Centre for Reconciliation besides his being a former sub-dean and canon for Reconciliation Ministry. He was practically unopposed as he walked into the office of the archbishop of Canterbury with a sort of sure-footedness. Unsurprising as well was the goal he wanted to pursue in office—"reconciliation through mission."

Once in office, one of his first actions was to attend a "Faith in Conflict" conference at The Coventry Cathedral, London. It was like returning home. Though subtle, the conference projected a message. Side by side, an American bishop supporting same-sex "marriage" had been brought with an opposing rector from the ACNA. The lesson was clear, contained in one of the conference's conclusions—"those who disagree about sexuality can maintain Christian fellowship and cooperate in Christian mission."

Archbishop Welby followed the ground-testing step with a second, more telling one: his appointment of Canon David Porter as "canon of reconciliation." Apparently, this was the rebranding of a similar office created by his predecessor. The focus of the office was to assist with mediation of the crisis. Canon Porter's schedule was a carbon copy of his forerunner's. Its focus was "supporting creative ways for renewing conversations and relationships around deeply held differences within the Church of England and the Anglican Communion."

On the one hand, Welby had been projected as an opponent of "the blessing of same sex relationships in or by the church." He was promoted as an advocate of "retaining the biblical definition of marriage." Yet he didn't "see those who promote [same-sex marriage] as false teachers." Nor did he openly declare their position or action contrary to the Anglican Church's stand. Indeed, Welby's position was illogical, plagued by inconsistencies and contradictions. In a House of Lords speech, he had "indicated his support for same sex unions so long as they are not considered 'marriages.'" Clearly, he was confusing the issues.

On January 29, 2014, ten months into his leadership of the Anglican Communion, he further cast doubt on his sincerity in addressing the Communion's problem.[3] He wrote a letter, in conjunction with his York counterpart, to all primates in the Anglican Communion and, curiously, decided to send copies to the presidents of Nigeria and Uganda, the only two heads of state to receive what ought to have been internal

---

3. Oni, "Homosexuality: 'I Will Attend My Son's Gay Wedding Ceremony'- Archbishop"; "Archbishops Recall Commitment to Pastoral Care and Friendship for All, Regardless of Sexual Orientation"; https://en.wikipedia.org/wiki/Justin_Welby.

correspondence of the Communion. The letter read as though Welby was attempting to rewind the clock of the Anglican crisis back to the 1998 Lambeth Conference, when the defeated minority wrote a treacherous dissenting letter disowning the Communion's stand on human sexuality.

Archbishop Welby's letter began, "In recent days, questions have been asked about the Church of England attitude to new legislation in several countries that penalises people with same sex attraction." He highlighted "the common mind of the Primates of the Communion, as expressed in the Dromantine communique of 2005," in particular, their decision to "continue unreservedly to be committed to the pastoral support and care of the homosexual people." When Archbishop Welby took over leadership of the Anglican Communion, the gay crisis had gone on unabated for fifteen years. The eleven years preceding his assumption of office had witnessed a catastrophic impasse, with the standoffs getting worse, especially in connection with the grave events that had continued to occur in the Communion after the primates met in Dromantine, England.

Archbishop Williams had been able to summon vague, diplomatic language to his rescue instead of embarrassing himself publicly with politically or strategically incorrect statements. If he considered a statement to be prickly, he would allow a subordinate to make it. In contrast, Welby didn't seem to be schooled in that sort of diplomacy. Thus, when he singled out the Dromantine meeting without juxtaposing it with views the primates expressed in Dar es Salam, he was just being half clever.[4] If he thought that the Communion viewed Dromantine as binding, he should have also honored the primates' verdict in Dar es Salam concerning the two recalcitrant North American churches. By not putting the issues in a clear, contextual perspective, Welby tipped his hand, indicating openly the side he took regarding the Communion's crisis.

In fact, the sustained duplicity of Canterbury during the post-Dromantine period was the offense that pushed the Global South and GAFCON to withdraw from further participation in the Communion's activities until Canterbury summoned the courage to discipline the erring churches.[5] The same offense accounted for their holding GAFCON and the Lambeth Conference separately in 2008.[6] Five years later, there had been no progress on this issue. For Welby to revive Dromantine and feign amnesia about Dar es Salam made obvious his prejudice, which had been such a sore point under Archbishop Williams.

Every new administration tends to have its honeymoon period during which people are willing to excuse its missteps as part of an initial learning period. Regrettably,

4. Global South, "Global South Primates Meeting—Executive Summary of the Minutes of Meeting," Dar es Salam, Tanzania, from the archive and papers of the Archbishop Peter Akinola.

5. "Primates' Meeting Communique (Tanzania)—The Communique of the Primates' Meeting in Dar es Salam."

6. GAFCON, "Statement on Global Anglican Future"; GAFCON, "The Jerusalem Declaration," both from the papers and archive of the Most Rev. Peter Akinola.

Archbishop Welby's honeymoon was short-lived. His first major Communion-wide test arose from a meeting of the thirty-eight primates of the Church, which he convened in January 2016.[7] Most GAFCON/Global South leaders had read his lips and body language, and from the outset they did not place any trust or confidence in him. Consequently, the moment Welby mooted the primates meeting idea, a number expressed strong lack of interest in the get-together.[8] The champions of boycotting the meeting predicated their stand on: (1) Welby's inconsistencies and contradictions regarding the Bible; (2) his stand on the issue of homosexuality, which was in violation of the Communion's stand; and (3) his position on the recalcitrant North American churches, which showed nothing was going to change under him. To GAFCON and Global South primates, Welby's primate meeting would be no different than those in the past, a sort of Potemkin village.

The negative feelings were strong after eighteen years of orchestrated and deliberate frustration of the reconciliation process. The only hope was for Welby to break away from the duplicity of his predecessor, Archbishop Rowan Williams, a grand master of deception. From 2003 to 2006 he conned them, taking advantage of their gullibility until it became clear to all of them that "a clear pattern [had] emerged under him."

In his time, Williams' perfected style revolved around making public remarks about how deep the crisis within the Communion was. He would identify human sexuality as the main issue, going further to affirm the 1998 Lambeth Conference's decision. Giving the impression that he was going to maintain discipline within the Communion, he would insist on the inviolability of Lambeth Resolution 1.10 and other past agreements. Shrewdly, he would blame TEC (The Episcopal Church of America) and ACC (the Anglican Church of Canada) for the crisis. Williams would then plead with his colleagues to attend the primates meeting he was convening. He would prey on their sense of responsibility by publicly urging them to act in best interest of the Communion and attend the meeting, so that they might collectively seek ways of resolving the crisis.

The primates would respond positively, honoring their leader. Wisely but craftily, Williams would design the agenda while denying his colleagues the opportunity to see it ahead of time. Artfully, he would ensure that a substantial part of the meeting was devoted to common worship, reserving only a few moments for critical discussion. At the end, there would be elaborate photo sessions. The primates would be pictured together in worship, during conversations, and in a group photograph. A group of primates would be constituted to draft the official communique, with the communique's working group comprising a blend of primates friendly to TEC and the ACC. A communique would then be issued with specific demands from TEC and the ACC. Of course, TEC and the ACC would ignore the demands, and, if pressed to

---

7. https://en.wikipedia.org/wiki/Justin_Welby.
8. Atwood, "High Noon in Lusaka."

take action, Williams would plead helplessness, hiding under a lack of legal or constitutional power to discipline the errant churches.

Meanwhile, TEC and the ACC would be invited again to the next primates meeting. Similarly, they would continue to attend meetings of other organs of the Communion like the Lambeth Council (whenever it was held) and the Anglican Communion
Council. The archbishop would plead for continued dialogue, understanding, and restraint, particularly from the Global South leaders. This trajectory became the pattern.
Nothing had changed nor did the biblically faithful group detect a change in the offing.

"This pattern has held steady," they observed. Rather than serve the useful purpose of assisting to resolve the Anglican crisis, the primates meetings had served to
further the interest of one person only—Archbishop Rowan Williams. "Each meeting," the primates contended, "provided an opportunity for Archbishop Williams to
present himself as struggling to keep the Communion together amidst the demands
of the 'extremists' on both sides." But this had been a well-crafted lie, fed ingeniously
to the public. The propaganda had almost achieved its Machiavellian aim. Meanwhile,
behind the scenes, the archbishop was unrelenting in his attempt to divide, confuse,
and conquer the Global South leaders, thinking that their vulnerability and weakness
predisposed them to easy conquest.

The tragedy was that Archbishop Welby was unwilling to distance himself from
the foul system. "There is no basis for believing that his present invitation represents
any significant departure from the pattern set by his predecessor," affirmed those of
his colleagues opposed to sitting around a table with him. They also doubted "his
credentials as an evangelical," given that they had seen "no evidence of any change of
heart or mind on Archbishop Welby's part." In other words, Canterbury only had a
change of personality, not a change of regime.

Clear, however, was the fact the GAFCON/Global South leaders didn't need
Welby as much as he needed them. He was the one who wanted them desperately. To
them, therefore, the best way he could prove his sincerity of purpose was the "demo-
tion of TEC and the ACC." On this point, they didn't need anybody to tell them they
were jesters because they themselves were the first to doubt that their appeal would
be heeded. Sombrely, they acknowledged "there is virtually no hope for such an outcome." Those arguing against compromise insisted that if they remained "faithful to
scripture," they must deal a decisive "blow to the idea that heresy and orthodoxy can
coexist." The best of way of demonstrating that stand was "not to honour Archbishop
Welby's invitation."

Amid the raging controversy about boycotting the primates meeting, the primates of Nigeria and Uganda wrote separate letters to Archbishop Welby. Incidentally,
the Archbishop had singled out the two archbishops, Nicholas Okoh of Nigeria and
Stanley Ntagali of Uganda, for criticism in his earlier letter because their countries
had enacted laws "unfriendly" to homosexuals. In the main, too, their churches led
the provinces unrelentingly championing the anti-gay struggle. Okoh and Ntagali had

since become prominent leaders in GAFCON. (Okoh had succeeded Peter Akinola while Ntagali took over from the fiery Henry Orombi.) Neither had departed from the principled stand of his predecessor, and the duo had been entrusted with the leadership of GAFCON, as chairman and deputy chairman respectively.[9]

Okoh's letter of January 5, 2016, pledged to Welby his readiness, along with that of his colleagues in GAFCON, to honor the meeting Welby was convening.[10] He gave reasons why they had decided to shift from the position they had maintained for many years. Okoh said a major desire was "to find a way to resolve the spiritual and moral crisis that has beset the Communion." He explained his genuine interest as well as that of his colleagues in seeing the Anglican Church "mov[e] forward together in a renewed and restored Communion." There were provisos, however. The main condition was that any rapprochement must be "underpinned by robust commitments to biblical teaching and morality."

On the other hand, Ntagali's pastoral letter, written two days later on January 7, 2016, told bishops, clergy, and lay leaders within his Church of Uganda that GAFCON leaders had chosen to meet with the Canterbury archbishop.[11] He didn't want Ugandan Anglicans to see their decision as a betrayal. Ntagali said they did so in order "to discuss the future of the Anglican Communion." The GAFCON leaders, he wrote, were bending over backwards, and he wanted GAFCON's leaders to be understood in the light of Paul's exhortation in Ephesians 4:3—"Make every effort to keep the unity of the Spirit through the bond of peace." Hence, Ntagali insisted that they were going to England with hope there might be a resolution to the Anglian crisis during the four-day summit, January 11–15, 2016.

He assured his readers that he believed "the Archbishop of Canterbury understands that the first topic of conversation in the 'gathering' of Primates is the restoration of godly order in the Anglican Communion." The two sides, the GAFCON primates and the Canterbury archbishop, had a prior consultation where the GAFCON leaders told Welby they were "not in communion with the Episcopal Church USA or the Anglican Church of Canada." So their consenting to the London meeting was for the sole purpose of bringing the Communion back to its old order. If that failed, if "discipline and godly order is not restored," he assured his parishioners, he would have no choice other than to "uphold the Provincial Assembly's resolution and withdraw from the meeting."

It turned out that the meeting was a sheer waste of time. Their colleagues who had clamored for a boycott were right. And, as expected, the trouble didn't come from the GAFCON primates, but rather from the usual sources—Canterbury and the Communion's two axes of rebellion, The Episcopal Church of America and the

9. https://www.gafcon.org/about/history; https://www.gafcon.org/archive/201310; https://en.wikipedia.org/wiki/Stanley_Ntagali; Okoh, "Chairman's June 2016 Pastoral Letter."

10. GAFCON, "January 2016 Update," https://www.gafcon.org/news/january-2016-update.

11. Ntagali, "A Pastoral Message and Call to Prayer from Archbishop Stanley Ntagali."

Anglican Church of Canada. It was very unfortunate that this unique opportunity was frittered away again.

Over half of the thirty-eight primates at the table were new. More than half of them, twenty-one "had never been to a Primates meeting before." It was their first time to encounter each other, including the archbishop of Canterbury. The two leaders from the notorious churches, the presiding bishop of TEC, the Most Rev. Michael Curry, and his Canadian counterpart, Archbishop Fred Hiltz, were new as well.[12] Welby initially loosened things up a bit; he "let the Primates set their own agenda," for the agenda had developed into a major point of disagreement between former Archbishop Williams and his colleagues.[13] By 2010, the bulk of the primates had threatened to stop attending primates meetings unless they had some form of control or input regarding the agenda.

Welby conceded to the demand. The compromise had a therapeutic effect, producing some optimism about the possibility of a positive outcome attending their deliberations. Many of the primates in doubt were encouraged that they "did not feel manipulated" when the meeting began. Less animosity and suspicion pervaded the air at the meeting. A feeling of camaraderie was evident, and they felt motivated to speak candidly, honestly, fairly, and objectively. Also, there was no wall of race, region, color, and tongue to inhibit them from honest exchange. And no homosexual group was there to tug at the coattails of any of the primates.

In addition, no friction or irritation smoldered from the past conflict. Instead, a newness of spirit and atmosphere seemed to prevail, an ambiance of "give and take" that precipitated mutual respect in the once sharply divided house. As an example, despite the decision of the GAFCON primates to not be at the same table with the two intransigent churches, they still bent over backwards. They were ready to listen to the leaders of the errant churches and extend case-by-case consideration rather than insisting on total condemnation or blanket ban. Nevertheless, though the Anglican Church of Canada succeeded in being exempted from indictment because "it claimed that it has not altered its Marriage Canon," it seemed clear "that the Anglican Church of Canada, Scotland, Wales, Brazil and New Zealand are on the way to toeing the footsteps of TEC."

In the absence of convincing evidence to prove her guilt, the ACC got away with inconsequential punishment. The same, however, could not be said of TEC. Its crimes were proven beyond a reasonable doubt: "For a period of three years," before the rejuvenation of the primates meeting, sanctions had been imposed on the American church. A variety of bans and restrictions had been clamped on her. For instance, she

12. https://en.wikipedia.org/wiki/Michael_Curry_(bishop) accessed 04/12/16; Fred Hiltz http://www.anglican.ca/primate/.

13. Akinola, "Notes of a private & confidential conversation between The Most Rev'd Rowan Williams, Archbishop of Canterbury, and The Most Rev'd Peter J. Akinola, Primate of All Nigeria," from the archive and personal papers of Archbishop Peter Akinola.

was denied participation in the Ecumenical and Interfaith bodies that the Anglican Communion had established with other Christian groups and denominations. Similarly, too, its members had been blocked from the internal standing committees of the Communion as well as precluded from the decision-making organs of the Communion on issues that had to do with doctrine or policy. The unfortunate reality was that the measures, still, had failed to make the church remorseful.

There was no question about which of the Anglican churches had been the most recalcitrant. The General Convention of the American Episcopal Church, for instance, had just changed its marriage canon to recognize a union between any two people, whether of the same or opposite sex. Consequently, out of the thirty-eight global Anglican leaders at the meeting, "33 of the Primates wanted to see the Episcopal Church disciplined." And the call extended beyond a slap on the wrist or a pull on the ears. They were demanding a real spanking of the church, to see her reclaimed from her wayward ways. Accordingly, the primates decided that the American church should continue to face its old sanctions. It would also continue to be excluded from doctrinal, polity, and ecumenical conversations within the Communion. To put to rest doubts, the meeting insisted that the Scripture would remain the standard of measuring TEC's readiness to repent of its grievous errors.

So despite the bleak atmosphere cast by the attitude of the American church, the primates were hopeful that a new beginning could be forged from their gathering. In this regard, they requested Archbishop Welby "to appoint a Task Group to maintain conversation" between them. They were confident that if the steps suggested were followed, there was a possibility of "restoration of relationship, the rebuilding of mutual trust, [and] healing the legacy of hurt" in the Communion.

An African proverb maintains that a leopard does not change its skin, and the American church fit this observation perfectly—though millions of Anglicans worldwide had no knowledge of the extent to which the American church had mortgaged its soul to the homosexual movement. Even among the men sitting around the table in London at that moment, some did not understand the depth of the American church's perversion. The brand new American presiding bishop, Michael Curry, who had replaced Jefferts Schori couldn't deny the existence of a deeply-entrenched cabal in his church. Curry was attending the London gathering barely forty-one days after stepping into the shoes of the bulldozing Schori.

The 52-year-old Curry, an African American, was the first black to be elected to his position. You didn't have to be a genius to know why Curry was chosen to lead the American church at that period in her history. Accordingly, he had no real opposition, and victory came to him on the first ballot, where he received 121 of the 174 votes cast—a 70 percent majority over three other candidates. Curry's election took place at the church's 78th General Convention in Salt Lake City, Utah, the same meeting at which The Episcopal Church altered its marriage canon.

Curry was honest about what took place. He didn't deny that altering the marriage canon was tantamount to changing the core doctrine of marriage, and he did acknowledge that the larger Communion "would be upset about that." Curry was new, very fresh in office, and the incident showed how naïve he was about who really held the power. It had been a long time since the American presiding bishop had truly exercised the authority of office as an ecclesiastical and spiritual leader, and Curry was delusional if he thought things were going to be different. The cabal of the Episcopal Church was the real owner of power and authority in the church. They made and unmade presiding bishops. It didn't take long for Curry to realize he was merely a puppet.

The four-day London gathering over, Curry didn't return to a red carpet reception back home. He had goofed terribly on his first assignment. The powers behind his throne weren't expecting him to admit the American guilt so cheekily. He found himself thrown into "the shark pond here at home," noted an observer. The man who had talked humbly in London suddenly changed into the typical combative American Episcopal Church leader. He was transformed from the gentleman of London into an American cowboy, and he renounced his earlier statement. His new stand was to maintain that "changing the definition of marriage is not a change to core doctrine." He started talking big and looking down on his colleagues, questioning their authority in a snickering remark that "the Primates can only decide things that relate to the Primates Meeting." In other words, they had no powers to discuss and make decisions on the American church's intransigence. Wasn't he at the meeting? Why didn't he tell them that?

Meanwhile, back in England, Canterbury was facing its own stormy waves. The fence-mending exercise that Archbishop Welby was initiating hadn't gone well, try as he might. At "two different times at the Primates' Meeting," Welby had promised his colleagues, "I give you my word that I will follow the directions of this meeting." With Curry's new intransigence, Welby was caught in a trap. The American church and her leader's action had put him in a serious dilemma. His honeymoon was over, and it was time to confront his first test of leadership. Confronting him was whether he would act sincerely, honestly, fairly, and decisively as he had promised, or do otherwise. For Welby, a crisis of leadership loomed.

For their part, the primates, particularly those in the GAFCON and the Global South, had honored their freshly appointed leader by consenting to be part of his meeting. Once again, they had, in concert with their other colleagues, arrived at a set of critical decisions they considered the way toward resolving the Communion's crisis. Before them all, Archbishop Welby had promised to see that their resolutions were executed. But once again, the American church was revealing its arrogance, snubbing the worldwide Anglican Church's leaders contemptuously. Beyond the insult was the American church's effrontery of announcing that its representatives would be at the Anglican Consultative Council (ACC) meeting scheduled for later that year in Lusaka, Zambia!

The ACC was another important decision-making organ of the Communion. The primates at the London meeting had restated the ban of the American and Canadian churches from participation in the organization's activities. Now, gleefully and with characteristic insolence, the American church announced that its members would not only attend the ACC Lusaka meeting, but also that "they are going to participate and vote." The truth is that the Episcopal Church never put anything beyond its reach in the Communion. It possessed power, money, and influence, and could muscle, buy, or con its way as it deemed fit. Even with the ACC, it could boast of standing on a surer and firmer ground. The group was in its hands, especially its elected chair, the former bishop of Southern Malawi, James Tengatenga.

The side to which Tengatenga would throw the dice was indeed obvious. This stemmed from the fact that, in a replay of Archbishop Williams' controversial exoneration of the American church, Tengatenga similarly had given TEC a clean bill of health ahead of the meeting. The American church had guaranteed attendance. Tengatenga had endorsed its participation, saying, TEC "should be seated and should vote in Lusaka." The ACC chair had undertaken a coup against the primates, undermining their leadership—a slight that some observers blamed on the primates, saying they'd made a "strategic mistake not to get him on same side with" them. But had Archbishop Welby not promised his colleagues to follow through on all the decisions made?

There were those, however, who felt the real explanation of Tengatenga's snubbing of the primates' decision might require looking beyond the surface, and that perhaps a subtle or overt blackmail was involved. A while back, as the story went, Tengatenga wanted to change jobs.[14] He resigned from his diocese with the hope of taking a teaching appointment in the United States as a dean at Dartmouth. Tengatenga, however, attended the 1998 Lambeth Conference, where he had spoken against the aberrant lifestyle and cast his vote with the majority, which resulted in the defeat of homosexuality. While he had forgotten about the incident, the homosexual activists didn't forget his "transgression." Pronto, "his appointment evaporated." The former bishop and aspiring dean was thrown into the labor market, but not for long. TEC picked him up and employed him as an adjunct professor on a robust academic circuit across several seminaries. The formerly jobless Tengatenga had work and money to live a decent life. Would he have the courage, as someone asked, "to speak out against the ones who are paying his salary?" That would amount to biting the fingers feeding him, as an African proverb would aptly note.

In a way, as the source said, "he was compromised by the fact that the Episcopal Church pays him." Whatever game the ACC chair intended to play in Lusaka in favor of the American church would be of no effect on the GAFCON primates. That would not, however, be the case with American Presiding Bishop Curry and his Canterbury counterpart, Archbishop Justin Welby. For Curry, the time to learn he was merely a puppet dawned sooner rather than later. He had to begin acting and speaking with

14. Virtue, "The Delusional World of Bishop James Tengatenga."

political correctness all the time. Curry's burden was self-inflicted, for the leadership of the American church was never offered for nothing; it was always in exchange for personal principle and integrity.

Archbishop Welby's burden was of a different kind. The American insouciance occurred at a time when Welby was struggling to find his feet, a period during which he wanted desperately to win the confidence and trust of his colleagues, particularly the GAFCON primates. He wanted to rally them behind him at all costs, so it was unfortunate that the American church chose that time to reignite the Communion's fire. Now that the rebellion had been renewed, Welby was placed "in a very difficult spot" at the dawn of his tenure. The Communion's descent to the nadir of disrepute from its rich historical past could not be dissociated from Archbishop Williams' aiding and abetting of the rebels. He always found an alibi to justify his inaction, his failure to deal decisively with the offending churches of the West. Would Welby be different?

It's a pity that Archbishop Welby had no knowledge of the 1978 prophetic statement of Akinola's predecessor, Archbishop Joseph Adetiloye. The statement was made by the Nigerian church leader during that year's Lambeth Conference. Indeed, events preceding the declaration were regrettable in every way. During a plenary discussion, Adetiloye made his way to the microphone to discuss the issue at hand. For over thirty minutes, he was kept on his feet, standing without being recognized. The former Nigerian church leader was ignored. The presiding chair took no notice of the tall, ebony, black Nigerian primate. Instead, he kept moving from one Western speaker to another. A man of infinite patience, Adetiloye refused to give in to the insult. He maintained a stoic, regal perseverance. Eventually, there was no choice for the chair other than to recognize him, and give him the floor to speak.

Adetiloye betrayed no emotions as he took his turn. He was cool, calm, and controlled. "Here at this meeting," he began, "I have struggled to be recognized by the chair." He drew a deliberate pause. The opening sentence and short silence that followed had their effect. It helped focus his colleagues' attention on him. The dead silence in the hall suited him. It was what he wanted for the bombshell he intended to drop. Using the brief interval to sweep across the many different faces, he intoned pithily,

"But it will not always be this way forever."

He took another measured pause before releasing another volley.

"In ten years' time, 1988, the voice of the Africans will not only be allowed, it will be sought," Adetiloye said prophetically.

The prophesy came to pass in 1988. African Anglican Church leaders were not only sought, but their views were considered essential in the Communion before vital decisions were made at Lambeth Conferences. The thorny issue, for instance, at the 1988 Lambeth Conference was the ordination and consecration of women into the episcopate.[15] The Anglican Church leaders in Africa had no strong position regarding women's ordination. They were neither for nor against the idea. Their position

15. "Resolution 1–The Ordination or Consecration of Women to the Episcopate."

426

on the issue weighed heavily, however, on the decision reached. Africa contributed substantially to the 423 votes that helped the majority prevail over the minority, who recorded only 29 paltry votes. And at the end of the Lambeth Conference, Adetiloye had made another prediction when contributing to the closing remarks: "In 1998 The Global South bishops (especially those in Africa) will set the agenda."

That prediction came to pass as well. The Global South primates came to that year's Lambeth Conference better organized. Adetiloye had been elected as chair of the organization, and he imbued it with a sense of mission and direction. This time around, Anglican leaders from the southern hemisphere stood firmly in their determination to defend the Bible. The effect of their collective resolve was the "overwhelmingly passed Lambeth Resolution 1.10 affirming the historic Biblical position on human sexuality."

Unheard of was the way *Global South* leaders expressed themselves openly and boldly. Advocates of the homosexuality agenda in the Anglican Church were jolted by the way the Global South had used its collective influence. Based on previous developments, they had probably thought the Anglican Church would be easy prey to conquer, an easy wall to break and penetrate. But the Global South employed its muscle, resulting in an overwhelming 527 votes to defeat the 70 votes in favor of ordaining homosexuals as priests.[16] Indeed, for every one Anglican bishop supporting homosexuality, eight opposed the lifestyle that the Bible pronounces abhorrent.

Adetiloye retired one year later in 1999 as the Nigerian primate. The turning point that he predicted proved to be irreversible. In 2016, twenty-eight years after he had made that prophetic statement, the leaders of the Anglican Church in the developing countries, particularly in Africa, seemed to have gained in strength and doggedness in challenging ungodly agendas from their Western counterparts. With a resolute will, they were working hard to close the door to the new age of counterculture, sexual narcissism, and biblical revisionism that the Western nations were trying to foist on the Anglican Church.

Interestingly, Akinola, whose post-Adetiloye leadership helped nurture the African church into this position of strength, didn't start his priestly career until 1978, the same year Archbishop Adetiloye made that startling prediction. That was also the year Archbishop Williams was ordained into the priesthood. Similar parallels could also be noted between their successors—Archbishops Nicholas Okoh and Justin Welby. Both Okoh and Welby were yet to be ordained as priests in 1978. Okoh was ahead of Welby, however, in becoming a priest two years after Adetiloye's 1978 famous "Lambeth Declaration." As for Welby, he didn't find his way into the priesthood until 1989.

Akinola and Williams both attended the decisive 1998 Lambeth Conference, and by an act of providence, they also emerged as leaders of the Church. Akinola was elected to head the Nigerian church while Williams rose to the most prestigious position in the Church as its worldwide leader and spiritual father. Akinola was head

16. "Section H: Human Sexuality."

of the most formidable province in the Communion—the Church of Nigeria. The Nigerian church was great in number, possessed tremendous strength and dynamism, and resided in a country with strategic influence in world affairs. As Nigeria was the most populous black country in the world, the Church of Nigeria (Anglican Communion) had the largerst population of Anglicans throughout the world. Its over 18 million members represented more than one-third of the entire membership of global Church.[17] Within the Anglican Communion and in global religious circles, its visionary leadership commanded respect.

In the Anglican Church at large, the most dignified position for any leader is becoming the archbishop of Canterbury. The office is venerated, historically prestigious, and full of power, authority, and influence. As the global leader of the Anglican Church, the archbishop of Canterbury commands respect not only within Britain, but in countries around the world, where he is treated as a foreign head of state. The Anglicans are the third largest Christian denomination in the world, thus endowing the archbishop of Canterbury with the clout of an international spiritual leader. At both the institutional and individual level, the occupant of the office has enormous powers to exert on governments as well as nongovernmental organizations and corporations. That's a difference between Canterbury and any other province of the Anglican Communion.

Nevertheless, the Church of Nigeria and the archbishopric of Canterbury can be said to be dual strategic poles, crucial to the life of the Communion. Both are powerful institutions, strategically and dynamically. The types of leaders they have will impact the fortune of the global Church, as was the case with Akinola and Williams. Both men were strong characters. They also had conflicting viewpoints—convictions that seriously clashed—about the Church, and each was uncompromising in his belief. Nevertheless, Williams underrated Akinola and undermined his leadership capability seriously, thus deepening the crisis within the Church and imperilling its corporate existence. Perhaps, if Williams had taken a sip from Adetiloye's sage warning, he might have acted differently. Most certainly, the Anglican Church would have been better for it, having been spared the crisis that began, escalated, and remained intractable during Williams' tenure.

Unfortunately, Welby chose to walk in Williams' path. So far, he had not shown any ingenuity in approaching the problem differently. As noted earlier, when he was barely ten months in office, he wrote a disruptive letter with his York counterpart, one in which they singled out Nigeria and Uganda as the only two countries in the world to be reminded of the Anglican Communion's view that "the victimisation and diminishment of human beings whose affections happen to be ordered towards people of the same sex is anathema." Nigeria and Uganda were not on "Welby's anti-homosexual dishonor list" for nothing.

---

17. https://en.wikipedia.org/wiki/Anglican_Communion; http://anglican-nig.org/anglican-heritage-with-emphasis-on-the-church-of-nigeria-anglican-communion/.

The Anglican Church in the two countries had remained consistent in its opposition to the unilateral imposition of homosexuality on the Communion by the North American churches, aided and abetted by the archbishop of Canterbury. Beginning in 1997, Nigeria had been at the forefront of the crusade against selling the Anglican Church to this unbiblical lifestyle.[18] Furthermore, the Nigerian government, along with other critical sectors of Nigerian society, did not hide its dislike for any form of aberrant same-sex relationship. The Anglican Church in Nigeria and Nigeria as a country thus shared one mind on homosexuality. Perhaps Archbishop Williams knew it would be a waste of time to exert political influence on the country's leadership, so he left the onerous work of arm twisting to the British government.

Archbishop Welby took a different course from his predecessor. Or perhaps times and situations had opened new possibilities for him to explore. Therefore, it might not be a mystery why he included the Nigerian president as a recipient of his letter concerning the treatment of homosexuals. The move seemed to be calculated.

Five months after the scorching letter, Welby arrived in Abuja, Nigeria's federal capital.[19] The Wednesday, June 4, 2014, visit wasn't pastoral, and he wasn't a guest of the Nigerian church, unlike former Archbishop of Canterbury George Carey on his visit to Nigeria. Indeed, nearly a decade and a half separated the two visits, which would have made Welby's call a major event for the Nigerian church. But Welby's only host was Nigerian President Goodluck Jonathan, and their talks took place behind closed doors.

In a press conference with State House correspondents at Aso Villa, Nigeria's seat of power, the archbishop made a usual diplomatic statement. He said nothing about the worry he had expressed in his January letter to the Nigerian president. Rather, his reason for coming all the way from London was to express "his profound respect and deep love for Nigeria . . . to condole and to pray with President Jonathan." Ironically, Nigeria as a country and its president as an individual were not in the good graces of Britain and America at that particular time. President Jonathan had defied blackmails and pressures and signed the same-sex (prohibition) bill passed by the country's National Assembly into law on January 7, 2014.[20]

Whatever was said in the priviate discussion between Welby and the Nigerian president remained a secret between the two men. Nigeria had earlier refused to be blackmailed by British and American threats to deny her aid and development assistance if she kept refusing to make homosexuality a way of life in the country. It appeared that Welby didn't find Jonathan pliable or easy to be arm-twisted over the homosexuality issue either. Despite the numerous challenges to his regime, it was

18. Okoh, "Chairman's June 2016 Pastoral Letter"; Ntagali, "A Pastoral Message and Call to Prayer from Archbishop Stanley Ntagali."

19. Ejiofor, "Goodluck Jonathan Meets Archbishop of Canterbury Justin Welby."

20. Onuah, "Nigerian President Signs Anti-Gay Bill into Law."

obvious that the Jonathan's government couldn't be pressured to rescind the decision Nigeria had made as a sovereign country.

The Jonathan government ensured that the law banning homosexuality remained intact. But he lost his bid for reelection in 2015 and was succeeded by Gen. Muhammadu Buhari, the military leader who toppled the civilian government of Alhaji Shehu Shagari in 1983 and had ruled Nigeria with draconian power until 1985, when he was overthrown in a palace coup.[21] From all indications, Archbishop Welby desperately wanted Muhammadu Buhari's new government on his side, and he was always charming, even patronizing, in his presence. Even if Welby's intent was not to curtail the influence of the Nigerian church in her formidable leadership amid the Anglican crisis, a mutually reinforcing relationship between the Nigerian government and Canterbury certainly would speak volumes both locally and internationally. At home, it would send a message to the obstinate Nigerian church leaders that the song had changed. Internationally, the perception of the Nigerian church as a steadfast force in the crusade against the imposition of homosexuality on the Anglican Communion would have been dented and weakened.

Buhari was sworn into office on May 29, 2015. He might not have been an old-timer in the murky waters of international politics, but he was not a newcomer either. Events since his assumption of office suggested an effort by Welby to help him achieve a particular end in the Anglo-Nigerian relationship. First was Welby's attempt to break the ranks of the Nigerian church's leadership by appointing one of its archbishops to a top Communion position in London.

The man appointed was the Most Rev. Josiah Idowu-Fearon, and if it hadn't been him, Welby would have had no one else for his "man Friday" job.[22] Idowu-Fearon was an upgraded, higher version of Davis Mac-Iyalla, the white serpent in black skin. He was one of those singularly picked by Rowan Williams to serve on the 2003/2004 Lambeth Commission. Since then, he had not been short on strolls around the halls of power in Canterbury. He was installed a "Six Preacher," that is, a preaching priest, at Canterbury Cathedral by Archbishop Williams in 2007. This was in addition to the opportunity given him to teach at the Cathedral's International Study Centre.

Welby was enthroned March 21, 2013, as archbishop of Canterbury, and within thirty-eight days, he had come up with the trick to crack the hard-nut Nigerian church. Bringing Idowu-Fearon to Lambeth Palace on June 20, 2013, he gave him the Cross of St Augustine award, a recognition reserved for "those who have given long and exceptionally distinguished service to the Anglican Communion." Idowu-Fearon was honoured for his "pivotal role in advancing understanding between Christians and Muslims in Nigeria," helping to stem "the cycle of violence and misunderstanding" in that volatile section of the county. He was also esteemed for his work on the Tony Blair Faith Foundation. There is an obvious fact, however, that cannot be overlooked.

21. https://en.wikipedia.org/wiki/Muhammadu_Buhari.
22. https://en.wikipedia.org/wiki/Josiah_Idowu-Fearon.

Clearly, Welby wanted to make of Idowu-Fearon a phenomenon from Nigeria. He was from Kerinye, Kogi State, the border between the Northern and Southern parts of the country. His career in the priesthood, which began in 1971 at the age 22, was spent mostly in the Northern part of Nigeria. He had worked in the seat of the Muslim caliphate in Nigeria, Sokoto, when he was consecrated as a bishop in 1990. In 1998, he was unanimously elected the fourth bishop of the political capital of Northern Nigeria, Kaduna. Idowu-Fearon therefore knew the dynamics shaping power and politics in Nigeria, especially with regard to the centripetal and centrifugal forces of ethnicity and religion that are impossible to ignore in the country.

Working in Sokoto and originating from an area regarded as part of Northern Nigeria, he had the opportunity of relating with key religious leaders of the Islamic faith. Having his see at Kaduna, the center and capital of political activities in the Northern Nigeria, opened doors of interaction for him in the political sphere. Every Northern politician of note has a home in Kaduna. Intelligent and clever, Idowu-Fearon integrated himself with religious and political leaders. He built a scholarship base through promotion and advancement of knowledge on interfaith matters, particularly related to Christianity and Islam. His good relations with leaders in religion gained him friends at the top echelon of political, business, traditional, and religious leadership in Nigeria.

Political undercurrents were showing how the pendulum was going to swing in the 2015 Nigerian general elections. The Nigerian presidential election was held on March 29, 2015, and Buhari was elected in a straight defeat of the incumbent Jonathan. Four days after Buhari, a Northerner and Muslim became the president-elect of Nigeria. Idowu-Fearon was appointed as the new London-based Anglican Communion Office secretary general.[23] This was on Tuesday, May 2, 2015. Prior consultation was not made with the Church of Nigeria about the appointment by Canterbury. The Nigerian Church was rather taken aback by his selection. Idowu-Fearon had spent forty-four years in the priesthood and, at 66, was only four years away from retirement. Yet the new office to which he had just been appointed had a seven-year tenure. There were younger and brighter Nigerian priests, and the Nigerian church was displeased with Idowu-Fearon's appointment, chiefly over his treachery and his willingness to be bought cheaply by Canterbury at the market for mercenaries.

Clearly, his recruitment was to discredit the Church of Nigeria just as Davis Mac-Iyalla was procured by gay groups to bring Archbishop Akinola to international dishonor.[24] "I have never supported the law in Nigeria that criminalizes the gay community and I will never support it," Idowu-Fearon said in a public statement immediately after his appointment was announced.

23. Virtue, "Nigerian Bishop Appointed Next Secretary General of Anglican Communion Office."

24. See among others, Changing Attitude, "Davis Mac-Iyalla, Director of Changing Attitude Nigeria to visit UK," http://changingattitude.org.uk/archives/1601; "Davis Mac-Iyalla in Diocese of Newark."

Promptly the Nigerian church disowned him. His statement was described as a dishonest claim. The once revered church leader invited a disclaimer on himself, and the Church of Nigeria declared him a turncoat, with a caveat that he "represents himself at the ACC, and not the Church of Nigeria." Three top-ranking officials of the church—the registrar, Mr. Abraham N. Yisa; the episcopal secretary, the Rt. Rev. David O. C. Onuoha; and the general secretary of the church, Ven. Prof Israel 'Kelue Okoye—signed the powerful statement. The church asked the "ACC, the general public and the International Community . . . [to] . . . please note the stand of the Church of Nigeria."

Expectedly, the archbishop of Canterbury reacted to the Church of Nigeria's disowning of Idowu-Fearon. Welby denied all allegations of the Nigerian church and defended Idowu-Fearon's credentials.[25] He made him look like a prized possession, an acquired asset, describing him as the best out of thrity-one applicants who contested for the job from different parts of the world. Welby listed the candidates he defeated to have included five bishops. Keen was the competition, and Idowu-Fearon emerged the most outstanding "appointee from this transparent process." "It is very good news that he comes from the largest and one of the most vigorous Provinces of the Communion," the archbishop said patronisingly. Welby was merely garnishing the rotten beef, because his view ran contrary to the opinion of the Nigerian church leaders, who had advertised Idowu-Fearon's appointment as an appalling act of treachery and betrayal.

Though not admitting it publicly, the archbishop of Canterbury and his new secretary general of the ACO were under no illusions that his Nigerian colleagues would warmly embrace Idowu-Fearon. Indeed, there was a behind-the-scenes move to gain legitimacy for Idowu-Fearon by getting his colleagues to soft pedal their hard stand against his sellout.[26] A top Nigerian with political and international clout allegedly was procured to undertake the scheme. He had arranged a reception to celebrate Idowu-Fearon's appointment, with invitations extended to all his colleagues to attend the party. Not one of them honored the invitation. What happened to the sumptuous, elaborate menu prepared for the cocktail party could not be ascertained.

The rejection and negative public declaration did nothing to dissuade the former Nigerian church leader from accepting the new post. Idowu-Fearon began his duties as the seventh secretary general of the Anglican Consultative Council in July 2015. Interestingly, Idowu-Fearon was to work under the former bishop of Southern Malawi, James Tengatenga, the incumbent ACC chair. Tengatenga was a man familiar with the pawned integrity challenge of swallowing one's words in order to save his bread and butter. Incidentally, the American Episcopal Church didn't stop at corrupting individuals. It also kept the ACC afloat by sending it more than $1 million annually.

---

25. Archbishop of Canterbury, "Response to Church of Nigeria on Archbishop Josiah Idowu-Fearon."

26. This story was related by a very credible source who wanted to remain anonymous because of the personality involved and to avoid lowering his dignity in the international community.

Power, money, and position have always be the shortcut to human downfall. Idowu-Fearon wasn't new to Anglican Communion politics. He could decipher when and how to act with political correctness. He knew the toes that could be stepped on and the big ones that were better avoided. Clear however was the fact that he hadn't jumped the ship for nothing; nor was he shifting allegiance for the fun of it. Idowu-Fearon's major need was to destabilize the Church of Nigeria and use the opportunity of the subversion to break the Anglican Communion's impasse. He understood the place to begin the hatchet job. Of course, working from within the Nigerian church was completely out for him since the church had disowned him publicly.

On the other hand, the incoming Buhari government had opportunities to offer. Idowu-Fearon's northern background and experience gave him an advantage. They provided him weapons with which to switch the Nigerian government to the side of Canterbury. Luckily, Britain had always been a major partner of Nigeria as well as being her former colonial master. Thus, there was good ground for the new ACC secretary general to plant his feet in defence of homosexuality in Nigeria and beyond. Idowu-Fearondid did seem to press the right button with President Buhari from the inception of his government.

The president apparently wasn't informed about the Church of Nigeria's stand regarding the appointment of Idowu-Fearon, or if he was, he didn't care.[27] Apart from issuing, on behalf of the country, a congratulatory message to Idowu-Fearon, Buhari sent a personal emissary, Mallam Adamu Adamu, to deliver the special correspondence to the new appointee in London. The president praised the new ACC Secretary General for being "the first African to occupy the office." The September 05, 2015, letter came five months after the public disclaimer of the Church of Nigeria and with a claim that "all Nigerians were proud of his elevation into one of the most important offices in the world of faith." Embarrassingly, the President said, "It is our prayer that, in your new position, God uses you to counsel and move the entire worldwide Anglican Communion in the direction in which you have taken the Anglican Church in Nigeria." Of course, he had done no such thing.

Whoever the president's communication officials were, they probably knew the ends they wanted to achieve. The letter was full of flatteries, sure to make Idowu-Fearon's head swell, and encouraging the powers that be to think they had invested well: "You have lived up to your calling and attained your self-stated goals." It trumpeted Idowu-Fearon's fame in "creating a culture of respect for differences, a culture of accepting human beings for what they are, and playing down the things that divide them." It held him up as a model: "Our nation and the world will certainly be a better place if all men of God approach pastoral work with the same patience, compassion and fidelity to higher principles that you have exhibited in the various offices you have held." With the letter, Buhari polished the turncoat Nigerian Anglican church leader from being a prophet without honor in his own home into an international shining light.

27. "Buhari Congratulates Idowu-Fearon Over his New Appointment."

Not surprisingly, the president's letter was shrouded in utter secrecy from the media back home in Nigeria. Hardly was there media coverage or mention of it. However, it helped Idowu-Fearon. It bolstered his image, which had taken a dent from the April 30, 2015, disclaimer by the Church of Nigeria. On the other hand, it didn't seem that President Buhari understood the implications of what he had signed. He had put the Nigerian presidency behind an individual who did not believe in the law validly passed and legally assented to by his predecessor. The president had sworn to defend the constitution of the country and protect its laws. Somehow he had been carelessly misguided to the point of committing a constitutional infraction, even if the breach seemed inconsequential.

The Church of Nigeria decided to maintain silence, considering it pointless to contest the president's inaccuracies. The president might have acted ignorantly as he was illiterate concerning the affairs of the church. He had been misled into undertaking an act that was politically incorrect and inappropriate. Perhaps it was better for the church not to have taken issue with the government on the matter. It didn't look as if those behind the Idowu-Fearon-Canterbury plot would stop at anything to bend the hands of the church backwards on the gay issue.

Then out of the blue came a sizzling story with a screaming headline: "Former Nigerian Maximum Ruler, Abacha, Handed Millions To Anglican Church Leaders, Exclusive Documents Reveal."[28] The story was published on August 21, 2015, by *Sahara Reporters*, a New York based online medium. Apparently, it was a planted story, and the news medium had not deemed it necessary to apply the principles that should be the hallmark of any professional news outfit in handling such an explosive story. *Sahara Reporters* had based its story on "documents exclusively obtained," which were a government classified report. The report was entitled, "Investigation Report on Alleged Swindle of Public Funds–Late Gen. Sanni Abacha, former Nigerian Head of State & Alhaji Ismaila Gwarzo, former National Security Adviser."

The medium had cited its source as a "top government official," which meant someone deliberately leaked the highly classified security report to *Sahara Reporters*. Characteristic of a press without ethics, the news medium willfully slanted the story with an apparent aim of scandalizing the Church of Nigeria (CON) and, particularly, Archbishop Akinola. The intention of the story was unmistakable. The introduction to the story claimed sensationally "that former military ruler, Sanni Abacha, gave millions of dollars in public funds to leaders of the Anglican Church of Nigeria during his brutal reign." In subsequent paragraphs, it reported the specific amount given to the church as "$1,021,388." Akinola was said to have taken delivery of the money, which he "claimed to have handed over to . . . the Primate of the Anglican Church of Nigeria, Archbishop J. Abiodun Adetiloye, who had reportedly requested for the funds from Mr. Abacha's regime to assist Nigeria's Anglican bishops in attending the decennial conference."

28. "Former Nigerian Maximum Ruler, Abacha, Handed Millions To Anglican Church Leaders, Exclusive Documents Reveal."

The *Sahara Reporters* and the *Daily Telegraph* of London were practicing the same profession. The two media houses, however, did not share the same international best practices. What one news medium was looking for as the outcome of its investigative story was different from what the other desired. The *Daily Telegraph*, seemingly, was interested in the truth of Archbishop Justin Welby's birth. On the other hand, the quest of the *Sahara Reporters* was muckraking and scandalizing, exposing the past and current leaders of the Church of Nigeria to public opprobrium. Did the medium know it had been used? Or was it part of a grand conspiracy? The unfortunate part was that the story relied on an investigation conducted in 1999 by President Olusegun Obasanjo's government. The Obasanjo government had two terms to sort the matter out, an ample opportunity for it to raise questions if there were any. After him, there had been two other governments—of Presidents Umar Musa Yar'Adua and Goodluck Jonathan—and they had raised no eyebrow either. Exhuming the report from the government's archive and dusting it of dirt, especially when the Nigerian church was confronting pro-homosexuality forces in and out of the Anglican Church, smelled of a rat.

There were two principal characters mentioned in the story: Archbishop Akinola and the late Archbishop Abiodun Adetiloye. Obviously, Adetiloye was dead, but Akinola was alive and could explain what happened. That was what the principle of fair hearing required in journalism, to give an accused person opportunity to state his case. The *Daily Telegraph* demonstrated this by giving Archbishop Welby a chance to know the truth and state his side of the story. The same opportunity was denied Akinola. But as providence would have it, though Archbishop Adetiloye had long joined the Saints Triumphant, he had, however, clarified the matter while alive. He had spoken on the issue during an interview in the process of gathering materials for the biography of Archbishop Akinola in 2007. Adetiloye's exact words were, "With all the bad things that Abacha did . . . he sponsored our trip to the last Lambeth Conference, the entire Church of Nigeria."[29] The fourteenth Lambeth Conference took place July 16-August 4, 2008, at the University of Kent's Canterbury campus. Adetiloye had led the sixty-member Nigerian delegation to the Conference. He died December 14, 2012, three years preceding the malicious report. As wisdom would dictate in reaction to muckraking stories, Akinola and the leadership of the CON simply ignored the scurrilous report. They dismissed it for what it was: arrant nonsense. Expectedly, the story went the eventual way of every thoughtless story—a natural death. No media outlet in Nigeria reported the story apart from the *Sahara Reporters*.

As for Canterbury, President Buhari's endorsement of Archbishop Idowu-Fearon was a morale booster and hope-lifter. All these incidents had preceded Archbishop Welby's convening of a London meeting with all Anglican primates in January 2016.[30]

---

29. Interview with the Most Rev. Abiodun Adetiloye, the retired Primate of Church of Nigeria, at his house in Lagos on May 28, 2007.

30. GAFCON, "January 2016 Update."

The Anglican Church leader seemingly was assembling a war cabinet and had strategically selected his foot soldiers. First was Bishop Tengatenga, the ACC chair, and now was the addition of Archbishop Idowu-Fearon to be his secretary general at the ACC. Does anybody require special knowledge to interpret why the archbishop gave two Africans strategic positions in a crucial administrative organ of the global Church? The tactic was a perfect scheme to divide and conquer GAFCON and the Global South as the two men would have no choice other than to be fifth columnists, caring less about the position of their kinsmen on matters concerning the Anglican crisis.

Indeed, Idowu-Fearon was eager to deliver his assignment, which did not spare efforts at subversion of the Nigerian church. Contrary to all outward pretensions, everyone in the Communion knew that as long as the Nigerian church maintained her uncompromising stand on the issue of homosexuality, the matter would remain foreclosed in the Anglican Communion. There would be little or no room for Canterbury and her cohorts to move in lining up the Communion behind them. Given his knowledge and experience, Idowu-Fearon knew where the work should begin—with manipulation of the new Nigerian government. Incidentally, the Nigerian church leader, Archbishop Nicholas Okoh, was fully aware of the enormity of the battle that had been passed on to him. Amid the unfolding events, therefore, he remained unperturbed.

As had been related, Okoh was in London, January 11–15, 2016, for the weeklong primates gathering.[31] On his return, he only managed to suffer the weekend before letting people know what transpired at the roundtable with Welby. Okoh's "Statement to the Church of Nigeria on the outcomes of Primates 2016," issued on January 18, 2016, was very succinct: "We are yet to be convinced that the restrictions imposed on TEC will be implemented . . . The bottom line is that nothing has changed." With a stroke of the pen, he slammed the door shut once again on any possible hope of the situation being normalized. "We are not going back on our stand," the statement reiterated.

The straightforward statement turned into ashes the dream of those who thought the Nigerian church's resolve could be weakened through deft political moves. Okoh's message hit the target with the right force. But Canterbury would not give up. Rather than face the reality of the situation by addressing the issues dividing them honestly and sincerely, Archbishop Welby chose instead to go on a wild goose chase, courting Nigeria's President Muhammadu Buhari like a beautiful bride. At every opportunity, the global Anglican Church leader would fawn over and be obsequious with the septuagenarian Nigerian leader.

When former British Prime Minister David Cameron committed a diplomatic gaffe by insulting Nigeria before her majesty, the queen, President Buhari couldn't

---

31. "Archbishop Nicholas Okoh issues a Statement to the Church of Nigeria on the outcomes of Primates 2016,"
https://www.gafcon.org/news/archbishop-nicholas-okoh-issues-a-statement-to-the-church-of-nigeria-on-the-outcomes-of.

have had a better ambassador at large and plenipotentiary than the archbishop of Canterbury.[32] On May 8, 2016, Cameron had gone to brief the queen on an international corruption summit that the UK government was organizing. Nigeria was one of the countries invited to participate in the conference. During the process of briefing the British monarch, Cameron had dropped a bombshell. It was a quip, a rib-cracking pun. He had told the queen that among the expected attendees were "leaders of 'fantastically corrupt' nations." Naturally, the prime minister had made specific mention of Nigeria as being on the list. Archbishop Welby quickly rose to the defence of his friend. Welby and Cameron had both been at the briefing, and swiftly he had countered the prime minister's claim, saying of his friend Buhari to the queen: "This one is not corrupt." (Of course, rightly, one magazine had described the Canterbury archbishop's statement as an "invaluable testimonial . . . to the Nigerian leader.")

To much media acclaim, Welby had been a regular visitor to the Nigerian leader whenever he was visiting Britain. He made no pretensions about making the visits a matter of public knowledge. And if they raised speculations so be it. It's difficult, however, to determine what Welby hoped to achieve for the Anglican Communion with his kowtowing, for the key to resolution of the Anglican crisis is not in Buhari's hands. It is in the custody of the archbishop. It is up to him to decide whether he wants to end the Communion's crisis or keep playing the ostrich game like his predecessor. As an observer candidly notes about the archbishop, "He has a tough row to hoe."

Archbishop Welby is confronted with hard choices from which he cannot run. The politicking of the past has not helped resolve the Anglican crisis. Of this he is very much aware. He has to face the truth and reality. Only the truth will set the Anglican Church free, and that truth starts with Canterbury honestly coming to terms with the reality facing it. Only by admitting the truth to himself can Archbishop Welby find a solution to the festering Anglican problem he inherited. The Global Anglican Future Conference (GAFCON) had indicated its unwavering and inflexible stand on the critical issue dividing the Communion. The group has been stout, consistent, and persistent for years about ways to bring the impasse to an end. Within GAFCON, a new generation of leaders has replaced the pioneering generation without any sign of abandoning the principled stand. Over the years, therefore, the Anglican Communion has witnessed many failed opportunities to resolve the crisis, leading to a deepening gulf between leaders that continues to pull the Church asunder.

The reform and realignment precipitated by disagreement in the Church in 2008 is steadily crystallizing into a permanent feature. The Anglican house is divided. On one side are the pro-GAFCON groups while Canterbury is on the other. In 2008, at the inception of GAFCON, the Communion leadership's attitude seemingly was "let's wait and see." Over 1,100 participants converged in Jerusalem for that maiden historical and epochal event. Besides the conference giving birth to GAFCON as a landmark

---

32. "Buhari Meets Archbishop of Canterbury, Welby"; "Buhari Meets the Archbishop Who Saved Him."

movement within the Anglican house, it also sent a powerful statement regarding how fractured Anglican unity had become across the world. Any doubts about GAFCON's staying power have been erased. The 2013 GAFCON further punched holes in the idea that the Conference could be ephemeral. Attendance climbed to more than 1,300. The success, however, was beyond the numerical strength. GAFCON 2013 had profound effects on the Anglican Communion. It marked the emergence of an obverse side of the Anglican Communion worldwide, another face of legitimate Anglicanism and Anglican identity globally.

GAFCON met again in 2018, marking three occasions within the space of ten years that Anglicans sharing common doctrinal and scriptural views came together.[33] Unfortunately, Canterbury had had no opportunity to assemble all the Anglican leaders as used to occur at the decennial Lambeth Conference. Though Lambeth was due in 2018, the archbishop of Canterbury postponed it by two years. Ironically, this same suggestion drew scoffing from Welby's predecessor, Rowan Williams, during a private meeting between him and Akinola in 2007. The latter had pleaded fervently, reasoning with Williams to move the Conference forward so that tempers could cool and ways found to address the angst of the Global South primates who were threatening to boycott Lambeth. It appears that the two Anglican leaders share the trait of obstinancy. As Archbishop Williams pretended the concerns of his colleagues from the Globlal South did not matter, the same attitude of nonchalance was demonstrated by Archbishop Welby. He pretended not to hear cries of his GAFCON counterparts.

In a fashion resembling what happened in 1997 and 2007, when Global South leaders convened Encounters to chart a course ahead of the 1998 and 2008 Lambeth Conferences, the third GAFCON was convoked against an analogous background. Well attended with close to 1,950 representatives from 50 countries, the gathering was made up of 316 bishops, 669 clergy, and 965 laity. GAFCON members were brought back to Jerusalem as during the maiden conference. For one week, June 17–22, 2018, the gathering discussed and, at the end, sent a serious notice of warning to the archbishop of Canterbury. This was the same way the 2008 GAFCON had notified Archbishop Williams about the potential boycott of the Lambeth Conference by members of the group if he failed to address the core issues dividing the Communion.

This time around, Welby received his own warning about the possibility of that situation repeating itself. Two key demands were made from him. The first was that he should invite "as full members to Lambeth 2020 bishops of the Province of the Anglican Church in North America and the Province of the Anglican Church in Brazil." The second was that he should exclude "those Provinces which have endorsed by word or deed sexual practices which are in contradiction to the teaching of Scripture and Resolution 1.10 of the 1998 Lambeth Conference, unless they have repented of their actions and reversed their decisions." Without resolution of the two issues, the

---

33. GAFCON, "Letter to the Churches—GAFCON Assembly 2018," https://www.gafcon.org/kigali-2020/letters-to-the-churches.

conference urged "GAFCON members to decline the invitation to attend Lambeth 2020." In addition, they were urged not to participate in "all other meetings of the Instruments of Communion."[34]

The only things that appeared to have changed in the two decades of the Anglican crisis were dates and dramatis personae. Like Archbishop Williams, the response of Welby was to snub and scorn the entreaties of his colleagues. Whether they liked it or not, the 2020 Lambeth Conference would hold. From July 23 to August 2, 2020, Anglican bishops worldwide would be brought to London. And in the same haughty manner with which his predecessor spoke with finality, he too ruled out the possibility of going back. The invited bishops and their spouses would be returning to the University of Kent, which hosted the 2008 edition. About 1,232 bishops with their spouses had been invited, including bishops in same-sex unions. Bishops in same-sex unions at the Lambeth Conference?

The last time, Williams didn't even have the audacity to try that. Archbishop Welby's skill must have extended to fishing in troubled waters. While red carpets were rolled out for same-sex bishops, he was unequivocal, on the other hand, that the bishops who remained faithful to the Communion's doctrine and canon, but whom he referred to as "members of breakaway Anglican Churches," were barred from the Conference.[35] However, they were free to look through the window as observers![36]

Can anything change in the Anglican crisis? It's doubtful. In an April 2019 letter to all Anglican leaders worldwide about the Conference, Archbishop Welby made an oblique reference to the GAFCON leaders, saying, "But if you do choose to decline the invitation to be present at the Lambeth Conference your voice and view will not be ignored, it will simply not be heard."[37] Yet, the theme he had chosen for the 2020 Lambeth Conference was: God's Church for God's World: Walking, Listening and Witnessing Together.

On their part, the GAFCON leaders expressed regret at being pushed into an unwilling position once more, forced to boycott the 2020 Lambeth Conference. At the 2018 GAFCON, they had resolved that "if godly order in the Communion had not been restored," if the archbishop refused to effect "necessary changes that fell within his power and responsibility," they would be compelled to excuse themselves from the Lambeth gathering. Of course, all the archbishop's decisions and actions since then had reinforced the unsavory situations.

34. "Letter to the Churches—GAFCON Assembly 2018."

35. https://www.lambethconference.org/; https://www.anglicannews.org/news/2019/06/more-than-1000-bishops-and-their-spouses-book-for-the-lambeth-conference-2020.aspx; https://www.anglicannews.org/news/2019/04/lambeth-conference-2020-over-500-bishops-in-39-anglican-communion-churches-register.aspx; https://www.anglicanjournal.com/750000-grant-gives-major-boost-to-lambeth-conference-2020/.

36. https://www.gafcon.org/news/lambeth-2020-descends-into-confusion.

37. Welby, "Lambeth Conference 2020—God's Church for God's World: Walking, Listening and Witnessing Together."

Therefore, they were compelled "to call together a meeting of bishops of the Anglican Communion in June of 2020." "Kigali 2020" as the gathering would be known, would convene under the theme: "Consecrated to Christ." The GAFCON leaders intended to bring together "all bishops of the Anglican Communion who subscribe to the Jerusalem Declaration and Lambeth Resolution 1.10." From June 9–14, 2020, one month ahead of Lambeth, the Rwandan capital would host the congregation of orthodox Anglican Church leaders from all parts of the world. The GAFCON leaders who met in Sydney, Australia, the first week of May 2019 (weeks after the Archbishop Welby's letter) were the primates of Rwanda, Nigeria, Uganda, Myanmar, the Indian Ocean, Kenya, Congo, Chile, South America, the head of the biblical, orthodox Church of Brazil, and Archbishop Foley Beach of the Anglican Church of North America. None was happy with the development, but they considered their action inevitable. As their jointly signed communique said, they considered it unfair to have their bishops "deprived of faithful fellowship while we wait for order in the Communion to be restored."[38]

Order? Order in the Anglican Communion? Who will bring the direly needed "order" to the beleaguered Anglican Church? Who? Who? When? And who can provide the answer?

---

38. Handley, "Next Lambeth Conference—and its Rival."

Bibilography

Oral Interviews

Ademo, Ade (2007, October 12). Interview and transcription by Akin Enilolobo. Interview conducted at his OAU Quarters, Abuja, FCT, Nigeria.

Ademowo, Ephraim (The Most Rev.) The Archbishop of Lagos. (2007, June 27). Interview and transcription by Akin Enilolobo. Interview conducted at the Archbishop's Palace, Marina, Lagos.

Adetiloye, Abiodun (The Most Rev.) The retired Archbishop, Primate & Metropolitan, Church of Nigeria (Anglican Communion). (2007, May 28). Interview and transcription by Akin Enilolobo, Interview conducted at his Lekki home, Lagos.

Akinde, Adebayo Dada (The Most Rev. [Prof]), The Archbishop Lagos Province & member Board of Trustees of Peter Akinola Foundation (PAF). (2007, June 27). Interview and transcription by Akin Enilolobo. Interview conducted at Episcopal House, St. Judes' Cathedral, Ebutte-Metta, Lagos.

Akinkugbe, Modupe Dorcas (Mrs.) Member Board of Trustees, Peter Akinola Foundation (PAF). (2016, September 14). Interview and transcription by the author. Interview conducted through the telephone from Abeokuta with the interviewee in Abuja.

Akinola, Peter (The Most Rev.) Archbishop, Primate & Metropolitan, Church of Nigeria (CON) Anglican Communion. (Various times in 2006 and 2007) Interviews and transcriptions by Akin Enilolobo. Interviews variously conducted in Abuja and Abeokuta. (2011, July 23 & 24) Interview and transcription by author. Interviews conducted at interviewee's house in Abeokuta. (December 25, 2013) Interview and transcription by the author. Interview conducted at interviewee's house.

Efobi, Christian (The Rt. Rev.) Bishop of Aguata Diocese. (2007, September 14, 2007). Interview and transcription by Akin Enilolobo. Interview conducted at Osun Diocese Retreat Centre, Osogbo, Osun State.

Karibi-Whyte, A. G. (Hon Justice) Chancellor of Abuja Diocese and later Church of Nigeria. (2007, June 8). Interview and transcription by Akin Enilolobo. Interview at his Lagos home.

Kattey, Ignatius (The Rt. Rev.) Bishop of Niger Delta North Diose, Rivers State & member PAF Board. (2007, September 14). Interview conducted by Akin Enilolobo. Interview conducted at Osun Diocese Retreat Centre, Osogbo, Osun State.

Ogbonyomi, T. E. (The Rt. Rev.) Retired bishop of Northern Nigeria and later Kaduna Diocese. (2007, May 25). Interview and transcription by Akin Enilolobo. Interview at his Kabba home, Kogi State.

Pepple, Ammal (Ms.) Former Head of Service of Nigeria, later minister in the federal cabinet as well as member of the Abuja Diocese. (2007, October 12). Interview and transcriptions by Akin Enilolobo. In Interview conducted at her Mabuchi Quarters, Abuja.

Sonekan, Ernest (Chief) Former Nigeria Head of State. (Date unstated) Responded through a filled-questionnaire submitted by Akin Enilolobo to him at his Lagos home.

Books

Agbaje, A. A. *Abiodun Lagos: A Blossomy Tree in the Desert – A Biography of Joseph Abiodun Adetiloye*. Lagos: CSS Limited, 2001.

Anglican Communion Office. *The Lambeth Commission of Communion – The Windsor Report 2004*. London: Anglican Communion Office, 2004.

Asaju, Dapo. *In Defence of Christian Orthodoxy (A Collection of Articles)*. Produced for the Conference of Chancellors and Registrars, Church of Nigeria. Abeokuta: Crowther Theological Publishers, 2013.

Boer, R. Harry. *A Short History of the Early Church*. Ibadan: Daystar, 1976.

The Church of Nigeria (Anglican Communion). *Church Year Calendar 2007*. Lagos: The Church of Nigeria, 2007.

Fafowora, O. Oladapo. *The Cathedral Church of Christ, Marina, Lagos (1867–2007)*. Lagos: CSS Bookshops Ltd., 2008.

Gbesan, Gbenga & Akin Enilolobo. *In The World But Not of The World – Collected Charges and Speeches of Peter J. Akinola*. Abeokuta: Gbenga Gbesan & Associates, 2009.

Gbesan, Gbenga. *Peter Jasper Akinola: Before the Mission – A Biography*. Abeokuta: Gbenga Gbesan & Associates, 2009.

Oxford Centre for Mission Studies and The American Anglican Council. *Lambeth Directory – The Worldwide Anglican Communion 1998*. Carlisle, UK: Jeremy Mudditt, 1998.

Peter Akinola Foundation. *4 Main Initiatives of PAF*. Abeokuta: PAF, 2011.

———. *Inroad Industrial Institute Prospectus*. Abeokuta: PAF, 2013.

———. *Consolidated Annual Reports 2011 – 2015*. Abeokuta: PAF, 2015.

Taiwo, C. O. *Joseph Abiodun Adetiloye – The Visionary Primate*. Lagos: CSS Limited, 1999.

Woodliff, George F. "Rediscovering Christian Orthodoxy in Episcopal Anglicanism." In *The Lambeth Commission on Communion*, 429–525. 2004. https://www.anglicancommunion.org/media/100345/The-Lambeth-Commission-on-Communion.pdf

Articles & Websites

Akinola, Peter. "A Statement On The Church Of England's Response To Civil Partnerships By The Primate of All Nigeria." August 2005. Abuja: The Church of Nigeria (Anglican Communion).

———. "Why I Object to Homosexuality and Same-Sex Unions." *Virtue Online.* https://virtueonline.org/why-i-object-homosexuality-and-same-sex-unions-peter-akinola.

Anis, Mouneer. "Archbishop Mouneer Anis To TEC HoB - Address of Archbishop Mouneer Anis to the TEC House of Bishops meeting in New Orleans." *Global South Anglican Online.* September 22, 2007. http://www.globalsouthanglican.org/index.php/blog/comments/archbishop_mouneer_anis_to_tec_hob.

———. "Bishop Mouneer Anis Reflections on the Joint Standing Committee (JSC) 29/02/08 - 04/03/08," *Global South Anglican Online.* March 17, 2008. http://www.globalsouthanglican.org/index.php/blog/comments/bishop_mouneer_anis_reflections_on_the_joint_standing_committee_jsc.

"Anti-Gay Pressures in Anglican Church." *The Punch.* May 25, 2007, p. 16.

Bates, Stephen. "No schism for now: Williams get tough on liberals to save the church." *The Guardian.* February 19, 2007, http://www.guardian.co.uk/religion/Story/0,,2016971,00.html.

———. "God's Squad – Stephen Bates on the Predicament Tearing Anglicanism Apart." *The Guardian.* May 22, 2009. https://www.theguardian.com/books/2009/may/23/rowan-williams-rowans-rule.

"Bishop of Singapore Slams Other Provinces for 'Departing from the Faith.'" *Anglican Journal.* October 1, 1999. https://www.anglicanjournal.com/bishop-of-singapore-slams-other-provinces-for-departing-from-the-faith-646/.

Boyer, Peter J. "A Church Asunder." *The New Yorker.* April 10, 2006. https://www.newyorker.com/magazine/2006/04/17/a-church-asunder.

"Buhari congratulates Idowu-Fearon over his new appointment." *Vanduard.* September 05, 2015. https://www.vanguardngr.com/2015/09/buhari-congratulates-idowu-fearon-over-his-new-appointment/.

"Buhari Meets Archbishop of Canterbury, Welby." *This Day.* June 14, 2016. http://www.thisdaylive.com/index.php/2016/06/14/buhari-meets-archbishop-of-canterbury-welby/.

Butt, Riazat "Lambeth Conference: Archbishop Blames Liberals for Church Rift." *The Guardian.* August 3, 2008. https://www.theguardian.com/world/2008/aug/04/anglicanism.religion.

Church of Nigeria. "Anglicans Set To Renew Links With Chinese Christians As Archbishops Pay Mission Exploratory Visit." September 29, 2006. http://nianglicannews.blogspot.com.

Conger, George. "Behind the Scenes at the Primates' Meeting: Part 2." *Church of England Newspaper.* March 4, 2005, p. 5.

———. "Three U.S. Bishops Invited to Primates' Meeting, Third Episcopal Bishop Invited to Primates' Meeting." *The Living Church.* January 29, 2007. www.americananglican.org.

Conlon, Michael. "Anglican Church Turmoil Over Gay Issues Deepens." *Reuters.* May 8, 2007. https://www.reuters.com/article/us-episcopals-split/anglican-church-turmoil-over-gay-issues-deepens-idUSN0737733620070508.

Doughty, Steve. "I Sometimes Question if God Exists: Archbishop of Canterbury Admits he Sometimes Has Moments of Doubts." *Virtue Online.* September 17, 2014. https://virtueonline.org/i-sometimes-question-if-god-exists-archbishop-canterbury-admits-he-sometimes-has-moments-doubt.

Ejiofor, Clement. "Goodluck Jonathan Meets Archbishop of Canterbury Justin Welby." *Legit.* June 4, 2014. https://www.legit.ng/67609.html.

Episcopal News Service. https://www.episcopalnewsservice.org.

Gledhill, Ruth. "For God's Sake." *The Times*. July 5, 2007. https://www.thetimes.co.uk/article/for-gods-sake-mqdmclhwb2b.

———. "Rowan Williams 'Hated' Being Archbishop of Canterbury." *Christian Today*. June 23, 2014. http://www.christiantoday.com/article/rowan.williams.hated.being.archbishop.of.canterbury/38355.htm.

Gove, Michael "The Tide Is Turning: Justin Welby Interviewed." *The Spectator*. December 12, 2015. http://www.spectator.co.uk/2015/12/the-tide-is-turning-in-this-country-justin-welby-interviewed/.

Griggs, Ian and Cole Moreton. "Gay Bishop Defies his Lambeth Conference Ban...Gene Robinson Wasn't Invited But He's Coming Anyway." *The Independent*. July 12, 2008. http://www.independent.co.uk/news/uk/home-news/gay-bishop-defies-his-lambeth-conference-ban-866487.html.

Gunn, Stephen. "Sunday: Akinola Missed Out." *Inclusive Church*. February 18, 2007. http://inclusive-churh.org.uk.

Gyamfi, Charles Coffie. "Gun Men Kidnap Ex-Anglican Primate, Peter Akinola." *The Guardian*. December 25, 2013. Vol. 30, No.12, 781.

———. "Kidnapping: 'My Story' by Primate Akinola," *The Guardian*. December 27, 2013. Vol. 30, No.12, 782.

Handley, Paul. "Next Lambeth Conference – and its Rival." *Church Times*. May 10, 2019. https://www.churchtimes.co.uk/articles/2019/10-may/news/world/next-lambeth-conference-and-its-rival.

"How I Was Denied Entry into Jordan – Akinola." *Anglicans Ablaze*. July 4, 2008. https://anglicansablaze.blogspot.com/2008/07/how-i-was-denied-entry-into-jordan.html.

Institute on Religion and Democracy. "IRD Supports CANA – All Orthodox Anglicans on Eve of Bishop Martyn Minns' Installation." May 4, 2007. http://www.christiannewswire.com/news/411583031.html.

"Issues in Human Sexuality – A Statement by the House of Bishops of the General Synod of the Church of England, December 1991." London: Church House Publishing.

Kennebi Preye, et al. *The Jewel*. Vol. 1. *No*.1. 2014. Edited by Ajibade Odunayo. A publication of the trainees of the Peter Akinola Foundation Centre for Youth Industrial Training. Abeokuta, Ogun State, Nigeria.

Mason, Bruce. "Latest AAC Upate on Plano, TX Meeting." *Free Republic*. September 26, 2003. http://www.freerepublic.com/focus/f-religion/990345/posts.

McLaughlin, Kay Collier. "The Rev. Katharine Jefferts Schori Elected to Be 26th Presiding Bishop of the Episcopal Church; First Female Presiding Bishop and Primate." News from General Convention, Episcopal Diocese of Lexington. 2006.

Moore, Charles and Gordon Rayner. "Justin Welby: DNA Test Reveals My Secret Father Was Sir Winston Churchill's Private Secretary." *The Telegraph*. April 8, 2016. http://www.telegraph.co.uk/news/2016/04/08/justin-welby-dna-test-reveals-my-secret-father-was-sir-winston-c/.

Ojo, Olalekan. "Akinola Named Among 100 Influential People on Earth." *The Punch*. May 8, 2007, p 9.

Oni, Olamide. "Homosexuality: 'I Will Attend My Son's Gay Wedding Ceremony'-Archbishop." *Pulse*. November 12, 2015. http://pulse.ng/religion/homosexuality-i-will-attend-my-sons-gay-wedding-ceremony-archbishop-id4452183.html.

Onuah, Felix. "Nigerian President Signs Anti-Gay Bill Into law." *Reuters*. January 13, 2014. http://www.reuters.com/article/nigeria-gay-idUSL6N0KN2PP20140113.

Pepinster, Catherine. "Rowan's Rule, By Rupert Shortt." *The Independent*. January 9, 2009. http://www.independent.co.uk/arts-entertainment/books/reviews/rowans-rule-by-rupert-shortt-1232972.html.

Rusbridger, Alan. "Interview: Rowan Williams." *The Guardian*. March 21, 2006. https://www.theguardian.com/world/2006/mar/21/religion.uk.

Sagay, I. J. "From Carpenter to Primate." *The Guardian*. October 1, 2006. https://web.archive.org/web/20120205180658/http://www.anglican-nig.org/sagaywrites.htm.

Sahara Reporters. "Former Nigerian Maximum Ruler, Abacha, Handed Millions To Anglican Church Leaders, Exclusive Documents Reveal." *Sahara Reporters*. August 21, 2015. http://saharareporters.com/2015/08/21/former-nigerian-maximum-ruler-abacha-handed-millions-anglican-church-leaders-exclusive.

Sanghani, Radhika. "Church of England Creating 'Pagan Church' to Recruit Members." *The Telegraph*. June 21, 2013. https://www.telegraph.co.uk/news/religion/10133906/Church-of-England-creating-pagan-church-to-recruit-members.html.

Snow, Deborah. "Exit Jensen, Enigma and True Believer." *The Sydney Morning Herald*. June 15, 2013. https://www.smh.com.au/national/exit-jensen-enigma-and-true-believer-20130614-2o9hw.html.

Steere, Tania. "Oh Buddha! Ex-Archbishop Rowan Williams Reveals He Meditates for 40 Minutes Every Day to Clear His Mind for Prayer." *Daily Mail*. July 2, 2014. https://www.dailymail.co.uk/news/article-2678815/Oh-Buddha-Ex-archbishop-Rowan-reveals-meditates-40-minutes-day-help-clear-mind-prayers.html.

Thomas, Anne. "Anglican Head: US Church has 'Pushed the Boundaries.'" *Christian Today*. August 24, 2016. http://www.christiantoday.com/article/anglican.head.us.church.has.pushed.the.boundaries/7357.htm?print=1.

Thompson, Damian. "Giles Fraser: The Church's Own Radical Cleric Will Still Have a Voice." *The Telegraph*. October 28, 2011. https://www.telegraph.co.uk/news/religion/8854463/Giles-Fraser-The-Churchs-own-radical-cleric-will-still-have-a-voice.html.

Van Biema, David. (2007) "Peter Akinola." *Time*. May 03, 2007. http://content.time.com/time/specials/2007/time100/article/0,28804,1595326_1615513_1614655,00.html.

Voice Of America. "Anglican Church of Nigeria Installs Bishop From America." Archive and Papers of the Most Rev. Peter Akinola.

Warren, Rick. "Archbishop Peter Akinola – The Strength of a Lion." *Time*. April 30, 2006. Reprinted in *Global South Anglican*. http://globalsouthanglican.org/comments/archbishop_peter_akinola_the_strength_of_a_lion_in_time_100_list_of_people.

Other Internet Sources

"Who is Doing the Dividing?" http://www.beliefnet.com/Faiths/Christianity/2004/02/Who-Is-Doing-The-Dividing.aspx?p=7.

"40 Days of Discernment – Updated Timeline of Defining Actions." http://www.wearestandrews.com/resources/40-days-of-discernment.aspx?ArticleId=221.

"A Brief History of Integrity." https://www.rci.rutgers.edu/~lcrew/pubd/briefhist.html.

"A Pastoral Statement to Lesbian and Gay Anglicans from Some Member Bishops of the Lambeth Conference." August 5, 1998. http:justus.anglican.org/resources/Lambeth1998/pasttment.html.

"AAC and Christ Church Announce Soaring Registration Numbers for 'A Place to Stand' Gathering. Latest AAC Update on Plano, TX Meeting, September 26, 2003." http://www. freerepublic.com/focus/f-religion/990345/posts.

"AAC's Anderson Among Four New CANA Bishops: TLC 9.13.07." September 14, 2007. https://geoconger.wordpress.com/2007/09/14/aacs-anderson-among-four-new-cana-bishops-tlc-91307/.

"About The Bishop Peter Awelewa Adebiyi." *Church of Nigeria website.* http://www. dioceseoflagoswest.org/paadebiyi/bishopFlash.html.

Ackerman, Keith. "San Joaquin: Bishop John David Schofield Dies." *Virtue* Online. October 30, 2013. http://www.virtueonline.org/san-joaquin-bishop-john-david-schofield-dies.

"Advocate Makes History Again with a Masterly Performance." *The Herald.* August 17, 1997. http://www.heraldscotland.com/news/12296137.Advocate_makes_history_again_with_a_masterly_performance/.

"African Anglican Bishops' Joint Statement Responds to Windsor Report: 'Homosexuality Is Clearly Un-Biblical, Unnatural and Definitely Un-African.'" October 30, 2004. http:// www.christiantoday.com/article/african.anglican.bishops.joint.statement.responds. to.windsor.report/1627.htm.

Akueth, Michael Mading. "Bishop Nathaniel Garang Anyieth: The Spiritual Leader of Our Time." *PaanLuel Wel Media.* June 17, 2015. https://paanluelwel.com/2015/06/17/ bishop-nathaniel-garang-the-spiritual-leader-of-our-time/.

Anglican Church in North America. "Our Genesis." http://anglicanchurch.net/media/acna_our_genesis_june_2009.pdf.

"Anglican Church in North America: Reaching North America with the Transforming Love of Jesus Christ – The Most Reverend Robert W. Duncan." http://www.anglicanchurch. net/media/acna_archbishop_duncan_biography_01.12_.11_.pdf.

"Anglican Mainstream – Who We Are." http://anglicanmainstream.org/anglican-mainstream-who-we-are/.

"Archbishop Duncan Announces Two Appointments." http://www.anglicanchurch.net/?/ main/page/564.

"Archbishop Njongonkulu of Cape Town Declares Same-Sex Marriages Unchristian." December 9, 2004. www.changingattitude.org.uk.

"Archbishop of Canterbury Arrives." *Modern Ghana.* July 24, 2003. https://www. modernghana.com/news/37932/1/archbishop-of-canterbury-arrives.html.

Atwood, Bill. "High Noon in Lusaka." *GAFCON website.* March 8, 2016. https://www.gafcon. org/news/high-noon-in-lusaka.

Baim, Tracy. "Activist Jim Wickliff Dies." *Windy City Times.* September 18, 2002. http://www. windycitymediagroup.com/lgbt/Activist-Jim-Wickliff-Dies/22237.html.

Bates, Stephen, "A Match Made in Heaven." *The Guardian.* September 22, 2006. https://www. theguardian.com/commentisfree/2006/sep/22/anopportunitymissed.

"Bishop Andrus of California: Same Sex marriage Guidelines." June 9, 2008. http://www. episcopalcafe.com/bishop_andrus_of_california_same_sex_marriage_guidelines/ retrieved.

"Bishop Armstrong Dies." *Diocesan Press Service.* May 6, 1964. http://episcopalarchives.org/ cgi-bin/ENS/ENSpress_release.pl?pr_number= XXI-14.

"Bishop Eames Elected Primate Of Ireland." *Episcopal News Service.* February 20, 1986. http://episcopalarchives.org/cgibin/ENS/ENSpress_release.pl?pr_number=86029\.

"Bishop Johnson Found Dead." *The Living Church.* January 29, 1995. http://episcopalarchives. org/cgibin/the_living_church/TLCarticle.pl?volume=210&issue=5&article_id=10.

"Bishop Lyman Ogilby, 'One of the Great Missionary Bishops of the Church,' Dead at 68." November 8, 1990. http://episcopalarchives.org/cgibin/ENS/ENSpress_release.pl?pr_number=90294 .

"Bishop Theuner's legacy." Reprinted from *The Concord Monitor.* November 10, 2013. http:// www.episcopalcafe.com/bishop_theuners_legacy/.

"Bishops Urged to Reconsider Ordination Plans." *Diocesan Press Service.* July 25, 1974. http:// episcopalarchives.org/cgi-bin/ENS/ENSpress_release.pl?pr_number=74199.

"Buhari Congratulates Idowu-Fearon Over His New Appointment." *Vanguard.* September 05, 2015. http://www.vanguardngr.com/2015/09/buhari-congratulates-idowu-fearon-over-his-new-appointment/.

Brachear, Manya A. "Message to Episcopalians." *Chicago Tribune.* June 04, 2007. http:// articles.chicagotribune.com/2007-6-04/news/0706040003_1_anglican-church-archbishop-peter-akinola-gay-man.

"Buhari Meets the Archbishop Who Saved Him." *The News.* May 13, 2016. https://www. thenewsnigeria.com.ng/2016/05/13/buhari-meets-the-archbishop-who-saved-him/.

Carlson, Richard. "Who Is Davis Mac-Iyalla And Why Is He Here?" *New Civilization News.* May 22, 2007. http://www.newciv.org/nl/newslog.php/_v45/__show_article/_a000063-00437.htm.

"Charges Filed Against Four Bishops." *Diocesan Press Service.* September 23, 1974. http:// episcopalarchives.org/cgi-bin/ENS/ENSpress_release.pl?pr_number=74242.

Christian Concern. "'No Unity at the Expense of Truth': A Response to Justin Welby's Presidential Address." *GAFCON website.* February 17, 2016. https://www.gafcon.org/ news/no-unity-at-the-expense-of-truth-a-response-to-justin-welbys-presidential-address.

Cohen, Tamara. "Church of England Ends Ban on Gay Clergy in Civil Partnerships Becoming Bishops (But They Must Remain Celibate)." *Daily Mail.* January 4, 2013. http://www. dailymail.co.uk/news/article-2257265/Church-England-ends-ban-gay-clergy-civil-partnerships-bishops-remain-celibate.html.

"Commission Appointed by Archbishop of Canterbury Rowan Williams: A Preliminary Analysis by Progressive Episcopalians of Pittsburgh." October 30, 2003. http:// progressiveepiscopalians.com.

Cooper, Michael. "Bishop David E. Johnson, 61, Dies From Gunshot." *New York Times.* January 17, 1995. http://www.nytimes.com/1995/01/17/obituaries/bishop-david-e-johnson-61-dies-from-gunshot.html.

"Criteria for Selection for the Ordained Ministry in the Church of England." 2014. https:// www.churchofengland.org/media/1274926/criteria%20document%20-%20web.pdf.

"Davis Mac-Iyalla in Diocese of Newark: Nigerian Activist Tells His Story." *Telling Secrets.* June 11, 2007. http://telling-secrets.blogspot.com.ng/2007/06/davis-mac-iyalla-in-diocese-of-newark.html.

"Defiance: Archbishop Desmond Tutu Daughter Marries Lesbian Lover." *Pulse.* http:// pulse.ng/gist/defiance-archbishop-desmond-tutu-daughter-marries-lesbian-lover-id4521184.html.

"Dissenting Episcopal Bishop Pittsburgh Bishop Robert Duncan on CNN." *Virtue Online.* http://www.virtueonline.org/dissenting-episcopal-bishop-robert-duncan-cnn.

Dolbee, Sandi. "A House Divided Carries On." *San Diego Tribune.* September 16, 2006. http://www.sandiegouniontribune.com/uniontrib/20060916/news_1c16church.html.

"Dr. Leland W. F. Stark Dies; A Retired Episcopal Bishop." *New York Times.* May 13, 1986. http://www.nytimes.com/1986/05/13/obituaries/dr-leland-w-f-stark-dies-a-retired-episcopal-bishop.html.

Duin, Julia. "Bishop to Retire After Lackluster Tenure." *The Washington Times.* February 1, 2010, http://www.washingtontimes.com/news/2010/feb/01/bishop-to-retire-after-lackluster-tenure/?page=2.

Dyer, Mark. "From Bishop Mark Dyer: Statement on Windsor Report." *Episcopal News Service.* October 18, 2004. http://archive.episcopalchurch.org/3577_52926_ENG_HTM.htm.

"Eleven Women Ordained Episcopal Priests." *Diocesan Press Service.* July 31, 1974. http://episcopalarchives.org/cgi-bin/ENS/ENSpress_release.pl?pr_number=74200.

"Episcopal Bishop Zabriskie Dies." *Las Vegas Sun.* September 16, 1999. http://lasvegassun.com/news/1999/sep/16/episcopal-bishop-zabriskie-dies/.

Eyoboka, Sam. "Nigeria: African Anglicans Bishops' Bold Statement On Gay Marriages." *Vanguard.* October 31, 2004. http://allafrica.com/stories/200411010468.html.

Fox, Lisa. "Schofield's Closet?" *My Manner of Life.* November 22, 2006. http://my-manner-of-life.blogspot.com.ng/2006/11/schofields-closet.html.

"From Columbus: Anglican Leaders Reflect Favorably on Jefferts Schori Election." *Episcopal News Service.* June 18, 2006. http://archive.episcopalchurch.org/3577_76171_ENG_HTM.htm.

"The 1972 Gay Rights Platform." *All Things Queer.* http://www.rslevinson.com/gaylesissues/features/collect/onetime/bl_platform1972.htm.

Gledhill, Ruth. "Lambeth Conference in Jeopardy Over Homosexuality Row." *Christian Today.* October 1, 2014. http://www.christiantoday.com/article/lambeth.conference.in.jeopardy.over.homosexuality.row/41141.htm.

Grundy, Trevor. "Mugabe Fuels 'Reformation' Against Gays." *The Scotsman.* September 5, 2004. http://scotlandonsunday.scotsman.com/index.cfm?id=1045722004.

Haley A. S. "Charges Filed Against +Bruno by Clergy and Parishioners." *Anglican Curmudgeon.* July 14, 2015. https://accurmudgeon.blogspot.com/2015/07/charges-filed-against-bruno-by-clergy.html.

Harrison, Judy. "First Female Episcopal Bishop in Maine Passes Shepherd's Staff." *Bangor Daily News.* September 14, 2008. http://bangordailynews.com/2008/09/14/news/first-female-episcopal-bishop-in-maine-passes-shepherdrsquos-staff/.

Hills, Carol. "It Just Got Even Tougher to be Gay in Nigeria." *PRI.* January 14, 2014. http://www.pri.org/stories/2014-11-14/it-just-got-even-tougher-be-gay-nigeria.

Hirsley, Michael. "Episcopalians Approve Guidelines That Conflict on Homosexuality." *Chicago Tribune.* August 25, 1994. http://articles.chicagotribune.com/1994-98-25/news/9408250233_1_pastoral-teaching-bishop-john-spong-teaching-on-human-sexuality.

House of Lords Proceedings. "Civil Partnerships Bill [HL]." *UK Parliament website.* January 25, 2002. http://www.publications.parliament.uk/pa/ld200102/ldhansrd/vo020125/text/20125-21.htm#column_1691.

"January 2016 Update." *GAFCON website.* January 5, 2016. https://www.gafcon.org/news/january-2016-update.

Kallsen, Kevin. "Lambeth Conference Cancelled." *Anglican Ink*. September 30, 2014. http://www.anglican.ink/article/lambeth-conference-cancelled retrieved.

"Kirkley Named Nominee for Suffragan Bishop of Los Angeles." *Diocese of California*. August 2, 2009. http://www.diocal.org/pcn/DioNews/kirkley-named-nominee-suffragan-bishop-los-angeles.

"Lambeth Diary: Anglicans in Turmoil." *BBC News*. August 4, 2008. http://news.bbc.co.uk/2/hi/uk_news/7509125.stm.

"Lambeth: South Asia Bishops Take Stand Against Homosexuality. Call for Humility and Healing and Walk Calvary Road." *Virtue Online*. http://www.virtueonline.org/lambeth-south-asia-bishops-take-stand-against-homosexuality.

LeVay, Simon. "Queer Science: The Use and Abuse of Research into Homosexuality." *Washington Post*.http://www.washingtonpost.com/wp-srv/style/longterm/books/chap1/queersscience.htm.

Makinana, Andisiwe. "Tutu Gay Wedding Creates Conundrum for Anglican Church." *City Press*. January 18, 2016. http://city-press.news24.com/News/tutu-gay-wedding-creates-conundrum-for-anglican-church-20160118.

Matson, Dale. "A Man Of Joy, Courage and Prayer: Bishop John David Schofield RIP." *Soundings*. October 30, 2013. http://sanjoaquinsoundings.blogspot.com/2013/10/a-man-of-joy-courage-and-prayer-bishop.html.

"Mentor, Predecessor to Episcopal Church's First Openly Gay Bishop Dies." November 10, 2013. https://3riversepiscopal.blogspot.com/2013/11/mentor-predecessor-to-episcopal-churchs.html?m=0.

Meyer, Graham. "Mysteries of the Washington National Cathedral." *Washingtonian*. September 1, 2007. http://www.washingtonian.com/articles/arts-events/mysteries-of-the-washington-national-cathedral/.

Murphy, Caryle. "Episcopal Bishop to Bless Gay Priest's Union in Md." *The Washington Post*. May 29, 2004. http://www.washingtonpost.com/wp-dyn/articles/A64490–2004May28.html.

Nai-Chu Poon, Michael. "A Vision for the Fellowship of Anglican Churches." *Kiwianglo's Blog*. July 26, 2012. https://kiwianglo.wordpress.com/2012/07/26/fr-michael-poon-singapore-looks-to-the-future-of-anglicanism/.

"New Top Episcopal Bishop Challenged on Her Resume." *WorldNetDaily*. August 1, 2006. https://www.wnd.com/2006/08/37277/#YJqUulqGC2t5ueWF.99%20http://www.wnd.com/2006/08/37277/.

Nigeria Population Census 1991 Analysis. http://www.population.gov.ng/images/the_elderly.pdf and http://www.indexmundi.com/nigeria/demographics_profile.html.

"Nigerian Anglican Archbishop Ignatius Kattey Kidnapped." *The Telegraph*. September 10, 2013. http://www.telegraph.co.uk/news/worldnews/africaandindianocean/nigeria/10297824/Nigerian-Anglican-Archbishop-Ignatius-Kattey-kidnapped.html.

"Nigeria's Anti-Gay Bill Causes Protests." *Afrol News*. March 1, 2010. http://www.afrol.com/articles/24541.

Oakley, Nicola and Jon Dean. "Man Who Had UK's First Civil Partnership Recalls Tragic Moment his Partner Passed Away Just Hours Later." *Mirror*. December 3, 2015. http://www.mirror.co.uk/news/uk-news/man-who-uks-first-civil-6945150.

"Obasanjo Chides Same Sex Marriage, Homosexuality." *Sudan Tribune*. October 27, 2004. http://www.sudantribune.com/spip.php?article6193.

Okoh, Nicholas. "Chairman's June 2016 Pastoral Letter." *GAFCON website*. June 4, 2016. https://www.gafcon.org/news/chairmans-june-2016-pastoral-letter.

Otufodunrin, Lekan. "Lagos: Williams Absent at African Bishops Conference." *Virtue Online*. October 26, 2004. http://www.virtueonline.org/lagos-williams-absent-african-bishops-conference.

Packer, J. I. "Who We Are and "Where We Stand." *GAFCON website*. October 16, 2007. https://www.gafcon.org/resources/who-we-are-and-where-we-stand.

"Plea to Silent Church Leaders: Oppose 'Jail the Gays' Law." *Erasing 76 Crimes*. January 22, 2014. https://76crimes.com/2014/01/22/plea-to-silent-church-leaders-oppose-jail-the-gays-law/.

Polgreen, Lydia and Laurie Goodstein. "At Axis of Episcopal Split, an Anti-Gay Nigerian." *New York Times*. December 25, 2006. http://www.nytimes.com/2006/12/25/world/africa/25episcopal.html?pagewanted=2&_r=1.

"Pomp and Colour Marks the Launch of the Strategic Plan." *Anglican Communion News Service*. February 23, 2007. https://www.anglicannews.org/news/2007/02/pomp-and-colour-marks-the-launch-of-the-strategic-plan.aspx.

Renner, Gerald. "Homosexual Issue Splits Episcopal Leaders." *The Hartford Courant*. July 21, 1991. http://articles.courant.com/1991–97-21/news/0000213950_1_church-leaders-homosexual-episcopal-general-convention/2.

"Resolution 1 - The Ordination or Consecration of Women to the Episcopate." 1988 Lambeth Conference. http://www.anglicancommunion.org/resources/document-library/lambeth-conference/1988/resolution-1-the-ordination-or-consecration-of-women-to-the-episcopate?author=Lambeth+Conference&year=1988.

"Response to Church of Nigeria on Archbishop Josiah Idowu-Fearon." *Archbishop of Canterbury website*. June 26, 2015. http://www.archbishopofcanterbury.org/articles.php/5578/response-to-the-church-of-nigeria-on-archbishop-josiah-idowu-fearon.

"Retired Bishops Stark And Hogg Die." *Episcopal News Service*. May 15, 1986. http://www.episcopalarchives.org/cgi-bin/ENS/ENSpress_release.pl?pr_number=86111.

"Retired Indianapolis Bishop Edward Jones Dies at 78." *The Episcopal Church*. July 30, 2007. www.episcopalchurch.org/library/article/retired-indianapolis-bishop-edward-jones-dies-78.

Scaife, Janice Beetle. "Desmond Tutu's Daughter Follows in Father's Footsteps." *The Episcopal Church website*. June 8, 2003. http://www.episcopalchurch.org/library/article/desmond-tutus-daughter-follows-fathers-footsteps.

"Section H: Human Sexuality." 2008 Lambeth Conference. http://www.anglicancommunion.org/resources/document-library/lambeth-conference/2008/section-h-human-sexuality?author=Lambeth+Conference&year=2008.

Shoffman, Mark. "Gay Group Slams Archbishop of Canterbury for 'Appeasing Homophobia.'" *Pink News*. April 24, 2006. https://www.pinknews.co.uk/2006/04/24/gay-group-slams-archbishop-of-canterbury-for-appeasing-homophobia/.

Smith, Peter. "Bishop Duncan Retiring from Anglican Post." *Pittsburgh Post-Gazette*. November 8, 2015. http://www.postgazette.com/local/region/2015/11/08/Bishop-Duncan-retiring-from-Anglican-post/stories/201511080183 retrieved 13/12/15.

Stannard, Ed. "Hero or Heretic, Spong Won't Be Forgotten." *Episcopal Life*. http://arc.episcopalchurch.org/episcopal-life/Spong.html.

Steele, Dominic. "Dr Peter Jensen on the Future of the Anglican Communion." *GAFCON website.* January 17, 2016. http://gafcon.org/2016/01/httpwww-dominicsteele-comblog2016117pfj/.

"The Most Revd. Nicholas Dikeriehi Orogodo Okoh." *Church of Nigeria.* https://anglican-nig.org/the-primate/.

"The Most Reverend Datuk Yong Ping Chung, 2nd Archbishop of the Province of South East Asia." *Anglican Communion News Service.* February 24, 2000. http://www.anglicannews.org/news/2000/02/biography-of-the-new-archbishop-of-south-east-asia.aspx.

Thomas, Anne. "Anglican Head: US Church has 'Pushed the Boundaries.'" *Christian Today.* August 24, 2016. http://www.christiantoday.com/article/anglican.head.us.church.has.pushed.the.boundaries/7357.htm?print=1.

Turner, Philip. "An Open Letter to Rev. Prof. Stephen Noll." *The Anglican Communion Institute.* August 2, 2007. http://www.anglicancommunioninstitute.com/2007/08/an-open-letter-to-rev-prof-stephen-noll/.

"Two More Bishops Nominated for Presiding Bishop. Jenkins, Duque Agree to Nomination by Petition." *Episcopal News Service.* March 19, 2006. http://archive.episcopalchurch.org/3577_72967_ENG_HTM.htm.

Virtue, David W. "Changing Attitude Spins Disinformation on Homosexuality to Anglican Communion." *Virtue Online.* January 3, 2008. http://www.virtueonline.org/changing-attitude-spins-disinformation-homosexuality-anglican-communion.

———. "The Delusional World of Bishop James Tengatenga." *Virtue Online.* November 19, 2014. https://virtueonline.org/delusional-world-bishop-james-tengatenga.

———. "General Convention: What Ails Bishop Stacy Sauls Ails Episcopalians." *Virtue Online.* July 21, 2012. http://www.virtueonline.org/general-convention-what-ails-bishop-stacy-sauls-ails-episcopalians.

———. "The Mind and Mission of Anglican Archbishop Robert Duncan." *Virtue Online.* October 12, 2009. http://www.virtueonline.org/mind-and-mission-anglican-archbishop-robert-duncan.

———. "Netherlands: Daughter of Archbishop Desmond Tutu Ties Knot with Woman Professor." *Virtue Online.* January 1, 2016. http://www.virtueonline.org/netherlands-daughter-archbishop-desmond-tutu-ties-knot-woman-professor.

Waring, Steve. "Retired Bishop William Cox to be Tried by Ecclesiastical Court." *Global South Anglican Online.* March 21, 2007. http://www.globalsouthanglican.org/index.php/blog/comments/retired_bishop_william_cox_to_be_tried_by_ecclesiastical_court.

Whalon, Pierre. "The Ghost of Bishop Pike, Revisited." *Anglicans Online.* March 20, 2005. http://anglicansonline.org/resources/essays/whalon/PikesGhost.html.

"Williams to Visit Africa." *Wales Online.* July 22, 2003. http://www.walesonline.co.uk/news/uk-news/williams-to-visit-africa-2478815.

Woo, Elaine. "George Barrett; Episcopal Bishop Defied Church to Ordain 4 Women Priests." *Los Angeles Times.* December 05, 2000. http://articles.latimes.com/2000/dec/05/local/me-61379.

Yafugborhi, Egufe. "Police Lied About My Rescue – Archbishop Kattey." *Vanguard.* September 19, 2013. https://www.vanguardngr.com/2013/09/police-lied-about-my-rescue-archbishop-kattey/.

www.ingramcontent.com/pod-product-compliance
Lightning Source LLC
Chambersburg PA
CBHW081426270326
41932CB00019B/3106